Fodor's 04

WASHINGTON, D.C.

D1621452

Where to Stay and Eat
for All Budgets

Must-See Sights
and Local Secrets

Ratings You Can Trust

Fodor's Travel Publications   New York, Toronto, London, Sydney, Auckland
www.fodors.com

FODOR'S WASHINGTON, D.C. 2004
Editor: John D. Rambow

Editorial Production: David Downing
Editorial Contributors: Susanna M. Carey, Kristi Delovitch, Robin Dougherty, Satu Hummasti, Karyn-Siobhan Robinson, Mitch Tropin, Elizabeth A. Whisler, CiCi Williamson
Maps: David Lindroth *cartographer;* Robert Blake and Rebecca Baer, *map editors*
Design: Fabrizio La Rocca, *creative director;* Guido Caroti, *art director;* Melanie Marin, *senior picture editor*
Production/Manufacturing: Robert B. Shields
Cover Photo (View from the Lincoln Memorial): Catherine Karnow

ISBN 1–4000–1274–0

ISSN 0743–9741

SPECIAL SALES

Fodor's Travel Publications are available at special discounts for bulk purchases for sales promotions or premiums. Special editions, including personalized covers, excerpts of existing guides, and corporate imprints, can be created in large quantities for special needs. For more information, contact your local bookseller or write to Special Markets, Fodor's Travel Publications, 1745 Broadway, New York, New York 10019. Inquiries from Canada should be directed to your local Canadian bookseller or sent to Random House of Canada, Ltd., Marketing Department, 2775 Matheson Boulevard East, Mississauga, Ontario L4W 4P7. Inquiries from the United Kingdom should be sent to Fodor's Travel Publications, 20 Vauxhall Bridge Road, London SW1V 2SA, England.

AN IMPORTANT TIP & AN INVITATION

Although all prices, opening times, and other details in this book are based on information supplied to us at press time, changes occur all the time in the travel world, and Fodor's cannot accept responsibility for facts that become outdated or for inadvertent errors or omissions. So **always confirm information when it matters,** especially if you're making a detour to visit a specific place. Your experiences—positive and negative—matter to us. If we have missed or misstated something, **please write to us.** We follow up on all suggestions. Contact the Washington, D.C., editor at editors@fodors.com or c/o Fodor's at 1745 Broadway, New York, New York 10019.

DESTINATION D.C.

t's hard to anticipate the impact of Washington, D.C. As you enter town, iconic buildings you've seen a thousand times on computer monitors and TV screens now stand before you: the Washington Monument, the Lincoln and Jefferson memorials, the White House, the Capitol. Rising majestically from the low city, and often flanked by sweeping lawns, they inspire awe. Washington is more than just a seat of power, but it is this power that people notice first. It's not just in its buildings. Just as striking, almost palpable, is the energy that comes from its people. Congressional staff rush around Capitol Hill, motorcades speed down side streets, politicians jockey for position on the Senate floor, and reporters lie in wait on the White House lawn. But when working hours are over, most of the city turns quiet and reflective. Take a stroll on the Mall one night when moonlight washes over the monuments. Pause to contemplate the grandeur of it all. Ready or not, you will be moved. Have a wonderful trip!

Karen Cure

Karen Cure, Editorial Director

CONTENTS

Maps

CloseUps

ABOUT THIS BOOK

SELECTION	Our goal is to cover the best properties, sights, and activities in their category, as well as the most interesting communities to visit. We make a point of including local food-lovers' hot spots as well as neighborhood options, and we avoid all that's touristy unless it's really worth your time. You can go on the assumption that everything you read about in this book is recommended wholeheartedly by our writers and editors. Flip to On the Road with Fodor's to learn more about who they are. It goes without saying that no property mentioned in the book has paid to be included.
RATINGS	Orange stars ★ denote sights and properties that our editors and writers consider the very best in the area covered by the entire book. These, the best of the best, are listed in the Fodor's Choice section in the front of the book. Black stars ★ highlight the sights and properties we deem Highly Recommended, the don't-miss sights within any area. Fodor's Choice and Highly Recommended options are listed on the title page of each chapter. Use the index to find complete descriptions. Sights pinpointed with numbered map bullets ❶ in the margins tend to be more important than those without bullets.
SPECIAL SPOTS	Pleasures & Pastimes focuses on types of experiences that reveal the spirit of the destination. Watch for Off the Beaten Path sights. Some are out of the way, some are quirky, and all are worth your while. If the munchies hit while you're exploring, look for Need a Break? suggestions.
TIME IT RIGHT	Wondering when to go? Check On the Calendar up front and chapters' Timing sections for weather and crowd overviews and best days and times to visit.
SEE IT ALL	Use Fodor's exclusive Great Itineraries as a model for your trip. (For a good overview of the entire destination, follow those that begin the book, or mix regional itineraries from several chapters.) In cities, Good Walks guide you to important sights in each neighborhood; ☞ indicates the starting points of walks and itineraries in the text and on the map.
BUDGET WELL	Hotel and restaurant price categories from ¢ to $$$$ are defined in the opening pages of each chapter—expect to find a balanced selection for every budget. For attractions, we always give standard adult admission fees; reductions are usually available for children, students, and senior citizens. Look in Discounts & Deals in Smart Travel Tips for information on destination-wide ticket schemes.
BASIC INFO	Smart Travel Tips lists travel essentials for the entire area covered by the book; region-specific basics end the Side Trips chapter. To find the best way to get around, see individual modes of travel ("Car Travel," "Train Travel") for details. We assume you'll check Web sites or call for particulars.
ON THE MAPS	Maps throughout the book show you what's where and help you find your way around. Black and orange numbered bullets ❶❶ in the text correlate to bullets on maps.

BACKGROUND	In general, we give background information within the chapters in the course of explaining sights as well as in **CloseUp** boxes and in **Understanding D.C.** at the end of the book. To get in the mood, review the suggestions in **Books & Movies**.
DON'T FORGET	**Restaurants** are open for lunch and dinner daily unless we state otherwise; we mention dress only when there's a specific requirement and reservations only when they're essential or not accepted—it's always best to book ahead. Unless otherwise noted, **Hotels** have private baths, phones, TVs, and air-conditioning and operate on the European Plan (a.k.a. EP, meaning without meals). We always list facilities but not whether you'll be charged extra to use them, so when pricing accommodations, find out what's included.
SYMBOLS	

Many Listings

★ Fodor's Choice

★ Highly recommended

⊠ Physical address

✢ Directions

🗐 Mailing address

☎ Telephone

🖷 Fax

⊕ On the Web

✉ E-mail

🎫 Admission fee

☉ Open/closed times

▶ Start of walk/itinerary

Ⓜ Metro stations

⊟ Credit cards

Outdoors

🏌 Golf

⛺ Camping

Hotels & Restaurants

🖃 Hotel

⇋ Number of rooms

⚴ Facilities

🍽 Meal plans

✕ Restaurant

⚴ Reservations

🏛 Dress code

🚭 Smoking

🍷 BYOB

✕🖃 Hotel with restaurant that warrants a visit

Other

☕ Family-friendly

🛈 Contact information

⇨ See also

⊠ Branch address

☞ Take note

ON THE ROAD WITH FODOR'S

A trip takes you out of yourself. Concerns of life at home completely disappear, driven away by more immediate thoughts—about, say, what marvels will beguile the next day, or where you'll have dinner. That's where Fodor's comes in. We make sure that you know all your options, so that you don't miss something that's around the next bend just because you didn't know it was there. Because the best memories of your trip might well have nothing to do with what you came to Washington, D.C., to see, we guide you to sights large and small all over town. You might set out to explore the corridors of "our nation's attic," the Smithsonian, but back at home you find yourself unable to forget strolling through the elegant gardens of Georgetown or being awestruck at the Vietnam Veterans Memorial. With Fodor's at your side, serendipitous discoveries are never far away.

Our success in showing you every corner of the District is a credit to our extraordinary writers. Although there's no substitute for travel advice from a good friend who knows your style, our contributors are the next best thing—the kind of people you would poll for travel advice if you knew them.

Susanna M. Carey, the freelance publications consultant and writer who updated our Smart Travel Tips, divides her time between her clients and her 2½-year-old daughter, Charlotte. After living and working in and around Washington for more than 12 years, she has seen nearly every sight in the city and looks forward to gaining a new perspective through the eyes of a preschooler.

Where to Eat chapter updater Kristi Delovitch is a resident of Capitol Hill. Over the past year, she has conducted over 70 wine and food tastings in D.C. restaurants, embassies, and hotels. She began her writing career as a news reporter and has recently written travel programs that have aired on PBS. Kristi also wrote portions of the upcoming Fodor's Where to Weekend Around Washington, D.C.

Our updater for the Where to Stay and Shopping chapters, Robin Dougherty, a native Washingtonian, recently moved back to D.C. after living in Miami and Boston. When she's not working on her book column for the Boston Globe, she spends time shopping and hoping for an excuse to stay in a great hotel.

Karyn-Siobhan Robinson checked out the nightlife and arts scenes and updated the non-D.C. portions of our Exploring chapter. She is a reporter, part-time actor, and essayist. Karyn has lived in the Dupont Circle neighborhood since 1991 and is working on her first novel.

Native Washingtonian Mitch Tropin, who updated the Sports & the Outdoors chapter, has been a dedicated runner for 25 years. A senior editor for a national news organization, he spends lunch hours running the streets and parks of D.C. in search of new routes. Mitch also writes for a number of local running publications.

Georgetown resident Elizabeth A. Whisler updated the District portions of the Exploring chapter. While living in Belfast, she worked on the Fodor's Ireland guide. Whisler works at the Pentagon for the congressional relations office of the U.S. Air Force.

CiCi Williamson has been a food and travel writer and syndicated newspaper columnist for more than two decades. The author of six books, she updated the Side Trips chapter. A resident of McLean, Virginia, and the daughter of a U.S. Naval officer, her inherited wanderlust has enticed her to visit every U.S. state and more than 80 countries on six continents.

It's often said that Washington doesn't have any old-fashioned neighborhoods, the way, for example, nearby Baltimore does. Although it's true that Washingtonians are not given to huddling together on their front stoops, each area of the city does have a clearly defined personality, and some, such as Capitol Hill, can even feel like a small town.

The Mall

With nearly a dozen diverse museums ringing an expanse of green, the Mall is the closest thing the capital has to a theme park—but here, almost everything is free. Lindbergh's *Spirit of St. Louis,* the Hope Diamond, Julia Child's kitchen, dinosaurs galore, and myriad other modern and classical artifacts await you. Of course, the Mall is more than just a front yard for all these museums: it's a picnicking park and a running path, an outdoor stage for festivals and fireworks, and America's town green.

The Monuments

Punctuating the capital like a huge exclamation point is the Washington Monument. The Jefferson Memorial's rotunda rises beside the Tidal Basin, where you can rent paddleboats and admire more than 200 cherry trees, gifts from Japan and the focus of a festival each spring. The Lincoln Memorial has a somber statue of the seated president gazing out over the Reflecting Pool. The Vietnam Veterans Memorial's black granite panels reflect the sky, the trees, and the faces of those looking for the names of loved ones. The popular Franklin Delano Roosevelt Memorial covers seven meandering acres near the Jefferson Memorial.

The White House Area

In a city full of immediately recognizable images, perhaps none is more familiar than the White House. In the neighborhood are some of the city's oldest houses and two important art galleries: the Renwick Gallery—the Smithsonian's museum of American decorative arts—and the Corcoran Gallery of Art, known for its collections of photography, European impressionist paintings, and post-war American art.

Capitol Hill

Anchoring this neighborhood is the Capitol, where the Senate and the House have met since 1800. But the Hill is more than just the center of government. There are charming residential blocks here, lined with Victorian row houses and a fine assortment of restaurants, bars, and shops. Union Station, Washington's train depot, has vaulted and gilded ceilings, arched colonnades, statues of Roman legionnaires, and a mall and movie theater complex. Also in this area are the Supreme Court, the Library of Congress, and the Folger Shakespeare Library.

Old Downtown & Federal Triangle

In what was once Downtown—the area within the diamond formed by Massachusetts, Louisiana, Pennsylvania, and New York avenues—are Chinatown, Ford's Theatre, and several important museums. At the National Archives, the original Declaration of Independence, the Constitution, and the Bill of Rights are on display. The National Building Museum, formerly know as the Pension Building, has the largest columns in the world as well as displays devoted to architecture. Other museums include the National Museum of Women in the Arts, the National Portrait Gallery, and the Smithsonian American Art Museum. The Old Post Office Pavilion is also here, as is the International Spy Museum.

Georgetown

The capital's wealthiest neighborhood (and one that's attractive to architecture buffs) is always hopping. Restaurants, bars, nightclubs, and boutiques line the narrow crowded streets. Originally used for shipping, the C&O Canal today is a part of the National Park system: walkers follow the towpath and canoeists paddle the calm waters; you can also go on a leisurely mule-drawn trip aboard a canal barge. Washington Harbour is a riverfront development of restaurants, offices, apartments, and upscale shops; Georgetown Park is a multilevel shopping extravaganza; and Georgetown University is the oldest Jesuit school in the country. Dumbarton Oaks's 10 acres of formal gardens make it one of the loveliest spots in Washington.

Dupont Circle

Fashionable, vibrant Dupont Circle has a cosmopolitan air due partly to its many restaurants, shops, and specialty bookstores; it's also home to the most visible segment of Washington's gay community. The exclusive Kalorama neighborhood (Greek for "beautiful view") is a peaceful, tree-lined enclave filled with embassies and luxurious homes. For a glimpse of the beautiful view, look down over Rock Creek Park—1,800 acres of green—which has a planetarium, an 18-hole golf course, and equestrian and bicycle trails. The Phillips Collection is also here; its best-known paintings include Auguste Renoir's *Luncheon of the Boating Party,* Edgar Degas's *Dancers at the Bar,* and a self-portrait of Paul Cézanne.

Foggy Bottom

Foggy Bottom—an appellation earned years ago when smoke from factories combined with swampy air to produce a permanent fog along the waterfront—has three main claims to fame: the State Department, the Kennedy Center, and George Washington University. Watergate, one of the world's most legendary apartment–office complexes, is notorious for the events that took place here on June 17, 1972. As Nixon aides sat in a motel across the street, five men were caught trying to bug the headquarters of the Democratic National Committee.

Cleveland Park & the National Zoo

Tree-shaded Cleveland Park, in northwest Washington, has attractive houses and a suburban character. Its Cineplex Odeon Uptown is a marvelous 1930s art deco movie house. The National Zoological Park, part of the Smithsonian Institution, is one of the foremost zoos in the world. Star denizens include Komodo dragons and two giant pandas.

Upper Massachusetts Avenue

This area, to the north of Georgetown and close to the National Zoo, is best known for Washington National Cathedral, finally completed in 1990 after more than 80 years of construction.

Adams-Morgan

One of Washington's most ethnically diverse and interesting neighborhoods, Adams-Morgan holds many offbeat restaurants and shops, and cool bars and clubs. The neighborhood's grand 19th-century apartment buildings and row houses as well as its bohemian atmosphere have attracted young urban professionals, the businesses that cater to them, and the attendant parking and crowd problems.

Arlington, Virginia

Two attractions here—both linked to the military and accessible by Metro—make Arlington a part of any complete visit to the nation's capital: Arlington National Cemetery and the U.S. Marine Corps War Memorial.

Alexandria, Virginia

Alexandria's history is linked to the most significant events and personages of the colonial, revolutionary, and Civil War periods. This colorful past is still alive on the cobbled streets; on the revitalized waterfront, where clipper ships dock and artisans display their wares; and in restored 18th- and 19th-century homes, churches, and taverns. The history of African-Americans in Alexandria and Virginia from 1749, when the city was founded, to the present is recounted at the Alexandria Black History Resource Center, near Robert E. Lee's boyhood home.

GREAT ITINERARIES

You could easily spend several weeks exploring Washington, D.C., but if you're here for just a short period, make sure to plan your time carefully. The following suggested itineraries (one set is geared specifically for those traveling with children) can help you structure your visit efficiently.

Washington in 3 to 5 Days

Days 1 and 2 Spend both days on the Mall. Visit all the museums that interest you—a few standouts are the National Museum of Natural History, the National Air and Space Museum, and the U.S. Holocaust Memorial Museum. Take time out for a leisurely paddleboat ride in the Tidal Basin.

Day 3 Explore Georgetown. There are sights to see, but people come here mainly to watch other people, shop, eat, and bar-hop.

Day 4 Head to the National Zoo.

Day 5 Split your last day between Adams-Morgan and Dupont Circle. As upscale as Georgetown, these two neighborhoods have unusual shops, restaurants, and clubs. Ethnic food and crafts abound, especially in Adams-Morgan; both areas also have an assortment of art galleries.

Washington in 3 to 5 Days—with Children

Days 1 and 2 Spend both days on the Mall, checking out the museums and monuments that interest you and your kids. Even children who can't read the Gettysburg Address etched on the walls of the Lincoln Memorial can recognize the building from its picture on the back of a penny. At the Vietnam Veterans Memorial, children old enough to hold a pencil can make rubbings of the names (paper and pencils are available at the site). Consider investing in Tourmobile tickets for a respite from walking while still seeing the attractions. For breaks, ride the carousel on the Mall or sit by the fountain in the National Gallery of Art Sculpture Garden.

Day 3 Older children may enjoy morning tours of the Bureau of Engraving and Printing and the Capitol before heading off to the National Zoo. If you have younger children, start and end the day at the zoo. On cold or hot days, take advantage of the numerous indoor animal houses. If little ones wear out, you can rent strollers.

Days 4 and 5 Plan on a visit to the Capital Children's Museum, where you can expect to spend at least three hours. If you and your children still have stamina, grab a bite to eat at Union Station on your way to the National Postal Museum. On your final day, take older children to the International Spy Museum, followed by a trip to the Washington Navy Yard or Old Town Alexandria. With younger children, see creatures of the deep at the National Aquarium, followed by a trip to Glen Echo Park for a play or puppet show. On Day

Washington in 1 Day

Head for the Mall. Start at either end—the Capitol or the Lincoln Memorial—and walk leisurely to the opposite end. You won't have time to see everything along the way, but you'll walk past or have in sight most of the attractions Washington is famous for: the Lincoln Memorial, the Korean War Veterans Memorial, the Vietnam Veterans Memorial, the Tidal Basin and Jefferson Memorial, the Washington Monument (and, to the north, the White House), most of the Smithsonian museums, the National Gallery of Art, and the Capitol.

Washington in 1 Day—with Children

Head right to the Washington Monument, where both directions yield a breathtaking view of the Mall. From here head to the National Air and Space Museum; on the way, you can stop to ride a painted pony at the carousel near the Smithsonian castle or perhaps take a few minutes to wander through the Hirshhorn Museum and Sculpture Garden. If you still have time, visit either the National Museum of American History or the National Museum of Natural History; both have hands-on children's exhibits that are open most afternoons.

WHEN TO GO

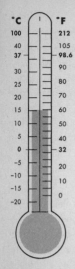

°C		°F
100		212
40		105
37		98.6
30		90
25		80
20		70
15		60
10		50
5		40
0		32
-5		20
-10		10
-15		0
-20		

Climate

Washington has two delightful seasons: spring and autumn. In spring, the city's ornamental fruit trees are budding, and its many gardens are in bloom. By autumn, most of the summer crowds have left and you can enjoy the sights in peace. Summers can be uncomfortably hot and humid. Winter weather is often bitter, with a handful of modest snowstorms that somehow bring this southern city to a standstill. When lawmakers break for recess (at Thanksgiving, Christmas, Easter, July 4, the entire month of August, and other holiday periods), the city seems a little less vibrant.

Forecasts Weather Channel Connection ☎ 900/932–8437, 95¢ per minute from a Touch-Tone phone ⊕ www.weather.com.

WASHINGTON, D.C.

Jan.	47F	8C	May	76F	24C	Sept.	79F	26C
	34	1		58	14		61	16
Feb.	47F	8C	June	85F	29C	Oct.	70F	21C
	31	1		65	18		52	11
Mar.	56F	13C	July	88F	31C	Nov.	56F	13C
	38	3		70	21		41	5
Apr.	67F	19C	Aug.	86F	30C	Dec.	47F	8C
	47	8		39	68		32	0

ON THE CALENDAR

The following festivals and other events, sponsored by various organizations throughout D.C., go some way toward representing the city's local, regional, and national pride. Check out ⊕ www.washington.org, the Web site of the Washington, D.C., Convention and Tourism Corporation, for more information about these and other events throughout the year.

ONGOING

Late Apr.–mid-Aug.	During the **Twilight Tattoo Series** (☎ 703/696–3399), the 3rd U.S. Infantry, the U.S. Army Band, the Drill Team, and the Old Guard Fife and Drum Corps play on the Ellipse grounds Wednesdays at 7 PM.

WINTER

Mid-Nov.–late Dec.	*A Christmas Carol* (☎ 202/347–4833 ⊕ www.fordstheatre.org) returns each year to Ford's Theatre.
Dec.	The **National Christmas Tree Lighting/Pageant of Peace** (☎ 202/619–7222) is accompanied by music and caroling. In mid-December, the president lights the tree at dusk on the Ellipse. For the next few weeks the Ellipse grounds host choral performances, a Nativity scene, a Yule log, and a display of lighted Christmas trees representing each U.S. state and territory.
Early Dec.	The **National Cathedral Christmas Celebration and Services** (☎ 202/537–6200 ⊕ www.nationalcathedral.org) has carols, pageants, and choral performances. The **Campagna Center's Annual Scottish Christmas Walk** (☎ 703/549–0111) salutes Alexandria's Scottish heritage with a parade, bagpipers, house tours, and crafts.
Mid-Dec.	**Old Town Christmas Candlelight Tours** (☎ 703/838–4242) visit Alexandria's Gadsby's Tavern Museum, the Lyceum, Lee-Fendall House, and Carlyle House. Included in the tour are music and refreshments. Military bands perform at the **People's Christmas Tree Lighting** on the west side of the Capitol.
Mid–late Dec.	*The Nutcracker* (☎ 202/362–3606) is performed by the Washington Ballet at Warner Theatre.
Mid-Jan.	**Martin Luther King Jr.'s birthday** is celebrated with speeches and dance and choral performances.
Late Jan.–early Feb.	The **Chinese Lunar New Year Festival** explodes in Chinatown with firecrackers and a dragon-led parade.
Feb.	**African-American History Month** (☎ Martin Luther King Jr. Library 202/727–1186) brings special events, exhibits, and cultural programs.
Mid-Feb.	A wreath-laying ceremony and a reading of the Gettysburg Address takes place at the Lincoln Memorial on February 12, **Lincoln's birthday** (☎ 202/619–7222). A wreath-laying ceremony is held at the Frederick Douglass National Historic Site to commemorate **Frederick Douglass's birthday** (☎ 202/619–7222 or 202/426–5961). **George Washington's birthday** (☎ 703/838–9270) is celebrated over Presidents' Day weekend with a parade and a reenactment of his farewell address in Old Town Alexandria, a Birthnight Banquet and Ball at Gadsby's Tavern Museum, a birthday celebration and wreath-laying

ceremony at Mt. Vernon, and Revolutionary War reenactments at Fort Ward Park.

Early Mar.	The Spring Antiques Show (☎ 301/933–9433; 202/547–9215 during the show ⊕ www.shador.com) at the D.C. Armory hosts as many as 200 dealers the first weekend in March.
Mid-Mar.	St. Patrick's Day (☎ 202/637–2474 ⊕ www.dcstpatsparade.com) begins with a parade down Constitution Avenue at noon. The following days feature theater, folk music, and dance concerts. Alexandria's St. Patrick's Day parade (☎ 703/237–2199) usually takes place the weekend before the parade in Washington. The Bach Marathon (☎ 202/363–2202) honors Johann Sebastian's birthday. Ten organists each play the pipe organ at Chevy Chase Presbyterian Church from 2 to 7. A catered German dinner follows the marathon.

SPRING

Mar. or Apr.	The White House Easter Egg Roll (☎ 202/456–2200 or 202/208–1631 ⊕ www.whitehouse.gov) brings children ages three to six to the White House lawn on Easter Monday.
Late Mar.–early Apr.	The Smithsonian Kite Festival (☎ 202/357–3030 ⊕ www.si.edu), for kite makers and fliers of all ages, is held on the Washington Monument grounds. The two-week-long National Cherry Blossom Festival (☎ 202/547–1500 ⊕ www.nationalcherryblossomfestival.org) opens with a Japanese lantern-lighting ceremony at the Tidal Basin.
Mid-Apr.	Thomas Jefferson's birthday (☎ 202/619–7222) is marked by military drills and a wreath-laying service at his memorial on April 13. The White House Spring Garden & Grounds Tour (☎ 202/456–2200 or 202/208–1631 ⊕ www.whitehouse.gov) takes in the Jacqueline Kennedy Rose Garden and the South Lawn. During the event, military bands perform.
Mid–late Apr.	The Georgetown House Tour (☎ 202/338–2287 ⊕ www.georgetownhousetour.com) gives you the chance to view private homes. Admission includes high tea at historic St. John's Georgetown Parish Church. During the Alexandria Garden Tour (☎ 800/644–7776 ⊕ www.vagardenweek.org), six private gardens and another half-dozen historical sights are open to the public, with afternoon tea at the Athenaeum.
Late Apr.	The Smithsonian Craft Show (☎ 202/357–2700 ⊕ www.smithsoniancraftshow.org) exhibits one-of-a-kind objects by 120 top U.S. artisans.
Late Apr.–early May	The D.C. International Film Festival (☎ 202/628–3456 ⊕ www.filmfestdc.org) shows films from all over the world; each year a different region is highlighted. Tickets are required.
Early May	The National Cathedral Flower Mart (☎ 202/537–2937 ⊕ www.nationalcathedral.org/cathedral/flowermart) salutes a different country each year with flower booths and crafts. The Georgetown Garden Tour (☎ 202/333–3921) shows off more than a dozen private gardens in one of the city's most historic neighborhoods.

Early–mid-May	Baltimore is all abuzz around the running of the Preakness Stakes, the middle jewel in horse racing's Triple Crown. The Preakness Celebration (☎ 410/837–3030 ⊕ www.preaknesscelebration.org) includes a balloon festival, parade, and music.
Mid-May	The Joint Service Open House (☎ 301/981–4600 ⊕ www.andrews. af.mil) at Andrews Air Force Base in Maryland includes two days of static aircraft and weapons displays, parachute jumps, and the navy's Blue Angels or the army's Golden Knights.

SUMMER

Late May	The Memorial Day Concert (☎ 202/619–7222), by the National Symphony Orchestra at 8 PM on the Capitol's West Lawn, officially welcomes summer to D.C. Memorial Day at Arlington National Cemetery (☎ 703/607–8052) includes a wreath-laying ceremony at the Tomb of the Unknowns, services at the Memorial Amphitheatre featuring military bands, and a presidential keynote address. Memorial Day at the U.S. Navy Memorial (☎ 202/737–2300 Ext. 768) has wreath-laying ceremonies as well as an outdoor evening concert by the navy band. Memorial Day at the Vietnam Veterans Memorial (☎ 202/619–7222) is commemorated with a wreath-laying ceremony and a concert by the National Symphony. Come to Alexandria's Memorial Day Jazz Festival (☎ 703/883–4686) for big-band music performed by local musicians.
Early June	The Alexandria Red Cross Waterfront Festival (☎ 703/549–8300 Ext. 500 ⊕ www.waterfrontfestival.org) promotes the American Red Cross and recognizes Alexandria's rich maritime heritage. Tall ships are open for visits, and there are arts-and-crafts displays and a blessing of the fleet. The first Saturday in June is reserved for the world's largest 5-km (3.1-mi) race, The Race for the Cure, which takes place in downtown Washington and takes runners around the Capitol building. The number of entrants always exceeds 50,000.
June	During the two weeks of its Free for All (☎ 202/547–1122 Washington Shakespeare Theatre ⊕ www.shakespearetheatre.org), the Washington Shakespeare Theatre company mounts free, nightly performances at the open-air Carter Barron Amphitheater in Rock Creek Park.
Early–mid-June	The Capital Jazz Fest (☎ 301/218–0404 or 888/378–3378) is a weekend showcase for such contemporary performers as David Sanborn and Grover Washington Jr. It's held in Manassas, Virginia.
June–July	The free performances held as part of the National Cathedral's Summer Festival of Music (☎ 202/537–6200) include everything from Renaissance choral music to contemporary instrumental fare.
June–Aug.	The Military Band Summer Concert Series (☎ 202/433–2525, 703/696–3399, 202/433–4011, or 202/767–5658) is held on Tuesday evenings at various locations throughout the Washington area and Friday evenings on the west steps of the Capitol at 8 PM. Every August the *1812 Overture* is performed with real cannons at the Sylvan Theater, at the base of the Washington Monument.

Late June–early July	The Smithsonian's **Folklife Festival** (☎ 202/357–2700 ⊕ www.folklife. si.edu) is held on the National Mall. It celebrates various cultures through music, arts and crafts, and food.
July 4	The **Independence Day Celebration** (☎ 202/619–7222) includes a grand parade past many monuments. In the evening, the National Symphony Orchestra gives free performances on the Capitol's West Lawn; this is followed by fireworks over the Washington Monument.
Late July	The **Korean War Armistice Day Ceremony** (☎ 202/619–7222) remembering the 1953 cease fire includes a formal wreath-laying ceremony at the Korean War Veterans Memorial. The **Virginia Scottish Games** (☎ 703/912–1943 ⊕ www.vascottishgames.org) include Highland dancing, bagpipes, athletic contests, fiddling competitions, animal events, and a British antique auto show. The games are held on the grounds of the Episcopal High School in Alexandria.
Early Sept.	The **Labor Day Weekend Concert** (☎ 202/619–7222 National Park Service; 202/467–4600 Kennedy Center) by the National Symphony Orchestra takes place on the Capitol's West Lawn. At the free **John F. Kennedy Center's Open House** (☎ 202/467–4600 ⊕ www.kennedy-center.org) there are events by musicians, dancers, and other performers. The **National Black Family Reunion Celebration** (☎ 202/737–0120) includes free performances by nationally renowned R&B and gospel singers, exhibits, and food on the Washington Monument grounds. **Adams Morgan Day** (☎ 202/789–7000 ⊕ www.adamsmorganday.org) celebrates family and community diversity with a large neighborhood street festival.
Mid-Sept.	The **Constitution Day Commemoration** (☎ 202/501–5000 or 301/837–1700) observes the anniversary of the signing of the Constitution. Events include a naturalization ceremony, speakers, and concerts.
FALL	
Late Sept.	The **National Cathedral Open House** (☎ 202/537–2378) is a chance to share in Cathedral-related crafts, music, and activities.
Oct.	**Art-O-Matic** (☎ 202/661–7589 ⊕ www.artomatic.org) showcases the work of hundreds of local painters, sculptors, filmmakers, writers, dancers, poets, and musicians. For each year's festival, an unlikely site becomes an art gallery for a month.
Early Oct.	The **"Taste of D.C." Festival** (☎ 202/724–5430 ⊕ www.washington.org) presents dishes (and the chance to taste them) from many different D.C. eateries.
Late Oct.	The **White House Fall Garden & Grounds Tour** (☎ 202/456–2200 or 202/208–1631 ⊕ www.whitehouse.gov), like a similar event in spring, gives you an upclose view of places that can normally be seen only on TV or on the wrong side of a fence. The **Marine Corps Marathon** (☎ 703/690–3431 or 800/786–8768 ⊕ www.marinemarathon.com) attracts thousands of world-class runners on the fourth Sunday in October. **Theodore Roosevelt's birthday** (☎ 202/619–7222) is celebrated on Roosevelt Island with tours of the island, exhibits, and family activities. The **Washington**

International Horse Show (⊕ www.wihs.org) is D.C.'s major equestrian event.

Mid-Nov.   **Veterans' Day** (☎ 703/607–8052 Cemetery Visitors Center; 202/ 619–7222 National Park Service) services take place at Arlington National Cemetery, the Vietnam Veterans Memorial, and the U.S. Navy Memorial. A wreath-laying ceremony is held at 11 AM at the Tomb of the Unknowns.

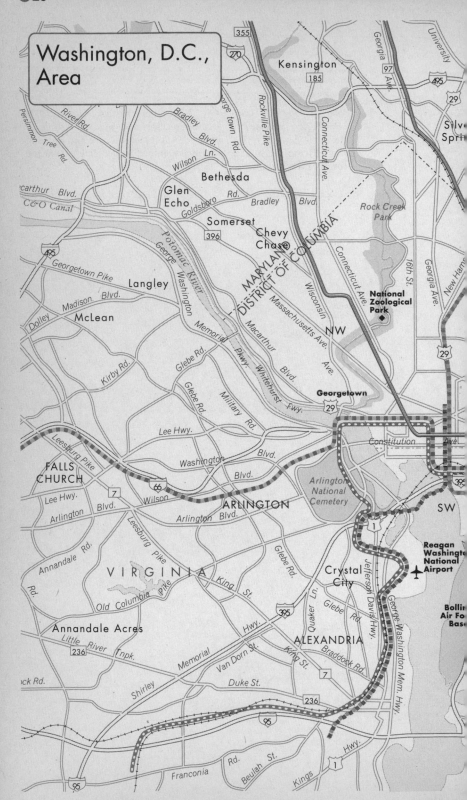

Washington, D.C., Area

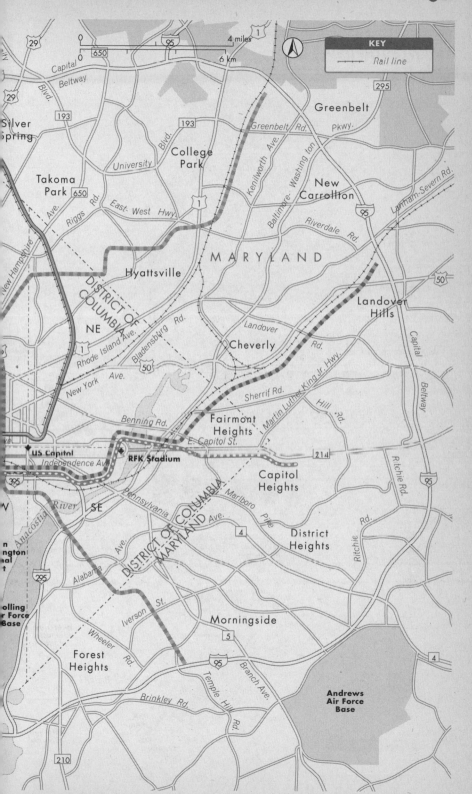

KEY

Rail line

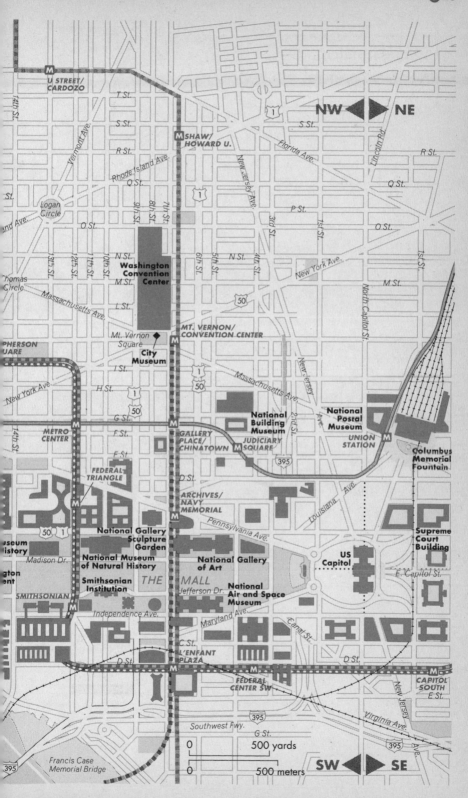

NW ◀▶ NE

U STREET/ CARDOZO

T St.

S St.

R St.

Rhode Island Ave.

Q St.

SHAW/ HOWARD U.

Florida Ave.

S St.

R St.

Vermont Ave.

New Jersey Ave.

Q St.

Logan Circle

O St.

P St.

O St.

1st St.

13th St.

12th St.

11th St.

10th St.

N St.

9th St.

8th St.

7th St.

6th St.

5th St.

4th St.

3rd St.

New York Ave.

M St.

Washington Convention Center

Thomas Circle

Massachusetts Ave.

M St.

L St.

N St.

North Capitol St.

Mt. Vernon/ CONVENTION CENTER

Mt. Vernon Square

City Museum

I St.

H St.

G St.

Massachusetts Ave.

2nd St.

New Jersey Ave.

National Postal Museum

PHERSON QUARE

New York Ave.

METRO CENTER

F St.

E St.

GALLERY PLACE/ CHINATOWN

National Building Museum

JUDICIARY SQUARE

UNION STATION

Columbus Memorial Fountain

14th St.

FEDERAL TRIANGLE

D St.

ARCHIVES/ NAVY MEMORIAL

Pennsylvania Ave.

Louisiana Ave.

Supreme Court Building

National Gallery Sculpture Garden

Madison Dr.

National Museum of Natural History

Smithsonian Institution

National Gallery of Art

US Capitol

E. Capitol St.

useum istory

gton ent

THE MALL

Jefferson Dr.

National Air and Space Museum

SMITHSONIAN

Independence Ave.

Maryland Ave.

Canal St.

C St.

L'ENFANT PLAZA

D St.

D St.

FEDERAL CENTER SW

CAPITOL SOUTH

E St.

New Jersey Ave.

Southwest Fwy.

G St.

Virginia Ave.

Francis Case Memorial Bridge

0		500 yards
0		500 meters

SW ◀▶ SE

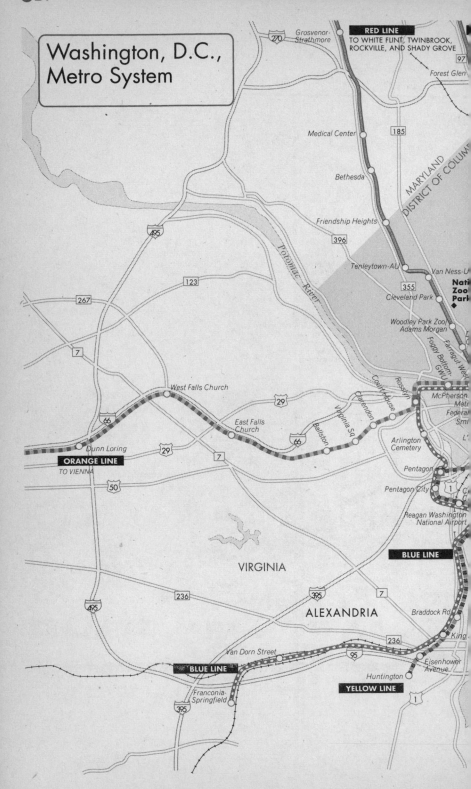

Washington, D.C., Metro System

RED LINE
TO WHITE FLINT, TWINBROOK,
ROCKVILLE, AND SHADY GROVE

Grosvenor-Strathmore

Forest Glen

Medical Center

Bethesda

Friendship Heights

Tenleytown-AU

Van Ness-U

Nati
Zoo
Park

Cleveland Park

Woodley Park Zoo/
Adams Morgan

Foggy Bottom-
GWU

Rosslyn

Court House

McPherson
Metr
Federal
Smi

Farragut West

West Falls Church

Clarendon

Virginia Sq

Arlington
Cemetery

East Falls Church

Ballston

Dunn Loring

Pentagon

ORANGE LINE
TO VIENNA

Pentagon City

Reagan Washington
National Airport

BLUE LINE

VIRGINIA

ALEXANDRIA

Braddock Rd

King

Van Dorn Street

BLUE LINE

Eisenhower
Avenue

Franconia-
Springfield

Huntington

YELLOW LINE

MARYLAND

DISTRICT OF COLUM

Potomac River

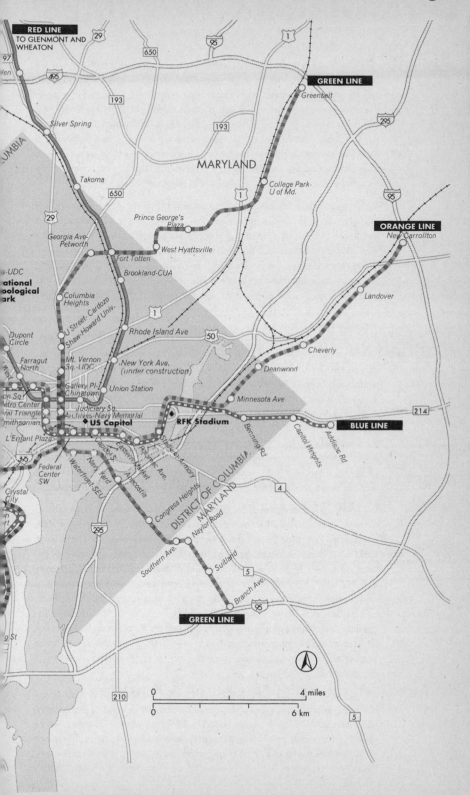

RED LINE
TO GLENMONT AND WHEATON

GREEN LINE

Greenbelt

MARYLAND

Silver Spring

Takoma

College Park-
U of Md.

ORANGE LINE
New Carrollton

Prince George's
Plaza

Georgia Ave-
Petworth

West Hyattsville

Landover

Fort Totten

Brookland-CUA

-UDC

ational
oological
ark

Columbia
Heights

U Street-Cardozo
Shaw-Howard Univ.

Rhode Island Ave

Cheverly

Dupont
Circle

Farragut
North

Mt. Vernon
Sq.-UDC

New York Ave.
(under construction)

Deanwood

Gallery Pl-
Chinatown

Union Station

Minnesota Ave

BLUE LINE

etro Center
ral Triangle
mithsonian

Judiciary Sq.

Archives-Navy Memorial

US Capitol

RFK Stadium

Benning Rd

Capitol Heights

Addison Rd

L'Enfant Plaza

Navy Yard

Eastern Market

Stadium-Armory

Federal
Center
SW

Waterfront-SEU

Anacostia

Congress Heights

DISTRICT OF COLUMBIA

Crystal
City

MARYLAND

Naylor Road

g St

Southern Ave.

Suitland

GREEN LINE

Branch Ave.

0   4 miles

0   6 km

PLEASURES & PASTIMES

Architecture
Washington National Cathedral, the sixth-largest cathedral in the world, will impress even the most hardened cathedral viewer with its Gothic arches, flying buttresses, and imaginative stonework. The open interior of the massive redbrick National Building Museum, one of the city's great spaces, has been the site of inaugural balls for more than 100 years. The eight central Corinthian columns are the largest in the world, rising to a height of 75 feet. This enormous edifice, once called the Pension Building, is devoted to architecture and the building arts. It outlines the capital's architectural history, from its monuments to its residential neighborhoods.

Washington has many buildings of architectural interest, filled with exquisite period furniture, draperies, and china. The DAR Museum has 33 period rooms decorated in styles representative of various U.S. states as well as a 33,000-item collection of colonial and Federal silver, china, porcelain, and glass. The Renwick Gallery, the Smithsonian's museum of American decorative arts, has exquisitely designed and crafted utilitarian items, as well as objects created out of such traditional crafts materials as fiber and glass. Displays include Shaker furniture, enamel jewelry, and the opulently furnished Victorian-style Grand Salon.

Canals, Rapids & Cliffs
C&O Canal National Historical Park has one end in Georgetown and the other in Cumberland, Maryland. Canoeists paddle the canal's "watered" sections, while hikers and bikers use the 12-foot-wide towpath that runs alongside it. In warmer months you can hop a mule-drawn canal boat for an hour-long trip. You can also walk over a series of bridges to Olmsted Island in the middle of the Potomac for a spectacular view of the falls. The waters of the Potomac River cascade dramatically over a steep jagged gorge, creating the spectacle that gives the 800-acre Great Falls Park its name. Hikers follow trails, climbers scale the rock faces leading down to the water, and experienced kayakers shoot the rapids.

Great Gardens
The paths of the Constitution Gardens wind through groves of trees, around a lake—a memorial to signers of the Declaration of Independence—and past the sobering Vietnam Veterans Memorial. Dumbarton Oaks's 10 acres of formal gardens, in a variety of styles, are some of the loveliest in the city. The grounds of Marjorie Merriweather Post's Georgian-style Hillwood House have a French-style parterre (ornamental garden), a rose garden, a Japanese garden, paths through azaleas and rhododendrons, and a greenhouse containing 5,000 orchids. Exotic water lilies, lotuses, hyacinths, and other water-loving plants thrive at the Kenilworth Aquatic Gardens, a sanctuary of quiet pools and marshy flats. The gardens are home to a variety of wetland animals, including turtles, frogs, muskrats, and some 40 species of birds.

Military Memorials, Museums & Parades
Washington is a fitting spot to honor those who served and fell in defense of our country. More than 200,000 veterans are buried in Arlington National Cemetery, where you can trace America's history through the aftermath of its battles. The guard at the Tomb of the Unknowns is changed frequently with a precise ceremony. Near the cemetery is the U.S. Marine Corps War Memorial, where there's

a sunset parade in summer. Next to the statue that serves as the Navy Memorial is the Naval Heritage Center, where you can look up the service records of navy veterans.

Some Washington monuments may move you to tears—notably the Vietnam Veterans Memorial, a quietly shining black granite wall, half sunk into the lawn and inscribed with the names of more than 58,000. Daniel Chester French's statue of Abraham Lincoln keeps vigil from inside his Parthenon-like memorial, providing solace in troubled moments to Washingtonians great and small.

Official Washington

Political buffs will want to visit Capitol Hill and the Supreme Court. Because the terror attacks of 2001 led the White House, the FBI Building, and other popular buildings to close their doors temporarily to many visitors, you may want to supplement your tour of exteriors with visits to related museums connected to statesmanship and nation-building, including the International Spy Museum.

The soul of the nation takes tangible form in stone as you walk the streets south, east, and west of Union Station, the grand beaux arts rail terminal that even today welcomes thousands to Washington. The city's power grid is focused on the White House. Across the street and a heartbeat away is the vice president's office in the Old Executive Office Building, which resembles a giant wedding cake. A close look at the glorious Capitol, which has a grand and inspiring rotunda, is almost mandatory.

World-Class Museums

Even if D.C. were not the seat of the U.S. government, the city would remain first class for its museums alone. So often their names include "national," implying that the very best of America is inside. Many are part of the Smithsonian Institution. In its National Air and Space Museum you can touch a moon rock and see numerous spiky spacecraft. The Smithsonian's National Museum of Natural History houses more than 120 million specimens, plus an insect zoo. The National Museum of American History has George Washington's false teeth and the original Star-Spangled Banner. Elsewhere, the city's art makes the senses reel. Among the masterworks in the National Gallery of Art is Leonardo's pensive *Ginevra de'Benci*. The cozier Phillips Collection houses Bonnard's *Open Window* and other treasures. Close by but a world away in mood is the U.S. Holocaust Memorial Museum, a shattering testament to man's inhumanity to man.

FODOR'S CHOICE

Fodor's Choice
★

The sights, restaurants, hotels, and other travel experiences on these pages are our editors' top picks—our Fodor's Choices. They're the best of their type in the area covered by the book—not to be missed and always worth your time. In the destination chapters that follow, you will find all the details.

LODGING

$$$$	**Hotel Monaco,** Downtown. This relative newcomer, inside what was once the Tariff Commission Building, is whimsically decorated and gaining a reputation for attentive service.
$$–$$$$	**George Washington University Inn,** Foggy Bottom. The centrally located George Washington has rooms furnished in a colonial style.
$$–$$$$	**Hotel Madera,** Dupont Circle. Among embassies and other hotels, the Madera has a high proportion of rooms with great views.
$–$$$	**Doubletree Guest Suites,** Downtown. Close to the Kennedy Center and Georgetown and with a pool on the roof, this all-suites hotel is a great place to relax and to plan your next outing.

BUDGET LODGING

$–$$$	**Holiday Inn Select Bethesda.** A handy place to spend the night, the Holiday Inn provides shuttle service to the National Institutes of Health and the Naval Medical Center.
$–$$	**Hotel Tabard Inn,** Dupont Circle. Lived-in and far from glitzy, the Tabard is made up of three Victorian houses. The rooms here vary widely in size and price.
¢–$	**Woodley Park Guest House.** Close to the Woodley Park Metro stop, this bed-and-breakfast is friendly and attractive.

RESTAURANTS

$$$$	**Citronelle,** Georgetown. In this embodiment of California chic, the kitchen's glass front lets you watch the chefs scurrying to and fro as they prepare, say, leek-encrusted salmon steak topped by a crisp fried-potato lattice.
$$$$	**Inn at Little Washington,** Washington, VA. Since 1978 Patrick O'Connell and his partner have been turning out New American food that wins raves from all and sundry.
$$$$	**L'Auberge Chez François,** Great Falls, VA. The soufflés and the other traditional fare are worth a trip to this large Alsation restaurant.
$$$–$$$$	**Galileo,** Downtown. A spacious, popular Italian restaurant, Galileo makes everything in house, from bread sticks to mozzarella.
$$–$$$$	**Jaleo,** Downtown and Bethesda, VA. At this lively Spanish bistro you can make a meal out of the many hot and cold tapas (appetizer-size dishes). The entrées, including grilled fish and paella, are equally good.
$$–$$$$	**Zaytinya,** Downtown. The ingredients and techniques of Turkey, Greece, and Lebanon come through in little dishes served at this popular Downtown spot.

BUDGET RESTAURANTS

$–$$	**Sushi-Ko,** Georgetown. Look to the daily specials when you're ordering at the best Japanese eatery in D.C.—the dishes are always creative.
¢–$	**Ben's Chili Bowl,** U St. corridor. This longtime veteran of U Street serves some of the best chili dogs you're likely to come across. Extra-late hours make it that much more easy to fit a "half-smoke" or a regular in—and maybe even some cheese fries.
¢–$	**Pizzeria Paradiso.** Both the Dupont Circle original and the larger Georgetown branch serve well executed, delicious Italian basics, including *panini*, salads, and gelato as well as the pizza that's made them famous.

HISTORY

Capitol. Home of the Senate and the House of Representatives and reminiscent of the Roman Pantheon in design, the marble Capitol is an architectural marvel filled with frescoes and statues.

Georgetown University. The Gothic spires of Georgetown's older buildings make the country's oldest Jesuit school look medieval.

Mount Vernon. Here you can tour the plantation workshops and reconstructed slave quarters as well as the kitchen, the carriage house, the gardens, and the tomb of George and Martha Washington. The sweeping Potomac views are a bonus.

U.S. Naval Academy. Crisply uniformed midshipmen populate the 329 scenic acres of this institution, alongside the Severn River in Annapolis, Maryland.

Washington National Cathedral. Like its 14th-century counterparts, this 20th-century cathedral has a nave, flying buttresses, transepts, and vaults that were built stone by stone.

MONUMENTS

Franklin Delano Roosevelt Memorial. With its waterfalls, wide walkways, and inspiring messages, this rambling memorial is ideal for contemplation.

Jefferson Memorial. Jefferson always admired the Pantheon in Rome, so architect John Russell Pope drew from the same source when he designed this graceful memorial facing the Tidal Basin.

Lincoln Memorial. Many consider the Lincoln Memorial the city's most inspiring monument. The somber Daniel Chester French statue of the seated president, in the center, gazes out over the Reflecting Pool.

Tomb of the Unknowns. At this moving shrine in Arlington National Cemetery, soldiers from the Army's U.S. 3rd Infantry keep watch around the clock.

Vietnam Veterans Memorial. Maya Lin's black-granite memorial is a stark tribute to those who died in this war.

MUSEUMS

National Air and Space Museum. At the most-visited museum in the world, you'll find displays of the airplanes and spacecraft that have made history. The flight-simulating IMAX movies are not to be missed.

National Gallery of Art. John Russell Pope's domed West Building and I. M. Pei's East Building house one of the world's finest collections of paintings, sculptures, and graphics.

Phillips Collection. It's as beloved for its well-known impressionist and modern paintings as for its relaxed atmosphere and knowledgeable guards.

U.S. Holocaust Memorial Museum. In a clear and often graphic fashion, this moving museum tells the stories of the 11 million people killed by the Nazis.

SMART TRAVEL TIPS

Finding out about your destination before you leave home means you won't squander time organizing everyday minutiae once you've arrived. You'll be more streetwise when you hit the ground as well, better prepared to explore the aspects of Washington, D.C., that drew you here in the first place. The organizations in this section can provide information to supplement this guide; contact them for up-to-the-minute details, and consult the A to Z sections in the Side Trips chapter for facts on the various topics as they relate to the areas around D.C. Happy landings!

ADDRESSES

Although it may not appear so at first glance, there's a system to addresses in D.C., albeit one that's a bit confusing. The city is divided into the four quadrants of a compass (NW, NE, SE, SW), with the U.S. Capitol building at the center. If someone tells you to meet them at 6th and G, ask them to specify the quadrant, because there are actually four different 6th and G intersections (one per quadrant). Within each quadrant, numbered streets run north–south, and lettered streets run east–west (the letter J is skipped). The streets form a fairly simple grid—for instance, 900 G Street NW is the intersection of 9th and G streets in the NW quadrant of the city. Likewise, if you count the letters of the alphabet, skipping J, you can get a good approximation of an address for a numbered street or diagonal state-named avenue. For instance, 1200 Connecticut Avenue NW is close to M Street, M being the 12th letter of the alphabet if you skip J.

All the city avenues are named after U.S. states and run diagonally. If all that's too much to keep track of, you can usually find a helpful resident, police officer, or uniformed business district representative to lend a hand.

AIR TRAVEL TO & FROM WASHINGTON

BOOKING

When you book, **look for nonstop flights** and **remember that "direct" flights stop at least once.** Try to avoid connecting flights, which require a change of plane. Two airlines may operate a connecting flight jointly, so ask whether your airline operates every segment of the trip; you may find that the carrier you prefer flies you only part of the way. To find more booking tips and to check prices and make on-line flight reservations, log on to www.fodors.com.

CARRIERS

All major airlines fly into BWI, Ronald Reagan Washington National, and Dulles airports, except America West, which doesn't fly into Dulles.

Of the smaller airlines, Air Tran flies to Dulles and Midwest Express flies to National. Southwest has service to BWI.

▶ **Major Airlines Air Canada** ☎ 888/422-7533 ⊕ www.aircanada.ca. **America West** ☎ 800/235-9292 ⊕ www.americawest.com. **American** ☎ 800/433-7300 ⊕ www.aa.com. **Continental** ☎ 800/525-0280 ⊕ www.continental.com. **Delta** ☎ 800/221-1212 ⊕ www.delta.com. **Northwest** ☎ 800/225-2525 ⊕ www.nwa.com. **United** ☎ 800/241-6522 ⊕ www.united.com. **US Airways** ☎ 800/428-4322 ⊕ www.usairways.com.

▶ **Smaller Airlines Air Tran** ☎ 800/825-8538 ⊕ www.airtran.com. **Midwest Express** ☎ 800/452-2022 ⊕ www.midwestexpress.com. **Southwest** ☎ 800/435-9792 ⊕ www.southwest.com.

CHECK-IN & BOARDING

Always **find out your carrier's check-in policy.** Plan to arrive at the airport about two hours before your scheduled departure time for domestic flights and 2½ to 3 hours before international flights. You may need to arrive earlier if you're flying from one of the busier airports or during peak air-traffic times. To avoid delays at airport-security checkpoints, try not to wear any metal. Jewelry, belt and other buckles, steel-toe shoes, barrettes, and underwire bras are among the items that can set off detectors.

Assuming that not everyone with a ticket will show up, airlines routinely overbook planes. When everyone does, airlines ask for volunteers to give up their seats. In return, these volunteers usually get a several-hundred-dollar flight voucher, which can be used toward the purchase of another ticket, and are rebooked on the next flight out. If there are not enough volunteers, the airline must choose who will be denied boarding. The first to get bumped are passengers who checked in late and those flying on discounted tickets, so **get to the gate and check in as early as possible,** especially during peak periods.

Always **bring a government-issued photo I.D. to the airport;** even when it's not required, a passport is best.

CUTTING COSTS

The least expensive airfares to Washington, D.C., are priced for round-trip travel and must usually be purchased in advance. Airlines generally allow you to change your return date for a fee; most low-fare tickets, however, are nonrefundable. It's smart to **call a number of airlines and check the Internet;** when you are quoted a good price, **book it on the spot**—the same fare may not be available the next day, or even the next hour. Always **check different routings** and look into using alternate airports. Also, price off-peak flights, which may be significantly less expensive than others. Travel agents, especially low-fare specialists (⇨ Discounts & Deals), are helpful.

Consolidators are another good source. They buy tickets for scheduled flights at reduced rates from the airlines, then sell them at prices that beat the best fare available directly from the airlines. Sometimes you can even get your money back if you need to return the ticket. Carefully read the fine print detailing penalties for changes and cancellations, purchase the ticket with a credit card, and **confirm your consolidator reservation with the airline.**

When you **fly as a courier,** you trade your checked-luggage space for a ticket deeply subsidized by a courier service. There are restrictions on when you can book and how long you can stay. Some courier companies list with membership organizations, such as the Air Courier Association and the International Association of Air Travel Couriers; these require you to become a member before you can book a flight.

Many airlines, singly or in collaboration, offer discount air passes that allow foreigners to travel economically in a particular country or region. These visitor passes usually must be reserved and purchased before you leave home. Information about passes often can be found on most airlines' international Web pages, which tend to be aimed at travelers from outside the carrier's home country. Also, try typing the name of the pass into a search engine, or search for "pass" within the carrier's Web site.

▶ **Consolidators AirlineConsolidator.com** ☎ 888/468-5385 ⊕ www.airlineconsolidator.com,

for international tickets. **Best Fares** ☏ 800/576-8255 or 800/576-1600 🌐 www.bestfares.com, $59.90 annual membership. **Cheap Tickets** ☏ 800/377-1000 or 888/922-8849 🌐 www.cheaptickets.com. **Expedia** ☏ 800/397-3342 or 404/728-8787 🌐 www.expedia.com. **Hotwire** ☏ 866/468-9473 or 920/330-9418 🌐 www.hotwire.com. **Now Voyager Travel** ✉ 45 W. 21st St., 5th floor, New York, NY 10010 ☏ 212/459-1616 🖷 212/243-2711 🌐 www.nowvoyagertravel.com. **Onetravel.com** 🌐 www.onetravel.com. **Orbitz** ☏ 888/656-4546 🌐 www.orbitz.com. **Priceline.com** 🌐 www.priceline.com. **Travelocity** ☏ 888/709-5983, 877/282-2925 in Canada, 0870/111-7060 in the U.K. 🌐 www.travelocity.com.
🚩 Courier Resources **Air Courier Association/Cheaptrips.com** ☏ 800/282-1202 🌐 www.aircourier.org or www.cheaptrips.com; $29 annual membership. **International Association of Air Travel Couriers** ☏ 308/632-3273 🌐 www.courier.org; $45 annual membership.

ENJOYING THE FLIGHT

State your seat preference when purchasing your ticket, and then repeat it when you confirm and when you check in. For more legroom, you can request one of the few emergency-aisle seats at check-in, if you are capable of lifting at least 50 pounds—a Federal Aviation Administration requirement of passengers in these seats. Seats behind a bulkhead also offer more legroom, but they don't have under-seat storage. Don't sit in the row in front of the emergency aisle or in front of a bulkhead, where seats may not recline.

Ask the airline whether a snack or meal is served on the flight. If you have dietary concerns, **request special meals when booking.** These can be vegetarian, low-cholesterol, or kosher, for example. It's a good idea to pack some healthful snacks and a small (plastic) bottle of water in your carry-on bag. On long flights, try to maintain a normal routine, to help fight jet lag. At night, **get some sleep.** By day, **eat light meals, drink water** (not alcohol), and **move around the cabin** to stretch your legs. For additional jet-lag tips consult *Fodor's FYI: Travel Fit & Healthy* (available at bookstores everywhere).

Smoking policies vary from carrier to carrier. Many airlines prohibit smoking on all of their flights; others allow smoking only on certain routes or certain departures. Ask your carrier about its policy.

FLYING TIMES

A flight to D.C. from New York takes a little less than an hour. It's about 1½ hours from Chicago, 3 hours from Denver or from Dallas, and 5 hours from San Francisco. Those flying from London can expect a trip of about 6 hours, and it's an 18-hour flight from Sydney.

HOW TO COMPLAIN

If your baggage goes astray or your flight goes awry, complain right away. Most carriers require that you **file a claim immediately.** The Aviation Consumer Protection Division of the Department of Transportation publishes *Fly-Rights,* which discusses airlines and consumer issues and is available on-line. You can also find articles and information on mytravelrights.com, the Web site of the nonprofit Consumer Travel Rights Center.
🚩 Airline Complaints **Aviation Consumer Protection Division** ✉ U.S. Department of Transportation, C-75, Room 4107, 400 7th St. SW, Washington, DC 20590 ☏ 202/366-2220 🌐 airconsumer.ost.dot.gov. **Federal Aviation Administration Consumer Hotline** ✉ For inquiries: FAA, 800 Independence Ave. SW, Washington, DC 20591 ☏ 800/322-7873 🌐 www.faa.gov.

RECONFIRMING

Check the status of your flight before you leave for the airport. You can do this on your carrier's Web site, by linking to a flight-status checker (many Web booking services offer these), or by calling your carrier or travel agent.

AIRPORTS & TRANSFERS

The major gateways to D.C. are **Ronald Reagan Washington National Airport** (DCA), in Virginia, 4 mi south of downtown Washington; **Dulles International Airport** (IAD), 26 mi west of Washington; and **Baltimore-Washington International Airport** (BWI) in Maryland, about 30 mi to the northeast.
🚩 Airport Information **Baltimore-Washington International Airport** ☏ 410/859-7100 🌐 www.bwiairport.com. **Dulles International Airport** ☏ 703/572-2700 🌐 www.mwaa.com. **Ronald Reagan Washington National Airport** ☏ 703/417-8000 🌐 www.mwaa.com.

AIRPORT TRANSFERS

If you're coming into Ronald Reagan Washington National Airport, have little to carry, and are staying at a hotel near a subway stop, it makes sense to take the Metro. The station is within walking distance of the baggage claim area, but a free airport shuttle bus runs between the Metro station and Terminal A. The Metro ride downtown takes about 20 minutes and costs $1.20–$2, depending on the time of day and your end destination.

By bus: The Washington Flyer Coach Service provides a convenient link between Dulles Airport and the West Falls Church (VA) Metro station. The 20-minute ride is $8 one-way or $14 round-trip; buses run every half hour. Discounts are available for groups of 3 or more, people over age 55, and international students. All coaches are disabled-accessible. Fares may be paid with cash or credit card; children under age six ride free.

The Washington Metropolitan Area Transit Authority operates an express Metro bus service between Dulles and downtown.

Reagan National, Dulles, and BWI airports are served by SuperShuttle, which will take you to a specific hotel or residence. Make reservations at the ground transportation desk. Fares vary depending on the destination. The 20-minute ride from Reagan National to downtown averages $9–$13; the 45-minute ride from Dulles runs $22–$25; the 65-minute ride from BWI averages $28–$30; drivers accept major credit cards in addition to cash. The length of the ride varies depending on traffic and the number of stops that need to be made.

By private car: **Private Car** has two counters at BWI Airport and charges approximately $70 plus a 15% tip for up to four passengers traveling from there to downtown; or call ahead to have a car waiting for you at Reagan National (approximately $45 plus 15% tip) or Dulles (approximately $85 plus 15% tip). Reservations are a good idea.

By taxi: Expect to pay about $14 to get from Ronald Reagan National Airport to downtown, $50–$65 from Dulles, and $58–$65 from BWI. A $1.50 airport surcharge is added to the total at all airports. A $1 surcharge is added to the total for travel during rush hour. (Be aware that unscrupulous cabbies prey on out-of-

towners, so if the fare strikes you as astronomical, get the driver's name and cab number and threaten to call the D.C. Taxicab Commission.)

By train: Free shuttle buses carry passengers between airline terminals and the train station at BWI Airport. Amtrak and Maryland Rail Commuter Service (MARC) trains run between BWI and Washington's Union Station from around 6 AM to 10 PM. The cost of the 30-minute ride is $20–$32 on an Amtrak train and $5 on a MARC train, which only runs on weekdays.

? Taxis & Shuttles **Amtrak** ☎ 800/872-7245 ⊕ www.amtrak.com. **D.C. Taxicab Commission** ☎ 202/645-6018. **Maryland Rail Commuter Service (MARC)** ☎ 800/325-7245 ⊕ www.mtamaryland.com. **SuperShuttle** ☎ 800/258-3826 or 202/296-6662 ⊕ www.supershuttle.com. **Washington Flyer** ☎ 888/927-4359 or 703/572-8400 ⊕ www.washfly.com. **Washington Metropolitan Area Transit Authority (WMATA)** ☎ 202/637-7000; 202/638-3780 TDD ⊕ www.metroopensdoors.com.

BIKE TRAVEL

D.C. is a fairly bike-friendly city. Except for the ire provoked by the sometimes reckless local bike messengers, cars and bicycles coexist peacefully. It's best to avoid riding during rush hour, if possible. On weekends and holidays, sections of Rock Creek Park are closed to motorists, making it safe for bikers, rollerbladers, and walkers alike.

During normal non-rush hours (all times except weekdays 7 AM–10 AM and 4 PM–7 PM) the Metro system allows riders to bring bicycles aboard any car of the train. Bicycles are not allowed on the Metro on days when large crowds are expected, such as the Fourth of July. In addition, the fronts of all Metro buses are equipped with racks that can hold up to two bikes. The racks may be used for no additional charge throughout the day, including rush hour (riders are responsible for securing and removing their own bikes).

The Washington Area Bicyclists Association has information on local bike laws, where to ride, and maps of bike trails on its Web site.

? Bike Maps **Washington Area Bicyclists Association** ☎ 202/628-2500 ⊕ www.waba.org.

BIKES IN FLIGHT

Most airlines accommodate bikes as luggage, provided they are dismantled and boxed; check with individual airlines about packing requirements. Some airlines sell bike boxes, which are often free at bike shops, for about $15 (bike bags can be considerably more expensive). International travelers often can substitute a bike for a piece of checked luggage at no charge; otherwise, the cost is about $100. U.S. and Canadian airlines charge $40–$80 each way.

BUS TRAVEL TO & FROM WASHINGTON

Washington's Greyhound bus terminal, a major one for the company, is approximately four blocks north of Union Station.

PAYING

You can purchase your ticket 10 days in advance via the Internet, or pay for your ticket in the station before you board the bus. Greyhound accepts cash and all major credit cards.

🚌 Bus Information **Greyhound Ticket Center** ✉ 1005 1st. St. NE ☎ 202/289-5154; 800/229-9424 tickets, 800/229-9424 fares and schedules ⊕ www.greyhound.com.

BUS TRAVEL WITHIN WASHINGTON

The red, white, and blue Washington Metropolitan Area Transit Authority (WMATA) Metrobuses crisscross the city and nearby suburbs. Although most of the major monuments and museums are at or near a Metro rail station, some neighborhoods and popular sites, including Georgetown, the National Cathedral, and the National Zoo, are better reached by bus.

FARES & SCHEDULES

All bus rides within the District are $1.20. All-day passes are available on the bus for $3.

Complete bus and Metro maps for the metropolitan D.C. area, which note museums, monuments, theaters, and parks, can be purchased for $1.50 at the Metro Center or at map stores.

Free bus-to-bus transfers, good for two hours, are available on buses. In Metro stations rail-to-bus transfers must be picked up before boarding the train.

There's a transfer charge (35¢ on regular Metrobus routes and $1.65 on express routes) when boarding the bus. Transfers are free for senior citizens. There are no bus-to-rail transfers.

🚌 Bus Information **Metro Center rail station** ✉ 11th and G Sts. NW ☎ No phone. **Washington Metropolitan Area Transit Authority** ☎ 202/637-7000; 202/638-3780 TDD ⊕ www.wmata.com.

PAYING

Buses require either exact change or tokens available for purchase inside the Metro Center train station sales office, open weekdays from 7:30 AM to 6:30 PM.

BUSINESS HOURS

MUSEUMS & SIGHTS

Museums are usually open daily 10–5:30; some have later hours on Thursday. Many private museums are closed Monday or Tuesday, and some museums in government buildings are closed weekends. The Smithsonian often sets extended spring and summer hours for some of its museums.

SHOPS

Stores are generally open Monday–Saturday 10–6. Some have extended hours on Thursday and many open Sunday anywhere from 10 to noon and close at 5 or 6.

CAMERAS & PHOTOGRAPHY

With so much pomp and circumstance in D.C., there's no dearth of photo opportunities. But how do you make your pictures of oft-photographed memorials and ceremonies unique? When shooting structures, look at postcards to see what the pros have done. Snap a few shots from the same angle and with the same light as the commercial photos, and then add your own flourishes through different perspectives, juxtapositions, and light effects.

For monuments and buildings, take a few shots in which you zoom in on particular elements. Try to capture details with light coming from the side so they have more definition. Put your zoom lens away and experiment with a wide-angle lens for up-close (perhaps even upward) shots of building exteriors; look for dramatic lines and angles. Then step back and take a few straightforward, sweeping shots. For parades or ceremonies, arrive early and find a spot with clear sight lines (a hill, steps of a nearby building, a balcony). Zoom in on reactions in the crowd, particularly the expressions on children's faces. Try shooting distinctive uniforms or costumes; look for items in the procession that express its theme.

The *Kodak Guide to Shooting Great Travel Pictures* (available at bookstores everywhere) is loaded with tips.

F **Photo Help Kodak Information Center** ☎ 800/242-2424 ⊕ www.kodak.com.

EQUIPMENT PRECAUTIONS

Don't pack film and equipment in checked luggage, where it is much more susceptible to damage. X-ray machines used to view checked luggage are extremely powerful and therefore are likely to ruin your film. Try to **ask for hand inspection of film,** which becomes clouded after repeated exposure to airport X-ray machines, and **keep videotapes and computer disks away from metal detectors.** Always **keep film, tape, and computer disks out of the sun.** Carry an extra supply of batteries, and **be prepared to turn on your camera, camcorder, or laptop** to prove to airport security personnel that the device is real.

CAR RENTAL

Rates in Washington, D.C., begin at $31 a day and $110 a week for an economy car with air-conditioning, an automatic transmission, and unlimited mileage. This does not include airport facility fees or the tax on car rentals, which is 8%–11.5% depending on the place from which you're renting.

F **Major Agencies Alamo** ☎ 800/327-9633 ⊕ www.alamo.com. **Avis** ☎ 800/331-1212, 800/879-2847, or 800/272-5871 in Canada; 0870/606-0100 in the U.K.; 02/9353-9000 in Australia; 09/526-2847 in New Zealand ⊕ www.avis.com. **Budget** ☎ 800/527-0700; 0870/156-5656 in the U.K. ⊕ www.budget.com. **Dollar** ☎ 800/800-4000; 0124/622-0111 in the U.K., where it's affiliated with Sixt; 02/9223-1444 in Australia ⊕ www.dollar.com. **Hertz** ☎ 800/654-3131; 800/263-0600 in Canada; 0870/844-8844 in the U.K.; 02/9669-2444 in Australia; 09/256-8690 in New Zealand ⊕ www.hertz.com. **National Car Rental** ☎ 800/227-7368; 0870/600-6666 in the U.K. ⊕ www.nationalcar.com.

CUTTING COSTS

For a good deal, **book through a travel agent who will shop around.** Also, **price**

local car-rental companies—whose prices may be lower still, although their service and maintenance may not be as good as those of major rental agencies—and **research rates on the Internet.** Remember to ask about required deposits, cancellation penalties, and drop-off charges if you're planning to pick up the car in one city and leave it in another. If you're traveling during a holiday period, also make sure that a confirmed reservation guarantees you a car.

INSURANCE

When driving a rented car you are generally responsible for any damage to or loss of the vehicle. You also may be liable for any property damage or personal injury that you may cause while driving. Before you rent, see what coverage you already have under the terms of your personal auto-insurance policy and credit cards.

For about $9 to $25 a day, rental companies sell protection, known as a collision- or loss-damage waiver (CDW or LDW), that eliminates your liability for damage to the car; it's always optional and should never be automatically added to your bill. In most states you don't need a CDW if you have personal auto insurance or other liability insurance. However, **make sure you have enough coverage to pay for the car.** If you do not have auto insurance or an umbrella policy that covers damage to third parties, purchasing liability insurance and a CDW or LDW is highly recommended.

REQUIREMENTS & RESTRICTIONS

In Washington you must be 25 to rent a car, although some companies may allow those age 21–25 to rent after paying a surcharge. Employees of major corporations and military or government personnel on official business may also be able to rent a car even if they're under age 25.

SURCHARGES

Before you pick up a car in one city and leave it in another, **ask about drop-off charges or one-way service fees,** which can be substantial. Note, too, that some rental agencies charge extra if you return the car before the time specified in your contract. To avoid a hefty refueling fee, **fill the tank just before you turn in the car,** but be aware that gas stations near the rental outlet may overcharge. It's almost never a deal to buy the tank of gas that's in the car when you rent it; the understanding is that you'll return it empty, but some fuel usually remains. Surcharges may apply if you take the car outside the area approved by the rental agency. You'll pay extra for child seats (about $6 a day), which are compulsory for children under five, and usually for additional drivers (about $10 per day).

CAR TRAVEL

A car is often a drawback in Washington. Traffic is horrendous, especially at rush hours, and driving is often confusing, with many lanes and some entire streets changing direction suddenly during rush hour. Even longtime residents carry maps in their cars to help navigate confusing traffic circles and randomly arranged one-way streets. The traffic lights stymie some visitors; most lights don't hang down over the middle of the streets but stand at the sides of intersections.

EMERGENCY SERVICES

Dial 911 to report accidents on the road and to reach police, the highway patrol, or the fire department. For police nonemergencies, dial 311.

🚔 U.S. Park Police ☎ 202/619-7300.

GASOLINE

As a rule, gas stations are hard to find in the District, especially in the areas around Pennsylvania Avenue area and the National Mall. Gas also tends to be slightly higher in the District than it is in Maryland or Virginia.

LAY OF THE LAND

Interstate 95 skirts D.C. as part of the Beltway, the six- to eight-lane highway that encircles the city. The eastern half of the Beltway is labeled both I–95 and I–495; the western half is just I–495. If you're coming from the south, take I–95 to I–395 and cross the 14th Street Bridge to 14th Street in the District. From the north, stay on I–95 south. Take the exit to Washington, which will place you onto the Baltimore–Washington (B-W) Parkway heading south. The B-W Parkway will turn into New York Avenue, taking you into downtown Washington, D.C.

Interstate 66 approaches the city from the southwest. You can get downtown by taking I–66 across the Theodore Roosevelt Bridge to Constitution Avenue.

Interstate 270 approaches Washington from the northwest before hitting I–495. To get downtown, take I–495 east to Connecticut Avenue south, toward Chevy Chase.

PARKING

Parking in Washington is an adventure; the police are quick to tow away or immobilize with a "boot" any vehicle parked illegally. If you find you've been towed from a city street, call ☎ 202/727–5000 or log on to ⊕ www.dmv.washingtondc.gov. Since the city's most popular sights are within a short walk of a Metro station anyway, it's best to **leave your car at the hotel.** Touring by car is a good idea only for visiting sights in Maryland or Virginia.

Most of the outlying, suburban Metro stations have parking lots, though these fill quickly with city-bound commuters. If you plan to park in one of these lots, arrive early, armed with lots of quarters.

Private parking lots downtown often charge around $5 an hour and $20 a day. There's free, three-hour parking around the Mall on Jefferson, Madison, and Ohio drives, though these spots are almost always filled. You can park free—in some spots all day—in parking areas off Ohio Drive near the Jefferson Memorial and south of the Lincoln Memorial on Ohio Drive and West Basin Drive in West Potomac Park.

RULES OF THE ROAD

Always **strap children under a year old or under 20 pounds into approved rear-facing child-safety seats in the back seat.** In Washington, D.C., children weighing 20–40 pounds must also ride in a car seat in the back, although it may face the front. Children cannot sit in the front seat of a car until they are at least 4 years old and weigh over 80 pounds.

In D.C., you may turn right at a red light after stopping if there's no oncoming traffic. When in doubt, wait for the green. Be alert for one-way streets, "no left turn" intersections, and blocks closed to car traffic.

Although there's no specific law in Washington outlawing the use of handheld mobile phones while operating a vehicle, some drivers who have done so have been cited for "failure to pay full time and attention while operating a motor vehicle." Another action for which a driver could be cited under this law is applying makeup while driving.

Radar detectors are illegal in Washington, D.C., and Virginia.

During rush hour (6–9 AM and 4–7 PM), HOV (high-occupancy vehicles) lanes on I-395 and I-95 are reserved for cars with three or more persons. All the lanes of I-66 inside the beltway are reserved for cars carrying two or more during rush hour, as are some of the lanes on the Dulles Toll Road and on I-270.

CHILDREN IN WASHINGTON

Washington has many activities that appeal to the younger set. To get some ideas, consult the Friday *Washington Post* "Weekend" section. Its "Carousel" listings include information on plays, puppet shows, concerts, storytelling sessions, nature programs, and events at the Capital Children's Museum. *Washington Parent,* a free monthly available at many supermarkets and libraries, is another good source. Finally, *Fodor's Around Washington, D.C. with Kids* (available in bookstores everywhere) can help you plan your days together.

Also, don't forget to visit information desks. Many museums have exhibits designed for children and/or docents (trained guides) who conduct kid-friendly tours. In addition, many sights have special printed children's guides, allowing kids to take pencil in hand, for example, and go on "scavenger hunts" to pick out the shapes and patterns in modern artwork.

If you are renting a car, don't forget to **arrange for a car seat** when you reserve. For general advice about traveling with children, consult *Fodor's FYI: Travel with Your Baby* (available in bookstores everywhere). ⏺ Local Information **Washington Parent** ☎ 301/320-2321 ⊕ www.washingtonparent.com.

BABY-SITTING

Most large hotels and those with concierges can arrange baby-sitting (or even the opportunity to have sitters take your children sightseeing) with a D.C.-area child-care agency. These agencies perform in-depth interviews and background checks of all their sitters, and some provide references. Rates average about $15 an hour (usually with a four-hour minimum) for one child, with additional children about $1 more per hour. Some agencies charge more to sit for additional, nonrelated children; some also charge a daily fee of about $35 or more above and beyond the cost of the sitter. In addition, you may need to pay for the sitter's transportation and/or parking costs. Agencies can usually arrange last-minute child care, but advance notice is appreciated. Mothers' Aides Inc. counts teachers among its sitters. White House Nannies, in business since 1985, charges a $35 referral fee. ⏺ Agencies **Mothers' Aides Inc.** ⏺ 5618 Ox Rd., Suite B, Fairfax Station, VA 22039 ☎ 703/250-0700 ⊕ www.mothersaides.com. **White House Nannies** ✉ 7200 Wisconsin Ave., Suite 409, Bethesda, MD 20814 ☎ 301/652-8088 or 800/270-6266 ⊕ www.whitehousenannies.com.

FLYING

Experts agree that it's a good idea to use safety seats aloft for children weighing less than 40 pounds. Airlines set their own policies: if you use a safety seat, U.S. carriers usually require that the child be ticketed, even if he or she is young enough to ride free, because the seats must be strapped into regular seats. And even if you pay the full adult fare for the seat, it may be worth it, especially on longer trips. Do **check your airline's policy about using safety seats during takeoff and landing.** Safety seats are not allowed everywhere in the plane, so get your seat assignments as early as possible.

When reserving, request children's meals or a freestanding bassinet (not available at all airlines) if you need them. But note that bulkhead seats, where you must sit to use the bassinet, may lack an overhead bin or storage space on the floor.

SIGHTS & ATTRACTIONS

Places that are especially appealing to children are indicated by a rubber-duckie icon (🦆) in the margin.

CONCIERGES

Concierges, found in many hotels, can help you with theater tickets and dinner reservations: a good one with connections may be able to get you seats for a hot show or prime-time dinner reservations at the restaurant of the moment. You can also turn to your hotel's concierge for help with travel arrangements, sightseeing plans, services ranging from aromatherapy to zipper repair, and emergencies. **Always tip** a concierge who has been of assistance (⇨ Tipping).

CONSUMER PROTECTION

Whether you're shopping for gifts or purchasing travel services, **pay with a major credit card** whenever possible, so you can cancel payment or get reimbursed if there's a problem (and you can provide documentation). If you're doing business with a particular company for the first time, **contact your local Better Business Bureau and the attorney general's offices** in your state and (for U.S. businesses) the company's home state as well. Have any complaints been filed? Finally, if you're buying a package or tour, always **consider travel insurance** that includes default coverage (⇨ Insurance).

BBBs Better Business Bureau of Metro Washington DC and Eastern Pennsylvania ⊠ 1411 K St., NW, 10th fl., Washington, DC 20005-3404 ☎ 202/393-8000 🖷 202/393-1198 ⊕ www.mybbb.org. **Council of Better Business Bureaus** ⊠ 4200 Wilson Blvd., Suite 800, Arlington, VA 22203 ☎ 703/276-0100 🖷 703/525-8277 ⊕ www.bbb.org.

CUSTOMS & DUTIES

IN AUSTRALIA

Australian residents who are 18 or older may bring home A$400 worth of souvenirs and gifts (including jewelry), 250 cigarettes or 250 grams of cigars or other tobacco products, and 1,125 ml of alcohol (including wine, beer, and spirits). Residents under 18 may bring back A$200 worth of goods. Members of the same family traveling together may pool their allowances. Prohibited items include meat products. Seeds, plants, and fruits need to be declared upon arrival.

Australian Customs Service 🖉 Regional Director, Box 8, Sydney, NSW 2001 ☎ 02/9213-2000 or 1300/363263; 02/9364-7222 or 1800/803-006 quarantine-inquiry line 🖷 02/9213-4043 ⊕ www.customs.gov.au.

IN CANADA

Canadian residents who have been out of Canada for at least seven days may bring in C$750 worth of goods duty-free. If you've been away fewer than seven days but more than 48 hours, the duty-free allowance drops to C$200. If your trip lasts 24 to 48 hours, the allowance is C$50. You may not pool allowances with family members. Goods claimed under the C$750 exemption may follow you by mail; those claimed under the lesser exemptions must accompany you. Alcohol and tobacco products may be included in the seven-day and 48-hour exemptions but not in the 24-hour exemption. If you meet the age requirements of the province or territory through which you reenter Canada, you may bring in, duty-free, 1.5 liters of wine or 1.14 liters (40 imperial ounces) of liquor or 24 12-ounce cans or bottles of beer or ale. Also, if you meet the local age requirement for tobacco products, you may bring in, duty-free, 200 cigarettes and 50 cigars. Check ahead of time with the Canada Customs and Revenue Agency or the Department of Agriculture for policies regarding meat products, seeds, plants, and fruits.

You may send an unlimited number of gifts (only one gift per recipient, however) worth up to C$60 each duty-free to Canada. Label the package UNSOLICITED GIFT—VALUE UNDER $60. Alcohol and tobacco are excluded.

Canada Customs and Revenue Agency ⊠ 2265 St. Laurent Blvd., Ottawa, Ontario K1G 4K3 ☎ 800/461-9999, 204/983-3500, or 506/636-5064 ⊕ www.ccra.gc.ca.

IN NEW ZEALAND

All homeward-bound residents may bring back NZ$700 worth of souvenirs and gifts; passengers may not pool their allowances, and children can claim only the concession on goods intended for their own use. For those 17 or older, the duty-free allowance also includes 4.5 liters of wine or beer; one 1,125-ml bottle of spirits; and either 200 cigarettes, 250 grams of tobacco, 50 cigars, or a combination of the three up to 250 grams. Meat products, seeds, plants, and fruits must be declared upon arrival to the Agricultural Services Department.

New Zealand Customs ⊠ Head office: The Customhouse, 17–21 Whitmore St., Box 2218, Wellington ☎ 09/300-5399 or 0800/428-786 ⊕ www.customs.govt.nz.

IN THE U.K.

From countries outside the European Union, including the United States, you may bring home, duty-free, 200 cigarettes or 50 cigars; 1 liter of spirits or 2 liters of fortified or sparkling wine or liqueurs; 2 liters of still table wine; 60 ml of perfume; 250 ml of toilet water; plus £145 worth of other goods, including gifts and souvenirs. Prohibited items include meat products, seeds, plants, and fruits.

🔢 **HM Customs and Excise** ✉ Portcullis House, 21 Cowbridge Rd. E, Cardiff CF11 9SS ☎ 0845/010-9000 or 0208/929-0152; 0208/929-6731 or 0208/910-3602 complaints ⊕ www.hmce.gov.uk.

DISABILITIES & ACCESSIBILITY

The Metro has excellent facilities for visitors with vision and hearing impairments or mobility problems. Virtually all streets have wide, level sidewalks with curb cuts, though in Georgetown the brick-paved terrain can be bumpy. Most museums and monuments are accessible to visitors using wheelchairs.

The Smithsonian publishes an access guide to all its museums; "Dial-a-Museum" lists museum hours and daily activities. At all Smithsonian museums wheelchairs are available for use free of charge and on a first-come, first-served basis.

LODGING

Despite the Americans with Disabilities Act, the definition of accessibility seems to differ from hotel to hotel. Some properties may be accessible by ADA standards for people with mobility problems but not for people with hearing or vision impairments, for example.

If you have mobility problems, ask for the lowest floor on which accessible services are offered. If you have a hearing impairment, check whether the hotel has devices to alert you visually to the ring of the telephone, a knock at the door, and a fire/emergency alarm. Some hotels provide these devices without charge. Discuss your needs with hotel personnel if this equipment isn't available, so that a staff member can personally alert you in the event of an emergency.

If you're bringing a guide dog, get authorization ahead of time and write down the name of the person with whom you spoke.

RESERVATIONS

When discussing accessibility with an operator or reservations agent, **ask hard questions.** Are there any stairs, inside *or* out? Are there grab bars next to the toilet *and* in the shower/tub? How wide is the doorway to the room? To the bathroom? For the most extensive facilities meeting the latest legal specifications, **opt for newer accommodations.** If you reserve through a toll-free number, consider also calling the hotel's local number to confirm the information from the central reservations office. Get confirmation in writing when you can.

SIGHTS & ATTRACTIONS

You can expect that all federal buildings, museums, and sites will be completely accessible. To check the accessibility of a place you plan to visit, head to the Web site DisabilityGuide.org, which covers the Washington metro area. The site covers such issues as accessible entrances, rest rooms, water fountains, and telephones; permit-only parking spaces; elevators; and accommodations for people with hearing and visual impairments. The organization also publishes a printed version of its guide.

🔢 **Complaints Aviation Consumer Protection Division** (⇨ Air Travel) for airline-related problems. **Departmental Office of Civil Rights** ✉ For general inquiries, U.S. Department of Transportation, S-30, 400 7th St. SW, Room 10215, Washington, DC 20590 ☎ 202/366-4648 🖷 202/366-9371 ⊕ www.dot.gov/ost/docr/index.htm. **Disability Rights Section** ✉ NYAV, U.S. Department of Justice, Civil Rights Division, 950 Pennsylvania Ave. NW, Washington, DC 20530 ☎ ADA information line 202/514-0301 or 800/514-0301; 202/514-0383 TTY; 800/514-0383 TTY ⊕ www.ada.gov. **U.S. Department of Transportation Hotline** ☎ For disability-related air-travel problems, 800/778-4838; 800/455-9880 TTY.

🔢 **Resources DisabilityGuide.org** ✉ 21618 Slidell Rd., Boyds, MD 20841 ☎ 301/528-8664 ⊕ www.disabilityguide.org. **Smithsonian** ☎ 202/357-2700; 202/357-2020 "Dial-a-Museum"; 202/357-1729 TDD ⊕ www.si.edu.

TRAVEL AGENCIES

In the United States, the Americans with Disabilities Act requires that travel firms serve the needs of all travelers. Some agencies specialize in working with people with disabilities.

🔢 Travelers with Mobility Problems **Access Adventures/B. Roberts Travel** ✉ 206 Chestnut Ridge

Rd., Scottsville, NY 14624 ☎ 585/889-9096 ⊕ www.brobertstravel.com ✉ dltravel@prodigy. net, run by a former physical-rehabilitation counselor. **Accessible Vans of America** ✉ 9 Spielman Rd., Fairfield, NJ 07004 ☎ 877/282-8267, 888/282-8267, 973/808-9709 reservations 🖷 973/808-9713 ⊕ www.accessiblevans.com. **CareVacations** ✉ No. 5, 5110-50 Ave., Leduc, Alberta, Canada, T9E 6V4 ☎ 780/986-6404 or 877/478-7827 🖷 780/986-8332 ⊕ www.carevacations.com, for group tours and cruise vacations. **Flying Wheels Travel** ✉ 143 W. Bridge St., Box 382, Owatonna, MN 55060 ☎ 507/451-5005 🖷 507/451-1685 ⊕ www. flyingwheelstravel.com.

▪ Travelers with Developmental Disabilities **Sprout** ✉ 893 Amsterdam Ave., New York, NY 10025 ☎ 212/222-9575 or 888/222-9575 🖷 212/222-9768 ⊕ www.gosprout.org.

DISCOUNTS & DEALS

Be a smart shopper and **compare all your options** before making decisions. A plane ticket bought with a promotional coupon from travel clubs, coupon books, and direct-mail offers or purchased on the Internet may not be cheaper than the least expensive fare from a discount ticket agency. And always keep in mind that what you get is just as important as what you save.

DISCOUNT RESERVATIONS

To save money, **look into discount reservations services** with Web sites and toll-free numbers, which use their buying power to get a better price on hotels, airline tickets (⇨ Air Travel), even car rentals. When booking a room, always **call the hotel's local toll-free number** (if one is available) rather than the central reservations number—you'll often get a better price. Always ask about special packages or corporate rates.

▪ Airline Tickets **Air 4 Less** ☎ 800/AIR4LESS, low-fare specialist.

▪ Hotel Rooms **Accommodations Express** ☎ 800/444-7666 or 800/277-1064 ⊕ www. accommodationsexpress.com. **Central Reservation Service (CRS)** ☎ 800/555-7555 or 800/548-3311 ⊕ www.crshotels.com. **Hotels.com** ☎ 800/246-8357 ⊕ www.hotels.com. **Quikbook** ☎ 800/789-9887 ⊕ www.quikbook.com. **RMC Travel** ☎ 800/245-5738 ⊕ www.rmcwebtravel.com. **Steigenberger Reservation Service** ☎ 800/223-5652 ⊕ www.srs-worldhotels.com. **Turbotrip.com** ☎ 800/473-7829 ⊕ www.turbotrip.com.

PACKAGE DEALS

Don't confuse packages and guided tours. When you buy a package, you travel on your own, just as though you had planned the trip yourself. Fly/drive packages, which combine airfare and car rental, are often a good deal. In cities, ask the local visitor's bureau about hotel packages that include tickets to major museum exhibits or other special events.

GAY & LESBIAN TRAVEL

There's a gay and lesbian presence in the Dupont Circle area as well as in Adams-Morgan, Mount Pleasant, Logan Circle, and Capitol Hill. Residents of the District tend to be tolerant, but the millions of visitors who come each year may not be; exercise good judgment. And despite all the political activism, gay Washingtonians have a reputation for being conservative, so something unobjectionable in San Francisco's Castro or New York's East Village might draw stares at the local bars, stores, and restaurants.

For details about the gay and lesbian scene, consult *Fodor's Gay Guide to the USA* (available in bookstores everywhere).

▪ Gay- & Lesbian-Friendly Travel Agencies **Different Roads Travel** ✉ 8383 Wilshire Blvd., Suite 520, Beverly Hills, CA 90211 ☎ 323/651-5557 or 800/429-8747 (Ext. 14 for both) 🖷 323/651-3678 ✉ lgernert@tzell.com. **Kennedy Travel** ✉ 130 W. 42nd St., Suite 401, New York, NY 10036 ☎ 212/840-8659, 800/237-7433 🖷 212/730-2269 ⊕ www. kennedytravel.com. **Now, Voyager** ✉ 4406 18th St., San Francisco, CA 94114 ☎ 415/626-1169 or 800/255-6951 🖷 415/626-8626 ⊕ www.nowvoyager. com. **Skylink Travel and Tour** ✉ 1455 N. Dutton Ave., Suite A, Santa Rosa, CA 95401 ☎ 707/546-9888 or 800/225-5759 🖷 707/636-0951; serving lesbian travelers.

HOLIDAYS

Washington officially observes only federal holidays: New Year's Day (Jan. 1); Martin Luther King Jr. Day (3rd Mon. in Jan.); Presidents' Day (3rd Mon. in Feb.); Memorial Day (last Mon. in May); Independence Day (July 4); Labor Day (1st Mon. in Sept.); Columbus Day (2nd Mon. in Sept.); Veterans' Day (Nov. 11); Thanksgiving Day (4th Thurs. in Nov.); and Christmas Day (Dec. 25).

INSURANCE

The most useful travel-insurance plan is a comprehensive policy that includes coverage for trip cancellation and interruption, default, trip delay, and medical expenses (with a waiver for preexisting conditions).

Without insurance you'll lose all or most of your money if you cancel your trip, regardless of the reason. Default insurance covers you if your tour operator, airline, or cruise line goes out of business. Trip-delay covers expenses that arise because of bad weather or mechanical delays. Study the fine print when comparing policies.

U.K. residents can buy a travel-insurance policy valid for most vacations taken during the year in which it's purchased (but check preexisting-condition coverage).

Always **buy travel policies directly from the insurance company**; if you buy them from a cruise line, airline, or tour operator that goes out of business you probably won't be covered for the agency or operator's default, a major risk. Before making any purchase, **review your existing health and home-owner's policies** to find what they cover away from home.

 Travel InsurersIn the U.S.: **Access America** ✉ 6600 W. Broad St., Richmond, VA 23230 ☎ 800/284-8300 🖶 804/673-1491 or 800/346-9265 ⊕ www.accessamerica.com. **Travel Guard International** ✉ 1145 Clark St., Stevens Point, WI 54481 ☎ 715/345-0505 or 800/826-1300 🖶 800/955-8785 ⊕ www.travelguard.com.

FOR INTERNATIONAL TRAVELERS

For information on customs restrictions, *see* Customs & Duties.

CAR RENTAL

When picking up a rental car, non-U.S. residents need a reservation voucher for any prepaid reservations that were made in the traveler's home country, a passport, a driver's license, and a travel policy that covers each driver.

CAR TRAVEL

In the D.C. area, gasoline costs $1.75–$2 a gallon. Stations are plentiful. Most stay open late (24 hours along large highways and in big cities), except in rural areas, where Sunday hours are limited and where you may drive long stretches without a refueling opportunity. Highways are well paved. Interstate highways—limited-access, multilane highways whose numbers are prefixed by "I–"—are the fastest routes. Interstates with three-digit numbers encircle urban areas, which may have other limited-access expressways, freeways, and parkways as well. Tolls may be levied on limited-access highways. So-called U.S. highways and state highways are not necessarily limited-access but may have several lanes.

Along larger highways, roadside stops with rest rooms, fast-food restaurants, and sundries stores are well spaced. State police and tow trucks patrol major highways and lend assistance. If your car breaks down on an interstate, pull onto the shoulder and wait for help, or have your passengers wait while you walk to an emergency phone (available in most states). If you carry a cell phone, dial *55, noting your location on the small green roadside mileage markers.

Driving in the United States is on the right. **Obey speed limits** posted along roads and highways. Watch for lower limits in small towns and on back roads. The District of Columbia requires front-seat passengers to wear seat belts. On weekdays between 6 and 10 AM and again between 4 and 7 PM **expect heavy traffic.** To encourage carpooling, some freeways have special lanes for so-called high-occupancy vehicles (HOV)—cars carrying more than one passenger.

Bookstores, gas stations, convenience stores, and rest stops sell maps (about $3) and multiregion road atlases (about $10).

CURRENCY

The dollar is the basic unit of U.S. currency. It has 100 cents. Coins are the copper penny (1¢); the silvery nickel (5¢), dime (10¢), quarter (25¢), and half-dollar (50¢); and the golden $1 coin, replacing a now-rare silver dollar. Bills are denominated $1, $5, $10, $20, $50, and $100, all green and identical in size; designs vary. In addition, you may come across a $2 bill, but the chances are slim. The exchange rate at this writing is US$1.65 per British pound, 0.73 per Canadian dollar, 0.65 per Australian dollar, and 0.58 per New Zealand dollar.

ELECTRICITY

The U.S. standard is AC, 110 volts/60 cycles. Plugs have two flat pins set parallel to each other.

EMBASSIES

▶ **Australia** ✉ 1601 Massachusetts Ave. NW ☎ 202/797-3000.
▶ **Canada** ✉ 501 Pennsylvania Ave. NW ☎ 202/682-1740.
▶ **New Zealand** ✉ 37 Observatory Circle NW ☎ 202/328-4800.
▶ **United Kingdom** ✉ 3100 Massachusetts Ave. NW ☎ 202/588-7800.

EMERGENCIES

For police, fire, or ambulance, **dial 911** (0 in rural areas).

INSURANCE

Britons and Australians need extra medical coverage when traveling overseas.
▶ **Insurance Information** In the U.K.: **Association of British Insurers** ✉ 51 Gresham St., London EC2V 7HQ ☎ 020/7600-3333 ⊟ 020/7696-8999 ⊕ www.abi.org.uk. In Australia: **Insurance Council of Australia** ✉ Insurance Enquiries and Complaints, Level 3, 56 Pitt St., Sydney, NSW 2000 ☎ 1300/363683 or 02/9251-4456 ⊟ 02/9251-4453 ⊕ www.iecltd.com.au. In Canada: **RBC Insurance** ✉ 6880 Financial Dr., Mississauga, Ontario L5N 7Y5 ☎ 800/565-3129 ⊟ 905/813-4704 ⊕ www.rbcinsurance.com. In New Zealand: **Insurance Council of New Zealand** ✉ Level 7, 111-115 Customhouse Quay, Box 474, Wellington ☎ 04/472-5230 ⊟ 04/473-3011 ⊕ www.icnz.org.nz.

MAIL & SHIPPING

You can buy stamps and aerograms and send letters and parcels in post offices. Stamp-dispensing machines can occasionally be found in airports, bus and train stations, office buildings, drugstores, and the like. You can also deposit mail in the stout, dark blue, steel bins at strategic locations everywhere and in the mail chutes of large buildings; pickup schedules are posted. You can deposit packages at public collection boxes as long as the parcels are affixed with proper postage and weigh less than one pound. Packages weighing one or more pounds must be taken to a post office or handed to a postal carrier.

For mail sent within the United States, you need a 37¢ stamp for first-class letters weighing up to 1 ounce (23¢ for each additional ounce) and 23¢ for postcards.

You pay 80¢ for 1 ounce airmail letters and 70¢ for airmail postcards to most other countries; to Canada and Mexico, you need a 60¢ stamp for a 1-ounce letter and 50¢ for a postcard. An aerogram—a single sheet of lightweight blue paper that folds into its own envelope, stamped for overseas airmail—costs 70¢.

To receive mail on the road, have it sent c/o General Delivery at your destination's main post office (use the correct five-digit ZIP code). You must pick up mail in person within 30 days and show a driver's license or passport.

PASSPORTS & VISAS

When traveling internationally, **carry your passport** even if you don't need one (it's always the best form of I.D.) and **make two photocopies of the data page** (one for someone at home and another for you, carried separately from your passport). If you lose your passport, promptly call the nearest embassy or consulate and the local police.

Visitor visas aren't necessary for Canadian or European Union citizens, or for citizens of Australia who are staying fewer than 90 days.
▶ **Australian Citizens Passports Australia** ☎ 131-232 ⊕ www.passports.gov.au. **U.S. Consulate General** ✉ MLC Centre, Level 59, 19-29 Martin Pl., Sydney, NSW 2000 ☎ 02/9373-9200; 1902/941-641 fee-based visa-inquiry line ⊕ www.usembassy-australia.state.gov/sydney.
▶ **Canadian Citizens Passport Office** ✉ To mail in applications: 200 Promenade du Portage, Hull, Québec J8X 4B7 ☎ 819/994-3500, 800/567-6868, 866/255-7655 TTY ⊕ www.ppt.gc.ca.
▶ **New Zealand Citizens New Zealand Passports Office** ✉ For applications and information, Level 3, Boulcott House, 47 Boulcott St., Wellington ☎ 0800/22-5050 or 04/474-8100 ⊕ www.passports.govt.nz. **Embassy of the United States** ✉ 29 Fitzherbert Terr., Thorndon, Wellington ☎ 04/462-6000 ⊕ usembassy.org.nz. **U.S. Consulate General** ✉ Citibank Bldg., 3rd fl., 23 Customs St. E, Auckland ☎ 09/303-2724 ⊕ usembassy.org.nz.
▶ **U.K. Citizens U.K. Passport Service** ☎ 0870/521-0410 ⊕ www.passport.gov.uk. **American Consulate General** ✉ Queen's House, 14 Queen St., Belfast, Northern Ireland BT1 6EQ ☎ 028/9032-8239 ⊟ 028/9024-8482 ⊕ www.usembassy.org.uk. **American Embassy** ✉ For visa and immigration information (enclose an SASE), Consular Information Unit, 24 Grosvenor Sq., London W1 1AE ✉ To submit an application via mail, Visa Branch,

5 Upper Grosvenor St., London W1A 2JB ☎ 09068/200-290 recorded visa information; 09055/444-546 operator service, both with per-minute charges; 0207/499-9000 main switchboard ⊕ www.usembassy.org.uk.

TELEPHONES

All U.S. telephone numbers consist of a three-digit area code and a seven-digit local number. Within many local calling areas, you dial only the seven-digit number. Within some area codes, you must dial "1" first for calls outside the local area. To call between area-code regions, dial "1" then all 10 digits; the same goes for calls to numbers prefixed by "800," "888," "866," and "877"—all toll free. For calls to numbers preceded by "900" you must pay—usually dearly.

For international calls, dial "011" followed by the country code and the local number. For help, dial "0" and ask for an overseas operator. The country code is 61 for Australia, 64 for New Zealand, 44 for the United Kingdom. Calling Canada is the same as calling within the United States. Most local phone books list country codes and U.S. area codes. The country code for the United States is 1.

For operator assistance, dial "0." To obtain someone's phone number, call directory assistance at 555-1212 or occasionally 411 (free at public phones). To have the person you're calling foot the bill, phone collect; dial "0" instead of "1" before the 10-digit number.

At pay phones, instructions often are posted. Usually you insert coins in a slot (usually 25¢–50¢ for local calls) and wait for a steady tone before dialing. When you call long-distance, the operator tells you how much to insert; prepaid phone cards, widely available in various denominations, are easier. Call the number on the back, punch in the card's personal identification number when prompted, then dial your number.

MAIL & SHIPPING

National Capitol Station is open 7 AM–midnight on weekdays and 7 AM–8 PM on weekends.

🚹 Post Offices **National Capitol Station** ✉ 2 Massachusetts Ave. NE 20002 ☎ 202/523-2368 ⊕ www.usps.gov.

MEDIA

NEWSPAPERS & MAGAZINES

Several publications have calendars of entertainment events. The *Washington Post* (⊕ www.washingtonpost.com) "Weekend" section comes out on Friday, and its "Guide to the Lively Arts" is printed daily. On Thursday, look for the *Washington Times* ⊕ www.washingtontimes.com "Weekend" section and the free weekly *Washington CityPaper* (⊕ www.washingtoncitypaper.com). Also consult the "Where & When" section in the monthly *Washingtonian* magazine (⊕ www.washingtonian.com)

RADIO & TELEVISION

WETA 90.9 plays classical music during the day and NPR and other news programming in the morning and evening. WAMU 88.5 FM has a public-radio format, with NPR programs and call-in shows. WPFW 89.3 FM, a noncommercial Pacifica station, broadcasts leftist news, jazz, and world music. WKYS 93.9 FM plays hip-hop and R&B. WMZQ 98.7 FM plays country. Mix 107.3 FM plays adult contemporary music. Z104.1 FM plays modern rock. WGMS 103.5 FM is a classical station. WTOP 1500 AM has news, traffic, and weather.

Washington's major TV stations are NBC 4 (WRC), ABC 7 (WJLA), CBS 9 (WUSA), Fox 5 (WTTG), News Channel 8 (a local 24-hour news channel), and two local PBS stations, channels 26 (WETA) and 22 (WMPT).

METRO TRAVEL

The WMATA provides bus and subway service in the District and in the Maryland and Virginia suburbs. The Metro, opened in 1976, is one of the country's cleanest and safest subway systems. It begins operation at 5:30 AM on weekdays and 8 AM on weekends. The Metro closes on Saturday and Sunday mornings at 2 AM and at midnight other days. On Saturday and Sunday mornings, some train service ends slightly before 2 AM, so you should plan to arrive at least 10 minutes before the last train is scheduled to leave. During the weekday rush hours (5:30–9:30 AM and 3–7 PM), trains come along every three to six minutes. At other times and on weekends and holidays, trains run about every 12–15 minutes.

FARES & SCHEDULES

The Metro's base fare is $1.20; the actual price you pay depends on the time of day and the distance traveled. Up to two children under age five ride free when accompanied by a paying passenger.

Buy your ticket at the Farecard machines; they accept coins and crisp $1, $5, $10, or $20 bills. If the machine spits your bill back out at you, try folding and unfolding it lengthwise before asking someone for help. The Farecard should be inserted into the turnstile to enter the platform. Make sure you **hang onto the card**—you'll need it to exit at your destination.

Some Washingtonians report that the Farecard's magnetic strip interferes with the strips on ATM cards and credit cards, so **keep the cards separated in your pocket or wallet.**

 Metro Information **Washington Metropolitan Area Transit Authority (WMATA)** 202/637-7000 or 202/628-8973; 202/638-3780 TTY; 202/962-1195 Lost and Found www.wmata.com.

MONEY MATTERS

Washington is an expensive city, one that's comparable to New York. On the other hand, many attractions, including most of the museums, are free.

A cup of coffee in D.C. costs $1 at a diner or $4 at an upscale café; a sandwich will set you back $4.50–$7. Taxi rides cost upward of $5 depending on your destination. Prices throughout this guide are given for adults. Substantially reduced fees are almost always available for children, students, and senior citizens. For information on taxes, *see* Taxes.

ATMS

Most ATMs in the Washington, D.C., area are linked to national networks that let you withdraw money from your checking account or take a cash advance from your credit card account for an additional fee. ATMs can be found at most banks, in many grocery stores, and in some major tourist attractions. For more information on ATM locations that can be accessed with your particular account, call the phone number found on the back of your ATM or debit card.

CREDIT CARDS

Throughout this guide, the following abbreviations are used: **AE**, American Express; **D**, Discover; **DC**, Diners Club; **MC**, MasterCard; and **V**, Visa.

 Reporting Lost Cards **American Express** 800/441-0519. **Diners Club** 800/234-6377. **Discover** 800/347-2683. **MasterCard** 800/622-7747. **Visa** 800/847-2911.

PACKING

In your carry-on luggage, **pack an extra pair of eyeglasses or contact lenses and enough of any medication** you take to last a few days longer than the entire trip. You may also ask your doctor to write a spare prescription using the drug's generic name, as brand names may vary from country to country. In luggage to be checked, **never pack prescription drugs, valuables, or undeveloped film.** And don't forget to carry with you the addresses of offices that handle refunds of lost traveler's checks. Check *Fodor's How to Pack* (available at on-line retailers and bookstores everywhere) for more tips.

To avoid customs and security delays, carry medications in their original packaging. Don't pack any sharp objects in your carry-on luggage, including knives of any size or material, scissors, and corkscrews, or anything else that might arouse suspicion.

To avoid having your checked luggage chosen for hand inspection, don't cram bags full. The U.S. Transportation Security Administration suggests packing shoes on top and placing personal items you don't want touched in clear plastic bags.

CHECKING LUGGAGE

You're allowed to carry aboard one bag and one personal article, such as a purse or a laptop computer. Make sure what you carry on fits under your seat or in the overhead bin. Get to the gate early, so you can board as soon as possible, before the overhead bins fill up.

Baggage allowances vary by carrier, destination, and ticket class. On international flights, you're usually allowed to check two bags weighing up to 70 pounds (32 kilograms) each, although a few airlines allow checked bags of up to 88 pounds (40 kilograms) in first class. Some international carriers don't allow more than 66 pounds (30 kilograms) per bag in business class and 44 pounds (20 kilograms) in economy. On domestic flights, the limit is usually 50 to 70 pounds (23 to 32 kilograms) per bag. In general, carry-on bags shouldn't exceed 40 pounds (18 kilograms). Most airlines won't accept bags that weigh more than 100 pounds (45 kilograms) on domestic or international flights. Check baggage restrictions with your carrier before you pack.

Airline liability for baggage is limited to $2,500 per person on flights within the United States. On international flights it amounts to $9.07 per pound or $20 per kilogram for checked baggage (roughly $640 per 70-pound bag), with a maximum of $634.90 per piece, and $400 per passenger for unchecked baggage. You can buy additional coverage at check-in for about $10 per $1,000 of coverage, but it often excludes a rather extensive list of items, shown on your airline ticket.

Before departure, **itemize your bags' contents** and their worth, and label the bags with your name, address, and phone number. (If you use your home address, cover it so potential thieves can't see it readily.) Include a label inside each bag and **pack a copy of your itinerary.** At check-in, **make sure each bag is correctly tagged** with the destination airport's three-letter code. Because some checked bags will be opened for hand inspection, the U.S. Transportation Security Administration recommends that you leave luggage unlocked or use the plastic locks offered at check-in. TSA screeners place an inspection notice inside searched bags, which are re-sealed with a special lock.

If your bag has been searched and contents are missing or damaged, file a claim with the TSA Consumer Response Center as soon as possible. If your bags arrive damaged or fail to arrive at all, file a written report with the airline before leaving the airport.

⚡ Complaints U.S. Transportation Security Administration Consumer Response Center ☎ 866/289-9673 ⊕ www.tsa.gov.

REST ROOMS

Rest rooms are available in hotels, restaurants, tourist attractions, and department stores. In upscale restaurants, ask before you enter.

SAFETY

D.C. is a fairly safe city, but as with any metropolitan area it's best to be alert and aware. Tourist areas and train stations are heavily patrolled by the city's numerous police affiliations. At night, stay in highly populated areas, and avoid dark streets and alleys. Panhandlers can be aggressive and may respond with verbal insults, but are otherwise usually harmless. If someone threatens you with violence for money, it's best to hand it over without a fight and seek police help later.

LOCAL SCAMS

The only likely scam you'll encounter in D.C. is an elaborate story from a panhandler. In order to evoke sympathy, a well-dressed panhandler may pretend to have lost his wallet and need money to get home or a woman may say she needs cab fare to take a sick child to the hospital. A simple, "I'm sorry," is usually enough to send them on their way, or you may suggest they call the police for help.

SENIOR-CITIZEN TRAVEL

To qualify for age-related discounts, **mention your senior-citizen status up front** when booking hotel reservations (not when checking out) and before you're seated in restaurants (not when paying the bill). Be sure to have identification on hand. When renting a car, ask about promotional car-rental discounts, which can be cheaper than senior-citizen rates.

⚡ Educational Programs Elderhostel ⊠ 11 Ave. de Lafayette, Boston, MA 02111-1746 ☎ 877/426-8056; 978/323-4141 international callers; 877/426-2167 TTY 📠 877/426-2166 ⊕ www.elderhostel.org. **Interhostel** ⊠ University of New Hampshire, 6 Garrison Ave., Durham, NH 03824 ☎ 603/862-1147 or 800/733-9753 📠 603/862-1113 ⊕ www.learn. unh.edu.

SIGHTSEEING TOURS

BICYCLE TOURS

Bike the Sites Tours has knowledgeable guides leading daily tours of 55 Washington landmarks; these tours are geared to the occasional exerciser. Bicycles, helmets, snacks, and water bottles are included. Prices are $40 for adults; $30 for children 12 and under. The national

Adventure Cycling Association offers regional tours.

🚲 **Adventure Cycling Association** ☎ 800/755-2453 ⊕ www.adventurecycling.org. **Bike the Sites Tours** ☎ 202/966-8662 ⊕ www.bikethesites.com.

BOAT TOURS

Capitol River Cruises offers 50-minute sightseeing tours aboard the *Nightingale* and *Nightingale II*, Great Lakes boats from the 1950s. Beverages and light snacks are available for purchase. Cruises board daily every hour on the hour beginning at 11 AM (April through October). Prices are $10 for adults and $5 for children (ages 3 to 12).

The enclosed boat called *Nina's Dandy* cruises up the Potomac to Georgetown. Lunch cruises board weekdays starting at 11 AM. Dinner cruises board daily at 6:30 PM. Prices are $33–$38 for lunch and $67.50–$80.50 for dinner.

From March through October, D.C. Ducks offers 90-minute tours in converted World War II amphibious vehicles. After an hour-long road tour of prominent sights, the tour moves from land to water, as the vehicle is piloted into the waters of the Potomac for a 30-minute boat's-eye view of the city. Tickets are $26 for adults, $13 for children ages 4 to 12, and free for those under 3.

Odyssey III, a long, sleek vessel specially built to fit under the Potomac's bridges, departs from the Gangplank Marina at 6th and Water streets SW. Lunch, dinner, or Saturday and Sunday brunch cruises are among the options. Tickets start at $36 and go up to $90. This upscale, glass-enclosed vessel serves elegant food; jackets are requested for men at dinner. The *Spirit of Washington* offers lunch and dinner cruises and sightseeing tours to Mount Vernon; prices range from $31 to $84 depending on the type of cruise and the time of year.

🚲 **Fees & Schedules Capitol River Cruises** ☎ 301/460-7447 or 800/405-5511 ⊕ www.capitolrivercruises.com. *Dandy* ✉ Prince St., between Duke and King Sts., Alexandria, VA ☎ 703/683-6076 or 703/683-6090 ⊕ www.dandydinnerboat.com. **D.C. Ducks** ☎ 202/832-9800 ⊕ www.historictours.com. *Odyssey III* ✉ 600 Water St. SW ☎ 202/488-6010 or 800/946-7245 ⊕ www.odysseycruises.com. *Spirit of Washington* ✉ Pier 4, 6th and Water Sts. SW ☎ 866/211-3811 ⊕ www.spiritcruises.com.

BUS TOURS

All About Town, Inc. has half-day, all-day, two-day, and twilight bus tours that drive by some sights and stop at others. Tours leave from various downtown locations and hotels. An all-day tour costs $36, a half-day tour costs $26, and a twilight tour costs $26.

Capital Entertainment Services offers guided sightseeing bus tours that focus on African-American history. Tours are $20 for a three-hour tour.

Gray Line's four-hour tour of Washington, Embassy Row, and Arlington National Cemetery leaves Union Station at 8:30 AM (late June–late October) and 2 PM (year-round; adults $30, children $15); tours of Mount Vernon and Alexandria depart at 8:30 AM (year-round) and 2 PM (late June–late October; adults $30, children $15). An all-day trip combining both tours leaves at 8:30 AM (year-round; adults $50, children $25).

The DC Heritage Tourism Coalition's bus tours are generally devoted to examining particular neighborhoods in depth rather than trying to cover the city all at once. Recent tours have includes "Duke Ellington's DC," a tour of the Shaw and U-Street area; and "Washington in the Civil War."

🚌 **Fees & Schedules All About Town, Inc.** ☎ 301/856-5556 ⊕ www.allabouttown.com ✉ aatc@aol.com. **Capital Entertainment Services** ✉ 3629 18th St. NE, Washington, DC 20018 ☎ 202/636-9203 ⊕ www.washington-dc-tours.com. **DC Heritage Tourism Coalition** ✉ 1250 H Street NW, 10th fl., Washington, DC 20005 ☎ 202/828-9255 ⊕ www.dcheritage.org. **Gray Line** ☎ 301/386-8300 or 800/862-1400 ⊕ www.graylinedc.com.

ORIENTATION TOURS

Old Town Trolley Tours, orange-and-green motorized trolleys, take in the main downtown sights and also head into Georgetown and the upper northwest. Tickets are $26 for adults and $13 for children. Tourmobile buses, authorized by the National Park Service, make 25 stops at more than 40 historical sites between the Capitol and Arlington National Cemetery. Tickets are $18 ($8 for children ages 3–11).

🚌 **Fees & Schedules Old Town Trolley Tours** ☎ 202/832-9800 ⊕ www.historictours.com. **Tourmobile** ☎ 202/554-5100 or 888/868-7707 ⊕ www.tourmobile.com.

PRIVATE GUIDES

Private tours can be arranged through the Guide Service of Washington and A Tour de Force. Sonny Odom offers custom photography tours.

F Fees & Schedules **Guide Service of Washington** ⊠ 733 15th St. NW, Suite 1040, Washington, DC 20005 ☎ 202/628-2842 ⊕ www.dctourguides.com. **Sonny Odom** ⊠ 2420F S. Walter Reed Dr., Arlington, VA 22206 ☎ 703/379-1633 ⊕ www. sonnyodom.photoreflect.com. **A Tour de Force** ⌂ Box 2782, Washington, DC 20013 ☎ 703/525-2948 ⊕ www.atourdeforce.com.

SPECIAL-INTEREST TOURS

Special tours of some government buildings can be arranged through your representative's or senator's office. Limited numbers of these so-called VIP tickets are available, so **plan up to six months in advance of your trip.**

Tours of the *Washington Post* are conducted on Mondays; reservations are required two to six weeks in advance.

Gross National Product's Scandal Tours, led by members of the GNP comedy troupe, last two hours and cover scandals from George Washington to George Bush. Held year-round, the tours cost $30 per person; reservations are required.

F Fees & Schedules **Bureau of Engraving and Printing** ⊠ 14th and C Sts. SW ☎ 202/874-2330 or 866/874-2330 ⊕ www.moneyfactory.com. **DC Heritage Tourism Coalition** ☎ 202/661-7581 ⊕ www. dcheritage.org. **Gross National Product's Scandal Tours** ☎ 202/783-7212 ⊕ www.gnpcomedy.com. **State Department Diplomatic Reception Rooms** ⊠ 23rd and C Sts. NW ☎ 202/647-3241; 202/736-4474 TDD. **Voice of America** ⊠ 330 Independence Ave. SW ☎ 202/619-3919 ⊕ www.voa.gov. **Washington, D.C., Post Office** ⊠ Brentwood Rd. NE between Rhode Island and New York Aves. ☎ 202/636-2148. *The Washington Post* ⊠ 1150 15th St. NW ☎ 202/334-7969 ⊕ www.washpost.com.

WALKING TOURS

Guided walks and bus tours of neighborhoods in Washington and communities outside the city are routinely offered by the Smithsonian Resident Associates Program; advance tickets are required. Tour D.C. specializes in walking tours of Georgetown and Dupont Circle/Embassy Row, covering historical topics such as the Civil War and the underground railroad and featuring the Kennedys' Georgetown. Anecdotal History Tours leads tours in Georgetown, Adams-Morgan, Capitol Hill to the White House, as well as tours of the Lincoln assassination sites and the homes of former presidents.

The DC Heritage Tourism Coalition's guided walking tours cover the history and architecture of neighborhoods from the southwest waterfront to points much farther north: "Before Harlem, There Was U Street," for instance, takes you back to the days when U Street was Washington's "Black Broadway." The self-guided "Civil War to Civil Rights: Downtown Heritage Trail" highlights historic sites with markers.

F Fees & Schedules **Anecdotal History Tours** ⊠ 9009 Paddock La., Potomac, MD 20854 ☎ 301/294-9514 ⊕ www.dcsightseeing.com. **DC Heritage Tourism Coalition** ⊠ 1250 H Street NW, 10th fl., Washington, DC 20005 ☎ 202/828-9255 ⊕ www. dcheritage.org. **National Park Service** ⊠ 1100 Ohio Dr. SW, Washington, DC 20242 ☎ 202/619-7222 ⊕ www.nps.gov. **Smithsonian Resident Associates Program** ☎ 202/357-3030 ⊕ www. residentassociates.org. **Tour D.C.** ⊠ 1912 Glen Ross Rd., Silver Spring, MD 20910 ☎ 301/588-8999 ⊕ www.tourdc.com.

STUDENTS IN WASHINGTON

F I.D.s & Services **STA Travel** ⊠ 10 Downing St., New York, NY 10014 ☎ 212/627-3111, 800/777-0112 24-hr service center ☎ 212/627-3387 ⊕ www.sta. com. **Travel Cuts** ⊠ 187 College St., Toronto, Ontario M5T 1P7, Canada ☎ 800/592-2887 in the U.S., 416/979-2406 or 866/246-9762 in Canada ☎ 416/979-8167 ⊕ www.travelcuts.com.

TAXES

Area hotel taxes are 14.5% in Washington, 12% in Maryland, and 9.75% in Virginia.

SALES TAX

Sales tax is 5.75% in D.C., 5% in Maryland, and 3.5% in Virginia.

TAXIS

You can hail a taxi on the street just about anywhere in the city. However, you will probably have to phone for a cab if you find yourself in a more residential area.

Taxis in the District are not metered; they operate instead on a zone system. **Before you set off, ask your cab driver how much the fare will be.** The basic single rate for traveling within one zone is $4. There's an extra $1.50 charge for each additional passenger and a $1 surcharge during the 7–9:30 AM and 4–6:30 PM rush hours. Bulky suitcases are charged at a higher rate, and a $1.50 surcharge is tacked on when you phone for a cab. Maryland and Virginia taxis are metered but are not allowed to take passengers between points in D.C.

⌗ Taxi Companies Diamond Cab ☎ 202/332–6200. **Taxi Transportation** ☎ 202/398–0512 is an affiliation of 14 cab companies. **Yellow Cab** ☎ 202/544–1212.

TIME

Washington, D.C., is in the eastern time zone. It's 3 hours ahead of Los Angeles, 1 hour ahead of Chicago, 5 hours behind London, and 15 hours behind Sydney.

TIPPING

At restaurants a 15% tip is standard for waiters; up to 20% may be expected at more expensive establishments. The same goes for taxi drivers, bartenders, and hairdressers. Coat-check operators usually expect $1–$2; bellhops and porters should get 50¢–$1 per bag; hotel maids in upscale hotels should get about 4%–5% of the pre-tax room rate per day of your stay.

On package tours, conductors and drivers usually get $10 per day from the group as a whole; check whether this has already been figured into your cost. For local sightseeing tours, you may individually tip the driver-guide a few dollars if he or she has been helpful or informative. Ushers in theaters, museum guides, and gas station attendants do not expect tips.

A concierge typically receives a tip of $5 to $10, with an additional gratuity for special services or favors.

TOURS & PACKAGES

Because everything is prearranged on a prepackaged tour or independent vacation, you spend less time planning—and often get it all at a good price.

BOOKING WITH AN AGENT

Travel agents are excellent resources. But it's a good idea to collect brochures from several agencies, as some agents' suggestions may be influenced by relationships with tour and package firms that reward

them for volume sales. If you have a special interest, find an agent with expertise in that area; the American Society of Travel Agents (ASTA; ⇨ Travel Agencies) has a database of specialists worldwide. You can log on to the group's Web site to find an ASTA travel agent in your neighborhood.

Make sure your travel agent knows the accommodations and other services of the place being recommended. Ask about the hotel's location, room size, beds, and whether it has a pool, room service, or programs for children, if you care about these. Has your agent been there in person or sent others whom you can contact?

Do some homework on your own, too: local tourism boards can provide information about lesser-known and small-niche operators, some of which may sell only direct.

BUYER BEWARE

Each year consumers are stranded or lose their money when tour operators—even large ones with excellent reputations—go out of business. So **check out the operator.** Ask several travel agents about its reputation, and try to **book with a company that has a consumer-protection program.** (Look for information in the company's brochure.) In the United States, members of the National Tour Association and the United States Tour Operators Association are required to set aside funds to cover payments and travel arrangements in the event that the company defaults. It's also a good idea to choose a company that participates in the American Society of Travel Agents' Tour Operator Program; ASTA will act as mediator in any disputes between you and your tour operator.

Remember that the more your package or tour includes, the better you can predict the ultimate cost of your vacation. Make sure you know exactly what is covered, and **beware of hidden costs.** Are taxes, tips, and transfers included? Entertainment and excursions? These can add up.

⌗ Tour-Operator Recommendations American Society of Travel Agents (⇨ Travel Agencies). **National Tour Association (NTA)** ✉ 546 E. Main St., Lexington, KY 40508 ☎ 859/226–4444 or 800/682–8886 ⊟ 859/226–4404 ⊕ www.ntaonline.com. **United States Tour Operators Association (USTOA)** ✉ 275 Madison Ave., Suite 2014, New York, NY 10016 ☎ 212/599–6599 ⊟ 212/599–6744 ⊕ www.ustoa.com.

TRAIN TRAVEL

More than 80 trains a day arrive at Washington, D.C.'s Union Station. Acela, Amtrak's high-speed service, travels from D.C. to New York in 2½ hours and from D.C. to Boston in 6½ hours.

FARES & SCHEDULES

Amtrak tickets and reservations are available at Amtrak stations, by telephone, through travel agents, or on-line. Amtrak schedule and fare information can be found at Union Station as well as on-line. **⌚ Train Information** Amtrak ☎ 800/872-7245 ⊕ www.amtrak.com. **MARC** ☎ 800/325-7245 ⊕ www.mtamaryland.com. **Union Station** ✉ 50 Massachusetts Ave. NE ☎ 202/371-9441 ⊕ www. unionstationdc.com. **Washington Metropolitan Area Transit Authority (WMATA)** ☎ 202/637-7000 or 202/638-3780; 202/628-8973 TDD ⊕ www. wmata.com.

RESERVATIONS

Amtrak has both reserved and unreserved trains available. If you plan to travel during peak times, such as a Friday night or near a holiday, you'll need to **get a reservation and a ticket in advance.** Some trains at nonpeak times are unreserved, with seats assigned on a first-come, first-served basis.

TRAVEL AGENCIES

A good travel agent puts your needs first. Look for an agency that has been in business at least five years, emphasizes customer service, and has someone on staff who specializes in your destination. In addition, **make sure the agency belongs to a professional trade organization.** The American Society of Travel Agents (ASTA)—the largest and most influential in the field with more than 20,000 members in some 140 countries—maintains and enforces a strict code of ethics and will step in to help mediate any agent-client disputes involving ASTA members if necessary. ASTA (whose motto is "Without a travel agent, you're on your own") also maintains a Web site that includes a directory of agents. (If a travel agency is also acting as your tour operator, *see* Buyer Beware *in* Tours & Packages.) **⌚ Local Agent Referrals** American Society of Travel Agents (ASTA) ✉ 1101 King St., Suite 200, Alexandria, VA 22314 ☎ 703/739-2782; 800/965-2782 24-hr hot line ⎙ 703/739-3268 ⊕ www.

astanet.com. **Association of British Travel Agents** ✉ 68-71 Newman St., London W1T 3AH ☎ 020/7637-2444 ⎙ 020/7637-0713 ⊕ www.abta.com. **Association of Canadian Travel Agencies** ✉ 130 Albert St., Suite 1705, Ottawa, Ontario K1P 5G4 ☎ 613/237-3657 ⎙ 613/237-7052 ⊕ www.acta.ca. **Australian Federation of Travel Agents** ✉ Level 3, 309 Pitt St., Sydney, NSW 2000 ☎ 02/9264-3299 ⎙ 02/9264-1085 ⊕ www.afta.com.au. **Travel Agents' Association of New Zealand** ✉ Level 5, Tourism and Travel House, 79 Boulcott St., Box 1888, Wellington 6001 ☎ 04/499-0104 ⎙ 04/499-0786 ⊕ www. taanz.org.nz.

VISITOR INFORMATION

Learn more about foreign destinations by checking government-issued travel advisories and country information. For a broader picture, consider information from more than one country.

The Washington, D.C., Convention and Tourism Corporation offers a free, 128-page publication, titled *The Official Visitors' Guide*, full of sightseeing tips, maps, and contacts. The Washington WMTA publishes a metro and bus-system guide.

The National Portrait Gallery and the Smithsonian American Art Museum are closed for renovations until July 2006. All Smithsonian museums and the National Zoo are open every day of the year except Christmas; admission is free. **⌚ Events & Attractions** National Park Service ☎ 202/619-7275 "Dial-A-Park" park information. **Smithsonian** ☎ 202/357-2700; 202/357-2020 "Dial-a-Museum"; 202/357-1729 TDD ⊕ www.si. edu. **White House Visitor Center** ✉ Baldrige Hall, Dept. of Commerce: 1450 S. Pennsylvania Ave. NW, Washington, DC 20230 ☎ 202/208-1631 ⊕ www.nps.gov/whho. **⌚ Tourist Information** D.C. Visitor Information Center ✉ Reagan Bldg., 1300 Pennsylvania Ave. NW, Washington, DC 20004 ☎ 202/328-4748 ⊕ www.dcvisit.com. **Washington, D.C., Convention and Tourism Corporation** ✉ 1212 New York Ave. NW, Suite 600, Washington, DC 20005 ☎ 202/789-7000 or 800/422-8644 ⊕ www.washington.org. **Washington MTA** ☎ 202/637-7000 ⊕ www. metroopensdoors.com. **⌚ Government Advisories** Australian Department of Foreign Affairs and Trade ☎ 02/6261-1299 Consular Travel Advice Faxback Service ⊕ www.dfat. gov.au. **Consular Affairs Bureau of Canada** ☎ 800/267-6788 or 613/944-6788 ⊕ www.voyage. gc.ca. **New Zealand Ministry of Foreign Affairs and Trade** ☎ 04/439-8000 ⊕ www.mft.govt.nz.

U.K. Foreign and Commonwealth Office ⊠ Travel Advice Unit, Consular Division, Old Admiralty Bldg., London SW1A 2PA ☎ 020/7008-0232 or 020/7008-0233 ⊕ www.fco.gov.uk/travel.

f National Parks **National Park Service (NPS)** ⊠ Office of Public Affairs, National Capital Region 1100 Ohio Dr. SW, Washington, DC 20242 ☎ 202/619-7222 ⊕ www.nps.gov.

f State Information **State of Maryland** ⊠ Office of Tourist Development, 217 E. Redwood St., 9th fl., Baltimore, MD 21202 ☎ 410/767-3400 or 800/634-7386 ⊕ www.mdisfun.org. **Virginia Tourism Corporation** ⊠ Headquarters: 901 E. Byrd St., Richmond, VA 23219 ☎ 804/786-4484 or 804/786-2051 ⊕ www.virginia.org ⊠ Walk-in office ⊠ 1629 K St. NW, Washington, DC 20006 ☎ 202/872-0523 or 800/934-9184.

WEB SITES

Do check out the World Wide Web when planning your trip. You'll find everything from weather forecasts to virtual tours of famous cities. Be sure to **visit Fodors.com**
(⊕ www.fodors.com), a complete travel-planning site. You can research prices and book plane tickets, hotel rooms, rental cars, vacation packages, and more. In addition, you can post your pressing questions in the Travel Talk section. Other planning tools include a currency converter and weather reports, and there are loads of links to travel resources.

The Library of Congress's site (⊕ www.cweb.loc.gov) covers current and upcoming exhibitions, visitor information, and vast, fascinating on-line exhibits. At the National Park Service, (⊕ www.cr.nps.gov/NR/travel/wash), the maps, photos, and concise but thorough descriptions take you beyond the obvious destinations. First-Gov's portal (⊕ www.firstgov.gov) takes you to national, state, and local government sites. At ⊕ www.vietvet.org, poems, photographs, and personal stories pay tribute to the Vietnam Veterans Memorial and the lives it memorializes.

EXPLORING WASHINGTON

1

FODOR'S CHOICE

Capitol, Capitol Hill

Franklin Delano Roosevelt Memorial, The Mall

Georgetown University, Georgetown

Jefferson Memorial, The Mall

Lincoln Memorial, The Mall

National Air and Space Museum, The Mall

National Gallery of Art, West Building, The Mall

Tomb of the Unknowns, Arlington, VA

United States Holocaust Memorial Museum, The Mall

Vietnam Veterans Memorial, The Mall

Washington National Cathedral, Cleveland Park

HIGHLY RECOMMENDED

Arlington National Cemetery, Arlington, VA

National Gallery of Art, East Building, The Mall

National Museum of Natural History, The Mall

Phillips Collection, Dupont Circle

Washington Monument, The Mall

White House

Updated by
Elizabeth A.
Whisler and
Karyn-Siobhan
Robinson

THE BYZANTINE WORKINGS of the federal government; the sound-bite–ready oratory of the well-groomed politician; the murky foreign policy pronouncements issued from Foggy Bottom: they all cause many Americans to cast a skeptical eye on anything that happens "inside the Beltway." Washingtonians take it all in stride, though, reminding themselves that, after all, those responsible for political hijinks don't come *from* Washington, they come *to* Washington. Besides, such ribbing is a small price to pay for living in a city whose charms extend far beyond the bureaucratic. World-class museums and art galleries (nearly all of them free), tree-shaded and flower-filled parks and gardens, bars and restaurants that benefit from a large and creative immigrant community, and nightlife that seems to get better with every passing year are as much a part of Washington as floor debates or filibusters.

This city, which calls to mind politicking, back-scratching, and delicate diplomatic maneuvering, is itself the result of a compromise. Tired of its nomadic existence after having set up shop in eight locations, Congress voted in 1785 to establish a permanent federal city. Northern lawmakers wanted the capital on the Delaware River, in the North; Southerners wanted it on the Potomac, in the South. A deal was struck when Virginia's Thomas Jefferson agreed to support the proposal that the federal government assume the war debts of the colonies if New York's Alexander Hamilton and other Northern legislators would agree to locate the capital on the banks of the Potomac. George Washington himself selected the site of the capital, a diamond-shape, 100-square-mi plot that encompassed the confluence of the Potomac and Anacostia rivers, not far from his estate at Mount Vernon. To give the young city a head start, Washington included the already thriving tobacco ports of Alexandria, Virginia, and Georgetown, Maryland, in the District of Columbia. In 1791, Pierre-Charles L'Enfant, a French engineer who had fought in the Revolution, created the classic plan for the city.

It took the Civil War—and every war thereafter—to energize the city, by attracting thousands of new residents and spurring building booms that extended the capital in all directions. Streets were paved in the 1870s, and the first streetcars ran in the 1880s. Memorials to famous Americans like Lincoln and Jefferson were built in the first decades of the 20th century, along with the massive Federal Triangle, a monument to thousands of less-famous government workers.

Despite the growth and the important role that African-Americans have played in Washington's history (black mathematician Benjamin Banneker surveyed the land with Pierre-Charles L'Enfant), this city continues to struggle for full racial and ethnic equality. It's a city of other unfortunate contrasts: citizens of the capital of the free world couldn't vote in a presidential election until 1964, weren't granted limited home rule until 1974, and are now represented in Congress by a single nonvoting delegate. Today many Washington automobile license plates are imprinted with the slogan TAXATION WITHOUT REPRESENTATION, protesting the district's lack of status in Congress. Homeless people sleep on steam grates next to multimillion-dollar government buildings. But violent crime, although it still exists, is down (as it is in many other big cities) from the drug-fueled violent days of the late 1980s and early 1990s. Although it's little consolation to those affected, most crime is restricted to neighborhoods far from the areas visited by tourists.

There's no denying that Washington, the world's first planned capital, is also one of its most beautiful. And although the federal government dominates many of the city's activities and buildings, there are places where you can leave politics behind. Washington is a city of vistas—

pleasant views that shift and change from block to block, a marriage of geometry and art. Unlike other large cities, Washington isn't dominated by skyscrapers, largely because in 1910 Congress passed a height-restrictions act to prevent federal monuments from being overshadowed by commercial construction. Its buildings stretch out gracefully and are never far from expanses of green. Like its main industry, politics, Washington's design is a constantly changing kaleidoscope that invites contemplation from all angles.

THE MALL

The Mall is the heart of almost every visitor's trip to Washington. With nearly a dozen museums ringing the expanse of green, it's the closest thing the capital has to a theme park (unless you count the federal government itself, which has uncharitably been called "Disneyland on the Potomac"). You may have to stand in an occasional line, but unlike the amusements at the real Disneyland, almost everything you'll see here is free. You may, however, need free, timed-entry tickets to some sites like the Washington Monument, the Capitol, and the Holocaust Museum. These are usually available at the museum information desk or by phone, for a service charge, from Ticketmaster (☎ 202/432–7328).

Of course, the Mall is more than just a front yard for these museums. Bounded on the north and south by Constitution and Independence avenues and on the east and west by 3rd and 14th streets, it's a picnicking park, a jogging path, an outdoor stage for festivals and fireworks, and America's town green. Nine of the Smithsonian Institution's fourteen D.C. museums lie within these boundaries.

It wasn't always this way. In the middle of the 19th century, horticulturist Andrew Jackson Downing took a stab at converting the Mall into a large, English-style garden, with carriageways curving through groves of trees and bushes. This was far from the "vast esplanade" L'Enfant had in mind, and by the dawn of the 20th century the Mall had become an eyesore. It was dotted with sheds and bisected by railroad tracks. There was even a railroad station at its eastern end.

In 1900 Senator James McMillan, chairman of the Committee on the District of Columbia, asked a distinguished group of architects and artists to come up with ways to improve Washington's park system. The McMillan Commission, which included architects Daniel Burnham and Charles McKim, landscape architect Frederick Law Olmsted, and sculptor Augustus Saint-Gaudens, didn't confine its recommendations to parks; its 1902 report would shape the way the entire capital looked for decades. The Mall received much of the group's attention and is its most stunning accomplishment. L'Enfant's plan was rediscovered; the sheds, railroad tracks, and carriageways were removed; and Washington finally had the monumental core it had been denied for so long.

Numbers in the text correspond to numbers in the margin and on The Mall map.

a good walk

Start your tour of the museums on the Mall in the **Smithsonian Institution Building** ❶▶ (also known as the Castle), where the Smithsonian Information Center can orient you and help you plan your time. Walk east on Jefferson Drive to the **Arts and Industries Building** ❷, which holds changing exhibits—mostly cultural—from the Smithsonian and other institutions. The **Hirshhorn Museum and Sculpture Garden** ❸, which exhibits modern and contemporary art and has outdoor sculpture gardens, is the next building to the east on Jefferson Drive.

Cleveland Park & the
National Zoo

Adams-Morgan

Upper
Massachusetts Ave.

Dupont Circle

Georgetown

Massachusetts Ave.

California St.

S St.

R St.

Decatur Pl.

R St.

Sheridan
Circle

Q St.

Dupont
Circle

Church St.

P St.

Scott
Circle

N St.

Rock Creek

M St.

29

M St.

New Hampshire Ave.

L St.

Washington
Circle

L St.

K St.

C&O Canal

White hurst Fwy.

Pennsylvania

The White
House Area

Francis Scott
Key Bridge

H St.

The Wh
Hous

Theodore
Roosevelt
Island

Virginia Ave.

G St.

F St.

E St.

D St.

C St.

The
Ellips

George Washington Memorial Pkwy.

Vietnam
Veterans
Memorial

Constitution Ave.

NW

Foggy Bottom

SW

50

Lincoln
Memorial

Reflecting Pool

George

Wn. St. Parkway

Arlington Memorial

Bridge

Independence Ave.

Kutz
Bridge

Tidal Basin

Lady Bird Johnson Park

Columbia
Island

West

Potomac Park

W. Basin Dr.

FDR
Memorial

Inlet
Bridge

Memorial Dr.

Potomac River

ARLINGTON
NATIONAL
CEMETERY

Arlington

VIRGINIA

To
Old Town
Alexandria

The Monuments

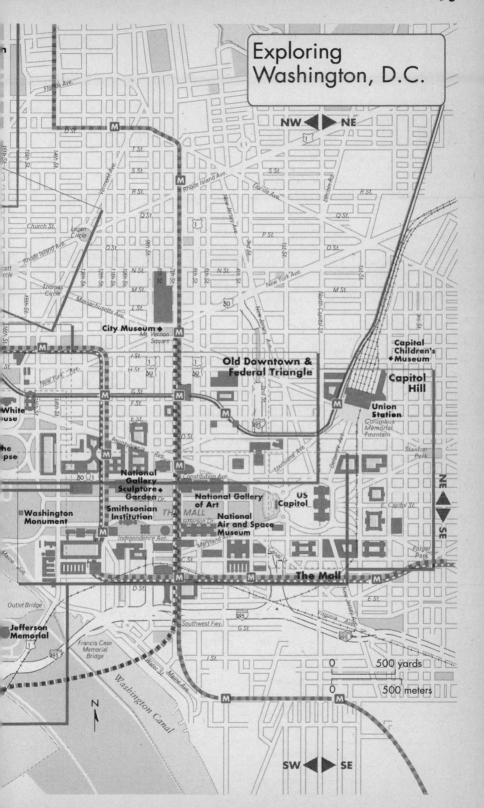

Exploring Washington, D.C.

NW ◄► NE

Florida Ave.

D St.

T St.

S St.

R St.

Rhode Island Ave.

Florida Ave.

Q St.

Church St.

Logan Circle

Q St.

P St.

New Jersey Ave.

3rd St.

1st St.

Q St.

Rhode Island Ave.

Thomas Circle

N St.

New York Ave.

Massachusetts Ave.

N St.

M St.

50

M St.

L St.

11th St.

10th St.

9th St.

8th St.

7th St.

6th St.

5th St.

4th St.

City Museum ◆

Mt. Vernon Square

Lincoln Rd.

R St.

Q St.

North Capitol St.

1st St.

Capital Children's ◆ Museum

Capitol Hill

I St.

Old Downtown & Federal Triangle

H St.

G St.

2nd St.

Union Station

Columbus Memorial Fountain

White House

New York Ave.

F St.

E St.

Pennsylvania Ave.

D St.

395

Louisiana Ave.

Delaware Ave.

Stanton Park

the pse

National Gallery Sculpture ◆ Garden

Madison Dr.

Constitution Ave.

US Capitol

E. Capitol St.

NE

SE

Washington Monument

Smithsonian Institution

THE MALL

National Gallery of Art

Jefferson Dr.

National Air and Space Museum

Maryland Ave.

Folger Park

Independence Ave.

C St.

Canal St.

The Mall

Outlet Bridge

D St.

E St.

Maine Ave.

Jefferson Memorial

395

Francis Case Memorial Bridge

Southwest Fwy.

395

G St.

Virginia Ave.

New Jersey Ave.

Water St.

Maine Ave.

I St.

0   500 yards

0   500 meters

N

Washington Canal

SW ◄► SE

CloseUp

THE CITY'S ARCHITECT

THE LIFE OF Pierre-Charles L'Enfant, architect of the city of Washington, has all the elements of a television miniseries: handsome, idealistic, 22-year-old Parisian volunteer in the American war for independence; rises to rank of major of engineers; becomes popular with fellow officers (and their wives); becomes toast-of-the-town architect in New York City; is selected by President George Washington to plan the new Federal City; gets fired amid controversy; dies bitter and broke; is vindicated posthumously.

L'Enfant was educated as an architect and engineer in France. At least two of his teachers profound influenced his career and, ultimately, his plan for Washington. He learned painting from his father, who was a battle-scene and landscape painter, and he studied landscape architecture with Andre LeNotre, who designed the gardens at Versailles. After Congress voted in 1785 to create a permanent Federal City, L'Enfant enthusiastically wrote to George Washington in 1789 with an offer to create a capital "magnificent enough to grace a great nation." He got the job, and arrived in Washington in 1791 to survey the land with black mathematician Benjamin Banneker.

L'Enfant's 1791 plan borrowed much from Versailles, with ceremonial circles and squares, a grid pattern of streets, and broad, diagonal avenues. He described Jenkins Hill, the gentle rise on which he intended to erect the "Congress House," as "a pedestal waiting for a monument." He envisioned the area west of the Congress House as a "Grand Avenue, 400 feet in breadth, and about a mile in length, bordered with gardens, ending in a slope from the houses on each side." (This is the area we now know as the Mall.)

Pennsylvania Avenue was to be a broad, grand, uninterrupted straight line running from the Capitol to the site chosen for the Executive Mansion. (The construction of the Treasury Building in 1836 ruined this straight sight line.) The area just north of the White House was to be part of "President's Park" (it was basically the president's front yard). But in yet another change to L'Enfant's plans, Thomas Jefferson, concerned that large, landscaped White House grounds weren't befitting that area be turned into a public park (now Lafayette Park).

Congress authorized a monument to George Washington in 1783. L'Enfant chose a site at the spot where a line drawn west from the Capitol crossed one drawn south from the White House. But marshy conditions at his original site required moving the position of the monument 100 yards southeast to firmer ground. A stone marker just north of the monument denotes L'Enfant's original site.

Though skillful at city planning, the headstrong L'Enfant had trouble with the game of politics. Things went slightly awry early on when L'Enfant had difficulty with the engravers of the city plan, they got worse when he expressed his resentment at dealing with Secretary of State Thomas Jefferson rather than the President, and they hit rock bottom when he enraged the city commissioners by tearing down a manor house being constructed where he had planned a street. The house belonged to Daniel Carroll—one of the commissioners. Only 11 months after his hire, L'Enfant was let go by Jefferson. L'Enfant continued to work as an architect, but when he died in 1825, he was poor and bitter, feeling he hadn't been recognized for his genius. His contributions to the city were finally recognized when, in 1909, amid much ceremony, his body was moved from his original burial site in Maryland to Arlington Cemetery at the request of the Washington, D.C., board of commissioners.

Cross 7th Street to reach the **National Air and Space Museum ❹**, one of the most visited museums in the world. Continue east on Jefferson Drive to 4th Street past the construction site bounded by 3rd and 4th streets and Independence Avenue and Jefferson Drive SW, where the Smithsonian's National Museum of the American Indian is scheduled to open in 2004; the planned 3-acre site of the National Garden is just beyond. The conservatory of the **U.S. Botanic Garden,** newly renovated, is on the right at Maryland Avenue and 1st Street SW. Walk north past the Capitol Reflecting Pool and cross 3rd Street to get to the **National Gallery of Art, East Building ❺**, which generally displays 19th- and 20th-century works. Next door, the **National Gallery of Art, West Building ❻** exhibits works from the 13th to the 20th centuries. If you're visiting in winter and are up for a little exercise, you can cross 7th Street and put on skates in the National Gallery Sculpture Garden Ice Rink; it's a cooling fountain in summer. Exit on Madison Drive to the **National Museum of Natural History ❼**, which has some 124 million objects in its collection. The next building to the west is the **National Museum of American History ❽**, which contains everything from Lincoln's death mask to Julia Child's kitchen.

Go south on 14th Street, crossing the Mall and Independence Avenue, to the **United States Holocaust Memorial Museum ❾**, a powerful reminder of humanity's capacity for evil. One block to the south is the **Bureau of Engraving and Printing ❿**, the source of all U.S. paper money. Head back north up 14th Street, cross Independence Avenue, and turn right, passing below overpasses connecting the two buildings of the **Department of Agriculture ⓫**. Just across 12th Street is the **Freer Gallery of Art ⓬**, which holds a collection of Asian treasures. East of the Freer, off Independence Avenue, are the winding brick paths and wooden benches of the 4-acre Enid Haupt Memorial Garden. The garden sits mostly on two underground museums, the **Arthur M. Sackler Gallery ⓭**, sister museum to the Freer, and the **National Museum of African Art ⓮**, with objects from hundreds of African cultures.

TIMING Don't try to see all the Mall's attractions in a day. Few people have the stamina for more than a half day of museum or gallery going at a time; children definitely don't. To avoid mental and physical exhaustion, try to devote at least two days to the Mall. Do the north side one day and the south the next. Or split your sightseeing on the Mall into a walking day, when you take in the scenic views and enjoy the architecture of each museum (the Mall museums are free, so a quick peek inside doesn't cost anything), and a museum day, when you go back to spend time with the exhibits that catch your interest. Afterward, plan something relaxing that doesn't require more walking—picnicking or getting a snack in one of the many museum cafeterias may make more sense than, say, shopping.

What to See

⓭ **Arthur M. Sackler Gallery.** When Charles Freer endowed the gallery that bears his name, he insisted on a few conditions: objects in the collection could not be loaned out, nor could objects from outside the collections be put on display. Because of the restrictions it was necessary to build a second, complementary museum to house the Asian art collection of Arthur M. Sackler, a wealthy medical researcher and publisher who began collecting Asian art as a student in the 1940s. Sackler allowed Smithsonian curators to select 1,000 items from his ample collection and pledged $4 million toward the construction of the museum. The collection includes works from China, Southeast Asia, Korea, Tibet, and Japan. Articles in the permanent collection include Chinese ritual bronzes, jade ornaments from the 3rd millennium BC, Persian manuscripts, and Indian paintings in gold, silver, lapis lazuli, and malachite. The lower level connects to the Freer Gallery of Art. ⊠ *1050 Independence Ave. SW, The Mall* ☎ *202/357–2700; 202/357–1729 TDD* ⊕ *www.asia.si. edu* ☜ *Free* ⊙ *Daily 10–5:30* Ⓜ *Smithsonian.*

② Arts and Industries Building. In 1876 Philadelphia hosted the U.S. International Exposition in honor of the nation's Centennial. After the festivities, scores of exhibitors donated their displays to the federal government. To house the objects that had suddenly come its way, the Smithsonian commissioned this redbrick-and-sandstone structure. Designed by Adolph Cluss, the building was originally called the United States National Museum, the name that's still engraved above the doorway. The second Smithsonian museum to be constructed, it was finished in 1881, just in time to host President James Garfield's inaugural ball.

The Arts and Industries Building's artifacts were eventually moved to other museums as the Smithsonian grew. It was restored to its original appearance and reopened during the Bicentennial celebrations. Today the building houses changing exhibits, a working fountain in the rotunda surrounded by a horticultural exhibit and geometric stencils in rich Victorian colors, a museum shop, and the Discovery Theater for children. The Smithsonian carousel is right outside. ⊠ *900 Jefferson Dr. SW, The Mall* ☎ *202/357–2700; 202/357–1500 Discovery Theater show times and ticket information; 202/357–1729 TDD* ⊕ *www.si.edu* ☜ *Free* ⊙ *Daily 10–5:30* Ⓜ *Smithsonian.*

⑩ Bureau of Engraving and Printing. The bureau turns out some 38 million dollars worth of currency a day. Paper money has been printed here since 1914, when the bureau relocated from the redbrick-towered Auditors Building at the corner of 14th Street and Independence Avenue. In addition to all the paper currency in the United States, stamps, military certificates, and presidential invitations are printed here, too. Tours usually last 35 minutes. From March through September, same-day timed-entry passes are issued starting at 8 AM at the Raoul Wallenberg Place SW entrance. ⊠ *14th and C Sts. SW, The Mall* ☎ *202/874–3188* ⊕ *www.bep.treas.gov* ☜ *Free* ⊙ *Sept.–May, weekdays 9–2; June–Aug., weekdays 9–2 and 5–6:30* Ⓜ *Smithsonian.*

⑪ Department of Agriculture. Although there's little of interest inside, this complex is too gargantuan to ignore. The offices of the governmental agency responsible for setting and carrying out the nation's agricultural policies are divided up between two buildings. The older white-marble building, on the north side of Independence Avenue, was begun in 1903. Its cornices on the north side depict forests as well as grains, flowers, and fruits—some of the vegetation the department keeps an eye on. The newer building (built between 1930 and 1936) south of Independence Avenue covers two city blocks. ⊠ *Independence Ave. between 12th and 14th Sts. SW, The Mall* ⊕ *www.usda.gov* Ⓜ *Smithsonian.*

⑫ Freer Gallery of Art. One of the world's finest collections of masterpieces from Asia, the Smithsonian's Freer Gallery of Art was made possible by an endowment from Detroit industrialist Charles L. Freer, who retired in 1900 and devoted the rest of his life to collecting art. Opened in 1923, four years after its benefactor's death, the collection includes more than 27,000 works of art from the Far and Near East. The Asian porcelains, Japanese screens, Chinese paintings and bronzes, Korean stoneware, Islamic manuscripts, and other items date from Neolithic times to the 20th century.

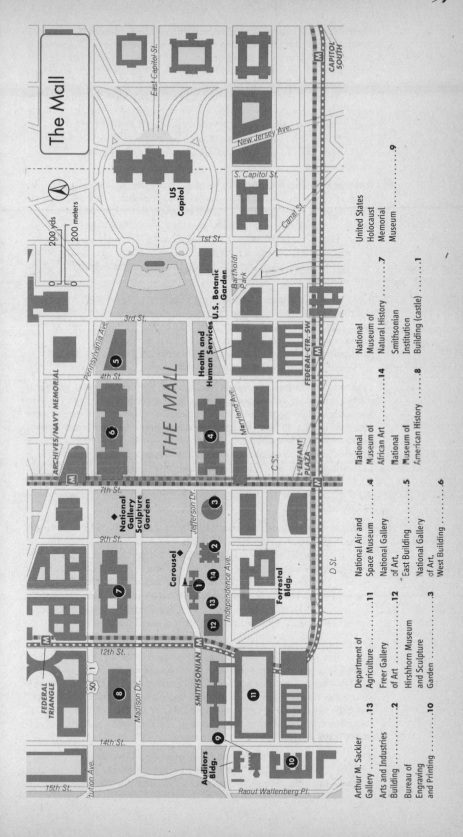

The Mall

US Capitol

THE MALL

National Gallery
Sculpture Garden

U.S. Botanic Garden

Health and Human Services

Auditors Bldg.

Forrestal Bldg.

FEDERAL TRIANGLE

ARCHIVES/NAVY MEMORIAL

SMITHSONIAN

FEDERAL CTR. SW

L'ENFANT PLAZA

CAPITOL SOUTH

Carousel

200 yds
200 meters

East Capitol St.
New Jersey Ave.
S. Capitol St.
Canal St.
1st St.
Bartholdi Park
3rd St.
Pennsylvania Ave.
4th St.
Maryland Ave.
C St.
7th St.
9th St.
Jefferson Dr.
Independence Ave.
D St.
12th St.
Madison Dr.
14th St.
15th St.
Raoul Wallenberg Pl.

Freer's friend James McNeill Whistler introduced him to Asian art, and the American painter is represented in the vast collection. On display is the Peacock Room, a blue-and-gold dining room decorated with painted leather, wood, and canvas. It was designed by Whistler for a British shipping magnate. Freer paid $30,000 for the entire room and moved it from London to the United States in 1904. The works of other American artists Freer felt were influenced by the Far East are also on display. A lower-level exhibition gallery connects the building to the Arthur M. Sackler Gallery. ⊠ *12th St. and Jefferson Dr. SW, The Mall* ☎ *202/357–2700; 202/357–1729 TDD* ⊕ *www.asia.si.edu* ⊠ *Free* ☉ *Daily 10–5:30* Ⓜ *Smithsonian.*

❸ **Hirshhorn Museum and Sculpture Garden.** Inside this striking round building from 1974 are some 12,000 works of art donated and bequeathed by Joseph H. Hirshhorn, a Latvian immigrant who made his fortune in this country running uranium mines. American artists such as Edward Hopper, Willem de Kooning, Andy Warhol, and Richard Diebenkorn are represented, as are modern European and Latin American masters, including Francis Bacon, Piet Mondrian, Jean Dubuffet, and Joan Miró.

The Hirshhorn's impressive sculpture collection is displayed throughout the museum, as well as on the lawns and granite surfaces of the fountain plaza. Indoors and out, the display includes works by Henry Moore, Alexander Calder, and Alberto Giacometti. Across Jefferson Drive, in the sunken Sculpture Garden, the highlights are Henri Matisse's *Backs I–IV* and Auguste Rodin's *Burghers of Calais.*

Dubbed "the Doughnut on the Mall" by its detractors, the cylindrical, reinforced-concrete building designed by Gordon Bunshaft is a fitting home for contemporary art. The severe exterior lines of the museum were softened a bit in 1992 when its plaza was relandscaped by James Urban. Grass and trees provide a soft backdrop for such work as Juan Munoz's bronze *Conversation Piece,* an ensemble of five beanbag-like figures. ⊠ *Independence Ave. and 7th St. SW, The Mall* ☎ *202/357–2700; 202/ 633–8043 TDD* ⊕ *www.hirshhorn.si.edu* ⊠ *Free* ☉ *Museum daily 10–5:30, sculpture garden 7:30–dusk* Ⓜ *Smithsonian or L'Enfant Plaza (Maryland Ave. exit).*

☾ ❹ **National Air and Space Museum.** Opened in 1976, this museum attracts
FodorsChoice more than 9 million people each year. Its 23 galleries tell the story of
★ aviation from the earliest human attempts at flight. Suspended from the ceiling like plastic models in a child's room are dozens of aircraft, including the *Wright 1903 Flyer,* which Wilbur Wright piloted over the sands of Kitty Hawk, North Carolina; Charles Lindbergh's *Spirit of St. Louis;* the X-1 rocket plane in which Chuck Yeager broke the sound barrier; and an X-15, the first aircraft to exceed Mach 6.

Other highlights include a backup model of the Skylab orbital workshop that you can walk through; the *Voyager,* the airplane that Dick Rutan and Jeana Yeager flew nonstop around the world in 1986; and the Lockheed Vega that Amelia Earhart piloted in 1932: it was the first solo transatlantic flight by a woman. You can also see a piece of the moon: a 4-billion-year-old slice of rock collected by *Apollo 17* astronauts. A permanent exhibition on the history of the scientific study of the universe is on the first floor.

Don't let long lines deter you from seeing a show in the museum's Lockheed Martin IMAX Theater. Films shown on the five-story-high screen—including the now-classic *To Fly!, Straight Up: Helicopters in*

Action, and *Space Station 3-D,* for which special viewing glasses are provided—employ swooping aerial scenes that make you feel as if you've
left the ground. Purchase tickets up to two weeks in advance or as soon
as you arrive (prices vary); then tour the museum. Upstairs, the Albert
Einstein Planetarium is the first in the world to employ all-dome digital technology to create a feeling of movement through space.

At the end of 2003, the **National Air and Space Museum Steven F. Udvar-
Hazy Center** will open at Washington Dulles International Airport in
northern Virginia. The facility will display more than 200 aircraft, 135
spacecraft, and rockets, satellites, and experimental flying machines. Many
of the functions of the **Paul E. Garber Facility** in suburban Maryland
have been transferred here. ⊠ *Independence Ave. and 6th St. SW, The
Mall* ☏ *202/357–1729; 202/357–1686 movie information; 202/357–
1729 TDD* ⊕ *www.nasm.si.edu* ✆ *Free, IMAX $7.50, planetarium $7.50*
☉ *Daily 10–5:30* Ⓜ *Smithsonian.*

need a
break?

A fast-food–style restaurant at the eastern end of the National Air
and Space Museum, the **Wright Place** (☏ 202/357–4700), is open
weekdays 7:30–5 and weekends 9–5 (if the museum is not yet open
for the day, enter through the glass doors at the east end of the
museum). It's operated by McDonald's, and although at first glance it
looks like the offerings are mostly burgers and fries, you can also find
pizza from Donato's, scrambled eggs and roast chicken from Boston
Market, and Caesar and green salad. Two ice cream kiosks are set
among the tables. On the second level is the upscale **Mezza Café**,
serving Lavazza coffee, muffins, scones, and fruit salad as well as
wine and beer. There's also a small Lavazza stand outside, on the
west terrace of the museum.

★ ☺ ⑤ **National Gallery of Art, East Building.** The atrium is dominated by Alexander Calder's mobile *Untitled,* and the galleries display modern and contemporary art, although you'll also find major temporary exhibitions
that span many years and artistic styles. Permanent works include Pablo
Picasso's *The Lovers* and *Family of Saltimbanques,* four of Matisse's
cutouts, Miró's *The Farm,* and Jackson Pollock's *Lavender Mist.*

The East Building opened in 1978 in response to the changing needs of
the National Gallery. The trapezoidal shape of the site prompted architect
I. M. Pei's dramatic approach: two interlocking spaces shaped like triangles provide room for galleries, auditoriums, and administrative offices. Although the building's triangles contrast sharply with the
symmetrical classical facade and gentle dome of the West Building, both
structures are constructed of pink marble from the same Tennessee
quarries. Despite its severe angularity, Pei's building is inviting. The axe-
blade-like southwest corner has been darkened and polished smooth by
thousands of hands irresistibly drawn to it.

To reach the East Building from the West Building, take the underground
concourse, lined with gift shops, a café, and a cafeteria. But to appreciate Pei's impressive, angular East Building, enter it from outside rather
than from underground. Exit the West Building through its eastern doors,
and cross 4th Street. (As you cross, look to the north: seeming to float
above the Doric columns and pediment of the D.C. Superior Court are
the green roof and redbrick pediment of the National Building Museum,
four blocks away.) ⊠ *Constitution Ave. between 3rd and 4th Sts. NW,
The Mall* ☏ *202/737–4215; 202/842–6176 TDD* ⊕ *www.nga.gov*
✆ *Free* ☉ *Mon.–Sat. 10–5, Sun. 11–6* Ⓜ *Archives/Navy Memorial.*

⑥ **National Gallery of Art, West Building.** The two buildings of the National
FodorsChoice Gallery hold one of the world's foremost collections of paintings,
★ sculptures, and graphics. If you want to view the museum's holdings
in (more or less) chronological order, it's best to start your exploration
in the West Building. The rotunda, with 24 marble columns surrounding a fountain topped with a statue of Mercury, sets the stage
for the masterpieces on display in more than 100 galleries. A tape-
recorded tour of the building's better-known holdings is available for
a $5 rental fee on the main floor adjacent to the rotunda. If you'd rather
explore on your own, get a map at one of the two art information desks;
one is just inside the Mall entrance (off Madison Drive), and the other
is near the Constitution Avenue entrance on the ground floor. The Micro
Gallery near the rotunda maintains computerized information on
more than 1,700 works of art from the permanent collection. Touch-
screen monitors provide access to color images, text, animation, and
sounds to help you better understand—and appreciate—the works on
display.

The National Gallery's permanent collection includes works from the
13th to 20th centuries. A comprehensive survey of Italian paintings and
sculpture includes *The Adoration of the Magi,* by Fra Angelico and Filippo Lippi, and *Ginevra de'Benci,* the western hemisphere's only painting by Leonardo da Vinci. Flemish and Dutch works, displayed in
paneled rooms, include *Daniel in the Lions' Den,* by Peter Paul Rubens,
and a self-portrait by Rembrandt. The Chester Dale Collection comprises
works by such Impressionists as Edgar Degas, Claude Monet, Auguste
Renoir, and Mary Cassatt. Salvador Dalí's *Last Supper* is also in this
building.

The **National Gallery of Art Sculpture Garden** is between 7th and 9th
streets along the Mall. Granite walkways take you through the garden,
which is planted with shade trees, flowering trees, and perennials. Sculptures on display from the museum's permanent collection include Roy
Lichtenstein's playful *House I,* Alexander Archipenko's *Woman Comb-
ing Her Hair;* Miró's *Personnage Gothique, Oiseau-Eclair;* and Isamu
Noguchi's *Great Rock of Inner Seeking.* The huge central fountain becomes a skating rink during the winter.

Opened in 1941, the domed West Building was a gift to the nation from
Andrew Mellon. (The dome was one of architect John Russell Pope's
favorite devices. He also designed the Jefferson Memorial and the National Archives, which has a half-domed rotunda.) A wealthy financier
and industrialist, Mellon served as secretary of the treasury under three
presidents and as ambassador to the United Kingdom. He first came
to D.C. in 1921 and lived for many years near Dupont Circle, in a building that today houses the National Trust for Historic Preservation. Mellon had long collected great works of art, acquiring some on his frequent
trips to Europe. In 1930 and 1931, when the Soviet government was
short on cash and selling off many of its art treasures, Mellon bought
more than $6 million worth of old masters, including Raphael's *The
Alba Madonna* and Sandro Botticelli's *Adoration of the Magi.* Mellon
promised his collection to America in 1936, the year before his death.
He also donated the funds for the construction of the huge gallery and
resisted suggestions it be named after him. ⊠ *Constitution Ave. between
4th and 7th Sts. NW, The Mall* ☎ *202/737–4215; 202/842–6176 TDD*
⊕ *www.nga.gov* ⊠ *Free* ☉ *Mon.–Sat. 10–5, Sun. 11–6* Ⓜ *Archives/
Navy Memorial.*

need a
break?

For a quick, casual meal, try the **Cascade Café**, in the concourse between the East and West buildings of the National Gallery of Art. Open 10–3 Monday to Saturday and 11:30–4 Sunday, it carries sandwiches and salads, as well as espresso and *gelato* (Italian-style ice cream) that's made in-house. The **Garden Café** (☎ 202/215–5966), in a picturesque spot on the ground floor of the National Gallery's West Building, gracefully combines food and art by presenting dishes related to current exhibitions, as well as traditional American fare. It's open 11–3 Monday to Saturday and noon–6:30 Sunday. The **Pavilion Café** has indoor and outdoor seating and a panoramic view of landscaping in the National Gallery of Art Sculpture Garden. On offer are specialty pizzas and sandwiches. From September through May it's open 10–5 Monday to Saturday and 11–6 Sunday; from June through August it's open 10–6 Monday to Thursday and Saturday, 10–8 Friday, and 11–6 Sunday.

National Museum of African Art. Opened in 1987, this unique underground building houses galleries, a library, photographic archives, and educational facilities. The museum's rotating exhibits present African visual arts, including sculpture, textiles, photography, archaeology, and modern art. Long-term installations explore the sculpture of sub-Saharan Africa, the art of Benin, pottery of Central Africa, the archaeology of the ancient Nubian city of Kerma, and the artistry of everyday objects. The museum's educational programs include films with contemporary perspectives on African life, storytelling programs, festivals, and hands-on workshops for families, all of which bring Africa's oral traditions, literature, and art to life. Workshops and demonstrations by African and African-American artists offer a chance to meet and talk to practicing artists. If you're traveling with children, look for the museum's free guide to the permanent "Images of Power and Identity" exhibition. ✉ *950 Independence Ave. SW, The Mall* ☎ *202/357–2700; 202/357–1729 TDD* ⊕ *www.nmafa.si.edu* ✉ *Free* ⊙ *Daily 10–5:30* Ⓜ *Smithsonian.*

National Museum of American History. Opened in 1964 as the National Museum of History and Technology and renamed in 1980, the museum explores America's cultural, political, technical, and scientific past. The incredible diversity of artifacts helps the Smithsonian live up to its nickname, "the Nation's attic." This is the museum that displays Muhammad Ali's boxing gloves, Judy Garland's ruby slippers from *The Wizard of Oz,* and the Bunkers' living-room furniture from *All in the Family.*

You can wander for hours on the museum's three floors. Exhibits on the first floor emphasize the history of science and technology and include farm machines, automobiles, and a 280-ton steam locomotive. The permanent "Science in American Life" exhibit shows how science has shaped American life through such breakthroughs as the mass production of penicillin, the development of plastics, and the birth of the environmental movement. Another permanent exhibit looks at 19th-century life in three communities: industrial-age Bridgeport, Connecticut; the Jewish immigrant community in Cincinnati, Ohio; and African-Americans living in Charleston, South Carolina. Also here are Lewis and Clark's compass and a life mask of Abraham Lincoln. The second floor is devoted to U.S. social and political history and has an exhibit on everyday American life just after the Revolution. A permanent exhibit, "First Ladies: Political Role and Public Image," displays gowns worn by presidential wives, but it goes beyond fashion to explore the women behind the satin, lace, and brocade. The third floor has installations on money, musical instruments, and photography.

Be sure to check out Horatio Greenough's statue of the first president (near the west-wing escalators on the second floor). Commissioned by Congress in 1832, it was intended to grace the Capitol Rotunda. It was there for only a short while, however, since the toga-clad likeness proved shocking to some legislators, who grumbled that it looked as if the father of our country had just emerged from a bath. If you want a more interactive visit, check out the Hands on History Room, where you can try some 30 activities, such as pedaling a high-wheeler bike or plucking an old stringed instrument. In the Hands on Science Room you can conduct one of 25 experiments, including testing a water sample and exploring DNA fingerprinting. ⊠ *Constitution Ave. and 14th St. NW, The Mall* ☎ *202/357–2700; 202/357–1729 TDD* ⊕ *www. americanhistory.si.edu* ✉ *Free* ☉ *Daily 10–5:30; call for hrs of Hands on History and Hands on Science rooms* Ⓜ *Smithsonian or Federal Triangle.*

need a break?

The **Palm Court** (☎ 202/357–2700), on the first floor of the National Museum of American History, is designed like an old-fashioned ice cream parlor. A good place for lunch, the restaurant is open 10–5:30 daily. The National Museum is also the perfect place for souvenirs. In the four stores in the building, you can purchase presidential souvenirs, reproductions of newspapers with notable headlines, and even personalized dog tags.

★ ☺ ❼ **National Museum of Natural History.** This is one of the great natural history museums in the world, filled with bones, fossils, stuffed animals, and other natural delights—124 million specimens in all. It was constructed in 1910, and two wings were added in the 1960s.

The first-floor rotunda is dominated by a stuffed, 8-ton, 13-foot-tall African bull elephant, one of the largest ever found. (The tusks are fiberglass; the original ivory ones were far too heavy for the stuffed elephant to support.) Off to the right is the popular **Dinosaur Hall.** Fossilized skeletons here range from a 90-foot-long diplodocus to a tiny *Thescelosaurus neglectus* (a small dinosaur so named because its disconnected bones sat for years in a college drawer before being reassembled).

Beyond the Dinosaur Hall is the newest permanent exhibition, **African Voices.** It shows the influence of Africa's peoples and culture with refreshingly up-to-date displays, including a Somali camel herder's portable house, re-creations of markets in Ghana (housewares, cola nuts, and yams are for sale), a Tunisian wedding tunic, and artifacts showing the Yoruba influence on Afro-Brazilian culture.

Renovation of the west wing, which houses displays of birds, mammals, and sea life, was completed in 2003. It is here that you can handle elephant tusks, petrified wood, seashells, rocks, feathers, and other items from nature.

The highlight of the second floor is the **Janet Annenberg Hooker Hall of Geology, Gems and Minerals.** Objects on display include a pair of Marie Antoinette's earrings, the Rosser Reeves ruby, spectacular crystals and minerals, and, of course, the Hope Diamond, a blue gem found in India and reputed to carry a curse (Smithsonian guides are quick to pooh-pooh this notion).

Also on the second floor is the **O. Orkin Insect Zoo,** named for the pest-control magnate who donated the money to modernize the exhibits. Here you can view at least 60 species of live insects, and there are tarantula feedings Tuesday through Friday at 10:30, 11:30, and 1:30.

The second IMAX theater on the Mall—the other is in the National Air and Space museum—is the Samuel C. Johnson IMAX theater, which shows two- and three-dimensional natural-history films, including the 3-D movie: *T-REX*. The theater is also open Friday evenings from 6 for the "IMAX Jazz Café," an evening of live entertainment, food, and special IMAX films not shown during the day. Tickets for the theater can be purchased at the museum box office. ✉ *Constitution Ave. and 10th St. NW, The Mall* ☎ *202/357–2700; 202/357–1729 TDD* ⊕ *www.mnh. si.edu* ✉ *Free, IMAX $7.50* ☉ *Museum daily 10–5:30; Discovery Corner Tues.–Fri. noon–2:30, weekends 10:30–3:30; Discovery Corner passes distributed starting at 11:45 weekdays, 10:15 weekends* Ⓜ *Smithsonian or Federal Triangle.*

► ❶ **Smithsonian Institution Building.** The first Smithsonian museum constructed, this red sandstone, Norman-style building is better known as the Castle. It was designed by James Renwick, the architect of St. Patrick's Cathedral in New York City. Although British scientist and founder James Smithson had never visited America, his will stipulated that should his nephew, Henry James Hungerford, die without an heir, Smithson's entire fortune would go to the United States, "to found at Washington, under the name of the Smithsonian Institution, an establishment for the increase and diffusion of knowledge." The museums on the Mall are the Smithsonian's most visible example of this ideal, but the organization also sponsors traveling exhibitions and maintains research posts in such outside-the-Beltway locales as the Chesapeake Bay and the tropics of Panama.

Smithson died in 1829, Hungerford in 1835, and in 1838 the United States received $515,169 worth of gold sovereigns. After eight years of congressional debate over the propriety of accepting funds from a citizen of another country, the Smithsonian Institution was finally established on August 10, 1846. The Castle building was completed in 1855 and originally housed all of the Smithsonian's operations, including the science and art collections, research laboratories, and living quarters for the institution's secretary and his family. The statue in front of the Castle's entrance is not of Smithson but of Joseph Henry, the scientist who served as the institution's first secretary. Smithson's body was brought to America in 1904 and is entombed in a small room to the left of the Castle's Mall entrance.

Today the Castle houses Smithsonian administrative offices as well as the **Smithsonian Information Center,** which can help you get your bearings and decide which attractions you want to visit. A 24-minute video provides an overview of the Smithsonian museums and the National Zoo, and monitors display information on the day's events. Interactive touch-screen displays provide more detailed information on the museums as well as other attractions in the capital. The center opens at 9 AM, an hour before the other museums, so you can plan your day without wasting sightseeing time. ✉ *1000 Jefferson Dr. SW, The Mall* ☎ *202/357–2700; 202/ 357–1729 TDD* ⊕ *www.si.edu* ✉ *Free* ☉ *Daily 9–5:30* Ⓜ *Smithsonian.*

❾ **United States Holocaust Memorial Museum.** Museums usually celebrate the
FodorśChoice best that humanity can achieve, but this James Ingo Freed–designed mu-
★ seum instead documents the worst. A permanent exhibition tells the stories of the millions of Jews, Gypsies, Jehovah's Witnesses, homosexuals, political prisoners, mentally ill, and others killed by the Nazis between 1933 and 1945. Striving to give a you-are-there experience, the graphic presentation is as extraordinary as the subject matter: upon arrival, you are issued an "identity card" containing biographical information on a real person from the Holocaust. As you move through the museum, you

read sequential updates on your card. The museum recounts the Holocaust through documentary films, video- and audiotaped oral histories, and a collection that includes such items as a freight car like those used to transport Jews from Warsaw to the Treblinka death camp, and the Star of David patches that Jewish prisoners were made to wear. Like the history it covers, the museum can be profoundly disturbing; it's not recommended for children under 11, although "Daniel's Story," in a ground-floor exhibit not requiring tickets, is designed for children ages 8 and up. Plan to spend two to three hours here. After this powerful experience, the adjacent Hall of Remembrance provides a space for quiet reflection. In addition to the permanent exhibition, the museum also has a multimedia learning center, a resource center for students and teachers, a registry of Holocaust survivors, and occasional special exhibitions. Same-day timed-entry passes (distributed on a first-come, first-served basis at the 14th Street entrance starting at 10 AM or available through tickets.com) are necessary for the permanent exhibition. ✉ *100 Raoul Wallenberg Pl. SW, enter from Raoul Wallenberg Pl. or 14th St. SW, The Mall* ☎ *202/488–0400; 800/400–9373 tickets.com* ⊕ *www.ushmm. org* ⊠ *Free* ⊙ *Daily 10–5:30* Ⓜ *Smithsonian.*

THE MONUMENTS

Washington is a city of monuments. In the middle of traffic circles, on tiny slivers of park, and at street corners and intersections, statues, plaques, and simple blocks of marble honor the generals, politicians, poets, and statesmen who helped shape the nation. The monuments dedicated to the most famous Americans are west of the Mall on ground reclaimed from the marshy flats of the Potomac. This is also the location of Washington's greatest single display of cherry trees, gifts from Japan.

Numbers in the text correspond to numbers in the margin and on The Monuments map.

a good walk

Start with the tallest of them all, the 555-foot **Washington Monument** ❶ ▶, at the western end of the Mall. Then walk southwest past the building site of the National WWII Memorial and cross Independence Avenue to the **Tidal Basin** ❷. The path that skirts the basin leads to the Outlet Bridge and the **Jefferson Memorial** ❸. Continue along the sidewalk that hugs the Tidal Basin. Cross Inlet Bridge, bear right, and enter the **Franklin Delano Roosevelt Memorial** ❹; you'll be going through in reverse, but this won't spoil your enjoyment of the memorial's drama. Exit the memorial through its entrance and bear right on West Basin Drive. At the next traffic light, cross Independence Avenue and walk left toward the **Korean War Veterans Memorial** ❺, in a grove of trees called Ash Woods.

Your next stop is the **Lincoln Memorial** ❻, which resembles a Greek temple. After visiting it, walk down its steps and to the left to the **Vietnam Veterans Memorial** ❼. From there take the path that passes the **Vietnam Women's Memorial** ❽ on your way to the **Constitution Gardens** ❾. Walk north to Constitution Avenue and head east to the stone **Lockkeeper's House** ❿ at the corner of Constitution Avenue and 17th Street, an artifact from a failed waterway.

TIMING Allow four or five hours to tour the monuments. This includes time to relax on a park bench and to grab a snack from either a vendor or one of the snack bars east of the Washington Monument and near the Lincoln Memorial. If you're visiting during the first two weeks in April, take some extra time around the Tidal Basin and the Washington Monument to marvel at the cherry blossoms. From mid-April through November, you might want to set aside an hour for a relaxing paddleboat ride in the Tidal Basin. In summer, if it's an extremely hot day, you may want to hop a Tourmobile bus and travel between the monuments in air-conditioned comfort.

What to See

off the beaten path

THE AWAKENING – J. Seward Johnson Jr.'s colossal aluminum sculpture of a bearded giant with head and limbs breaking through the ground is great fun—especially for kids. The 70-foot-tall work was installed at the southern tip of East Potomac Park for a sculpture exhibition in 1980. ⊠ *Hains Pt., East Potomac Park, Southwest.*

❾ Constitution Gardens. Many ideas were proposed to develop this 50-acre site. It once held "temporary" buildings erected by the navy before World War I and not removed until after World War II. President Nixon is said to have favored something resembling Copenhagen's Tivoli Gardens. The final design was a little plainer, with paths winding through groves of trees and, on the lake, a tiny island paying tribute to the signers of the Declaration of Independence, their signatures carved into a low stone wall. In 1986 President Reagan proclaimed the gardens a living legacy to the Constitution; in that spirit, a naturalization ceremony for new citizens now takes place here each year. ⊠ *Constitution Ave. between 17th and 23rd Sts. NW* ⊕ *www.nps.gov/coga* Ⓜ *Foggy Bottom.*

need a break?

At the circular **snack bar** just west of the Constitution Gardens lake you can get hot dogs, potato chips, candy bars, soft drinks, and beer at prices lower than those charged by most street vendors.

☾ East Potomac Park. This 328-acre finger of land extends from the Tidal Basin between the Washington Channel to the east and the Potomac River to the west. Facilities include playgrounds, picnic tables, tennis courts, swimming pools, a driving range, two 9-hole golf courses, miniature golf, and an 18-hole golf course. Double-blossoming cherry trees line Ohio Drive and bloom about two weeks after the single-blossoming variety that attracts throngs to the Tidal Basin each spring. *The Awakening* sculpture is on Hains Point, at the tip of the park, where the Anacostia River merges with the Potomac. ⊠ *Maine Ave. SW heading west, or Ohio Dr. heading south (follow signs carefully); Ohio Dr. closed to traffic on summer weekends and holidays 3 PM–6 AM.* ☎ *202/619–7222* Ⓜ *Smithsonian.*

☾ ❹ Franklin Delano Roosevelt Memorial. This monument, designed by Lawrence

Fodor's Choice ★

Halprin, was unveiled in 1997. The 7½-acre memorial to the 32nd president employs waterfalls and reflection pools, four outdoor gallery rooms—one for each of Roosevelt's terms as president—and 10 bronze sculptures. The granite megaliths that connect the galleries are engraved with some of Roosevelt's most famous quotes, including, "The only thing we have to fear is fear itself." Although today the memorial is one of the most popular in the District, a delight to toddlers as well as to those who remember FDR firsthand, the FDR Memorial has had its share of controversy. Roosevelt is not portrayed with his omnipresent cigarette nor is he pictured in a wheelchair, which he used for the last 24 years of his life, after he contracted polio. However, a wheelchair that FDR used is now exhibited in the visitor center, and this D.C. memorial was the first purposely designed to be wheelchair accessible. It is also the first to honor a first lady; a bronze statue of Eleanor Roosevelt (without *her* trademark, a fur boa), stands in front of the United Nations symbol. ⊠ *West side of Tidal Basin, The Mall* ☎ *202/426–6841* ⊕ *www.nps.gov/fdrm* ☒ *Free* ☉ *24 hrs; staffed daily 8 AM–midnight* Ⓜ *Smithsonian.*

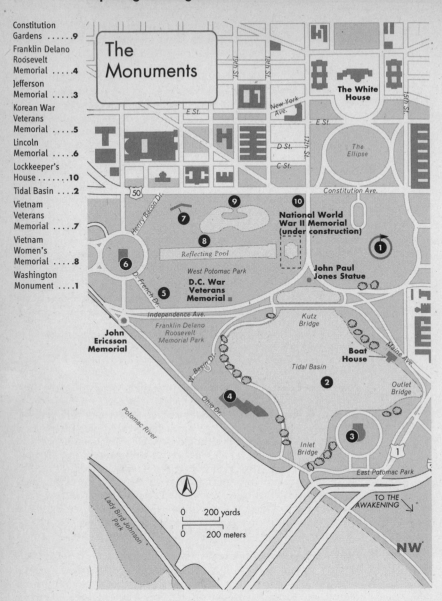

③ **Jefferson Memorial.** The monument honoring the third president of the

Fodor'sChoice United States incorporates his own architectural taste in its design. Jef-

★ ferson had always admired the Pantheon in Rome—the rotundas he designed for the University of Virginia were inspired by its dome—so the
memorial's architect, John Russell Pope, drew from the same source. In
the 1930s Congress decided that Jefferson deserved a monument positioned as prominently as those in honor of Washington and Lincoln, so
workers scooped and moved tons of river bottom to create dry land on
this spot directly south of the White House. Dedicated in 1943, it houses
a statue of Jefferson, and its walls are lined with inscriptions based on
the Declaration of Independence and his other writings. One of the best
views of the White House can be seen from its top steps. ⊠ *Tidal Basin,
south bank, The Mall* ☎ *202/426–6821* ⊕ *www.nps.gov/thje* ☒ *Free*
☉ *Daily 8 AM–midnight* Ⓜ *Smithsonian.*

A CITY OF STATUES

WITH MORE EQUESTRIAN STATUES *than any other city in the nation, green-streaked stone and metal men atop steeds are everywhere, watching the city from traffic circles, squares, and parks. The statues proliferated in the 19th century; Civil War generals who went into politics seemed virtually assured of this legacy—regardless of their success in either endeavor. Some of the statues reveal more than stories of men in battle.

Henry James wrote of America's first equestrian statue, "the most prodigious of all Presidential effigies, Andrew Jackson, as archaic as a Ninevite king, prancing and rocking through the ages." Standing in Lafayette Square across from the White House, the statue of Jackson is by sculptor Clark Mills, who had never seen an equestrian statue, much less created one. In order to get the proportions of the rearing horse correct, Mills had a horse trained to remain in an upright position so he could study the anatomy of its muscles. Though the statue is much acclaimed, some critics have argued that it's too small for the park, and should be replaced with the statue of George Washington (also by Mills) that currently stands in Foggy Bottom's Washington Circle.

Directly up 16th Street from Lafayette Square at Massachusetts and Rhode Island avenues is a statue of Lt. Gen. Winfield Scott (1786–1866), in the circle bearing his name. "Old Fuss and Feathers" was to be shown atop his favorite mount, a lightweight mare. That is, until right before the statue was cast, when some of Scott's descendents decided that a stallion would be a more appropriate horse to ride into battle (regardless of historical accuracy). The sculptor, H. K. Brown, was forced to give the horse a last-minute sex change.

Farther up Massachusetts Avenue, at 23rd Street, is a statue of Civil War Gen. Philip Henry Sheridan, also in a circle bearing his name. The piece is by Gutzon Borglum, who completed more than 170 public statues, including the head of Abraham Lincoln in the Capitol Rotunda, and whose final work was the presidential faces on Mount Rushmore. The statue of the leader riding Rienzi (who was later renamed "Winchester" for Sheridan's victory there) stands in the type of circle Pierre-Charles L'Enfant envisioned in his plan for Washington—a small, formal park where avenues come together surrounded by isolated houses and buildings.

The statue of Gen. William Tecumseh Sherman at 15th Street and Treasury Place is often overlooked—in summer, the general's head is obscured by trees, and all year long he presents his back and his mount's hindquarters to passersby. walking. He's positioned where he is thought to have stood while reviewing the Union troops on their victorious return from Georgia. The bar at the Hotel Washington, which affords some of the best views of the city, is also the place for a good look at Sherman.

A long-held theory says that the number of raised legs on the mount of an equestrian statue reveals how the rider died: one leg raised means the rider died of wounds sustained in battle, two legs raised means the rider died in battle, and four feet on the ground means the rider died of natural causes. Actually, though, it isn't true. Of the more than 30 equestrian statues in Washington, only about a third (including Scott, Sheridan, and Sherman, but not Jackson) are true to the "code."*

— Lisa Greaves

⑤ Korean War Veterans Memorial. Dedicated in 1995, this memorial to the 1.5 million United States men and women who served in the Korean War highlights the high cost of freedom. The statue group in the triangular Field of Service depicts 19 multiethnic soldiers on patrol in rugged Korean terrain. They're heading toward an American flag. To the south of the soldiers stands a 164-foot-long granite wall etched with the faces of 2,400 unnamed service men and women with a silver inlay reading FREEDOM IS NOT FREE. The adjacent Pool of Remembrance honors all who were killed, captured, wounded, or missing in action; it's a quiet spot for contemplation. ⊠ *West end of Mall at Daniel French Dr. and Independence Ave., The Mall* ☎ *202/619–7222* ⊕ *www.nps.gov/kwvm* ⊡ *Free* ⊙ *Daily 8* AM–*midnight* Ⓜ *Foggy Bottom.*

⑥ Lincoln Memorial. Nowadays many people consider the Lincoln Memorial the most inspiring monument in the city. This was not always the case. Although today it would be hard to imagine D.C. without the Lincoln and Jefferson memorials, both were criticized when first built. The Jefferson Memorial was dubbed "Jefferson's muffin"; critics lambasted the design as outdated and too similar to that of the Lincoln Memorial. Some also complained that the Jefferson Memorial blocked the view of the Potomac from the White House. Detractors of the Lincoln Memorial thought it inappropriate that the humble Lincoln be honored with what amounts to a modified but nonetheless rather grandiose Greek temple. The white Colorado-marble memorial was designed by Henry Bacon and completed in 1922. The 36 Doric columns represent the 36 states in the Union at the time of Lincoln's death; the names of the states appear on the frieze above the columns. Above the frieze are the names of the 48 states in the Union when the memorial was dedicated. (Alaska and Hawaii are represented with an inscription on the terrace that leads up to the memorial.)

FodorsChoice
★

Daniel Chester French's somber statue of the seated president, in the center of the memorial, gazes out over the Reflecting Pool. Although the 19-foot-high sculpture looks as if it were cut from one huge block of stone, it's actually composed of 28 interlocking pieces of Georgia marble. (The memorial's original design called for a 10-foot-high sculpture, but experiments with models revealed that a statue that size would be lost in the cavernous space.) Inscribed on the south wall is the Gettysburg Address, and on the north wall is Lincoln's second inaugural address. Above each inscription is a mural painted by Jules Guerin: on the south wall is an angel of truth freeing a slave; the unity of North and South are depicted opposite. The memorial served as a fitting backdrop for Martin Luther King Jr.'s "I Have a Dream" speech in 1963.

Many visitors look only at the front and inside of the Lincoln Memorial, but there is much more to explore. On the lower level is the Lincoln Museum, a small exhibit financed with pennies collected by schoolchildren. There's also a set of windows that overlooks the huge structure's foundation. Stalactites (hanging from above) and stalagmites (rising from below) have formed underneath the marble tribute to Lincoln. Although visiting the area around the Lincoln Memorial during the day allows you to take in an impressive view of the Mall to the east, the best time to see the memorial itself is at night. Spotlights illuminate the outside, and inside light and shadows play across Lincoln's gentle face. ⊠ *West end of Mall, The Mall* ☎ *202/426–6895* ⊕ *www. nps.gov/linc* ⊡ *Free* ⊙ *24 hrs; staffed daily 8* AM–*midnight* Ⓜ *Foggy Bottom.*

⑩ Lockkeeper's House. The stone Lockkeeper's House is the only remaining monument to Washington's unsuccessful experiment with a canal.

The waterway's lockkeeper lived here until the 1870s, when the waterway was covered over with B Street (renamed Constitution Avenue in 1932). The house is not open to visitors. ⊠ *Constitution Ave. and 17th St., The Mall* Ⓜ *Federal Triangle, 5 blocks east on 12th St.*

❷ **Tidal Basin.** This placid pond was part of the Potomac until 1882, when portions of the river were filled in to improve navigation and create additional parkland. At the **boathouse** (☎ 202/479–2426), on the northeast bank of the Tidal Basin, you can rent paddleboats during the warmer months. Rental cost is $8 per hour for a two-person boat, $16 per hour for a four-person boat. The boathouse is open from mid-March through October from 10 to 6.

Two grotesque sculpted heads on the sides of the Inlet Bridge can be seen as you walk along the sidewalk that hugs the basin. The inside walls of the bridge also sport two other interesting sculptures: bronze, human-headed fish that spout water from their mouths. The bridge was refurbished in the 1980s at the same time the chief of the park, Jack Fish, was retiring. Sculptor Constantine Sephralis played a little joke: these fish heads are actually Fish's head.

Once you cross the bridge, continue along the Tidal Basin to the right. This route is especially scenic when the cherry trees are in bloom. The first batch of these trees arrived from Japan in 1909. The trees were infected with insects and fungus, however, and the Department of Agriculture ordered them destroyed. A diplomatic crisis was averted when the United States politely asked the Japanese for another batch, and in 1912 Mrs. William Howard Taft planted the first tree. The second was planted by the wife of the Japanese ambassador, Viscountess Chinda. About 200 of the original trees still grow near the Tidal Basin. (These cherry trees are the single-flowering Akebeno and Yoshino variety. Double-blossom Fugenzo and Kwanzan trees grow in East Potomac Park and flower about two weeks after their more-famous cousins.)

The trees are now the centerpiece of Washington's Cherry Blossom Festival, held each spring since 1935. The festivities are kicked off by the lighting of a ceremonial Japanese lantern that rests on the north shore of the Tidal Basin, not far from where the first tree was planted. The once-simple celebration has grown over the years to include concerts, martial-arts demonstrations, and a parade. Park-service experts try their best to predict exactly when the buds will pop. The trees are usually in bloom for about 10–12 days in late March or early April. When winter refuses to release its grip, the parade and festival are held anyway, without the presence of blossoms, no matter how inclement the weather. And when the weather complies and the blossoms are at their peak at the time of the festivities, Washington rejoices. ⊠ *Bordered by Independence Ave. and Maine Ave., The Mall.* Ⓜ *Smithsonian.*

need a break? If you've worked up an appetite at the Tidal Basin, head four blocks down Maine Avenue to the **Maine Avenue Seafood Market,** where vendors sell fresh fish and shellfish. Seven restaurants stretch along the avenue, including local seafood powerhouse Phillips Flagship. All have terraces overlooking the Washington Channel and the motorboats, houseboats, and sailboats moored here.

❼ **Vietnam Veterans Memorial.** Renowned for its power to evoke reflection, **Fodor's**Choice the Vietnam Veterans Memorial was conceived by Jan Scruggs, a for-★ mer infantry corporal who had served in Vietnam. The stark design by Maya Lin, a 21-year-old Yale architecture student, was selected in a 1981 competition. Upon its completion in 1982, the memorial was decried by some veterans as a "black gash of shame." With the addition of Frederick Hart's realistic statue of three soldiers and a flagpole south of the wall, most critics were won over.

The wall is one of the most-visited sites in Washington, its black granite panels reflecting the sky, the trees, and the faces of those looking for the names of friends or relatives who died in the war. The names of more than 58,000 Americans are etched on the face of the memorial in the order of their deaths. Directories at the entrance and exit to the wall list the names in alphabetical order. For help in finding a name, ask a ranger at the blue-and-white hut near the entrance. Thousands of offerings are left at the wall each year: letters, flowers, medals, uniforms, snapshots. The National Park Service collects these and stores them in a warehouse in Maryland. Some of the items are also on display at the National Museum of American History. Many of those visiting the memorial bring paper and crayons or charcoal to make rubbings of the names of their loved ones. Tents are often set up near the wall by veterans groups; some provide information on soldiers who remain missing in action, and others are on call to help fellow vets and relatives deal with the sometimes overwhelming emotions that grip them when visiting the wall for the first time. ⊠ *Constitution Gardens, 23rd St. and Constitution Ave. NW, The Mall* ☎ *202/634–1568* ⊕ *www.nps.gov/vive* ✉ *Free* ⊙ *24 hrs; staffed daily 8 AM–midnight* Ⓜ *Foggy Bottom.*

❽ **Vietnam Women's Memorial.** After years of debate over its design and necessity, the Vietnam Women's Memorial, honoring the women who served in that conflict, was finally dedicated on Veterans' Day 1993. Sculptor Glenna Goodacre's stirring bronze group depicts two uniformed women caring for a wounded male soldier while a third woman kneels nearby. The eight trees around the plaza commemorate each of the women in the military who died in Vietnam. ⊠ *Constitution Gardens, southeast of Vietnam Veterans Memorial, The Mall* ⊕ *www.nps.gov/vive/commem.htm* Ⓜ *Foggy Bottom.*

★ ☾ ⚑ ❶ **Washington Monument.** At the western end of the Mall, the 555-foot, 5-inch Washington Monument punctuates the capital like a huge exclamation point. Visible from nearly everywhere in the city, it's truly a landmark.

In 1833, after years of quibbling in Congress, a private National Monument Society was formed to select a designer and to search for funds to construct this monument. Robert Mills's winning design called for a 600-ft-tall decorated obelisk rising from a circular colonnaded building. The building at the base was to be an American pantheon, adorned with statues of national heroes and a massive statue of Washington riding in a chariot pulled by snorting horses.

Because of the marshy conditions of L'Enfant's original site, the position of the monument was shifted to firmer ground 100 yards southeast. (If you walk a few steps north of the monument you can see the stone marker that denotes L'Enfant's original axis.) The cornerstone was laid in 1848 with the same Masonic trowel Washington himself had used to lay the Capitol's cornerstone 55 years earlier. The National Monument Society continued to raise funds after construction was begun, soliciting subscriptions of $1 from citizens across America. It also urged states, organizations, and foreign governments to contribute memorial stones for the construction. Problems arose in 1854, when members of the anti–Roman Catholic Know-Nothing party stole a block donated by Pope Pius IX, smashed it, and dumped its shards into the Potomac. This action, combined with a lack of funds, and the onset of the Civil

War, kept the monument at a fraction of its final height, open at the top, and vulnerable to the rain. A clearly visible ring about a third of the way up the obelisk testifies to this unfortunate stage of the monument's history: although all of the marble in the obelisk came from the same Maryland quarry, the stone used for the second phase of construction came from a different stratum and is of a slightly different shade.

In 1876 Congress finally appropriated $200,000 to finish the monument, and the Army Corps of Engineers took over construction, thankfully simplifying Mills's original design. Work was finally completed in December 1884, when the monument was topped with a 7½-pound piece of aluminum, at that time one of the most expensive metals in the world. Four years later the monument was opened to visitors, who rode to the top in a steam-operated elevator. (Only men were allowed to take the 20-minute ride; it was thought too dangerous for women, who as a result had to walk up the stairs if they wanted to see the view.)

The view from the top takes in most of the District and parts of Maryland and Virginia. You are no longer permitted to climb the more than 800 steps leading to the top. (Incidents of vandalism and a number of heart attacks on the steps convinced the park service that letting people walk up on their own wasn't a good idea.)

To avoid the formerly long lines of people waiting for the minute-long elevator ride up the monument's shaft, the park service now uses a free timed-ticket system. A limited number of tickets are available at the kiosk on 15th Street daily beginning half an hour before the monument opens, though in spring and summer lines start well before then. Tickets are good during a specified half-hour period. ⊠ *Constitution Ave. and 15th St. NW, The Mall* ☎ *202/426–6840; 800/967–2283 for up to 6 advance tickets* ⊕ *www.nps.gov/wamo* ✉ *Free, advance tickets require a $2 service and handling fee per ticket* ⊘ *Memorial Day–Labor Day, daily 8 AM–11:45 PM; Labor Day–Memorial Day, daily 9 4:15* Ⓜ *Smithsonian.*

West Potomac Park. Between the Potomac and the Tidal Basin, West Potomac Park is best known for its flowering cherry trees, which bloom only two weeks in late March or early April. During the rest of the year, West Potomac Park is just a nice place to relax, play ball, or admire the views at the Tidal Basin.

THE WHITE HOUSE AREA

In a world full of recognizable images, few are better known than the whitewashed, 132-room mansion at 1600 Pennsylvania Avenue. The residence of perhaps the single most powerful person on the planet, the White House has an awesome majesty, having been the home of every U.S. president but George Washington. This is where the buck stops in America and where the nation turns in times of crisis. After having a look at the White House, strike out into the surrounding streets to explore the president's neighborhood, which includes some of the city's oldest houses.

Numbers in the text correspond to numbers in the margin and on the White House Area map.

a good walk

Your first stop should be the **White House Visitor Center** ❶ ⌐ at 14th and E streets. Walk north four blocks on 15th Street, and then turn left to the **White House** ❷. Across Pennsylvania Avenue is **Lafayette Square** ❸, full of statues, trees, and flowers. Beyond the park, on H Street, is the golden-domed **St. John's Episcopal Church** ❹, the so-called Church of the Presidents. Head west on H Street to Jackson Place and the Federal-style

Decatur House ❺, built in 1818 for a pirate-fighter. Walk down Jackson Place to Pennsylvania Avenue and turn right to the **Renwick Gallery** ❻, another member of the Smithsonian family of museums, and its neighbor Blair House, used as a residence by visiting heads of state. Go south on 17th Street past the **Eisenhower Executive Office Building** ❼, which once held the State, War, and Navy departments. At the corner of 17th Street and New York Avenue is the **Corcoran Gallery of Art** ❽, one of the few large, non-Smithsonian museums in Washington. Proceed one block west on New York Avenue to the unusually shaped **Octagon Museum** ❾, with exhibits on the architecture and history of Washington. A block south on 18th Street is the **Department of the Interior** ❿, decorated with 1930s murals illustrating the department's work as overseer of most of the country's federally owned land and natural resources.

Walk back east on E Street to 17th Street to the three buildings of the American Red Cross, one of which has three Tiffany stained-glass windows. A block south is Memorial Continental Hall, headquarters of the Daughters of the American Revolution and the location of the **DAR Museum** ⓫, which has 33 rooms decorated in period styles. Just across C Street (to the south of Continental Hall) is the headquarters of the **Organization of American States** ⓬, in the House of the Americas. Behind the House of the Americas is the **Art Museum of the Americas** ⓭, a small gallery with works by 20th-century Latin American artists. Head east on Constitution Avenue and take the first left after 17th Street, following the curving drive that encircles the **Ellipse** ⓮. Take E Street east to 15th Street; then turn left and pass between the mammoth **William Tecumseh Sherman Monument** ⓯ on the left and **Pershing Park** ⓰ on the right. Continue north up 15th Street to the impressive **Treasury Building** ⓱.

TIMING   Touring the area around the White House could easily take you a day, depending on how long you visit each of the museums along the way. The walk itself might take half a day or longer. If you enjoy history, you may be more interested in Decatur House, the DAR Museum, and the Octagon Museum. If art is your passion, devote the hours to the Corcoran and Renwick galleries instead.

What to See

American Red Cross. The national headquarters for the American Red Cross is composed of three buildings. The primary one, a neoclassical structure of blinding-white marble built in 1917, commemorates the service and devotion of the women who cared for the wounded on both sides during the Civil War. Its Georgian-style board-of-governors hall has three stained-glass windows designed by Louis Comfort Tiffany. The building at 1730 E Street NW, dedicated to the women of World War I, houses the American Red Cross Visitor Center and has six galleries that explain the organization's work, from what happens to the blood you donate to how the Red Cross assists the military and provides disaster relief both at home and abroad. ✉ *430 17th St. NW, White House area* ◔ *8:30–4* Ⓜ *Farragut West.*

⓭ **Art Museum of the Americas.** Changing exhibits highlight 20th-century Latin American artists in this small gallery, part of the Organization of American States. The museum also screens documentaries on South and Central American art. A garden, open to the public, connects the Art Museum and the OAS building. ✉ *201 18th St. NW, White House area* ☎ *202/458–6016* ⊕ *www.oas.org* ✂ *Free* ◔ *Tues.–Sun. 10–5* Ⓜ *Farragut West.*

Blair House. A green canopy marks the entrance to Blair House, the residence used by heads of state visiting Washington. Harry S. Truman lived

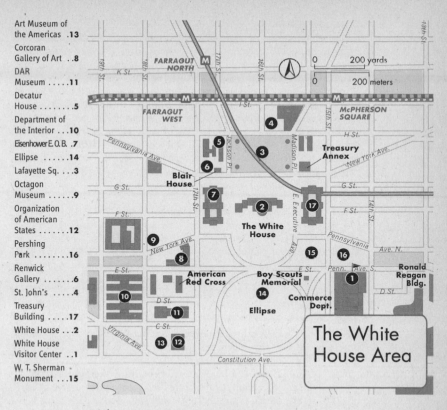

The White
House Area

here from 1948 to 1952 while the White House was undergoing much-needed renovations. A plaque on the fence honors White House policeman Leslie Coffelt, who died in 1950 when Puerto Rican separatists attempted to assassinate President Truman at this site. The house is closed to the public. ⊠ *1651 Pennsylvania Ave., White House area* Ⓜ *McPherson Square.*

Boy Scouts Memorial. Near the Ellipse stands this statue of a uniformed Boy Scout flanked by a male figure representing Patriotism and a female figure holding the light of faith. ⊠ *East of Ellipse, near 15th St. NW, White House area* Ⓜ *McPherson Square.*

❽ **Corcoran Gallery of Art.** The Corcoran is Washington's largest nonfederal art museum, as well as its first art museum. The beaux arts building, its copper roof green with age, was designed by Ernest Flagg and completed in 1897. (The museum's first home was in what is now the Renwick Gallery.) The gallery's permanent collection of 14,000 works includes paintings by the greatest of the early American portraitists: John Copley, Gilbert Stuart, and Rembrandt Peale. The Hudson River School is represented by such works as *Mount Corcoran* by Albert Bierstadt and Frederic Church's *Niagara.* There are also portraits by John Singer Sargent, Thomas Eakins, and Mary Cassatt. The Walker Collection shows late-19th- and early 20th-century European paintings, including works by Gustave Courbet, Claude Monet, Camille Pissarro, and Pierre-Auguste Renoir. Dutch, Flemish, and French Romantic paintings are on display at the Clark Collection, as is the restored 18th-century Salon Doré that was once part of the Hotel de Clermont in Paris. Be sure to see Samuel Morse's *Old House of Representatives* and Hiram Powers's *Greek Slave,* which scandalized Victorian society. (The latter, a statue of a nude woman with her wrists chained, was considered so shocking that separate viewing hours were established for men and women; children under 16 weren't allowed to see it at all.) Photography and works by contemporary American artists are also among the Corcoran's strengths. The Corcoran College of Art and Design, housed in the museum, is the only four-year art college in the Washington area. The **Winder Building** (✉ 604 17th St., White House area), one block north, was erected in 1848 as one of the first office blocks in the capital. It served as the headquarters of the Union Army during the Civil War. ✉ *500 17th St. NW, White House area* ☏ *202/639–1700* ⊕ *www.corcoran. org* ✉ *$5, free all day Mon. and Thurs. after 5* ⊙ *Mon., Wed., and Fri.–Sun. 10–5; Thurs. 10–9; tours of permanent collection Mon., Wed., and Fri. at noon; weekends at 10:30 AM, noon, and 2:30 PM; Thurs. at 7:30 PM* Ⓜ *Farragut West or Farragut North.*

need a break?

The Corcoran Gallery's **Café des Artistes** (☏ 202/639–1700) has a lunch menu of salads, light entrées, desserts, and a refreshing assortment of fruit and vegetable shakes. The café also serves Continental breakfast and an English tea with scones and clotted cream and light fare on Thursday, when the museum is open late. Sunday brunch, when gospel singers perform, is very popular.

Ⓒ ⓫ **DAR Museum.** The headquarters of the Daughters of the American Revolution, the beaux arts Memorial Continental Hall was the site of the DAR's annual congress until the larger Constitution Hall was built around the corner. An entrance on D Street leads to the DAR Museum. Its 33,000-item collection includes fine examples of colonial and Federal furniture, textiles, quilts, silver, china, porcelain, stoneware, earthenware, and glass. Thirty-three period rooms are decorated in styles representative of various U.S. states, ranging from an 1850 California adobe parlor to a New Hampshire attic filled with toys from the 18th and 19th centuries. Two galleries—one of them permanent—hold decorative arts. Tours are available weekdays 10–2:30 and Sunday 1–5. During the "Colonial Adventure" tours, held the first and third Sundays of the month at 1:30 and 3 from September through May, costumed docents use the objects on display to teach children ages five to seven about day-to-day life in colonial America. Make reservations at least 10 days in advance. ✉ *1776 D St. NW, White House area* ☏ *202/879–3241* ⊕ *www.dar.org* ✉ *Free* ⊙ *Weekdays 8:30–4, Sun. 1–5* Ⓜ *Farragut West.*

❺ **Decatur House.** Designed by Benjamin Latrobe, Decatur House was built for naval hero Stephen Decatur and his wife, Susan, in 1819. A redbrick Federal-style building on the corner of H Street and Jackson Place, it was the first private residence on Lafayette Square (the White House doesn't really count as *private*). Decatur had earned the affection of the nation in battles against the British and the Barbary pirates. Planning to start a political career, he used the money Congress awarded him for his exploits to build this home near the White House. Tragically, only 14 months after he moved in, Decatur was killed in a duel with James Barron, a disgruntled former navy officer who held Decatur responsible for his court-martial. Later occupants of the house included Henry Clay, Martin Van Buren, and the Beales, a prominent Western family whose modifications of the building include a parquet floor with the state seal of California. The house, now operated by the National Trust for Historic Preservation, has a first floor furnished as it was in Decatur's time. The second floor is done in the Victorian style favored by the Beales, who owned it until 1956 (thus making Decatur House both the first and last private residence on the square). The museum shop around the corner (entrance on H Street) sells books, postcards, and gifts.

Many of the row houses along Jackson Place date from the pre–Civil War or Victorian period; even the more modern additions, though—such as those at 718 and 726—are designed to blend with their more historic neighbors. Count Rochambeau, aide to General Lafayette, is honored with a statue at Lafayette Square's southwest corner. ✉ *748 Jackson Pl. NW, White House area* ☎ *202/842–0920* ⊕ *www.decaturhouse.org* 🖾 *Free* ⊙ *Tues.–Fri. 10–3, weekends noon–4; tours on the hr and ½ hr* Ⓜ *Farragut West.*

❿ Department of the Interior. Designed by Waddy B. Wood, the Department of the Interior was the first large federal building with escalators and central air-conditioning and the most modern government building in the city when it was built in 1937. The outside of the building is somewhat plain, but the inside holds many artworks that reflect the department's work. Along the hallways are heroic oil paintings of dam construction, gold panning, and cattle drives. A guided tour takes you past more of the three-dozen murals throughout the building. Reservations for the tour are required at least two weeks in advance. The **Department of the Interior Museum** (☎ 202/208–4743), on the first floor, displays more of its artwork holdings. You can enter the building at its E Street or C Street doors; adults must show photo I.D. The small museum tells the story of the Department of the Interior, a huge agency dubbed "the Mother of Departments" because from it grew the departments of Agriculture, Labor, Education, and Energy. Soon after it opened in 1938, the museum became one of the most popular attractions in Washington; evening hours were maintained even during World War II. The museum is open weekdays from 8:30 to 4:30, and the third Saturday of the month, from 1 to 4; admission is free.

Today the Department of the Interior oversees most federally owned land and natural resources. Exhibits in the museum outline the work of the Bureau of Land Management, the U.S. Geological Survey, the Bureau of Indian Affairs, the National Park Service, and other department branches. The museum retains a New Deal–era flavor that carries through to its meticulously created dioramas of historic events and American locales. Depending on your tastes, this makes the place either quaint or outdated. The Indian Craft Shop across the hall from the museum sells Native American pottery, dolls, carvings, jewelry, baskets, and books. ✉ *C and E Sts. between 18th and 19th Sts. NW, White House area* ⊕ *www.doi.gov* 🖾 *Free* Ⓜ *Farragut West.*

❼ Eisenhower Executive Office Building. Once one of the most detested buildings in the city, the Eisenhower Executive Office Building (still called the Old Executive Office Building by locals) is now one of the most beloved. It was built between 1871 and 1888 as the State, War, and Navy Building, headquarters of those three executive-branch offices. Its architect, Alfred B. Mullett, styled it after the Louvre, but detractors quickly criticized the busy French Empire design—with a mansard roof, tall chimneys, and 900 freestanding columns—as an inappropriate counterpoint to the Greek Revival Treasury Building that sits on the other side of the White House. A 1930 plan was approved by Congress to replace the exterior in a Greek Revival style, but was shelved in 1933 due to the depressed economy. The granite edifice may look like a wedding cake, but its high ceilings and spacious offices make it popular with occupants, who include members of the executive branch. Nine presidents, including both Roosevelts, Richard Nixon, and George Bush have had offices here during their careers. The former office of the secretary of the navy is done in the opulent style of the turn of the 20th century; it has been an office for every vice president (except Hubert Humphrey) since Lyndon B. Johnson. The building has hosted numerous historic events: it was here that Secretary of State Cordell Hull met with Japanese diplomats after the bombing of Pearl Harbor, and it was the site of both the first presidential press conference in 1950 and the first televised press conference five years later. Tours have been suspended indefinitely; call ahead if you're planning a visit. ⊠ *East side of 17th St., west of White House, White House area* ☎ *202/395–5895* Ⓜ *Farragut West.*

⑭ **Ellipse.** From this expanse of lawn you can see the Washington Monument and the Jefferson Memorial to the south and the red-tile roof of the Department of Commerce to the east, with the tower of the Old Post Office sticking up above it. To the north you have a good view of the rear of the White House (the Ellipse was once part of its backyard); the rounded portico and Harry Truman's second-story porch are clearly visible. The White House's south lawn, also visible, is a heliport for *Marine One,* the president's helicopter. It's on the northern edge of the Ellipse that the National Christmas Tree is put up each year. In early December the president lights it during a festive ceremony that marks the official beginning of the holiday season. On spring and summer Wednesday evenings at 7, the U.S. Army holds a Twilight Tattoo of musical marching and gun salutes here.

The Ellipse's rather weather-beaten **gatehouse** (at the corner of Constitution Avenue and 17th Street) once stood on Capitol Hill. It was designed in 1828 by Charles Bulfinch, the first native-born American to serve as architect of the Capitol, and was moved here in 1874 after Frederick Law Olmsted redesigned the Capitol grounds. A twin of the gatehouse stands at Constitution Avenue and 15th Street. The **Boy Scouts Memorial** is nearby. ⊠ *Bounded by Constitution Ave. and E, 15th, and 17th Sts., White House area* Ⓜ *Farragut West or McPherson Square.*

❸ **Lafayette Square.** With such an important resident across the street, the National Capital Region's National Park Service gardeners lavish extra attention on this square's trees and flower beds. It's an intimate oasis amid downtown Washington.

When Pierre-Charles L'Enfant proposed the location for the Executive Mansion, the only building north of what is today Pennsylvania Avenue was the Pierce family farmhouse, which stood at the northeast corner of the present square. An apple orchard and a family burial ground were the area's two other features. During the construction of the White House, workers' huts and a brick kiln were set up, and soon residences began popping up around the square (though sheep would continue to graze on it for years). Soldiers camped in the square during the War of 1812 and the Civil War, turning it at both times into a muddy pit. Today, protesters set their placards up in Lafayette Square, jockeying for positions that face the White House. Although the National Park Service can't restrict the protesters' freedom of speech, it does try to limit the size of their signs.

In the center of the park—and dominating the square—is a large **statue of Andrew Jackson.** Erected in 1853 and cast from bronze cannons that Jackson captured during the War of 1812, this was the second equestrian statue made in America. (The first one, of King George III, was in New York City. Colonists melted it down for bullets during the Revolutionary War.)

Jackson's is the only statue of an American in the park. The other statues are of foreign-born soldiers who helped in America's fight for independence. In the southeast corner is the park's namesake, the **Marquis** de **Lafayette,** the young French nobleman who came to America to fight in the Revolution. When Lafayette returned to the United States in 1824 he was given a rousing welcome, being wined and dined in the finest homes and showered with gifts of cash and land.

The colonnaded building across Madison Place at the corner of Pennsylvania Avenue is an annex to the Treasury Department. The modern redbrick building farther on, at 717 Madison Place, houses judicial offices. Its design, with squared-off bay windows, is echoed in the taller building that rises behind it and in the **New Executive Office Building** on the other side of Lafayette Square. Planners in the '20s recommended that the private houses on Lafayette Square, many built in the Federal style, be torn down and replaced with a collection of uniform neoclassical-style government buildings. A lack of funds providentially kept the neighborhood intact, and demolition was not even scheduled until 1957. In the early '60s Jacqueline Kennedy intervened and asked that the historic town houses and residential character be saved. A new plan devised by John Carl Warnecke set the large office buildings behind the historic row houses.

The next house down, yellow with a second-story ironwork balcony, was built in 1828 by Benjamin Ogle Tayloe. During the McKinley administration, Ohio senator Marcus Hanna lived here, and the president's frequent visits earned it the nickname the "Little White House." Dolley Madison lived in the Cutts-Madison House, next door, after her husband died. Both the Tayloe and Madison houses are now part of the U.S. Court of Claims complex.

A bit further north on Madison Place is a statue of **Thaddeus Kosciuszko,** the Polish general who fought alongside American colonists against the British. ✉ *Bounded by Pennsylvania Ave., Madison Pl., H St., and Jackson Pl., White House area* Ⓜ *McPherson Square.*

need a break?

Bernard Baruch, adviser to Woodrow Wilson and other presidents, used to eat his lunch in Lafayette Park; you can, too. Nearby, **Loeb's Restaurant** (✉ 15th and I Sts. NW, White House area ☎ 202/371–1150) is a New York–style deli that serves salads and sandwiches to eat there or to go.

❾ Octagon Museum. Why this six-sided building is named the Octagon remains a subject of debate. Some say it's because the main room is a circle, and was built by rounding out the angles of an eight-sided room; others say it's for the eight angles formed by the odd shape of the six walls—an old definition of an octagon. Designed by Dr. William Thornton (the Capitol's architect), it was built for John Tayloe III, a wealthy Virginia plantation owner, and was completed in 1801. Thornton chose the unusual shape to conform to the acute angle formed by L'Enfant's intersection of New York Avenue and 18th Street.

After the White House was burned in 1814, the Tayloes invited James and Dolley Madison to stay in the Octagon. It was in a second-floor study that the Treaty of Ghent, ending the War of 1812, was ratified. By the late 1800s the building was used as a rooming house. In the 20th century the house served as the headquarters of the American Institute of Architects before the construction of AIA's rather unexceptional building behind it. It's now the Museum of the American Architectural Foundation.

A renovation in the 1960s revealed the intricate plaster molding and the original 1799 Coade stone mantels (named for the woman who invented a now-lost method of casting crushed stone). A far more thorough restoration, completed in 1996, returned the Octagon to its 1815 appearance, topped off by a historically accurate, cypress-shingle roof with balustrade. The galleries inside host changing exhibits on architecture, city planning, and Washington history and design. ⊠ *1799 New York Ave. NW, White House area* ☎ *202/638-3105* ⊕ *www. archfoundation.org* ⊠ *$5* ☉ *Tues.–Sun. 10–4* Ⓜ *Farragut West or Farragut North.*

⑫ **Organization of American States.** The headquarters of the Organization of American States, which is made up of nations from North, South, and Central America, contains a patio adorned with a pre-Columbian–style fountain and lush tropical plants. This tiny rain forest is a good place to rest when Washington's summer heat is at its most oppressive. The upstairs Hall of the Americas contains busts of generals and statesmen from the 34 OAS member nations, as well as each country's flag. The OAS runs the Art Museum of the Americas. ⊠ *17th St. and Constitution Ave. NW, White House area* ☎ *202/458-3000* ⊕ *www.oas.org* ⊠ *Free* ☉ *Weekdays 9–5:30* Ⓜ *Farragut West.*

⑯ **Pershing Park.** A quiet, sunken garden honors General John J. "Black Jack" Pershing, the first to hold the title General of the Armies, a rank Congress created in 1919 to recognize his military achievements. Engravings on the stone walls recount pivotal campaigns from World War I, where Pershing commanded the American expeditionary force and conducted other military exploits. Ice-skaters glide on the square pool here in winter. ⊠ *15th St. and Pennsylvania Ave., White House area* Ⓜ *McPherson Square.*

need a break? One block north of Pershing Park is the venerable **Hotel Washington** (⊠ 515 15th St. NW, White House area ☎ 202/638-5900 ⊕ www. hotelwashington.com), where the view from the rooftop Sky Top Terrace—open May to October—is one of the best in the city. Drinks, coffee, and a light menu are available.

⑥ **Renwick Gallery.** The Renwick Gallery of the Smithsonian American Art Museum remains at the forefront of the crafts movement, and its collection includes exquisitely designed and made utilitarian items, as well as objects created out of such traditional crafts media as fiber and glass. The words "Dedicated to Art" are engraved above the entrance to the French Second Empire–style building, designed by architect James Renwick in 1859 to house the art collection of Washington merchant and banker William Wilson Corcoran. Corcoran was a Southern sympathizer who spent the duration of the Civil War in Europe. While he was away, the government pressed his unfinished building into service as a quartermaster general's post.

In 1871 the Corcoran, as it was then called, opened as the first private art museum in the city. Corcoran's collection quickly outgrew the building, and in 1897 it was moved to what's now the Corcoran Gallery of Art. After a stint as the U.S. Court of Claims, the building Renwick designed was restored, renamed after its architect, and opened in 1972 as the Smithsonian's Museum of American Crafts. Although crafts such as handwoven rugs and delicately carved tables were once considered less "artistic" than, say, oil paintings and sculptures, they have long since come into their own. Not everything in the museum is Shaker furniture and enamel jewelry, though. The second-floor Grand Salon is still furnished in the opulent Victorian style Corcoran favored when his collection adorned its walls. ⊠ *Pennsylvania Ave. at 17th St. NW, White*

House area ☎ *202/357–2531; 202/357–1729 TDD* ⊕ *www.americanart. si.edu* ▣ *Free* ⊙ *Daily 10–5:30* Ⓜ *Farragut West.*

④ St. John's Episcopal Church. The golden-domed so-called Church of the Presidents sits across Lafayette Park from the White House. Every president since Madison has visited the church, and many worshiped here regularly. Built in 1816, the church was the second building on the square. Benjamin Latrobe, who worked on both the Capitol and the White House, designed it in the form of a Greek cross, with a flat dome and a lantern cupola. The church has been altered somewhat since then; additions include the Doric portico and the cupola tower. You can best sense the intent of Latrobe's design while standing inside under the saucer-shape dome of the original building. Not far from the center of the church is Pew 54, where visiting presidents are seated. The kneeling benches of many of the pews are embroidered with the presidential seal and the names of several chief executives. Brochures are available inside for self-guided tours. ✉ *16th and H Sts. NW, White House area* ☎ *202/347–8766* ▣ *Free* ⊙ *Weekdays 9–3; guided tours by appointment* Ⓜ *McPherson Square.*

⑰ Treasury Building. Once used to store currency, this is the largest Greek Revival edifice in Washington. Robert Mills, the architect responsible for the Washington Monument and the Patent Office (now the Smithsonian American Art Museum), designed the grand colonnade that stretches down 15th Street. Construction of the Treasury Building started in 1836 and, after several additions, was finally completed in 1869. Its southern facade has a **statue of Alexander Hamilton,** the department's first secretary. The Andrew Johnson Suite was used by Johnson as the executive office while Mrs. Lincoln moved out of the White House. Other vestiges of its earlier days are the two-story marble Cash Room and a 19th-century burglarproof vault lining. Tours have been suspended indefinitely; call ahead if you're planning a visit ✉ *15th St. and Pennsylvania Ave. NW, White House area* ☎ *202/622–0896; 202/ 622–0692 TDD* Ⓜ *McPherson Square or Metro Center.*

> **need a break?**
> The **Bonkay** (✉ 727 15th St. NW, lower level, White House area ☎ 202/737–1515) restaurant has a lunchtime sushi buffet. The luxurious **Old Ebbitt Grill** (✉ 675 15th St. NW, White House area ☎ 202/347–4800) is a popular watering spot for journalists and TV news correspondents. About a block from the Treasury Building is a glittering urban mall, the **Shops** (✉ National Press Bldg., F and G Sts. between 13th and 14th Sts. NW, White House area), which houses full-service restaurants as well as faster and cheaper fare in its top-floor food court.

★ ☺ ② White House. This "house" surely has the best-known address in the United States: 1600 Pennsylvania Avenue. Pierre-Charles L'Enfant called it the President's House; it was known formally as the Executive Mansion; and in 1902 Congress officially proclaimed it the White House after long-standing common usage of that name. Irishman James Hoban's plan, based on the Georgian design of Leinster Hall in Dublin and of other Irish country houses, was selected in a 1792 contest. The building wasn't ready for its first occupant, John Adams, the second U.S. president, until 1800: George Washington, who seems to have slept everyplace else, never stayed here. The building has undergone many structural changes since then. Andrew Jackson installed running water. James Garfield put in the first elevator. Between 1948 and 1952, Harry Truman had the entire structure gutted and restored, adding a second-story porch to the south portico. Each family that has called the White House home has left its imprint on the 132-room mansion.

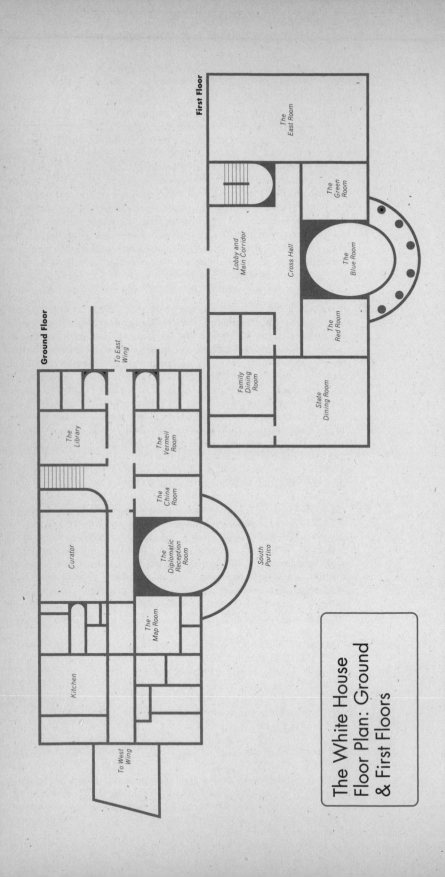

First Floor

The East Room

Lobby and Main Corridor

Cross Hall

The Green Room

The Blue Room

The Red Room

Family Dining Room

State Dining Room

Ground Floor

To East Wing

The Library

The Vermeil Room

The China Room

Curator

The Diplomatic Reception Room

The Map Room

Kitchen

South Portico

To West Wing

The White House
Floor Plan: Ground
& First Floors

Selected public rooms on the ground floor and first floor are open to visitors who make arrangements in advance through their member of Congress. The tour includes several rooms on the ground floor and, on the State Floor, the large white-and-gold **East Room,** the site of presidential social events. In 1814 Dolley Madison saved the room's full-length portrait of George Washington from torch-carrying British soldiers by cutting it from its frame, rolling it up, and spiriting it out of the White House. (Dolley, not a fool, also rescued her own portrait.) One of Abraham Lincoln's sons once harnessed a pet goat to a chair and went for a ride through the East Room during a reception.

The Federal-style **Green Room,** named for the moss-green watered silk that covers its walls, is used for informal receptions and "photo opportunities" with foreign heads of state. Notable furnishings here include a New England sofa that once belonged to Daniel Webster and portraits of Benjamin Franklin, John Quincy Adams, and Abigail Adams. The president and his guests are often shown on TV sitting in front of the Green Room's English Empire mantel, engaging in what are generally described as "frank and cordial" discussions.

The elliptical **Blue Room,** the most formal space in the White House, is furnished with a gilded Empire-style settee and chairs that were ordered by James Monroe. (Monroe asked for plain wooden chairs, but the furniture manufacturer thought such unadorned furnishings too simple for the White House and took it upon himself to supply chairs more in keeping with their surroundings.) The White House Christmas tree is placed in this room each year. (Another well-known elliptical room, the president's **Oval Office,** is in the West Wing of the White House, along with other executive offices.)

The **Red Room** is decorated as an American Empire–style parlor of the early 19th century, with furniture by the New York cabinetmaker Charles-Honoré Lannuier. The marble mantel is the twin of the one in the Green Room.

The **State Dining Room,** second in size only to the East Room, can seat 140 people. It's dominated by G. P. A. Healy's portrait of Abraham Lincoln, painted after the president's death. The stone mantel is inscribed with a quote from one of John Adams's letters: "I pray heaven to bestow the best of blessings on this house and all that shall hereafter inhabit it. May none but honest and wise men ever rule under this roof." In Teddy Roosevelt's day a stuffed moose head hung over the mantel. ⊠ *1600 Pennsylvania Ave. NW, Downtown* ☎ *202/208–1631; 202/456–7041 24-hr information line* ⊕ *www.whitehouse.gov* Ⓜ *Federal Triangle.*

▶ **①** **White House Visitor Center.** The visitor center is in charge of handing out White House tickets. All tours must be arranged by a member of Congress, and they may be cancelled at any time without notice. Updates on the situation are available through the Web or by calling the information line. On display at the center are photographs, artifacts, and videos that relate to the White House's construction, decor, and residents. ⊡ *1450 Pennsylvania Ave. NW* ⊠ *Entrance: Department of Commerce's Baldrige Hall, E St. between 14th and 15th Sts., White House area* ☎ *202/208–1631; 202/456–7041 24-hr information line* ⊕ *www. nps.gov/whho* 🖃 *Free* ☉ *Daily 7:30–4* Ⓜ *Federal Triangle.*

⑮ **William Tecumseh Sherman Monument.** Sherman, whose Atlanta Campaign in 1864 cut a bloody swath of destruction through the Confederacy, was said to be the greatest Civil War general, as the sheer size of this massive monument, set in a small park, would seem to attest. ⊠ *Bounded by E and 15th Sts., East Executive Ave., and Alexander Hamilton Pl., White House area* Ⓜ *Federal Triangle.*

CAPITOL HILL

The people who live and work on "the Hill" do so in the shadow of the edifice that lends the neighborhood its name: the gleaming white Capitol. More than just the center of government, however, the Hill also includes charming residential blocks lined with Victorian row houses and a fine assortment of restaurants, bars, and shops. Capitol Hill's exact boundaries are disputed: it's bordered to the west, north, and south by the Capitol, H Street NE, and I Street SE, respectively. Some argue that Capitol Hill extends east to the Anacostia River, others say that it ends at 14th Street near Lincoln Park. The neighborhood does in fact seem to extend its boundaries as urban pioneers and members of Capitol Hill's active historic-preservation movement restore more and more 19th-century houses.

The Capitol serves as the point from which the city is divided into quadrants: northwest, southwest, northeast, and southeast. North Capitol Street, which runs north from the Capitol, separates northeast from northwest; East Capitol Street separates northeast and southeast; South Capitol Street separates southwest and southeast; and the Mall (Independence Avenue on the south and Constitution Avenue on the north) separates northwest from southwest.

Numbers in the text correspond to numbers in the margin and on the Capitol Hill map.

a good walk

Start your exploration of the Hill at the beautifully restored **Union Station ❶ ▶**. You can take a side trip to the Pope John Paul II Cultural Center and the National Shrine of the Immaculate Conception by taking the Metro from Union Station to Brookland–Catholic University. For a detour to the Capital Children's Museum, take two escalators up from the station's Amtrak concourse to the parking garage and follow signs for Friendship Bridge. Turn right on the bridge and walk left at Third Street to reach the museum entrance. If you're staying on the main tour, head to the **National Postal Museum ❷**, across the street from the arcade to the right of the main Union Station exit. Just east of the station is the **Thurgood Marshall Federal Judiciary Building ❸**, with a spectacular atrium. Follow Delaware Avenue from the Columbus fountain directly in front of Union Station. On the left you pass the Russell Senate Office Building (1st Street and Constitution Avenue NE); note the way the stone below the second-story windows resembles twisted lengths of fringed cloth. To the right, a block west on Constitution Avenue, is the **Robert A. Taft Memorial ❹**. Behind it, on the triangle formed by New Jersey and Louisiana avenues and D Street NW, is the **National Japanese American Memorial to Patriotism**; its granite walls honor the Japanese-American soldiers who fought in World War II and also list the 10 internment camps where 120,000 Japanese-Americans were held from 1942 to 1945. Heading southward again, cross Constitution Avenue to the **Capitol ❺**, where Congress decides how to spend your federal tax dollars. Walk down Capitol Hill and out the westernmost exit to the white-marble **Peace Monument ❻**. Walking south on 1st Street NW, you pass the Capitol Reflecting Pool, the **Grant Memorial ❼**, and the **James Garfield Memorial ❽**. Across Maryland Avenue is the **United States Botanic Garden ❾**, an indoor museum of orchids, cacti, and other flora. The ornate **Bartholdi Fountain ❿** is in a park across Independence Avenue. Continue east on

Independence Avenue, walking back up Capitol Hill past the Rayburn, Longworth, and Cannon House office buildings, to the Jefferson Building of the **Library of Congress** ⑪.

Continue on 1st Street NE to the **Supreme Court Building** ⑫, near East Capitol Street. One block north, at the corner of Constitution Avenue and 2nd Street, is the redbrick **Sewall-Belmont House** ⑬, from 1800. For a taste of the residential side of the Hill, follow Maryland Avenue to Stanton Park; then walk two blocks south on 4th Street NE to A Street NE. The **Frederick Douglass Townhouse** ⑭ is between 3rd and 4th streets. The houses on the **south side of East Capitol Street** ⑮ are a sampling of the different architectural styles on the Hill. At the corner of 3rd and East Capitol streets stands the **Folger Shakespeare Library** ⑯, the world's foremost collection of works by and about the playwright.

If you'd like to make a side trip to visit the Navy and Marine Corps sites on Capitol Hill, head east on East Capitol Street to 8th Street SE and take the bus south to I Street SE, in front of the **Marine Corps Barracks.** Walk under the highway overpass to the **Washington Navy Yard** complex, enter from the gate at 9th and M streets SE, and follow signs for the Navy Art Museum, Navy Art Gallery, Marine Corps Historical Center, and the USS *Barry.*

TIMING Touring Capitol Hill should take you about four hours, allowing for about an hour each at the Capitol, the Botanic Garden, and the Library of Congress. If you want to see Congress in action, bear in mind that the House and Senate are usually not in session during August. Supreme Court cases are usually heard October through April, Monday through Wednesday of two weeks in each month. The side trip to the two sites near Catholic University, the Pope John Paul II Cultural Center and the National Shrine of the Immaculate Conception, will take about half a day. The side trip to the Navy and Marine sites takes a similar amount of time, about four hours. A detour to the Capitol Children's Museum takes a full morning or afternoon.

What to See

⑩ **Bartholdi Fountain.** Frédéric-Auguste Bartholdi, sculptor of the Statue of Liberty, created this delightful fountain, some 30 foot tall, for the Philadelphia International Exposition of 1876. The aquatic monsters, sea nymphs, tritons, and lighted globes all represent the elements of water and light. The U.S. Government purchased the fountain after the exposition and placed it on the grounds of the old Botanic Garden on the Mall. It was moved to its present location in 1932 and was restored in 1986. The surrounding Bartholdi Park, which has benches and dense plantings, fills with brown-baggers at lunchtime. ✉ *1st St. and Independence Ave. SW, The Mall* Ⓜ *Federal Center.*

🄲 **Capital Children's Museum.** This sprawling, hands-on museum full of culture, science, and crafts keeps kids ages 1 through 12 busy. Children can "drive" a Metrobus, stage a puppet show, or enclose themselves in huge soap bubbles. The museum has in-depth exhibitions on the cultures of Mexico and Japan, including a spectacular Mexican plaza re-created in the museum's three-story atrium. Kids can board a replica of a bullet train, sit cross-legged in a Japanese living room, and leaf through kanji-filled schoolbooks in a Japanese-style classroom. Scientists age 6 and up may perform experiments led by "stand-up" chemists at the chemical science center. The museum is a bit frayed around the edges, but it's the comfortable sort of wear and tear achieved through the inquisitive hands of countless youngsters. The only refreshments available are from vending machines in a lunchroom. Daily activities are posted at

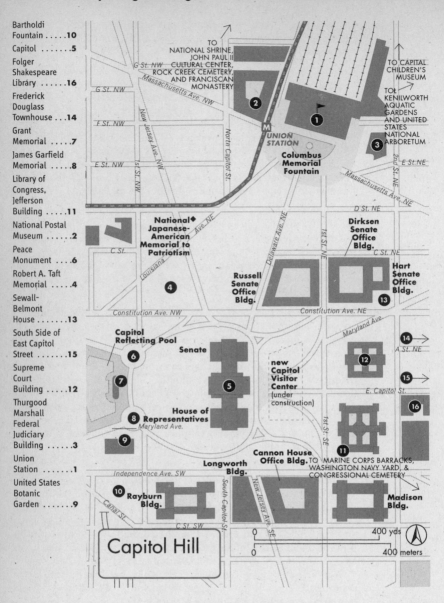

Capitol Hill

the entrance. ✉ 800 3rd St. NE, Capitol Hill ☎ 202/675–4120 ⊕ www.
ccm.org ✉ $7 ☉ Daily 10–5 Ⓜ Union Station.

⑤ Capitol. Before heading to the Capitol, pay a little attention to the
grounds, landscaped in the late 19th century by Frederick Law Olmsted, a co-creator of New York City's Central Park. On these 68 acres
are both the city's tamest squirrels and the highest concentration of TV
news correspondents, jockeying for a good position in front of the
Capitol for their "stand-ups." A few hundred feet northeast of the
Capitol are two cast-iron car shelters, left from the days when horse-
drawn trolleys served the Hill. Olmsted's six pinkish, bronze-top lamps
directly east from the Capitol are worth a look, too.

The design of the building itself was the result of a competition held in
1792; the winner was William Thornton, a physician and amateur ar-

FodorsChoice ★

United States Capitol: Second-Floor Plan

0   30 yards

0   30 meters

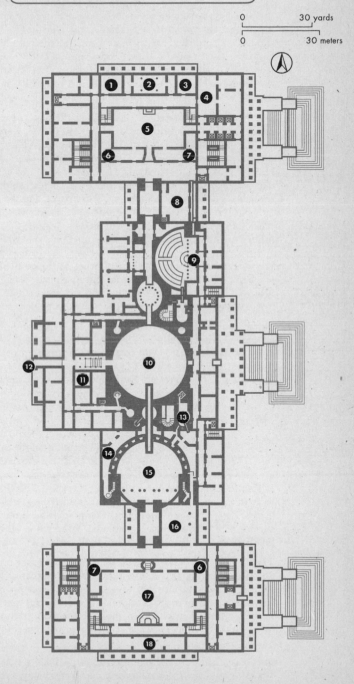

chitect from the West Indies. With its central rotunda and dome, Thornton's Capitol is reminiscent of Rome's Pantheon. This similarity must have delighted the nation's founders, who sought inspiration from the principles of the Republic of Rome.

The cornerstone was laid by George Washington in a Masonic ceremony on September 18, 1793, and in November 1800, both the Senate and the House of Representatives moved down from Philadelphia to occupy the first completed section: the boxlike portion between the central rotunda and today's north wing. (Subsequent efforts to find the cornerstone Washington laid have been unsuccessful, though when the east front was extended in the 1950s, workers found a knee joint thought to be from a 500-pound ox that was roasted at the 1793 celebration.) By 1807 the House wing had been completed, just to the south of what's now the domed center, and a covered wooden walkway joined the two wings.

The "Congress House" grew slowly and suffered a grave setback on August 24, 1814, when British troops led by Sir George Cockburn marched on Washington and set fire to the Capitol, the White House, and numerous other government buildings. (Cockburn reportedly stood on the House Speaker's chair and asked his men, "Shall this harbor of Yankee democracy be burned?" The question was rhetorical; the building was torched.) The wooden walkway was destroyed and the two wings gutted, but the walls were left standing after a violent rainstorm doused the flames. Fearful that Congress might leave Washington, residents raised money for a hastily built "Brick Capitol" that stood where the Supreme Court is today. Architect Benjamin Henry Latrobe supervised the rebuilding, adding such American touches as the corncob-and-tobacco-leaf capitals to columns in the east entrance of the Senate wing. He was followed by Boston-born Charles Bulfinch, and in 1826 the Capitol, its low wooden dome sheathed in copper, was finished.

North and south wings were added in the 1850s and 1860s to accommodate a growing government trying to keep pace with a growing country. The elongated edifice extended farther north and south than Thornton had planned, and in 1855, to keep the scale correct, work began on a taller, cast-iron dome. President Lincoln was criticized for continuing this expensive project while the country was in the throes of the Civil War, but he called the construction "a sign we intend the Union shall go on." This twin-shell dome, a marvel of 19th-century engineering, rises 285 feet above the ground and weighs 4,500 tons. It expands and contracts up to 4 inches a day, depending on the outside temperature. The allegorical figure atop the dome, often mistaken for Pocahontas, is called *Freedom*. Sculptor Thomas Crawford had first planned for the 19½-foot-tall bronze statue to wear the cloth liberty cap of a freed Roman slave, but Southern lawmakers, led by Jefferson Davis, objected. An "American" headdress composed of a star-encircled helmet surmounted with an eagle's head and feathers was substituted. A light just below the statue burns whenever Congress is in session.

The Capitol has continued to grow. In 1962 the east front was extended 33½ feet, creating 100 additional offices. Preservationists have fought to keep the west front from being extended, since it's the last remaining section of the Capitol's original facade. A compromise was reached in 1983, when it was agreed that the facade's crumbling sandstone blocks would simply be replaced with stronger limestone.

Tours of the Capitol start under the center of the **Rotunda's** dome. At the dome's center is Constantino Brumidi's 1865 fresco, *Apotheosis of Washington*. The figures in the inner circle represent the 13 original states;

those in the outer ring symbolize arts, sciences, and industry. The flat, sculpture-style frieze around the Rotunda's rim depicts 400 years of American history and was started by Brumidi in 1877. While painting Penn's treaty with the Indians, the 74-year-old artist slipped on the 58-foot-high scaffold and almost fell off. Brumidi managed to hang on until help arrived, but he died a few months later from the shock of the incident. The work was continued by another Italian, Filippo Costaggini, but the frieze wasn't finished until American Allyn Cox added the final touches in 1953.

The Rotunda's eight immense oil paintings are of scenes from American history. The four scenes from the Revolutionary War are by John Trumbull, who served alongside George Washington and painted the first president from life. Twenty-nine people have lain in state or in honor in the Rotunda, including nine presidents, from Abraham Lincoln to Lyndon Baines Johnson. The most recently honored were the two U.S. Capitol policemen killed in the line of duty in 1998.

South of the Rotunda is **Statuary Hall,** once the legislative chamber of the House of Representatives. The room has an architectural quirk that maddened early legislators: a slight whisper uttered on one side of the hall can be heard on the other. (This parlor trick doesn't always work; sometimes the hall is just too noisy.) When the House moved out, Congress invited each state to send statues of two great deceased citizens for placement in the former chamber. Because the weight of the accumulated statues threatened to cave the floor in, some of the sculptures were dispersed to other spots in the Capitol.

To the north, on the Senate side, is the chamber once used by the Supreme Court and, above it, the splendid Old Senate Chamber (closed until further notice), both of which have been restored. In the Brumidi Corridor (also closed until further notice), on the ground floor of the Senate wing, frescoes and oil paintings of birds, plants, and American inventions adorn the walls and ceilings. Intricate, Brumidi-designed bronze stairways lead to the second floor. The Italian artist also memorialized several American heroes, painting them inside trompe l'oeil frames. Some frames were left blank. The most recent one to be filled, in 1987, honors the crew of the space shuttle *Challenger.*

Due to construction of the **Capitol Visitor Center,** a three-level subterranean education and information area beneath the east side of the building scheduled to open in 2005, tours begin on the west front of the Capitol in a special screening facility. They run Monday through Saturday from 9:30 AM to 3:30 PM. The free timed-entry tickets are distributed, one ticket per person, starting at 8:15 AM. Free gallery passes to watch the House or Senate in session can only be obtained from your senator or representative's office; both chambers are closed to the public when Congress is not in session. Note that there is a strict limit to the baggage and possessions that can be brought into the building: there are no facilities for checking personal belongings. If you're planning a visit, call ahead to check the status of tours and access; security measures may change. ✉ *East end of Mall, Capitol Hill* ☎ *202/224–3121 Capitol switchboard; 202/225–6827 guide service* ⊕ *www.aoc.gov* ✉ *Free* Ⓜ *Capitol South or Union Station.*

Congressional Cemetery. Established in 1807 "for all denomination of people," the Congressional Cemetery was the first national cemetery created by the government. Notables buried here include U.S. Capitol architect William Thornton, Marine Corps march composer John Philip Sousa, Civil War photographer Mathew Brady, and FBI director J.

Edgar Hoover. There are also 76 members of Congress, many of them beneath ponderous markers. A brochure for a self-guided walking tour is available at the office and in a mailbox near the main gate. ⊠ *1801 E St. SE, Capitol Hill* ☎ *202/543–0539* ⊕ *www.congressionalcemetery. org* ⊙ *Daily dawn–dusk; office Mon.–Wed. and Fri.* Ⓜ *Stadium Armory or Potomac Avenue.*

⑯ Folger Shakespeare Library. The Folger Library's collection of works by and about Shakespeare and his times is second to none. The white-marble art deco building, designed by architect Paul Philippe Cret and dedicated in 1932, is decorated with scenes from the Bard's plays. Inside is a reproduction of an inn-yard theater—the site for performances of chamber music, baroque opera, and Shakespearean plays—and a gallery, designed in the manner of an Elizabethan Great Hall, which hosts rotating exhibits from the library's collection. Henry Clay Folger, the library's founder, was Standard Oil's president and chairman of the board. ⊠ *201 E. Capitol St. SE, Capitol Hill* ☎ *202/544–7077* ⊕ *www.folger. edu* ☜ *Free* ⊙ *Mon.–Sat. 10–4* Ⓜ *Capitol South.*

> **off the beaten path**

FRANCISCAN MONASTERY AND GARDENS – Not far from the National Shrine of the Immaculate Conception, this Byzantine-style Franciscan monastery contains facsimiles of such Holy Land shrines as the Grotto of Bethlehem and the Holy Sepulchre. Underground are reproductions of the catacombs of Rome. The rose gardens are especially beautiful. Take the Metro here from Union Station. The monastery and shrine are about the same distance from the metro, but in opposite directions. ⊠ *14th and Quincy Sts. NE, Catholic University* ☎ *202/526–6800* ⊕ *www.myfranciscan.com* ☜ *Free* ⊙ *Daily 9–5, catacombs tour on the hr (except noon) Mon.–Sat. 9–4, Sun. 1–4* Ⓜ *Brookland/Catholic University.*

⑭ Frederick Douglass Townhouse. In the first Washington home of the fiery abolitionist and writer are two restored rooms containing Douglass memorabilia. The rest of the structure houses the Hall of Fame for Caring Americans. ⊠ *316–320 A St. NE, Capitol Hill* ☎ *202/544–6130* ☜ *Free* ⊙ *By appointment only.*

> **off the beaten path**

GLENWOOD CEMETERY – Not too far from Catholic University is Glenwood. The cemetery has its share of notable residents, including the artists Constantino Brumidi, responsible for much of the Capitol building's beauty (among other things, he painted the frescoes adorning the inside of the great dome), and Emanuel Leutze, painter of *Washington Crossing the Delaware.* More striking are the tombstones of two more-obscure citizens: Benjamin Greenup was the first firefighter killed on duty in Washington, and he's honored with an obelisk carved with his death scene. Teresina Vasco, a child who died at age two after playing with matches, is immortalized sitting in her favorite rocking chair. ⊠ *2219 Lincoln Rd. NE, Catholic University* ☎ *202/667–1016* ⊙ *Daily dawn–dusk; office weekdays 9:30–3:30* Ⓜ *Brookland/Catholic University.*

❼ Grant Memorial. The 252-foot-long memorial to the 18th American president and commander in chief of the Union forces during the Civil War is one of the largest sculpture groups in the city. The pedestal statue of Ulysses S. Grant on horseback displays his composure in the face of chaos. The soldiers and horses are notable for their realism; sculptor Henry Shrady spent 20 years researching and completing the memorial. ⊠ *Near 1st St. and Maryland Ave. SW, Capitol Hill* Ⓜ *Federal Center.*

8 James Garfield Memorial. Near the Grant Memorial and the United States Botanic Garden is a memorial to the 20th president of the United States. James Garfield was assassinated in 1881 after only a few months in office. His bronze statue stands on a pedestal with three other bronze figures seated around it; one bears a tablet inscribed with the words LAW, JUSTICE, AND PROSPERITY. Garfield's two primary claims to fame were that he was the last log-cabin president and that his was the second presidential assassination (Lincoln's was first), ending the second-shortest presidency (the shortest was William Henry Harrison's, killed by pneumonia less than a month into his term in office). ⊠ *1st St. and Maryland Ave. SW, Capitol Hill* Ⓜ *Federal Center.*

> **off the beaten path**

KENILWORTH AQUATIC GARDENS – Exotic water lilies, lotuses, hyacinths, and other water-loving plants thrive in this 14-acre sanctuary of quiet ponds and marshy flats. The gardens' wetland animals include turtles, frogs, beavers, spring azure butterflies, and some 40 species of birds. In July nearly everything blossoms; early morning is the best time to visit, when day-bloomers are just opening and night-bloomers have yet to close. ⊠ *Anacostia Ave. and Douglas St. NE, Anacostia* ☎ *202/426–6905* ⊕ *www.nps.gov/nace/keaq* ⊠ *Free* ⊙ *Gardens open daily 6:30–4; visitor center daily 8–4; garden tour summer weekends at 9, 11, and 1.*

⓫ Library of Congress. One of the world's largest libraries, the Library of Congress contains some 115 million items, of which only a quarter are books. The remainder includes manuscripts, prints, films, photographs, sheet music, and the largest collection of maps in the world. Also part of the library is the Congressional Research Service, which, as the name implies, works on special projects for senators and representatives.

Built in 1897, the copper-domed 1897 Thomas Jefferson Building is the oldest of the three buildings that make up the library. Like many other structures in Washington, the library was criticized when it was completed. Detractors felt its design, based on the Paris Opera House, was too florid. Congressmen were even heard to grumble that its dome—topped with the gilt "Flame of Knowledge"—competed with that of their Capitol. It's certainly decorative, with busts of Dante, Goethe, Nathaniel Hawthorne, and other great writers perched above its entryway. The *Court of Neptune,* Roland Hinton Perry's fountain at the base of the front steps, rivals some of Rome's best fountains.

Provisions for a library to serve members of Congress were originally made in 1800, when the government set aside $5,000 to purchase and house books that legislators might need to consult. This small collection was housed in the Capitol but was destroyed in 1814, when the British burned the city. Thomas Jefferson, then in retirement at Monticello, offered his personal library as a replacement, noting that "there is, in fact, no subject to which a Member of Congress may not have occasion to refer." Jefferson's collection of 6,487 books, for which Congress eventually paid him $23,950, laid the foundation for the great national library. (Sadly, another fire in 1851 destroyed two-thirds of Jefferson's books.) By the late 1800s it was clear that the Capitol could no longer contain the growing library, and the Jefferson Building was constructed. The **Adams Building,** on 2nd Street behind the Jefferson, was added in 1939. A third structure, the **James Madison Building,** opened in 1980; it's just south of the Jefferson Building, between Independence Avenue and C Street. Less architecturally interesting than the Jefferson building, the Adams does attract visitors for evening literary readings and small exhibitions, which are open from 8:30 AM to

6 PM. The U.S. Copyright Office, in Room 401, is where all copyright registrations are issued.

The Jefferson Building opens into the Great Hall, richly adorned with mosaics, paintings, and curving marble stairways. The grand, octagonal Main Reading Room, its central desk surrounded by mahogany readers' tables under a 160-foot-high domed ceiling, may inspire some researchers and overwhelm others. Computer terminals have replaced card catalogs, but books are still retrieved and dispersed the same way: readers (18 years or older) hand request slips to librarians and wait patiently for their materials to be delivered. Researchers aren't allowed in the stacks, and only members of Congress and other special borrowers can check books out. Items from the library's collection—which includes one of only three perfect Gutenberg Bibles in the world—are on display in the Jefferson Building's second-floor Southwest Gallery and Pavilion. ⊠ *Jefferson Bldg., 1st St. and Independence Ave. SE, Capitol Hill* ☎ *202/707–4604, 202/707–5000, or 202/707–6400* ⊕ *www.loc.gov* ✇ *Free* ⊙ *Mon.–Sat. 10 AM–5:30 PM; reading room hrs may extend later. Free tours Mon.–Sat. 10:30 AM, 11:30 AM, 1:30 PM, 2:30 PM, and weekdays 3:30 PM* Ⓜ *Capitol South.*

need a break? It's easy to grab a bite near the Library of Congress. The sixth-floor dining halls of the library's **Madison Building** offer great views and inexpensive fare to the public weekdays from 9 to 10:30 and from 12:30 to 3. Or head for the south side of Pennsylvania Avenue SE, between 2nd and 4th streets, which is lined with restaurants and bars frequented by those who live and work on the Hill. **Le Bon Café** (⊠ 210 2nd St. SE, Capitol Hill ☎ 202/547–7200) is a cozy French bistro that serves excellent coffees, pastries, and light lunches. **Bullfeathers** (⊠ 410 First St. SE, Capitol Hill ☎ 202/543–5005), which has a 40-foot-long bar, has been serving beer and burgers to members of the House since 1980.

Marine Corps Barracks and Commandant's House. The Marine Corps Barracks, the nation's oldest continuously active Marine installation, is the home of the Marine Band. On Friday evenings from May to August, you can attend the hour-long ceremony given on the parade deck by the U.S. Marine Band (the "President's Own") and the Drum and Bugle Corps (the "Commandant's Own"). Entry to the grounds at other times is by tour only. ⊠ *8th and I streets SE, Capitol Hill* ☎ *202/433–4173* ⊕ *www.mbw.usmc.mil* ✇ *Free.* ⊙ *Public concerts May–Aug., 9 PM; the line for general admission tickets begins to form at 7 PM, or reserve tickets in advance by phone. Tours Mon.–Thurs. 10 AM and 1 PM by advance phone reservation only* Ⓜ *Eastern Market.*

🖑 ❷ **National Postal Museum.** The Smithsonian's stamp collection, housed here, consists of a whopping 11 million stamps. Exhibits, underscoring the important part the mail has played in the development of America, include horse-drawn mail coaches, railway mail cars, airmail planes, and a collection of philatelic rarities. The National Museum of Natural History may have the Hope Diamond, but the National Postal Museum has the container used to mail the priceless gem to the Smithsonian. The family-oriented museum has more than 40 interactive and touch-screen exhibits. The museum takes up only a portion of what is the old Washington City Post Office, designed by Daniel Burnham and completed in 1914. Nostalgic odes to the noble mail carrier are inscribed on the exterior of the marble building; one of them, "The Letter," eulogizes the "Messenger of sympathy and love / Servant of parted friends / Consoler of the lonely / Bond of the scattered family / Enlarger of the common life." ⊠ *2 Massa-*

chusetts Ave. NE, Capitol Hill ☎ *202/357–2700; 202/357–1729 TDD* ⊕ *www.si.edu/postal* ⊠ *Free* ⊘ *Daily 10–5:30* Ⓜ *Union Station.*

off the
beaten
path

NATIONAL SHRINE OF THE IMMACULATE CONCEPTION – The largest Catholic church in the United States, the National Shrine of the Immaculate Conception was begun in 1920 and built with funds contributed by every parish in the country. Dedicated in 1959, the shrine is a blend of Romanesque and Byzantine styles, with a bell tower that recalls that of St. Mark's in Venice. Take the Metro here from Union Station; the shrine is about a half mile from the station, halfway to the Pope John Paul II Cultural Center. ⊠ *400 Michigan Ave. NE, Catholic University* ☎ *202/526–8300* ⊕ *www. nationalshrine.com* ⊘ *Apr.–Oct., daily 7–7; Nov.–Mar., daily 7–6; Sat. vigil mass at 5:15; Sun. mass at 7:30, 9, 10:30, noon, 1:30 (in Latin), and 4:30* Ⓜ *Brookland/Catholic University.*

❻ Peace Monument. A white-marble memorial depicts America in the form of a woman grief-stricken over sailors lost at sea during the Civil War; she's weeping on the shoulder of a second female figure representing History. The plaque inscription refers movingly to Navy personnel who "fell in defence of the union and liberty of their country 1861–1865." ⊠ *Traffic circle at 1st St. and Pennsylvania Ave. NW, The Mall.* Ⓜ *Union Station.*

Pope John Paul II Cultural Center. Part museum, part place of pilgrimage, the Pope John Paul II Cultural Center is a spectacular architectural embodiment of the Roman Catholic church's desire to celebrate its charismatic leader and its rich artistic tradition. Themes covered include church and papal history, representations of the Virgin Mary, Polish heritage, and the Catholic tradition of community activism. These are explored through traditional displays of art and artifacts as well as with audiovisual presentations and interactive computer stations. The center is about a mile from the Metro and can easily be combined with a visit to the National Shrine of the Immaculate Conception. ⊠ *3900 Harewood Rd. NE, Catholic University* ☎ *202/635–5400* ⊕ *www.jp2cc.org* ⊠ *$8* ⊘ *Tues.–Sat. 10–5, Sun. noon–5* Ⓜ *Brookland/Catholic University.*

❹ Robert A. Taft Memorial. Rising above the trees in the triangle formed by Louisiana, New Jersey, and Constitution avenues, a monolithic carillon pays tribute to the longtime Republican senator and son of the 27th president. ⊠ *Constitution and New Jersey Aves. NW, Capitol Hill* Ⓜ *Union Station.*

Rock Creek Cemetery. Rock Creek, the city's oldest cemetery, is administered by the city's oldest church, St. Paul's Episcopal, which erected its first building in 1712. (A single brick wall is all that remains of the original structure.) Many beautiful and imposing monuments are in the cemetery. The best known and most moving honors Marion Hooper "Clover" Adams, wife of historian Henry Adams; she committed suicide in 1885. Sculptor Augustus Saint-Gaudens created the enigmatic figure of a seated, shroud-draped woman, calling it *The Peace of God That Passeth Understanding,* though it's best known simply as "Grief." It may be the most moving sculpture in the city. ⊠ *Rock Creek Church Rd. and Webster St. NW, Northwest* ☎ *202/829–0585* ⊘ *Daily 7:30–dusk.*

⓭ Sewall-Belmont House. Built in 1800 by Robert Sewall, this is one of the oldest homes on Capitol Hill. Today it's the headquarters of the National Woman's Party. A museum inside chronicles the early days of the women's movement and the history of the house; there's also a library open to researchers by appointment. From 1801 to 1813 Secretary of the Treasury Albert Gallatin lived here; he finalized the details of the Louisiana Purchase in his front-parlor office. This building was the only private house in Washington that the British set on fire during their invasion of 1814. They did so after a citizen fired on advancing British troops from an upper-story window (a fact later documented by the offending British general's sworn testimony, 30 years later, on behalf of the Sewalls in their attempt to secure war reparations from the U.S. government). This shot was, in fact, the only armed resistance the British met that day. The house is filled with period furniture and portraits and busts of such suffragists as Lucretia Mott, Elizabeth Cady Stanton, and Alice Paul, who drafted the first version of the Equal Rights Amendment in 1923. ⊠ *144 Constitution Ave. NE, Capitol Hill* ☎ *202/546–3989* ⊕ *www.sewallbelmont.org* ✉ *Suggested donation $3* ☉ *Tours on the hr Tues.–Fri. 11–3, Sat. noon–4* Ⓜ *Union Station.*

⑮ South Side of East Capitol Street. Walk along East Capitol Street, the border between the northeast and southeast quadrants of the city, for a sample of the residential area of the Hill. The house on the corner of East Capitol Street, No. 329, has a striking tower with a bay window and stained glass. Next door are two Victorian houses with iron trim below the second floor. No. 317, an antebellum Greek Revival frame house, sits behind a tidy garden. ⊠ *Between 3rd and 4th Sts. SE, Capitol Hill* Ⓜ *Capitol South or Union Station.*

⑫ Supreme Court Building. It wasn't until 1935 that the Supreme Court got its own building: a white-marble temple with twin rows of Corinthian columns designed by Cass Gilbert. In 1800 the justices arrived in Washington along with the rest of the government but were for years shunted around various rooms in the Capitol; for a while they even met in a tavern. William Howard Taft, the only man to serve as both president and chief justice, was instrumental in getting the court a home of its own, though he died before it was completed.

The Supreme Court convenes on the first Monday in October and remains in session until it has heard all of its cases and handed down all of its decisions (usually the end of June). On Monday through Wednesday of two weeks in each month, the justices hear oral arguments in the velvet-swathed court chamber. Visitors who want to listen can choose to wait in either of two lines. One, the "three- to five-minute" line, shuttles you through, giving you a quick impression of the court at work. If you choose the other, and you'd like to stay for the whole show, it's best to be in line by 8:30 AM. The main hall of the Supreme Court is lined with busts of former chief justices; the courtroom itself is decorated with allegorical friezes. ⊠ *1 1st St. NE, Capitol Hill* ☎ *202/479–3000* ⊕ *www.supremecourtus.gov* ✉ *Free* ☉ *Weekdays 9–4:30* Ⓜ *Union Station or Capitol South.*

❸ Thurgood Marshall Federal Judiciary Building. If you're in the Union Station neighborhood, it's worth taking a moment to peer inside the signature work of architect Edward Larabee Barnes. The atrium encloses a garden of bamboo five stories tall. ⊠ *1 Columbus Circle NE, Capitol Hill* Ⓜ *Union Station.*

▶❶ Union Station. With a 96-foot-high coffered ceiling gilded with 8 pounds of gold leaf, the city's train station is one of the capital's great spaces. Back in 1902 the McMillan Commission—charged with suggesting ways to improve the appearance of the city—recommended that the many train lines that sliced through the capital share one depot. Union Station, opened in 1908, was the first building completed under the commission's plan. Chicago architect and commission member Daniel H. Burnham patterned the station after the Roman Baths of Diocletian (AD 305).

For many coming to Washington, the capital city is first seen framed through the grand station's arched doorways. In its heyday, during World War II, more than 200,000 people passed through the building daily. By the '60s, however, the decline in train travel had turned the station into an expensive white-marble elephant. It was briefly, and unsuccessfully, transformed into a visitor center for the Bicentennial; but by 1981 rain was pouring in through its neglected roof, and passengers boarded trains at a ramshackle depot behind the station.

The Union Station you see today is the result of a restoration, completed in 1988, intended to begin a revival of Washington's east end. Between train travelers and visitors to the shops, restaurants, and a nine-screen movie theater, 70,000 people a day pass through the beaux arts building. The jewel of the structure is its main waiting room. Forty-six statues of Roman legionnaires, one for each state in the Union when the station was completed, ring the grand room. The statues were the subject of controversy when the building was first opened. Pennsylvania Railroad president Alexander Cassatt (brother of artist Mary) ordered sculptor Louis Saint-Gaudens (brother of sculptor Augustus) to alter the statues, convinced that the legionnaires' skimpy outfits would upset female passengers. The sculptor obligingly added a shield to each figure, obscuring any offending body parts.

The east hall, now filled with vendors, is decorated with Pompeiian-style tracery and plaster walls and columns painted to look like marble. The station also has a secure presidential waiting room, now restored. This room was by no means frivolous: 20 years before Union Station was built, President Garfield was assassinated in the public waiting room of the old Baltimore and Potomac terminal on 6th Street.

The **Columbus Memorial Fountain,** designed by Lorado Taft, sits in the plaza in front of Union Station. A caped, steely eyed Christopher Columbus stares into the distance, flanked by a hoary, bearded figure (the Old World) and an Indian brave (the New). ⊠ *50 Massachusetts Ave. NE, Capitol Hill* ☏ *202/289–1908* ⊕ *www.unionstationdc.com* Ⓜ *Union Station.*

need a break? On Union Station's lower level are more than 20 food stalls with everything from pizza to sushi. There are several restaurants throughout the station, the largest of which is **America** (☏ 202/682–9555), with a menu of regional foods that lives up to its expansive name. The two-level **Center Cafe,** in the main hall of Union Station, is a perfect spot for people-watching.

☝ ❾ **United States Botanic Garden.** This glistening, plant-filled oasis, established by Congress in 1820, is the oldest botanic garden in North America. The Palm House conservatory is the center of attention. Now called the Jungle, it houses rainforest plants and includes walkways 24 feet above ground. With equal attention paid to science and aesthetics, the Botanic Garden contains plants from all around the world, with an emphasis on tropical and economically useful plants, desert plants, and orchids. On a 3-acre plot immediately to the west, the new **National Garden** is being constructed. It's scheduled to open in 2005. ⊠ *1st St. and Maryland Ave. SW, Downtown* ☏ *202/225–8333* ⊕ *www.usbg.gov* ⊠ *Free* ☉ *Daily 10–5* Ⓜ *Federal Center SW.*

> **off the beaten path**

UNITED STATES NATIONAL ARBORETUM – During azalea season (mid-April through May), this 444-acre oasis is a blaze of color. In early summer, clematis, peonies, rhododendrons, and roses bloom. At any time of year, the 22 original Corinthian columns from the U.S. Capitol, re-erected here in 1990, are striking. The arboretum is ideal for a relaxing stroll or scenic drive. On weekends, a tram tours the Arboretum's curving roadways at 10:30, 11:30, 1, 2, 3, and 4; tickets are $3. The **National Herb Garden** and the **National Bonsai Collection** are also here. ✉ *3501 New York Ave. NE, Northeast* ☎ *202/245-2726* ⊕ *www.usna.usda.gov* ✒ *Free* ⊙ *Arboretum and herb garden daily 8–5, bonsai collection daily 10–3:30* Ⓜ *Weekends only, Union Station, then X6 bus (runs every 40 minutes); weekdays, Stadium/Armory, then B2 bus to Bladensburg Rd. and R St.*

ℂ **Washington Navy Yard.** A 115-acre historic district with its own street system, the Washington Navy Yard is the Navy's oldest outpost on shore. Established in 1799 as a shipbuilding facility and converted to weapons production by the mid-19th century, it gradually fell into disuse over the next hundred years. In the early '60s the Navy Yard was revived as an administrative center. The **Navy Museum** (☎ 202/433–4882 Navy Museum; 202/433–3377 USS Barry ⊕ www.history.navy.mil), in Building 76, chronicles the history of the U.S. Navy from the Revolution to the present. Exhibits range from the fully rigged foremast of the USS *Constitution* (better known as "Old Ironsides") to a U.S. Navy Corsair fighter plane dangling from the ceiling. All around are models of fighting ships, working periscopes, displays on battles, and portraits of the sailors who fought them. The decommissioned U.S. Navy destroyer *Barry* floats a few hundred yards away in the Anacostia River. In front of the museum is a collection of guns, cannons, and missiles. Call ahead to schedule a free weekday highlights tour. Hours for the Navy Museum are after Labor Day through March, weekdays 9–4; from April through Labor Day, weekdays 9–5. The USS *Barry* is open weekdays 10–4. The **Navy Art Gallery** (☎ 202/433–3815 ⊕ www.history.navy.mil), in Building 67, exhibits navy-related paintings, sketches, and drawings, many created during combat by navy artists. The bulk of the collection illustrates World War II. Hours for the Navy Art Gallery are Wednesday through Friday 9–4. The **Marine Corps Museum** (☎ 202/433–3840 ⊕ www.hqmc.usmc.mil), within the Marine Corps Historical Center in Building 58, tells the story of the corps from its inception in 1775 to its role in Desert Storm. Artifacts—uniforms, weapons, documents, photographs—outline the growth of the corps, including its embrace of amphibious assault and the strategy of "vertical envelopment" (helicopters, to you and me). The Marine Corps Museum is open Monday and Wednesday through Friday 10–4; during the Evening Parade season (May to August), the museum remains open on Fridays until 8. ✉ *Main Gate, 9th and M Sts. SE, Capitol Hill* ✒ *Free* Ⓜ *Eastern Market.*

OLD DOWNTOWN & FEDERAL TRIANGLE

Just because Washington is a planned city doesn't mean the plan was executed flawlessly. Pierre-Charles L'Enfant's design has been alternately shelved and rediscovered several times in the past 200 years. Nowhere have the city's imperfections been more visible than on L'Enfant's grand thoroughfare, Pennsylvania Avenue. By the early '60s it had become a national disgrace; the dilapidated buildings that lined it were pawn shops and cheap souvenir stores. While riding up Pennsylvania

Avenue in his inaugural parade, a disgusted John F. Kennedy is said to have turned to an aide and said, "Fix it!" Washington's downtown—once within the diamond formed by Massachusetts, Louisiana, Pennsylvania, and New York avenues—had its problems, too, many the result of riots that rocked the capital in 1968 after the assassination of Martin Luther King Jr. In their wake, many businesses left the area and moved north of the White House.

In recent years developers have rediscovered "old downtown," and buildings are now being torn down or remodeled at an amazing pace. After several false starts, Pennsylvania Avenue is shining once again. This walk explores the old downtown section of the city, then swings around to check the progress on the monumental street that links the Capitol with the President's House. (Note: where E Street meets Pennsylvania Avenue, the intersection creates an odd one-block stretch that looks like Pennsylvania Avenue but is technically E Street. Buildings usually choose to associate themselves with the more prestigious-sounding "Pennsylvania Avenue" rather than "E Street.")

Numbers in the text correspond to numbers in the margin and on the Old Downtown and Federal Triangle map.

a good walk

Start at the redbrick **National Building Museum** ❶ ▶, the site of inaugural balls for more than 100 years. Across F Street from the National Building Museum is Judiciary Square, where city and federal courthouses, as well as the **National Law Enforcement Officers Memorial** ❷ are located. Walk over to 6th Street and up to H Street to Washington's tiny Chinatown, home to the **Surratt Boarding House** ❸, a meeting place for those planning Abraham Lincoln's assassination. The Friendship Arch spans H Street at 7th Street and marks the entrance to **Chinatown** ❹.

Continue west on H Street and right on 13th Street to the **National Museum of Women in the Arts** ❺, with works dating from the Renaissance to the present. Across the street is the InterAmerican Development Bank Cultural Center, with changing exhibits by artists from member countries in Latin America and the Caribbean. Walking south to 12th and G streets, you pass Hecht's, the downtown area's last remaining major department store. The city's largest public library, the **Martin Luther King Jr. Memorial Library** ❻, is at 9th and G streets. Two of the Smithsonian's non-Mall museums, the National Portrait Gallery on the south and the Smithsonian American Art Museum on the north, are in the **Old Patent Office Building** ❼; due to major renovations, both museums are closed through 2005. Just across the F Street pedestrian mall and to the left is the Hotel Monaco, which is housed in the **Tariff Commission Building**. At 800 F Street NW is the **International Spy Museum** ❽, made up of renovated older buildings and a modern addition.

Turn left off F Street onto 10th Street to **Ford's Theatre** ❾, where Abraham Lincoln was shot. The place where he died, the **Petersen House** ❿, is across the street. Follow Pennsylvania Avenue three blocks west to **Freedom Plaza** ⓫, where there's a statue of Revolutionary War hero General Casimir Pulaski. Across E Street from the plaza is Washington's oldest stage, the National Theatre.

The cluster of limestone government buildings south of Freedom Plaza between 15th Street, Pennsylvania Avenue, and Constitution Avenue is Federal Triangle. The triangle includes, from west to east, the Department of Commerce Building, home of the **National Aquarium** ⓬; the John A. Wilson Building; the **Ronald Reagan Building and International Trade Center** ⓭; the **Old Post Office** ⓮; the Internal Revenue Service Building; the Department of Justice (the **J. Edgar Hoover Federal Bureau of Investi-**

gation Building ⑮ is across Pennsylvania Avenue and not actually part of the Federal Triangle); the **National Archives** ⑯; and the **Apex Building** ⑰, home of the Federal Trade Commission. The white-stone-and-glass building across Pennsylvania Avenue is the **Canadian Embassy** ⑱. The intersection of 7th Street and Pennsylvania and Indiana avenues has numerous statues and memorials and a fountain. Across 7th Street, near the General Winfield Scott Hancock memorial, is the **Navy Memorial** ⑲, consisting of the *Lone Sailor* and a huge map carved into the plaza.

TIMING   Although many of the attractions on this walk are places you look at rather than enter, it's still an all-day affair. You may or may not think the best time to visit the National Aquarium is for the shark feedings (Monday, Wednesday, and Saturday at 2), piranha feedings (Tuesday, Thursday, and Sunday at 2), or alligator feedings (Friday at 2), when the frenzy of the crowds jockeying to see the action often rivals that inside the tanks.

What to See

off the
beaten
path

ANACOSTIA MUSEUM AND CENTER FOR AFRICAN AMERICAN HISTORY AND CULTURE – The richness of African-American culture is on display in this Smithsonian museum and research facility in southeast Washington's Anacostia neighborhood. The museum's facade uses traditional African design elements: brickwork patterns evoke West African *kente* cloth, and the concrete cylinders reference the stone towers of Zimbabwe and are ornamented with diamond patterns like those found on the adobe houses of Mali. Special exhibitions showcase fine art—photography, painting, sculpture—as well as crafts, social history, and popular culture. ⊠ *1901 Fort Pl. SE, Anacostia* ☎ *202/287–3306* ⊕ *www.si.edu/anacostia* ⊠ *Free* ⊘ *Daily 10–5* Ⓜ *Anacostia, then W2/W3 bus.*

⑰ **Apex Building.** The triangular Apex Building, completed in 1938, is the home of the Federal Trade Commission. The relief decorations over the doorways on the Constitution Avenue side depict agriculture (the harvesting of grain, by Concetta Scaravaglione) and trade (two men bartering over an ivory tusk, by Carl Schmitz). Michael Lantz's two heroic statues, on either side of the rounded eastern portico, each depict a muscular, shirtless workman wrestling with a wild horse and represent man controlling trade. Just across 6th Street is a three-tier fountain decorated with the signs of the zodiac; it's a memorial to Andrew Mellon. As secretary of the treasury, Mellon construction of the $125 million Federal Triangle. (A deep-pocketed philanthropist, Mellon was the driving force behind the National Gallery of Art, just across Constitution Avenue.) ⊠ *7th St. and Pennsylvania Ave. NW, Downtown* Ⓜ *Archives/Navy Memorial.*

⑱ **Canadian Embassy.** A spectacular edifice constructed of stone and glass, the Canadian Embassy was designed by Arthur Erickson and completed in 1988. The columns of the rotunda represent Canada's 12 provinces and territories. Inside, a gallery periodically displays exhibits on Canadian culture and history. ⊠ *501 Pennsylvania Ave. NW, The Mall* ☎ *202/682–1740* ⊕ *www.canadianembassy.org* ⊠ *Free* ⊘ *Weekdays 9–5 during exhibitions only* Ⓜ *Archives/Navy Memorial.*

❹ **Chinatown.** If you don't notice you're entering Washington's compact Chinatown by the Chinese characters on the street signs, the ornate, 75-foot-wide **Friendship Arch** spanning H Street might clue you in. Though Chinatown's main cross-streets may appear somewhat down-at-the-heels, this area borders many blocks undergoing revitalization, and it's

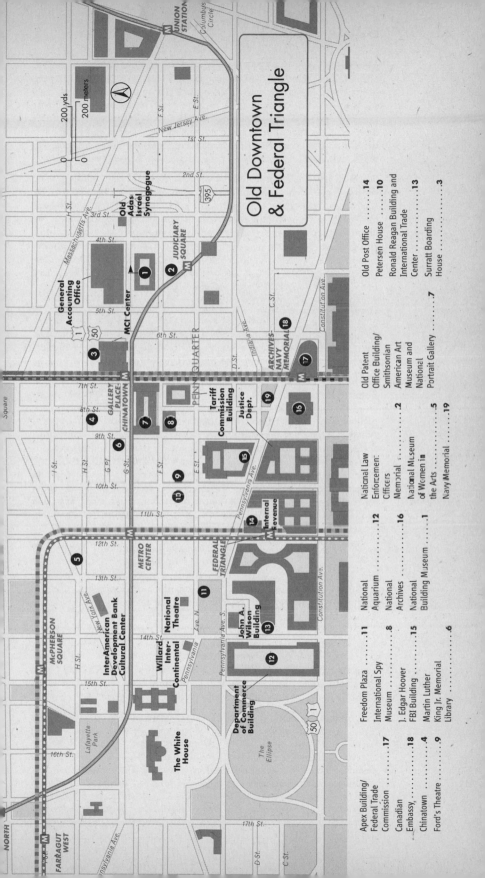

still the place to go for Chinese food in the District. Cantonese, Szechuan, Hunan, and Mongolian are among the regional styles you'll find here. Nearly every restaurant has a roast duck hanging in the window, and the shops here sell Chinese food, arts and crafts, and newspapers. Most interesting are traditional pharmacies purveying folk medicines such as dried eels, powdered bones, and unusual herbs for teas and broths believed to promote health, longevity, and sexual potency. ✉ *Bounded by G, H, 5th, and 8th Sts., Downtown* Ⓜ *Gallery Place/Chinatown.*

City Museum. The beautiful beaux arts Carnegie Library building, once Washington's Central Public Library, underwent a spectacular renovation before reopening in 2003. It's the only museum devoted to the nation's capital. Run by the Historical Society of Washington, D.C., the facility includes a library and a reading room, an archaeology exhibit, and galleries for multimedia presentations on Washington's neighborhoods, ethnic groups, and prehistory. ✉ *801 K St. NW, Downtown* ☎*202/785–2068* ⊕*www.hswdc.org* ☒*$3* ⊙ *Tues.–Sun. 10–5* Ⓜ *Gallery Place/Chinatown or Mt. Vernon Square/UDC.*

Federal Triangle. To the south of Freedom Plaza, this mass of government buildings was constructed between 1929 and 1938. Notable are the Department of Commerce, which holds the National Aquarium; the John A. Wilson Building; the Old Post Office; the Internal Revenue Service Building; the Department of Justice; the National Archives; and the Apex Building, which houses the Federal Trade Commission.

Before Federal Triangle was developed, government workers were scattered throughout the city, largely in rented offices. Looking for a place to consolidate this workforce, city planners hit on the area south of Pennsylvania Avenue, which was known as "Murder Bay" for its notorious collection of rooming houses, taverns, tattoo parlors, and brothels. A uniform classical architectural style, with Italianate red-tile roofs and interior plazas reminiscent of the Louvre, was chosen for the building project. Federal Triangle's planners envisioned interior courts filled with plazas and parks, but the needs of the motorcar foiled any such grand plans. ✉ *15th St. and Pennsylvania and Constitution Aves., Downtown.* Ⓜ *Federal Triangle.*

ⓒ ❾ **Ford's Theatre.** In 1859, Baltimore theater impresario John T. Ford leased the First Baptist Church building that stood on this site and turned it into a successful music hall. The building burned down late in 1863, and Ford built a new structure on the same spot. The events that occurred less than two years later would shock the nation and close the theater. On night of April 14, 1865, during a performance of *Our American Cousin,* John Wilkes Booth entered the state box and shot Abraham Lincoln in the back of the head. The stricken president was carried across the street to the house of tailor William Petersen. Charles Augustus Leale, a 23-year-old surgeon, was the first man to attend to the president. To let Lincoln know that someone was nearby, Leale held his hand throughout the night. Lincoln died the next morning.

The federal government bought Ford's Theatre in 1866 for $100,000 and converted it into office space. It was remodeled as a Lincoln museum in 1932 and was restored to its 1865 appearance in 1968. The basement museum contains artifacts such as Booth's pistol and the clothes Lincoln was wearing when he was shot. The theater itself continues to present a complete schedule of plays; *A Christmas Carol* is an annual holiday favorite. ✉ *511 10th St. NW, Downtown* ☎ *202/426–6924* ⊕ *www.nps.gov/foth* ☒ *Free* ⊙ *Daily 9–5; theater closed to visitors during rehearsals and matinees (generally Thurs. and weekends);*

Lincoln museum in basement remains open at these times Ⓜ *Metro Center or Gallery Place.*

> **off the beaten path**

FREDERICK DOUGLASS NATIONAL HISTORIC SITE – Cedar Hill, the Anacostia home of abolitionist Frederick Douglass, was the first Black National Historic Site that Congress designated. Douglass, a former slave who delivered rousing abolitionist speeches at home and abroad, resided here from 1877 until his death in 1895. The house has a wonderful view of Washington across the Anacostia River and contains many of Douglass's personal belongings. A short film on his life is shown at a nearby visitor center. Reservations are required for tours. To get here, take the B2 bus from the Anacostia Metro stop. ✉ *1411 W St. SE, Anacostia* ☎ *202/426–5961; 800/967–2283 tour reservations* ⊕ *www.nps.gov/frdo* 🎟 *$3* ⊙ *Mid-Oct.–mid-Apr., daily 9–4, last tour at 3; mid-Apr.–mid-Oct., daily 9–5, last tour at 4; tours on the hr, except noon* Ⓜ *Anacostia.*

⑪ Freedom Plaza. In 1988, Western Plaza was renamed Freedom Plaza in honor of Martin Luther King Jr. The east end is dominated by a statue of General Casimir Pulaski, a Polish nobleman who led an American cavalry corps during the Revolutionary War and who was mortally wounded in 1779 at the Siege of Savannah. He gazes over a plaza inlaid with a detail from L'Enfant's original 1791 plan for the Federal City. The "President's Palace" and the "Congress House" are outlined in bronze and the Mall is represented by a green lawn. Cut into the edges are quotations about the capital city, not all of them complimentary. To compare L'Enfant's vision with today's reality, stand in the middle of the map's Pennsylvania Avenue and look west. L'Enfant had planned an unbroken vista from the Capitol to the White House, but the Treasury Building, begun in 1836, ruined the view. Turning to the east, you'll see the U.S. Capitol sitting on the former Jenkins Hill.

There's a lot to see and explore in the blocks near Freedom Plaza. The beaux arts Willard Inter-Continental is on the corner of 14th Street and Pennsylvania Avenue NW. Just north of Freedom Plaza, on F Street between 13th and 14th streets, are The Shops, a collection of stores in the **National Press Building,** itself the address for dozens of media organizations. The Shops' upstairs Food Hall has sit-down restaurants and fast-food places. Washington's oldest stage, the National Theatre, also overlooks the plaza. ✉ *Bounded by 13th, 14th, and E Sts. and Pennsylvania Ave., Downtown* Ⓜ *Federal Triangle.*

Interamerican Development Bank Cultural Center. Founded in 1959, the IADB finances economic and social development in Latin America and the Caribbean. Its small cultural center hosts changing exhibits of paintings, sculptures, and artifacts from member countries. It's across the street from the National Museum of Women in the Arts. ✉ *1300 New York Ave. NW, Downtown* ☎ *202/623–1000 or 202/623–3774* ⊕ *www.iadb.org* 🎟 *Free* ⊙ *Weekdays 11–6* Ⓜ *Metro Center.*

❽ International Spy Museum. Cryptologists, masters of disguise, and former officials of the CIA, FBI, and KGB are among the advisers of this museum, which displays the largest collection of spy artifacts anywhere in the world. Fittingly, it's just a block away from FBI headquarters. Fans of novelist John Le Carré will revel in exhibits such as the School for Spies, which describes what makes a good spy and how they are trained; the Secret History of History, about spying from biblical times to the early 20th century; Spies Among Us, about spying in the world wars; War of the Spies, devoted to sophisticated Cold War spy techniques; and

21st-Century Spying, in which espionage experts analyze the latest spy trends. Five buildings, some dating from the 19th century, were combined to create the museum complex; one, the Warder-Atlas building, held Washington's Communist party in the 1940s. A large gift shop, a café, and the restaurant Zola are here as well. ⊠ *800 F St. NW, Downtown* ☎ *202/393–7798* ⊕ *www.spymuseum.org* ⊠ *$11* ◯ *Apr.–Oct., daily 10–8; Nov.–Mar., daily 10–6* Ⓜ *Gallery Place/Chinatown.*

🐾 ⓯ **J. Edgar Hoover Federal Bureau of Investigation Building.** Though tours of the building's interior have been suspended indefinitely, it's still worth walking past this hulking structure, decried from birth as hideous. Even Hoover himself is said to have called it the "ugliest building I've ever seen." Opened in 1974, it hangs over 9th Street like a poured-concrete Big Brother. Those hoping for a dose of espionage history can walk a block to the International Spy Museum. ⊠ *10th St. and Pennsylvania Ave. NW, Downtown* ☎ *202/324–3447* ⊕ *www.fbi.gov* Ⓜ *Federal Triangle or Gallery Place/Chinatown.*

John A. Wilson Building. Renamed in honor of the late city council chairman, this beaux arts structure, formerly known as the District Building, was built in 1908 and listed on the National Register of Historic Places in 1972. ⊠ *Federal Triangle, 1350 Pennsylvania Ave. NW, Downtown* ⊕ *www.fbi.gov* Ⓜ *Federal Triangle.*

❻ **Martin Luther King Jr. Memorial Library.** The only D.C. building designed by Mies van der Rohe, one of the founders of modern architecture, this squat black building at 9th and G streets is the largest public library in the city. A mural on the first floor depicts events in the life of the Nobel Prize–winning civil rights activist and reverend. Used books are almost always on sale at bargain prices in the library's gift shop. ⊠ *901 G St. NW, Downtown* ☎ *202/727–1111* ⊠ *Free* ◯ *Mon.–Thurs. 10–9, Fri. and Sat. 10–5:30, Sun. 1–5* Ⓜ *Gallery Place/Chinatown.*

🐾 **MCI Center.** The Washington Wizards, Washington Mystics, and Georgetown Hoyas play basketball here, and the Washington Capitals get out on the ice during hockey season. This is also the site of concerts and shows—including ice-skating extravaganzas and the circus. ⊠ *601 F St. NW, between 6th and 7th Sts., Downtown* ☎ *202/628–3200 MCI Center; 202/432–7328 Ticketmaster* Ⓜ *Gallery Place/Chinatown.*

🐾 ⓬ **National Aquarium.** The western base of Federal Triangle between 14th and 15th streets is the home of the Department of Commerce, charged with promoting U.S. economic development and technological advancement. When it opened in 1932 it was the world's largest government office building. It's a good thing there's plenty of space; incongruously, the National Aquarium is housed inside. Established in 1873, it's the country's oldest public aquarium, with more than 1,200 fish and other creatures—such as eels, sharks, and alligators—representing 270 species of fresh- and saltwater life. The exhibits look somewhat dated, but the easy-to-view tanks, accessible touching pool (with crabs and sea urchins), low admission fee, and general lack of crowds make this a good, low-key outing with children. ⊠ *14th St. and Constitution Ave. NW, Downtown* ☎ *202/482–2825* ⊕ *www.nationalaquarium.com* ⊠ *$3* ◯ *Daily 9–5, last admission at 4:30; sharks fed Mon., Wed., and Sat. at 2; piranhas fed Tues., Thurs., and Sun. at 2; alligators fed Fri. at 2* Ⓜ *Federal Triangle.*

⓰ **National Archives.** If the Smithsonian Institution is the nation's attic, the Archives is its basement. The Archives bears responsibility for important government documents and other items; the Declaration of Independence, the Constitution, and the Bill of Rights are on display in the building's rotunda, in a case made of bulletproof glass, equipped with green filters and filled with helium gas (to protect the irreplaceable documents). At night and on Christmas—the only day the Archives is closed—the cases and documents are lowered into a vault. Other objects in the Archives' vast collection include bureaucratic correspondence, veterans' and immigration records, treaties, Richard Nixon's resignation letter, and the rifle Lee Harvey Oswald used to assassinate John F. Kennedy.

The Archives fills the area between 7th and 9th streets and Pennsylvania and Constitution avenues on Federal Triangle. Beside it is a small park with a modest memorial to Franklin Roosevelt. The desk-size piece of marble on the sliver of grass is exactly what the president asked for (though this didn't stop fans of the 32nd president from building the grand memorial at the Tidal Basin). Designed by John Russell Pope, the Archives was erected in 1935 on the site of the old Center Market. This large block had been a center of commerce since the early 1800s. At that time, barges were unloaded here, when Constitution Avenue was still the City Canal. A vestige of this mercantile past lives on in the name given to the two semicircular developments across Pennsylvania Avenue from the Archives—Market Square. Residential development continues to further enliven this stretch of Pennsylvania Avenue.

Head to the Constitution Avenue side of the Archives. All the sculpture that adorns the building was carved on site, including the two statues that flank the flight of steps facing the Mall, *Heritage* and *Guardianship,* by James Earle Fraser. Fraser also carved the scene on the pediment, which represents the transfer of historic documents to the recorder of the Archives. (Like nearly all pediment decorations in Washington, this one bristles with electric wires designed to thwart the advances of destructive starlings.) Call at least three weeks in advance to arrange a behind-the-scenes tour. ✉ *Constitution Ave. between 7th and 9th Sts. NW, Downtown* ☎ *202/501–5000; 202/501–5205 tours* ⊕ *www.nara. gov* ✆ *Free* ☉ *Apr.–Labor Day, daily 10–9; Labor Day–Mar., daily 10–5:30; tours weekdays at 10:15 and 1:15* Ⓜ *Archives/Navy Memorial.*

☜ ⚑ ❶ **National Building Museum.** The open interior of this mammoth redbrick edifice is one of the city's great spaces and has been the site of many an inaugural ball. (The first ball was for Grover Cleveland in 1885; because the building wasn't finished at the time, a temporary wooden roof and floor were built.) The eight central Corinthian columns are among the largest in the world, rising to a height of 75 feet. Although they resemble Siena marble, each is made of 70,000 bricks that have been covered with plaster and painted. For years, the annual *Christmas in Washington* TV special has been filmed in this breathtaking hall.

Formerly known as the Pension Building, it was erected between 1882 and 1887 to house workers who processed the pension claims of veterans and their survivors, an activity that intensified after the Civil War. The architect was U.S. Army Corps of Engineers general Montgomery C. Meigs, who took as his inspiration Rome's Palazzo Farnese. The museum is devoted to architecture and the building arts: recent exhibits have covered home improvement in 20th-century America, the preservation of Mount Vernon, and tools as an art form. The hands-on displays here are great for kids.

Before entering the building, walk down its F Street side. The terra-cotta frieze by Caspar Buberl between the first and second floors depicts soldiers marching and sailing in an endless procession around the building. Architect Meigs lost his eldest son in the Civil War, and, though the frieze depicts Union troops, he intended it as a memorial to all who were killed in the bloody war. Meigs designed the Pension Building with workers' comfort in mind. Note the three "missing" bricks under each window that allowed for air to circulate and helped keep the building cool. Tours are offered at 12:30 Monday through Wednesday; 11:30, 12:30, 1:30 Thursday through Saturday; and 12:30 and 1:30 Sunday. Family programs are available at 2:30 Saturdays and Sundays. ⊠ *401 F St. NW, between 4th and 5th Sts., Downtown* ☎ *202/272–2448* ⊕ *www.nbm. org* ✉ *Free* ☉ *Mon.–Sat. 10–5, Sun. 11–5* Ⓜ *Judiciary Square.*

② **National Law Enforcement Officers Memorial.** This 3-foot-high wall bears the names of more than 15,000 American police officers killed in the line of duty since 1792. On the third line of panel 13W are the names of six officers killed by William Bonney, better known as Billy the Kid. J. D. Tippit, the Dallas policeman killed by Lee Harvey Oswald, is honored on the ninth line of panel 63E. Some of the most recent additions include the names of the 71 officers who died in the terror attacks of 2001. Two blocks from the memorial is a visitor center with exhibits on its history. Computers there allow you to look up officers by name, date of death, state, and department. A small shop sells souvenirs. Call to arrange for a free tour. In 2000, President Clinton authorized a bill to allow the construction of a National Law Enforcement Museum which is scheduled for completion in 2008. ⊠ *605 E St. NW, Downtown* ☎ *202/737–3400* ⊕ *www.nleomf.com* ✉ *Free* ☉ *Weekdays 9–5, Sat. 10–5, Sun. noon–5* Ⓜ *Gallery Place/Chinatown.*

⑤ **National Museum of Women in the Arts.** Works by female artists from the Renaissance to the present are showcased at this museum. The beautifully restored 1907 Renaissance Revival building was designed by Waddy B. Wood; ironically, it was once a Masonic temple, for men only. In addition to displaying traveling shows, the museum has a permanent collection that includes paintings, drawings, sculpture, prints, and photographs by Georgia O'Keeffe, Mary Cassatt, Élisabeth Vigée-Lebrun, Frida Kahlo, and Camille Claudel. ⊠ *1250 New York Ave. NW, Downtown* ☎ *202/783–5000* ⊕ *www.nmwa.org* ✉ *$8* ☉ *Mon.–Sat. 10–5, Sun. noon–5* Ⓜ *Metro Center.*

National Portrait Gallery. This museum is in the Old Patent Office Building along with the Smithsonian American Art Museum. A major renovation of the building, set to last through 2005, means that the gallery is closed. ⊠ *8th and F Sts. NW, Downtown* ☎ *202/357–2700; 202/357–1729 TDD* ⊕ *www.npg.si.edu* ☉ *Closed during renovation* Ⓜ *Gallery Place/Chinatown.*

National Theatre. Except for brief periods spent as a movie house, the National Theatre been mounting plays in this location since 1835. Helen Hayes saw her first play here at the age of six; she then vowed to become an actress. If you plan ahead, you can take a free tour that includes the house, stage, backstage, wardrobe room, dressing rooms, the area under the stage, the Helen Hayes Lounge, and the memorabilia-filled archives. Tours are given for a minimum of 10 people, and only when there is no show; make reservations at least two weeks in advance. ⊠ *1321 Pennsylvania Ave. NW, intersection of 13th and E Sts., Downtown* ☎ *202/783–3370* ⊕ *www.nationaltheatre.org* ✉ *Free* Ⓜ *Metro Center.*

⑲ **Navy Memorial.** A huge outdoor plaza, this memorial includes a granite map of the world and a 7-foot statue, *The Lone Sailor*. In summer, military bands perform on its concert stage. Next to the memorial, in the Market Square East Building, is the Naval Heritage Center, which has a gift shop and the Navy Log Room, where you can use computers to look up the service records of navy veterans. The 242-seat, wide-screen Arleigh & Roberta Burke Theater shows a rotating series of historical sea service movies at noon. A memorial to General Winfield Scott Hancock, whose forces repelled Pickett's Charge at Gettysburg, is in the park adjacent to the Navy Memorial. ⊠ *701 Pennsylvania Ave. NW, Downtown* ☎ *202/737–2300* ⊕ *www.lonesailor.org* 🎞 *Films free* ☉ *Naval Heritage Center Mar.–Nov., Mon.–Sat. 9:30–5* Ⓜ *Archives/Navy Memorial.*

Old Adas Israel Synagogue. This is the oldest synagogue in Washington. Built in 1876 at 6th and G streets NW, the redbrick federal Revival–style building was moved to its present location in 1969 to make way for an office building. Exhibits in the Lillian and Albert Small Jewish Museum inside explore Jewish life in Washington. ⊠ *701 3rd St. NW, Downtown* ☎ *202/789–0900* 🎞 *Suggested donation $3* ☉ *Museum Sun.–Thurs. noon–4* Ⓜ *Judiciary Square.*

❼ **Old Patent Office Building.** The two Smithsonian museums that share the Old Patent Office Building's space are closed through 2005 because of its renovation. The National Portrait Gallery, which has presidential portraits, *Time* magazine covers, and Civil War photographs, paintings, and prints, is on the south side. The Smithsonian American Art Museum, with displays on Early American and western art, is on the north.

Construction of the south wing, designed by Washington Monument architect Robert Mills, started in 1836. When the huge Greek Revival quadrangle was completed in 1867 it was the largest building in the country. Many of its rooms housed glass display cabinets filled with the scale models that were required to accompany patent applications.

During the Civil War, the Patent Office, like many other buildings in the city, was turned into a hospital. Among those caring for the wounded here were Clara Barton and Walt Whitman. In the 1950s the building was threatened with demolition to make way for a parking lot, but the efforts of preservationists saved it. ⊠ *G St. between 7th and 9th Sts., Downtown* ⊕ *www.nps.gov.opot* Ⓜ *Gallery Place/Chinatown.*

🖐 ⓮ **Old Post Office.** When it was completed in 1899, this Romanesque structure on Federal Triangle was the largest government building in the District, the first with a clock tower, and the first with an electric power plant. Despite these innovations, it earned the sobriquet "old" after only 15 years, when a new District post office was constructed near Union Station. When urban planners in the '20s decided to impose a uniform design on Federal Triangle, the Old Post Office was slated for demolition. The fanciful granite building was saved first because of a lack of money during the Depression, then thanks to the intercession of preservationists. Major renovation was begun in 1978, and in 1983 the Old Post Office Pavilion—an assortment of shops and restaurants inside the airy central courtyard—opened.

Park service rangers who work at the Old Post Office consider the observation deck in the clock tower one of Washington's best-kept secrets. Although not as tall as the Washington Monument, it offers nearly as impressive a view. Even better, it's usually not as crowded, the windows are bigger, and—unlike the monument's windows—they're open, allowing cool breezes to waft through. (For self-guided tours, use the entrance at 12th Street and Pennsylvania Avenue and take the glass elevator to the 9th floor.) On the way down be sure to look at the Congress Bells, cast at the same British foundry that made the bells in London's Westminster Abbey. The bells are rung to honor the opening and closing of Congress and on other important occasions, such as when the Redskins win the Super Bowl.

Cross 10th Street from the Old Post Office Pavilion. Look to your left at the delightful trompe l'oeil mural on the side of the **Lincoln Building** two blocks up. It appears as if there's a hole in the building. There's also a portrait of the building's namesake. ⊠ *12th St. and Pennsylvania Ave. NW, Downtown* ☎ *202/606–8691 tower; 202/289–4224 pavilion* ⊕ *www.oldpostofficedc.com* ☜ *Free* ⊙ *Tower early May–early Sept., weekdays 9–7:45, Sat. 10–7:45, Sun. 10–6; early Sept.–early May, weekdays 9–5, weekends 9–6* Ⓜ *Federal Triangle.*

Pennsylvania Avenue. The capital's most historically important thoroughfare repeatedly threads through sightseeing walks. Newly inaugurated presidents travel west on Pennsylvania Avenue en route to the White House. Thomas Jefferson started the parade tradition in 1805 after taking the oath of office for his second term. He was accompanied by a few friends and a handful of congressmen. Four years later James Madison made things official by instituting a proper inaugural celebration. The flag holders on the lampposts are clues that Pennsylvania Avenue remains the city's foremost parade route. With the Capitol at one end and the White House at the other, the avenue symbolizes both the separation and the ties between these two branches of government.

When Pennsylvania Avenue first opened in 1796, it was an ugly, dangerous bog. Attempts by Jefferson to beautify the road by planting poplar trees were only partially successful: many were chopped down by fellow citizens for firewood. In the mid-19th century, crossing the rutted thoroughfare was treacherous, and rainstorms often turned the street into a river. The avenue was finally paved with wooden blocks in 1871.

At the convergence of 7th Street and Pennsylvania and Indiana avenues is a multitude of statues and monuments. The **Grand Army of the Republic** memorial pays tribute to the soldiers who won the Civil War. Less conventional is the nearby **Temperance Fountain,** which has a heron on its top. It was designed and built in the 19th century by Henry D. Cogswell, a teetotaling physician who hoped the fountain, which once dispensed ice-cold water, would help lure people from the evils of drink.

Redevelopment has rejuvenated Pennsylvania Avenue and the neighboring **Penn Quarter,** the name given to the mix of condominiums, apartments, retail spaces, and restaurants in the blocks bounded by Pennsylvania Avenue and 6th, 9th, and G streets. In addition to the Hotel Monaco and the International Spy Museum, the area also contains the Lansburgh complex, at the corner of 8th and E streets. Built around three existing buildings (including the defunct Lansburgh department store), the complex includes the Shakespeare Theatre, a 447-seat space. Ⓜ *Archives/Navy Memorial.*

🔟 **Petersen House.** Lincoln died in the house of William Petersen, a tailor, on the morning of April 15, 1865, after being shot at Ford's Theatre the night before. You can see the restored front and back parlors of the house, as well as the bedroom where the president died. Call in advance for tour times. ⊠ *516 10th St. NW, Downtown* ☎ *202/426–6830* ⊕ *www.nps.gov/foth* ☜ *Free* ⊙ *Daily 9–5* Ⓜ *Metro Center or Gallery Place/Chinatown.*

need a break? Around the corner and across the street from Petersen House is the **Hard Rock Cafe** (⊠ 999 E St. NW, Downtown ☎ 202/737–7625 ⊕ www.hardrock.com), serving hearty American food and a modest selection of beers. They're also selling lots of those famous T-shirts. (The gift shop opened a full year before the restaurant did.) This is a popular spot, so if you're not up to waiting in line, try to arrive early.

⑬ Ronald Reagan Building and International Trade Center. This $818 million, 3.1-million-square-foot colossus is the largest federal building to be constructed in the Washington area since the Pentagon, and the first to be designed for use by both the government and the private sector. A blend of classical and modern architecture, the Indiana limestone structure replaced what for 50 years had been an enormous parking lot, an eyesore that interrupted the flow of the buildings of Federal Triangle. At present, the Reagan Building houses the Environmental Protection Agency, the U.S. Customs Service, and USAID. The **D.C. Visitor Information Center** (☎ 202/328–4748 ⊕ www.dcvisit.com), located here, is a convenient place to pick up brochures, see a free historical video, and get tickets for tours or evening performances. There's also a multilingual touch-screen computer kiosk with information about the city (the same machine lets you send a free e-mail postcard with your photo to anyone in the world). Hours for the visitor center and its gift shop are 8–6 weekdays and 8–5 Saturday. The building has a food court on the lower level, and a theatrical group, the Capitol Steps, performs works of political satire here on Friday and Saturday nights. You may just catch a glimpse of Washington Wizard, Michael Jordan, at his restaurant Jordans, which is also here. ✉ *1300 Pennsylvania Ave. NW, Downtown* ▧ *Free* Ⓜ *Federal Triangle.*

Smithsonian American Art Museum. This museum (formerly the National Museum of American Art) is housed in the Old Patent Office Building, which is under major renovation through 2005. The museum and the National Portrait Gallery, which share the building, are closed during the renovation, but the Smithsonian American Art Museum continues its public presence through its Web site and a full program at the Renwick Gallery. ✉ *8th and G Sts. NW, Downtown* ☎ *202/357–2700; 202/357–1729 TDD* ⊕ *www.americanart.si.edu* Ⓜ *Gallery Place/Chinatown.*

❸ Surratt Boarding House. A plaque by the front door attests that it was here that John Wilkes Booth and his coconspirators plotted the assassination of Abraham Lincoln. The current occupant of the building is the Wok & Roll Chinese restaurant. ✉ *604 H St. NW, Downtown* Ⓜ *Gallery Place/Chinatown.*

Tariff Commission Building (Old General Post Office). The Tariff Commission Building, designed by Robert Mills and finished in 1866, is one of three historic structures to occupy the same site. When the Capitol was burned by the British in 1814, Congress met temporarily in a hotel that stood here. Another earlier building housed the nation's first public telegraph office, operated by Samuel F. B. Morse. It now houses the Hotel Monaco. ✉ *700 F St. NW, Downtown* Ⓜ *Gallery Place/Chinatown.*

Willard Inter-Continental. There was a Willard Hotel on this spot long before this ornate structure was built in 1901. The original Willard was *the* place to stay in Washington if you were rich or influential (or wanted to give that impression). Abraham Lincoln stayed there while waiting to move into the nearby White House. Julia Ward Howe stayed there during the Civil War and wrote "The Battle Hymn of the Republic" after gazing down from her window to see Union troops drilling on Pennsylvania Avenue. It's said the term "lobbyist" was coined to describe the favor seekers who would buttonhole President Ulysses S. Grant in the hotel's public rooms. The second Willard, with a mansard roof dotted with circular windows, was designed by Henry Hardenbergh, architect of New York's Plaza hotel. Although it was just as opulent as the hotel it replaced, it fell on hard times after World War II. In 1968 it closed, standing empty until 1986, when it reopened, amid much fanfare, after an ambitious restoration. The Willard's rebirth is one of the most visible successes of the Pennsylvania Avenue Development Corporation, the organization charged with reversing the decay of America's Main Street. ⊠ *1401 Pennsylvania Ave. NW, Downtown* ☎ *202/ 628–9100 or 800/327–0200* ⊕ *www.washington.interconti.com.*

GEORGETOWN

Long before the District of Columbia was formed, Washington's oldest and wealthiest neighborhood, was a separate city with a harbor full of ships and warehouses filled with tobacco. Washington has filled in around Georgetown over the years, but the former tobacco port retains an air of aloofness. Its narrow streets, which don't conform to Pierre-Charles L'Enfant's plan for the Federal City, host a great deal of foot traffic and an active nightlife.

The area that would come to be known as George (after George II), then George Towne and, finally, Georgetown, was part of Maryland when it was settled in the early 1700s by Scottish immigrants, many of whom were attracted to the region's tolerant religious climate. Georgetown's position—at the farthest point up the Potomac that's accessible by boat—made it an ideal transit and inspection point for farmers who grew tobacco in Maryland's interior. In 1789 the state granted the town a charter, but two years later Georgetown—along with Alexandria, its counterpart in Virginia—was included by George Washington in the Territory of Columbia, site of the new capital.

While Washington struggled, Georgetown thrived. Wealthy traders built their mansions on the hills overlooking the river; merchants and the working class lived in modest homes closer to the water's edge. In 1810 a third of Georgetown's population was African-American—both free people and slaves. The Mt. Zion United Methodist Church on 29th Street is the oldest organized black congregation in the city. When the church stood at 27th and P streets, it was a stop on the Underground Railroad (the original building burned down in the mid-1800s). Georgetown's rich history and success instilled in all its citizens a feeling of pride that still lingers today. (When Georgetowners thought the dismal capital was dragging them down, they asked to be given back to Maryland, the way Alexandria was given back to Virginia in 1845.) Tobacco eventually became a less important commodity, and Georgetown became a milling center, using water power from the Potomac. When the Chesapeake & Ohio (C&O) Canal was completed in 1850, the city intensified its milling operations and became the eastern end of a waterway that stretched 184 mi to the west. The canal took up some of the slack when Georgetown's harbor began to fill with silt and the port lost business to Alexandria and Baltimore, but the canal never became the success it was meant to be.

In the years that followed, Georgetown was a far cry from the fashionable spot it is today. Clustered near the water were a foundry, a fish market, paper and cotton mills, and a power station for the city's streetcar system, all of which made Georgetown a smelly industrial district. It still had its Georgian, federal, and Victorian homes, though, and when the New Deal and World War II brought a flood of newcomers to Washington, Georgetown's tree-shaded streets and handsome brick houses were rediscovered. Pushed out in the process were many of Georgetown's renters, which included many of its black residents.

Today some of Washington's most famous citizens call Georgetown home, including former *Washington Post* editor Ben Bradlee, political pundit George Stephanopoulos, Democratic Presidential candidates Senator Joe

Lieberman and Senator John Kerry, and celebrity biographer Kitty Kelley. Georgetown's historic preservationists are among the most vocal in the city. Part of what the activists want protection from is the crush of people who descend on their community every night. This is one of Washington's main areas for restaurants, bars, nightclubs, and trendy boutiques. On M Street and Wisconsin Avenue, you can indulge just about any taste and take home almost any upscale souvenir. Harder to find is a parking place.

Georgetown owes some of its charm and separate growth to geography. This town-unto-itself is separated from Washington to the east by Rock Creek. On the south it's bordered by the Potomac, on the west by Georgetown University. How far north does Georgetown reach? Probably not much farther than the large estates and parks above R Street, though developers and real estate agents would be happy to include in Georgetown all the land up to the Canadian border if it increased the value of property along the way.

There's no Metro stop in Georgetown, so you have to take a bus or taxi or walk to this part of Washington. It's about a 15-minute walk from the Dupont Circle or Foggy Bottom Metro station. Perhaps the best transportation deal in Georgetown is the Georgetown Metro Connection. These little blue buses have two routes, one along Wisconsin Avenue and K Street to the Foggy Bottom Metro and the second along M Street to the Dupont Circle and Rosslyn Metros. Buses run daily every 10 minutes. Other options include the G2 Georgetown University bus, which goes west from Dupont Circle along P Street, and the 34 and 36 Friendship Heights buses, which leave from 22nd and Pennsylvania and deposit you at 31st and M.

Numbers in the text correspond to numbers in the margin and on the Georgetown map.

a good
walk

Georgetown's largest and grandest estates occupy the northern part of the neighborhood, commanding fine views of Rock Creek to the east and of the Potomac River below. If you're in the mood for a stroll, the best way to get to the estates is to walk north either on Wisconsin Avenue (the bustling commercial route) or a block east, on 31st Street (a quieter residential street). Otherwise, start your exploration of Georgetown at 31st and M streets, in front of the **Old Stone House** ❶ ☞, possibly Washington's only pre-Revolutionary building. From the Old Stone House, cross over M Street to Thomas Jefferson Street (between 30th and 31st streets). The 200-year-old, two-story brick structure at No. 1058 was built as a **Masonic Lodge** ❷. Follow Thomas Jefferson Street as it passes over the **C&O Canal** ❸, whose towpath and waters are now used by runners, bikers, and canoeists. In spring and summer, you can take a mule-drawn canal boat ride. Cross K Street to **Washington Harbour** ❹, a development that includes waterfront restaurants, offices, apartments, and pricey shops. Across the street at 31st and K streets is the site, no longer recognizable, that's thought to be the location of Suter's Tavern, where George Washington made the land deal that became the District of Columbia. The original building was torn down during the late 19th century. Nearby, the three Francis Dodge warehouses along Wisconsin Avenue, built around 1830, make a good backdrop for a photo. Up Wisconsin Avenue, across the street, stands the Gothic Revival Grace Episcopal Church.

Cross the canal again at Wisconsin Avenue. At 1066 Wisconsin Avenue, Papa Razzi restaurant inhabits the building that was once the Vigilant Firehouse, built in 1840. Near the door of the restaurant, a plaque reads BUSH, THE OLD FIRE DOG, DIED OF POISON, JULY 5TH, 1869, R.I.P. Nearby is a simple granite obelisk honoring the men who built the C&O Canal. At the intersection of Wisconsin Avenue and M Street—the heart of Georgetown—turn left to the Victorian-style Shops at Georgetown Park (3222 M Street NW), that rarest of rarities: an architecturally attractive shopping mall. Both M Street and Wisconsin Avenue are lined with restaurants and boutiques selling just about anything you could want, from the latest fashions to antique furniture and jewelry—but don't expect any bargains. Continue along M Street to the Markethouse, an 1865 brick building currently occupied by Dean & Deluca, the fancy food store. M Street west leads to the Key Bridge into Rosslyn, Virginia. A house owned by Francis Scott Key, author of the national anthem, was demolished in 1947 to make way for the bridge that would bear his name. The **Francis Scott Key Memorial Park** ➎ lies at the foot of the D.C. side of Key Bridge.

To head to the residential area, continue on M Street past the old brick streetcar barn at No. 3600 (now offices), turn right, and climb the 75 *Exorcist* steps ➏. You can see that it would be a truly terrifying fall, especially when being hurled by a demon. If you're not up to the climb, walk up 34th Street instead. **Halcyon House** ➐ was built in 1763 by the first secretary of the navy. The beautiful campus of **Georgetown University** ➑, the oldest Jesuit school in the country, is a few blocks to the west. **Cox's Row** ➒, a group of five Federal houses between 3339 and 3327 N Street, was built in 1817 by a former mayor of Georgetown. The redbrick house at 3307 N Street was the home of then-Senator John F. Kennedy and his family before they moved downtown to 1600 Pennsylvania Avenue.

Turn left onto Potomac Street and walk a block up to O Street, several blocks of which still have cobblestones and trolley tracks. **St. John's Church** ➓ was built in 1809. Cross Wisconsin Avenue and go up 31st Street to Q Street, where through the trees you can see **Tudor Place** ⓫, a neoclassical mansion with a dramatic domed portico. Walk up 32nd Street to **Dumbarton Oaks** ⓬, a former estate that contains two excellent art collections and 10 acres of formal gardens. Three other sylvan retreats lie north of Dumbarton Oaks. Dumbarton Oaks Park sprawls to the north and west of the estate, Montrose Park lies to the east, and farther east is **Oak Hill Cemetery** ⓭, overlooking Rock Creek. Walk south on 28th Street past the 200-year-old Georgian manor house **Evermay** ⓮, now a private home with lovely grounds. Around the corner on Q Street is **Dumbarton House** ⓯, headquarters of the National Society of the Colonial Dames of America. It's filled with magnificent period antiques.

TIMING You can easily spend a pleasant day in Georgetown, partly because some sights (Tudor Place, Dumbarton Oaks, Oak Hill Cemetery, Evermay, and Dumbarton House) are somewhat removed from the others and partly because the street scene, with its intriguing shops and people-watching, invites you to linger. Georgetown is almost always crowded. It's not very car-friendly either, especially at night; driving and parking are usually difficult. The wise take the Metro to Foggy Bottom or Dupont Circle and then walk 15 minutes from there, or take a bus or taxi.

What to See

🐾 ➌ **C&O Canal.** This waterway kept Georgetown open to shipping after its harbor had filled with silt. George Washington was one of the first to advance the idea of a canal linking the Potomac with the Ohio River across the Appalachians. Work started on the C&O Canal in 1828, and when it opened in 1850, its 74 locks linked Georgetown with Cumberland, Maryland, 184 mi to the northwest (still short of its intended destina-

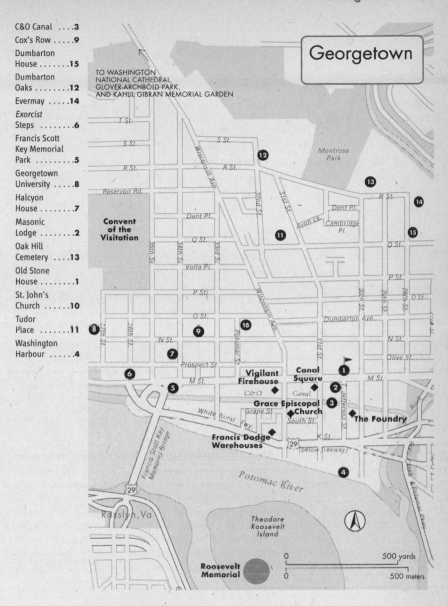

tion). Lumber, coal, iron, wheat, and flour moved up and down the canal, but it was never as successful as its planners had hoped it would be. Many of the bridges spanning the canal in Georgetown were too low to allow anything other than fully loaded barges to pass underneath, and competition from the Baltimore & Ohio Railroad eventually spelled an end to profitability. Today the canal is a part of the National Park System, and walkers follow the towpath once used by mules while canoeists paddle the canal's calm waters. Between April and November you can go on a mule-drawn trip aboard the *Georgetown* canal boat. Tickets for the rides, which last about an hour, are available across the canal, next to the Foundry. Barge rides are also available at Great Falls, at the end of MacArthur Boulevard, in nearby Potomac, Maryland. Barge rides are given late March through mid-June and early September through early November, Wednesday to Friday at 11 and 2:30, and on weekends at

11, 1, 2:30, and 4. From mid-June through early September, barge rides are Wednesday to Friday at 11, 1, and 2:30, and on weekends at 11, 1, 2:30, and 4; the cost is $8. ⊠ *Canal Visitor Center, 1057 Thomas Jefferson St. NW, Georgetown* ☎ *202/653–5190.*

Canal Square. This 1850s warehouse was converted into a retail and office complex in the 1970s, retaining much of the original brickwork. In the interior courtyard are retail shops and several art galleries, notably the small but innovative **Museum of Contemporary Art** (☎ 202/342–6230 ⊕ www.mocadc.org). ⊠ *1054 31st St. NW, Georgetown.*

⑨ Cox's Row. Architecture buffs, especially those interested in federal and Victorian houses, enjoy wandering along the redbrick sidewalks of upper Georgetown. The average house here has two signs on it: a brass plaque notifying passersby of the building's historic interest and a window decal that warns potential burglars of its state-of-the-art alarm system. To get a representative taste of the houses in the area, walk along the 3300 block of N Street. The group of five federal houses between 3339 and 3327 N Street is known collectively as Cox's Row, after Colonel John Cox, a former mayor of Georgetown, who built them in 1817 and resided at 3339. The flat-front, redbrick federal house at 3307 N Street was the home of then-Senator John F. Kennedy and his family before the White House beckoned.

⑮ Dumbarton House. Its symmetry and the two curved wings on its north side make Dumbarton, built around 1800, a distinctive example of Federal architecture. The first occupant of the house, Joseph Nourse, was registrar of the U.S. Treasury. Other well-known Americans have spent time here, including Dolley Madison, who stopped here when fleeing Washington in 1814. One hundred years later, the house was saved from demolition by being moved 100 ft up the hill, when Q Street was cut through to the Dumbarton Bridge. Since 1928, it has served as the headquarters of the National Society of the Colonial Dames of America.

Eight rooms inside Dumbarton House have been restored to Federal-period splendor, with period furnishings such as mahogany American Chippendale chairs, hallmark silver, Persian rugs, and a breakfront cabinet filled with rare books. Other notable items include Martha Washington's traveling cloak, a British soldier's red coat, and a 1789 Charles Willson Peale portrait of the children of Benjamin Stoddert, the first secretary of the navy (the portrait has a view of Georgetown harbor in the background). In order to see the house's interior, you must take the 45-minute guided tour. ⊠ *2715 Q St. NW, Georgetown* ☎ *202/337–2288* ☞ *Suggested donation $3* ☉ *Labor Day–July, Tues.–Sat. 10–1; last tour at 12:15. Tours at 10:15, 11:15, and 12:15.*

⑫ Dumbarton Oaks. Don't confuse Dumbarton Oaks with the nearby Dumbarton House. In 1944 one of the most important events of the 20th century took place here, when representatives of the United States, Great Britain, China, and the Soviet Union met in the music room to lay the groundwork for the United Nations.

Career diplomat Robert Woods Bliss and his wife, Mildred, bought the property in 1920 and set about taming the sprawling grounds and removing later 19th-century additions that had obscured the federal lines of the 1801 mansion. In 1940 the Blisses gave the estate to Harvard University, which maintains world-renowned collections of Byzantine and pre-Columbian art here. Both collections are small but choice, reflecting the enormous skill and creativity going on at roughly the same time on two sides of the Atlantic. The Byzantine collection includes beautiful examples of both religious and secular items executed in mosaic, metal, enamel, and ivory. Pre-Columbian works—artifacts and textiles from Mexico and Central and South America by such peoples as the Aztec, Maya, and Olmec—are arranged in an enclosed glass pavilion designed by Philip Johnson. Also on view to the public are the lavishly decorated music room and selections from Mrs. Bliss's collection of rare illustrated garden books.

If you have even a mild interest in flowers, shrubs, trees, and magnificent natural beauty, visit Dumbarton Oaks's 10 acres of formal gardens, one of the loveliest spots in Washington (enter at 31st and R streets). Planned by noted landscape architect Beatrix Farrand, the gardens incorporate elements of traditional English, Italian, and French styles such as a formal rose garden, an English country garden, and an Orangery (circa 1810). A full-time crew of a dozen gardeners toils to maintain the stunning collection of terraces, geometric gardens, tree-shaded brick walks, fountains, arbors, and pools. Plenty of well-positioned benches make this a good place for resting weary feet, too. ⊠ *1703 32nd St. NW, Georgetown* ☎ *202/339–6401 or 202/339–6400* ☉ *Art collections Tues.–Sun. 2–5. Gardens Apr.–Oct., daily 2–6; Nov.–Mar., daily 2–5.*

⓴ **Evermay.** A Georgian manor house built around 1800 by real estate speculator Samuel Davidson, Evermay is almost hidden by its black-and-gold gates and high brick wall. Davidson wanted it that way. He sometimes took out advertisements in newspapers warning sightseers to avoid his estate "as they would a den of devils or rattlesnakes." The mansion is in private hands, but its grounds are occasionally opened for garden tours. ⊠ *1623 28th St. NW, Georgetown.*

⓺ **Exorcist Steps.** The heights of Georgetown to the north above N Street contrast with the busy jumble of the old waterfront. To reach the higher ground you can walk up M Street, past the old brick streetcar barn at No. 3600 (now a block of offices), turn right, and climb the 75 steps that figured prominently in the horror movie *The Exorcist*. If you prefer a less-demanding climb, walk up 34th Street instead. ⊠ *M and 36th Sts., Georgetown.*

The Foundry. This building gets its name from the machine shop that was here from 1856 to 1866. It housed several businesses after that, and around the turn of the 19th century it was a veterinary hospital for mules that worked on the canal. In 1976 the Foundry was reborn as a mall, with restaurants, art galleries, and a movie theater (renovated in 2003). ⊠ *1055 Thomas Jefferson St. NW, Georgetown.*

need a break? If the crowds of Georgetown become overwhelming, step into **Ching Ching Cha** (⊠ 1063 Wisconsin Ave. NW Georgetown ☎ 202/333–8288), a Chinese teahouse where tranquillity reigns supreme. In addition to tea, lunch and dinner may be ordered from a simple menu with light, healthy meals presented in lacquer boxes.

Francis Dodge Warehouses. The last three buildings at the foot of the west side of Wisconsin Avenue are reminders of Georgetown's mercantile past. They were built around 1830 by trader and merchant Francis Dodge. Note the heavy stone foundation of the southernmost warehouse, its star-end braces, and the broken hoist in the gable end. According to an 1838 newspaper ad, Georgetown shoppers could visit Dodge's grocery to buy such items as "Porto Rico Sugar, Marseilles soft-shelled Almonds and Havanna Segars." Although the traders of yesteryear have been replaced by small nonprofit organizations, the buildings don't look as if they house modern offices, and their facades make an interesting snapshot. ⊠ *1000–1002 Wisconsin Ave. NW, Georgetown.*

⑤ **Francis Scott Key Memorial Park.** A small, noisy park near the Key Bridge honors the Washington attorney who "by the dawn's early light" penned the national anthem during the War of 1812. Key was inspired when he saw that the British's night bombardment of Ft. McHenry in Baltimore harbor had failed to destroy the fort's flag. A replica of the 15-star, 15-stripe flag flies over the park 24 hours a day (the original is on display at the National Museum of American History). Here, Georgetown's quaint demeanor contrasts with the silvery skyscrapers of Rosslyn, Virginia, across the Potomac. ⊠ *M St. between 34th St. and Key Bridge, Georgetown.*

⑧ **Georgetown University.** Founded in 1789 by John Carroll, first American bishop and first archbishop of Baltimore, Georgetown is the oldest
Fodor's Choice
★ Jesuit school in the country. About 12,000 students attend Georgetown, known now as much for its perennially successful basketball team as for its fine programs in law, medicine, foreign service, and the liberal arts. When seen from the Potomac or from Washington's high ground, the Gothic spires of Georgetown's older buildings give the university an almost medieval look. ⊠ *37th and O Sts., Georgetown* ☎ *202/687–5055* ⊕ *www.georgetown.edu.*

Grace Episcopal Church. In the mid- to late 19th century, the Gothic Revival Grace Episcopal Church served the boatmen and workers from the nearby C&O Canal. The area was then one of the poorest in Georgetown. ⊠ *1041 Wisconsin Ave. NW, Georgetown* ☎ *202/333–7100* ☉ *Services Sat. 6 PM and Sun. 8:30 and 10 AM.*

⑦ **Halcyon House.** Built in 1783 by Benjamin Stoddert, the first secretary of the navy, Halcyon House has been the object of many subsequent additions and renovations. It's now a motley assortment of architectural styles. Prospect Street, where the house is set, gets its name from the fine views it affords of the waterfront and the river below. The house is closed to the public. ⊠ *34th and Prospect Sts., Georgetown.*

② **Masonic Lodge.** A two-story brick structure, Georgetown's Masonic Lodge, which isn't open to visitors, was built around 1810. Freemasonry, the world's largest secret society, was started by British stonemasons and cathedral builders as early as the 14th century; the fraternal order now has a much broader international membership that has included U.S. presidents—among them George Washington—as well as members of Congress. It's no accident that the Freemasons chose Georgetown to be the site of a lodge. Although Georgetown today is synonymous with affluence, for most of its history it was a working-class city, and the original names of its streets—Water Street, Canal Road, Fishing Lane—attest to the past importance of traditional trades to the region's economy. The area south of M Street (originally called Bridge Street because of the bridge that spanned Rock Creek to the east) was inhabited by tradesmen, laborers, and merchants who were good candidates for expanding the Masons' ranks. Among the lodge's interesting details are a pointed facade and recessed central arch, features that suggest the society's traditional attachment to the building arts. ⊠ *1058 Thomas Jefferson St., Georgetown.*

Montrose Park. Originally owned by 19th-century rope-making magnate Richard Parrot, this tract of land was purchased by Congress in the early part of this century "for the recreation and pleasure of the people." A popular spot for locals out with their toddlers and dogs, the park is good for an outing or short break. There are tennis courts, a swing set, and picnic tables. ⊠ *3001 R St. NW, Georgetown.*

⑬ Oak Hill Cemetery. Oak Hill Cemetery's funerary obelisks, crosses, and gravestones spread out over four landscaped terraces on a hill overlooking Rock Creek. Near the brick and sandstone gatehouse entrance is an 1850 Gothic-style chapel designed by Smithsonian Castle architect James Renwick. Across from the chapel is the resting place of actor, playwright, and diplomat John H. Payne, who is remembered today primarily for his song "Home Sweet Home." A few hundred feet to the north is the circular tomb of William Corcoran, founder of the Corcoran Gallery of Art, who donated the land for the cemetery. Cameras and backpacks are forbidden in the cemetery. ✉ *3001 R St. NW, Georgetown* ☎ *202/ 337–2835* ☞ *Free* ⊙ *Weekdays 10–4.*

▶ ❶ Old Stone House. What was early American life like? Here's the capital's oldest window into the past. Work on this fieldstone house, thought to be Washington's oldest surviving building, was begun in 1764 by a cabinetmaker named Christopher Layman. The house, now a museum, was used as both a residence and a place of business by a succession of occupants. Five of the house's rooms are furnished with the simple, sturdy artifacts—plain tables, spinning wheels, and so forth—of 18th-century middle-class life. The National Park Service maintains the house and its lovely gardens in the rear, which are planted with fruit trees and perennials. ✉ *3051 M St. NW, Georgetown* ☎ *202/426–6851* ☞ *Free* ⊙ *Wed.–Sun. 10–4*

⑩ St. John's Church. West of Wisconsin Avenue, a several-blocks-long stretch of O Street has remnants from an earlier age: cobblestones and streetcar tracks. Residents are so proud of the cobblestones that newer concrete patches have been scored to resemble them. Prominent in this section of Georgetown is one of the oldest churches in the city, St. John's Church, built in 1796 and attributed to Dr. William Thornton, architect of the Capitol. Interior alterations reflect a Victorian, rather than federal, style. St. John's is also noted for its stained-glass windows, including a small Tiffany. ✉ *3240 O St. NW, Georgetown* ☎ *202/ 338–1796* ⊙ *Services Sun. at 9 and 11, Thurs. at 11:30.*

⑪ Tudor Place. Stop at Q Street between 31st and 32nd streets; look through the trees to the north, at the top of a sloping lawn; and you'll see the neoclassical Tudor Place, designed by Capitol architect Dr. William Thornton and completed in 1816. On a house tour you'll see Francis Scott Key's desk, items that belonged to George Washington, and spurs belonging to soldiers who were killed in the Civil War. The grounds contain many specimens planted in the early 19th century. The house was built for Thomas Peter, son of Georgetown's first mayor, and his wife, Martha Custis, Martha Washington's granddaughter. It was because of this connection to the president's family that Tudor Place came to house many items from Mount Vernon. The yellow stucco house is interesting for its architecture—especially the dramatic, two-story domed portico on the south side—but its familial heritage is even more remarkable: Tudor Place stayed in the same family for 178 years, until 1983, when Armistead Peter III died. Before his death, Peter established a foundation to restore the house and open it to the public. Tour reservations are advised. ✉ *1644 31st St. NW, Georgetown* ☎ *202/965–0400* ⊕ *www.tudorplace.org* ☞ *House and garden tour, suggested donation $6* ⊙ *House tour Tues.–Fri. at 10, 11:30, 1, and 2:30; Sat. hourly 10–4; last tour at 3. Garden Nov.–Mar. and June–Aug., Mon.–Sat. 10–4; Apr. and May and Sept.–Oct., Mon.–Sat. 10–4, Sun. noon–4.*

❹ Washington Harbour. Stately columns and the liberal use of glass in its construction are hallmarks of Washington Harbour, a six-acre glittering postmodern riverfront development designed by Arthur Cotton

Moore. Included are such restaurants as the two-story Sequoia, Tony & Joe's Seafood Place, and the Riverside Grille, as well as offices, apartments, and upscale shops. Highlights of the central plaza are a large fountain and a futuristic, lighthouselike structure made up of four towering white columns. Several restaurants offer outdoor dining. From the edge of Washington Harbour you can see the Watergate complex and Kennedy Center to the east; meanwhile you can hear the waters of the Potomac gently lap at the edge of the dock. Those who prefer the water to the streets often arrive by boat, docking just yards from outdoor diners. At night, the area sparkles like a Christmas scene, with hundreds of twinkling white lights. ⊠ *3000 K St. NW, Georgetown.*

DUPONT CIRCLE

Three of Washington's main thoroughfares intersect at Dupont Circle: Connecticut, New Hampshire, and Massachusetts avenues. With a small, handsome park and a splashing fountain in the center, Dupont Circle is more than an island around which traffic flows, making it an exception among Washington circles. The activity spills over into the surrounding streets, one of the liveliest, most vibrant neighborhoods in D.C.

Development near Dupont Circle started during the post–Civil War boom of the 1870s. As the city increased in stature, the nation's wealthy and influential citizens began building their mansions near the circle. The area underwent a different kind of transformation in the middle of the 20th century, when the middle and upper classes deserted Washington for the suburbs, and in the 1960s the circle became the starting point for rowdy, litter-strewn marches sponsored by countercultural groups. Today the neighborhood is once again fashionable, and its many restaurants, offbeat shops, coffeehouses, art galleries, and specialty bookstores lend it a distinctive, cosmopolitan air. Stores and clubs catering to the neighborhood's large gay community are abundant.

Numbers in the text correspond to numbers in the margin and on the Dupont Circle map.

a good walk

Start your exploration in **Dupont Circle** ❶ ► itself, which has a large central fountain. Carefully cross the circle traffic and head southwest down New Hampshire Avenue to the **Heurich House Museum** ❷, built by a beer magnate. Cross New Hampshire Avenue and go onto O Street. Not all the homes here are mansions, but the typical brick Victorian row houses on this block tend to be large. Turn right on 21st Street to admire the opulent **Walsh-McLean House** ❸, which isn't open to tours. Head west on Massachusetts Avenue to No. 2118, **Anderson House** ❹, which holds the art and treasures a former diplomat collected during his travels.

Head west on Q Street to the **Bison Bridge** ❺, so called because of its four bronze statues of the shaggy horned beasts. Walk north on 23rd Street and pass between two embassies, those of Turkey and Romania, both on Sheridan Circle. This area of Massachusetts Avenue, going either direction from the circle, is known as Embassy Row, with the various nations' flags flying in front of their respective embassies. Turn left on Massachusetts Avenue and walk north one block, where the **Cameroon Embassy** ❻ is housed in a fanciful mansion. Turn right on S Street and go past the statue of Irish patriot Robert Emmet, dedicated in 1966 to celebrate the 50th anniversary of Irish independence. The former home of the 28th president, the **Woodrow Wilson House** ❼, is a few hundred feet down S Street. Right next door is the **Textile Museum** ❽, founded by Bristol-Myers heir George Hewitt Myers to house and show some of his 17,000 textiles and carpets.

From the Textile Museum, walk north on 23rd Street until it dead-ends at the Tudor mansion at **2221 Kalorama Road** ❾, now the residence of the French ambassador. Turn right, and as you walk up Kalorama, the large beige building on the left near Connecticut Avenue is the Chinese Embassy. Turn right down Connecticut Avenue. On the left at 1919 Connecticut is the Washington Hilton & Towers, the site of John Hinckley's 1981 assassination attempt on Ronald Reagan (the shots were fired at the entrance on T Street NW). Go left on R Street for two blocks to the **National Museum of American Jewish Military History** ❿. Follow R Street back across Connecticut Avenue to the **Fondo Del Sol Visual Arts Center,** a nonprofit center featuring art, poetry, and music of the Americas. Walk south on 21st Street and discover some of the many private art galleries in the area.

One of Washington's great art museums is the **Phillips Collection** ⓫ at 21st and Q streets, filled with Impressionist and modern art masterpieces. The neighborhood surrounding the Phillips has a large concentration of art galleries that hold evening receptions the first Friday of the month. Continue east on Q Street, and then turn right at Connecticut to the circle. Follow Massachusetts Avenue east to the National Trust for Historic Preservation (18th St. and Massachusetts Ave.), which isn't open to the public; however, a quick peek at the circular lobby gives you an idea of the lavish world its onetime residents inhabited. At the corner of 16th Street is the **Australian Embassy,** which has occasional art exhibits. And now you've arrived at yet another circle—**Scott Circle** ⓬, with its equestrian statue of General Winfield Scott, who served in the military from the presidency of Jefferson through to Lincoln.

Take a slight detour along N Street to Vermont Avenue to visit **Mary McLeod Bethune Council House** ⓭, a museum named after the founder of the Nationla Council of Negro Women. Follow Vermont Avenue south to Thomas Circle and turn right on M Street. After a block, the **Metropolitan African Methodist Episcopal Church** ⓮ is on your left. Continue on M Street to 17th Street, to the headquarters of the **National Geographic Society** ⓯, which has a very interactive museum. The **Charles E. Sumner School Museum and Archives** ⓰, across M Street from the National Geographic offices, was built in 1872 as a school for black children. It's now used mainly for conferences, but it also has a permanent exhibit on the history of the city's public school system. Head up 17th Street to Rhode Island Avenue and walk a half block west to **St. Matthew's Cathedral** ⓱, the seat of Washington's Catholic archbishop. John F. Kennedy frequently went to church here, which also was the site of his funeral mass.

TIMING   Visiting the Dupont Circle area takes at least half a day, although you can find things to keep you busy all day. The most time-consuming sites are probably the Phillips Collection, the National Geographic Society's Explorers Hall, and Anderson House, although the Textile and the American Jewish Military History museums can be captivating as well.

What to See

❹ **Anderson House.** A palatial home that's a mystery even to many longtime Washingtonians, Anderson House isn't an embassy, though it does have a link to that world. Larz Anderson was a diplomat whose career included postings to Japan and Belgium. Anderson and his heiress wife, Isabel, toured the world, picking up objects that struck their fancy. They filled their residence, which was constructed in 1905, with the booty of their travels, including choir stalls from an Italian Renaissance church, Flemish tapestries, and a large—if spotty—collection of Asian art. All this remains in the house for you to see.

In accordance with the Andersons' wishes, the building also serves as the headquarters of a group to which Larz belonged: the Society of the Cincinnati. The oldest patriotic organization in the country, the society was formed in 1783 by a group of officers who had served with George Washington during the Revolutionary War. The group took its name from Cincinnatus, a distinguished Roman farmer who, circa 500 BC, led an army against Rome's enemies and later quelled civil disturbances in the city. After each success, rather than seek the political power that could have easily been his, he returned to the simple life on his farm. The story impressed the American officers, who saw in it a mirror of their own situation: they, too, would leave the battlefields to get on with the business of forging a new nation. (One such member went on to name the city in Ohio.) Today's members are direct descendants of those American revolutionaries.

Many of the displays in the society's museum focus on the colonial period and the Revolutionary War. One room—painted in a marvelous trompe l'oeil style that makes the walls seem as if they're covered with sculpture—is filled with military miniatures from the United States and France. (Because of the important role France played in defeating the British, French officers were invited to join the society. Pierre-Charles L'Enfant, "Artist of the Revolution" and planner of Washington, designed the society's eagle medallion.)

The house is often used by the federal government to entertain visiting dignitaries. Amid the glitz, glamour, beauty, and patriotic spectacle of the mansion are two painted panels in the solarium that depict the Andersons' favorite motorcar sightseeing routes around Washington. ⊠ 2118 Massachusetts Ave. NW, Dupont Circle ☎ 202/785–2040 ▣ Free ⊘ Tues.–Sat. 1–4 Ⓜ Dupont Circle.

Australian Embassy. Many foreign embassies in Washington host art exhibits or cultural programs open to the public. One of the best galleries is at the Australian Embassy, which periodically displays masterpieces from Down Under. If you're lucky, you might see aboriginal artifacts and dot paintings of striking originality and beauty, as well as contemporary landscapes and portraits with a uniquely Australian character. ⊠ 1601 Massachusetts Ave. NW, Dupont Circle ☎ 202/797–3000 ⊕ www.austemb.org ▣ Free ⊘ Weekdays 9–5 by appointment only Ⓜ Dupont Circle.

❺ Bison Bridge. Tour guides at the Smithsonian's National Museum of Natural History are quick to remind you that America never had buffalo; the big, shaggy animals that roamed the plains were bison. (True buffalo are African and Asian animals of the same family.) Although it's officially the Dumbarton Bridge, locals call it the Bison Bridge because of the four bronze statues designed by A. Phimister Proctor. The sides of the structure, which stretches across Rock Creek Park into Georgetown, are decorated with busts of Native Americans, the work of architect Glenn Brown, who, along with his son Bedford, designed the bridge in 1914. The best way to see the busts is to walk the footpath along Rock Creek. ⊠ 23rd and Q Sts. NW, Dupont Circle and Georgetown Ⓜ Dupont Circle.

❻ Cameroon Embassy. The westernmost of the beaux arts mansions built along Massachusetts Avenue around 1900 now houses the Cameroon Embassy. The building is a fanciful castle with a conical tower, bronze weather vane, and intricate detailing around the windows and balconies. ⊠ 2349 Massachusetts Ave. NW, Dupont Circle Ⓜ Dupont Circle.

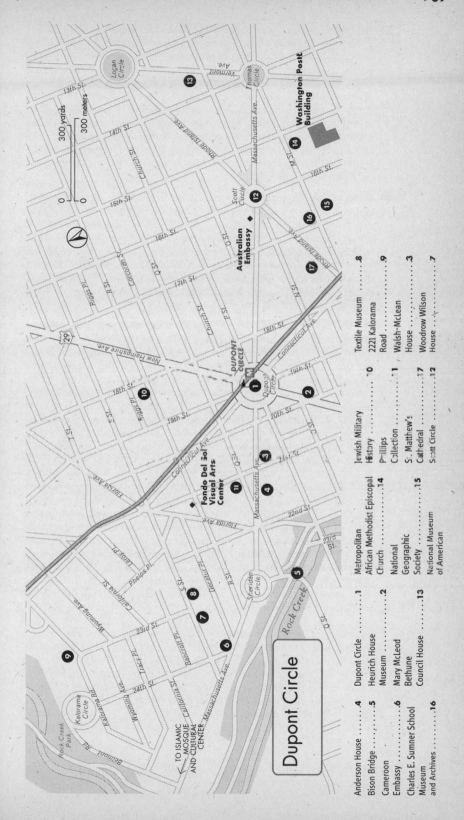

Dupont Circle

⑯ Charles E. Sumner School Museum and Archives. Built in 1872 for the education of black children, the school takes its name from the Massachusetts senator who delivered a blistering attack against slavery in 1856 and was savagely caned as a result by a congressman from South Carolina. The building was designed by Adolph Cluss, who created the Arts and Industries Building on the Washington Mall. It's typical of the District's Victorian-era public schools. Beautifully restored in 1986, the school serves mainly as a conference center, though it hosts changing art exhibits and houses a permanent collection of memorabilia relating to the city's public school system. ⊠ *1201 17th St. NW, Downtown* ☎ *202/442-6060* ☜ *Free* ⊙ *Mon.–Sat. 10–5; often closed for conferences* Ⓜ *Farragut North.*

► **❶ Dupont Circle.** Originally known as Pacific Circle, this hub was the westernmost circle in Pierre-Charles L'Enfant's original design for the Federal City. The name was changed in 1884, when Congress authorized construction of a bronze statue honoring Civil War hero Admiral Samuel F. Dupont. The statue fell into disrepair, and Dupont's family—who had never liked it anyway—replaced it in 1921. The marble fountain that stands in its place, with allegorical figures Sea, Stars, and Wind, was created by Daniel Chester French, the sculptor of Lincoln's statue in the Lincoln Memorial.

As you look around the circumference of the circle, you can see the peculiar constraints within which architects in Washington must work. Since a half dozen streets converge on Dupont Circle, the buildings around it are, for the most part, wedge-shaped and set on plots of land formed like massive slices of pie. Only two of the great houses that stood on the circle in the early 20th century remain today. The Renaissance-style house at **15 Dupont Circle**, next to P Street, was built in 1903 for Robert W. Patterson, publisher of the *Washington Times-Herald*. Patterson's daughter, Cissy, who succeeded him as publisher, was known for hosting parties that attracted such notables as William Randolph Hearst, Douglas MacArthur, and J. Edgar Hoover. In 1927, while Cissy was living in New York City and the White House was being refurbished, Calvin Coolidge and his family stayed here. While they did, they received American aviator Charles Lindbergh; some of the most famous photographs of Lindy were taken as he stood on the house's balcony and smiled down at the crowds below. In 1948 Cissy willed the house to the American Red Cross, and the Washington Club, a private club, bought it from the organization in 1951. The **Sulgrave Club**, at the corner of Massachusetts Avenue, with its rounded apex facing the circle, was also once a private home and is now a private club as well. ⊠ *Intersection of Connecticut, Massachusetts, and New Hampshire Aves.* Ⓜ *Dupont Circle.*

need a break? Connecticut Avenue near Dupont Circle is chockablock with restaurants. At **Kramerbooks and Afterwords** (⊠ 1517 Connecticut Ave. NW, Dupont Circle ☎ 202/387–1400), you can relax over dinner or a drink after browsing through the volumes on display. For lunch or a light dinner (or just a cup of tea and an oatmeal cookie), visit **Teaism** (⊠ 2009 R St. NW, Dupont Circle ☎ 202/667–3827). In addition to several dozen varieties of tea, there's also a selection of seafood and vegetarian entrées, many available in bento boxes and all seasoned with tea.

Fondo Del Sol Visual Arts Center. A nonprofit museum devoted to the cultural heritage of Latin America and the Caribbean, the Fondo Del Sol Visual Arts Center has changing exhibitions covering contemporary, pre-

Columbian, and folk art. The museum also offers a program of lectures, concerts, poetry readings, exhibit tours, and an annual summer festival featuring salsa and reggae music. ✉ *2112 R St., Dupont Circle* ☎ *202/483-2777* ⊕ *www.dkmuseums.com/fondo* ☜ *$3* ☉ *Tues.–Sat. 12:30–5* Ⓜ *Dupont Circle.*

② **Heurich House Museum.** This opulent Romanesque Revival was the home of Christian Heurich, a German orphan who made his fortune in the beer business. Heurich's brewery was in Foggy Bottom, where the Kennedy Center stands today. Brewing was a dangerous business in the 19th century, and fires more than once reduced Heurich's brewery to ashes. Perhaps because of this he insisted that his home, completed in 1894, be fireproof; in fact, it was the first building in Washington with residential fireproofing. Although 17 fireplaces were installed—some with onyx facings, one with the bronze image of a lion staring out from the back—not a single one ever held a fire.

Heurich must have taken the proverbs seriously. He drank his beer every day, had three wives (in succession), and lived to be 102. (In 1986 Heurich's grandson Gary started brewing the family beer again. Though it's made in Utica, New York, he vows to someday build another Heurich brewery near Washington.)

After Heurich's widow died in 1955, the house was turned over to the Historical Society of Washington, D.C. The society used the house until 2003, when it was sold in preparation for a move into the new City Museum in the Old Downtown area. The new owners, descendants of Christian Heurich, intend to use the house for special events and as a museum. ✉ *1307 New Hampshire Ave. NW, Dupont Circle* Ⓜ *Dupont Circle.*

> **need a break?** The Dupont Circle branch of **Pan Asian Noodles and Grill** (✉ 2020 P St. NW, Dupont Circle ☎ 202/872-8889) is one of two locations in Washington. Both offer reasonably priced Asian noodle dishes.

⑬ **Mary McLeod Bethune Council House.** Exhibits in this museum focus on the achievements of African-American women, including Mary McLeod Bethune, who founded Florida's Bethune-Cookman College, established the National Council of Negro Women, and served as an adviser to President Franklin D. Roosevelt. ✉ *1318 Vermont Ave. NW, Dupont Circle* ☎ *202/673-2402* ☜ *Free* ☉ *Mon.–Sat. 10–4* Ⓜ *McPherson Square.*

⑭ **Metropolitan African Methodist Episcopal Church.** Completed in 1886, the Gothic-style Metropolitan African Methodist Episcopal Church has become one of the most influential African-American churches in the city. Abolitionist orator Frederick Douglass worshiped here, and Bill Clinton chose the church for both of his inaugural prayer services. ✉ *1518 M St. NW, Downtown* ☎ *202/331-1426* Ⓜ *Farragut North.*

☝ ⑮ **National Geographic Society.** Founded in 1888, the society is best known for its yellow-border magazine. The society has sponsored numerous expeditions throughout its 100-year history, including those of admirals Peary and Byrd and underwater explorer Jacques Cousteau. Explorers Hall, entered from 17th Street, is the magazine come to life. It invites you to learn about the world in a decidedly interactive way: you can experience everything from a mini tornado to video touch screens that explain geographic concepts and then quiz you on what you've learned. The most dramatic events take place in Earth Station One Interactive Theatre, a 72-seat amphitheater that sends the audience on a journey around the world. The centerpiece is a hand-painted globe, 11 foot in diameter, that floats and spins on a cushion of air, showing off differ-ent features of the planet. ✉ *17th and M Sts. NW, Dupont Circle* ☎*202/857–7588; 202/857–7689 group tours* ☒*Free* ☉ *Mon.–Sat. 9–5, Sun. 10–5* Ⓜ *Farragut North.*

⑩ National Museum of American Jewish Military History. The museum's focus is on American Jews in the military, who have served in every war the nation has fought. On display are weapons, uniforms, medals, recruit-ment posters, and other military memorabilia. The few specifically re-ligious items—a camouflage yarmulke, rabbinical supplies fashioned from shell casings and parachute silk—underscore the sometimes strange de-mands placed on religion during war. ✉ *1811 R St. NW, Dupont Cir-cle* ☎ *202/265–6280* ☒ *Free* ☉ *Weekdays 9–5, Sun. 1–5* Ⓜ *Dupont Circle.*

★ **⑪ Phillips Collection.** The first permanent museum of modern art in the coun-try, the masterpiece-filled Phillips Collection is unique both in origin and content. In 1918 Duncan Phillips, grandson of a founder of the Jones and Laughlin Steel Company, started to collect art for a museum that would stand as a memorial to his father and brother, who had died within 13 months of each other. Three years later what was first called the Phillips Memorial Art Gallery opened in two rooms of this Georgian Revival house near Dupont Circle.

Not interested in a painting's market value or its faddishness, Phillips searched for works that impressed him as outstanding products of a par-ticular artist's unique vision. Holdings include works by Georges Braque, Paul Cézanne, Paul Klee, Henri Matisse, and John Henry Twachtman; the museum's collection of the work of Pierre Bonnard is the largest in the country. The exhibits change regularly. The collection's best-known paintings include Renoir's *Luncheon of the Boating Party, Repentant Peter* by both Goya and El Greco, *A Bowl of Plums* by 18th-century artist Jean-Baptiste Siméon Chardin, Degas's *Dancers at the Bar,* and Vincent van Gogh's *Entrance to the Public Garden at Arles.* A self-por-trait of Cézanne was the painting Phillips said he would save first if the gallery caught fire. During the 1920s, Phillips and his wife, Marjorie, started to support American Modernists such as John Marin, Georgia O'Keeffe, and Arthur Dove.

The Phillips is a comfortable museum. Works of an artist are often grouped together in "exhibition units," and, unlike most other galleries (where uniformed guards appear uninterested in the masterpieces around them), the Phillips employs students of art, many of whom are artists them-selves, to sit by the paintings and answer questions.

On Thursday the museum stays open late for live jazz, gallery talks, and a cash bar. From September to May, the museum hosts a Sunday after-noon concert series at 5 in the music room. It's free with museum ad-mission. Construction, begun in 2003 and scheduled for completion at the end of 2005, means that many of the major works are off-site, on tour at other museums. ✉ *1600 21st St. NW, Dupont Circle* ☎ *202/ 387–2151* ⊕ *www.phillipscollection.org* ☒ *$7.50* ☉ *Sept.–May, Tues., Wed., Fri., and Sat. 10–5, Thurs. 10–8:30, Sun. noon–7; June–Aug., Tues., Wed., Fri., and Sat. 10–5, Thurs. 10–8:30, Sun. noon–5. Tour Wed. and Sat. at 2. Gallery talk 1st and 3rd Thurs. at 12:30* Ⓜ *Dupont Circle.*

⑰ St. Matthew's Cathedral. John F. Kennedy frequently worshiped in this Renaissance-style church, the seat of Washington's Roman Catholic diocese, and in 1963 Kennedy's funeral mass was held within its richly decorated walls. Set in the floor, directly in front of the main altar, is a memorial to the slain president: "Here rested the remains of President

Kennedy at the requiem mass November 25, 1963, before their removal to Arlington where they lie in expectation of a heavenly resurrection." A memorial to nuns who served as nurses during the Civil War is across Rhode Island Avenue. ⊠ *1725 Rhode Island Ave. NW, Dupont Circle* ☎ *202/347-3215* ⬛ *Free* ⊙ *Weekdays and Sun. 7–6:30, Sat. 8–6:30; tour usually Sun. at 2:30* Ⓜ *Farragut North.*

⓬ **Scott Circle.** The equestrian statue of General Winfield Scott (1786–1866), who pioneered the use of light artillery in the Mexican War, was cast from cannons captured during that conflict. On the west side of the traffic circle is a statue of fiery orator Daniel Webster. If you walk to the south side of the circle and look down 16th Street, you'll get a familiar view of the columns of the White House, six blocks away. Across the circle is a memorial to S. C. F. Hahnemann, founder of homeopathy and the namesake of Hahnemann Medical School in Philadelphia. His statue sits in a recessed wall, his head surrounded by a mosaic of colorful tiles. ⊠ *Massachusetts and Rhode Island Aves. and 16th St., Downtown* Ⓜ *Archives/Navy Memorial.*

❽ **Textile Museum.** In the 1890s, George Hewitt Myers, a heir to the Bristol-Myers fortune, purchased his first Oriental rug for his dorm room at Yale. Later, Myers lived two houses down from Woodrow Wilson, at 2310 S Street, in a home designed by John Russell Pope, architect of the National Archives and the Jefferson Memorial. Myers bought the Waddy B. Wood–designed house next door, at No. 2320, and opened his museum to the public in 1925. Today the collection includes more than 17,000 textiles and carpets. Rotating exhibits are taken from a permanent collection of historic and ethnographic items that include Coptic and pre-Columbian textiles, Kashmir embroidery, and Turkman tribal rugs. At least one show of modern textiles—such as quilts or fiber art—is mounted each year. ⊠ *2320 S St. NW, Kalorama* ☎ *202/667 0441* ⊕ *www.textilemuseum.org* ⬛ *Suggested donation $5* ⊙ *Mon.–Sat. 10–5, Sun. 1–5; highlight tour Sept.–May, Wed. and weekends at 1:30* Ⓜ *Dupont Circle.*

❾ **2221 Kalorama Road.** S Street is an informal dividing line between the Dupont Circle area to the south and the Kalorama neighborhood to the north. The name for this peaceful, tree-filled enclave—Greek for "beautiful view"—was contributed by politician and writer Joel Barlow, who bought the large tract in 1807. Kalorama is filled with embassies and luxurious homes. The Tudor mansion at 2221 Kalorama Road, where 23rd Street runs into Kalorama Road, was built in 1911 for mining millionaire W. W. Lawrence, but since 1936 it has been the residence of the French ambassador. For a taste of the beautiful view that so captivated Barlow, walk west on Kalorama Road, and then turn right on Kalorama Circle. At the bottom of the circle you can look down over Rock Creek Park, the finger of green that pokes into northwest Washington.

❸ **Walsh-McLean House.** Tom McLean was an Irish prospector who made a fortune in Colorado gold and came to Washington to show it all off. The city on the Potomac was the perfect place to establish a presence for America's late-19th-century nouveau riche. It was easier to enter "society" in the nation's planned capital than in more established cities like New York or Philadelphia, and wealthy industrialists and entrepreneurs flocked here. Walsh announced his arrival with this 60-room mansion. His daughter, Evalyn Walsh-McLean, the last private owner of the Hope Diamond (now in the National Museum of Natural History), was one of the city's leading hostesses. Today the house is used as an embassy by the Indonesian government and isn't open for tours. ⊠ *2020 Massachusetts Ave. NW, Dupont Circle* Ⓜ *Dupont Circle.*

off the
beaten
path

WASHINGTON POST BUILDING – Although the newspaper is no longer printed here, the claim to fame of the main *Washington Post* building when it opened in 1951 was that the printing plant and editorial offices were stacked so compactly in one small downtown location. You can see the newsroom that broke the Watergate story on a 45-minute guided tour of the building, which is otherwise not open to the public. In addition to the newsroom, there's a small museum dedicated to the history of the newspaper and old and new printing processes. For the guided tour, you must reserve a spot by phone two to six weeks in advance. ⊠ *1150 15th St. NW, Downtown* ☎ *202/334–7969* ⊕ *www.washingtonpost.com* ▣ *Free* ☉ *Tours Mon. on the hr 10–3.*

❼ Woodrow Wilson House. Until the Clintons bought a house here, Wilson was the only president who stayed in D.C. after leaving the White House. (He's still the only president buried in the city, inside the National Cathedral.) He and his second wife, Edith Bolling Wilson, retired in 1920 to this Georgian Revival designed by Washington architect Waddy B. Wood. (Wood also designed the Department of the Interior and the National Museum of Women in the Arts.) The house was built in 1915 for a carpet merchant.

President Wilson suffered a stroke toward the end of his second term, in 1919, and he lived out the last few years of his life on this quiet street. Edith made sure he was comfortable; she had a bed constructed that was the same dimensions as the large Lincoln bed Wilson had slept in while in the White House. She also had the house's trunk lift (a sort of dumbwaiter for trunks) converted to an Otis elevator so the partially paralyzed president could move from floor to floor. When the streetcars stopped running in 1962 the elevator stopped working; it had received its electricity directly from the streetcar line.

Wilson died in 1924. Edith survived him by 37 years. After she died in 1961, the house and its contents were bequeathed to the National Trust for Historic Preservation. On view inside are such items as a Gobelins tapestry, a baseball signed by King George V, and the shell casing from the first shot fired by U.S. forces in World War I. The house also contains memorabilia related to the history of the short-lived but influential League of Nations, including the colorful flag Wilson hoped would be adopted by that organization. ⊠ *2340 S St. NW, Kalorama* ☎ *202/ 387–4062* ▣ *$5* ☉ *Tues.–Sun. 10–4* Ⓜ *Dupont Circle.*

FOGGY BOTTOM

The Foggy Bottom area of Washington—bordered roughly by the Potomac and Rock Creek to the west, 20th Street to the east, Pennsylvania Avenue to the north, and Constitution Avenue to the south—has three main claims to fame: the State Department, the Kennedy Center, and George Washington University. In 1763 a German immigrant named Jacob Funk purchased this land, and a community called Funkstown sprang up on the Potomac. This nickname is only slightly less amusing than the present one, which is derived from the wharves, breweries, lime kilns, and glassworks that were near the water. Smoke from these factories combined with the swampy air of the low-lying ground to produce a permanent fog along the waterfront.

The smoke-belching factories ensured work for the hundreds of German and Irish immigrants who settled in Foggy Bottom in the 19th century. By the 1930s, however, industry was on the way out, and Foggy

Bottom had become a poor part of Washington. The opening of the State Department headquarters in 1947 reawakened middle-class interest in the neighborhood's modest row houses. Many of them are now gone, and Foggy Bottom today suffers from a split personality: its tiny, one-room-wide row houses sit next to large, mixed-use developments.

Although the Foggy Bottom neighborhood has its own Metro stop, many attractions are a considerable distance away. If you don't relish long walks or time is limited, check the Foggy Bottom map to see if you need to make alternate travel arrangements to visit specific sights.

Numbers in the text correspond to numbers in the margin and on the Foggy Bottom map.

a good walk

Start your exploration near the Foggy Bottom Metro station at 23rd and I streets. The sprawling campus of **George Washington University** ❶ ☞ covers much of Foggy Bottom south of Pennsylvania Avenue between 19th and 24th streets. Walk west from the Metro station on the I Street pedestrian mall, and then turn left on New Hampshire Avenue. At Virginia Avenue you run into the **Watergate** ❷ apartment-office complex, forever a part of our language for the role it played in the downfall of a president. Walk south on New Hampshire Avenue, past the Saudi Arabian Embassy, to the **John F. Kennedy Center for the Performing Arts** ❸, Washington's premier cultural center. Walk back up New Hampshire Avenue; then turn right on G Street, right on Virginia Avenue (follow the outstretched arm of the statue of Benito Juárez, the 19th-century Mexican statesman), and right on 23rd Street. The Pan American Health Organization, American headquarters of the World Health Organization, is at 23rd Street and Virginia Avenue, in the circular building that looks like a huge car air filter. Two blocks down 23rd Street is the massive **Department of State** ❹, which has impressive reception rooms filled with museum-quality furnishings.

Follow 23rd Street to Constitution Avenue and turn left. On the south side of Constitution are the Lincoln and Vietnam Veterans memorials. The John Russell Pope–designed **American Pharmaceutical Association** ❺ building sits at the corner of Constitution Avenue and 23rd Street. One block east is the **National Academy of Sciences** ❻, which has a bust of Einstein outside. You can tour the white-marble **Federal Reserve Building** ❼ to find out exactly what it is the Fed does. Turn left on 20th Street. Crossing Virginia Avenue and continuing north on 20th Street takes you back onto the campus of George Washington University. To the right—near No. 1901—are the only two remaining 18th-century row houses that made up the **Seven Buildings** ❽. The modern glass office building at **2000 Pennsylvania Avenue NW** ❾ incorporates a row of hollowed-out and refurbished Victorian houses as part of its facade. Across Pennsylvania Avenue, on the small triangle where I Street intersects it, is the **Arts Club of Washington** ❿, a one-time home of James Monroe. Walk north on 20th Street to the **Klutznick National Jewish Museum Collection and Gallery** ⓫ at 2020 K Street NW. The museum is inside the headquarters of B'nai B'rith.

TIMING   Foggy Bottom is a half-day walk. Touring the State Department and the Federal Reserve Building should take about two hours. It takes a fair amount of time to walk between sites, because this area isn't as densely packed with points of interest as are most others.

What to See

❺ **American Pharmaceutical Association.** You might think the American Pharmaceutical Association is a rather odd sightseeing recommendation, even just for a casual glance as you're passing. But aside from the fact that the white-marble building was designed in 1934 by noted architect John Russell Pope, who also designed the Lincoln Memorial and the National Gallery of Art, the American Pharmaceutical Association is as much a symbol of modern Washington as any government edifice. It's the home of one of more than 3,000 trade and professional associations (some as obscure as the Cast Iron Soil Pipe Institute and others as well-known as the AARP) that have chosen the capital for their headquarters, eager to represent their members' interests before the government. ⊠ *Constitution Ave. and 23rd St., Foggy Bottom* ☎ *202/429–7565* Ⓜ *Foggy Bottom.*

⑩ **Arts Club of Washington.** Built in 1806 by Timothy Caldwell, this federal-style house was once the residence of James Monroe and since 1916 has been the headquarters of the Arts Club, a nonprofit organization dedicated to the promotion of the arts in the nation's capital. Exhibits in the Monroe House and adjoining MacFeely House galleries represent many styles, with the work of local artists well represented. ⊠ *2017 I St. NW, Foggy Bottom* ☎ *202/331–7282* ▩ *Free* ☾ *Tues.–Fri. 10–5, Sat. 10–2* Ⓜ *Farragut West.*

❹ **Department of State.** The foreign policy of the United States is formulated and administered by battalions of brainy analysts in the huge Department of State Building (often referred to as the State Department), which also serves as the headquarters of the United States Diplomatic Corps. All is presided over by the secretary of state, who is fourth in line for the presidency (after the vice president, speaker of the House, and president *pro tempore* of the Senate) should the president be unable to serve. On the top floor are the opulent Diplomatic Reception Rooms, decorated like the great halls of Europe and the rooms of colonial American plantations. The furnishings include a Philadelphia highboy, a Paul Revere bowl, and the desk on which the Treaty of Paris, which ended the Revolutionary War, was signed in 1783. The largest room has a specially loomed carpet so heavy and large it had to be airlifted in by helicopter. The rooms are used 15–20 times a week to entertain foreign diplomats and heads of state; you can see them, too, but you need to register for a tour three months in advance. The tours are recommended for those 13 and over. ⊠ *2201 C St. NW, Foggy Bottom* ☎ *202/647–3241; 202/736–4474 TDD* ⊕ *www.state.gov* ▩ *Free* ☾ *Tours weekdays at 9:30, 10:30, and 2:45* Ⓜ *Foggy Bottom.*

❼ **Federal Reserve Building.** This imposing marble edifice, its bronze entryway topped by a massive eagle, was designed by Folger Library architect Paul Cret. Its appearance seems to say "Your money's safe with us." Even so, there's no money here (The Fed sets interest rates and thereby seeks to keep the economy on track). The building's stately facade belies a friendlier interior, with a varied collection of art and four special art exhibitions every year. A 45-minute tour includes a film that explains the Fed's origins and mission. *Enter on* ⊠ *20th St. and Constitution Ave. NW, Foggy Bottom* ☎ *202/452–3000; 202/452–3149 building tours; 202/452–3686 art tours.* ⊕ *www.federalreserve.gov* ▩ *Free* ☾ *Weekdays 11–4 during art exhibitions (tours of permanent art collection by appointment only); building tour Thurs. at 2:30* Ⓜ *Foggy Bottom.*

▶❶ **George Washington University.** George Washington had always hoped the capital would hold a renowned university. He even left 50 shares of stock in the Patowmack Canal Co. to endow it. Congress never acted upon his wishes, however, and it wasn't until 1822 that the university that would eventually be named after the first president began to take shape. The private Columbian College in the District of Columbia opened that year with the aim of training students for the Baptist ministry. In 1904

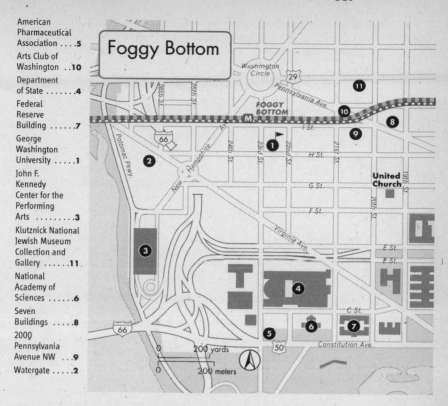

the university shed its Baptist connections and changed its name to George Washington University. In 1912 it moved to its present location and since that time has become the second largest landholder in the District (after the federal government). Students have ranged included from J. Edgar Hoover and Jacqueline Bouvier. In addition to residing in modern university buildings, GWU occupies many 19th-century houses. ✉ *South of Pennsylvania Ave. between 19th and 24th Sts., Foggy Bottom* ☎ *202/994–1000* ⊕ *www.gwu.edu* Ⓜ *Foggy Bottom.*

❸ **John F. Kennedy Center for the Performing Arts.** Thanks to the Kennedy Center, Washington regularly hosts world-class performers. Prior to 1971, Washington after dark was primarily known for cocktail parties, not culture. The opening of the Kennedy Center in that year instantly established the capital as a locale for culture on an international scale. Concerts, ballets, opera, musicals, and drama are presented in the center's five theaters, and movies are screened periodically in the American Film Institute's theater.

The idea for a national cultural center had been proposed by President Eisenhower in 1955. John F. Kennedy had also strongly supported the idea, and after his assassination it was decided to dedicate the center to him. Some critics have called the center's square design unimaginative—it has been dubbed the cake box that the more decorative Watergate came in—but no one can deny that the building's big. The Grand Foyer, lighted by 18 1-ton Orrefors crystal chandeliers, is 630 foot long. (Even at this size it's mobbed at intermission.) Many of the center's furnishings were donated by foreign countries: the chandeliers came from Sweden; the tapestries on the walls came from Brazil, France, and Mexico; and the 3,700 tons of white Carrara marble for the interior and exterior of the building were a gift from Italy. Flags fly in the Hall of Nations and the Hall of States, and in the center of the foyer is a 7-foot-high, bronze, oddly textured bust of Kennedy by sculptor Robert Berks.

In addition to the regular performances in the five theaters, each year the Kennedy Center also produces festivals that highlight different musical traditions and cultures. The hugely popular annual open house is a free, daylong extravaganza of theater, dance, and music, with nonstop entertainment both indoors and outdoors. There also are free performances every evening at 6 on the Millennium Stage.

Two restaurants on the Roof Terrace Level range from casual fare to more formal dining. It can get noisy as jets fly overhead to nearby Ronald Reagan National Airport, but you can get one of the city's better views from the terrace: to the north are Georgetown and the National Cathedral; to the west, Theodore Roosevelt Island and Rosslyn, Virginia; and to the south, the Lincoln and Jefferson memorials. ⊠ *New Hampshire Ave. and Rock Creek Pkwy. NW, Foggy Bottom* ☎ *202/467–4600* ⊕ *www.kennedy-center.org* ✉ *Free* ☉ *Daily 10–until end of last show* Ⓜ *Foggy Bottom (free shuttle-bus service every 15 min to and from Kennedy Center on performance days).*

⑪ Klutznick National Jewish Museum Collection and Gallery at B'nai B'rith. This gallery, inside B'nai B'rith International's headquarters and available for viewing only by advance reservation, displays highlights of the collection upon which B'nai B'rith plans to found a National Jewish Museum in Washington. Key objects on display from the museum's permanent collection include George Washington's 1790 letter to a Rhode Island synagogue promising that the U.S. will give "to Bigotry No Sanction" as well as an international selection of artifacts celebrating the contributions of Jewish people. Call for information about cultural and educational programs. This exhibition space replaces the former B'nai B'rith Klutznick Museum in Dupont Circle. ⊠ *2020 K St. NW, Foggy Bottom* ☎ *202/857–6513* ⊕ *bbi.koz.com* ✉ *$5* ☉ *Mon.–Thurs. noon–3 by advance reservation only, Sun. hrs by appointment only* Ⓜ *Foggy Bottom or Farragut West.*

⑥ National Academy of Sciences. Inscribed in Greek under the cornice is a quotation from Aristotle on the value of science—appropriate for a building that houses the offices of the National Academy of Sciences, the National Academy of Engineering, the Institute of Medicine, and the National Research Council. There are often free art exhibits here—not all of them relating to science—and, from September to May, free Sunday afternoon concerts. In front of the academy is Robert Berks's sculpture of Albert Einstein, done in the same mashed-potato style as the artist's bust of JFK in the Kennedy Center. ⊠ *2100 C St. NW, Foggy Bottom* ☎ *202/334–2436* ⊕ *www.nationalacademies.org/nas/arts* ✉ *Free* ☉ *Weekdays 9–5* Ⓜ *Foggy Bottom.*

⑧ Seven Buildings. Only two structures remain of the string of 18th-century row houses known as the Seven Buildings. One of the five were demolished served as President Madison's executive mansion after the British burned the White House in 1814. The two survivors are now dwarfed by the taller office block behind them and have been integrated into the Mexican Embassy, which is at 1911 Pennsylvania Avenue NW. ⊠ *Near 1901 Pennsylvania Ave., Foggy Bottom* Ⓜ *Foggy Bottom.*

⑨ 2000 Pennsylvania Avenue NW. It's a shame that so many important historical buildings fail to survive as a city matures. The row of residences on Pennsylvania Avenue between 20th and 21st streets escaped the fate of the Seven Buildings by being incorporated—literally—into the present. The Victorian houses have been hollowed out and refurbished to serve as the entryway for a modern glass office structure at 2000 Pennsylvania Avenue. The backs of the buildings are under the sloping roof of the development, preserved as if in a terrarium. Ⓜ *Foggy Bottom.*

United Church. Foggy Bottom's immigrant past is still part of the present at the United Church. Built in 1891 for blue-collar Germans in the neighborhood, the church still conducts services in German the first and third Sunday of every month at 9:30, September through May. ✉ *1920 G St. NW, Foggy Bottom* ☎ *202/331–1495* Ⓜ *Foggy Bottom.*

❷ **Watergate.** Thanks to the events that took place on the night of June 17, 1972, the Watergate is possibly the world's most notorious apartment-office complex. As President Richard Nixon's aides E. Howard Hunt Jr. and G. Gordon Liddy sat in the Howard Johnson Motor Lodge across the street, five of their men were caught trying to bug the Democratic National Committee, headquartered on the sixth floor, in an attempt to subvert the democratic process on behalf of the then-president of the United States. A marketing company occupies the space today.

The suffix "-gate" is attached to any political scandal nowadays, but the Watergate itself was named after a monumental flight of steps that led down to the Potomac behind the Lincoln Memorial. The original Watergate was the site of band concerts until plane noise from nearby Ronald Reagan National Airport made the locale impractical.

Even before the break-in, the Watergate—which opened in 1965—was well known in the capital. Within its curving lines and behind its "toothpick" balusters have lived some of Washington's most famous—and infamous—citizens, including attorney general John Mitchell and presidential secretary Rose Mary Woods of Nixon White House fame as well as such D.C. insiders as Jacob Javits, Alan Cranston, Bob and Elizabeth Dole, Monica Lewinsky, and National Security Advisor Condoleezza Rice. The embassies of Brunei and Yemen are also in the Watergate. ✉ *2600 Virginia Ave. NW, Foggy Bottom* Ⓜ *Foggy Bottom.*

CLEVELAND PARK & THE NATIONAL ZOO

Cleveland Park, a tree-shaded neighborhood in northwest Washington, owes its name to onetime summer resident Grover Cleveland and its development to the streetcar line that was laid along Connecticut Avenue in the 1890s. President Cleveland and his wife, Frances Folson, escaped the heat of downtown Washington in 1886 by establishing a summer White House on Newark Street between 35th and 36th streets. Many prominent Washingtonians followed suit. When the streetcar came through in 1892, construction in the area snowballed. Developer John Sherman hired local architects to design houses and provided amenities such as a fire station and a streetcar-waiting lodge to entice home buyers out of the city and into "rural" Cleveland Park. Today the neighborhood's attractive houses and suburban character are popular with Washington professionals. (The Clevelands' retreat no longer stands, but on the same block is Rosedale, an 18th-century estate that was the home of another famous summer visitor, young Cuban refugee Elian Gonzalez, in 2000.)

Numbers in the text correspond to numbers in the margin and on the Cleveland Park & the National Zoo map.

a good walk

Start your exploration at the Cleveland Park Metro station at Connecticut Avenue and Ordway Street NW. The colonial-style Park and Shop on the east side of Connecticut Avenue was Washington's first shopping center with off-street parking. The art deco style is well represented by many of the buildings and apartments along some of the main thoroughfares in northwest Washington, including Connecticut Avenue. The **Cineplex Odeon Uptown** ❶ ▶, a marvelous art deco movie house from 1936, is a reminder of the days when movie theaters were something other than boring little boxes. Continue south on Connecticut Avenue, where you cross a sliver of Rock Creek Park, via a bridge decorated with eight art deco lights. Off to your left is the city's finest art deco apartment house, the **Kennedy-Warren** ❷, with stylized carved eagles flanking the driveways. Follow Connecticut Avenue two more blocks to the **National Zoological Park** ❸, another member of the Smithsonian family. Tian Tian and Mei Xiang, the zoo's most famous residents, are among a handful of giant pandas in the United States.

Stately old apartment buildings line Connecticut Avenue south of the zoo. Cross Cathedral Avenue and enter the Woodley Park section of the city. The cross-shape **Wardman Tower** ❹, at the corner of Connecticut Avenue and Woodley Road, was built in 1928 as a luxury apartment building. Once known for its famous residents, it's now part of the Marriott Wardman Park hotel. Get back on the Metro and ride two stops to Van Ness to visit Hillwood Museum and Gardens, a mansion with beautiful gardens.

TIMING   The amount of time you spend at the zoo depends on you. Popular visiting times are during the elephant-training session at 11 and the sea-lion training demonstration at 11:30.

What to See

▶ ❶   **Cineplex Odeon Uptown.** If you're in the mood for a movie during your stay and want to see it in a grand entertainment palace of yesteryear, the Cineplex Odeon Uptown is the place to go. Jack Valenti, the president of the Motion Picture Association of America, says that the huge single screen "is probably the best we have in this town." Unlike most of the nation's other old theaters, which have been chopped up and transformed into multiplexes, this art deco theater, the only one of its kind left in Washington, has remained true to its origins. There's an inviting balcony. ✉ *3426 Connecticut Ave. NW, Cleveland Park* ☎ *202/966–5400 or 202/966–5401* Ⓜ *Cleveland Park.*

off the beaten path

HILLWOOD MUSEUM AND GARDENS – Hillwood House, cereal heiress Marjorie Merriweather Post's 40-room Georgian mansion, contains a large collection of 18th- and 19th-century French and Russian decorative art that includes gold and silver work, icons, tapestries, porcelain, and Fabergé eggs. Also on the estate are a dacha (summer cottage) filled with Russian objects and an Adirondacks-style cabin that houses Native American artifacts. The 25-acre estate grounds are composed of lawns, formal French and Japanese gardens, greenhouses, and paths that wind through plantings of azaleas, laurels, and rhododendrons. Make reservations for the house tour well in advance. ✉ *4155 Linnean Ave. NW, Northwest* ☎ *202/686–5807 or 202/686–8500* ⛩ *House and grounds $10* ☉ *House tours Mar.–Jan., Tues.–Sat. 9–5* Ⓜ *Van Ness/UDC.*

❷   **Kennedy-Warren.** Lovers of art deco won't want to miss the Kennedy-Warren. The apartment house is a superb example of the style, with such period detailing as decorative aluminum panels and a streamlined en-

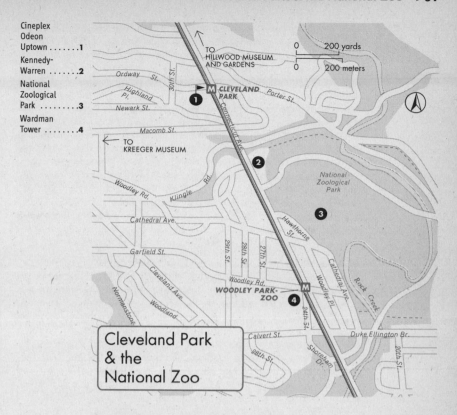

Cleveland Park
& the
National Zoo

tryway, stone griffins under the pyramidal copper roof, and stylized carved eagles flanking the driveways. Perhaps in keeping with its elegant architecture, this is one of the last apartment buildings in town still to have a doorman. ⊠ *3133 Connecticut Ave. NW, Cleveland Park* Ⓜ *Cleveland Park.*

off the beaten path

KREEGER MUSEUM – You need to travel by car or taxi to the Kreeger Museum. Its cool white domes and elegant lines stand in stark contrast to the traditional feel of the rest of the Foxhall Road neighborhood. The building, designed by Philip Johnson, was once the home of GEICO insurance executive David Lloyd Kreeger and his wife, Carmen. The collection includes works by Renoir, Degas, Cézanne, and Munch, as well as traditional African artifacts. ⊠ *2401 Foxhall Rd. NW, Foxhall* ☎ *202/338–3553* ⊕ *www. kreegermuseum.com* ⊠ *$5* ⊙ *Open Sat. 10–4. Tours (reservation required) Tues.–Fri. 10:30 and 1:30, Sat. 10:30.*

Ⓒ ❸ **National Zoo.** Part of the Smithsonian Institution, the National Zoo is one of the foremost zoos in the world. Created by an Act of Congress in 1889, the 163-acre park was designed by landscape architect Frederick Law Olmsted, the man who designed the U.S. Capitol grounds. (Before the zoo opened in 1890, live animals used as taxidermists' models had been kept on the Mall.) For years the zoo's most famous residents were the giant pandas Hsing-Hsing and Ling-Ling, gifts from China in 1972. Both are gone now, but panda fans can welcome Tian Tian and Mei Xiang, who arrived from China in 2001. They receive visitors from 9 to 6 May through mid-September and 9 to 4:30 mid-September through April; expect a wait when the zoo is busy.

Throughout the zoo, innovative compounds show many animals in nat-
uralistic settings, including the Great Flight Cage—a walk-in aviary in
which birds fly unrestricted from May to October (they're moved indoors
during the colder months). The Reptile Discovery Center, the Bird Resource Center, and an exhibition called "How Do You Zoo" all teach
children about biology. The most ambitious addition to the zoo is Ama-
zonia, a reproduction of a South American rain-forest ecosystem. Fish
swim behind glass walls, while overhead, monkeys and birds flit from
tree to tree. In 2001, ring-tailed and red-fronted lemurs were installed in
an exhibit called Lemur Island. The Cheetah Conservation Area is a grassy
compound with a family of the world's fastest cats. The American Prairie
exhibit includes some grasses that are toweringly tall, and examines the
resurgence of the bison, nearly killed off in the 19th century. ⊠ *3001
Connecticut Ave. NW, Woodley Park* ☎ *202/673–4800 or 202/673–4717*
⊕ *www.si.edu/natzoo* ⊠ *Free, parking $5* ⊙ *May–mid-Sept., daily 6 AM–8
PM; mid-Sept.–Apr., daily 6–6. Zoo buildings open at 10 and close before the zoo closes* Ⓜ *Cleveland Park or Woodley Park/Zoo.*

❹ **Wardman Tower.** At the corner of Connecticut Avenue and Woodley
Road is the cross-shape, Georgian-style tower built by developer Harry
Wardman in 1928 as a luxury apartment building. Washingtonians
called the project "Wardman's Folly," convinced no one would want to
stay in a hotel so far from the city—some 25 blocks from the White House;
most upscale residential buildings, especially older ones, are within a
few blocks. Contrary to predictions, however, Wardman Tower was famous for its well-known residents, who included Dwight D. Eisenhower, Herbert Hoover, Clare Booth Luce, Dean Rusk, Earl Warren, and
Caspar Weinberger. It's now part of the Marriott Wardman Park hotel.
⊠ *2660 Woodley Rd. NW, Woodley Park* Ⓜ *Woodley Park/Zoo.*

Woodley Park. The stretch of Connecticut Avenue south of the National
Zoo is bordered by venerable apartment buildings. Passing Cathedral
Avenue (the first cross street south of the zoo entrance), you enter a part
of town known as Woodley Park. Like Cleveland Park to the north, Wood-
ley Park grew as the streetcar advanced into this part of Washington.
In 1800 Philip Barton Key, uncle of Francis Scott Key, built Woodley, a
Georgian mansion on Cathedral Avenue between 29th and 31st streets.
The white stucco mansion was the summer home of four presidents: Van
Buren, Tyler, Buchanan, and Cleveland. It's now owned by the private
Maret School. Ⓜ *Woodley Park/Zoo.*

UPPER MASSACHUSETTS AVENUE

Several good sights, including the National Cathedral, are on the portion of Massachusetts Avenue that's to the north of Georgetown. To get
here via public transportation, take the Friendship Heights bus, which
travels north along Wisconsin Avenue in Georgetown.

*Numbers in the text correspond to numbers in the margin and on the
Upper Massachusetts Avenue map.*

What to See

❺ **Glover-Archbold Park.** Groves of beeches, elms, and oaks flourish at this
183-acre park, which is part of the Rock Creek system. A 3½-mi nature trail runs the length of Glover-Archbold, a gift to the city in 1924.
⊠ *Garfield St. and New Mexico Ave. NW, Georgetown* Ⓜ *Friendship
Heights.*

❶ **Islamic Mosque and Cultural Center.** The Muslim faithful are called to prayer
five times a day from atop the 162-foot-high minaret of the Islamic

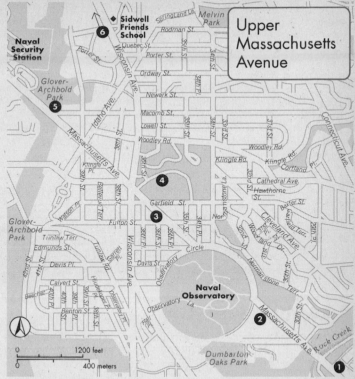

Mosque and Cultural Center. The ornate interior is filled with deep-pile Persian rugs and covered with Arabic art. Each May the Muslim Women's Association sponsors a bazaar, with crafts, clothing, and food for sale. Visitors wearing shorts will not be admitted to the mosque; women must wear scarves to cover their heads. ⊠ *2551 Massachusetts Ave. NW, Dupont Circle* ☎ *202/332–8343* ☉ *Center daily 10–5; mosque open for all 5 prayers, dawn–after sunset.*

② **Kahlil Gibran Memorial Garden.** This tiny urban park combines Western and Arabian symbols; it's perfect for contemplation. From the Massachusetts Avenue entrance, a stone walk bridges a grassy swale. Further on are limestone benches, engraved with sayings from Gibran, that curve around a fountain and a bust of the Lebanese-born poet. ⊠ *3100 block of Massachusetts Ave. NW, Woodley Park.*

③ **St. Sophia Cathedral.** The Greek Orthodox St. Sophia Cathedral is noted for the handsome mosaic work on the interior of its dome. The cathedral holds a festival of Greek food and crafts each spring and fall. ⊠ *Massachusetts Ave. at 36th St. NW, Cleveland Park* ☎ *202/333–4730* ☉ *Service Sun. at 9:30.*

⑥ **Washington Dolls' House and Toy Museum.** A collection of American and imported dolls, dollhouses, toys, and games—most from the Victorian period—fills a compact museum founded in 1975 by a dollhouse historian. Miniature accessories, dollhouse kits, and antique toys and games are on sale in the museum's shops. ⊠ *5236 44th St. NW, Chevy Chase* ☎ *202/244–0024* ⊴ *$4* ☉ *Tues.–Sat. 10–5, Sun. noon–5* Ⓜ *Friendship Heights.*

❹ **Washington National Cathedral.** Construction of Washington National
Fodor'sChoice Cathedral—the sixth-largest cathedral in the world—started in 1907 and
★ finished in 1990, when the building was consecrated. Like its 14th-century Gothic counterparts, the stunning National Cathedral (officially the Cathedral Church of St. Peter and St. Paul) has a nave, flying buttresses, transepts, and vaults that were built stone by stone. It's adorned with fanciful gargoyles created by skilled stone carvers. The tomb of Woodrow Wilson, the only president buried in Washington, is on the south side of the nave. The expansive view of the city from the Pilgrim Gallery is exceptional. The cathedral is Episcopal but has hosted services of many denominations.

On the grounds of the cathedral is the compact, English-style **Bishop's Garden.** Boxwoods, ivy, tea roses, yew trees, and an assortment of arches, bas-reliefs, and stonework from European ruins provide a restful counterpoint to the cathedral's towers. ⊠ *Wisconsin and Massachusetts Aves. NW, Cleveland Park* ☎ *202/537–6200; 202/537–6207 tour information* ⊕ *www.cathedral.org* ✉ *Suggested tour donation $3* ⊙ *Early May–early Sept., weekdays 10–5, Sat. 10–4:30, Sun. 8–5; early Sept.–early May, daily 10–5. Sun. services at 8, 9, 10, 11, and 4; evening prayer daily at 4:30; tours every 15 mins Mon.–Sat. 10–11:30 and 12:45–3:15, Sun. 12:45–2:30.*

ADAMS-MORGAN

To the young, the hip, and the cool, Washington has the reputation of being a rather staid town, more interested in bureaucracy than bling-bling, with all the vitality of a seersucker suit. It may have the Hope Diamond, these detractors say, but that's about the only thing that really sparkles. What they mean, of course, is that Washington isn't New York City. And thank goodness, say Washingtonians, who wouldn't want to give up their clean subway, comfortable standard of living, or place in the political spotlight, even if it did mean being able to get a decent corned beef sandwich or a martini at three in the morning. Besides, Washington does have Adams-Morgan. It may not be the Lower East Side, but it's close enough in spirit to satisfy all but the most hardened black-clad cynics.

Adams-Morgan (roughly, the blocks north of Florida Avenue, between Connecticut Avenue and 16th Street NW) is Washington's most ethnically diverse neighborhood. And as is often the case, that means it's one of Washington's most interesting areas—a United Nations of cuisines, offbeat shops, and funky bars and clubs. The name itself, fashioned in the 1950s by neighborhood civic groups, serves as a symbol of the area's melting pot character: it's a conjunction of the names of two local schools, the predominantly white Adams School and the largely black Morgan School. Today Adams-Morgan also has every shade in between, with large Latin American and West African populations.

The neighborhood's grand 19th-century apartment buildings and row houses, along with its fun character, have attracted young professionals, the businesses that cater to them, the attendant parking and crowd problems, and the rise in real estate values. All this has caused some long-time Adams-Morganites to wonder if their neighborhood is in danger of becoming another Georgetown.

Adams-Morgan already has one thing in common with Georgetown: there's no Metro stop. It's a pleasant 15-minute walk from the Woodley Park/Zoo Metro station: walk south on Connecticut, then turn left on Calvert Street, and cross over Rock Creek Park on the Duke Ellington Bridge. Or you can get off at the Dupont Circle Metro stop and walk east to (and turn left onto) 18th Street. The heart of Adams-Morgan is at the crossroads of Adams Mill Road, Columbia Road, and 18th Street.

Numbers in the text correspond to numbers in the margin and on the Adams-Morgan map.

a good walk

Some walks are most enjoyable if followed in the suggested sequence, but in this case it's probably more fun to wander from the path to make your own discoveries. Begin by walking east on Calvert Street from the Woodley Park/Zoo Metro stop and turning left on Columbia Road. At tables stretched along the street, vendors hawk watches, leather goods, knockoff perfumes, CDs, sneakers, clothes, and handmade jewelry. The store signs—Casa Lebrato, Urgente Express (the business specializes in shipping to and from Central America)—are a testament to the area's Latin flavor; on these blocks you hear as much Spanish as you do English.

Cross Columbia at Ontario Road and backtrack west. On Saturday morning a market springs up on the plaza in front of the Suntrust bank, at the southwest corner of 18th and Columbia, with vendors selling fruits, vegetables, flowers, and fresh bread.

If Columbia Road east of 18th is Adams-Morgan's Latin Quarter, 18th Street south of Columbia is its restaurant corridor. In the next few blocks are restaurants serving the dishes from China, Mexico, India, El Salvador, Ethiopia, France, the Caribbean, Thailand, Argentina, Italy, South America, Vietnam, and, believe it or not, the United States. If you can't make up your mind, there's even a palm reader who can help decide what your stomach has in store.

You can also feed your hunger for the outré or offbeat with the shops on 18th Street. Here you'll find such collectibles as Mission furniture, Russel Wright crockery and Fiesta ware, aerodynamic art deco armchairs, Bakelite telephones, massive chromium toasters, kidney-shape coffee tables, skinny neckties, and oddball salt-and-pepper shakers. On the west side of 18th Street are antiques shops as well as secondhand shops set up in alleys or warehouses. Nearby is the **District of Columbia Arts Center ❶** ⌐, a combination art gallery and performance space.

On 16th Street there are several points of interest, including the **All Souls' Unitarian Church ❷**, the **Mexican Cultural Institute ❸**, the **Meridian House and the White-Meyer House ❹**, and the **House of the Temple ❺**. Hop on an S2 or S4 bus toward Silver Spring to visit the National Museum of Health and Medicine.

Of course, one measure of any neighborhood is the tone it takes when the sun goes down. In the spring and summer, restaurants open their windows or set out tables on the sidewalks. Those lucky enough to have rooftop seating find diners lining up to eat under the stars. Washington can be notoriously hot in the summer, but one of Adams-Morgan's charms has always been that its slight elevation wraps it in cooling breezes. Although the neighborhood's bar and club scene isn't as varied as its restaurant scene, there are some standouts. Remember that the last trains leave the Woodley Park Metro station at around midnight. If that's too early for you, be prepared to take a cab.

TIMING If you're in a shopping mood, a wander around Adams-Morgan can occupy the better part of an afternoon. And if you take advantage of the restaurants and nightlife here, there's no telling when your head will hit the pillow.

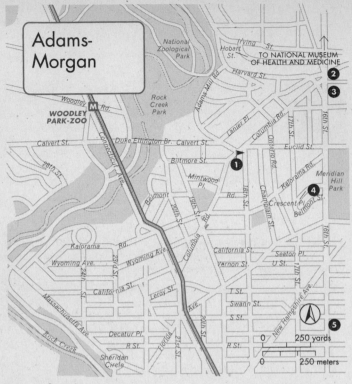

What to See

2 All Souls' Unitarian Church. The design of All Souls', erected in 1924, is based on that of St. Martin-in-the-Fields in London. ⊠ *16th and Harvard Sts. NW, Adams-Morgan* ☎ *202/332–5266* ☉ *Tues.–Thurs. 10–6; Sun. service at 10:50 AM.*

1 District of Columbia Arts Center. A combination art gallery and performance space, the DCAC exhibits the work of local artists and is the host of offbeat plays and performance art. ⊠ *2438 18th St. NW, Adams-Morgan* ☎ *202/462–7833* ⊠ *Gallery free, performance costs vary* ☉ *Wed.–Sun. 2–7, Fri.–Sat. 2–10, and during performances (generally Thurs.–Sun. 7–midnight).*

5 House of the Temple. A dramatic Masonic shrine, the House of the Temple was patterned after the Mausoleum at Halicarnassus, in present-day Turkey. Tours are available on a drop-in basis. ⊠ *1733 16th St. NW, Adams-Morgan* ☎ *202/232–3579* ⊠ *Free* ☉ *Tour weekdays 8–2.*

4 Meridian House and the White-Meyer House. Meridian International Center, a nonprofit institution promoting international understanding, owns two handsome mansions designed by John Russell Pope. The 30-room Meridian House was built in 1920 by Irwin Boyle Laughlin, scion of a Pittsburgh steel family and former ambassador to Spain. The Louis XVI–style home is furnished with parquet floors, ornamental iron grillwork, handsome moldings, period furniture, tapestries, and a garden planted with European linden trees. Next door is the Georgian-style house built for Henry White (former ambassador to France) that was later the home of the Meyer family, publishers of the *Washington Post*. The first floors of both houses are open to the public and hold periodic art exhibits with an international flavor. ⊠ *1630 and 1624 Crescent Pl. NW, Adams-Morgan* ☎ *202/667–6800* ☒ *Free* ☉ *Wed.–Sun. 2–5.*

③ **Mexican Cultural Institute.** This glorious Italianate house, designed by Nathan Wyeth and George A. Fuller, architects of the West Wing of the White House, housed the Embassy of Mexico until 1989. It's now the site of the Mexican Cultural Institute, which promotes Mexican art, culture, and science. Exhibits have included works by such 19th- and 20th-century Mexican artists as Diego Rivera, José Clemente Orozco, David Alfaro, and Juan O'Gorman. ⊠ *2829 16th St. NW, Adams-Morgan* ☎ *202/728–1628* ☒ *Free* ☉ *Tues.–Sat. 11–5:30.*

off the
beaten
path

NATIONAL MUSEUM OF HEALTH AND MEDICINE – Open since the 1860s, this medical museum illustrates medicine's fight against injury and disease. Included are displays on the Lincoln and Garfield assassinations and one of the world's largest collections of microscopes. Because some exhibits are fairly graphic (the wax surgical models and the preserved organs come to mind), the museum may not be suitable for young children or the squeamish. To get here from Adams-Morgan, catch Bus S2 or S4 to Silver Spring on 16th Street. ⊠ *Walter Reed Army Medical Center, 6825 16th St. NW, Adams-Morgan* ☎ *202/782–2200* ☒ *Free* ☉ *Open daily 10–5:30.*

☖ **Rock Creek Park.** The 1,800 acres on either side of Rock Creek have provided a cool oasis for D.C. residents ever since Congress set them aside in 1890. Bicycle routes and hiking and equestrian trails wind through the groves of dogwoods, beeches, oaks, and cedar, and 30 picnic areas are scattered here and there. Rangers at the **Nature Center and Planetarium** (⊠ south of Military Rd., 5200 Glover Rd. NW, Northwest ☎ 202/ 426–6829) introduce the park and keep track of daily events; guided nature walks leave from the center weekends at 2. The center and planetarium are open Wednesday through Sunday from 9 to 5. Landscape architect Horace Peaslee created oft-overlooked **Meridian Hill Park** (⊠ 16th and Euclid Sts., Adams-Morgan), a noncontiguous section of Rock Creek Park, after a 1917 study of the parks of Europe. As a result, it contains elements of parks in France (a long, straight mall bordered with plants), Italy (terraces and wall fountains), and Switzerland (a lower-level reflecting pool based on one in Zurich). It's also unofficially known as Malcolm X Park in honor of the civil rights leader, who once spoke here. Drug activity once made it unwise to visit Meridian Hill alone: it's somewhat safer now, but avoid it after dark. ☎ 202/ 282–1063 park information.

ARLINGTON

The Virginia suburb of Arlington County was once part of the District of Columbia. Carved out of the Old Dominion when Washington was created, it was returned to Virginia along with the rest of the land west of the Potomac in 1845. Washington hasn't held a grudge, though, and there are two attractions in Arlington—both linked to the military—that should be a part of any complete visit to the nation's capital: Arlington National Cemetery and the U.S. Marine Corps War Memorial. Both are accessible by Metro, and a trip across the Potomac to Arlington is a very worthwhile half day of sightseeing.

Numbers in the text correspond to numbers in the margin and on the Arlington, VA, map.

To begin your exploration, take either a 10-minute Metro ride from downtown or walk across Memorial Bridge (southwest of the Lincoln Memorial) to **Arlington National Cemetery** ❶ ☞. The visitor center has detailed maps, and the staff can help you find specific graves. Next to the visitor center is the Women in Military Service for America Memorial. West of the visitor center are the **Kennedy graves** ❷, where John F. Kennedy, two of his children who died in infancy, and his wife, Jacqueline Bouvier Kennedy Onassis, are buried. Long before it was a cemetery, this land was part of the 1,100-acre estate of George Washington Parke Custis, a descendant of Martha and (by marriage) George Washington whose daughter married Robert E. Lee. The Lees lived in **Arlington House** ❸, a fine example of Greek Revival architecture. Walk south on Crook Walk past row upon row of simple white headstones, following the signs to the **Tomb of the Unknowns** ❹, where the remains of unknown servicemen from Korea and both world wars are buried. Steps from the Tomb of the Unknowns is **Section 7A** ❺, where many distinguished veterans are buried. To reach the sites at the northern end of the cemetery and to make your way into the city of Arlington, first walk north along Roosevelt Drive to Schley Drive (past the Memorial Gate); then turn right on Custis Walk to the Ord and Weitzel Gate. On your way you pass **Section 27** ❻, where 3,800 former slaves are buried. Leave the cemetery through the Ord and Weitzel Gate, cross Marshall Drive carefully, and walk to the 49-bell **Netherlands Carillon** ❼, where, even if your visit doesn't coincide with a performance, you can enjoy a good vista of Washington. To the north is the **United States Marine Corps War Memorial** ❽, better known as the Iwo Jima Memorial, which honors all Marines who lost their lives while serving their country.

TIMING Visiting all the sites at Arlington National Cemetery could take a half day or longer, depending on your stamina and interest.

What to See

❸ **Arlington House.** It was in Arlington that the two most famous names in Virginia history—Washington and Lee—became intertwined. George Washington Parke Custis—raised by Martha and George Washington, his grandmother and step-grandfather—built Arlington House (also known as the Custis-Lee Mansion) between 1802 and 1817 on his 1,100-acre estate overlooking the Potomac. After his death, the property went to his daughter, Mary Anna Randolph Custis. In 1831, Mary married Robert E. Lee, a graduate of West Point. For the next 30 years they lived at Arlington House.

In 1861 Lee was offered command of the Union forces. He declined, insisting that he could never take up arms against his native Virginia. The Lees left Arlington House that spring, never to return. Federal troops crossed the Potomac not long after that, fortified the estate's ridges, and turned the home into the Army of the Potomac's headquarters. Arlington House and the estate were confiscated in May 1864 and sold to the federal government when the Lees failed to pay $92.07 in property taxes in person. (Survivors of General Lee were eventually compensated for the land.) Union forces built three fortifications on the land, and 200 nearby acres were set aside as a national cemetery. Sixty-five soldiers were buried there on June 15, 1864, and by the end of the Civil War more than 16,000 headstones dotted Arlington plantation's hills. Soldiers from the Revolutionary War and the War of 1812 were reinterred at Arlington as their bodies were discovered in other resting places.

The building's heavy Doric columns and severe pediment make Arlington House one of the area's best examples of Greek Revival architecture. The plantation home was designed by George Hadfield, a young En-

LEE, THE REBEL GENERAL

ROBERT E. LEE (1807–70) is a tragic figure in American history. Lee felt forced by principle and his family connections to lead a rebellion that resulted in more than half a million deaths and left the South in ruins. The only greater tragedy might have been if the Confederate States of America had won independence, which very probably would have led to even further political fractures and endless fighting among half a dozen nations across North America.

The youngest of the seven children of Revolutionary War hero Colonel Henry ("Light-Horse Harry") Lee, Robert Edward Lee was born to Ann Hill Carter at Stratford Plantation on Virginia's genteel Northern Neck. His family tree is a chart of the Old Dominion's leading families, crowned by his marriage to Martha Washington's great-granddaughter, Mary Anna Randolph Custis. Light-Horse Harry's relative poverty left the boy unable to afford a private education. Lee sought and won appointment to West Point, and there began the legend of his prowess: he rose to corps adjutant, the highest cadet rank; stood second in the Class of 1829; and never received a single demerit over the course of the four years. Advancement in the peacetime army was slow, even after he transferred from the elite engineer corps to the casualty-prone cavalry, and Lee still was but a captain when the Mexican War began in 1846. There his skill at military engineering, his strength and powers of endurance, and his great personal bravery caused his commander, General Winfield Scott, to describe Lee as "the very best soldier I ever saw in the field."

When the Civil War broke out in the spring of 1861, Scott advised President Abraham Lincoln to offer Colonel Lee command of the Union Army. Lee agonized but finally concluded that "I cannot raise my hand against my native state" and resigned his federal commission. Then, although he despised slavery, the root cause of the conflict, he offered his sword to the South. Union troops quickly overtook his house, and the plantation was converted into a refuge for fleeing slaves and a graveyard that eventually became Arlington National Cemetery. Lee was appointed military advisor to President Jefferson Davis, receiving a field command only after Confederate general Joseph E. Johnston was wounded in 1862. Lee so harried Union general George McClellan in the bloody Seven Days Battles that McClellan went into camp and abandoned any attempt to further menace the Confederate capital of Richmond.

Lee renamed his force the Army of Northern Virginia and launched a series of campaigns in which, by vigorous movement and audacious tactics, he repeatedly defeated superior Union forces. His troops so revered their gentle, soft-spoken leader that for his sake they would attempt, and often accomplish, the impossible. Lincoln was forced to fire one commanding general after another until he found the fierce bulldog he needed, Ulysses S. Grant. Finally, in the spring of 1865, Grant smashed his way into Richmond and defeated Lee.

At the age of 58, ailing and penniless, Lee began a new career as president of Washington College (now Washington and Lee University), in Lexington, Virginia. There his powerful personality, prestige, and progressive ideas, and his deep loyalty to the United States, produced southern leaders whose influence was sorely needed during Reconstruction. Lee died in 1870 and was entombed in a crypt beneath the college chapel.

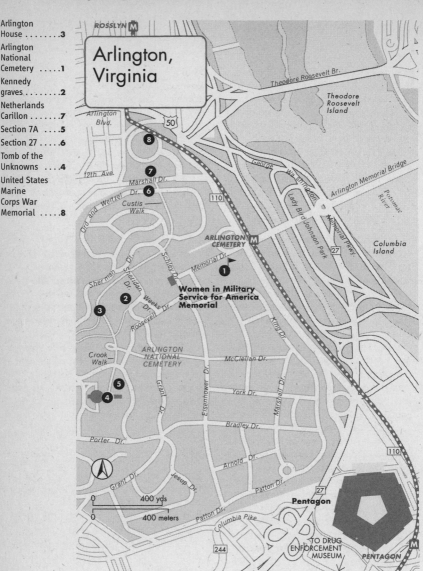

Arlington, Virginia

glish architect who, for a while, supervised construction of the Capitol. The view of Washington from the front of the house is superb. In 1955 Arlington House was designated a memorial to Robert E. Lee. It looks much as it did in the 19th century, and a quick tour takes you past objects once owned by the Custises and the Lees.

In front of Arlington House, next to a flag that flies at half staff whenever there's a funeral in the cemetery, is the flat-top **grave of Pierre-Charles L'Enfant,** designer of the Federal City. ⊠ *Between Lee and Sherman Drs.* ☎ *703/235–1530 or 703/557–0613* ⊠ *Free* ☉ *Daily 9:30–4:30.*

★ ► ❶ **Arlington National Cemetery.** More than 250,000 American war dead, as well as many notable Americans (among them presidents William Howard Taft and John F. Kennedy, General John Pershing, and Admiral Robert E. Peary), are interred in these 612 acres across the Potomac

River from Washington, established as the nation's cemetery in 1864. While you're at Arlington there's a good chance you might hear the clear, doleful sound of a trumpet playing taps or the sharp reports of a gun salute. Approximately 20 funerals are held daily (it's projected that the cemetery will be filled in 2020). Although not the largest cemetery in the country, Arlington is certainly the best known, a place where you can trace America's history through the aftermath of its battles.

To get here, you can take the Metro, travel on a Tourmobile bus, or walk across Arlington Memorial Bridge (southwest of the Lincoln Memorial). If you're driving, there's a large paid parking lot at the skylighted visitor center on Memorial Drive. Stop at the center for a free brochure with a detailed map of the cemetery. If you're looking for a specific grave, the staff can consult microfilm records and give you directions to it. You should know the deceased's full name and, if possible, his or her branch of service and year of death.

Tourmobile tour buses leave from just outside the visitor center April through September, daily 8:30–6:30, and October through March, daily 8:30–4:30. You can buy tickets here for the 40-minute tour of the cemetery, which includes stops at the Kennedy grave sites, the Tomb of the Unknowns, and Arlington House. Touring the cemetery on foot means a fair bit of hiking, but it can give you a closer look at some of the thousands of graves spread over these rolling Virginia hills. If you decide to walk, head west from the visitor center on Roosevelt Drive and then turn right on Weeks Drive. ⊠ *West end of Memorial Bridge* ☎ *703/607–8052 to locate a grave* ⊕ *www.arlingtoncemetery.com* ✉ *Cemetery free, parking $3.75 for the first 3 hrs. Tourmobile $5.25* ☉ *Apr.–Sept., daily 8–7; Oct.–Mar., daily 8–5.*

off the beaten path

DRUG ENFORCEMENT ADMINISTRATION MUSEUM – Just across the street from the Fashion Centre at Pentagon City—a destination in itself for shoppers—is the DEA Museum, within the U.S. Drug Enforcement Administration's headquarters. It explores the impact of drugs on American society, starting with quaint 19th-century ads for opium-laced patent medicines and "cocaine tooth drops" (opiates, cannabis, and cocaine were unregulated then). But documentation of these addictive substances' medical dangers, as well as the corrosive political effect of the opium trade, which China detested, is hard-hitting. A similar contrast is found between the period feel of artifacts from a 1970s head shop and displays on the realities of present-day drug trafficking. ⊠ *700 Army Navy Dr., at Hayes St.* ☎ *202/307–3463* ⊕ *www.deamuseum.org* ✉ *Free* ☉ *Tues.–Fri. 10–4* Ⓜ *Pentagon City.*

❷ Kennedy graves. An important part of any visit to Arlington National Cemetery is a visit to the graves of John F. Kennedy and other members of his family. JFK is buried under an eternal flame near two of his children, who died in infancy, and his wife, Jacqueline Bouvier Kennedy Onassis. The graves are a short walk west of the visitor center. Across from them is a low wall engraved with quotations from Kennedy's inaugural address. The public has been able to visit JFK's grave since 1967; it's now the most-visited grave site in the country. Nearby, marked by a simple white cross, is the grave of his brother Robert Kennedy. ⊠ *Sheridan and Weeks Drs.*

❼ Netherlands Carillon. A visit to Arlington National Cemetery affords the opportunity for a lovely and unusual musical experience, thanks to a 49-bell carillon presented to the United States by the Dutch people in

1960 in gratitude for aid received during World War II. Guest carillon players perform on Saturday afternoon May through September and on July 4. Times vary; call for details. For one of the most inclusive views of Washington, look to the east across the Potomac. From this vantage point, the Lincoln Memorial, the Washington Monument, and the Capitol appear in a side-by-side formation. ⊠ *Meade and Marshall Drs.* ☎ *703/289–2500.*

Pentagon. This office building, the headquarters of the United States Department of Defense, is the largest in the world. The Capitol could fit into any one of its five wedge-shape sections. Approximately 23,000 military and civilian workers arrive daily. Astonishingly, this mammoth office building was completed in 1943 after fewer than two years of construction.

The structure was reconstructed following the September 2001 crash of hijacked American Airlines Flight 77 into the northwest side of the building. The damaged area was removed in just over a month, and rebuilding proceeded rapidly (in keeping with the speed of the original construction). Renovations on all areas damaged by the terrorist attack were completed by spring 2003.

Tours of the building are given on a very limited basis to educational groups by advance reservation; tours for the general public have been suspended indefinitely. ⊠ *I–395 at Columbia Pike and Rte. 27* ☎ *703/ 695–1776* ⊕ *www.defenselink.mil/pubs/pentagon.*

❺ Section 7A. Many distinguished veterans are buried in this area of Arlington National Cemetery near the **Tomb of the Unknowns,** including boxing champ Joe Louis, ABC newsman Frank Reynolds, actor Lee Marvin, and World War II fighter pilot Colonel "Pappy" Boyington. ⊠ *Crook Walk near Roosevelt Dr.*

❻ Section 27. More than 3,800 former slaves are buried in this part of Arlington National Cemetery. They're all former residents of Freedman's Village, which operated at the Custis-Lee estate for more than 30 years beginning in 1863 to provide housing, education, and employment training for ex-slaves who had traveled to the capital. In the cemetery, the headstones are marked with their names and the word "Civilian" or "Citizen." Buried at Grave 19 in the first row of Section 27 is William Christman, a Union private who died of peritonitis in Washington on May 13, 1864. He was the first soldier interred at Arlington National Cemetery during the Civil War. ⊠ *Ord and Weitzel Dr. near Custis Walk.*

off the
beaten
path

THEODORE ROOSEVELT ISLAND – The island wilderness preserve in the Potomac River has 2½ mi of nature trails through marshland, swampland, and upland forest. It's an 88-acre tribute to the conservation-minded 26th president. Cattails, arrowarum, pickerelweed, willow, ash, maple, and oak all grow on the island, which is also a habitat for frogs, raccoons, birds, lizards, and the occasional red or gray fox. The 17-foot bronze statue of Roosevelt, reachable after a long walk toward the center of the woods, was done by Paul Manship. A pedestrian bridge connects the island to a parking lot on the Virginia shore, which is accessible by car from the northbound lanes of the George Washington Memorial Parkway. ⊠ *From downtown D.C., take Constitution Ave. west across the Theodore Roosevelt Bridge to George Washington Memorial Pkwy. north and follow signs or walk or bike across the Bridge beginning at the Kennedy Center* ☎ *703/289–2500 for park info* ▣ *Free* ☼ *Island daily dawn–dusk* Ⓜ *Rosslyn.*

④ Tomb of the Unknowns. Many countries established a memorial to their
Fodor'sChoice war dead after World War I. In the United States, the first burial at the
★ Tomb of the Unknowns took place at Arlington National Cemetery on
November 11, 1921, when the Unknown Soldier from the "Great War"
was interred under the large white-marble sarcophagus. Unknown servicemen killed in World War II and Korea were buried in 1958. The unknown serviceman killed in Vietnam was laid to rest on the plaza on
Memorial Day 1984 but was disinterred and identified in 1998. Officials then decided to leave the Vietnam War unknown crypt vacant. Soldiers from the Army's U.S. 3rd Infantry ("The Old Guard") keep watch
over the tomb 24 hours a day, regardless of weather conditions. Each
sentinel marches exactly 21 steps, then faces the tomb for 21 seconds,
symbolizing the 21-gun salute, America's highest military honor. The
guard is changed with a precise ceremony during the day—every half
hour from April through September and every hour the rest of the year.
At night the guard is changed every hour.

The Memorial Amphitheater west of the tomb is the scene of special
ceremonies on Veterans Day, Memorial Day, and Easter. Decorations
awarded to the unknowns by foreign governments and U.S. and foreign
organizations are displayed in an indoor trophy room. Across from the
amphitheater are memorials to the astronauts killed in the *Challenger*
shuttle explosion and to the servicemen killed in 1980 while trying to
rescue American hostages in Iran. Rising beyond that is the mainmast
of the USS *Maine,* the American ship that was sunk in Havana Harbor
in 1898, killing 299 men and sparking the Spanish-American War.
⊠ *End of Crook Walk.*

⑧ United States Marine Corps War Memorial. Better known simply as "the
Iwo Jima," this memorial, despite its familiarity, has lost none of its power
to stir the emotions. Honoring Marines who have given their lives since
the Corps was formed in 1775, the statue, sculpted by Felix W. de Weldon, is based on Joe Rosenthal's Pulitzer Prize–winning photograph of
five Marines and a Navy corpsman raising a flag atop Mt. Suribachi on
the Japanese island of Iwo Jima on February 19, 1945. By executive order,
a real flag flies 24 hours a day from the 78-foot-high memorial. On Tuesday evening at 7 from late May to late August there's a Marine Corps
sunset parade on the grounds of the memorial. On parade nights a free
shuttle bus runs from the Arlington Cemetery visitors' parking lot.

North of the memorial is the Arlington neighborhood of Rosslyn. Like
parts of downtown Washington and Crystal City farther to the south,
Rosslyn is almost empty at night, once the thousands of people who work
there have gone home. Its tall buildings provide a bit of a skyline, but
this has come about with some controversy: some say the silvery, wing-
shape Gannett Buildings are too close to the flight path followed by jets
landing at Ronald Reagan National Airport.

Women in Military Service for America Memorial. What is now this memorial next to the visitor center was once the Hemicycle, a huge carved retaining wall faced with granite at the entrance to Arlington National
Cemetery. Built in 1932, the wall was restored, with stairways added
leading to a rooftop terrace. Inside are 16 exhibit alcoves showing the
contributions that women have made to the military—from the Revolutionary War to the present—as well as the history of the memorial itself. A 196-seat theater shows films and is used for lectures and
conferences. A computer database has pictures, military histories, and
stories of thousands of women veterans. A fountain and reflecting pool
front the classical-style Hemicycle and entry gates.

ALEXANDRIA

Just a Metro ride (or bike ride) from Washington, Alexandria attracts those who seek a break from the monuments and hustle-and-bustle of the District. Here you can encounter America's colonial heritage. Founded in 1749 by Scottish merchants eager to capitalize on the booming tobacco trade, Alexandria emerged as one of the most important colonial ports. Alexandria has been associated with the most significant events and personages of the colonial, revolutionary, and Civil War periods. In Old Town, this colorful past is revived through restored 18th- and 19th-century homes, churches, and taverns; on the cobbled streets; and on the revitalized waterfront, where clipper ships dock and artisans display their wares.

One way to reach Alexandria is to take the Metro to the King Street stop (about 25 minutes from Metro Center) and walk about 10 blocks on King Street, going away from the Masonic memorial. To drive here, take either the George Washington Memorial Parkway or Jefferson Davis Highway (Route 1) south from Arlington.

Numbers in the text correspond to numbers in the margin and on the Old Town Alexandria, VA, map.

a good walk

Start your walk through Old Town at the Alexandria Convention & Visitors Association, in **Ramsay House ❶** ▶, the oldest house in Alexandria. Across the street, near the corner of Fairfax and King streets, is the **Stabler-Leadbeater Apothecary ❷**, the country's second-oldest apothecary. It was the equivalent of a corner drugstore to Alexandrians, including George Washington and the Lee family. Two blocks south on Fairfax Street, just beyond Duke Street, stands the **Old Presbyterian Meetinghouse ❸**, where Scottish patriots met during the Revolutionary War. Walk back up Fairfax Street one block and turn right on Prince Street to Gentry Row, the block between Fairfax and Lee streets. The striking edifice at the corner of Prince and Lee streets is the **Athenaeum ❹**. Many of the city's sea captains built their homes on the block of Prince Street between Lee and Union, which became known as **Captain's Row ❺**. Walk a block north on Union to King Street, where there are many shops and restaurants. One of Alexandria's most popular attractions is the **Torpedo Factory Art Center ❻**, a collection of art studios and galleries in a former munitions plant (on Union at the foot of King Street). Also here is the Alexandria Archaeology Museum, with exhibits of artifacts found during excavations in Alexandria. Take Cameron Street away from the river. **Carlyle House ❼**, built in 1753, is at the corner of Cameron and North Fairfax streets.

One block west along Cameron, at Royal Street, is **Gadsby's Tavern Museum ❽**, where Washington attended parties. Continue west on Cameron Street for two blocks, turn right on St. Asaph Street and walk up to Oronoco Street. Two historic Lee homes are on the short stretch of Oronoco between North Washington and St. Asaph streets. On the near side of Oronoco is the **Lee-Fendall House Museum ❾**; the **boyhood home of Robert E. Lee ❿** is across Oronoco on the St. Asaph Street corner.

Although they were a tiny minority, there were in fact 52 free blacks living in Alexandria in 1790. This population grew to become a significant factor in Alexandria's successful development. The **Alexandria Black History Resource Center ⓫**, two blocks north and two blocks west of Lee's boyhood home, tells the history of African-Americans in Alexandria and Virginia. Head back to North Washington Street and go south to the corner of Queen Street. The **Lloyd House ⓬**, a fine example of Georgian architecture, is owned by the City of Alexandria. At the corner of Cameron and North Washington streets, one block south, stands the Georgian country-style **Christ Church** ⑬.ˑWalk south two blocks to the **Lyceum** ⑭ at the corner of South Washington and Prince streets; it now houses two art galleries and a museum focusing on local history. The Confederate Statue is in the middle of South Washington and Prince streets, and two blocks to the west on South Alfred Street is the **Friendship Fire House** ⑮, restored and outfitted like a typical 19th-century firehouse. It's a long walk (or a quick ride on Bus 2 or 5 west on King Street) but worth the trouble to visit the **George Washington Masonic National Memorial** ⑯ on Callahan Drive at the King Street Metro station 1 mi west of the center of the city. In good weather, the open ninth-floor observation deck allows for good views.

TIMING   The Alexandria tour should take about four hours, not counting a trip to the George Washington Masonic National Memorial. A visit to the memorial adds about another hour and a half if you walk there and take the guided tour. If you're traveling by Metro, plan to finish your visit at the memorial and then get on the Metro at the King Street station.

What to See

⓫ **Alexandria Black History Resource Center.** The history of African-Americans in Alexandria and Virginia from 1749 to the present is recounted here. The federal census of 1790 recorded 52 free blacks living in the city, and the port town was one of the largest slave exportation points in the South, with at least two bustling slave markets. ⊠ *638 N. Alfred St., Old Town Alexandria* ☎ *703/519–3391 or 703/838–4356* ⊡ *Free* ☉ *Tues.–Sun. 9–4.*

❹ **Athenaeum.** One of the most noteworthy structures in Alexandria, the Athenaeum is a striking, reddish-brown Greek Revival edifice at the corner of Prince and Lee streets. It was built as a bank in the 1850s. The building is open most Friday afternoons from noon to 3 as a volunteer-staffed gallery showing ongoing art exhibits. ⊠ *201 Prince St., Old Town Alexandria.*

❿ **Boyhood Home of Robert E. Lee.** The childhood home in Alexandria of the commander in chief of the Confederate forces, Robert E. Lee, is a fine example of a 19th-century town house with federal architecture. The house was sold in 2000 to private owners who have made it their home. It's no longer open to visitors, but some of the home's furnishings are displayed at the Lyceum. ⊠ *607 Oronoco St., Old Town Alexandria.*

❺ **Captain's Row.** Many of Alexandria's sea captains once lived on this block. The cobblestones in the street were allegedly laid by Hessian mercenaries who had fought for the British during the Revolution and were held in Alexandria as prisoners of war. ⊠ *Prince St. between Lee and Union Sts., Old Town Alexandria.*

❼ **Carlyle House.** The grandest of Alexandria's older houses, Carlyle House was patterned after a Scottish country manor house. The structure was completed in 1753 by Scottish merchant John Carlyle. This was General Braddock's headquarters and the place where he met with five royal governors in 1755 to plan the strategy and funding of the early campaigns of the French and Indian War. ⊠ *121 N. Fairfax St., Old Town Alexandria* ☎ *703/549–2997* ⊡ *$4* ☉ *Tues.–Sat. 10–5, Sun. noon–5, guided tour every ½ hr.*

⓭ **Christ Church.** Both Washington and Lee were pewholders in this Episcopal church. (Washington paid £36 and 10 shillings—a lot of money

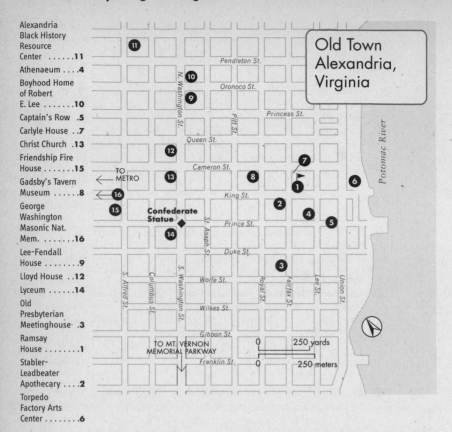

in those days—for Pew 60.) Built in 1773, Christ Church is a good example of Georgian church architecture. It has a fine Palladian window, an interior balcony, and an English wrought-brass-and-crystal chandelier. Docents give tours during visiting hours. ⊠ *118 N. Washington St., Old Town Alexandria* ☎ *703/549–1450* ✉ *Free* ☉ *Mon.–Sat. 9–4, Sun. 2–4.*

Confederate Statue. In 1861, when Alexandria was occupied by Union forces, the 800 soldiers of the city's garrison marched out of town to join the Confederate Army. In the middle of Washington and Prince streets stands a statue marking the point at which they assembled. In 1885 Confederate veterans proposed a memorial to honor their fallen comrades. This statue, based on John A. Elder's painting *Appomattox,* is of a lone soldier glumly surveying the battlefields after General Robert E. Lee's surrender. The names of 100 Alexandria Confederate dead are carved on the base.

⑮ Friendship Fire House. Alexandria's showcase firehouse is outfitted in typical 19th-century firefighting fashion. ⊠ *107 S. Alfred St., Old Town Alexandria* ☎ *703/838–3891* ✉ *Free* ☉ *Fri. and Sat. 10–4, Sun. 1–4.*

⑧ Gadsby's Tavern Museum. This museum is housed in the old City Tavern and Hotel, which was a center of political and social life in the late 18th century. George Washington went to birthday celebrations in the ballroom here. A tour takes you through the taproom, dining room, assembly room, ballroom, and communal bedrooms. Friday evening tours visit the same rooms but are led by a costumed guide using a candlelit lantern. ⊠ *134 N. Royal St., Old Town Alexandria* ☎ *703/838–4242* ✉ *$4, lantern tour $5* ☉ *Oct.–Mar., Tues.–Sat. 11–4, Sun. 1–4, last tour* *at 3:15; Apr.–Sept., Tues.–Sat. 10–5, Sun. 1–5, last tour at 4:15; tours 15 mins before and after the hr. Lantern tour Mar.–Nov., Fri. 7–9:30.*

⓰ George Washington Masonic National Memorial. Because Alexandria, like Washington, has no really tall buildings, the spire of this memorial dominates the surroundings. The building fronts King Street, one of Alexandria's major east–west arteries; from the ninth-floor observation deck you get a spectacular view of Alexandria, with Washington in the distance. The building contains furnishings from the first Masonic lodge in Alexandria, in which George Washington was a member; he became a Mason in 1752 and was a Worshipful Master, a high rank, at the same time he served as president. ✉ *101 Callahan Dr., Old Town Alexandria* ☎ *703/683–2007* ✑ *Free* ⊙ *Daily 9–5; 50-min guided tour of building and deck daily at 9:30, 10:30, 11:30, 1, 2, 3, and 4.*

❾ Lee-Fendall House Museum. The short block of Alexandria's Oronoco Street between Washington and St. Asaph streets is the site of two Lee-owned houses. One is the Lee-Fendall House, the home of several illustrious members of the Lee family, and the other is the boyhood home of Robert E. Lee. The Lee-Fendall House is decorated with Victorian furnishings and some Lee pieces. ✉ *614 Oronoco St., Old Town Alexandria* ✑ *$4* ⊙ *Feb.–mid-Dec., Tues.–Sat. 10–4, Sun. 1–4; sometimes closed weekends.*

⓬ Lloyd House. A fine example of Georgian architecture, Lloyd House was built in 1797 and is owned by the City of Alexandria. The interior is no longer open to the public, so it can only be admired from outside. ✉ *220 N. Washington St., Old Town Alexandria.*

⓮ Lyceum. Built in 1839, the Lyceum served as a library, a Civil War hospital, a residence, and an office building. It was restored in the 1970s and now houses two galleries with exhibits on the history of Alexandria, a third gallery with changing exhibits, and a gift shop. Some travel information for the entire state is also available here. ✉ *201 S. Washington St., Old Town Alexandria* ☎ *703/838–4994* ⊕ *www.alexandriahistory.org* ✑ *Free* ⊙ *Mon.–Sat. 10–5, Sun. 1–5.*

❸ Old Presbyterian Meetinghouse. Built in 1774, the Old Presbyterian Meetinghouse was, as its name suggests, more than a church. It was a gathering place in Alexandria vital to Scottish patriots during the Revolution. Eulogies for George Washington were delivered here on December 29, 1799. In a corner of the churchyard is the Tomb of the Unknown Soldier of the American Revolution. ✉ *321 S. Fairfax St., Old Town Alexandria* ☎ *703/549–6670* ⊕ *www.opmh.org* ✑ *Free* ⊙ *Sanctuary weekdays 9–3; key available at church office at 316 S. Royal St.*

▶ ❶ Ramsay House. The best place to start a tour of Alexandria's Old Town is at the **Alexandria Convention & Visitors Association,** in Ramsay House, the home of the town's first postmaster and lord mayor, William Ramsay. The structure is believed to be the oldest house in Alexandria. Travel counselors here provide brochures and maps for self-guided walking tours and can also give you a 24-hour permit for free parking at any two-hour metered spot. Daily guided walking tours are at 10:30 AM Monday through Saturday and 2 PM Sunday; tickets are $10. ✉ *221 King St., Old Town Alexandria* ☎ *703/838–4200 or 800/388–9119; 703/838–6494 TDD* ⊕ *www.funside.com* ⊙ *Daily 9–5.*

❷ Stabler-Leadbeater Apothecary. Once patronized by George Washington and the Lee family, Alexandria's Stabler-Leadbeater Apothecary is the second-oldest apothecary in the country (the oldest is reputedly in Bethlehem, PA). Some believe that it was here, on October 17, 1859, that

Lt. Col. Robert E. Lee received orders to lead Marines sent from the Washington Barracks to help suppress John Brown's insurrection at Harper's Ferry (then part of Virginia). The shop now houses a small museum of 18th- and 19th-century apothecary memorabilia, including one of the finest collections of apothecary bottles in the country (some 800 bottles in all). ✉ *105– 107 S. Fairfax St., Old Town Alexandria* ☎ *703/ 836–3713* 🖅 *$2.50* ☉ *Mon.–Sat. 10–4, Sun. 1–5.*

❻ Torpedo Factory Art Center. Torpedoes were manufactured here by the U.S. Navy during World War I and World War II. Now the building houses the studios and workshops of about 160 artists and artisans and has become one of Alexandria's most popular attractions. You can view the workshops of printmakers, jewelry makers, sculptors, painters, and potters, and most of the art and crafts are for sale. The Torpedo Factory also houses the **Alexandria Archaeology Program** (☎ 703/838–4399 ⊕ www.alexandriaarchaeology.org), a city-operated research facility devoted to urban archaeology and conservation. Artifacts from excavations in Alexandria are on display here. Admission is free; Tuesday through Friday 10–3, Saturday 10–5, and Sunday 1–5. ✉ *105 N. Union St., Old Town Alexandria* ☎ *703/838–4565* ⊕ *www.torpedofactory. org* 🖅 *Free* ☉ *Daily 10–5.*

AROUND WASHINGTON

The city and environs of Washington (including parts of Maryland and Virginia) are dotted with worthwhile attractions that are outside the walks in this chapter. You may find some intriguing enough to go a little out of your way to visit. The nearest Metro stop is noted only if it's within reasonable walking distance of a given sight.

Bethesda, Maryland

Bethesda was named in 1871 after the Bethesda Meeting House, which was built by the Presbyterians. Their house of worship's name alludes to the biblical pool of Bethesda, which had great healing power. Today, people seek healing in Bethesda at the U.S. Naval Regional Medical Center and the National Institutes of Health, and meet here to enjoy the burgeoning restaurant scene. While Bethesda has changed from a small community into an urban destination, time has stood still east of Bethesda in much of Chevy Chase, a town of exclusive country clubs, elegant houses, and huge trees.

McCrillis Gardens and Gallery. This premier shade garden has choice ornamental trees and shrubs. Bulbs, ground cover, and shade-loving perennials add ongoing color and texture. The gallery shows work from area artists. ✉ *6910 Greentree Rd.* ☎ *301/365–1657* ⊕ *www.mc-mncppc. org/parks/brookside/mccrillis.htm* 🖅 *Free* ☉ *Gardens daily 10–dusk, gallery Tues.–Sun. noon–4.*

Montgomery County Farm Woman's Cooperative Market. This market is one of the remaining vestiges of Montgomery County's agricultural society. In the midst of the Great Depression, women gathered goods from their gardens to sell in Bethesda to residents of the District of Columbia and its growing suburbs. Today the tradition continues. Baked goods, fresh fruits and vegetables, crafts, and flea-market goods are still sold in a low, white building in the midst of high-rise office buildings. (A view of the market in the 1930s is depicted in a mural on the wall of the Bethesda Post Office at 7400 Wisconsin Avenue.) ✉ *7155 Wisconsin Ave.* ☎ *301/652–2291* ⊕ *montgomerycountymd.com/events/*

montgomery_market.htm ⊙ *Wed. and Sat. 7–3, outdoor flea market Wed. and weekends 7–5* Ⓜ *Bethesda.*

National Institutes of Health (NIH). One of the world's foremost biomedical research centers, with a sprawling 300-acre campus, the NIH offers tours for the public, including an orientation tour at the NIH Visitor Information Center and one at the National Library of Medicine. Although best known for its books and journals—there are more than 5 million—the National Library of Medicine also houses historical medical references dating from the 11th century. A library tour includes a look at historical documents, the library's databases, and their "visible human," which provides a view of everything from how the kneecap works to how physicians use surgical simulators. The guides have some useful advice on how to start medical research (to do any research, you must arrive at least an hour and a half before closing time). ⊠ *Visitor Information Center, 9000 Rockville Pike, Bldg. 10, Bethesda* ☏ *301/ 496–1776* ⊠ *National Library of Medicine, 8600 Rockville Pike, Bldg. 38A* ☏ *301/496–6308* ⊕ *www.nih.gov* 🖾 *Free* ⊙ *Call for tour times and library hrs* Ⓜ *Medical Center.*

Strathmore Hall Arts Center. Local and national artists exhibit in the galleries and musicians perform year-round at this mansion built around 1900. A free series that includes poetry, music, art talks, and demonstrations takes place on Wednesday evening (call ahead for specific hours). On Tuesday and Thursday during the summer, concert goers spread out on the expansive lawn to listen to free concerts—everything from classical to Cajun and Brit pop. Strathmore's Tea is served in a well-lit wood-panel salon, Tuesday and Wednesday at 1. During July and August, "Backyard Theater" performers entertain children. ⊠ *10701 Rockville Pike* ☏ *301/530–0540* ⊕ *www.strathmore.org* 🖾 *Free, Backyard Theater $6, tea $17 (reservations essential)* ⊙ *Mon., Tues., Thurs., and Fri. 10–4, Wed. 10–9, Sat. 10–3* Ⓜ *Grosvenor/Strathmore.*

Elsewhere in Maryland

Brookside Gardens. A 50-acre garden within Wheaton Regional Park, Brookside includes several distinct gardens: azalea, rose, yew, formal, fragrance, Japanese-style, and trial. Brookside also has two conservatories for year-round floral enjoyment. A horticultural reference library is in the airy visitor center. ⊠ *1500 Glenallan Ave., Wheaton* ☏ *301/ 949–8230* ⊕ *www.mc-mncppc.org/parks/brookside* 🖾 *Free.*

Ⓒ **College Park Aviation Museum.** One of College Park's claims to fame is the world's oldest continuously operating airport. Opened in 1909, it has been the site of numerous aviation firsts. Orville and Wilbur Wright tested military planes here, and their presence is evident in the museum's early aviation memorabilia. The 27,000-square-foot museum has interactive exhibits and an animatronic Wilbur Wright. A full-scale reproduction of the 1911 Wright Model B Aeroplane is also here. ⊠ *1985 Corporal Frank Scott Dr., College Park* ☏ *301/864–6029* ⊕ *www. avialantic.com/collpark.html* 🖾 *$4* ⊙ *Daily 10–5.*

Ⓒ **Goddard Space Flight Center.** Goddard Space Flight Center was established in 1959 as NASA's first center devoted to the exploration of space. Since then, it has continued to take a leading role in Earth science, space science, and the development of cutting-edge technologies. The visitor center highlights Goddard's contributions to America's space program through exhibits and tours. The Main Gallery reflects the space program's legendary past and exciting future, and the Earth Science Gallery has earth science themes in a high-tech, 2,600 foot gallery. The Educator

Resource Center, on the 2nd floor, offers a variety of free teaching materials to educators. Only school groups are permitted access for the foreseeable future; call in advance to check status if planning a trip. ⊠ *Soil Conservation and Greenbelt Rds., Greenbelt* ☎ *301/286–8981* ⊕ *www. gsfc.nasa.gov* ⊠ *Free* ☉ *Daily 9–4, school groups only* Ⓜ *Greenbelt, then Bus T15, T16, or T17.*

Ⓒ **National Capital Trolley Museum.** A selection of the capital's historic trolleys have been rescued and restored and are now on display at a museum in suburban Maryland, along with streetcars from Europe and elsewhere in America. For a nominal fare you can go on a 2-mi ride through the countryside. ⊠ *1313 Bonifant Rd., between Layhill Rd. and New Hampshire Ave., Silver Spring* ☎ *301/384–6088* ⊕ *www.dctrolley. org* ⊠ *Trolley ride $2.50* ☉ *Jan.–Nov., weekends noon–5; plus mid-Mar.–mid-May, Thurs. and Fri. 10–2; mid-June–mid-Aug., Thurs. and Fri. 11–3; Oct.–Nov. 15, Thurs. and Fri. 10–2; Dec., weekends 5–9.*

National Cryptologic Museum. A 30-minute drive from Washington, Maryland's National Cryptologic Museum is a surprise, telling in a public way the anything but public story of "signals intelligence," the government's gleaning of intelligence from radio signals, messages, radar, and the cracking of other governments' secret codes. Connected to the supersecret National Security Agency, the museum recounts the history of intelligence from 1526 to the present. Displays include rare cryptographic books from the 16th century, items used in the Civil War, World War II cipher machines, and a Cray supercomputer of the sort that does the code work today. Newer exhibits include artifacts from intelligence programs of the Korean, Vietnam, and Cold wars and one of the earliest intelligence satellites. ⊠ *Colony Seven Rd. near Fort Meade (Baltimore–Washington Pkwy. to 32E; exit at 32W and follow detour signs for 32E, or call for directions)* ☎ *301/688–5849* ⊕ *www.nsa.gov/ museum* ⊠ *Free* ☉ *Weekdays 9–4, 1st and 3rd Sat. 10–2.*

Paul E. Garber Facility. A collection of Smithsonian warehouses in suburban Maryland, the Paul E. Garber Facility is where flight-related artifacts are stored and restored prior to their display at the National Air and Space Museum on the Mall. Many functions of this outpost will be transferred to the new **National Air and Space Museum Steven F. Udvar-Hazy Center** in Virginia, scheduled to open in December 2003, so call in advance if you're planning a visit. Among the approximately 140 aircraft you may see here are such historic craft as a Soviet MiG-15 from the Korean War and a Battle of Britain–era Hawker Hurricane IIC, as well as model satellites and assorted engines and propellers. A behind-the-scenes look at how the artifacts are preserved is included on a three-hour walking tour. Note: the tour is for ages 16 and up, and there's no heating or air-conditioning at the facility (and no rest-room stops once the three-hour tour begins), so plan accordingly. Reservations for a tour should be requested through the phone number below at least two weeks in advance; next-day reservations can sometimes be arranged. ⊠ *3904 Old Silver Hill Rd., at St. Barnabas Rd., Suitland* ☎ *202/357–1400* ⊕ *www.nasm.edu/nasm/garber* ⊠ *Free* ☉ *Tours weekdays at 10, weekends at 10 and 1.*

Temple of the Church of Jesus Christ of Latter-Day Saints. A striking Mormon temple in suburban Maryland—one of its white towers is topped with a golden statue of the Mormon angel and prophet Moroni—the Temple of the Church of Jesus Christ of the Latter-Day Saints has become a Washington landmark for the way it seems to rise up from the distance, appearing like a modern-day Oz. The temple is closed to non-Mormons, but the grounds and visitor center offer a lovely view of the white-marble temple and surroundings. Tulips, dogwoods, and azaleas bloom in the 57-acre grounds each spring. In December, Washingtonians enjoy the Festival of Lights—300,000 of them—and a live nativity scene. ✉ *9900 Stoneybrook Dr., Kensington* ☎ *301/587–0144* ⊕ *www. washingtonlds.org* ⊙ *Grounds and visitor center daily 10–9.*

Elsewhere in Virginia

(☉) **Flying Circus Airshow.** Stunt flying and wing walking are among the attractions at the Flying Circus Airshow. Billing itself as the only remaining barnstorming show in the country, the Flying Circus operates out of a Virginia aerodrome about 90 minutes by car from Washington. Biplane rides are available before and after the show. In addition to the airshow, special events—like model rocket day, antique car day, motorcycle day, and hot rod day—are held most Sundays. Call ahead for attraction information. ✉ *Rte. 17, Bealeton (between Fredericksburg and Warrenton)* ☎ *540/439–8661* ⊕ *www.flyingcircusairshow.com* ☛ *$10* ⊙ *May–Oct., Sun.; gates open at 11, show starts at 2:30.*

National Air and Space Museum Steven F. Udvar-Hazy Center. Two hangar-size exhibition spaces at Washington Dulles International Airport make up the latest outpost of the National Air and Space Museum. The new center is scheduled to open in December 2003 in celebration of the 100th anniversary of the Wright Brothers' first flight at Kitty Hawk. More than 300 aircraft and spacecraft will be displayed here in halls that soar to 103 feet. Highlights include the *Enola Gay,* a Lockheed SR-71 Blackbird, the Space Shuttle Orbiter *Enterprise,* and numerous missiles, satellites, and rocket engines. Those who manage to leave the National Air and Space Museum on the Mall still wishing for more will be satisfied here—the exhibition floor space at this outpost is 25 percent larger than that in the original building, which itself seems vast. The new museum will house restaurants, a large-screen theater, museum shops, and an observation deck for viewing airport traffic as well as restoration facilities for vintage aircraft. Call for hours if you're planning a visit. ✉ *Washington Dulles International Airport* ☎ *202/357–1729* ⊕ *www. nasm.si.edu* ☛ *Free* ⊙ *10–5:30; call in advance to confirm hrs.*

WHERE TO EAT

FODOR'S CHOICE

Ben's Chili Bowl, U Street corridor

Citronelle, Georgetown

Galileo, Downtown

Inn at Little Washington, Washington, VA

Jaleo, Downtown and Bethesda, MD

L'Auberge Chez François, Great Falls

Pizzeria Paradiso, Dupont Circle and Georgetown

Sushi-Ko, Georgetown

Zaytinya, Downtown

HIGHLY RECOMMENDED

Café Atlántico, Downtown

Cashion's Eat Place, Adams-Morgan

Firefly, Dupont Circle

Full Kee, Chinatown

Gerard's Place, Downtown

Mannequin Pis, Olney, MD

Rio Grande Café, Bethesda, MD

Taberna del Alabardero, Downtown

TenPenh, Downtown

Updated by
Kristi Delovitch

WEST AFRICAN DELICACIES that include *moi-moi* (black-eyed peas, toma-toes, and corned beef) and *nklakla* (tomato soup with goat). *Feijoada,* a rich Brazilian stew of black beans, pork, and smoked meats. Bouill-abaisse, the fish stew from France; Italian favorites such as fusilli with broccoli and roasted garlic; succulent lamb kabobs or crisp *falafel* (veg-etable fritters) from the Middle East, crunchily addictive Vietnamese spring rolls, spicy Carolina shrimp (eat them with steaming white grits), and some of the finest marbled steaks and butter-soft roast beef this side of the Mississippi. These dishes are just a few of the top dishes you'll find around the nation's capital.

As the host to visitors and new residents from around the word, Wash-ington gains a constant infusion of different cultures. Despite the dearth of ethnic neighborhoods and the kinds of restaurant districts found in many other cities, you *can* find almost any type of food here, from Burmese to Ethiopian. Even the city's French-trained chefs, who have tradition-ally set the standard in fine dining, have been turning to health-conscious contemporary cuisine, spicy southwestern recipes, or appetizer-size Spanish tapas for inspiration.

Eighteenth Street NW extending south from Columbia Road is wall-to-wall restaurants. In this section of Adams-Morgan, small ethnic spots open and close frequently, and it's worth taking a walk down the street to see what looks new and interesting. Although the area has retained some of its Latin American identity, the new eating establishments tend to be Asian, contemporary, Italian, and Ethiopian. Parking can be im-possible on weekends. The nearest Metro stop, Woodley Park/Zoo, is a 10- to 15-minute walk. Although this is a relatively safe stroll at night, it may be more convenient to take a cab. Woodley Park has culi-nary temptations of its own, with a lineup of popular ethnic restaurants right by the Metro.

"Downtown" covers everything between Georgetown and Capitol Hill. The "new downtown," centered at Connecticut Avenue and K Street, has many of the city's blue-chip law firms and deluxe eateries—places that feed expense-account diners and provide the most elegance, most attentive service, and often the best food. But "old downtown," farther east, is where the action is these days. Restaurants of all stripes (usu-ally casual and moderately priced) have sprung up to serve the crowds that attend games at the MCI Center. The entire downtown area, how-ever, has been in a state of flux gastronomically, with famed restaurants closing their doors and new ones blossoming. Trendy microbrewery-restaurants and cigar lounges are part of the new wave, and Chinatown has been suffering as rents go up and long-standing favorite restaurants are forced to go out of business or relocate.

Chinatown itself, centered on G and H streets NW between 6th and 8th, is the city's one officially recognized ethnic enclave. Here Burmese, Thai, and other Asian cuisines add variety to the many traditional Chi-nese restaurants. The latter entice you with huge, brightly lit signs and offer such staples as beef with broccoli or spicy *kung pao* chicken with roasted peanuts. But discriminating diners will find far better food at the smaller, less obvious restaurants.

Capitol Hill has a number of bars that cater to Congressional types who need to fortify themselves with food and drink after a day spent run-ning the country. Dining options are augmented by Union Station, which contains some decent—if pricey—restaurants. It also has a large food court for quick bites that range from barbecue to sushi.

Dupont Circle, which lies south from U Street and north from K Street, contains a cluster of restaurants. You can also find many cafés, most with outdoor seating. The District's better gay-friendly establishments are here, especially along 17th Street. Chains such as Starbucks have put fancy coffee on every corner, but long-established espresso bars, like the 24-hour Kramerbooks and Afterwords, as well as Teaism's three locations, are a better source for breakfast and light or late fare.

In Georgetown, whose central intersection is Wisconsin Avenue and M Street, white-tablecloth establishments are next to hole-in-the-wall joints. The closest Metro stop is Foggy Bottom, a 15- to 20-minute walk away; consult the Georgetown map before you set out, and consider taking a cab. Restaurants in the adjacent West End—bounded roughly by Rock Creek Park to the west, N Street to the north, 20th Street to the east, and K Street to the south—are worth checking out as well. North from Georgetown on Wisconsin Avenue, there's a cluster of good restaurants in the Glover Park area, including the city's best sushi bar, Sushi-Ko.

In the 1930s and 1940s, the U Street corridor, which begins just down the hill from 18th Street, was the place to enjoy a late-night drink and hear jazz greats such as Duke Ellington, Billie Holliday, and Charlie Parker. After decades of neglect and devastation from riots in the 1960s, the area saw a burst of revitalization. With some of the hippest bars in the District, quirky vintage stores, small but lively nightclubs, and numerous cafés, the neighborhood draws a young crowd day and night. The area is still rough around the edges, however, so use caution. Restaurants stay open late on weekend nights and serve everything from burgers to gourmet pizza to Ethiopian dishes at low prices. The U Street vicinity is known for excellent fried-fish spots, like **Webb's Southern Food** (✉ 1361 U St. NW, U St. corridor ☎ 202/462–3474) which unfortunately doesn't have seating.

Intriguing restaurant districts also thrive outside the city limits and are accessible by the Metro. Eateries in downtown Bethesda, Maryland, have southwestern dishes, classic Spanish cuisine, and good old American diner food and are said to be luring the cognoscenti from Georgetown. Bethesda is just a 20-minute drive from Georgetown up Wisconsin Avenue; by Metro it's a 15- to 20-minute ride from Metro Center to the Bethesda Metro stop and a 5-minute ride from the Foggy Bottom Metro stop.

Virginia has its ritzy Georgetown equivalent in quaint, historic Old Town Alexandria. And bragging rights to some of the greater D.C. area's best Asian restaurants go to Arlington, where Wilson Boulevard is lined with popular Vietnamese establishments and branches of D.C. restaurants. The Clarendon Metro station makes these Asian restaurants readily accessible, but the King Street Metro station is, unfortunately, a 15-minute walk from most Old Town Alexandria eateries.

Adams-Morgan/Woodley Park

African

$ ✕ **Meskerem.** Ethiopian restaurants abound in Adams-Morgan, but Meskerem is distinctive for its bright, appealingly decorated dining room and the balcony, where you can eat Ethiopian-style, seated on the floor on leather cushions, with large woven baskets for tables. Entrées are served family-style on a large tray lined with *injera,* a thin sourdough bread; scoop up mouthful-size portions of the hearty dishes with extra injera. Specialties include stews made with spicy *berbere* chili sauce; *kitfo,* buttery beef served very rare or raw like steak tartare; and a tangy, green-

2

Getting There
Most restaurants are easily accessible by Metro, some are not. Details on Metro stops are provided when this form of public transportation is realistic for the average traveler.

Good Brews
The Washington area is home to several noteworthy microbreweries and brew pubs. At the Capitol City Brewing Company brewpubs' four locations, you'll find ales, pilsners, and lagers. The Old Heurich Brewing Company makes the Foggy Bottom line of beers, which is available at select bars, restaurants, and stores in the area. Alexandria's Shenandoah Brewing Company is a microbrewery whose beers have won awards.

A number of popular wines are bottled just outside Washington in Loudoun County, Virginia: the area has seven vineyards available for tours and tastings.

Hotel Hot Spots
For fine dining, don't overlook restaurants in the city's luxury hotels. The Occidental Grill in the Willard Inter-Continental, Maestro in the Ritz at Tysons Corner, Citronelle at the Latham, Bistro Bis inside the Hotel George, and the newly opened Fahrenheit at the Georgetown Ritz are all noteworthy. The food is often artful and fresh.

Of course, such attention to detail comes at a price. One less expensive way to experience these nationally recognized restaurants is a weekday lunch. Also look for restaurants sprouting up in new or restored hotels around the city, especially in the downtown area around the MCI Center. Notables include Poste at The Hotel Monaco, Firefly at The Hotel Madera and 15 Ria at The Washington Terrace Hotel.

Reservations
It's always a good idea to make reservations; we mention them only when they're essential or are not accepted. However, even when reservations are not accepted, large groups should call ahead. All restaurants we list are open daily for lunch and dinner unless stated otherwise. Dress is mentioned only when men are required to wear a jacket or a jacket and tie, but gentlemen may be more comfortable wearing jackets and/or ties in $$$ and $$$$ restaurants, even when there is no formal dress code.

The Writing on the Wall
Look for recent reviews in *Washingtonian* magazine, the *Washington Post*, the *Washington Times*, and www.chowhound.com. Proud restaurant owners display good reviews on doors or in windows.

Prices
The restaurants we list are the cream of the crop in every price range.

WHAT IT COSTS				
	$$$$	**$$$**	**$$**	**$**	**¢**
AT DINNER	over $32	$22–$32	$15–$22	$7–$15	under $7

Prices are per person for a main course at dinner.

chili–vinaigrette potato salad. ⊠ *2434 18th St. NW, Adams-Morgan*
☎*202/462–4100* ⌕ *Reservations essential* ▭*AE, DC, MC, V* Ⓜ *Woodley Park/Zoo.*

¢–$ ✕ **Bukom Café.** Sunny African pop music, palm fronds, *kente* cloth, and
a spicy West African menu all brighten this narrow, two-story dining
room. Entrées range from *egussi* (goat with melon seeds) and *kumasi*
(chicken in a peanut sauce) to vegetarian dishes such as *jollof* (rice and
fried plantains). Live reggae and calypso keeps this place hopping at night.
⊠ *2442 18th St. NW, Adams-Morgan* ☎ *202/265–4600* ▭*AE, D, MC,
V* ⊘ *No lunch* Ⓜ *Woodley Park/Zoo.*

Asian

$ ✕ **Saigon Gourmet.** Service is brisk and friendly at this popular, French-
influenced Vietnamese restaurant. The neighborhood patrons return for
the ultracrisp *cha-gio* (spring rolls), the savory *pho* (beef broth), seafood
soups, and the delicately seasoned and richly sauced entrées. Shrimp Saigon
also includes pork in its peppery marinade, and another Saigon dish—
grilled pork with rice crepes—is a Vietnamese variation on Chinese
moo shu. ⊠ *2635 Connecticut Ave. NW, Woodley Park* ☎ *202/265–
1360* ⌕ *Reservations essential* ▭*AE, D, DC, MC, V* Ⓜ *Woodley
Park/Zoo.*

Cajun/Creole

¢–$ ✕ **Bardia's New Orleans Café.** Locals swarm to this cozy café, where the
great food is accompanied by jazz tunes. Seafood, whether batter-fried,
blackened, or sautéed, is always a winner. The house favorite is the
blackened catfish ($11). Po'boy sandwiches (subs on French bread) are
always reasonably priced, fresh, and huge. Breakfast items, served all day,
include traditional eggs Benedict or eggs New Orleans style, with fried
oysters, crabmeat, and hollandaise: they're both very tasty. Don't leave
without trying the outstanding beignets (fried puffs of dough sprinkled
with powdered sugar). ⊠ *2412 18th St. NW, Adams-Morgan* ☎ *202/
234–0420* ⌕ *Reservations not accepted* ▭*AE, MC, V* Ⓜ *Woodley
Park/Zoo.*

Contemporary

$$–$$$$ ✕ **New Heights.** This inviting restaurant has 11 large windows that over-
look nearby Rock Creek Park. The sophisticated contemporary cook-
ing blends the bold flavors of Asia and the Southwest into the traditional
dishes of the American repertoire. Oysters may be potato-encrusted and
served with a chive-and-shallot crème fraîche. An unusual item is roasted
skate wings stuffed with Jonah crab, spinach, and jasmine rice. Sunday
brunch in this lovely room is a particular treat. ⊠ *2317 Calvert St. NW,
Woodley Park* ☎ *202/234–4110* ▭ *AE, D, DC, MC, V* ⊘ *No lunch
Mon.–Sat.* Ⓜ *Woodley Park/Zoo.*

★ $$–$$$ ✕ **Cashion's Eat Place.** Walls are hung with family photos and tables
are jammed with regulars feasting on up-to-date, home-style cooking
in Ann Cashion's very personal restaurant. The menu changes daily,
but roast chicken, steak, and seafood are frequent choices. Side dishes,
such as garlicky mashed potatoes or buttery potatoes Anna, sometimes
upstage the main course. If it's available, don't miss the chocolate ter-
rine prepared by pastry chef Beth Christianson: it's five layers of wal-
nuts, caramel, mousse, and ganache. A big local attraction is Sunday
brunch, when many entrées are a fraction of the normal price. ⊠ *1819
Columbia Rd. NW, Adams-Morgan* ☎ *202/797–1819* ⌕ *Reservations
essential* ▭ *MC, V* ⊘ *Closed Mon. No lunch Tues.–Sat.* Ⓜ *Woodley
Park/Zoo.*

$–$$$ ✕ **Felix.** It may look more like a nightclub than a restaurant (there's neon
outside and a stylized mural of the city behind the bar), but Felix is se-

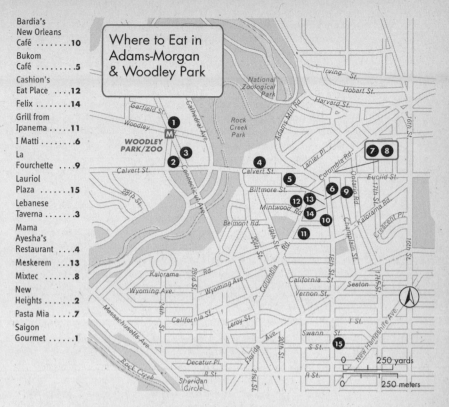

Where to Eat in
Adams-Morgan
& Woodley Park

rious about the food it serves. Start with tuna tartare with miso and a
side of tomatillos and kumquats. A popular entrée is Alaskan halibut
beside a bed of risotto made with Israeli couscous and fava beans. On
Fridays, try an unexpected treat—challah, matzo-ball soup, and brisket.
At 11 PM on Friday and Saturday, Felix brings its nightclub side to the
fore: there's live music, and the downstairs lounge starts serving upscale
bar food. ⊠ 2406 18th St. NW, Adams-Morgan ☎ 202/483–3549
⊟ AE, DC, MC, V ⊘ No lunch Ⓜ Woodley Park/Zoo.

French

$–$$$ ✕ La Fourchette. On a block in Adams-Morgan where restaurants seem
to open and close weekly, La Fourchette has stayed in business for
nearly a quarter of a century by offering good-quality bistro food at rea-
sonable prices. Most of the menu consists of daily specials like venison
with shallots and pepper sauce, chicken in beurre blanc, or even sweet-
breads in a mushroom-cream sauce. La Fourchette looks as a bistro should,
with an exposed-brick wall, a tin ceiling, bentwood chairs, and quasi-
postimpressionist murals. The weekend brunch attracts diners with its
quality food at very reasonable prices. ⊠ 2429 18th St. NW, Adams-
Morgan ☎ 202/332–3077 ⊟ AE, DC, MC, V Ⓜ Woodley Park/Zoo.

Italian

$–$$ ✕ I Matti. Local restaurant entrepreneur and Italy native Roberto Donna
owns the much more expensive Galileo, downtown, in addition to this
less formal trattoria, which serves a varied menu of sophisticated dishes
to a largely neighborhood clientele. Pasta or thin, crisp pizzas make good
lunches or light snacks. Meat and fish dishes—which might include rab-
bit, veal, or *bollito misto* (beef, capon, and other meats cooked in a flavorful broth)—are pricier but well worth it. Service is often perfunctory,

particularly on busy weekend evenings. ⊠ *2436 18th St. NW, Adams-Morgan* ☎ *202/462–8844* ☐ *AE, DC, MC, V* ⊙ *No lunch* Ⓜ *Woodley Park/Zoo.*

$ ✕ **Pasta Mia.** Patrons don't seem to mind waiting their turn to eat in this affordable, 40-seat trattoria. Pasta Mia's southern Italian appetizers and entrées all cost around $10. Large bowls of steaming pasta are served with a generous layer of freshly grated Parmesan. Some best-sellers are fusilli with broccoli and whole cloves of roasted garlic, rich spinach fettuccine *verde*, and penne *arrabiata* (in spicy marinara sauce with olives). Tiramisu, served in a teacup, is an elegant way to finish your meal. ⊠ *1790 Columbia Rd. NW, Adams-Morgan* ☎ *202/328–9114* ⚲ *Reservations not accepted* ☐ *MC, V* ⊙ *Closed Sun. No lunch* Ⓜ *Woodley Park/Zoo.*

Latin American

$$ ✕ **Grill from Ipanema.** Brazilian cuisine is the focus at the Grill, from spicy seafood stews to grilled steak and other hearty meat dishes. Appetizers include fried yucca with spicy sausages and—for adventurous eaters—fried alligator. Former Second Lady Tipper Gore adores the *mexilhão á carioca*, garlicky mussels cooked in a clay pot. Traditional feijoada, the stew that's the national dish of Brazil, is served every day. ⊠ *1858 Columbia Rd. NW, Adams-Morgan* ☎ *202/986–0757* ⚲ *Reservations essential* ☐ *AE, D, DC, MC, V* ⊙ *No lunch weekdays* Ⓜ *Woodley Park/Zoo.*

$–$$ ✕ **Lauriol Plaza.** This longtime favorite on the border of Adams-Morgan and Dupont Circle serves Latin American, Cuban, and Spanish dishes—seviche, paella, fajitas, and so on—to enthusiastic crowds. Rustic entrées such as Cuban-style pork and *lomo saltado* (Peruvian-style strip steak with onions, tomatoes, and jalapeño peppers) are specialties. The dining room can get noisy, but the roof terrace is a popular alternative in good weather. The two hours of free parking for customers is especially enticing: this street may be the most difficult place to park in the city. ⊠ *1835 18th St. NW, Adams-Morgan* ☎ *202/387–0035* ⚲ *Reservations not accepted* ☐ *AE, D, DC, MC, V* Ⓜ *Dupont Circle.*

Mexican

$ ✕ **Mixtec.** Don't expect tortilla chips as a starter at this truly Mexican restaurant—it doesn't serve them. Mixtec's tacos *al carbón* lack the lettuce and cheese toppings of their fast-food counterparts: they consist simply of charcoal-grilled beef or pork, encased in fresh corn tortillas and accompanied by grilled spring onions. Fajitas, enchiladas, and seafood are cooked in the regional styles of Veracruz, Mazatlán, and Acapulco, which the menu does a good job of explaining. The *licuados* (fruit drinks) are refreshing complements to the sometimes spicy dishes. ⊠ *1792 Columbia Rd. NW, Adams-Morgan* ☎ *202/332–1011* ⚲ *Reservations not accepted* ☐ *MC, V* Ⓜ *Woodley Park/Zoo.*

Middle Eastern

$–$$ ✕ **Lebanese Taverna.** Arched ceilings, cedar panels etched with leaf patterns, woven rugs, and brass lighting fixtures give the Taverna a warm elegance. Start with an order of Arabic bread, baked in a wood-burning oven. Lamb, beef, chicken, and seafood are either grilled on kabobs, slow-roasted, or smothered with a garlicky yogurt sauce. A group can make a meal of the *mezza* platters—a mix of appetizers and sliced *shawarma* (spit-roasted lamb). ⊠ *2641 Connecticut Ave. NW, Woodley Park* ☎ *202/265–8681* ☐ *AE, D, DC, MC, V* Ⓜ *Woodley Park/Zoo.*

$ ✕ **Mama Ayesha's Restaurant.** Journalists and politicians frequent this family-run eatery for its reasonably priced fare. Staples such as chicken and lamb kabobs can be had for less than $12, baskets of complimentary pita bread are served hot, and the crisp falafel is among the best in town.

wallet you must've dropped at the museum: $110
video camera you misplaced in Georgetown: $499
two-way pager you forgot at the memorial: $189

replacing your card anywhere:
priceless

For everything from card replacement to cash advances
to locating the nearest ATM, call 1-800-MasterCard.

there are some things money can't buy.
for everything else there's MasterCard.®

Find America *with a Compass*

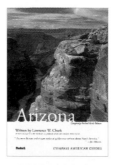

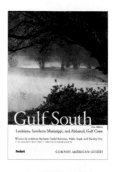

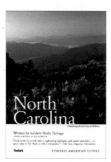

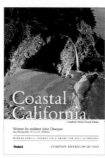

Written by local authors and illustrated throughout
with spectacular color images, Compass American
Guides reveal the character and culture of more than
40 of America's most fascinating destinations. Perfect
for residents who want to explore their own backyards
and for visitors who want an insider's perspective
on the history, heritage, and all there is to see and do.

Fodor's COMPASS AMERICAN GUIDES

At bookstores everywhere.

Weekends sometimes bring Arabic bands and belly dancing. ⊠ *1967 Calvert St. NW, Adams-Morgan* ☎ *202/232–5431* ⊟ *AE, D, DC, MC, V* Ⓜ *Woodley Park/Zoo.*

Capitol Hill

American

$$–$$$$ ✕ **The Capital Grille.** Just a few blocks from the U.S. Capitol, this New England steak house is a favorite among Republican congressmen. Politics aside, the cuisine, wine list, and surroundings are all top-shelf. Don't let the meat hanging in the window distract you from the fact that this restaurant has a lot more to offer than just meat and potatoes (though there are fine dry-aged porterhouse cuts and delicious cream-based potatoes). Don't miss the pan-fried calamari with hot cherry peppers, for instance. A second location in Tysons Corner has the same menu with a slightly different wine list. ⊠ *601 Pennsylvania Ave. NW, Capitol Hill* ☎ *202/737–6200* ⊕ *www.thecapitalgrille.com* ⌂ *Reservations essential* ⊟ *AE, D, DC, MC, V* ⊙ *No lunch weekends* Ⓜ *Navy Memorial/Archives.*

$$–$$$ ✕ **Monocle.** The nearest restaurant to the Senate side of the Capitol, Monocle is a great place to spot members of Congress at lunch and dinner. The regional American cuisine is rarely adventurous but is thoroughly reliable. The crab cakes, either as a platter or in a sandwich, are a specialty, and you might encounter specials such as pot roast or a first-rate fish dish. Still, the draw here is the old-style Capitol Hill atmosphere. ⊠ *107 D St. NE, Capitol Hill* ☎ *202/546–4488* ⊟ *AE, DC, MC, V* ⊙ *Closed weekends* Ⓜ *Union Station.*

$$–$$$ ✕ **Two Quail.** A welcome respite from the men's-club surroundings of traditional Capitol Hill eateries, this quaint, floral-pattern tearoom allows for power dining in surroundings that almost seem romantic. The seasonal menu has both hearty fare—Muscovy duck, pork loin, chicken stuffed with corn bread and pecans, game meats, filet mignon—and lighter seafood pastas and meal-size salads. The signature dish, Two Quail, is a pair of quail stuffed with raspberries, Brie, and French bread. Service can be leisurely. ⊠ *320 Massachusetts Ave. NE, Capitol Hill* ☎ *202/543–8030* ⊟ *AE, DC, MC, V* ⊙ *No lunch weekends* Ⓜ *Union Station.*

¢–$ ✕ **The Market Lunch.** A walk around the Capitol, a stroll though Eastern Market, and then a hefty pile of blueberry pancakes from Market Lunch make for a perfect Saturday morning or afternoon on the Hill. Locals wait in lines that circle the building for their turn to dine on ham, eggs, grits or pancakes in the morning or crab cakes, fried shrimp or fish for lunch. But don't be mistaken, this down-home food it is not a leisurely dining experience. To eat here on Saturday you must be in line by noon. Follow custom and order quickly, eat, and give up your seat for the next customer. ⊠ *North end of Eastern Market, 225 7th St. SE, Capitol Hill* ☎ *202/547–8444* ⊟ *No credit cards* ⊙ *Closed Mon. No dinner* Ⓜ *Eastern Market.*

¢–$ ✕ **Jimmy T's.** Five blocks from the Capitol, this D.C. institution is quietly tucked in the first floor of an old Capitol Hill row house. The small diner is packed daily with saucy waiters, talkative regulars and its two boisterous owners (who run the grill). Soak in the local culture or read the paper as you enjoy favorites such as grits, bacon, omelets, or the homey eggs Benedict, made with a toasted English muffin, a huge piece of ham, and lots of hollandaise sauce. Breakfast is served all day. ⊠ *501 East Capitol St. SE, Capitol Hill* ☎ *202/546–3646* ⊟ *No credit cards* ⊙ *Closed Sun.* Ⓜ *Eastern Market.*

Where to Eat in Washington

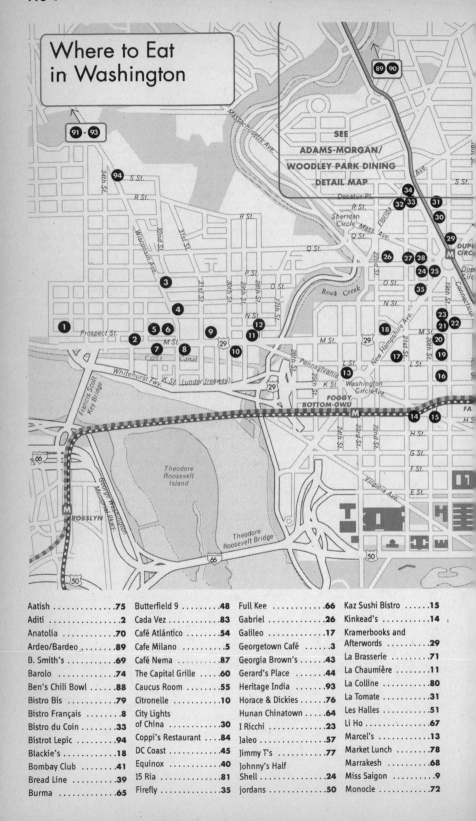

SEE
ADAMS-MORGAN/
WOODLEY PARK DINING
DETAIL MAP

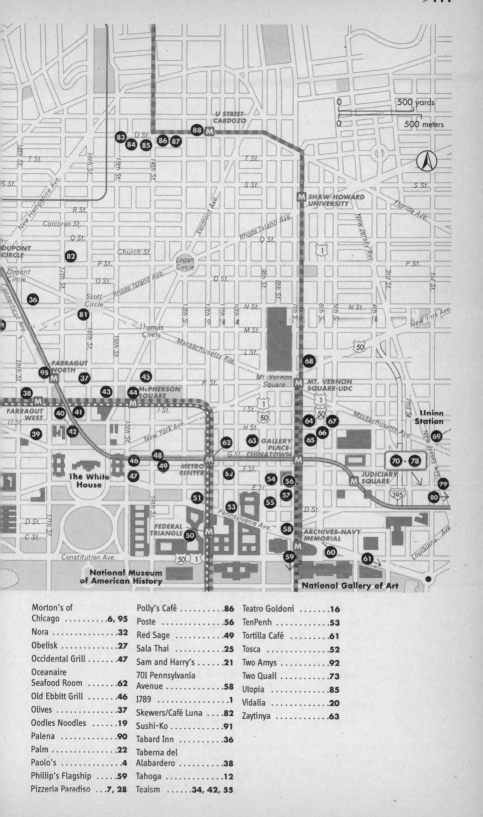

French

$$–$$$ ✕ **Bistro Bis.** A zinc bar, spacious brown leather booths, and a display kitchen with a glass front create great expectations at Bistro Bis, the second restaurant from the owner of the much-acclaimed Vidalia restaurant downtown. The seasonal menu seamlessly merges modern American standards with French bistro classics. For a first course, don't miss the onion tart Alsacienne, a crisp pastry topped with caramelized onions, bacon, Muenster cheese, and crème fraîche. Main-course hits include a grilled *escalope* (thin slice) of salmon with porcini mushrooms, braised oxtail, celery-root purée and bordelaise sauce. ⊠ *Hotel George, 15 E St. NW, Capitol Hill* ☎ *202/661–2700* ⚓ *Reservations essential* ▭ *AE, D, DC, MC, V* Ⓜ *Union Station.*

$$–$$$ ✕ **La Colline.** Chef Robert Gréault has worked to make La Colline one of the city's best French restaurants. The seasonal menu emphasizes fresh vegetables and seafood, from simple grilled preparations to fricassees and gratins with imaginative sauces. Some additional choices are duck in an orange sauce and veal with chanterelle mushrooms. ⊠ *400 N. Capitol St. NW, Capitol Hill* ☎ *202/737–0400* ▭ *AE, D, DC, MC, V* ◷ *Closed Sun. No lunch Sat.* Ⓜ *Union Station.*

$–$$$ ✕ **La Brasserie.** One of the Hill's most pleasant and satisfying restaurants for breakfast, lunch, or dinner, La Brasserie occupies two floors of adjoining town houses and has outdoor dining in the warmer months. The straightforward French menu changes seasonally, though poached salmon and breast of duck are always available. Likewise, the small, selective wine list changes often. The crème brûlée, served cold or hot with fruit, is superb. Neither breakfast nor lunch is served on Saturdays. ⊠ *239 Massachusetts Ave. NE, Capitol Hill* ☎ *202/546–9154* ▭ *AE, D, DC, MC, V* ◷ *No lunch Sat.* Ⓜ *Union Station.*

Indian

$ ✕ **Aatish.** *Aatish* means volcano, an appropriate name for a restaurant specializing in tandoori cooking—meats, seafood, vegetables, and breads are all cooked in the intense heat of a clay oven. What distinguishes this restaurant is the quality of its cooking: its samosa appetizer, made up of flaky pastry enclosing a spiced mixture of potatoes and peas, is a model of the form. The tandoori chicken is moist and delicious. Lamb dishes are also well-prepared, especially the lamb *karahi,* sautéed in a wok with ginger, garlic, tomatoes, vegetables, and spices. ⊠ *609 Pennsylvania Ave. SE, Capitol Hill* ☎ *202/544–0931* ⚓ *Reservations essential* ▭ *AE, D, MC, V* Ⓜ *Eastern Market.*

Italian

$$–$$$ ✕ **Barolo.** Chef Enzo Fargione, former sous-chef of Galileo, created this small restaurant's menu around the cuisine of his native Piedmont, in northwest Italy. Fargione has a sure hand with pastas (fettuccine with asparagus and black-truffle sauce), fish (baked salmon on a bed of asparagus), and game (quail with truffle-shallot sauce and a red pepper timbale). To end your meal, try the *panna cotta,* a creamy, gelatin-thickened dessert. ⊠ *223 Pennsylvania Ave. SE, Capitol Hill* ☎ *202/547–5011* ⚓ *Reservations essential* ▭ *AE, D, DC, MC, V* ◷ *Closed Sun. No lunch Sat.* Ⓜ *Capitol South.*

Salvadorian

¢–$ ✕ **Tortilla Cafe.** Right across from bustling Eastern Market, this small carry-out restaurant, where there are just a few tables, serves the best *pupusas* (rounded cornmeal dough stuffed with meat, cheese, or corn) in town. The menu is a mix of mostly Salvadorian and Mexican fare with favorites such as tamales, Peruvian seviche, and fried plantains served with sour cream and refried beans. If it's available, don't miss the homey

Salvadorian Stew made with large chunks of beef, celery, carrots, and potatoes. The café is open 10–7 weekdays and 7–7 weekends. ✉ *210 7th St. SE, Capitol Hill* ☎ *202/547–5700* ⌲ *Reservations not accepted* ▭ *AE, D, MC, V* Ⓜ *Eastern Market.*

Southern

\$\$–\$\$\$ ✗ **B. Smith's.** If you're in the mood for shrimp and grits, Southern-influenced B. Smith's is the spot for you. For appetizers, try the grilled cheddar cheese grits or the jambalaya—but skip the overly bready fried green tomatoes and the too-sweet sweet potatoes. The Swamp Thing entrée may not sound pretty, but this mix of mustard-seasoned shrimp and crawfish with collards is inspired. Seafood and anything with barbecue sauce are highly recommended. Desserts are comforting classics, slightly dressed up: coconut cake, warm bread pudding, and sweet-potato pecan pie. ✉ *Union Station, 50 Massachusetts Ave. NE, Capitol Hill* ☎ *202/289–6188* ⌲ *Reservations essential* ▭ *AE, D, DC, MC, V* Ⓜ *Union Station.*

¢ ✗ **Horace & Dickie's.** If you've ever had a craving for fried fish, then this is the place for you. The self-proclaimed home of the jumbo fish sandwich, this small, crowded restaurant has a loyal flock of regulars willing to wait in long lines for the \$4.35 sandwich that's made up of four pieces of fried fish on white bread. Make sure to pick up some of the Southern-style sides like macaroni and cheese, or get a slice of bean pie for dessert. The restaurant, which is carry-out only, is open until 2 AM Monday–Saturday and until 8 PM on Sunday, but use caution and visit during daylight hours. The neighborhood can be rough. ✉ *809 12th St. NE, Capitol Hill* ☎ *202/397–6040* ▭ *No credit cards.*

Turkish

\$–\$\$ ✗ **Anatolia.** As soft contemporary Turkish music plays, copper pails serving as lamp shades cast a warm light in this intimate restaurant run by a husband-and-wife team. Scoop up the appetizer spreads—such as sweet roasted eggplant or peppery hummus—with wedges of warm, grilled pita. In addition to standard kabobs, the *adana* kabob, made with lamb sausage specific to Turkey, is delicious. For dessert, try baklava and a cup of strong espressolike Turkish coffee. ✉ *633 Pennsylvania Ave. SE, Capitol Hill* ☎ *202/544–4753* ▭ *AE, D, MC, V* ☺ *Closed Sun. No lunch Sat.* Ⓜ *Eastern Market.*

Downtown

African

\$\$\$ ✗ **Marrakesh.** In a part of the city better known for auto-supply shops, Marrakesh provides a bit of Morocco with a fixed-price (\$32, not including drinks) feast shared by everyone at your table. Appetizers consist of a platter of three salads followed by *b'stella*, a chicken version of Morocco's traditional pie made with crisp layers of phyllo dough and seasoned with cinnamon. The first main course is chicken with lemon and olive. A beef or lamb dish is next, followed by vegetable couscous, fruit, mint tea, and pastries. Belly dancers perform nightly. Lunch is available for groups of 10 or more only, by reservation. ✉ *617 New York Ave. NW, Downtown* ☎ *202/393–9393* ⌲ *Reservations essential* ▭ *No credit cards* Ⓜ *Mt. Vernon/UDC.*

American

\$\$\$–\$\$\$\$ ✗ **Butterfield 9.** Light-color wood paneling, gleaming white linen, and stunning black-and-white photographs make Butterfield 9 one of the most elegant restaurants in town. Chef Martin Saylor's style of contemporary cooking glories in complexity. The menu changes every two months, but many of the imaginative appetizers—like foie gras atop a puffed-up pancake, rather like a Yorkshire pudding—have been hits, as have main courses like barbecued salmon on couscous, and filet mignon with a blue cheese, butter, and Port sauce, served with a crepe stuffed with potato and red onion. The peach shortcake and other seasonal desserts are both well worth a taste. ⊠ *600 14th St. NW, Downtown* ☎ *202/ 289–8810* ⌕ *Reservations essential* ⊟ *AE, D, DC, MC, V* ⊘ *No lunch weekends* Ⓜ *Metro Center.*

$$$–$$$$ ✕ **Caucus Room.** Here is the quintessential Washington political restaurant. The limited partnership that owns it includes a Democratic super-lobbyist and a former Republican National Committee chairman. The classy dark-wood and rich leather within make it perfect for business lunches or dinners, and the many private dining rooms are popular for political fund-raising events. The menu changes about three times a year, but you can count on finding prime steak, and seafood dishes that include sea bass and seared tuna dishes. ⊠ *401 9th St. NW, Downtown* ☎ *202/393–1300* ⊟ *AE, D, DC, MC, V* ⊘ *Closed Sun. No lunch weekends* Ⓜ *Navy Archives.*

$–$$$ ✕ **Old Ebbitt Grill.** People flock here to drink at the several bars, which seem to go on for miles, and to enjoy well-prepared buffalo wings, hamburgers, and Reuben sandwiches. The Old Ebbitt also has Washington's most popular raw bar, which serves farm-raised oysters from certified waters. Pasta is homemade, and daily fresh fish or steak specials are served until 1 AM. Despite the crowds, the restaurant never feels cramped, thanks to its well-spaced, comfortable booths. Service can be slow at lunch; if you're in a hurry, try the café-style Ebbitt Express next door. ⊠ *675 15th St. NW, Downtown* ☎ *202/347–4800* ⊟ *AE, D, DC, MC, V* Ⓜ *Metro Center.*

$–$$$ ✕ **15 Ria.** Ever since it opened in 2002, this small, cozy space with a fireplace and just over a dozen tables has been attracting a heavy after-work crowd and a neighborhood following. Chef Jamie Leed's fresh style of cooking, which emphasizes local ingredients and no-fuss preparation, sparkles in dishes like the four-inch-tall pear salad with aged goat cheese and the grilled fillet of rockfish (from Maryland's Eastern Shore). Take a chance and order the daily special. You're in good hands. ⊠ *Washington Terrace Hotel, 1515 Rhode Island Ave. NW, Downtown* ☎ *202/ 232–7000* ⊟ *AE, MC, V* Ⓜ *McPherson Square.*

Asian

★ $–$$$ ✕ **Full Kee.** Many locals swear by Full Kee, which has a competitive assortment of Cantonese-style roasted meats. Order from the house specialties, not the tourist menu; the meal-size soups garnished with roast meats are the best in Chinatown. Tried and true dishes include the steamed dumplings, crispy duck, eggplant with garlic sauce, and the sautéed leek flower. ⊠ *509 H St. NW, Chinatown* ☎ *202/371–2233* ⊟ *No credit cards* Ⓜ *Gallery Place/Chinatown.*

★ $–$$$ ✕ **TenPenh.** One of the closest restaurants to the White House, this hopping venue is always buzzing with socialites, political junkies, and politicians. Chef Jeff Tunks's menu draws from many Asian cuisines—Chinese, Thai, Vietnamese, even Filipino. Main courses range from the chef's signature Chinese smoked lobster to lamb chops with an Asian-influenced crust of pesto. Banana spring rolls with ginger ice cream and mango salsa is just one creation from pastry chef David Guas. ⊠ *10th St. and Pennsylvania Ave. NW, Downtown* ☎ *202/393–4500* ⌕ *Reservations essential* ⊟ *AE, D, DC, MC, V* ⊘ *Closed Sun.* Ⓜ *Navy Archives.*

$–$$$ ✕ **Hunan Chinatown.** One of Chinatown's most attractive and most attentive restaurants, Hunan uses fresh ingredients in its piping hot versions of familiar dishes. Try the fried dumplings, the tea-smoked duck, the Szechuan eggplant, and the crispy Hunan-style whole fish. ⊠ *624*

H St. NW, Chinatown ☎ *202/783–5858* ▤ *AE, D, DC, MC, V*
Ⓜ *Gallery Place/Chinatown.*

$–$$$ ✕ **Kaz Sushi Bistro.** Traditional Japanese cookery is combined with often inspired improvisations ("freestyle Japanese cuisine," in the words of chef–owner Kaz Okochi) at this serene location. For a first-rate experience, sit at the sushi bar and ask for whatever is freshest and best. The chef's years of experience preparing fugu—the legendarily dangerous blowfish, available only in winter—means you're in good hands, though the experience is pricey at $150 per person. It's not all sushi here: other innovations include sake-poached scallops with lemon-cilantro dressing. ⊠ *1915 I St. NW, Downtown* ☎ *202/530–5500* ▤ *AE, DC, MC, V* ◷ *Closed Sun. No lunch weekends* Ⓜ *Farragut West.*

$ ✕ **Teaism.** A stock of more than 50 teas (black, white, and green) imported from India, Japan, and Africa is the main source of pride for this tranquil tea house. But the tea doesn't outshine the healthy and delicious Japanese, Indian, and Thai food. Diners mix small dishes—tandoori kabobs, tea-cured salmon, Indian flat breads, salads, and various chutneys—to create meals or snacks. For the adventurous diner there's a juicy ostrich burger or *ochazuke,* green tea poured over seasoned rice. The smaller Connecticut Avenue branch is tucked neatly on a corner adjacent to Lafayette Park and the White House, a casual reprieve from neighboring high-priced restaurants. It's a perfect spot to grab lunch after touring the nation's power-center. Breakfast is served daily. The Connecticut Avenue location is closed on weekends. ⊠ *400 8th St. NW, Downtown* ☎ *202/638–7740* ▤ *AE, MC, V* Ⓜ *Navy/Archives* ⊠ *800 Connecticut Ave. NW, Downtown* ☎ *202/835–2233* ▤ *AE, MC, V* Ⓜ *Farragut West.*

¢–$ ✕ **Burma.** The country of Burma (now called Myanmar) is bordered by India, Thailand, and China, which gives a good indication of the cuisine at this Chinatown restaurant. Curry and tamarind share pride of place with lemon, cilantro, and soy seasonings. Batter-fried eggplant and squash are paired with complex, peppery sauces. Green-tea-leaf and other salads, despite their odd-sounding names and ingredients, leave the tongue with a pleasant tingle. Such entrées as mango pork and tamarind fish are equally satisfying. ⊠ *740 6th St. NW, 2nd floor, Downtown* ☎ *202/638–1280* ⬧ *Reservations essential* ▤ *AE, D, DC, MC, V* ◷ *No lunch weekends* Ⓜ *Gallery Place/Chinatown.*

¢–$ ✕ **Li Ho.** Head for unassuming Li Ho if you're seeking good Chinese food in satisfying portions. Kitchen specialties like duck soup with mustard greens and Singapore noodles, a rice-noodle dish seasoned with curry and bits of meat, are favorites among the lunchtime crowd. ⊠ *501 H St. NW, Downtown* ☎ *202/289–2059* ▤ *MC, V* Ⓜ *Gallery Place/ Chinatown.*

¢–$ ✕ **Oodles Noodles.** Packed from the day they opened and with long lines waiting for tables and takeout, these attractive Pan-Asian noodle houses have remarkably good Chinese, Japanese, Thai, Indonesian, Malaysian, and Vietnamese dishes; all are served on plates appropriate to the cuisine. Try the Thai drunken noodles, which are soused on sake; the Chinese clay-pot noodles; or the Vietnamese rice noodles with grilled chicken. ⊠ *1120 19th St. NW, Dupont Circle* ☎ *202/293–3138* ⬧ *Reservations essential* ▤ *AE, DC, MC, V* ◷ *Closed Sun.* Ⓜ *Farragut North.*

Contemporary

$$$–$$$$ ✕ **Equinox.** Chef Todd Gray headed the kitchen at Galileo, Washington's esteemed Italian restaurant, for seven years, but when he started his own place, the Virginia-born chef knew it had to be American. Both the furnishings and the food are simple and elegant. Fresh local ingredients speak for themselves: grilled quail with a truffle reduction, rare duck breast

served on a cabbage salad, crab cakes with diced mango, and barbe-
cued salmon with a sauce of roasted peppers and corn. The five-course
prix-fixe dinner option ($75, $100 with wine pairing) can be a good
way to be introduced to Gray's cooking. ⊠ *818 Connecticut Ave. NW,
Downtown* ☎ *202/331–8118* ⌘ *Reservations essential* ▱ *AE, DC, MC,
V* ☺ *No lunch Sat.* Ⓜ *Farragut West.*

$$$–$$$$ ✕ **Occidental Grill.** One of the most venerable restaurants in the city, the
popular Occidental Grill covers its walls with photos of politicians and
other notables who have come here for the food and the attentive ser-
vice. Tried and true dishes are best—chopped salad, grilled tuna, veal
meat loaf. Over half of the menu is seafood. ⊠ *Willard Inter-Continental,
1475 Pennsylvania Ave. NW, Downtown* ☎ *202/783–1475* ⌘ *Reser-
vations essential* ▱ *AE, DC, MC, V* Ⓜ *Metro Center.*

$$–$$$$ ✕ **Red Sage.** The multimillion-dollar southwestern interior at this upscale rancher's haven near the White House has a barbed-wire-and-lizard
theme and a pseudo-adobe warren of dining rooms. Upstairs at the Border Café, trendsetters can enjoy a comparatively inexpensive Tex-Mex
menu. Start with the ginger cured salmon, prepared in-house, and move
on to the always popular pecan-crusted chicken breast or pan-seared
yellowfin tuna. ⊠ *605 14th St. NW, Downtown* ☎ *202/638–4444*
▱ *AE, D, DC, MC, V* ☺ *No lunch Sun.* Ⓜ *Metro Center.*

$$–$$$ ✕ **DC Coast.** Chef Jeff Tunks's menu at this sophisticated downtown spot
brings the foods of three coasts—Atlantic, Gulf, and Pacific—to Washington. Try his version of the mid-Atlantic's best-known seafood deli-
cacy, crab cakes. They're among the best in town. If you're homesick
for New Orleans, try the gumbo, and for Pacific Rim cooking, you can't
beat the smoked lobster. The bar scene is one of the liveliest in the downtown area. ⊠ *1401 K St. NW, Downtown* ☎ *202/216–5988* ⌘ *Reservations essential* ▱ *AE, D, DC, MC, V* ☺ *Closed Sun. No lunch Sat.*
Ⓜ *McPherson Square.*

$$–$$$ ✕ **Poste.** Inside the trendy Hotel Monaco, Poste occupies a towering space
that until 1901 was the General Post Office. Now sifting through modern American fare, chef Jay Comfort conjures up dishes like seared ahi
tuna and foie gras with an acidic blackberry sauce. For a main course
try the steak frites: the 31-day dry aged strip loin served with flavorful,
wild mushrooms helps make the restaurant worthy of its self-proclaimed
title of modern brasserie. In warmer months drinks are served al fresco
in the striking courtyard where horses once parked with wagons of mail.
Valet parking is a steep $9. ⊠ *Hotel Monaco, 555 8th St. NW, Down-
town* ☎ *202/783–6060* ▱ *AE, D, DC, V* Ⓜ *Gallery Place/Chinatown.*

¢–$ ✕ **Bread Line.** Crowded, quirky, sometimes chaotic, this restaurant spe-
cializes in breads and bread-based foods and not only makes the city's
best baguette but also some of its best sandwiches. Owner Mark Fursten-
burg makes everything on the premises, from the breakfast bagels and
muffins to the ciabatta loaves for the tuna salad sandwich with preserved
lemons. It's best to arrive early or late to avoid the noontime rush. Outdoor seating is available in warmer months. ⊠ *1751 Pennsylvania Ave.
NW, Downtown* ☎ *202/822–8900* ⌘ *Reservations not accepted* ▱ *AE,
MC, V* ☺ *Closed weekends. No dinner* Ⓜ *Farragut West.*

Eclectic

$$$–$$$$ ✕ **Blackie's.** No longer the tour bus destination it was for decades,
Blackie's now has fine linens and valet parking. There remains, however,
the same hospitality and large portions that have made Blackie's famous
since it opened in the 1940s. The classic, and pricey, selection of aged
steaks is joined by eclectic options such as beef carpaccio with white truf-
fle oil and a significant selection of seafood. The massive space is divided
into five dining rooms, each with a distinct personality. The wine list has

200 bottles, and every night from 5:30–7 PM, that list is half price. ✉ *1217 22nd St. NW, Downtown* ☎ *202/333–1100* ⊕ *www.blackiesdc. com* ⌖ *Reservations essential* ▭ *AE, D, DC, MC, V.*

$$–$$$$ ✕ **jordans.** Many Washingtonians dine for sport, hoping to catch a glimpse of Michael Jordan while eating modern American cuisine that changes seasonally. Jordans is in the courtyard of the Ronald Reagan International Trade Building: park in the Trade Center's lot or use the valet parking that's available every evening on Pennsylvania Avenue. ✉ *1300 Pennsylvania Ave. NW, Downtown* ☎ *202/589–1223* ▭ *AE, D, DC, MC, V* ☺ *Closed Sun. No lunch Sat.* Ⓜ *Federal Triangle.*

$$$ ✕ **Kinkead's.** This multichambered restaurant has a raw bar downstairs and more-formal dining rooms upstairs. The open kitchen upstairs allows you to watch chef Robert Kinkead and company turn out an eclectic menu of mostly seafood dishes, inspired by Kinkead's New England roots and by the cooking of Asia and Latin America. Don't miss the signature dish, salmon encrusted with pumpkin seeds and served with a ragout of crab, shrimp, and corn. Save room for dessert—the chocolate and caramel sampler, which includes a chocolate-and-caramel soufflé, is a knockout. ✉ *2000 Pennsylvania Ave. NW, Foggy Bottom* ☎ *202/ 296–7700* ⌖ *Reservations essential* ▭ *AE, D, DC, MC, V* Ⓜ *Foggy Bottom/GWU.*

$$–$$$ ✕ **701 Pennsylvania Avenue.** Cuisine drawn from Italy, France, Asia, and the Americas graces the menu of this sleek restaurant, where an elegant meal might begin with tuna tartare topped with caviar or salmon seviche, progress to chicken on a bed of mashed potatoes or blue marlin on a black bean puree, and finish with chocolate-raspberry cake. In the Caviar Lounge, sample from caviar and tapas menus and more than 30 types of vodka. The three-course fixed-price ($24.95) pretheater dinner is popular, and convenient if you're attending a performance at the Shakespeare, National, Warner, or Ford's theater. Live jazz plays nightly. ✉ *701 Pennsylvania Ave. NW, Downtown* ☎ *202/393–0701* ⌖ *Reservations essential* ▭ *AE, MC, V* ☺ *No lunch weekends* Ⓜ *Archives/Navy Memorial.*

French

★ $$$–$$$$ ✕ **Gerard's Place.** Don't let the simplicity of the name cause you to underestimate this sophisticated spot owned by acclaimed French chef Gerard Pangaud. In the striking dining room you're served dishes with intriguing combinations of ingredients—to name a few: Gerard's signature poached lobster with a ginger, lime, and sauternes sauce; venison served with dried fruits and pumpkin and beet purees; or seared tuna with black olives and roasted red peppers. If your appetite and wallet are willing, you might try the five-course fixed-price ($85) dinner. ✉ *915 15th St. NW, Downtown* ☎ *202/737–4445* ⌖ *Reservations essential* ▭ *AE, DC, MC, V* ☺ *Closed Sun. No lunch Sat.* Ⓜ *McPherson Square.*

$–$$$$ ✕ **Les Halles.** This is about as close as you can come to a Parisian bistro without going to France. The cooking is plain and hearty, and the portions are large. The best first course is a sensational salad of *frisée* (a bitter salad green), bacon, and Roquefort cheese. Steak is the recommended main course, either the *onglet* (hanger steak) with the best fries in town or, for two, the gargantuan grilled rib. If you're lucky enough to visit in February, don't miss the Choûcroute Festival, when four different versions of this hearty meat-and-sauerkraut treat are offered. ✉ *1201 Pennsylvania Ave. NW, Downtown* ☎ *202/347–6848* ⌖ *Reservations essential* ▭ *AE, D, DC, MC, V* Ⓜ *Metro Center.*

Indian

$–$$ ✕ **Bombay Club.** One block from the White House, the beautiful Bombay Club tries to re-create a private club inhabited by 19th-century British colonials in India rather than the modern-day Beltway elite. Potted palms and a bright blue ceiling above white plaster moldings adorn the elegant and decorous dining room. On the menu are unusual seafood specialties and a large number of vegetarian dishes, but the real standouts are the breads and the seafood appetizers. The bar, furnished with rattan chairs and dark-wood paneling, serves hot hors d'oeuvres at cocktail hour. ⊠ *815 Connecticut Ave. NW, Downtown* ☏ *202/659–3727* ⌕ *Reservations essential* ⋔ *Jacket required* ▤ *AE, DC, MC, V* ⊙ *No lunch Sat.* Ⓜ *Farragut West.*

Italian

$$$–$$$$ ✕ **Galileo.** Sophisticated Piedmont-style cooking is served at the flagship
Fodor'sChoice restaurant of Washington entrepreneur–chef Roberto Donna. To get the
★ full Galileo experience, order an antipasto, a pasta, and a main course of grilled fish, game, or veal. Four-course ($60) and six-course ($80) fixed-price menus can be a good value. Donna cooks in his intimate restaurant within a restaurant, Laboratorio da Galileo, several nights a week. Snag one of the 25 seats for an up-close view of the master at work and a 12-course meal ($98 weekdays and $110 weekends). Reservations for the Laboratorio must be made months in advance. ⊠ *1110 21st St. NW, Downtown* ☏ *202/293–7191* ▤ *AE, D, DC, MC, V* ⊙ *No lunch weekends* Ⓜ *Foggy Bottom/GWU.*

$$$–$$$$ ✕ **Olives.** This D.C. outpost of celebrity chef Todd English plays to a crowded dining room at lunch and dinner. The upstairs room, which overlooks the open kitchen, is where the action is, but the spacious downstairs dining room is more comfortable, albeit formal. Hearty beginnings include English's signature butternut-squash–stuffed tortelli and a goat-cheese-and-onion tart topped with a boned quail. Most plates have so much going on that there are bound to be some hits and some misses, but the spit-roasted chicken is done well, as is the salmon atop a bowl of clam chowder. ⊠ *1600 K St. NW, Downtown* ☏ *202/452–1866* ⌕ *Reservations essential* ▤ *AE, DC, MC, V* ⊙ *Closed Sun. No lunch Sat.* Ⓜ *Farragut North.*

$$–$$$ ✕ **Teatro Goldoni.** Named for an 18th-century playwright, this elegant restaurant with a colorful Venetian-inspired interior is as much a showcase for chef Fabrizio Aielli's modern Italian cooking as it is for traditional Venetian cuisine. For a first course, try an unusual pasta dish, such as squid-ink noodles or cannelloni stuffed with shiitake mushroom puree. At the center of the menu is a selection of fresh fish, which may be grilled, roasted, or cooked in parchment paper Venetian style. There's also a wide selection of vegetarian entrées; there are more than 30 frozen vodkas at the bar. Live jazz plays Wednesday, Friday, and Saturday. ⊠ *1909 K St. NW, Downtown* ☏ *202/955–9494* ▤ *AE, D, DC, MC, V* ⊙ *Closed Sun. No lunch Sat.* Ⓜ *Farragut North.*

$$–$$$ ✕ **Tosca.** Chef Cesare Lanfranconi spent several years in the kitchen at Washington's best Italian restaurant, Galileo, before starting sleek and sophisticated Tosca. The food draws heavily from Lanfranconi's native Lake Como region of Italy, but isn't limited by it. Polenta topped with wild mushrooms is a great choice: the sweet corn taste is intense but tempered by the mushrooms' earthiness. Pasta dishes include a tasty ravioli stuffed with ricotta and crushed amaretto cookies. Save room for dessert, particularly the chef's updated version of tiramisu. ⊠ *1112 F St. NW, Downtown* ☏ *202/367–1990* ⌕ *Reservations essential* ▤ *AE, DC, MC, V* ⊙ *No lunch weekends* Ⓜ *Metro Center.*

Latin American

★ $$–$$$ ✕ **Café Atlántico.** The menu is always exciting and often adventurous at this *nuevo Latino* restaurant with friendly service. Guacamole made tableside by your waiter is unmistakably fresh. If they're available, try the scallops served with coconut crispy rice, ginger, squid and squid ink oil. The bar makes mean pisco sours and *caipirinhas,* made with *cachaça,* a sugar-cane brandy. Don't forget to check out the wines: you're unlikely to find a more extensive selection of South American wines anywhere else in the city. Café Atlántico offers a "Latino dim sum" option on weekends. For $34.95, you can get tapas-size portions of dishes like duck confit with passion fruit oil, pineapple shavings, and plantain powder. ✉ *405 8th St. NW, Downtown* ☎ *202/393–0812* ⚑ *Reservations essential* ▤ *AE, DC, MC, V* Ⓜ *Archives/Navy Memorial.*

Middle Eastern

$$–$$$ ✕ **Zaytinya.** After the booming success of chef Jose Andres's tapas
FodorsChoice restaurant Jaleo, he's trying his hand with mezze, tapas's Middle-East-
★ ern equivalent. Zaytinya, which means "olive oil" in Turkish, includes Turkish, Greek and Lebanese tastes in almost every dish. To get the full experience choose three or four of the appetizer-size mezze, such as the popular braised lamb dish with eggplant puree and cheese, or the baba ghanouj, made of pureed eggplant. Zaytinya is a great choice for vegetarians and meat-lovers alike—the menu pays equal attention to both. Reservations for times after 6:30 are not accepted; come prepared to wait on weekend evenings. ✉ *701 9th St. NW, Downtown* ☎ *202/638–0800* ▤ *AE, DC, MC, V* Ⓜ *Gallery Place/Chinatown.*

Seafood

$$–$$$$ ✕ **Oceanaire Seafood Room.** This outpost of a Minneapolis-based chain is beautiful, a throwback to another era, with dark wood paneling, semicircular red booths, white tablecloths, and a pink glow that makes everybody look their best. Oceanaire primarily distinguishes itself with first-rate ingredients; you see it at its best by ordering simply, picking from the list of fresh fish that heads the menu—perhaps lovely walleye pike or local rockfish. The portions are often big enough to feed a family of four. Oceanaire is a good time, and even better if you go with a group. ✉ *1201 F St. NW, Downtown* ☎ *202/347-2277* ⚑ *Reservations essential* ▤ *AE, D, DC, MC, V* ☉ *No lunch weekends* Ⓜ *Metro Center.*

$$–$$$$ ✕ **Phillip's Flagship.** The best of the enormous seafood restaurants that overlook the Capital Yacht Club's marina, Phillip's has cavernous rooms and capacious decks that are fully capable of accommodating the crowds from the tour buses that fill the parking lot. There's a sushi bar and seafood buffet Monday through Saturday, a party room with its own deck, and space for 1,400. Despite its size, the restaurant is distinguished by the quality of its raw materials, such as local fish and crab, which it acquires from a network of dealers built up over the years. ✉ *900 Water St. SW, Downtown* ☎ *202/488–8515* ▤ *AE, D, DC, MC, V* Ⓜ *L'Enfant Plaza.*

Southern

$–$$$ ✕ **Georgia Brown's.** An elegant "new South" eatery and a favorite hangout of local politicians, Georgia Brown's serves shrimp Carolina-style (head intact, with steaming grits on the side); beef tenderloin medallions with a bourbon–pecan sauce; thick, rich crab soup; and such specials as grilled salmon and slow-cooked green beans with bacon. Fried green tomatoes are filled with herb cream cheese, and a pecan pie is made with bourbon and imported Belgian dark chocolate. The airy, curving dining room has white honeycomb windows and an unusual ceiling ornamentation of bronze ribbons. ✉ *950 15th St. NW, Downtown* ☎ *202/393-4499* ▤ *AE, D, DC, MC, V* ⚑ *Reservations essential* ☉ *No lunch Sat.* Ⓜ *McPherson Square.*

Spanish

★ $$$–$$$$ ✕ **Taberna del Alabardero.** A lovely formal dining room, skillful service, and sophisticated cooking make this restaurant one of Washington's best.

Start with tapas: piquillo peppers stuffed with *bacalao* (salt cod) or roasted leg of duck in a phyllo pastry pouch. Proceed to a hefty bowl of gazpacho or white garlic soup and venture on to authentic paella and elegant Spanish country dishes. Ask the sommelier to pick a good Spanish wine to accompany your meal. Pineapple tart makes a light ending to rich fare. The plush interior and handsome bar help make things romantic, attracting a well-heeled clientele. ⊠ *1776 I St. NW, at 18th St., Downtown* ☎ *202/429–2200* ⌕ *Reservations essential* ⌂ *Jacket required* ⊟ *AE, D, DC, MC, V* ☉ *Closed Sun. No lunch Sat.* Ⓜ *Farragut West.*

$$–$$$$
Fodor$Choice
★

✕ **Jaleo.** You are encouraged to make a meal of the long list of tapas at this lively Spanish bistro, although entrées like paella are just as tasty. Tapas highlights include the *gambas al ajillo* (sautéed garlic shrimp), fried potatoes with spicy tomato sauce, and the grilled chorizo. Don't miss the crisp apple charlotte and the chocolate hazelnut torte. Dancers heat up the restaurant on Wednesdays. ⊠ *480 7th St. NW, Downtown* ☎ *202/628–7949* ⊟ *AE, D, DC, MC, V* Ⓜ *Gallery Place/Chinatown.*

Steak

$$$–$$$$
✕ **Morton's of Chicago.** Enjoy a steak on the patio at the downtown location of this national chain, one block from The Mayflower, a D.C. landmark hotel. In classic steak-house tradition, the emphasis is on quantity as well as quality; the New York strip and porterhouse steaks are well over a pound each. If you have an even larger appetite (or you plan to share), there's a 48-ounce porterhouse. Prime rib, lamb, veal, chicken, lobster, and grilled fish are also on the menu. ⊠ *1050 Connecticut Ave. NW, Downtown* ☎ *202/955–5997* ⊟ *AE, D, DC, MC, V* Ⓜ *Farragut North.*

Dupont Circle

American/Casual

$–$$
✕ **Kramerbooks and Afterwords.** A favorite neighborhood breakfast spot, this popular bookstore-cum-café is also a late-night haunt on weekends, when it's open around the clock. There's a simple menu with soups, salads, and sandwiches, but many people drop in just for cappuccino and dessert. The "dysfunctional family sundae"—a massive brownie soaked in amaretto with a plethora of divine toppings—is a local favorite. Live music, from rock to blues, is performed Wednesday through Sunday 10 PM to midnight. ⊠ *1517 Connecticut Ave. NW, Dupont Circle* ☎ *202/ 387–1462* ⌕ *Reservations not accepted* ⊟ *AE, D, MC, V* Ⓜ *Dupont Circle.*

Asian

$–$$$
✕ **City Lights of China.** The traditional Chinese fare and art-deco design at City Lights have made it a consistent pick on critics' lists. Less common specialties are shark's-fin soup and lamb in a tangy peppery sauce. Seafood items tend to be costly, but there are plenty of reasonably priced alternatives. For satisfying and inexpensive one-dish meals try the pickled-mustard-green soup with noodles and pork, or the *cha chang mein*, the Chinese counterpart to spaghetti with meat sauce. The mint-green booths and elegant silk-flower arrangements conjure up breezy spring days, even in the midst of a frenzied dinner rush. ⊠ *1731 Connecticut Ave. NW, Dupont Circle* ☎ *202/265–6688* ⊟ *AE, D, DC, MC, V* Ⓜ *Dupont Circle.*

$–$$
✕ **Sala Thai.** Who says Thai food has to be scalp-sweating hot? Sala Thai makes the food as spicy as you wish, but the chef is interested in flavor, not fire. Among the subtly seasoned dishes are *panang goong* (shrimp in curry–peanut sauce), chicken sautéed with ginger and pineapple, and flounder with a choice of four sauces. Mirrored walls and warm lights

soften this small downstairs dining room, as do the friendly service and largely neighborhood clientele. ✉ *2016 P St. NW, Dupont Circle* ☎ *202/ 872–1144* ⊟ *AE, D, DC, MC, V* Ⓜ *Dupont Circle.*

$ ✕ **Teaism.** This novel counterpoint to the many area coffee bars carries an impressive selection of more than 50 teas, which complement the small, tasty Japanese, Indian, and Thai dishes. *Bento* boxes—which contain a salad, entrée, rice—are full meals. Teaism is also a good place to enjoy a hot drink with ginger scones or other sweet treats. There are two additional branches downtown. ✉ *2009 R St. NW, Dupont Circle* ☎ *202/ 667–3827* ⊟ *AE, MC, V* Ⓜ *Dupont Circle.*

Contemporary

$$$ ✕ **Nora.** Although it bills itself as an organic restaurant, Nora is no collective-run juice bar. The food, like the quilt-decorated dining room, is sophisticated and attractive. Peppered beef carpaccio with manchego cheese is a good starter. Entrées such as seared rockfish with artichoke broth, grilled lamb chops with a white-bean sauce, and risotto with winter vegetables emphasize well-balanced, complex ingredients. At Nora's sister restaurant, **Asia Nora** (2213 M St. NW, Dupont Circle, ☎202/797–4860), organic ingredients are put to good use in Pan-Asian dishes. ✉*2132 Florida Ave. NW, Dupont Circle* ☎ *202/462–5143* ⌕ *Reservations essential* ⊟*AE, D, MC, V* ☯ *Closed Sun. No lunch* Ⓜ *Dupont Circle.*

$$–$$$ ✕ **Tabard Inn.** Fading portraits and overstuffed furniture make the lobby lounge of the Hotel Tabard Inn look like an antiques store, but the restaurant's culinary sensibility is thoroughly modern. The menu changes daily but consistently offers interesting seafood and vegetarian options. A popular entrée is the branzino, a flaky white fish, served with artichokes, preserved lemon, and lentils in an olive sauce. Vegetarian options might include a porcini risotto with kalamata olives, Roma tomatoes, and pesto. In good weather, you can dine in the courtyard. ✉ *1739 N St. NW, Dupont Circle* ☎ *202/331–8528* ⊟ *AE, DC, MC, V* Ⓜ *Dupont Circle.*

$$–$$$ ✕ **Vidalia.** There's a lot more to chef Jeffrey Buben's distinguished restaurant than the sweet Vidalia onion, which is a specialty in season. Inspired by the cooking and the ingredients of the South and the Chesapeake Bay region, Buben's version of New American cuisine revolves around the best seasonal fruits, vegetables, and seafood he can find. Don't miss the roasted onion soup with spoon bread, the shrimp on yellow grits, or the sensational lemon chess pie. ✉ *1990 M St. NW, Dupont Circle* ☎ *202/659–1990* ⊟*AE, D, DC, MC, V* ☯ *Closed Sun. July–Aug. No lunch weekends* Ⓜ *Dupont Circle.*

★ $–$$$ ✕ **Firefly.** The backlit, amber bar and birch-log wall keep things looking warm and natural at this showcase to contemporary American bistro food. Start with an upscale take on Italian sausages and onions with a caramelized onion and chorizo tart with mustard sauce and balsamic vinegar. More standard comfort food includes a slow grilled, thick-cut pork chop with cabbage and horseradish and braised short ribs with red wine and roasted vegetables. The small wine list is well chosen and fairly priced, made up mostly of California boutique labels. ✉ *Hotel Madera, 1310 New Hampshire Ave. NW, Dupont Circle* ☎ *202/861–1310* ⊟ *AE, D, DC, MC, V* Ⓜ *Dupont Circle.*

French

$–$$ ✕ **Bistrot du Coin.** An instant hit in its Dupont Circle neighborhood, this moderately priced French steak house is noisy, crowded, and great fun. The brainchild of Michel Verdon (formerly of Les Halles) and chef Yannis Felix has a monumental zinc bar and serves comforting traditional bistro fare. Mussels, as a starter, come in any of several preparations. Steaks, garnished with a pile of crisp fries, are the main attraction, but you might also try the duck-leg confit or tripe *à la niçoise* (a stew of tripe and fresh tomatoes). Wash it all down with a carafe of Beaujolais or Côtes du Rhone, or with a pitcher of Alsatian white. ⊠ *1738 Connecticut Ave. NW, Dupont Circle* ☎ *202/234–6969* ▤ *AE, D, DC, MC, V* Ⓜ *Dupont Circle.*

Italian

$$$$ ✕ **Obelisk.** Come here for the eclectic Italian cuisine. The only option, a five-course fixed-price ($58) menu that changes every day, combines traditional dishes with chef Peter Pastan's innovations. For the main course, you might try the lamb with garlic and sage or the braised grouper with artichoke and thyme. The minimally decorated dining room is tiny, with closely spaced tables. ⊠ *2029 P St. NW, Dupont Circle* ☎ *202/ 872–1180* ⌕ *Reservations essential* ▤ *DC, MC, V* ☾ *Closed Sun. and Mon. No lunch* Ⓜ *Dupont Circle.*

$$–$$$$ ✕ **i Ricchi.** An airy space with terra-cotta tiles, cream-color archways, and floral frescoes, i Ricchi remains a favorite of critics and upscale crowds for its earthy Tuscan cuisine, often prepared on its wood-burning grill or oven. Skewered shrimp and rolled pork roasted in wine and fresh herbs highlight the spring–summer menu. The fall–winter bill of fare brings grilled lamb chops, hearty soups, and sautéed beef filet. ⊠ *1220 19th St. NW, Dupont Circle* ☎ *202/835–0459* ⌕ *Reservations essential* 🏛 *Jacket required* ▤ *AE, DC, MC, V* ☾ *Closed Sun. No lunch Sat.* Ⓜ *Dupont Circle.*

$–$$$ ✕ **La Tomate.** A previously neglected corner near Dupont Circle has been transformed into a popular neighborhood Italian restaurant with an attractive garden-dining space. La Tomate is notable for its dependable pastas, traditional veal preparations, and friendly, if occasionally harried, service. ⊠ *1701 Connecticut Ave. NW, Dupont Circle* ☎ *202/ 667–5505* ▤ *AE, DC, MC, V* Ⓜ *Dupont Circle.*

$ ✕ **Pizzeria Paradiso.** The ever popular Pizzeria Paradiso sticks to crowd-
Fodor'sChoice pleasing basics: pizzas, *panini* (grilled sandwiches with fillings that in-
★ clude Italian cured ham and sun-dried tomatoes and basil), salads, and desserts. Although the standard pizza is satisfying, you can enliven things by ordering it with fresh buffalo mozzarella or unusual toppings such as potatoes, capers, and mussels. The intensely flavored gelato is a house specialty. A trompe l'oeil ceiling adds space and light to a simple interior. A larger location is in Georgetown. ⊠ *2029 P St. NW, Dupont Circle* ☎ *202/223–1245* ⌕ *Reservations not accepted* ▤ *DC, MC, V* Ⓜ *Dupont Circle.*

Latin American

$$–$$$ ✕ **Gabriel.** Traditional Latin American and Spanish dishes get a nouvelle approach at Gabriel. Pupusas, Salvadoran meat patties, are filled with chorizo; a starter of grilled sea scallops is served with lime, cilantro, and garlic cream. An extensive tapas buffet makes the bar a popular after-work hangout. The restaurant comes into its own with an outstanding Sunday brunch buffet, where you choose from the whole suckling pig, made-to-order quesadillas, and Mediterranean specialties like paella and cassoulet, in addition to traditional breakfast items. The dessert table is stacked with tiny fruit tarts, bread and rice pudding, mini crème brûlée, and cheesecake. ⊠ *Radisson Barceló Hotel, 2121 P St. NW, Dupont Circle* ☎ *202/956–6690* ⌕ *Reservations essential* ▤ *AE, D, DC, MC, V* ☾ *No lunch Mon.–Sat.* Ⓜ *Dupont Circle.*

Middle Eastern

$–$$ ✕ **Skewers/Café Luna.** As the name implies, the focus at Skewers is on kabobs, here served with almond-flaked rice or pasta. Lamb with egg-plant and chicken with roasted pepper are the most popular variations, but vegetable kabobs and skewers of filet mignon and seasonal seafood are equally tasty. With nearly 20 choices, the appetizer selection is huge. If the restaurant is too crowded, you can enjoy the cheap eats (chicken and avocado salad, mozzarella and tomato sandwiches, vegetable lasagna, pizza, and salads) downstairs at Café Luna or the reading room–coffeehouse upstairs at Luna Books. ⊠ *1633 P St. NW, Dupont Circle* ☎ *202/387–7400 Skewers; 202/387–4005 Café Luna* ▭ *AE, D, DC, MC, V* Ⓜ *Dupont Circle.*

Seafood

$–$$$ ✕ **Johnny's Half Shell.** It's almost always crowded, but Johnny's Half Shell is worth the wait. Owners John Fulchino and Ann Cashion (both of Cashion's Eat Place in Woodley Park) have created a modern version of the traditional mid-Atlantic seafood house. Here you can be comfortable ordering oysters on the half shell and a beer at the bar or settling into one of the roomy booths for a first course of the best fried oysters in town followed by local rockfish or broiled lobster. Don't miss the spectacular chocolate angel food cake with caramel sauce for dessert. ⊠ *2002 P St. NW, Dupont Circle* ☎ *202/296–2021* ⚑ *Reservations not accepted* ▭ *AE, MC, V* ☉ *Closed Sun.* Ⓜ *Dupont Circle.*

Steak

$$$–$$$$ ✕ **Sam and Harry's.** Cigar-friendly Sam and Harry's is understated, genteel, and packed at lunch and dinner. Miniature crab cakes are a good way to begin, but the real draws are prime meats like porterhouse and New York strip steak served on the bone. Seafood specials change daily; Maine lobster is one possibility. End the meal with warm pecan pie laced with melted chocolate or a "turtle cake," full of caramel and chocolate and big enough for two. ⊠ *1200 19th St. NW, Dupont Circle* ☎ *202/296–4333* ⚑ *Reservations essential* ▭ *AE, D, DC, MC, V* ☉ *Closed Sun. No lunch Sat.* Ⓜ *Dupont Circle.*

$–$$$ ✕ **Palm.** A favorite lunchtime hangout of power brokers, the Palm has walls papered with caricatures of the famous patrons who have dined here. Main attractions include gargantuan steaks and Nova Scotia lobsters, several kinds of potatoes, and New York cheesecake. But one of Palm's best-kept secrets is that it's also a terrific, old-fashioned Italian restaurant. Try the veal marsala for lunch or, on Thursday, the terrific shrimp in marinara sauce. ⊠ *1225 19th St. NW, Dupont Circle* ☎ *202/293–9091* ⚑ *Reservations essential* ▭ *AE, D, DC, MC, V* ☉ *No lunch weekends* Ⓜ *Dupont Circle.*

Georgetown/West End/Glover Park

American

$$$ ✕ **Palena.** Chef Frank Ruta and pastry chef Ann Amernick met while working in the White House kitchens; now they've joined forces to open this contemporary American restaurant, named for the Italian village where Ruta's great-grandmother lived. The French- and Italian-influenced menu changes seasonally. Sometimes Amernick and Ruta team up, as for an appetizer of crisp puff pastry with fresh sardines and greens. Ruta goes it alone with a veal chop with a barley-stuffed pepper and a pork chop with flavorful baked beans. Comforting desserts like a sprightly lemon–caramel tart or a chocolate torte are a perfect match for the earthy cooking. ⊠ *3529 Connecticut Ave. NW, Cleveland Park* ☎ *202/537–9250* ⚑ *Reservations essential* ▭ *AE, D, DC, MC, V* ☉ *Closed Sun. and Mon. No lunch* Ⓜ *Cleveland Park.*

$$–$$$ ✕ **Ardeo/Bardeo.** The trendy new-American Ardeo and its loungelike counterpart, Bardeo, sit side by side in the ever popular culinary strip of Cleveland Park. Ardeo is known for its sleek design, professional and

knowledgeable staff, and very creative menu. Bardeo has similar options in smaller portions. Everything is skillfully prepared, from standard choices of pan-roasted New Zealand rack of lamb to seared rare sesame tuna. The pecan-crusted soft-shell crab is a special treat. ⊠ *3311 Connecticut Ave. NW, Cleveland Park* ☎ *202/244–6750* ▤ *AE, D, MC, V* Ⓜ *Cleveland Park.*

$ ✕ **Georgetown Café.** With its unpretentious looks, cheap prices, and eclectic menu of classics, this café is a bit of an oddball for Georgetown. Students and other locals frequent it for the pasta, pizzas, kabobs, gyros, and such home-style American favorites as roast beef, baked chicken, and mashed potatoes. Closed only from 6 AM to 9 AM weekdays and open 24 hours on weekends, Georgetown Café is also good for a late-night snack. ⊠ *1623 Wisconsin Ave. NW, Georgetown* ☎ *202/333–0215* ⌔ *Reservations not accepted* ▤ *D, MC, V.*

Asian

$–$$ ✕ **Miss Saigon.** Shades of mauve and green, black art-deco accents, and potted palms decorate this Vietnamese restaurant, where careful attention is paid to presentation as well as to seasoning. Begin with crisp egg rolls or chilled spring rolls, then proceed to exquisite salads of shredded green papaya topped with shrimp or beef. Daily specials present the freshest seafood prepared in exciting ways. "Caramel"-cooked meats are standouts, as are the grilled meats. Prices are moderate, especially for lunch, but you may have to order several dishes to have your fill. ⊠ *3057 M St. NW, Georgetown* ☎ *202/333–5545* ▤ *AE, DC, MC, V* Ⓜ *Foggy Bottom/GWU.*

$–$$
Fodor'sChoice
★
✕ **Sushi-Ko.** At the city's best Japanese restaurant, daily specials are always innovative: sesame oil–seasoned trout is layered with crisp wonton crackers, and a sushi special might be salmon topped with a touch of mango sauce and a tiny sprig of dill. And you won't find ginger, mango, or green-tea ice cream at the local Baskin-Robbins. ⊠ *2309 Wisconsin Ave. NW, Georgetown* ☎ *202/333–4187* ⌔ *Reservations essential* ▤ *AE, MC, V* ☉ *No lunch Sat.–Mon.*

Belgian

$$$–$$$$ ✕ **Marcel's.** Chef Robert Wiedmaier trained in the Netherlands and Belgium, and in this, his first solo venture, his French-inspired Belgian cooking focuses on robust seafood and poultry preparations. Start with mussels, if they're available, and move on to perfectly seared diver scallops in saffron broth or tender roasted monkfish on a ragout of potatoes, olives, and onions. The roast chicken is a marvel, white and dark cooked separately to perfect tenderness and moistness. In season, be sure to order the fig tart with citrus crème anglaise and honey-cinnamon ice cream. ⊠ *2401 Pennsylvania Ave. NW, Foggy Bottom* ☎ *202/296–1166* ⌔ *Reservations essential* ▤ *AE, DC, MC, V* Ⓜ *Foggy Bottom/GWU.*

Contemporary

$$$$
Fodor'sChoice
★
✕ **Citronelle.** See all the action in the glass-front kitchen at chef Michel Richard's flagship California–French restaurant. The appetizers, which tend to the witty, might include "beignets" of foie gras coated with *kataifi* (shredded phyllo dough) and deep-fried. Main courses might include loin of venison with chestnuts, mushrooms, and a wine sauce or a breast of squab with truffle sauce. Desserts are luscious: a crunchy napoleon, with caramelized phyllo dough and creamy vanilla custard, is drizzled with butterscotch and dark chocolate. A chef's table in the kitchen gives those who have made reservations at least a month in advance a ringside seat. The prix-fixe menu ranges from $95 to $150. ⊠ *Latham Hotel, 3000 M St. NW, Georgetown* ☎ *202/625–2150* ⌔ *Reservations essential* 🏛 *Jacket required* ▤ *AE, D, DC, MC, V.*

$$-$$$$ ✕ **1789.** This elegant dining room, with Early American paintings and a fireplace, could easily be a room in the White House. But all the gentility is offset by the down-to-earth food. The soups, including the seafood stew and the rich black bean soup with unsweetened chocolate, are flavorful. Rack of lamb and filet of beef are specialties, and seared tuna stands out among the excellent seafood dishes. Service is fluid and attentive. Hazelnut chocolate bars with espresso sauce pep you up for a night on the town, or opt for the homier nectarine cobbler. ⊠ *1226 36th St. NW, Georgetown* ☎ *202/965–1789* ☖ *Reservations essential* 🏛 *Jacket required* ▤ *AE, D, DC, MC, V* ☉ *No lunch.*

$$-$$$ ✕ **Tahoga.** Beautifully prepared new-American cooking is elegantly presented at this relaxing spot. Main courses, modernized versions of American and French classics, might include roast chicken, braised lamb shank, bourbon-glazed pork chops, or chicken-fried beef tenderloin. The pretty garden is a lovely place for lunch. Take advantage of the lunchtime special: any wine on the list is half price. ⊠ *2815 M St. NW, Georgetown* ☎ *202/338–5380* ▤ *AE, DC, MC, V* ☉ *No lunch weekends.*

French

$$-$$$ ✕ **La Chaumière.** A favorite of Washingtonians seeking an escape from the hurly-burly of Georgetown, La Chaumière ("the thatched cottage") has the rustic charm of a French country inn, particularly in winter, when its central stone fireplace warms the room. Fish stew, mussels, and scallops are on the regular menu, and there are always several grilled fish specials. Venison and other hard-to-find meats round out the entrées. Many diners plan their meals around the specials, particularly the couscous on Wednesday and the cassoulet on Thursday. ⊠ *2813 M St. NW, Georgetown* ☎ *202/338–1784* ☖ *Reservations essential* ▤ *AE, DC, MC, V* ☉ *Closed Sun. No lunch Sat.*

$-$$$ ✕ **Bistro Français.** Washington's chefs head to Bistro Français for its minute steak or the sirloin with black pepper or red wine sauce. For many, the big draw is the rotisserie chicken. Daily specials may include *suprême* of salmon with broccoli mousse and beurre blanc. The restaurant is divided into two parts—the café side and the more formal dining room; the café menu has sandwiches and omelets in addition to entrées. The Bistro also has fixed-price lunches ($14.95), early and late-night dinner specials ($19.95), and all-you-can-eat brunches on weekends ($18.95). It stays open until 3 AM on weekday mornings, and 4 AM on weekends. ⊠ *3128 M St. NW, Georgetown* ☎ *202/338–3830* ▤ *AE, DC, MC, V.*

$$ ✕ **Bistrot Lepic.** Relaxed and upbeat, with bright yellow walls and colorful paintings, this small, crowded neighborhood bistro is named after chef–owner Bruno Fortin's favorite street in Paris. Though it's French in every regard—starting with the flirty servers—Lepic isn't exactly what Americans think of as a typical bistro: more traditional fare has been replaced with potato-crusted salmon served with French grapes and ouzo-grape sauce. The wine is all French, with many wines available by the glass. Neighborhood locals fill the 50 seats nightly, so call for reservations. ⊠ *1736 Wisconsin Ave. NW, Glover Park* ☎ *202/333–0111* ☖ *Reservations essential* ▤ *AE, D, DC, MC, V.*

Indian

$-$$$ ✕ **Heritage India.** You feel like a guest in a foreign land dining at this restaurant: there's an incredible attention to detail in everything from the tapestried chairs to the paintings of India to the traditional tandoori and curry dishes. *Tahli* (a variety plate, with rice, bread, and six or seven curries or meats separated into small bowls or compartments) is served on a silver platter with rice, lamb, chicken, and curries; the wine is presented in a small glass pitcher. Whatever you choose, the experience is as fascinating as the meal. ⊠ *2400 Wisconsin Ave. NW, Glover Park* ☎ *202/333–3120* ⌕ *Reservations essential* ▤ *AE, D, MC, V.*

$–$$ ✕ **Aditi.** The two-story dining room, where there are burgundy carpets and chairs and pastel walls with brass sconces—seems too elegant for a moderately priced Indian restaurant. The first floor is small, with a dramatic staircase leading to a larger room with windows that overlook the busy street. Tandoori and curry dishes are expertly prepared and not aggressively spiced; if you want your food spicy, request it. Rice *biryani* (chicken curry with yellow rice and saffron) entrées are good for lighter appetites. ⊠ *3299 M St. NW, Georgetown* ☎ *202/625–6825* ⌕ *Reservations essential* ▤ *AE, D, DC, MC, V.*

Italian

$$–$$$$ ✕ **Cafe Milano.** You're likely to rub shoulders with local socialites, sports figures, and visiting celebrities at Cafe Milano's crowded bar. Expect authentic, sophisticated Italian cooking and a pricey wine list. Specialties are pasta dishes like the elegant lobster with linguine, composed salads, and thin-crust pizzas. ⊠ *3251 Prospect St. NW, Georgetown* ☎ *202/333–6183* ▤ *AE, D, DC, MC, V.*

$–$$$ ✕ **Paolo's.** At one of the busiest corners in Georgetown, this bright and airy restaurant is always buzzing with life. It's great for people-watching from the outdoor patio or inside next to the brick pizza oven looking out of the large French windows. The modern Italian menu has daily specials as well as the standard fare of pizza, salads, and homemade pastas. For a twist, try espresso-rubbed steak salad. ⊠ *1303 Wisconsin Ave. NW, Georgetown* ☎ *202/333–7353* ▤ *AE, D, DC, MC, V.*

$ ✕ **Two Amys.** Judging from the long lines here, the best pizza in D.C. may have moved uptown. Simple recipes allow the ingredients to speak for themselves at this Neapolitan pizzeria. It's no surprise that Peter Pastan, owner of fine Italian restaurant Obelisk, is co-owner of this restaurant. You can taste his high standards in every bite. You may be tempted to go for the D.O.C. pizza (approved by the *Denominazione di Origine Controllata* as having authentic Neapolitan ingredients and methods of preparation), but don't hesitate to try the daily specials. This place is very child-friendly. ⊠ *3715 Macomb St. NW, Glover Park* ☎ *202/885–5700* ⌕ *Reservations not accepted* ▤ *MC, V* ☉ *Closed Mon.*

¢–$
FodorśChoice
★
✕ **Pizzeria Paradiso.** A newcomer to Georgetown, this is the second location of what might be the most popular pizzeria in town. The thin-crust pizzas are baked in a brick oven. In contrast with the Dupont Circle location this space is large and spacious, doubling the size of the original. This comfortable restaurant also includes a full bar. ⊠ *3282 M St. NW, Georgetown* ☎ *202/337–1245* ▤ *D, DC, MC, V.*

Steak

$$$–$$$$ ✕ **Morton's of Chicago.** A national steak-house chain that claims to serve the country's best beef, Morton's is always jumping. Several of the cuts of meat exceed 16 ounces, and there's even a 48-ounce porterhouse. Other choices include lamb, veal, chicken, lobster, and grilled fish. Morton's has additional branches downtown and in Vienna, Virginia. ⊠ *3251 Prospect St., Georgetown* ☎ *202/342–6258* ⌕ *Reservations essential* ▤ *AE, D, DC, MC, V* ☉ *No lunch.*

U Street

American

$–$$ ✕ **Polly's Café.** Tables can be hard to come by on weekend nights at Polly's Café, a cozy U Street oasis with a fireplace. That's when locals come to swill beer, eat better-than-average bar food (burgers, catfish tacos, chicken wings), and enjoy jukebox favorites from every era. A savory portobello mushroom "steak," crisp calamari, and Polly's own ample house salad are popular. The hearty brunch is one of Washington's best values. ⊠ *1342 U St. NW, U St. corridor* ☎ *202/265–8385* ⌦ *Reservations not accepted* ⊟ *MC, V* ☉ *No lunch weekdays* Ⓜ *U Street/Cardozo.*

¢–$ ✕ **Ben's Chili Bowl.** Long before U Street became hip, Ben's was serving
Fodor's Choice chili on hot dogs, chili on "half-smoke" sausages, chili on burgers, and
★ just plain chili. Add cheese fries if you dare. Faux-marble bar and shiny red vinyl stools give the impression that little has changed since the '50s, but turkey and vegetarian burgers and meatless chili are a nod to modern times. Ben's closes at 2 AM Monday through Thursday, at 4 AM on Friday and Saturday, and at 8 PM Sundays. Southern-style breakfast is served from 6 AM Monday through Friday and at 7 AM on Saturday. ⊠ *1213 U St. NW, U St. corridor* ☎ *202/667–0909* ⌦ *Reservations not accepted* ⊟ *No credit cards* Ⓜ *U Street/Cardozo.*

Eclectic

$–$$ ✕ **Utopia.** Here New Orleans meets Italy and the Mediterranean. Lamb couscous, seafood bisque, and pasta dishes such as the Chef's Advice (which combines shrimp, chicken, andouille sausage, and sweet peppers) are hits. Utopia has live music Thursday through Sunday with excellent jazz and Brazilian bands and a very reasonable $15 per person minimum. ⊠ *1418 U St. NW, U St. corridor* ☎ *202/483–7669* ⌦ *Reservations essential* ⊟ *AE, D, DC, MC, V* Ⓜ *U Street/Cardozo.*

$ ✕ **Cada Vez.** Inside what was once a post office, Cada Vez (Spanish for "every time") has a menu that combines traditional tastes in often unusual ways, such as the savory jerk chicken egg rolls or salmon stuffed with a rich shrimp mousse. Live music, frequently jazz, is performed nearly every night in the large, open space. ⊠ *1438 U St. NW, U St. corridor* ☎ *202/667–0785* ⊟ *AE, D, DC, MC, V* ☉ *Closed Sun. and Mon. No lunch.* Ⓜ *U Street/Cardozo.*

$ ✕ **Café Nema.** Somali, North African, and Middle Eastern cuisines are combined to form simple but flavorful entrées at Café Nema. Grilled chicken, lamb, and beef kabobs and salmon steak are paired with fresh vegetables and an outstanding curried basmati rice pilaf that has bits of caramelized onion, cloves, and raisins. *Sambousa* (flaky fried triangles of dough filled with curried vegetables or meat), hummus, and *baba ganoush* (eggplant puree) appetizers are well-prepared. There's a good selection of pastas, salads, and sandwiches. Live jazz plays Thursday nights. ⊠ *1334 U St. NW, U St. corridor* ☎ *202/667–3215* ⊟ *AE, D, DC, MC, V* Ⓜ *U Street/Cardozo.*

Italian

¢–$$ ✕ **Coppi's Restaurant.** An Italian bicycling motif permeates this restaurant, from the posters, photographs, and gear hanging on the walls to the monogrammed racing shirts worn by the staff. The wood oven–baked pizzas are delicious and adventurous. When it appears as a special, the pizza *ai funghi di bosco* (with white-oyster, shiitake, and cremini mushrooms) is a must. Fresh pasta topped with sauces made from local, organic produce is another favorite. ⊠ *1414 U St. NW, U St. corridor* ☎ *202/319–7773* ⊟ *AE, D, DC, MC, V* Ⓜ *U Street/Cardozo.*

Maryland Suburbs

American/Casual

¢–$ ✕ **Tastee Diner.** As 24-hour diners go, Tastee is a classic. Each branch is a sentimental favorite that invokes a sense of old-fashioned community appropriate to its location. Students and others on low budgets (or little sleep) ignore the dust and relish the coffee, which flows endlessly. ⊠ *7731 Woodmont Ave., Bethesda, MD* ☎ *301/652–3970* ⌦ *Reservations not* *accepted* ▭ *MC, V* Ⓜ *Bethesda* ✉ *8601 Cameron St., Silver Spring, MD* ☎ *301/589–8171* ⚱ *Reservations not accepted* ▭ *AE, MC, V* Ⓜ *Silver Spring.*

Belgian

★ **\$\$** ✕ **Mannequin Pis.**The last thing you'd expect from Olney, a small suburb 30 minutes north of Washington, is an elegant restaurant serving Northern Belgium cuisine. Chef and owner Bernard Dehaene, a native of Brussels, takes pride in the authenticity of his small, 45-seat restaurant. You won't find ketchup on the table and water is served only by request, he boasts. What can be expected is a huge selection of Belgium beer (about 50 types) and an arsenal of mussels served in over thirty sauces (\$8–\$18). One favorite is the Mussels Brussels, served in a broth of leek, house-smoked bacon, goat cheese, and beer. As for entrées, the menu changes monthly, but the rack of lamb and the organic chicken are good bets. Make weekend reservations two weeks in advance. ✉ *18064 Georgia Ave., Olney, MD* ☎ *301/570–4800* ⚱ *Reservations essential* ▭ *MC, V.*

Italian

¢–\$ ✕ **Pines of Rome.** Large, child-friendly, and inexpensive, this is the kind of neighborhood restaurant to seek out when you want dependable, comfortable food, not innovative cooking. Don't go for the pastas, which are ordinary at best. Regulars start with an order of white pizza to share and then choose from the list of specials—roast meats, including pork and veal, are served in enormous portions. The kitchen fries well; try the calamari or the soft-shell crabs if they're in season. ✉ *4709 Hampton La., Bethesda, MD* ☎ *301/657–8775* ▭ *AE, D, MC, V* Ⓜ *Bethesda.*

Seafood

\$–\$\$\$\$ ✕ **Crisfield.** Since it's about as elegant as a neighborhood barbershop, Crisfield's relatively high prices might seem absurd. But you get your money's worth with an eyeful of old Maryland frozen in time and some of the best no-nonsense seafood in the area. Crab cakes don't get any more authentic; they're presented with just enough structural imperfection to guarantee they're made by hand. The creamy, chunky clam chowder is rendered with similar, down-home care. The place retains an old-school charm; for maximum effect, sit at the bar, where the waiters shuck clams. ✉ *8012 Georgia Ave., Silver Spring, MD* ☎ *301/589–1306* ⚱ *Reservations not accepted* ▭ *AE, MC, V* ◷ *Closed Mon.* Ⓜ *Silver Spring.*

\$\$–\$\$\$ ✕ **Bethesda Crab House.** This modest restaurant is the best place in the Washington area to enjoy one of the Chesapeake Bay area's great delicacies—blue crabs, steamed with Old Bay seasoning. Order as many crabs as you want; when they're ready they'll be dumped on your paper-covered table. That's your clue to pick up a mallet and knife and attack the crustaceans. (The waiters gladly give instructions.) Settle back with a beer and some serious crab pickin'. The price varies with the time of year. It's a good idea to call in advance to reserve your crabs—the restaurant sometimes runs out. ✉ *4958 Bethesda Ave., Bethesda, MD* ☎ *301/652–3382* ▭ *MC, V* Ⓜ *Bethesda.*

\$\$–\$\$\$ ✕ **Black's Bar and Kitchen.** The bar and kitchen of this warehouse-like restaurant are separated by a glass divider, and the walls hold a clutter of barn doors, mounted fish, and old photos. Black's specializes in seafood as served on the Gulf Coast from Florida to Mexico. Oysters are a good place to start—on the half shell, wrapped in bacon and served in lemon butter, or baked with Parmesan cheese and garlic butter. Grilled yellowfin tuna is a hit, as is the spicy Vermillion Bay seafood stew. ✉ *7750 Woodmont Ave., Bethesda, MD* ☎ *301/652–6278* ▭ *AE, D, MC, V* Ⓜ *Bethesda.*

Southwestern

★ $–$$$ ✕ **Rio Grande Café.** Quail, goat, and other upscale Tex-Mex fare make it worth braving Rio Grande's crowds. Crates of Mexican beer stacked against the walls serve as decoration, as does a functioning perpetual-motion tortilla machine. Big portions make this a good spot for families. A young bar crowd likes to knock back the potent combination of frozen sangria and frozen margarita swirled in a frosted soda glass. ⊠ *4919 Fairmont Ave., Bethesda, MD* ☎ *301/656–2981* ⊟ *AE, D, DC, MC, V* ⌲ *Reservations not accepted* Ⓜ *Bethesda* ⊠ *231 Rio Blvd. Gaithersburg, MD* ☎ *240/632–2150* ⊟ *AE, D, DC, MC, V* ⌲ *Reservations not accepted.*

¢ ✕ **California Tortilla.** The biggest reason to wait with the crowds at lunchtime at California Tortilla is in its namesake—the massive, over-stuffed specialty tortilla. Their best seller is the blackened chicken Caesar, but there are lots of favorites. Don't miss the queso, a flavorful cheese dip. It's made in-house and is always served piping hot. Also make sure to test at least a few of the hot sauces—there are about 50 varieties on hand. ⊠ *4862 Cordell Ave., Bethesda, MD* ☎ *301/654–8226* ⊟ *MC, V* Ⓜ *Bethesda* ⊠ *7727 Tuckerman La., Potomac, MD* ☎ *301/765–3600* ⊟ *MC, V* ⊠ *199 East Montgomery Ave., Rockville, MD* ☎ *301/610–6500* ⊟ *MC, V* Ⓜ *Rockville.*

Spanish

$$–$$$$ ✕ **Jaleo.** Do you have a hard time deciding on just one dish? Then sample several at this lively eatery with an extensive menu of creative tapas and affordable Spanish wines. Among the more than 50 tapas are monk-fish with tomato and garlic, a plate of Spanish cheeses, and date-and-bacon fritters. If you don't like to graze, two popular entrées are the paella and *la plancha* (seared seafood with garlic and olive oil). Don't expect a quiet dinner here: the place is almost always packed with true-blue fans, and live dancing is performed Mondays and Tuesdays. ⊠ *7271 Woodmont Ave., Bethesda, MD* ☎ *301/913–0003* Ⓜ *Bethesda* ⊟ *AE, D, DC, MC, V.*

Fodor'sChoice
★

$–$$$ ✕ **Andalucia.** The spartan Rockville location of Andalucia (hidden in an office-and-shopping strip) was popular enough to spawn the more formally furnished Bethesda branch, which has a tapas bar and a tempting dessert cart. Zarzuela, a seafood stew, is a traditional specialty and is served at both locations. Classical Spanish guitarists perform weeknights, and there are live flamenco dancers on Thursdays at 8 PM. ⊠ *12300 Wilkins Ave., Rockville, MD* ☎ *301/770–1880* ⊟ *AE, D, DC, MC, V* ⊠ *4931 Elm St., Bethesda, MD* ☎ *301/907–0052* ⊟ *AE, D, DC, MC, V* ☉ *No lunch weekends* Ⓜ *Bethesda.*

Virginia Suburbs

Afghan

$ ✕ **Panjshir.** This restaurant's Falls Church location favors an interior of plush red and dark wood, while the Vienna branch is more into pinks—but both serve succulent kabobs of beef, lamb, and chicken, as well as fragrant stews (with or without meat) over impeccably cooked rice. Entrées come with Afghan salad and hearty bread. ⊠ *924 W. Broad St.,*

Falls Church, VA ☎ *703/536–4566* ▭ *AE, DC, MC, V* ☉ *Closed Sun.* ⊠ *224 Maple Ave. W., Vienna, VA* ☎ *703/281–4183* ▭ *AE, DC, MC, V* ☉ *No lunch Sun.*

American

$$–$$$ ✗ **Ashby Inn.** If there's a recipe for a perfect country inn, John and Roma Sherman have it. Head an hour west from D.C., and your reward is comfort food extraordinaire. Dishes are made with the freshest of local ingredients and presented in the most intimate of settings. Try the arugula salad with greens picked from the Inn's garden moments before serving. The roasted chicken, the first item ever offered on the menu, remains a sublime treat. Sunday brunch is from 12:30 to 2. ⊠ *692 Federal St., Paris, VA* ☎ *540/592–3900* ▭ *MC, V* ☉ *No lunch Mon.–Sat. No dinner Sun.*

$$–$$$ ✗ **The Capital Grille.** A small oasis of urban restaurants are tucked neatly in a pocket of high-end stores in the suburbs of Tysons Corner. Among them is the Capital Grille, which has fine dry-aged beef cuts and hearty, traditional sides. The menu is very similar to that of the branch that's a few blocks from the Capitol. ⊠ *1861 International Dr., McLean, VA* ☎ *703/448–3900* ▭ *AE, D, DC, MC, V* ☉ *No lunch weekends.*

$–$$$ ✗ **Carlyle Grand Cafe.** Whether you eat at the bustling bar or at the dining room upstairs, you'll find an imaginative, generous interpretation of modern American cooking. Start with the warm goat cheese and pecan salad, then progress to such entrées as braised lamb shank served with a savory bread pudding or the sea scallops served with a rock-shrimp-and-asparagus risotto. The banana pudding, made with candied vanilla wafers and caramel and chocolate sauces, is extremely popular. If you like the bread, you can buy more at the restaurant's own bakery, the Best Buns Bread Company, next door. ⊠ *4000 S. 28th St., Arlington, VA* ☎ *703/931–0777* ▭ *AE, D, DC, MC, V.*

$$–$$$ ✗ **Majestic Café.** A 1930s-era landmark that had been closed since 1978, the Majestic Café was reopened in 2002. The art-deco facade remains; inside, the café's appearance is in keeping with its '30s origins. The cooking style here moves between trendy American dishes and traditional Southern fare. Some of the best dishes are the sides, such as hush puppies with *remoulade* (a mayo-based sauce that includes shallots, garlic, tarragon, and chives), fluffy spoonbread, and stewed tomatoes. The restaurant is about eight blocks from the Metro. ⊠ *911 King St., Old Town Alexandria, Alexandria VA* ☎ *703/837–9117* ▭ *AE, D, DC, MC, V* ☉ *Closed Mon.* Ⓜ *King Street.*

Asian

$ ✗ **Café Dalat.** In the heart of Arlington's "Little Saigon," you can find low-priced Vietnamese fare in far-from-fancy but clean and pleasant Café Dalat, where service is extremely speedy. The sugarcane shrimp is very good, and *da ram gung* is a sinus-clearing dish of simmered chicken and ginger. All the appetizers are winners, in particular the crispy spring rolls and the tangy Vietnamese shrimp salad in lemon vinaigrette. ⊠ *3143 Wilson Blvd., Arlington, VA,* ☎ *703/276–0935* ▭ *MC, V* Ⓜ *Clarendon.*

$ ✗ **Little Viet Garden.** The patrons here swear by the spring rolls, beef-broth-and-glass-noodle soups, beef tips and potato stir-fried with onion in a smoky sauce, and crispy crepes stuffed with chicken, shrimp, bean sprouts, and green onion. In warm months reserve a table on the outdoor terrace bordered by a flower box–lined white fence. ⊠ *3012 Wilson Blvd., Arlington, VA* ☎ *703/522–9686* ▭ *AE, D, DC, MC, V* Ⓜ *Clarendon.*

¢ ✗ **Pho 75.** To refer to Pho 75's product as mere soup would be a disservice to the procession of flavors that comes with every mouthful—but that is essentially what *pho* is: a Hanoi-style beef soup packed with noodles and thinly sliced pieces of meat that are cooked in seconds by the steaming broth. A plate of fresh bean sprouts, mint leaves, lemon, and green chilies comes with every order: you can spice up your feast-in-a-bowl as you wish. Pho comes in either a large ($5.45) or small ($4.75) bowl, a remarkable bargain either way. ✉ *1771 Wilson Blvd., Suite B, Falls Church, VA* ☎ *703/204–1490* ⊟ *No credit cards.*

Barbecue

$–$$ ✕ **Red Hot & Blue.** Ribs are the specialty at this Memphis-style barbecue joint. They come "wet"—with sauce—or, when simply smoked, "dry." The delicious pulled-meat sandwiches and low prices lure hungry crowds. This chain has additional locations in Annapolis, Fairfax, Gaithersburg, and Laurel. ✉ *1600 Wilson Blvd., Arlington, VA* ☎ *703/276–7427* ⌂ *Reservations not accepted* ⊟ *AE, D, DC, MC, V* Ⓜ *Court House.*

Contemporary

$$$$ ✕ **Elysium at the Morrison House.** There's no sign on the street, but Elysium is worth seeking out. The restaurant is experimenting with a "chef of your own" format, which allows diners to personally design their own menu with the executive chef, tableside. The head chef visits each table giving diners a laundry list of the options in the kitchen. The diner and the chef then discuss preferences and dislikes in regards to the items. If you tell the chef, for example, that you love variations of tuna and handmade pasta, your entrée might be grilled tuna loin with tuna tartare and a side of risotto. The seven-course prix-fixe meal ($67), the only option, is $105 with an optional wine pairing. ✉ *Morrison House, 116 S. Alfred St., Alexandria, VA* ☎ *703/838–8000* ⊕ *www.morrisonhouse.com* ⌂ *Reservations essential* ⊟ *AE, DC, MC, V* ⊘ *No dinner Sun. and Mon.*

$$$$ ✕ **Inn at Little Washington.** A 90-minute drive from the District takes you
FodorsChoice into the Virginia countryside, past hills and farms. Entering the inn is
★ like being swept into a luxurious English country manor in a Merchant-Ivory film. Dinner (without wine) is $108 Sunday to Tuesday; $118 Wednesday to Friday and $148 Saturday. After a first course of tiny canapés, a soup follows—perhaps chilled fruit or creamy leek. Trout smoked over apple wood might come next. Desserts are fanciful and elegant, or choose the cheese plate, delivered on a lifesize, mooing plastic cow. ✉ *Middle and Main Sts., Washington, VA* ☎ *540/675–3800* ⌂ *Reservations essential* ⊟ *MC, V* ⊘ *Closed Tues. in Jan., Mar., July, and Aug.*

$$–$$$$ ✕ **Colvin Run Tavern.** Urban refinement in the suburbs? Well, if anyone was to achieve it, who better than D.C. restaurateur Robert Kinkead, founder of Kinkead's, a popular downtown seafood destination. Colvin Run divides its entrées evenly among seafood, poultry, and meat. The menu changes daily, with consistent options such as roasts (served from a tableside carving cart) and breast of squab with roasted foie gras. The four dining rooms were named by Kinkead to reflect the East Coast regions that inspire this cuisine (Nantucket, Shenandoah, Charleston, and Camden). ✉ *8045 Leesburg Pike, Vienna, VA* ☎ *703/356–9500* ⊕ *www.kinkead.com* ⊟ *AE, D, DC, MC, V* ⊘ *No lunch weekends.*

French

$$$$ ✕ **L'Auberge Chez François.** Tucked into the Virginia countryside, this
FodorsChoice sprawling restaurant serves the German-influenced cuisine of Alsace. The
★ decor is both romantic and kitschy—a fireplace dominates the main dining room, German knickknacks line the walls, and red-jacketed waiters courteously guide you through the meal. Sausage and foie gras served atop sauerkraut, red snapper in a pastry crust for two, and medallions of beef and veal are a few of the generously portioned, out-

standing entrées. You are asked in advance whether you'd like a souf-
flé. Say yes. ✉ *332 Springvale Rd., Great Falls, VA* ☎ *703/759–3800*
⚭ *Reservations essential* 🏛 *Jacket required* 🖃 *AE, D, DC, MC, V*
☺ *Closed Mon. No lunch.*

\$\$–\$\$\$ ✕ **La Bergerie.** One brother does the cooking and the other runs the din-
ing room of this elegant Old Town restaurant, which specializes in the
food of the Basque region of southern France. Try such robust dishes
as duck confit and *pipérade* (scrambled eggs with ham and green peppers), but don't neglect the specials, where some of brother Jean's most
imaginative cooking shows up. Main-course selections usually include
duck, venison, or lamb. Don't forget to order the dessert soufflés or apple
tart in advance. ✉ *218 N. Lee St., Alexandria, VA* ☎ *703/683–1007*
⚭ *Reservations essential* 🏛 *Jacket and tie* 🖃 *AE, D, DC, MC, V* ☺ *No
lunch Sun.*

Italian

\$\$\$\$ ✕ **Maestro.** Hotel dining has long had a bad name, but this restaurant
is trying hard to change that. Inside the state-of-the-art open kitchen,
Chef Fabio Trabocchi emphasizes both traditional Italian cooking and
what he calls *l'evolutione*, his creative takes on the classics. The menu
changes often, but you might find potato ravioli in black-truffle sauce
or oxtail tortellini. Desserts might be bonbons filled with rose, lavender, and peach ice cream, or a chocolate *delice* (chocolate custard
wrapped in a chocolate turban). Two courses (any combination) start
at \$54; the seven-course tasting menu is \$102. A brunch is offered on
Sunday. ✉ *Ritz-Carlton Tysons Corner, 1700 Tysons Blvd., Tysons
Corner, VA* ☎ *703/821–1515 or 703/917–5498* ⚭ *Reservations essential*
🖃 *AE, D, DC, MC, V* ☺ *Closed Mon.*

\$–\$\$ ✕ **Tempo.** In a renovated gas station, Tempo is an unlikely spot for up-
scale suburbanites to dine. But high ceilings and massive windows help
raise the tone of the bright, ornate dining room, and the attentive staff
fits the tony surroundings. Seafood, the kitchen's specialty, dominates
the mainly Northern-Italian menu. Both the sea scallops and the garlic-
and-rosemary–seasoned swordfish are invigorating. For starters, try the
smooth, peppery crab soup. ✉ *4231 Duke St., Alexandria, VA* ☎ *703/
370–7900* 🖃 *AE, D, DC, MC, V* ☺ *No lunch Sat.*

Southwestern

\$–\$\$\$ ✕ **Rio Grande Café.** This Tex-Mex haven is always packed with enthusiastic crowds. While you're waiting for a table order a "swirl," a mix
of frozen sangria and frozen margarita swirled in a frosted beer mug.
The menu goes well beyond standard Tex-Mex fare with grilled offerings like the sizzling fajitas and shrimp brochettes (shrimp, cheese, and
peppers wrapped in bacon) and exotic entrées like quail, goat, and lobster. Big portions and loud crowds make this a great spot for families.
✉ *4301 N. Fairfax Dr., Arlington, VA* ☎ *703/528–3131* 🖃 *AE, D, DC,
MC, V* ⚭ *Reservations not accepted* Ⓜ *Ballston* ✉ *1827 Library St.
Reston, VA* ☎ *703/904–0703* 🖃 *AE, D, DC, MC, V* ⚭ *Reservations
not accepted.*

WHERE TO STAY

FODOR'S CHOICE

Doubletree Guest Suites, Downtown

George Washington University Inn, Foggy Bottom

Holiday Inn Select Bethesda, Bethesda

Hotel Madera, Dupont Circle

Hotel Monaco, Downtown

Hotel Tabard Inn, Downtown

Woodley Park Guest House, Woodley Park

HIGHLY RECOMMENDED

Churchill Hotel, Dupont Circle

Fairmont Washington, Georgetown

Four Seasons Hotel, Georgetown

Hay-Adams Hotel, Downtown

Henley Park Hotel, Downtown

Hotel George, Capitol Hill

Hotel Washington, Downtown

Jefferson Hotel, Downtown

Jurys Normandy Inn, Adams-Morgan

Morrison House, Alexandria

Morrison-Clark Inn, Downtown

Ritz-Carlton Pentagon City, Arlington

Rouge Hotel, Dupont Circle

St. Regis, Downtown

Swissôtel Washington Watergate, Downtown

Willard Inter-Continental, Downtown

Updated by
Robin
Dougherty

Stay in the hotel where Martin Luther King wrote his "I Have a Dream" speech and become inspired to change history. Or sleep in a cozy bed-and-breakfast near the National Zoo and be able to easily pay a morning call to the pandas. Enjoy the history, grandeur, and White House views of the Hay-Adams or Willard Inter-Continental. Or stay up all night in the nightclubby lobby lounge of the Topaz.

Washington has the same broad range of digs of any major city, but also throws in some unique curves. In posh Downtown and Capitol Hill hotels, you can sign a guest register touched by diplomats and then sleep in beds where royalty have rested. You'll also be in walking distance of the National Mall, the Smithsonian, the Library of Congress, and the Capitol.

Penn Quarter, the part of Downtown near the MCI Center, is experiencing a revival. One of the city's newest hotels, the Hotel Monaco, is within the stern facade of the former Tariff Commission Building. But head inside, and you'll find playfully rendered interiors and tip-top service.

Make a reservation in Dupont Circle if you like being around hubbub and close to restaurants, bookstores, and galleries. Brand-name upscale lodgings such as Sofitel, Radisson, and Westin share the neighborhood with chic boutique hotels and B&Bs. For those looking for a respite on a quiet side street, the Hotel Tabard Inn offers its own eclectic kind of cozy, affordable comfort.

Whether you stay in Georgetown at the new Ritz-Carlton or at the Holiday Inn, you'll be able to get an upclose view of the tree-lined district best known for its wealthy and prominent residents. And although Foggy Bottom doesn't have many tourism destinations, staying here puts you close to the State Department and the Kennedy Center.

There are many appealing options in places you might not think to look. Hotels and inns on Connecticut Avenue north of Dupont Circle are close to the Zoo and the National Cathedral, as well as to the shopping and restaurant districts of Adams-Morgan and Dupont Circle. Bethesda hotels give you easy access to the National Institutes of Health, as well as the premier shopping areas of Friendship Heights and Georgetown. Hotels at the foot of Key Bridge in Virginia offer the great views of the District's skyline.

In Virginia, you can take advantage of reasonable prices and the convenience of the Metro, which eliminates the need for parking downtown. There is no true off season in the nation's capital, and lodging can certainly get expensive. The dip in tourism since 9/11, however, has meant that many hotels offer attractive packages, so keep your eyes open for bargains.

Capitol Hill

★ $$$$ ☒ **Hotel George.** At this hip Capitol Hill standout, guest rooms are bright and airy, and portraits of America's first president, by Andy Warhol protégé Steve Kaufman, adorn public areas. The boutique hotel has ample amenities for business travelers and is near Union Station and the Mall. Bistro Bis serves updated versions of classic French dishes. ☒ *15 E St. NW, Capitol Hill 20001* ☎ *202/347–4200 or 800/576–8331* 🖷 *202/347–4213* ⊕ *www.hotelgeorge.com* ➳ *139 rooms* ♦ *Restaurant, room service, in-room data ports, minibars, cable TV, in-room VCRs, gym, steam room, billiards, bar, lobby lounge, meeting rooms, parking (fee)* ⊟ *AE, D, DC, MC, V* Ⓜ *Union Station.*

3

Facilities

The properties listed were chosen because of their beauty, historical significance, location, or value. All hotels in the $$$ and $$$$ categories have concierges; some in the $$ group do, too. Because Washington is an international city with a diverse population and visitors from all over, many hotel staffs are multilingual. Every hotel has no-smoking rooms, and many have no-smoking floors.

We always list a property's facilities but not whether you'll be charged extra to use them, so when pricing accommodations, ask what's included. You can assume that all rooms have private baths, phones, TVs, and air-conditioning unless otherwise noted, and that all hotels operate on the European Plan (with no meals) unless we specify that they use the Continental Plan (CP, with a Continental breakfast), Breakfast Plan (BP, with a full cooked breakfast), Modified American Plan (MAP, with breakfast and dinner), or the Full American Plan (FAP, with all meals).

Reservations

With more than 63,000 guest rooms available in the area, you can almost always find a place to stay—though it's always prudent to reserve. Hotels often fill up with conventioneers, politicians in transit, families, and, in spring, school groups. Hotel rooms in D.C. can be particularly hard to come by during the Cherry Blossom Festival in late March or early April, and also in May, when so many graduate from college. Late October's Marine Corps Marathon also causes increased demand for rooms.

Parking

Hotels' parking fees range from free (usually, but not always, in the suburbs) to $24 (plus tax) per night. This sometimes involves valet parking, with its implied additional gratuities. Street parking is free on Sunday and usually after 6:30 PM. But there are often far more cars searching than there are spaces available, particularly downtown, in Georgetown, and in the upper Connecticut Avenue area. During weekday rush hours many streets are unavailable for parking; illegally parked cars are towed, and reclaiming a car is expensive and very inconvenient. *Read signs carefully*; some are confusing, and the ticket writers are quick.

Prices

Properties are assigned price categories based on the range between their least and most expensive standard double rooms at high season (excluding holidays).

If you're interested in visiting Washington at a calm, less expensive time—and if you can stand semitropical weather—come in August, during the Congressional recess. Rates also drop in late December and January, except around an inauguration.

If high-end prices aren't in your vacation budget, don't automatically assume that a stay in a fancy hotel is out of the question. Weekend, off-season, and special rates (such as American Automobile Association and American Association for Retired Persons discounts) can make rooms more affordable. During times of economic stress, hotels often employ special package rates to increase business, so a little bit of research can pay off in big savings.

WHAT IT COSTS				
$$$$	**$$$**	**$$**	**$**	**¢**
FOR 2 PEOPLE over $270	$205–$270	$150–$205	$100–$150	under $100

Prices are for two people in a standard double room in high season, excluding room tax (14.5% in D.C., 12.5% in MD, and 10.15% in VA). A $3.44 per-night energy charge is also applied to the total.

$$$$ ⌷ **Phoenix Park Hotel.** Named for a park in Dublin, this hotel is across the street from Union Station and only four blocks from the Capitol. A case in the lobby holds a collection of Waterford crystal. Regular rooms, which vary in size, have a Celtic theme, with Irish linen and original artwork. Three penthouse suites have balconies that overlook Union Station; three duplex suites have spiral staircases and fireplaces. At the Dubliner Pub, Irish entertainers perform nightly. ⊠ *520 N. Capitol St. NW, Capitol Hill 20001* ☎ *202/638–6900 or 800/824–5419* 🖷 *202/ 393–3236* ⊕ *www.phoenixparkhotel.com* ⤳ *144 rooms, 6 suites* ⟁ *Restaurant, room service, in-room data ports, minibars, some refrigerators, cable TV, exercise equipment, gym, health club, bar, pub, laundry service, business services, parking (fee)* ⊟ *AE, D, DC, MC, V* Ⓜ *Union Station.*

$$$$ ⌷ **Washington Court Hotel.** Terraced marble stairs lead to a contemporary atrium lobby with a skylight, waterfall, and glass elevator—you may also appreciate the inlaid wood and stained glass that are part of the hotel's original art deco elements. Guest accommodations are roomy, well appointed, and equipped with modern, luxurious furnishings. Convenient to Union Station, the hotel offers a wonderful view of the Capitol. ⊠ *525 New Jersey Ave. NW, Capitol Hill 20001* ☎ *202/628–2100* 🖷 *202/879–7918* ⊕ *www.washingtoncourthotel.com* ⤳ *252 rooms, 12 suites* ⟁ *Restaurant, room service, in-room data ports, cable TV, health club, bar, dry cleaning, laundry service, business services, parking (fee)* ⊟ *AE, D, DC, MC, V* Ⓜ *Union Station.*

$$–$$$ ⌷ **Capitol Hill Suites.** On a quiet residential street beside the Library of Congress, this all-suites hotel's proximity to the U.S. House of Representatives office buildings means that it's often filled with visiting lobbyists when Congress is in session. Guest rooms, which are actually renovated apartments, are large and cozy; there's a fireplace in the sun-filled lobby. ⊠ *200 C St. SE, Capitol Hill 20003* ☎ *202/543–6000, 800/ 424–9165, or 888/627–7811* 🖷 *202/547–2608* ⤳ *152 suites* ⟁ *In-room data ports, kitchenettes, refrigerators, cable TV, gym, health club, lobby lounge, dry cleaning, laundry service, business services, meeting rooms, parking (fee)* ⊟ *AE, D, DC, MC, V* Ⓜ *Capitol South* ⟦◯⟧ *CP.*

$–$$$ ⌷ **Holiday Inn on the Hill.** Expect clean, comfortable rooms and a friendly staff in this hotel, which is convenient to Union Station and the Capitol building. Hotel amenities include a Discovery Zone site for children, with supervised educational games, snacks, and contests. The Senators Sports Grille has a fine collection of D.C. baseball memorabilia, including photographs of various Senators players. ⊠ *415 New Jersey Ave. NW, Capitol Hill 20001* ☎ *202/638–1616 or 800/638–1116* 🖷 *202/638– 0707* ⊕ *www.holiday-inn.com/hotels/wasch* ⤳ *343 rooms, 4 suites* ⟁ *Restaurant, room service, in-room data ports, cable TV, pool, exercise equipment, gym, sauna, bar, children's programs (ages 4–14), laundry service, business services, meeting rooms, parking (fee)* ⊟ *AE, D, DC, MC, V* Ⓜ *Union Station.*

Downtown

$$$$ ⊡ **Grand Hyatt Washington.** In this fanciful high-rise hotel's atrium, a pianist plays Cole Porter tunes on a small island surrounded by a waterfall-fed blue lagoon. The location can't be beat—it's near the Washington Convention Center, two blocks from the MCI Center, and just steps from downtown shops and theaters. You can enter Metro Center—the hub of D.C.'s subway system—directly from the lobby. Rooms that face the atrium have windows that open indoors; if you don't want to be bothered by restaurant noise, ask for a room above the first few floors. Weekend brunch here is very popular. ⊠ *1000 H St. NW, Downtown 20001* ☎ *202/582–1234 or 800/233–1234* 🖷 *202/637–4781* ⊕ *www.grandwashington.hyatt.com* 🛏 *830 rooms, 58 suites* ⚘ *4 restaurants, room service, in-room data ports, minibars, cable TV, indoor pool, health club, 2 bars, business services, meeting rooms, parking (fee), no-smoking rooms* ⊟ *AE, D, DC, MC, V* Ⓜ *Metro Center.*

★ **$$$$** ⊡ **Hay-Adams Hotel.** Two famous Americans—statesman John Hay and historian Henry Adams—once owned homes on the site where this Italian Renaissance–style landmark structure now stands, near Lafayette Park and the White House. The interior is both contemporary and elegant. Many rooms have fireplaces and a view of the White House. An attentive staff assures warm, congenial service, including free car service (until 11:30 AM) to D.C. locations and airports. The Lafayette Room restaurant serves elegant contemporary American cuisine. ⊠ *1 Lafayette Sq. NW, Downtown 20006* ☎ *202/638–6600, 800/424–5054, or 800/853–6807* 🖷 *202/638–2716 or 202/638–3803* ⊕ *www.hayadams.com* 🛏 *125 rooms, 20 suites* ⚘ *Restaurant, room service, in-room data ports, minibars, some refrigerators, cable TV, bar, dry cleaning, laundry service, business services, parking (fee), some pets allowed* ⊟ *AE, D, DC, MC, V* Ⓜ *McPherson Square or Farragut North.*

$$$$
Fodor's Choice
★ ⊡ **Hotel Monaco.** Don't let its former incarnation as the Tariff Commission Building scare you away. Today, the property is a playfully designed boutique hotel. Service is attentive, rooms are brightly furnished in high-energy contemporary patterns, and the Monaco is happy to indulge you and your pets, too. The Poste Brasserie serves contemporary American cuisine. ⊠ *700 F St. NW, Downtown 20002* ☎ *202/628–7177 or 800/649–1202* 🖷 *202/628–7277* ⊕ *www.monaco-dc.com* 🛏 *184 rooms, 16 suites* ⚘ *Restaurant, room service, in-room data ports, in-room safes, gym, laundry service, concierge, parking (fee), some pets allowed* ⊟ *AE, D, DC, MC, V* Ⓜ *Gallery Place/Chinatown.*

★ **$$$$** ⊡ **Jefferson Hotel.** Federal-style elegance abounds at this small luxury hotel. American antiques and original art fill each room, which all have VCRs and CD players (the hotel has videos and CDs to borrow). A high staff-to-guest ratio ensures outstanding service—employees greet you by name, and laundry is hand-ironed and delivered in wicker baskets. The Jefferson restaurant, which serves American cuisine, is a favorite of high-ranking politicos and visiting film stars. The National Geographic Society's Explorer's Hall is next door. ⊠ *1200 16th St. NW, Downtown 20036* ☎ *202/347–2200 or 800/368–5966* 🖷 *202/331–8474* ⊕ *www.loewshotels.com* 🛏 *68 rooms, 32 suites* ⚘ *Restaurant, room service, in-room data ports, some microwaves, cable TV, in-room VCRs, bar, laundry service, business services, parking (fee)* ⊟ *AE, D, DC, MC, V* Ⓜ *Farragut North.*

$$$$ ⊡ **J. W. Marriott.** This modern flagship hotel has a prime location near the White House and next to the National Theatre. The capacious, columned lobby includes a four-story atrium, marble and mahogany accents, and Asian rugs. Rooms have dark-wood furnishings and burgundy and cream accents. The hotel has an entrance to the National Place mall,

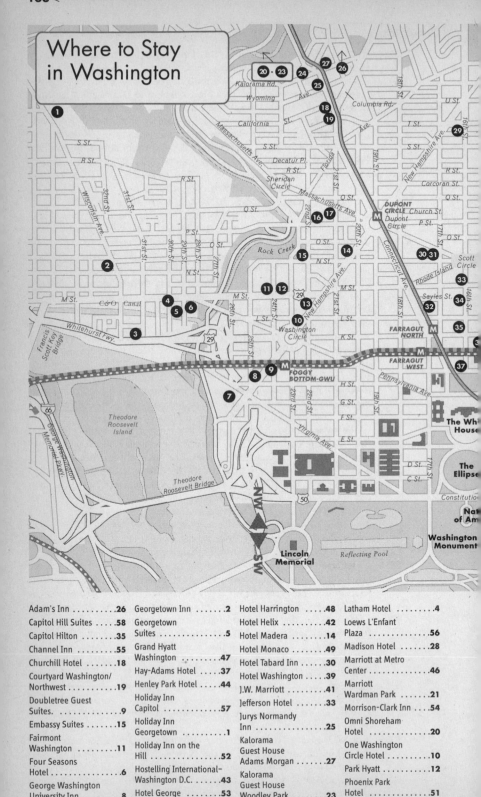

Where to Stay in Washington

CloseUp

WITH CHILDREN?

MAJOR CONVENTION HOTELS (and those on Capitol Hill and the waterfront) don't see many families. It's best to choose a hotel downtown, in Foggy Bottom, uptown, or in Maryland or Virginia. Also, the closer your hotel is to a Metro stop, the quicker you can hit the sightseeing trail.

Consider a stay at an all-suites hotel. This will allow you to spread out and, if you prepare your meals in a kitchenette, keep costs down. A pool may well be essential for a stay with children, and game rooms are a plus.

In Georgetown, the deluxe Four Seasons Hotel offers children's menus and activities, a Tea Time for Tots program, milk and cookies, Web TV, and electronic games in every room. Georgetown Suites has spacious, apartmentlike accommodations. The

Holiday Inn on the Hill is moderately priced and close to the Capitol, Union Station, and the Capital Children's Museum. The Embassy Suites in Foggy Bottom offers Nickelodeon packages (10%–20% discount with a Nick Pack at check-in). The hotel also has a video-game room and a Sony Playstation in every guest room.

Most hotels in Washington allow children under a certain age to stay in their parents' room at no extra charge, but others charge for them as extra adults; be sure to find out the cutoff age for children's discounts.

---

where there are 80 shops and 18 restaurants and cafés. ⊠ 1331 Pennsylvania Ave. NW, Downtown 20004 ☎ 202/393–2000 or 800/228–9290 🖶 202/626–6991 ⊕ www.marriotthotels.com/wasjw ⟿ 772 rooms, 42 suites ↺ 2 restaurants, room service, in-room data ports, in-room safes, some refrigerators, some cable TVs, indoor pool, gym, health club, hair salon, hot tub, massage, sauna, 2 bars, shops, dry cleaning, laundry service, business services, parking (fee) ▤ AE, D, DC, MC, V Ⓜ Metro Center.

$$$$ ▦ **Marriott at Metro Center.** Near the White House, MCI Center, and the Smithsonian museums, the Marriott's virtues include a marble lobby, commissioned artwork, and the popular Metro Grille and Regatta Raw Bar—a handsome two-level mahogany, oak, brass, and marble facility that serves new American cuisine. Rooms are typical of others in the Marriott chain. ⊠ 775 12th St. NW, Downtown 20005 ☎ 202/737–2200 🖶 202/347–5886 ⟿ 456 rooms, 3 suites ↺ Restaurant, grill, room service, in-room data ports, cable TV, indoor pool, gym, health club, hot tub, sauna, bar, dry cleaning, laundry service, business services, meeting rooms, parking (fee) ▤ AE, D, DC, MC, V Ⓜ Metro Center.

$$$$ ▦ **Renaissance Mayflower Hotel.** This 10-story hotel four blocks from the White House opened in 1925 for Calvin Coolidge's inauguration. Franklin Delano Roosevelt wrote "We have nothing to fear but fear itself" in Suite 776, and J. Edgar Hoover ate here at the same table every day for 20 years. Guest rooms are filled with antiques and have marble bathrooms. Contemporary Mediterranean cuisine is served at the Café Promenade restaurant amid silver, crystal, and artful flower arrangements. ⊠ 1127 Connecticut Ave. NW, Downtown 20036 ☎ 202/347–3000 or 800/468–3571 🖶 202/466–9082 ⊕ www.renaissancehotels.com ⟿ 660 rooms, 76 suites ↺ Restaurant, room service, in-room

data ports, refrigerators, cable TV, exercise equipment, gym, bar, laundry service, business services, parking (fee) ▭ *AE, D, DC, MC, V* Ⓜ *Farragut North.*

★ **$$$$** ▦ **St. Regis.** This luxurious hotel, in a bustling business sector near the White House, resembles an updated Italian Renaissance mansion. Amenities found in every room include cordless phones, Frette sheets, Bose radios, and bottled drinking water. The St. Regis Kids Program offers cookies and milk on arrival as well as accredited baby-sitting. The hotel's restaurant serves regional American cuisine. ✉ *923 16th St. NW, Downtown 20006* ☎ *202/638–2626 or 800/325–3535* 🖨 *202/638–4231* 🛏 *179 rooms, 14 suites* ♨ *Restaurant, room service, in-room data ports, in-room safes, minibars, refrigerators, cable TV, exercise equipment, gym, bar, lobby lounge, baby-sitting, business services, meeting rooms, parking (fee), some pets allowed* ▭ *AE, D, DC, MC, V* Ⓜ *McPherson Square.*

$$$$ ▦ **Sofitel Lafayette Square Washington.** If you've come to Washington to be in the center of things, this is a good choice. You can walk to the White House, the Mall museums, and National Theatre, and come back to plushly decorated rooms and a wealth of amenities. The multilingual staff is eager to please. The hotel restaurant, Cafe 15, serves French fare. ✉ *806 15th St. NW, Downtown 20005* ☎ *202/730–8800* 🖨 *202/730–8500* ⊕ *www.sofitel.com* 🛏 *220 rooms, 17 suites* ♨ *Restaurant, bar, room service, in-room data ports, in-room safes, minibars, health club, shop, business services, concierge, some pets allowed* ▭ *AE, D, DC, MC, V* Ⓜ *MacPherson Square.*

$$$$ ▦ **Washington Renaissance Hotel.** A 10-minute walk from the Smithsonian museums, the Renaissance was designed as a business hotel, with the requisite facilities and central location. If you stay here, you'll have free access to the 10,000-square-ft fitness center and its lap pool. The casual restaurant serves regional American food. ✉ *999 9th St. NW, Downtown 20001* ☎ *202/898–9000 or 800/228–9898* 🖨 *202/289–0947* ⊕ *www.renaissancehotels.com* 🛏 *797 rooms, 10 suites* ♨ *Restaurant, coffee shop, snack bar, room service, in-room data ports, minibars, refrigerators, cable TV, indoor pool, gym, health club, hot tub, sauna, 2 bars, business services, parking (fee), some pets allowed* ▭ *AE, D, DC, MC, V* Ⓜ *Chinatown.*

★ **$$$$** ▦ **Willard Inter-Continental.** Popular with those who expect nothing less than perfection, the Willard has long been a favorite of American presidents and other news-makers. Superb service and a wealth of amenities are a hallmark of the hotel, which is just two blocks from the White House. The spectacular beaux arts main lobby has great columns, sparkling chandeliers, mosaic floors, and elaborate ceilings. Period detail is reflected in the rooms, which have elegant yet comfortable turn-of-the-20th-century reproduction furniture, as well as sleek marble bathrooms. Some rooms look out on the Capitol building or the Washington Monument. The hotel's formal restaurant, the Willard Room, has won nationwide acclaim. ✉ *1401 Pennsylvania Ave. NW, Downtown 20004* ☎ *202/628–9100* 🖨 *202/637–7326* ⊕ *www.washington.interconti.com* 🛏 *299 rooms, 42 suites* ♨ *Restaurant, café, room service, in-room data ports, in-room safes, minibars, cable TV, gym, health club, 2 bars, dry cleaning, laundry service, business services, meeting rooms, parking (fee), some pets allowed* ▭ *AE, D, DC, MC, V* Ⓜ *Metro Center.*

$$$–$$$$ ▦ **Capitol Hilton.** Offering both exceptional access to downtown sights and the pleasant experiences that a well-run luxury hotel can provide, the Capitol Hilton also has an 11,000-square-ft health club and day spa. The well-appointed rooms have Biedermeier pieces. Baby-sitting and other child-friendly services are available. Fran O'Briens restaurant serves up chops and seafood, while the fare at Twigs includes American bistro stan-

CloseUp

LODGING ALTERNATIVES

Apartment Rentals

If you want a home base that's roomy enough for a family and comes with cooking facilities, consider a furnished rental. These can save you money, especially if you're traveling with a group. Home-exchange directories sometimes list rentals as well as exchanges.

International Agents *Hideaways International* (✉ 767 Islington St., Portsmouth, NH 03802 ☎ 603/430–4433 or 800/843–4433 🖶 603/430–4444 ⊕ www.hideaways.com), membership $129.

Rental Listings *Washington Post* (⊕ www.washingtonpost.com). *Washington City Paper* (⊕ www.washingtoncitypaper.com)

B&Bs

To find reasonably priced accommodations in small guest houses and private homes, try Bed & Breakfast Accommodations, Ltd., which is staffed weekdays 10–5. It handles about 85 different properties in the area.

Contacts *Bed and Breakfast Accommodations, Ltd.* (☎ 413/582–9888 or 877/893-3233 🖶 413/582–9669 ⊕ www.bedandbreakfastdc.com).

Home Exchanges

If you would like to exchange your home for someone else's, join a home-exchange organization, which will send you its updated listings of available exchanges for a year and will include your own listing in at least one of them. It's up to you to make specific arrangements.

Exchange Clubs *HomeLink International* (🖅 Box 47747, Tampa, FL 33647 ☎ 813/975-9825 or 800/638–3841 🖶 813/910-8144 ⊕ www.homelink. org); $110 yearly for a listing, on-line access, and catalog; $70 without catalog. *Intervac U.S.* (✉ 30 Corte San Fernando, Tiburon, CA 94920 ☎ 800/756–4663 🖶 415/435-7440 ⊕ www.intervacus. com); $105 yearly for a listing, on-line access, and a catalog; $50 without catalog.

Hostels

No matter what your age, you can save on lodging costs by staying at hostels. In some 4,500 locations in more than 70 countries around the world, Hostelling International (HI), the umbrella group for a number of national youth-hostel associations, offers single-sex, dorm-style beds and, at many hostels, rooms for couples and family accommodations. Membership in any HI national hostel association, open to travelers of all ages, allows you to stay in HI-affiliated hostels at member rates; one-year membership is about $28 for adults (C$35 for a two-year minimum membership in Canada, £13.50 in the U.K., A$52 in Australia, and NZ$40 in New Zealand); hostels charge about $10–$30 per night. Members have priority if the hostel is full; they're also eligible for discounts around the world, even on rail and bus travel in some countries.

Organizations *Hostelling International— USA* (✉ 8401 Colesville Rd., Suite 600, Silver Spring, MD 20910 ☎ 301/495–1240 🖶 301/495–6697 ⊕ www.hiayh. org). *Hostelling International—Canada* (✉ 205 Catherine St., Suite 400, Ottawa, Ontario K2P 1C3 ☎ 613/237–7884 or 800/663-5777 🖶 613/237–7868 ⊕ www.hihostels.ca). *YHA England and Wales* (✉ Trevelyan House, Dimple Rd., Matlock, Derbyshire DE4 3YH, U.K. ☎ 0870/870–8808, 0870/ 770–8868, 0162/959-2700 🖶 0870/ 770–6127 ⊕ www.yha.org.uk). *YHA Australia* (✉ 422 Kent St., Sydney, NSW 2001 ☎ 02/9261–1111 🖶 02/9261–1969 ⊕ www.yha.com.au). *YHA New Zealand* (✉ Level 4, Torrens House, 195 Hereford St., Box 436, Christchurch ☎ 03/379–9970 or 0800/278–299 🖶 03/365-4476 ⊕ www.yha.org.nz).

dards and tapas. ✉ *1001 16th St. NW, Downtown 20036* ☎ *202/393–
1000* 🖷 *202/639–5788* 🖅 *544 rooms, 16 suites* ⚒ *Restaurants, room
service, in-room data ports, refrigerators, cable TV, health club, hair salon,
bar, dry cleaning, laundry service, business services, parking (fee)* ▭ *AE,
D, DC, MC, V* Ⓜ *Union Station.*

$$$–$$$$ 🏨 **Madison Hotel.** Luxury and meticulous service prevail in the Madison, which is why the signatures of presidents, prime ministers, sultans, and kings fill the guest register. Deceptively contemporary on the outside, the 15-story building, four blocks from the White House, has a world-class collection of European and Asian antiques. The guest rooms are of average size; each of the suites is decorated individually. The Retreat restaurant serves high tea as well as three meals a day. ✉ *15th and
M Sts. NW, Downtown 20005* ☎ *202/862–1600 or 800/424–8577*
🖷 *202/785–1255* ⊕ *www.themadisonhotel.net* 🖅 *301 rooms, 52 suites*
⚒ *2 restaurants, room service, in-room data ports, minibars, refrigerators, cable TV, gym, massage, sauna, steam room, bar, business services, parking (fee)* ▭ *AE, DC, MC, V* Ⓜ *McPherson Square.*

★ $$$–$$$$ 🏨 **Morrison-Clark Inn.** The elegant merger of two 1864 Victorian town houses, this inn functioned as the Soldiers', Sailors', Marines' and Airmen's Club in the early 1900s. The antiques-filled public rooms have marble fireplaces, bay windows, 14-foot pier mirrors, and porch access, and one house has an ornate porch from 1917. Rooms have neoclassic, French country, or Victorian furnishings and come with soft bathrobes. American cuisine with southern and other regional accents is served at the inn's highly regarded restaurant, which has a popular brunch. ✉ *1015 L St. NW, Downtown 20001* ☎ *202/898–1200 or 800/332–
7898* 🖷 *202/289–8576* 🖅 *42 rooms, 12 suites* ⚒ *Restaurant, room service, in-room data ports, minibars, cable TV, in-room VCRs, exercise equipment, gym, dry cleaning, laundry service, business services, parking (fee)* ▭ *AE, D, DC, MC, V* 🍽 *CP* Ⓜ *Metro Center.*

★ $$$ 🏨 **Hotel Washington.** Since it opened in 1918, the Hotel Washington has been known for its view. Washingtonians bring out-of-towners to the outdoor rooftop bar (open May to October) for cocktails with a view: you can see the White House grounds and the Washington Monument. The hotel sprang from the drawing boards of John Carrère and Thomas Hastings, who designed the New York Public Library. Guest rooms have 18th-century mahogany reproductions and Italian marble bathrooms. Rooms in the interior portion of the hotel are small. ✉ *515 15th St.
NW, Downtown 20004* ☎ *202/638–5900* 🖷 *202/638–4275* ⊕ *www.
hotelwashington.com* 🖅 *344 rooms, 16 suites* ⚒ *2 restaurants, snack bar, room service, in-room data ports, cable TV, exercise equipment, gym, hair salon, sauna, bar, lobby lounge, dry cleaning, laundry service, business services, parking (fee), some pets allowed* ▭ *AE, D, DC, MC, V*
Ⓜ *Metro Center.*

$$ 🏨 **Hotel Helix.** The Helix serves up attitude along with hospitality. The theme here is fame, with blow-ups of pop culture figures ranging from Martin Luther King Jr. to Little Richard. Lava lamps, psychedelic prints, and others objects create a back-to-1965 effect. Some suites have bunk beds and flat-screen TVs with Nintendo and Web TV. The Helix Lounge serves American fare, including comfort food such as meat loaf. ✉ *1430
Rhode Island Ave. NW, Downtown 20002* ☎ *800/706–1202* 🖷 *202/
332–3519* ⊕ *www.hotelhelix.com* 🖅 *160 rooms, 18 suites* ⚒ *Restaurant, room TVs with video games, concierge, in-room safes, gym, parking* ▭ *AE, D, DC, MC, V* Ⓜ *McPherson Square.*

★ $$–$$$ 🏨 **Henley Park Hotel.** A Tudor-style building adorned with gargoyles, this National Historic Trust hotel has the cozy charm of an English country house. Rooms, decorated with Edwardian-style furnishings, are amply fitted with modern amenities. Tea is served daily at 4 PM. The hotel is close to the Washington Convention Center, the Smithsonian museums, and the MCI Sports Arena. The highly acclaimed Coeur de Lion restaurant offers an American menu. ✉ *926 Massachusetts Ave. NW, Downtown 20001* ☎ *202/638–5200 or 800/222–8474* ⊟ *202/638–6740* ⊕ *www.henleypark.com* ➔ *96 rooms, 17 suites* ⚭ *Restaurant, room service, in-room data ports, in-room safes, minibars, refrigerators, cable TV, bar, business services, parking (fee), some pets allowed* ⊟ *AE, D, DC, MC, V* Ⓜ *Metro Center or Gallery Place/Chinatown.*

¢ ▦ **Hotel Harrington.** One of Washington's oldest continuously operating hotels, the Harrington doesn't offer many frills, but it does have low prices and a location right in the center of everything. It's very popular with springtime high school bus tours and with families who like the two-bedroom, two-bathroom deluxe suites. ✉ *436 11th St. NW, Downtown 20004* ☎ *202/628–8140 or 800/424–8532* ⊟ *202/347–3924* ⊕ *www.hotelharrington.com* ➔ *246 rooms, 36 suites* ⚭ *Restaurant, cafeteria, room service, cable TV, hair salon, bar, pub, laundry facilities, business services, meeting rooms, parking (fee), some pets allowed* ⊟ *AE, D, DC, MC, V* Ⓜ *Metro Center.*

¢ ▦ **Hostelling International–Washington D.C.** This well-kept hostel has bunk beds, a small grocery, shared Internet access, and a living room. Rooms are generally dormitory style, without private bathrooms, but families can have their own room if the hostel is not full. Towels and linens are included in the rates. A communal TV room and kitchen are available to all. The maximum stay is 14 days and reservations are highly recommended. College-age travelers predominate, and July through August is the busiest period. ✉ *1009 11th St. NW, Downtown 20001* ☎ *202/737–2333* ⊟ *202/737–1508* ⊕ *www.hiwashingtondc.org* ➔ *270 beds without bath* ⚭ *Laundry facilities; no room phones, no room TVs, no smoking* ⊟ *D, MC, V* Ⓜ *Metro Center.*

Dupont Circle

★ **$$$–$$$$** ▦ **Churchill Hotel.** Head here for comfort and elegance right outside Dupont Circle. All rooms have a small work area, and the building's hilltop location means that many guest rooms have excellent views of Washington. The staff goes out of its way to be helpful; children under 12 stay for free. ✉ *1914 Connecticut Ave. NW, Dupont Circle 20009* ☎ *202/797–2000 or 800/424–2464* ⊟ *202/462–0944* ⊕ *www.thechurchillhotel.com* ➔ *70 rooms, 64 suites* ⚭ *Restaurant, room service, in-room data ports, in-room safes, cable TV, exercise equipment, gym, bar, dry cleaning, laundry service, business services, parking (fee)* ⊟ *AE, D, DC, MC, V* Ⓜ *Dupont Circle.*

$$$–$$$$ ▦ **Westin Fairfax Hotel.** Formerly the childhood home of Al Gore, the intimate Fairfax has an English hunt-club theme and complimentary butler service. It's near Dupont Circle, Georgetown, and the Kennedy Center, and rooms have views of Embassy Row, Georgetown, or the National Cathedral. ✉ *2100 Massachusetts Ave. NW, Dupont Circle 20008* ☎ *202/293–2100 or 800/325–3589* ⊟ *202/293–0641* ➔ *154 rooms, 59 suites* ⚭ *Restaurant, room service, in-room data ports, in-room safes, minibars, cable TV, in-room VCRs, gym, massage, sauna, bar, business services, meeting rooms, parking (fee)* ⊟ *AE, D, DC, MC, V* Ⓜ *Dupont Circle.*

$$–$$$ ▦ **Courtyard Washington/Northwest.** Excellent views of the skyline can be seen from many rooms in this hotel because of its elevation on upper Connecticut Avenue. In the compact but comfortable lobby, complimentary cookies and coffee are served each afternoon. ✉ *1900 Connecticut Ave. NW, Dupont Circle 20009* ☎ *202/332–9300 or 800/842–4211* ⊟ *202/328–7039* ➔ *147 rooms* ⚭ *Restaurant, in-room data* *ports, in-room safes, some minibars, cable TV, pool, exercise equipment, gym, hair salon, bar, lobby lounge, baby-sitting, dry cleaning, laundry facilities, laundry service, business services, meeting rooms, parking (fee)* ▤ *AE, D, DC, MC, V* Ⓜ *Dupont Circle.*

$$–$$$ 🏨 **Radisson Barceló Hotel.** Guest rooms are spacious, with large sitting areas and fluffy bedspreads, at this former apartment building near Dupont Circle and Georgetown. Spanish and Latin fare is served at the Gabriel restaurant, where the Sunday brunch spread—which includes delicacies like suckling pig as well as traditional American favorites—is legendary. ✉ *2121 P St. NW, Dupont Circle 20037* ☎ *202/293–3100 or 800/333–3333* 🖶 *202/857–0134* 🛏 *235 rooms, 65 suites* ⚭ *Restaurant, tapas bar, room service, in-room data ports, cable TV, pool, exercise equipment, gym, sauna, bar, business services, parking (fee)* ▤ *AE, D, DC, MC, V* Ⓜ *Dupont Circle.*

★ **$$–$$$** 🏨 **Rouge Hotel.** This hotel succeeds at bringing Florida's South Beach club scene to D.C. Guest rooms are decorated with swank eye-catching furniture that make them seem like an extension of the hip lobby lounge, where the bartenders are busy concocting sweet new drinks. Bar Rouge, the cocktail lounge, attracts club-going denizens at all hours and serves food nearly around the clock. ✉ *1315 16th St. NW, Dupont Circle 20036* ☎ *202/232–8000 or 800/368–5689* 🖶 *202/667–9827* ⊕ *www. rougehotel.com* 🛏 *137 rooms* ⚭ *Restaurant, café, room service, in-room data ports, in-room safes, some kitchenettes, minibars, some refrigerators, some cable TVs with video games, indoor pool, gym, health club, hair salon, massage, bar, lobby lounge, business services, parking (fee), some pets allowed* ▤ *AE, D, DC, MC, V* Ⓜ *Dupont Circle.*

$$–$$$ 🏨 **Topaz Hotel.** Although the street it's on is sedate, the reputation of the hotel itself is anything but. The hotel's New Age theme is expressed through the colorful walls and art, allusions to enlightenment, and the "power shakes" served in the morning. The popular (and loud) Topaz Bar draws people from all over town. ✉ *1733 N St. NW, Dupont Circle 20036* ☎ *202/393–3000 or 800/424–2950* 🖶 *202/785–9581* ⊕ *www. topazhotel.com* 🛏 *99 rooms* ⚭ *Restaurant, in-room data ports, in-room safes, kitchenettes, minibars, refrigerators, cable TV, bar, dry cleaning, laundry service, business services, meeting rooms, parking (fee)* ▤ *AE, D, DC, MC, V* ⵏⵐ *CP* Ⓜ *Dupont Circle.*

$–$$ 🏨 **Hotel Tabard Inn.** Three Victorian town houses were consolidated to
Fodor'sChoice form the Tabard, one of the oldest hotels in D.C. Although the wooden
★ floorboards are creaky, the hotel is charming, with well-worn Victorian and American Empire pieces filling the interior. Room sizes and facilities vary considerably—one guest room alternates as a private dining room, many rooms share bathrooms—as do the prices. Passes are provided to the nearby YMCA, which has extensive fitness facilities. The contemporary restaurant, with a cozy courtyard, is popular with locals. ✉ *1739 N St. NW, Dupont Circle 20036* ☎ *202/785–1277* 🖶 *202/785–6173* ⊕ *www.tabardinn.com* 🛏 *40 rooms, 25 with bath* ⚭ *Restaurant, in-room data ports, bar, lobby lounge, laundry facilities, business services, parking (fee), some pets allowed; no TV in some rooms* ▤ *AE, D, DC, MC, V* ⵏⵐ *CP* Ⓜ *Dupont Circle.*

$–$$ 🏨 **Windsor Inn.** Near tree-lined New Hampshire Avenue, this bed-and-breakfast is in one of Washington's most attractive neighborhoods. The Phillips Collection and the restaurants and shops of Dupont Circle are all within six blocks. The three-story inn is actually two buildings, and neither has an elevator. Rooms are small but pleasant, and have some amenities expected of larger hotels, like hair dryers and a morning newspaper. In the afternoon sherry is served in the downstairs lobby. ✉ *1842 16th St. NW, Dupont Circle 20009* ☎ *202/667–0300 or 800/423–9111* 🖶 *202/667–4503* 🛏 *36 rooms, 10 suites* ⚭ *Some refriger-*

ators, cable TV, lobby lounge, library, business services ☰ *AE, DC, MC, V* ⋮○⋮ *CP* Ⓜ *Dupont Circle.*

Georgetown

★ **$$$$** ⊡ **Four Seasons Hotel.** Impeccable service and a wealth of amenities have made this a favorite with celebrities, hotel connoisseurs, and families. Rooms are spacious and bright, with original art on the walls. Daily tea is served in the Garden Terrace restaurant. The formal Seasons restaurant offers traditional dishes with an elegant twist, as well as a popular Sunday brunch. ⊠ *2800 Pennsylvania Ave. NW, Georgetown 20007* ☎ *202/342–0444 or 800/332–3442* 🖷 *202/342–1673* ⊕ *www.fourseasons.com/washington* ⇆ *200 rooms, 60 suites* ⚭ *2 restaurants, room service, in-room data ports, in-room safes, minibars, cable TV, pool, gym, health club, hair salon, sauna, spa, bar, lobby lounge, children's programs, concierge, business services, parking (fee), some pets allowed* ☰ *AE, D, DC, MC, V* Ⓜ *Foggy Bottom.*

$$$$ ⊡ **Ritz-Carlton Georgetown.** Part of a mixed-use development that also includes condominiums and a movie theater, D.C.'s second Ritz-Carlton is smaller than its Foggy Bottom sister. Opened in 2003, this Ritz is built on the site of Georgetown's incinerator, right next to the C&O Canal: the smokestack's still there. The hotel is a stone's throw from the waterfront and just a block from M Street, Georgetown's main shopping street. The upper-level rooms that face south have amazing views of the Potomac. ⊠ *3100 South St. NW, Georgetown 20037* ☎ *202/912–4200* 🖷 *202/912–4199* ⊕ *www.ritzcarlton.com/hotels/georgetown* ⇆ *52 rooms, 29 suites* ⚭ *Restaurant, room service, in-room data ports, in-room safes, minibars, health club, bar, lobby lounge, laundry service, meeting rooms, cinema* ☰ *AE, D, DC, MC, V.*

$$$ ⊡ **Georgetown Inn.** Reminiscent of a gentleman's sporting club, this quiet, federal-era, redbrick hotel seems like something from the 1700s. Guest rooms are large and decorated in a colonial style. The hotel, in the heart of historic Georgetown, is near shopping, dining, galleries, and theaters. Free passes to a nearby fitness center are provided. The Daily Grill restaurant serves American cuisine. ⊠ *1310 Wisconsin Ave. NW, Georgetown 20007* ☎ *202/333–8900 or 800/424–2979* 🖷 *202/625–1744* ⊕ *www.georgetowninn.com* ⇆ *86 rooms, 10 suites* ⚭ *Restaurant, room service, in-room data ports, cable TV, gym, bar, business services, parking (fee)* ☰ *AE, D, DC, MC, V* Ⓜ *Foggy Bottom.*

$–$$$ ⊡ **Latham Hotel.** Many of the immaculate, beautifully decorated rooms at this small hotel on the area's fashionable main avenue have treetop views of the Potomac River and the C&O Canal. The hotel is a favorite of diplomats. The polished brass and glass lobby leads to Citronelle, one of the city's best French restaurants. ⊠ *3000 M St. NW, Foggy Bottom 20007* ☎ *202/726–5000 or 800/368–5922* 🖷 *202/337–4250* ⊕ *www.thelatham.com* ⇆ *143 rooms, 21 suites* ⚭ *Restaurant, coffee shop, room service, in-room data ports, cable TV, pool, bar, business services, parking (fee)* ☰ *AE, D, DC, MC, V* Ⓜ *Foggy Bottom.*

$$ ⊡ **Holiday Inn Georgetown.** On the edge of Georgetown, this Holiday Inn is a short walk from dining, shopping, Dumbarton Oaks, the National Cathedral, and Georgetown University. Many guest rooms have a scenic view of the Washington skyline. There's complimentary coffee every morning in the lobby. ⊠ *2101 Wisconsin Ave. NW, Georgetown 20007* ☎ *202/338–4600* 🖷 *202/338–4458* ⇆ *296 rooms, 4 suites* ⚭ *Restaurant, room service, in-room data ports, cable TV, pool, exercise equipment, gym, bar, laundry facilities, business services, meeting rooms, parking (fee), no-smoking floor* ☰ *AE, D, DC, MC, V* Ⓜ *Foggy Bottom.*

$–$$ 🏨 **Georgetown Suites.** If you consider standard hotel rooms cramped and overpriced, you'll find this establishment a welcome surprise. Consisting of two buildings a block apart in the heart of Georgetown, the hotel has suites of varying sizes. All have large kitchens with dishwashers and separate sitting rooms. ⊠ *1111 30th St. NW, Georgetown 20007* ☎ *202/298–7800 or 800/348–7203* 🖷 *202/333–5792* ⊕ *www. georgetownsuites.com* 🛏 *216 suites* ⅋ *In-room data ports, kitchens, microwaves, gym, dry cleaning, laundry facilities, laundry service, parking (fee)* ⊟ *AE, D, DC, MC, V* ⦿❘ *CP* Ⓜ *Foggy Bottom.*

Southwest

$–$$$$ 🏨 **Loews L'Enfant Plaza.** An oasis of calm above a Metro stop and a shopping mall, this hotel is two blocks from the Smithsonian museums and has spectacular views of the river, the Capitol, and monuments. Like other hotels in the Loews chain, this one is comfortably furnished and the staff is well trained and efficient. Business travelers in particular take advantage of its proximity to several government agencies (USDA, USPS, USIA, and DOT). All rooms have coffeemakers, and both bathrooms and bedrooms have TVs and phones. ⊠ *480 L'Enfant Plaza SW, Downtown 20024* ☎ *202/484–1000 or 800/223–0888* 🖷 *202/646–4456* 🛏 *348 rooms, 22 suites* ⅋ *Restaurant, room service, in-room data ports, minibars, refrigerators, cable TV, in-room VCRs, indoor pool, gym, health club, 2 bars, business services, parking (fee), some pets allowed* ⊟ *AE, D, DC, MC, V* Ⓜ *L'Enfant Plaza.*

$–$$$ 🏨 **Holiday Inn Capitol.** One block from the National Air and Space Museum, this large hotel is family friendly but also well equipped for business travelers. The downtown sightseeing trolley stops here, and you can buy discount tickets for NASM's IMAX movies at the front desk. If you buy a drink, you can avail yourself of the all-you-can-eat buffet from 4:30 to 6:30. ⊠ *550 C St. SW, Capitol Hill 20024* ☎ *202/479–4000* 🖷 *202/488–4627* 🛏 *505 rooms, 24 suites* ⅋ *Restaurant, food court, room service, in-room data ports, cable TV, pool, gym, bar, laundry facilities, business services, meeting rooms, parking (fee), no-smoking floor* ⊟ *AE, D, DC, MC, V* Ⓜ *L'Enfant Plaza.*

$–$$ 🏨 **Channel Inn.** The only hotel on Washington's waterfront, this property overlooks the Washington Channel, the marina, and the Potomac River. All rooms have a small balcony and are decorated with either Laura Ashley or similar-style fabrics. Public areas and meeting rooms are given a nautical motif through mahogany panels and marine artifacts. The terrace allows scenic cocktail quaffing and dining in warm weather. The Mall, Smithsonian, Treasury, and several other government offices are nearby. Access to a local health club is free. ⊠ *650 Water St. SW, Downtown 20024* ☎ *202/554–2400 or 800/368–5668* 🖷 *202/863–1164* ⊕ *www.channelinn.com* 🛏 *100 rooms, 4 suites* ⅋ *Restaurant, café, room service, in-room data ports, cable TV, pool, bar, meeting rooms, free parking* ⊟ *AE, D, DC, MC, V* Ⓜ *Waterfront.*

Northwest/Upper Connecticut Avenue

$$$$ 🏨 **Marriott Wardman Park.** With over a thousand rooms, this indomitable redbrick Victorian structure is the grand dame of Washington hotels. Off Connecticut Avenue, the Marriott has spectacular views of Rock Creek Park, and is a half-mile from Adams-Morgan and the National Zoo. Guest rooms and public areas of the older 10-story section are traditionally furnished. Rooms in the newer convention-ready main complex are contemporary, with chrome and glass touches and in-room data ports. ⊠ *2660 Woodley Rd. NW, Woodley Park 20008* ☎ *202/328–2000 or 800/228–9290* 🖷 *202/234–0015* ⊕ *www.wardmanpark.com*

↘ *1,338 rooms, 125 suites* ☊ *2 restaurants, coffee shop, room service, some in-room data ports, some refrigerators, cable TV, 2 pools, exercise equipment, gym, health club, spa, bar, pub, baby-sitting, laundry service, business services, convention center, meeting rooms, parking (fee), some pets allowed (fee)* ☰ *AE, D, DC, MC, V* Ⓜ *Woodley Park/Zoo.*

$$$$ ⊡ **Omni Shoreham Hotel.** An immense facility with seven ballrooms, this hotel has hosted the world's rich and famous since 1930, when its art deco– and Renaissance-style lobby opened for business. It's still a busy place, with black-tie political events held in its famed Regency ballroom on many nights. Rooms have cherry-wood furniture and marble-floor baths with phones and hair dryers. The hotel is a moderate walk from Rock Creek Park, Adams-Morgan, and the National Zoo. ⊠ *2500 Calvert St. NW, Woodley Park 20008* ☏ *202/234–0700 or 800/843–6664* ⊟ *202/756–5145* ↘ *836 rooms, 24 suites* ☊ *Restaurant, snack bar, room service, in-room data ports, minibars, cable TV, pool, gym, health club, bar, shops, dry cleaning, laundry service, business services, parking (fee), some pets allowed* ☰ *AE, D, DC, MC, V* Ⓜ *Woodley Park/Zoo.*

★ $–$$ ⊡ **Jurys Normandy Inn.** On a quiet street in the embassy area of Connecticut Avenue stands this small hotel. The cozy rooms come with coffeemakers and are attractively decorated with colonial reproduction furniture. Each Tuesday evening a wine-and-cheese reception is held for guests. Complimentary coffee and tea are available in the morning and afternoon. ⊠ *2118 Wyoming Ave. NW, Adams-Morgan 20008* ☏ *202/483–1350, 800/424–3729, or 800/842–3729* ⊟ *202/387–8241* ⊕ *www.jurysdoyle.com* ↘ *75 rooms* ☊ *In-room data ports, in-room safes, refrigerators, cable TV, library, parking (fee)* ☰ *AE, D, DC, MC, V* ⦿I *CP* Ⓜ *Dupont Circle.*

$–$$ ⊡ **Windsor Park Hotel.** The rooms are tiny and the hallways small, but the location (at the foot of Kalorama Circle overlooking Rock Creek Park) can't be beat. Those who don't mind a bit of a walk can easily get to the National Zoo, Dupont Circle, and Adams-Morgan, all within a mile of the hotel. Street parking can be difficult, but a reasonably priced garage is two blocks away. ⊠ *2116 Kalorama Rd. NW, Adams-Morgan 20008* ☏ *202/483–7700 or 800/247–3064* ⊟ *202/332–4547* ⊕ *www.windsorparkhotel.com* ↘ *38 rooms, 5 suites* ☊ *In-room data ports, refrigerators, cable TV, business services* ☰ *AE, D, DC, MC, V* ⦿I *CP* Ⓜ *Woodley Park/Zoo.*

¢–$ ⊡ **Adam's Inn.** This cozy and rustic bed-and-breakfast is in the heart of the city. Spread throughout three residential town houses, the inn is near Adams-Morgan, the zoo, and Dupont Circle. The Victorian-style rooms are small but comfortable. Many rooms share baths, but those that do also have a sink in the room. A shared kitchen and limited garage parking are available. Rooms don't have phones, but there are pay phones in the lobby, and the reception staff takes messages. ⊠ *1744 Lanier Pl. NW, Woodley Park 20009* ☏ *202/745–3600 or 800/578–6807* ⊟ *202/319–7958* ⊕ *www.adamsinn.com* ↘ *25 rooms, 15 with bath* ☊ *Laundry facilities, laundry service, business services, parking (fee); no room phones, no room TVs* ☰ *AE, D, DC, MC, V* ⦿I *CP* Ⓜ *Woodley Park/Zoo.*

¢–$ ⊡ **Woodley Park Guest House.** This comfortable, well-appointed B&B is right at the entrance to the Metro nearest the zoo, close to Adams-Morgan and Rock Creek Park, and therefore a short subway ride from downtown attractions. Conversation between guests is encouraged at the communal breakfast. ⊠ *2647 Woodley Rd. NW, Woodley Park 20008* ☏ *202/667–0218 or 800/667–0218* ⊟ *202/667–1080* ⊕ *www.woodleyparkguesthouse.com* ↘ *17 rooms, 11 with bath* ☊ *In-room data ports; no smoking* ☰ *AE, DC, MC, V* ⦿I *CP* Ⓜ *Woodley Park/Zoo.*

FodorśChoice
★

¢ 🏨 **Kalorama Guest House-Adams Morgan.** Like its sister property in Woodley Park, this Adams-Morgan location has been created out of old town houses, in this case ones built in 1905. The rooms, which vary in size, are furnished with 19th-century antiques. Bay windows and cozy furnishing are inside, and lively Adams-Morgan is outside. Dupont Circle is a 20-minute walk away. ⊠ *1845 Mintwood Pl. NW, Adams-Morgan 20008* ☎ *202/667–6369* 🖷 *202/319–1262* 🛏 *31 rooms, 14 with bath, 6 suites* ⚸ *Internet, parking (fee); no phones in some rooms, no TV in some rooms, no smoking* 🖭 *AE, DC, MC, V* ⫶◯⫶ *CP* Ⓜ *Woodley Park.*

¢ 🏨 **Kalorama Guest House–Woodley Park.** Two elegantly restored Victorian town houses make for comfortable and convenient lodging just north of Dupont Circle. Rooms vary in size and are furnished with 19th-century antiques. You can walk to the zoo and the National Cathedral from here. ⊠ *2700 Cathedral Ave. NW, Woodley Park 20008* ☎ *202/328–0860* 🖷 *202/328–8730* 🛏 *19 rooms, 13 with bath, 2 suites* ⚸ *Internet, parking (fee); no smoking* 🖭 *AE, DC, MC, V* ⫶◯⫶ *CP* Ⓜ *Woodley Park.*

West End/Foggy Bottom

★ $$$$ 🏨 **Fairmont Washington.** Contemporary and traditional meet at this stylish hotel at the Georgetown end of downtown Washington. The glassed-in lobby and about a third of the bright, airy rooms overlook the central courtyard and gardens—a popular spot for weddings. The informal Bistro restaurant serves contemporary American cuisine and has courtyard dining; there's a champagne brunch Sundays in the Colonnade room. The fitness center is one of the best in the city. ⊠ *2401 M St. NW, Georgetown 20037* ☎ *202/429–2400 or 877/222–2266* 🖷 *202/457–5010* ⊕ *www.fairmont.com* 🛏 *406 rooms, 9 suites* ⚸ *Restaurant, café, room service, in-room data ports, in-room safes, minibars, cable TV, indoor pool, gym, health club, hot tub, massage, sauna, steam room, racquetball, squash, bar, lobby lounge, business services, parking (fee), some pets allowed* 🖭 *AE, D, DC, MC, V* Ⓜ *Foggy Bottom/GWU.*

$$$$ 🏨 **Ritz-Carlton Washington, D.C.** Here you'll find everything you'd expect from a Ritz, as well as a Japanese water garden and the chance of catching a glimpse of basketball superstar (and Washington Wizards owner) Michael Jordan, who lives in the residence side of this hotel. Those staying here have lobby access to the shopping complex next door, as well as the complimentary use of the Sports Club/LA. Some rooms have private elevators. Both the White House and Georgetown are nearby. ⊠ *1150 22nd St. NW, Foggy Bottom 20037* ☎ *202/835–0500 or 800/241–3333* 🖷 *202/835–1588* 🛏 *267 rooms, 33 suites* ⚸ *Restaurant, café, room service, in-room data ports, in-room safes, refrigerators, cable TV, pool, gym, health club, hair salon, hot tub, massage, sauna, spa, steam room, bar, lobby lounge, baby-sitting, business services, parking (fee)* 🖭 *AE, D, DC, MC, V* Ⓜ *Foggy Bottom/GWU.*

$$$–$$$$ 🏨 **Embassy Suites.** Plants cascade over balconies beneath a skylight in this modern hotel's atrium, which is filled with classical columns, plaster lions, wrought-iron lanterns, waterfalls, and tall palms. Within walking distance of Georgetown, the Kennedy Center, and Dupont Circle, the suites here are suitable for both business travelers and families. Beverages are complimentary at the nightly manager's reception. The Italian restaurant, Panevino, serves lunch and dinner. ⊠ *1250 22nd St. NW, Downtown 20037* ☎ *202/857–3388 or 800/362–2779* 🖷 *202/293–3173* ⊕ *www.embassysuites.com* 🛏 *318 suites* ⚸ *Restaurant, room service, in-room data ports, minibars, microwaves, refrigerators, cable TV, indoor pool, exercise equipment, health club, hot tub, bar, laundry ser-*

vice, business services, parking (fee) ▣ *AE, D, DC, MC, V* ⍟ *BP*
Ⓜ *Foggy Bottom/GWU or Dupont Circle.*

$$–$$$$ 🏨 **George Washington University Inn.** This boutique hotel is in a quiet neigh-
FodorśChoice borhood a few blocks from the Kennedy Center, the State Department,
★ and George Washington University. Wrought-iron gates lead through a
courtyard up to the hotel's front entrance, where beveled glass doors
open into a small lobby floored in gray marble. Rooms, which vary in
size and configuration, have colonial-style furniture. The nearby Bally
fitness center is free for those staying here. ✉ *824 New Hampshire Ave.
NW, Foggy Bottom 20037* ☎ *202/337–6620 or 800/426–4455* 🖷 *202/
298–7499* ⊕ *www.gwuinn.com* ↰ *64 rooms, 31 suites* ⅃ *Restaurant,
room service, in-room data ports, some kitchenettes, microwaves, re-
frigerators, cable TV, hair salon, bar, laundry facilities, laundry service,
business services, meeting rooms, parking (fee)* ▣ *AE, DC, MC, V*
Ⓜ *Foggy Bottom/GWU.*

$$–$$$$ 🏨 **Hotel Madera.** In a quiet neighborhood of office buildings, embassies,
FodorśChoice and other fine hotels, this hotel is close to Dupont Circle as well as shops
★ and restaurants. Many rooms have excellent views of the city, Rock Creek
Park, and Georgetown. The adjoining L'Etoile Restaurant is open and
sunny, with outdoor dining in season. ✉ *1310 New Hampshire Ave.
NW, Dupont Circle 20036* ☎ *202/296–7600 or 800/368–5691* 🖷 *202/
293–2476* ⊕ *www.hotelmadera.com* ↰ *82 rooms* ⅃ *In-room data
ports, in-room safes, some kitchenettes, minibars, microwaves, refrigerators, cable TV, bar, business services, meeting rooms, parking (fee)*
▣ *AE, D, DC, MC, V* Ⓜ *Dupont Circle.*

$$–$$$$ 🏨 **One Washington Circle Hotel.** The combination of elegant rooms and
facilities and a coveted location makes this hotel a relative bargain. The
suites feel like well-furnished apartments, with separate bedrooms, liv-
ing rooms, dining areas, balconies, and some full kitchens. The Amer-
ican-style Circle Bistro is popular with locals who come for the food
and live music. ✉ *1 Washington Circle NW, Foggy Bottom 20037*
☎ *202/872–1680 or 800/424–9671* 🖷 *202/223–3961* ⊕ *www.
thecirclehotel.com* ↰ *151 suites* ⅃ *Restaurant, room service, in-room
data ports, some kitchens, minibars, refrigerators, cable TV, pool, gym,
bar, piano, dry cleaning, laundry facilities, laundry service, business
services, meeting rooms, parking (fee)* ▣ *AE, D, DC, MC, V* Ⓜ *Foggy
Bottom/GWU.*

$$–$$$$ 🏨 **Park Hyatt.** Original artworks, some by Picasso, Matisse, and Calder,
grace the guest rooms and public spaces of this luxurious modern hotel,
about four blocks from the eastern end of Georgetown and just off M
Street. Rooms have built-in armoires and goose-down duvets, and specially commissioned artwork. The Melrose restaurant, which specializes in seafood, has courtyard dining beside a cascading fountain. There's
also a Picasso at its entryway. ✉ *1201 24th St. NW, Foggy Bottom 20037*
☎ *202/789–1234 or 800/228–9000* 🖷 *202/457–8823* ↰ *93 rooms, 131
suites* ⅃ *Restaurant, café, room service, in-room data ports, refrigerators, cable TV, pool, gym, health club, hair salon, hot tub, massage, sauna,
spa, steam room, bar, lobby lounge, business services, parking (fee)*
▣ *AE, D, DC, MC, V* Ⓜ *Foggy Bottom/GWU.*

★ $$–$$$$ 🏨 **Swissôtel Washington Watergate.** The Watergate is on the Potomac River,
near the Kennedy Center and Georgetown. Originally intended as apart-
ments, the guest rooms are large, and all have walk-in closets, fax ma-
chines, and either full kitchens or wet bars. The restaurant Jeffrey's, a
favorite of Laura Bush, serves the food of Austin chef David Garrido,
who makes sophisticated Southwestern dishes. ✉ *2650 Virginia Ave.
NW, Downtown 20037* ☎ *202/965–2300 or 800/424–2736* 🖷 *202/337–
7915* ↰ *106 rooms, 146 suites* ⅃ *Restaurant, room service, in-room
data ports, in-room safes, some kitchens, minibars, refrigerators, cable*

TV, *indoor pool, gym, health club, hair salon, hot tub, massage, bar, business services, parking (fee), some pets allowed* ⊟ *AE, D, DC, MC, V* Ⓜ *Foggy Bottom/GWU.*

$–$$$ 🏨 **Doubletree Guest Suites.** Among the row houses on this stretch of
Fodor'sChoice New Hampshire Avenue, you might not realize at first how close you
★ are to the Kennedy Center and Georgetown. This all-suites hotel has
a tiny lobby, but its suites have full kitchens, separate bedrooms, and
living-dining areas with desks, dining tables, and sofa beds. The
rooftop pool provides a place to relax after sightseeing in the summer.
Guests receive chocolate-chip cookies upon arrival and have privileges
at a nearby health club. ⊠ *801 New Hampshire Ave. NW, Downtown
20037* ☎ *202/785–2000 or 800/222–8733* ☎ *202/785–9485* ✍ *105
suites* ⟁ *Room service, in-room data ports, kitchens, outdoor pool,
dry cleaning, laundry facilities, parking (fee)* ⊟ *AE, D, DC, MC, V*
Ⓜ *Foggy Bottom/GWU.*

Suburban Maryland

$$$$ 🏨 **Embassy Suites.** Shopping and sightseeing couldn't be more convenient
at this hotel, which is next to the Chevy Chase Pavilion mall and an el-
evator ride up from the Friendship Heights Metro Station. Each suite
includes a table suitable for dining and working. The fitness center has
more than 20 exercise stations and a personal trainer available at no
charge. Evening cocktails are offered daily in the sun-filled atrium. You
can only get dinner through room service, but many restaurants are on
the same block as the hotel. ⊠ *4300 Military Rd., Washington, DC 20015*
☎ *202/362 9300 or 800/362 2779* ☎ *202/686 3405* ⊕ *www.
embassysuites.com* ✍ *198 suites* ⟁ *Room service, indoor pool, health
club, laundry service, parking (fee), no-smoking rooms* ⊟ *AE, D, DC,
MC, V* Ⓜ *Friendship Heights* ¶◎¶ *BP.*

$$$ 🏨 **Hyatt Regency Bethesda.** The sights of downtown Washington are about
15 minutes by Metro from this hotel atop the Bethesda Metro station
on Wisconsin Avenue, the main artery between Bethesda and Georgetown. The atrium lobby has ferns and glass elevators. Some rooms have
fax machines. The Hyatt is an easy walk from Bethesda's burgeoning
restaurant district, and an adjacent plaza has a multiplex. ⊠ *1 Bethesda
Metro Center, 7400 block of Wisconsin Ave., Bethesda, MD 20814*
☎ *301/657–1234 or 800/233–1234* ☎ *301/657–6453* ✍ *390 rooms,
5 suites* ⟁ *Restaurant, café, room service, in-room data ports, cable TV,
indoor pool, exercise equipment, gym, health club, bar, lobby lounge,
laundry service, business services, convention center, meeting rooms, parking (fee)* ⊟ *AE, D, DC, MC, V* Ⓜ *Bethesda.*

$$–$$$ 🏨 **Four Points Sheraton.** Just south of the National Institutes of Health
and the Naval Medical Center, this hotel is particularly popular with
government employees and business travelers. But its heavily discounted
weekend rates attract vacationers who don't mind being just outside of
D.C. Rooms are bright and cheery, in rich navy with gold accents. The
hotel has an outdoor Olympic-size swimming pool and a washer, dryer,
and microwave on each floor. The popular Chatters Restaurant and Sports
Bar has wide-screen TVs, a pool table, a jukebox, and seasonal outdoor
dining. ⊠ *8400 Wisconsin Ave., Bethesda, MD 20814* ☎ *301/654–1000
or 800/272–6232* ☎ *301/986–1715* ✍ *164 rooms* ⟁ *Restaurant, in-
room data ports, refrigerators, pool, gym, hair salon, laundry facilities,
meeting rooms, parking (fee)* ⊟ *AE, D, DC, MC, V* ¶◎¶ *CP* Ⓜ *Medical Center.*

$$–$$$ 🏨 **Holiday Inn Chevy Chase.** Two blocks from the Friendship Heights Metro
on the D.C. border, this comfortable hotel is in the heart of the upscale
Chevy Chase shopping district. Dining options are plentiful—the Av-

enue Deli and Julian's restaurant are in the hotel, the nearby Chevy Chase Pavilion and Mazza Gallerie malls have family-style restaurants, and you'll find a wealth of good dining choices one Metro stop away in Bethesda or a 10-minute drive down Wisconsin Avenue into Georgetown. A large outdoor swimming pool is set near the hotel's beautiful rose garden terrace, a popular spot for weddings. ⊠ *5520 Wisconsin Ave., Chevy Chase, MD 20815* ☎ *301/656–1500* 🖷 *301/656–5045* 🗗 *203 rooms, 10 suites* ♨ *Restaurants, snack bar, room service, in-room data ports, cable TV, pool, gym, bar, laundry facilities, business services, meeting rooms, parking (fee), some pets allowed* ⊟ *AE, D, DC, MC, V* ¶◎¶ *CP* Ⓜ *Friendship Heights.*

$–$$$
Fodor'sChoice
★

🖭 **Holiday Inn Select Bethesda.** Slightly more upscale in appearance and services than its sibling in Chevy Chase, overnight stays at this inn promise comfort and convenience. The hotel provides a free shuttle to the nearby Metro, the National Institutes of Health, and the Naval Medical Center. ⊠ *8120 Wisconsin Ave., Bethesda, MD 20814,* ☎ *301/652–2000 or 877/888–3001* 🖷 *301/652–4525* 🗗 *269 rooms, 6 suites* ♨ *Restaurant, in-room data ports, cable TV, pool, exercise equipment, gym, bar, laundry facilities, business services, meeting rooms, parking (fee)* ⊟ *AE, D, DC, MC, V* ¶◎¶ *CP.*

$–$$$
🖭 **Marriott Residence Inn Bethesda Downtown.** In the heart of downtown Bethesda, this all-suites hotel caters primarily to business travelers who stay for several nights. But if you're looking for an affordable home-away-from-home, this is a great option. There are fully equipped kitchens—complete with standard-size refrigerator and dishwasher, plates, and utensils—and comfortable furnishings in the one- and two-bedroom suites. The many complimentary services also include grocery shopping, a breakfast buffet, and evening cocktail and dessert receptions. A number of restaurants are within walking distance. ⊠ *7335 Wisconsin Ave., Bethesda, MD 20814* ☎ *301/718–0200 or 800/331–3131* 🖷 *301/718–0679 or 301/913–0197* 🗗 *187 suites* ♨ *In-room data ports, kitchens, cable TV, pool, gym, sauna, laundry facilities, business services, airport shuttle, parking (fee)* ⊟ *AE, D, DC, MC, V* ¶◎¶ *CP.*

$$
🖭 **Bethesda Court Hotel.** Bright burgundy awnings frame the entrance to this comfortable, intimate, three-story Marriott property, where there's a lovely and well-tended courtyard. The relaxed hotel is two blocks from the Bethesda Metro and set back from busy Wisconsin Avenue. An evening tea with cookies and chocolates is complimentary, as are limousine service and shuttles to the National Institutes of Health. ⊠ *7740 Wisconsin Ave., Bethesda, MD 20814* ☎ *301/656–2100 or 800/874–0050* 🖷 *301/986–0375* ⊕ *www.tbchotels.com* 🗗 *75 rooms, 1 suite* ♨ *In-room data ports, in-room fax, in-room safes, refrigerators, cable TV, gym, laundry facilities, free parking* ⊟ *AE, D, DC, MC, V* ¶◎¶ *CP* Ⓜ *Bethesda.*

¢–$$
🖭 **American Inn of Bethesda.** At the north end of downtown Bethesda, the American Inn is five blocks from the Metro and is within walking distance of restaurants and nightclubs. Rooms at this budget-friendly hotel are clean, well-furnished, and bright. Guapo's restaurant, on the premises, serves moderately priced Tex-Mex fare. The hotel provides a free shuttle to the National Institutes of Health and the Naval Hospital. ⊠ *8130 Wisconsin Ave., Bethesda, MD 20814* ☎ *301/656–9300 or 800/323–7081* 🖷 *301/656–2907* ⊕ *www.american-inn.com* 🗗 *75 rooms, 1 suite* ♨ *Restaurant, in-room data ports, refrigerators, cable TV, pool, hair salon, bar, laundry facilities, laundry service, business services, meeting rooms, free parking* ⊟ *AE, D, DC, MC, V* ¶◎¶ *CP* Ⓜ *Bethesda.*

Suburban Virginia

★ $$$$ ⊞ **Ritz-Carlton Pentagon City.** The 18-story Ritz-Carlton at Pentagon City is more convenient to downtown Washington than many D.C. hotels. Guest rooms have mahogany furniture and lots of natural light. Public areas are decorated in a Virginia hunt country motif. Many upper rooms on the Potomac side have views of the monuments across the river. The lobby lounge serves meals and has an entrance to the Fashion Centre shopping mall, which has cinemas, a food court, 150 shops, and an underground Metro station. ✉ *1250 S. Hayes St., Arlington, VA 22202* ☎ *703/415–5000 or 800/241–3333* 🖷 *703/415–5060* ⊕ *www.ritzcarlton. com* 🛏 *345 rooms, 21 suites ⅁ Restaurant, room service, in-room data ports, in-room fax, in-room safes, minibars, cable TV, indoor pool, gym, health club, hot tub, massage, sauna, bar, lobby lounge, shops, laundry service, business services, convention center, meeting rooms, airport shuttle, parking (fee)* ⊟ *AE, D, DC, MC, V* Ⓜ *Pentagon City.*

$$$–$$$$ ⊞ **Embassy Suites Old Town Alexandria.** Adjacent to Alexandria's landmark George Washington Masonic Temple sits this modern all-suites hotel. There is a playroom for children. A free shuttle is available to transport you to the scenic Alexandria riverfront, which has shops and restaurants. A cooked-to-order breakfast is complimentary, as is the cocktail reception every evening. ✉ *1900 Diagonal Rd., Alexandria, VA 22314* ☎ *703/684–5900 or 800/362–2779* 🖷 *703/684–1403* 🛏 *268 suites ⅁ Restaurant, in-room data ports, refrigerators, cable TV, indoor pool, gym, hot tub, sauna, laundry service, business services, meeting rooms, parking (fee)* ⊟ *AE, D, DC, MC, V* ⋈ *BP* Ⓜ *King Street.*

$$–$$$$ ⊞ **Crystal City Marriott.** A business hotel in the heart of Crystal City, close to Ronald Reagan National Airport and the Pentagon, this Marriott is among a cluster of office buildings. The Smithsonian museums and Mall are just minutes away by Metro. The lobby, with lush plants, a marble floor, and art deco fixtures, is more luxurious than the rooms, which are tidy and have traditionally styled furniture. ✉ *1999 Jefferson Davis Hwy., Arlington, VA 22202* ☎ *703/413–5500 or 800/228–9290* 🖷 *703/413–0192* 🛏 *343 rooms, 15 suites ⅁ Restaurant, room service, in-room data ports, cable TV, indoor pool, exercise equipment, health club, hair salon, hot tub, sauna, bar, dry cleaning, laundry facilities, laundry service, business services, meeting rooms, airport shuttle, parking (fee)* ⊟ *AE, D, DC, MC, V* Ⓜ *Crystal City.*

$$–$$$$ ⊞ **Key Bridge Marriott.** A short walk across the Key Bridge from Georgetown, this Marriott is three blocks from a Metro stop, allowing for easy access to Washington's major sights. The hotel even provides a shuttle to the station. Rooms on the Potomac side have excellent Washington views, as does the rooftop restaurant. ✉ *1401 Lee Hwy., Arlington, VA 22209* ☎ *703/524–6400 or 800/228–9290* 🖷 *703/524–8964* 🛏 *588 rooms, 22 suites ⅁ 2 restaurants, room service, in-room data ports, microwaves, cable TV, indoor pool, exercise equipment, health club, hair salon, hot tub, 2 bars, lobby lounge, laundry facilities, laundry service, business services, meeting rooms, parking (fee)* ⊟ *AE, D, DC, MC, V* Ⓜ *Rosslyn.*

★ $$–$$$$ ⊞ **Morrison House.** The architecture, parquet floors, crystal chandeliers, decorative fireplaces, and furnishings of Morrison House are so faithful to the federal period (1790–1820) that it's often mistaken for a renovation rather than a structure built from scratch in 1985. The hotel blends Early American charm with modern conveniences. Some rooms have fireplaces, and all have four-poster beds. The popular and refreshing Elysium Restaurant serves American contemporary cuisine. The hotel is in the heart of Old Town Alexandria, seven blocks from the train and Metro stations. ✉ *116 S. Alfred St., Alexandria, VA*

22314 ☎ 703/838–8000 or 800/367–0800 ⓑ 703/684–6283 ⊕ *www. morrisonhouse.com* ☜ *42 rooms, 3 suites* ⚇ *2 restaurants, dining room, room service, in-room data ports, cable TV, in-room VCRs, bar, piano bar, parking (fee)* ▤ *AE, DC, MC, V* Ⓜ *King Street.*

$$–$$$ 🖭 **Hilton Arlington and Towers.** Traveling downtown is easy from this hotel, just above the Ballston Metro stop. Rooms make use of neutral colors and contemporary light-wood furniture, and all the suites have hot tubs. Entry to a nearby fitness club is available for a fee. The hotel has direct access via a skywalk to an adjacent shopping mall. ⊠ *950 N. Stafford St., Arlington, VA 22203* ☎ *703/528–6000 or 800/445–8667* ⓑ *703/812–5127* ☜ *204 rooms, 5 suites* ⚇ *Restaurant, in-room data ports, cable TV, bar, laundry service, business services, meeting rooms, parking (fee)* ▤ *AE, D, DC, MC, V* Ⓜ *Ballston.*

$$–$$$ 🖭 **Marriott Residence Inn Arlington Pentagon City.** The view across the Potomac of the D.C. skyline and the monuments is magnificent from this all-suites high-rise. Adjacent to the Pentagon, it's one block from the Pentagon City Fashion Centre mall, which has movies theaters, a food court, 150 shops, and a Metro stop. All suites have full kitchens with dishwashers, ice makers, coffeemakers, toasters, dishes, and utensils. Complimentary services include grocery shopping, daily newspaper, breakfast, light dinner Monday to Wednesday, dessert buffet on Thursday evening, and transportation to Ronald Reagan National Airport. ⊠ *550 Army Navy Dr., Arlington, VA 22202* ☎ *703/413–6630* ⓑ *703/418– 1751* ☜ *299 suites* ⚇ *Picnic area, in-room data ports, kitchens, microwaves, refrigerators, cable TV, indoor pool, exercise equipment, gym, hair salon, hot tub, dry cleaning, laundry facilities, laundry service, business services, meeting rooms, airport shuttle, parking (fee), no-smoking rooms* ▤ *AE, D, DC, MC, V* ⦿ *CP* Ⓜ *Pentagon City.*

$$ 🖭 **Holiday Inn Arlington at Ballston.** You can get in and out of Washington quickly from this hotel, two blocks from a Metro station. Especially comfortable for business travelers, rooms have spacious work spaces, plus coffee and tea makers. Sightseers can take advantage of the hotel's proximity to Arlington National Cemetery, Iwo Jima, and downtown monuments and museums. ⊠ *4610 N. Fairfax Dr., Arlington, VA 22203* ☎ *703/243–9800* ⓑ *703/527–2677* ☜ *219 rooms, 2 suites* ⚇ *Restaurant, room service, in-room data ports, cable TV with video games, pool, gym, bar, laundry facilities, business services* ▤ *AE, D, DC, MC, V* Ⓜ *Ballston.*

$–$$ 🖭 **Days Inn Crystal City.** On Route 1 between the Pentagon and National Airport, this eight-floor hotel is only four Metro stops from the Smithsonian. There is free shuttle service to nearby shops and Ronald Reagan National Airport. The Crystal City Underground—with its many shops and restaurants and a Metro stop—is a very short walk away. ⊠ *2020 Jefferson Davis Hwy., Rte. 1, Arlington, VA 22202* ☎ *703/920– 8600* ⓑ *703/920–2840* ⊕ *www.daysinn.com* ☜ *242 rooms, 3 suites* ⚇ *Restaurant, room service, in-room data ports, cable TV, pool, exercise equipment, gym, bar, laundry service, business services, airport shuttle, car rental, free parking* ▤ *AE, D, DC, MC, V* Ⓜ *Crystal City.*

$–$$ 🖭 **Holiday Inn Rosslyn.** Comfortable and affordable, this 17-story hotel is just two blocks from the Rosslyn Metro and a leisurely ¾-mi stroll across Key Bridge to Georgetown. Fort Myer and Arlington National Cemetery are very close. Each room has a balcony, but the hotel's best feature may be the view of Washington's monuments through the panoramic windows of the Vantage Point restaurant. ⊠ *1900 N. Fort Myer Dr., Arlington, VA 22209* ☎ *703/807–2000 or 800/368–3408* ⓑ *703/522–7480* ☜ *306 rooms, 28 suites* ⚇ *2 restaurants, café, in-room data ports, in-room safes, some refrigerators, cable TV, indoor pool, exercise equipment, health club, bar, dry cleaning, laundry facilities, laun-*

dry service, business services, meeting rooms, free parking ⊟ *AE, D, DC, MC, V* Ⓜ *Rosslyn.*

$–$$ ▦ **Quality Inn Iwo Jima.** Two blocks from the Marine Corps War Memorial and half a mile from the Rosslyn Metro, this budget hotel offers easy access to Georgetown, the Pentagon, and Ronald Reagan National Airport. The older original section of the hotel has outside entrances and larger rooms with double-sink bathrooms. The newer high-rise section has business-class rooms with work tables, data ports, and 25-inch TVs. ✉ *1501 Arlington Blvd., Rte. 50, Arlington, VA 22209* ☎ *703/ 524–5000, 800/221–2222, or 800/228–5151* 📠 *703/522–5484* 🛏 *141 rooms* ♻ *Restaurant, room service, in-room data ports, microwaves, cable TV, 2 pools (1 indoor), exercise equipment, gym, bar, laundry facilities, laundry service, free parking, some pets allowed (fee)* ⊟ *AE, D, DC, MC, V* Ⓜ *Rosslyn.*

¢–$ ▦ **Best Western Pentagon.** In the shadow of the world's largest office building, this hotel has free shuttle service to three nearby Metro stops and the attractions around them. Three two-story buildings have outside entrances and conventional motel rooms. The tower section has a restaurant and meeting rooms on the ground floor, and many of its guest rooms have nice views. ✉ *2480 S. Glebe Rd., Alexandria, VA 22206* ☎ *703/ 979–4400 or 800/426–6886* 📠 *703/685–0051* ⊕ *www.bestwestern. com* 🛏 *206 rooms* ♻ *Restaurant, room service, in-room data ports, in-room safes, cable TV, pool, gym, bar, laundry service, business services, airport shuttle, free parking* ⊟ *AE, D, DC, MC, V.*

¢ ▦ **Days Inn Pentagon.** A modestly priced, three-story lodging, this hotel is less than 2 mi from the Pentagon and Pentagon City Fashion Centre mall and a quick drive from the airport. Two Metro stations are nearby; the hotel can also be reached by a city bus that stops out front. Microwaves are available on request. Rincome, a Thai restaurant, is on the premises, and more than 50 other restaurants are within five blocks. ✉ *3030 Columbia Pike, Arlington, VA 22204* ☎ *703/521–5570* 📠 *703/271– 0081* ⊕ *www.daysinn.com* 🛏 *76 rooms* ♻ *Restaurant, room service, kitchenettes, microwaves, refrigerators, cable TV, pool, exercise equipment, gym, bar, laundry facilities, laundry service, business services, meeting rooms, free parking, no-smoking rooms* ⊟ *AE, D, DC, MC, V* 🍽 *CP* Ⓜ *Pentagon.*

NIGHTLIFE & THE ARTS

FODOR'S CHOICE

American Film Institute Silver Theatre, Silver Spring, MD

Blues Alley, Georgetown

JFK Center for the Performing Arts, Foggy Bottom

Smithsonian Institution, The Mall

Studio Theatre, Dupont Circle

Washington Opera, Foggy Bottom

HIGHLY RECOMMENDED

ARTS Arena Stage, Waterfront

Shakespeare Theatre, Downtown

Visions Cinema Bistro Lounge, Dupont Circle

Washington Ballet

NIGHTLIFE The Birchmere, Alexandria, VA

Brickskeller, Dupont Circle

Chi Cha Lounge, U Street corridor

Eighteenth Street Lounge, Dupont Circle

Habana Village, Adams-Morgan

HR-57, Logan Circle

Nation, Southeast

THE ARTS

By John F. Kelly
Revised by
Karyn-Siobhan
Robinson

In the past 40 years, D.C. has gone from being a cultural desert to a thriving arts center. The Kennedy Center, home of the National Symphony Orchestra (NSO), conducted by Leonard Slatkin, plays host to Broadway shows, ballet, modern dance, opera, and more. Placido Domingo, artistic director of the Washington Opera, has infused both international flair and talent into the cultural mix. Lines wrap around the block at the National Theatre for such big hit musicals as *Beauty and the Beast* and *The Full Monty*. Washington even has its own "off-Broadway," a half dozen or so plucky theaters scattered around the city that present new works and new twists on old works. Several art galleries, discussed in the "Shopping" chapter, have highly regarded chamber music series. And the service bands from the area's numerous military bases ensure an endless supply of John Philip Sousa–style music as well as rousing renditions of more contemporary tunes.

Several publications have calendars of entertainment events. The *Washington Post* "Weekend" section comes out on Friday, and its "Guide to the Lively Arts" is printed daily. On Thursday, look for the *Washington Times* "Weekend" section and the free weekly *Washington CityPaper*. Also consult the "City Lights" section in the monthly *Washingtonian* magazine. Tickets to most events are available by calling or visiting each theater's box office, or through the following ticket agencies.

Ticketmaster takes phone charges for events at most venues around the city. You can purchase Ticketmaster tickets in person at all Hecht's department stores. No refunds or exchanges are allowed. ☎ *202/432–7328 or 410/481–7328* ⊕ *www.ticketmaster.com.*

TicketPlace sells half-price, day-of-performance tickets for select shows; a "menu board" lists available performances. There's a 10% service charge per order. TicketPlace is also a full-price Ticketmaster outlet. It's closed on Sunday and Monday, but tickets for performances on those days are sold on Saturday. ⊠ *Old Post Office Pavilion, 1100 Pennsylvania Ave. NW, Downtown* ☎ *202/842–5387* ⊕ *www.cultural-alliance.org/tickets* Ⓜ *Federal Triangle.*

Tickets.com takes reservations for events at Arena Stage, Center Stage, Ford's Theatre, the Holocaust Museum, the 9:30 Club, and Signature Theater. It also has outlets in some Olsson's Books & Records. ☎ *703/218–6500* ⊕ *www.tickets.com.*

Concert Halls

Concert halls tend to focus on music, but many present all types of performances. It's not uncommon for a venue to present modern dance one week, a rock or classical music concert a week later, and a theatrical performance the next.

Cramton Auditorium. This 1,500-seat auditorium on the Howard University campus presents jazz, gospel, and R&B concerts. It's also the site of many special events. ⊠ *2455 6th St. NW, Howard University* ☎ *202/806–7194* Ⓜ *Shaw–Howard Univ.*

DAR Constitution Hall. Visiting musicians perform everything from jazz to pop to rap at the 3,700-seat Constitution Hall. ⊠ *18th and C Sts. NW, Downtown* ☎ *202/628–4780* Ⓜ *Farragut West.*

George Mason University. The glittering, ambitious Center for the Arts complex is here on the GMU campus in suburban Virginia. Music, ballet, and drama performances regularly take place in the 1,900-seat concert hall, the 500-seat proscenium Harris Theater, and the intimate 150-seat Black Box Theater. Also on campus is the 9,500-seat Patriot Center, site of pop acts and sporting events. ✉ *Rte. 123 and Braddock Rd., Fairfax, VA* ☎ *703/993–8888, 703/993–3000, or 202/432–7328* ⊕ *www.gmu.edu/cfa.*

Fodor'sChoice ★ **John F. Kennedy Center for the Performing Arts.** Any search for cultured entertainment should start here, whether you want to see an international symphony orchestra, a troupe of dancers, a Broadway musical, engaging children's theater, or a comedic whodunit. The "KenCen" is actually five stages under one roof: the Concert Hall, home of the National Symphony Orchestra (NSO); the Eisenhower Theater, usually used for drama; the Terrace Theater, a Philip Johnson–designed space that showcases chamber groups and experimental works; and the Theater Lab, home to cabaret-style performances (the audience-participation hit mystery *Shear Madness* has been playing there since 1987). You can catch a free performance every evening at 6 PM on the Millennium Stage in the center's Grand Foyer. At this writing, the 2,200-seat Opera House— a space for ballet, modern dance, opera, and large-scale musicals—is set to reopen at the end of 2003. On performance days, a free shuttle bus runs between the Center and the Foggy Bottom/GWU Metro stop. ✉ *New Hampshire Ave. and Rock Creek Pkwy. NW, Foggy Bottom* ☎ *202/467–4600 or 800/444–1324* ⊕ *www.kennedy-center.org* Ⓜ *Foggy Bottom/GWU.*

Lisner Auditorium. A 1,500-seat theater on the campus of George Washington University, Lisner Auditorium is the setting for pop, classical, and choral music shows, modern dance performances, and musical theater. ✉ *21st and H Sts. NW, Foggy Bottom* ☎ *202/994–6800* ⊕ *www.gwu. edu/~lisner* Ⓜ *Foggy Bottom/GWU.*

MCI Center. In addition to being the home of the Washington Capitals hockey and Washington Wizards basketball teams, this 19,000-seat arena also hosts concerts, ice-skating events, and the circus. In 2003, the World Figure Skating Championships were held here. Parking can be a problem, but the arena is near several Metro lines. ✉ *601 F St. NW, Chinatown* ☎ *202/628–3200* ⊕ *www.mcicenter.com* Ⓜ *Gallery Place/Chinatown.*

Merriweather Post Pavilion. An hour's drive north of Washington, Merriweather Post is an outdoor amphitheater with some covered seating. In warmer months it hosts big-name pop acts. ✉ *Broken Land Pkwy., Exit 18B, off Rte. 29 N, Columbia, MD* ☎ *301/982–1800 concert information; 301/596–0660 off-season* ⊕ *www.mppconcerts.com.*

National Gallery of Art. Free concerts by the National Gallery Orchestra, conducted by George Manos, and performances by visiting recitalists and ensembles are held in the venerable West Building's West Garden Court on Sunday nights from October to June. Most performances highlight classical music, though the program at April's American Music Festival is often jazz. Entry is first-come, first-served, with doors opening at 6 PM and concerts starting at 7. ✉ *6th St. and Constitution Ave. NW, The Mall* ☎ *202/842–6941 or 202/842–6698* ⊕ *www.nga.gov* Ⓜ *Archives/Navy Memorial.*

Nissan Pavilion at Stone Ridge. Cellar Door Productions, the country's largest concert promoter, built this 25,000-seat venue in rural Virginia, about an hour from downtown Washington, to host all types of music. ✉ *7800 Cellar Door Dr., Bristow, VA* ☎ *202/432–7328 or 703/754–6400* ⊕ *www.nissanpavilion.com.*

Fodor'sChoice ★ **Smithsonian Institution.** A rich assortment of music is presented at the Smithsonian. Jazz, musical theater, and popular standards are performed in the National Museum of American History. In the museum's third-floor Hall of Musical Instruments, musicians periodically play instruments from the museum's collection. The Smithsonian Associates sponsors programs that offer everything from a cappella groups to Cajun zydeco bands; all events require tickets and locations vary. The annual Smithsonian's Folk Life festival, held on the Mall, is one of the city's most anticipated events. In 2004 the maritime culture of the Mid-Atlantic region (from Long Island, New York, to the Outer Banks of North Carolina) will be featured. ✉ *1000 Jefferson Dr. SW, The Mall* ☎ *202/357–2700; 202/357–2020 recording; 202/357–3030 Smithsonian Associates* ⊕ *www.si.edu* Ⓜ *Smithsonian.*

Wolf Trap Farm Park. Just off the Dulles Toll Road, about a half hour from downtown, Wolf Trap is the only national park dedicated to the performing arts. On its grounds is the Filene Center, an outdoor theater where jazz, opera, ballet, and dance performances are held June through September. On performance nights, Metrorail operates a $3.50 round-trip shuttle bus between the West Falls Church Metro station and the Filene Center. The fare is exact change only, and the bus leaves 20 minutes after the show, or no later than 11 PM, whether the show is over or not. The rest of the year, the intimate indoor Barns at Wolf Trap hosts folk, jazz, rock, chamber, opera, and other music. ✉ *1551 Trap Rd., Vienna, VA* ☎ *703/255–1900; 703/938–2404 Barns at Wolf Trap* ⊕ *www.wolf-trap.org* Ⓜ *Vienna.*

Dance

Dance Place. A studio theater that presented its first performance in 1980, Dance Place hosts a wide assortment of modern and ethnic dance shows most weekends. It also conducts dance classes daily. ✉ *3225 8th St. NE, Brookland/CUA* ☎ *202/269–1600* ⊕ *www.danceplace.org* Ⓜ *Brookland/CUA.*

Joy of Motion. A dance studio by day, Joy of Motion is the home of several area troupes that perform in the studio's Jack Guidone Theatre by night, including City Dance Ensemble (modern), the Spanish Dance Ensemble (flamenco), and JazzDanz/dc. Two additional studios in Dupont Circle and Bethesda offer classes only. ✉ *5207 Wisconsin Ave. NW, Friendship Heights* ☎ *202/362–3042* ⊕ *www.joyofmotion.org* Ⓜ *Friendship Heights.*

★ **Washington Ballet.** Between September and May, this company presents classical and contemporary ballets—including works by such choreographers as George Balanchine, Choo-San Goh, and artistic director Septime Webre—at the Kennedy Center and the Warner Theatre. Each December the Washington Ballet performs *The Nutcracker.* ☎ *202/362–3606* ⊕ *www.washingtonballet.org.*

Film

AMC Union Station 9. Capitol Hill's AMC Union Station 9 has nine screens showing mainstream, first-run movies; validated, three-hour parking is available at an adjacent lot. ✉ *Union Station, 50 Massachusetts Ave. NE, Capitol Hill* ☎ *202/842–3757* Ⓜ *Union Station.*

Fodor'sChoice ★ **American Film Institute Silver Theatre & Cultural Center.** This state-of-the-art center for film is a restoration of architect John Eberson's Silver Theatre, built in 1938. The main screen seats 400 and maintains the art-deco looks of the original. The two other smaller screens both have stadium seating. ✉ *8633 Colesville Rd., Silver Spring* ☎ *301/495–6700* ⊕ *www.afi.com/Silver/Theatre* Ⓜ *Silver Spring.*

Arlington Cinema 'N' Drafthouse. Various libations, along with pizza, buffalo wings, nachos, and other snacks, are served during films at this cinema with table seating. Those under age 21 must be accompanied by a parent or guardian to to attend. ⊠ *2903 Columbia Pike, Arlington, VA* ☎ *703/486–2345.*

Cineplex Odeon Uptown. You don't find many like this old beauty anymore: one huge, multiplex-dwarfing screen; art deco flourishes instead of a bland, boxy interior; a wonderful balcony; and—in one happy concession to modernity—crystal-clear Dolby sound. ⊠ *3426 Connecticut Ave. NW, Cleveland Park* ☎ *202/966–5400 or 202/966–5401* Ⓜ *Cleveland Park.*

Filmfest DC. An annual citywide festival of international cinema, the DC International Film Festival, or Filmfest, as it is affectionately known, takes place in late April and early May at various venues throughout the city. ✆ *Box 21396, 20004* ☎ *202/724–5613* ⊕ *www.filmfestdc.org.*

General Cinema at Mazza Gallerie. Near the D.C.–Maryland border is the only movie theater in the area with stadium-seating and all-digital sound. In the smaller Club Cinema, moviegoers enjoy leather seats, a full-service bar, and sandwiches and snacks. Pampering like this doesn't come cheap: tickets are $9.50 for the main theater and $12.50 for the Club Cinema. ⊠ *5300 Wisconsin Ave. NW, 3rd fl., Friendship Heights* ☎ *202/537–9551* Ⓜ *Friendship Heights.*

Hirshhorn Museum & Sculpture Garden. If you love avant-garde and experimental film, check out the weekly movies—often first-run documentaries, features, and short films—shown here for free. ⊠ *Independence Ave. and 7th St. SW, The Mall* ☎ *202/357–2700* ⊕ *www.hirshhorn.si.edu* Ⓜ *Smithsonian or L'Enfant Plaza.*

Landmark's Bethesda Row Cinema. Art, foreign, and independent films can be found outside of D.C., thanks to this lush eight-screen art cinema with stadium seating. Look for fancy snacks (including imported chocolates), pastries from local bakeries, and a full coffee bar. ⊠ *7235 Woodmont Ave., Bethesda, MD* ☎ *301/652–7273* Ⓜ *Bethesda.*

Loews Georgetown. The newest movie palace in D.C. was once the Georgetown Incinerator—a 175-foot brick smokestack still looms over the lobby's center. Stadium seating, digital sound, comfy seats, and 14 huge screens all make for a prime movie-going experience. Wanna snuggle with your honey? It's not a problem here: the armrests between seats can be raised. ⊠ *3111 K St. NW, Georgetown* ☎ *202/274–1728* Ⓜ *Foggy Bottom.*

National Archives. Historical films are shown here daily. Call the information line or order a calendar of events for listings. ⊠ *Constitution Ave. between 7th and 9th Sts. NW, The Mall* ☎ *202/501–5000* Ⓜ *Archives/Navy Memorial.*

National Gallery of Art, East Building. Free classic and international films, often complementing exhibits, are shown in this museum's large auditorium. You can pick up a film calendar at the museum. ⊠ *Constitution Ave. between 3rd and 4th Sts. NW, The Mall* ☎ *202/737–4215* ⊕ *www.nga.gov* Ⓜ *Archives/Navy Memorial.*

National Geographic Society. Free educational films with a scientific, geographic, or anthropological focus are shown here weekly. ⊠ *17th and M Sts. NW, Dupont Circle* ☎ *202/857–7588* Ⓜ *Farragut North.*

★ **Visions Cinema Bistro Lounge.** Independent, foreign, and art films dominate the only independently owned theater in the city. In the Bistro, look for tasty Mediterranean, Middle Eastern, and Indian snacks alongside more standard movie fare. Sit at a table or take your snacks into the red-wall lounge, where you can nosh while gazing at the silent films running near a full bar. ⊠ *1927 Florida Ave. NW, Dupont Circle* ☎ *202/667–0090* ⊕ *www.visionsdc.com* Ⓜ *Dupont Circle.*

Music

Chamber Music

Corcoran Gallery of Art. Hungary's Takacs String Quartet and the Cleveland Quartet are among the chamber groups appearing in the Corcoran's Musical Evening Series, one Friday each month from October to May (there are also some summer offerings). Concerts are followed by a reception with the artists. ✉ *17th St. and New York Ave. NW, Downtown* ☎ *202/639–1700* ⊕ *www.corcoran.org* Ⓜ *Farragut West.*

Dumbarton Concerts. Held at Dumbarton United Methodist Church, the Dumbarton Concerts have hosted musicians such as the Sante Fe Guitar Quartet, Red Priest, and the Thibaud String trio. The church has been a part of Georgetown since 1772, congregating initially in a cooper's shop. The church has been in the current location since 1850. ✉ *3133 Dumbarton Ave. NW, Georgetown* ☎ *202/965–2000* ⊕ *www. dumbartonconcerts.org* Ⓜ *Foggy Bottom.*

Folger Shakespeare Library. The library's internationally acclaimed resident chamber music ensemble, the Folger Consort, regularly presents a selection of instrumental and vocal pieces from the medieval, Renaissance, and baroque periods. The season runs from October to May. ✉ *201 E. Capitol St. SE, Capitol Hill* ☎ *202/544–7077* ⊕ *www.folger. edu* Ⓜ *Union Station or Capitol South.*

National Academy of Sciences. Free performances are given fall through spring in the academy's 670-seat auditorium, which has almost perfect acoustics. Both the National Musical Arts Chamber Ensemble and the United States Marines Chamber Orchestra perform regularly. ✉ *2100 C St. NW, Downtown* ☎ *202/334–2436* ⊕ *www.nationalacademies. org* Ⓜ *Foggy Bottom/GWU.*

Phillips Collection. Duncan Phillips's mansion is more than an art museum. From September through May the long, paneled music room hosts Sunday-afternoon recitals. Chamber groups from around the world perform. Concerts begin at 5; arrive early for decent seats. ✉ *1600 21st St. NW, Dupont Circle* ☎ *202/387–2151* ⊕ *www.phillipscollection.org* Ⓜ *Dupont Circle.*

Choral Music

Basilica of the National Shrine of the Immaculate Conception. Choral and church groups occasionally perform at the largest Catholic church in the Americas. The Knights' Tower, a gift of the Knights of Columbus, rises 329 feet from ground level. The interior of the Great Upper Church is 399 feet long and can accommodate more than 6,000 worshipers. ✉ *400 Michigan Ave. NE, Brookland/CUA* ☎ *202/526–8300* ⊕ *www. nationalshrine.com* Ⓜ *Brookland/CUA.*

Choral Arts Society of Washington. The 190-voice Choral Arts Society choir performs a varied selection of classical pieces at the Kennedy Center from September to June. Three Christmas sing-alongs are scheduled each December. ☎ *202/244–3669.*

Washington National Cathedral. Choral and church groups frequently perform in this grand church. Admission is usually free. ✉ *Massachusetts and Wisconsin Aves. NW, Cleveland Park* ☎ *202/537–6207 or 202/537–6247* ⊕ *www.choralarts.org* Ⓜ *Tenleytown/AU.*

Opera & Classical

The *Washington Post* "Weekend" section is a good source for opera and classical performances.

In Series. Trademark cabaret, experimental chamber opera, performance-art productions, and Spanish musical theater (also known as *zarzuela*) are among the hallmarks of this burgeoning nonprofit company, which performs at various venues around the city. ☎ 202/237–9834 ⊕ www.inseries.org.

Opera Theater of Northern Virginia. During each of its three seasons (October, January and February, and May) this company stages an opera, sung in English, at an Arlington community theater. Each December the company also presents a one-act opera especially for young audiences. ☎ 703/528–1433.

Summer Opera Theater Company. An independent professional troupe, the Summer Opera Theater Company stages one opera in June and one in July. ✉ Hartke Theater, 620 Michigan Ave. NE, Brookland/CUA ☎ 202/526–1669 Ⓜ Brookland/CUA.

FodorśChoice **Washington Opera.** Seven operas—presented in their original languages
★ with English supertitles—are performed each season (September–May). After spending 2003 at DAR Constitution Hall, the company returns to the newly renovated Kennedy Center Opera House in spring 2004. Performances are often sold out to subscribers, but you can purchase returned tickets an hour before curtain time. Standing-room tickets for the fall season go on sale each Saturday at 10 AM for the following week's performances. ✉ John F. Kennedy Center for the Performing Arts., New Hampshire Ave. and Rock Creek Pkwy. NW, Foggy Bottom ☎ 202/295–2400 or 800/876–7372 ⊕ www.dc-opera.org Ⓜ Foggy Bottom/GWU.

Orchestra

National Symphony Orchestra. The season at the Kennedy Center is from September to June. In summer the NSO performs at Wolf Trap and gives free concerts at the Carter Barron Amphitheatre and, on Memorial Day and Labor Day weekends and July 4, on the West Lawn of the Capitol. The cheapest way to hear the NSO perform in the Kennedy Center Concert Hall is to get $19 second-tier side seats. ☎ 202/416–8100 ⊕ www.nationalsymphony.org.

Performance Series

Armed Forces Concert Series. From June to August, service bands from all four military branches perform Monday, Tuesday, Thursday, and Friday evenings on the East Terrace of the Capitol and several nights a week at the Sylvan Theater on the Washington Monument grounds. Concerts usually include marches, patriotic numbers, and some classical music. The air-force celebrity series features popular artists such as Earl Klugh and Keiko Matsui. The bands often perform free concerts at other locations throughout the year. ☎ 202/767–5658 Air Force; 703/696–3718 Army; 202/433–2525 Navy; 202/433–4011 Marines.

Carter Barron Amphitheatre. On Saturday and Sunday nights from mid-June to August this lovely, 4,250-seat outdoor theater in Rock Creek Park hosts pop, jazz, gospel, and rhythm-and-blues artists such as Chick Corea and Nancy Wilson. The National Symphony Orchestra also performs, and for two weeks in June the Shakespeare Theatre presents a free play by the Bard. ✉ 16th St. and Colorado Ave. NW ☎ 202/426–6837 ⊕ www.nps.gov/rocr/cbarron.htm.

District Curators. This independent, nonprofit organization presents adventurous contemporary performers from around the world in spaces around the city, mostly in summer (June–August). Much of the group's season is encompassed by its Jazz Arts Festival. Past artists have included Laurie Anderson, Philip Glass, the World Saxophone Quartet, and Cassandra Wilson. ☎ 202/723–7500.

Fort Dupont Summer Theater. The National Park Service presents national and international jazz artists at 8:30 on Friday and Saturday evenings from July to August at the outdoor Fort Dupont Summer Theater. Wynton Marsalis, Shirley Horne, and Ramsey Lewis are among the artists who have performed free concerts. ⊠ *Minnesota Ave. and Randall Circle SE, Southeast* ☎ *202/426–7723.*

Sylvan Theater. Military bands from all four branches usually perform al fresco at the Sylvan Theater from June to August, Tuesday, Thursday, Friday, and Sunday nights at 8 PM. Schedules are subject to change. ⊠ *Washington Monument grounds, 14th St. and Constitution Ave., The Mall* ☎ *202/426–6841* Ⓜ *Smithsonian.*

Transparent Productions. Composed of a small group of dedicated jazz connoisseurs, this nonprofit presenting organization regularly brings acclaimed avant-garde jazz musicians to intimate clubs and university stages. Past performers have included the Ethnic Heritage Ensemble, bassist William Parker, and saxophonist Steve Coleman. Tickets are usually in the $10 range, with 100% of the revenues going directly to the artists. ☎ *No phone* ⊕ *www.geocities.com/eyelounge/DC.*

Washington Performing Arts Society. This independent nonprofit organization books high-quality classical music, jazz, modern dance, and gospel and performance art into halls around the city. Past artists include Alvin Ailey American Dance Theater, Wynton Marsalis, Yo-Yo Ma, the Chieftains, Sweet Honey in the Rock, and Cecilia Bartoli. ☎ *202/833–9800* ⊕ *www.wpas.org.*

Theater & Performance Art

Commercial Theaters

★ **Arena Stage.** The city's most-respected resident company (established in 1950), Arena Stage was also the first non–New York company to win a Tony award. Arena Stage presents a mix of classic and recent productions in its three theaters: the Fichandler Stage, the proscenium Kreeger, and the cabaret-style Old Vat Room. ⊠ *6th St. and Maine Ave. SW, Waterfront* ☎ *202/488–3300* ⊕ *www.arenastage.org* Ⓜ *Waterfront.*

Ford's Theatre. Looking much as it did when President Lincoln was shot at a performance of *Our American Cousin,* Ford's hosts both dramas and musicals, many with family appeal. Dickens's *A Christmas Carol* is staged each year. ⊠ *511 10th St. NW, Downtown* ☎ *202/347–4833* ⊕ *www.fordstheatre.org* Ⓜ *Metro Center.*

Lincoln Theatre. From the 1920s to the 1940s, the Lincoln hosted the same performers as the Cotton Club and the Apollo Theatre in Harlem: Cab Calloway, Lena Horne, Duke Ellington. Today the 1,250-seater shows films and welcomes such acts as the Count Basie Orchestra and the Harlem Boys and Girls Choir. ⊠ *1215 U St. NW, U St. corridor* ☎ *202/328–6000* Ⓜ *U Street/Cardozo.*

National Theatre. Though it was once destroyed by fire and has been rebuilt several times throughout its life, the National Theatre has operated in the same location since 1835. It presents touring Broadway shows. From September through April, look for free children's shows on Saturday, and free Monday night shows that run the gamut from Asian dance to performance art to a cappella cabarets. ⊠ *1321 Pennsylvania Ave. NW, Downtown* ☎ *202/628–6161* ⊕ *www.nationaltheatre.org* Ⓜ *Metro Center.*

★ **Shakespeare Theatre.** Five plays—three by Shakespeare and two classics from the same era—are staged each year by this acclaimed troupe in a state-of-the-art, 450-seat space. For two weeks each June the company offers a free play under the stars at Carter Barron Amphitheatre. ⊠ *450 7th St. NW, Downtown* ☎ *202/547–1122* ⊕ *www.shakespearedc.org* Ⓜ *Gallery Place/Chinatown or Archives/Navy Memorial.*

Warner Theatre. One of Washington's grand theaters, this 1924 building hosts road shows, dance recitals, pop music, and the occasional comedy act. ⊠ *1299 Pennsylvania Ave. NW, Downtown* ☎ *202/783–4000* ⊕ *www.warnertheatre.com* Ⓜ *Metro Center.*

Small Theaters & Companies

Often performing in churches and other less-than-ideal settings, Washington's small companies present some beautifully staged and acted plays and musicals that can be every bit as enthralling as—and often more daring than—their blockbuster counterparts. No matter the size, all the companies in town compete fiercely for the Helen Hayes Award, Washington's version of the Tony. Several acclaimed alternative stages are on 14th Street NW and near Dupont Circle.

District of Columbia Arts Center. Known by area artists as DCAC, this cross-genre space shows changing exhibits in its gallery and presents avant-garde performance art and experimental plays in its small black-box theater. ⊠ *2438 18th St. NW, Adams-Morgan* ☎ *202/462–7833* ⊕ *www. dcartscenter.org* Ⓜ *Woodley Park/Zoo.*

Folger Shakespeare Library. Look for three to four productions a year of Shakespeare or Shakespeare-influenced works, all staged in the library's theater, which seats 250. It's a replica of the inn-yard theaters popular in Shakespeare's time. ⊠ *201 E. Capitol St. SE, Capitol Hill* ☎ *202/ 544–4600* ⊕ *www.folger.edu* Ⓜ *Union Station or Capitol South.*

Gala Hispanic Theatre. This company produces Spanish classics as well as contemporary and modern Latin American plays in both Spanish and English. ⊠ *1021 7th St. NW, Chinatown* ☎ *202/234–7174* ⊕ *www. galatheatre.org* Ⓜ *Archives/Navy Memorial.*

Glen Echo Park. The National Park Service has transformed this former amusement park into a thriving arts center. The Adventure Theater produces traditional plays and musicals every weekend. Plays are aimed at children ages 4 to 12, and families can spread out on carpeted steps. At the Puppet Company Playhouse, skilled puppeteers manipulate puppets in classic plays and stories Wednesday through Sunday. ⊠ *7300 MacArthur Blvd. NW, Glen Echo, MD* ☎ *301/492–6282; 301/320–5331 Adventure Theater; 301/320–6668 Puppet Co.* ⊕ *www.nps.gov/glec.*

Imagination Stage. Shows like *Cinderella Likes Rice and Beans* and *Amelia Bedelia* are produced here for children ages 4 to 12. Imagination Stage's state-of-the-art theater in Bethesda includes a digital media studio. Audience capacity expands from 150 to 450. Make reservations in advance. ⊠ *4908 Auburn Ave., Bethesda, MD* ☎ *301/961–6060* ⊕ *www.imaginationstage.org.*

Olney Theatre Center for the Arts. Musicals, comedies, and summer stock are presented in a converted barn, one hour from downtown on 14 acres in the Maryland countryside. The main stage season emphasizes 20th-century American classics, new works, area premieres, reinterpretations of classics, and musical theater. The free Summer Shakespeare Festival is eagerly anticipated by local theater lovers. ⊠ *2001 Olney–Sandy Spring Rd., Olney, MD* ☎ *301/924–3400* ⊕ *www.olneytheatre.org.*

Signature Theatre. This plucky group performs in a 136-seat black-box theater in a converted bumper-plating facility. Sondheim is a favorite with Signature, and Signature is said to be a favorite of Sondheim's, too. ⊠ *3806 S. 4 Mile Run Dr., Arlington, VA* ☎ *703/820–9771* ⊕ *www. sig-online.org.*

Source Theatre. Established plays with a sharp satirical edge and modern interpretations of classics are presented at this 125-seat theater. Every July and August, Source hosts the Washington Theater Festival, a series of new plays, many by local playwrights. ⊠ *1835 14th St. NW, U St. corridor* ☎ *202/462–1073* ⊕ *www.sourcetheatre.com* Ⓜ *U Street/ Cardozo.*

FodorsChoice **Studio Theatre.** One of the busiest groups in the city, this small independent
★ company has an eclectic season of classic and offbeat plays. Two 200-
seat theaters—the Mead and the Milton—as well as the 50-seat Sec-
ondstage (which stages particularly experimental works) are contained
in the spacious building in the up-and-coming Logan Circle area. ✉ *1333
P St. NW, Dupont Circle* ☎ *202/332–3300* ⊕ *www.studiotheatre.org*
Ⓜ *Dupont Circle.*

Washington Stage Guild. After Carroll Hall—the Guild's home of several decades—was demolished, this company moved to the Source Theatre. Classics are performed, in addition to more contemporary works;
Shaw is a specialty. ✉ *1835 14th St. NW, Dupont Circle* ☎ *240/582–
0050* Ⓜ *U Street/Cardozo.*

Woolly Mammoth. Unusual, imaginatively produced shows have earned
Woolly Mammoth good reviews and favorable comparisons to Chicago's
Steppenwolf. Bounced from its 13-year home at Logan Circle, the com-
pany has spent the last few years in temporary locations around town.
In the fall of 2004, the theater moves into a new 265-seat theater in Penn
Quarter near the MCI Center. ☎ *202/393–3939* ⊕ *www.*
woollymammoth.net.

NIGHTLIFE

From proper political appointees to blue-collar regulars in from the 'burbs,
Washington's watering holes, clubs, comedy venues, and intimate music
halls cater to all types of customers. Many places are clustered in key
areas, making a night of bar-hopping relatively easy. Georgetown has
dozens of bars, nightclubs, and restaurants on M Street east and west
of Wisconsin Avenue, and on Wisconsin Avenue north of M Street. Along
the 18th Street strip in Adams-Morgan, bordered by Columbia Road
and Florida Avenue, are several small live-music clubs, ethnic restaurants, and bars. The area west of Florida Avenue, along the U Street corridor—perhaps one of the hippest neighborhoods in the country—appeals
to young people looking for music from hip-hop to alt-rock to reggae.
Theatergoers seeking post-show entertainment once had to venture to
nearby Dupont Circle, but no more. The 14th Street strip from U Street
toward P Street has developed an eclectic, thriving nightlife of its own.
On a stretch of Pennsylvania Avenue between 2nd and 4th streets, you'll
find a half dozen Capitol Hill bars. And for a happenin' happy hour,
head to the intersection of 19th and M streets NW, near the lawyer- and
lobbyist-filled downtown.

D.C. may be a two-party town, but Washington audiences tend not to
draw party lines when it comes to music. This means that you can hear
funk at a rock club, blues at a jazz club, and calypso at a reggae club.
Washington was the birthplace of hard-core, a socially aware form of
punk rock music that has influenced young bands throughout the country. Go-go, an infectious, rhythmic music that mixes elements of hip-
hop, rhythm and blues, and funk, is another homegrown art form.
Punk and go-go shows can get rowdy, and the best place for curious
out-of-towners to experience these sounds may be at an outdoor summer music event.

The city's formerly sleepy suburbs have emerged in the past few years
to gain a nightlife of their own. Downtown Bethesda has a vibrant restaurant and club scene. In Northern Virginia, where exciting bars and
clubs render once-necessary trips to the city moot, the beautiful people
have a strong and resilient presence. Much of the suburban growth can
be traced to Washington's Metro system, which runs until 2 AM on weekend nights. Club-hoppers find plenty to do in the areas surrounding the

Clarendon and Ballston Metro stations in Virginia and the Bethesda stop in Maryland.

To check out the local scene, consult Friday's "Weekend" section in the *Washington Post* and the free weekly *Washington CityPaper*. The free *Metro Weekly* and *Women in the Life* magazines offer insights on gay and lesbian nightlife. It's also a good idea to call clubs ahead of time to find out what's on. Reservations are advised for comedy clubs; places where reservations are essential are noted.

Most bars in D.C. have cover charges for bands and DJs, generally on the weekends. Expect to pay anywhere from $5 to $15 for most dance clubs. Jazz and comedy clubs often have higher cover charges along with drink minimums. Last call in D.C. is 2 AM, and most bars and clubs close by 3 AM on the weekends and between midnight and 2 AM during the week. The exceptions are after-hours dance clubs and bars with kitchens that stay open late.

Acoustic, Folk & Country Clubs

Washington has a very active folk scene. For information on folk events—from contra dancing to storytelling to open singing—contact the **Folklore Society of Greater Washington** (☎ 202/546–2228 recorded information line ⊕ www.fsgw.org).

★ **The Birchmere.** This is one of the best places this side of the Blue Ridge Mountains to hear acoustic folk and bluegrass. Audiences come to listen, and the management politely insists on no distracting chatter. ✉ *3701 Mt. Vernon Ave., Alexandria, VA* ☎ *703/549–7500* ⊕ *www.birchmere.com.*

Soho Tea and Coffee. Quality singer-songwriters share the stage with poets and writers at Soho's open mike the second and fourth Wednesdays of every month (featured performances go on throughout the month). Other pluses: the café serves as a gallery space with changing monthly exhibits, stays open very late, and serves breakfast all day along with its regular menu of light fare. ✉ *2150 P St. NW, Dupont Circle* ☎ *202/463–7646* Ⓜ *Dupont Circle.*

Bars & Lounges

★ **Brickskeller.** This is *the* place to go when you want something more exotic than a Bud Lite. A list of more than 1,000 varieties of beer from around the world earned Brickskeller mention in *Guinness World Records 2003*. Servers actually have to go to "beer school" to land a job here. ✉ *1523 22nd St. NW, Dupont Circle* ☎ *202/293–1885* ⊕ *www.thebrickskeller.com* Ⓜ *Dupont Circle.*

Cap City Brewing Company. At the New York Avenue location of this microbrewery, a gleaming copper bar dominates the airy room. Consult the brew master's chalkboard to see what's on tap. The fabulous Postal Square location on Massachusetts Avenue has five 30-keg copper serving vessels in the center of the restaurant and a gorgeous vault door, left over from the days when the building was a post office. ✉ *1100 New York Ave. NW, Downtown* ☎ *202/628–2222* Ⓜ *Metro Center* ✉ *2 Massachusetts Ave. NE, Capitol Hill* ☎ *202/842–2337* Ⓜ *Union Station.*

Carpool. Andy Warhol meets General Motors is how *Billiards Digest* described this former-garage-turned-bar. Enjoy a brew and food from a kitchen run by the restaurant Rocklands, which makes some of the best barbecue in the area. Carpool has 16 pool tables, four dartboards, and a cigar room with a walk-in humidor. ✉ *4000 Fairfax Dr., Arlington, VA* ☎ *703/532–7665.*

★ **Chi Cha Lounge.** Groups of stylish young patrons relax on sofas and armchairs, while Latin jazz plays in the background. It gets packed on weekends, so come early to get a coveted sofa along the back wall, where it's easier to see and be seen. On the menu are Andean appetizers, homemade sangria, and cocktails; Sunday through Thursday, for a small price, you can smoke a hookah filled with imported honey-cured tobacco. ⊠ *1624 U St. NW, U St. corridor* ☎ *202/234–8400* Ⓜ *U Street/Cardozo.*

Dr. Dremo's Tap House. Nooks, couches, and a huge 6- by 9-foot TV (sneak downstairs for a peek) fill this former auto dealership. The bar has nine microbrews from the Bardo Brewery as well as 10 pool tables, two of which are outdoors. Nachos, bratwurst, and Italian sausage can be found on the pub-style menu. ⊠ *2001 Clarendon Blvd., Arlington, VA* ☎ *703/528–4660.*

Dragonfly. Minimalist white-and-chrome furnishings and sleek, mod, '60s bar stools set the tone at this bar frequented by youthful, beautiful people. Projections of kung-fu movies provide a pleasant distraction. The bar serves sushi, but the food here is more fashion accessory than nourishment. ⊠ *1215 Connecticut Ave. NW, Dupont Circle* ☎ *202/331–1715* Ⓜ *Dupont Circle.*

Dubliner. Cozy paneled rooms, thick Guinness, and nightly live entertainment make Washington's premier Irish pub popular among Capitol Hill staffers. ⊠ *520 N. Capitol St. NW, Capitol Hill* ☎ *202/737–3773* Ⓜ *Union Station.*

★ **Eighteenth Street Lounge (ESL).** Yes, it's hard to find. And yes, the guys at the door are intimidating (they ARE checking out your clothes), but don't let fear stop you. Fans of techno music flock here, the home of the ESL record label and the world-renowned DJs that make up Thievery Corporation. Inside are hardwood floors, candles, lush couches, and even a fireplace. ESL has never advertised: its success is due completely to word-of-mouth. ⊠ *1212 18th St. NW, Dupont Circle* ☎ *202/466–3922* ⊕ *www.eslmusic.com* Ⓜ *Dupont Circle.*

Fadó Irish Pub. Designed by Irish craftspeople with authentic Irish materials, Fadó is really four pubs in one: the Library, the Victorian Pub, the Gaelic, and the Cottage. Each spotlights an era of Irish pub culture. Live Irish acoustic music is performed every Sunday afternoon, and there's live Celtic rock on Wednesday and Saturday nights. Irish movies are shown Monday nights. ⊠ *808 7th St. NW, Chinatown* ☎ *202/789–0066* Ⓜ *Gallery Place/Chinatown.*

Felix. Cool, hip, and chic are the watchwords of the mixed and international crowd that haunts Felix. The sounds of live Latin jazz or funk often waft out to 18th Street. Be sure to sip one of the exotic cocktails while you check out the scene. ⊠ *2406 18th St. NW, Adams-Morgan* ☎ *202/483–3549* Ⓜ *Woodley Park/Zoo.*

Fishmarket. There's something different in just about every section of the Fishmarket—a multilevel, multiroom space in Old Town Alexandria—from piano-bar crooner to ragtime piano shouter to guitar strummer. The operative word here is *boisterous.* If you really like beer, order the largest size; it comes in a glass big enough to wash your face in. ⊠ *105 King St., Alexandria, VA* ☎ *703/836–5676.*

Galaxy Hut. Holiday lights out front mark this small yet intimate bar that hosts breaking bands from the area. The bar also hosts an ever-changing display of intriguing outsider art. ⊠ *2711 Wilson Blvd., Arlington, VA* ☎ *703/525–8646.*

Gazuza. The bar, whose name means "lust" in Castilian Spanish, attracts an eclectic and often attractive crowd that chats while house music throbs in the background. The interior, done in an aggressively modern style, fills up early. Don't miss the balcony, a prime people-watching spot.

✉ *1629 Connecticut Ave. NW, Dupont Circle,* ☎ *202/667–5500* Ⓜ *Dupont Circle.*

Hawk & Dove. The regulars at this friendly bar—set in a neighborhood dominated by the Capitol and the Library of Congress—include politicos, lobbyists, and well-behaved marines from a nearby barracks. The D.C.-based NBC series *The West Wing* regularly films scenes at this venerable standby. ✉ *329 Pennsylvania Ave. SE, Capitol Hill* ☎ *202/543–3300* Ⓜ *Eastern Market.*

Iota. The bands at Iota tend to play alt-country or stripped-down rock. The refreshingly unpretentious crowd comes mainly because they're fans of good music. Expect to fight your way to the bar—it gets crowded quickly. ✉ *2832 Wilson Blvd., Arlington, VA* ☎ *703/522–8340.*

Madam's Organ. Neon lights behind the bar and art from local artists add to the gritty, urban feel that infuses Madam's Organ. Uptight Hill staffers rub shoulders with dreadlocked bike messengers and college students pining for something a bit more adventurous than the staid offerings of Bethesda or Georgetown. ✉ *2461 18th St. NW, Adams-Morgan* ☎ *202/667–5370* Ⓜ *Woodley Park/Zoo.*

Mimi's American Bistro. What swiftly became a neighborhood sensation employs some of the city's most talented undiscovered performers, who work as "singing servers." Expect to be mesmerized by their renditions of beloved standards, campy torch songs, and fun pop tunes. The bar gets packed quickly, and the coveted plush couch is rarely vacant. ✉ *2120 P St. NW, Dupont Circle* ☎ *202/464–6464* ⊕ *www.mimisdc. com* Ⓜ *Dupont Circle.*

Ozio Restaurant & Lounge. There are four stories of hip coolness in this popular martini and cigar lounge. A humidor graces the first floor, along with cozy plush couches and art-deco furnishings. Three more floors have dancing and VIP service for the multiethnic, upscale crowd. Long lines of sharply dressed hipsters stretch in front on weekends. Dig out your fancy shoes—looks count here. ✉ *1813 M St. NW, Dupont Circle* ☎ *202/822–6000* Ⓜ *Dupont Circle.*

Tryst. At once ultrahip and unpretentious, this coffeehouse-bar serves freshly made waffles all day, as well as fancy Italian sandwiches and exotic coffee creations. Comfy chairs and couches fill the big open space, where you can sit for hours sipping a cup of joe (or a martini, in the evenings) and chatting or clacking away at your laptop. It can get noisy at night. ✉ *2459 18th St. NW, Adams-Morgan* ☎ *202/232–5500* Ⓜ *Woodley Park/Zoo.*

Uncle Jed's Roadhouse. Who knew that downtown Bethesda had such a laid-back, down-to-earth bar? Maybe everyone did. Expect long lines on the weekends at this fun-filled roadhouse. Jukeboxes blare rock and country, arcade games roar, and big screen TVs blast. Wind down from the fun with a brew and some down-home food; don't miss the ribs. ✉ *7525 Old Georgetown Rd., Bethesda, MD* ☎ *301/913–0026.*

Yacht Club. Enormously popular with well-dressed, 35-plus singles, this suburban Maryland lounge is the brainchild of an irrepressible entrepreneur who measures his success by the number of engagements and marriages spawned here. At last count it was in the vicinity of 118. The bar is open Wednesday through Saturday. ✉ *8111 Woodmont Ave., Bethesda, MD* ☎ *301/654–2396.*

Comedy Clubs

The number of comedy groups in Washington that welcome, indeed count on, the zany suggestions of audience members has mushroomed. These improvisation groups pop up at various venues, performing in the laughs-at-any-cost style of Chicago's Second City troupe, but many disappear as quickly as they appeared.

Capitol Steps. The musical political satire of this group of current and former Hill staffers is presented in the high-tech, 600-seat amphitheater of the Ronald Reagan Building and International Trade Center every Friday and Saturday at 7:30 PM, and occasionally at other spots around town. Tickets are available through Ticketmaster or from the D.C. Visitor Information Center. ✉ *Ronald Reagan Building and International Trade Center, 1300 Pennsylvania Ave. NW* ☎ *703/683–8330 Capitol Steps* ⊕ *www.capsteps.com* Ⓜ *Federal Triangle.*

ComedySportz. Two teams of improv artists go to work to make you laugh on Thursday, Friday, and Saturday nights. ✉ *Ballston Common Mall, 4238 Wilson Blvd., Arlington, VA* ☎ *703/486–4242* ⊕ *www.cszdc. com* Ⓜ *Ballston.*

Gross National Product. After years of aiming its barbs at the Democrats in *Clintoons* and *All the President's Women,* this satirical comedy troupe was most recently performing *Son of a Bush.* Their pieces are regularly updated with bits sure to annoy the sitting president. ☎ *202/783–7212* ⊕ *www.gnpcomedy.com.*

Improv. A heavyweight on the Washington comedy scene, the Improv is descended from the club that sparked the stand-up boomlet in New York City and across the country. Well-known headliners are common. ✉ *1140 Connecticut Ave. NW, Downtown* ☎ *202/296–7008* ⊕ *www. dcimprov.com* Ⓜ *Farragut North.*

Washington Improv Theater (WIT). Refreshingly, the WIT troupe's comedy tends not to focus strictly on Beltway politics, and relies heavily on audience suggestions. Their irreverent humor is performed to sellout crowds at area theaters and clubs. ☎ *202/244–8630 location and reservations* ⊕ *www.dcwit.com.*

Dance Clubs

Washington's dance clubs seem to be constantly re-creating themselves. A club might offer heavy "industrial" music on Wednesday, host a largely gay clientele on Thursday, and thump to the sounds of '70s disco on Friday. Club hoppers can choose from five club hubs: Georgetown; Adams-Morgan; U Street; the intersection of 18th and M streets, just south of Dupont Circle; and along 9th Street NW near Metro Center.

Dream. A four-story dance powerhouse looms over the industrial-feeling New York Avenue corridor far from downtown D.C. It's currently one of the most popular spots in town; Washington Wizards players and other celebs are frequently spotted in the VIP areas. The music ranges from hip-hop (on Fridays) to salsa, house, and trance. Avoid the headache of parking yourself and head directly for the valets. Dress to impress the doorman. ✉ *1350 Okie St. NE, Northeast/Ivy City* ☎ *202/232–2710* ⊕ *www.welcometodream.com.*

★ **Habana Village.** No matter what the temperature is outside, it's always balmy inside Habana Village. The tiny dance floor is packed nightly with couples moving to the latest salsa and merengue tunes. When it's time to cool down, you can head to one of several lounges in this converted four-story town house and relax in a wicker chair surrounded by potted palms. Be sure to order a *mojito,* the house special, made of white rum, sugar, and fresh crushed mint leaves. ✉ *1834 Columbia Rd. NW, Adams-Morgan* ☎ *202/462–6310* Ⓜ *Woodley Park/Zoo.*

Platinum. Known for years as the Bank, this multilevel, upscale dance venue always keeps up with the trends. The DJs play techno, hip-hop, house, and Latin music at the club, which has three dance floors and a VIP lounge. ✉ *915 F St. NW, Downtown* ☎ *202/393–3555* ⊕ *www. platinumclubdc.com/* Ⓜ *Metro Center.*

Polly Esther's. Polly Esther's is the Hard Rock Cafe of dance clubs, with outlets in New York, downtown D.C., and even Rockville, Maryland. Current tunes are spun, but '70s and '80s standbys are the crowd-pleasers. Catering to a crowd barely old enough to remember the tail end of the disco era, the club provides an unpretentious good time, especially for groups. Sing out loud to your favorite Bee Gees song while striking a John Travolta pose, and no one will look twice. Tennis shoes and baseball caps, however, do stand out, and are not considered appropriate attire. ✉ *605 12th St. NW, Downtown* ☎ *202/737–1970* Ⓜ *Metro Center.*

State of the Union. A young, eclectic crowd dressed in styles of today's casually hip are the regulars at State. Patrons tend to be serious music fans who come to dance or hold down a spot at the bar, while the city's best DJs spin a mix of hip-hop, house, jungle, and R&B. ✉ *1357 U St. NW, U St. corridor* ☎ *202/588–8926* Ⓜ *U Street/Cardozo.*

Gay & Lesbian Dance Clubs

Apex. The nightclub once known as Badlands is still a prime hotspot for gay men. An upgraded light show, mirrors and fog enhance the experience on the club's expanded dance floor. It's a bit easier to get a drink at the upstairs bar; while you're there, you might want to drop by the pool table for a game. Men will find a definite meat-market vibe here, but with less attitude than at larger nightclubs. ✉ *1415 22nd St. NW, Dupont Circle* ☎ *202/296–0505* Ⓜ *Dupont Circle.*

Club Chaos. You could walk right by this basement-level restaurant/nightclub if it weren't for all the guys spilling up the stairs into the street on Fridays and Saturdays. A young, chic lesbian crowd takes over on Wednesday, and Thursday is Latin night. ✉ *17th and Q Sts. NW, Dupont Circle* ☎ *202/232–4141* Ⓜ *Dupont Circle.*

Hung Jury. You can count on the women at the Hung Jury to make the most of the dance floor, where you're just as likely to hear the innuendo-laden lyrics of rapper Lil' Kim as you are an upbeat Top 40 dance track. ✉ *1819 H St. NW, Downtown* ☎ *202/785–8181* Ⓜ *Farragut West.*

Ziegfeld's. This club's clientele is made up mostly of gay men and straight women. Half the club is dedicated to drag shows, male strippers, and go-go boys, while on the other side of the club patrons dance to the latest house tracks. ✉ *1345 Half St. SE, Southeast* ☎ *202/554–5141* Ⓜ *Navy Yard.*

Jazz & Blues Clubs

The **D.C. Blues Society Hotline** (☎ 202/828–3028 ⊕ www.dcblues.org) is a clearinghouse for information on upcoming shows, festivals, and jam sessions in the metropolitan area. It also publishes a monthly newsletter.

Fodor'sChoice **Blues Alley.** The restaurant turns out Creole cooking, while on stage
★ you'll find such nationally known performers as Nancy Wilson, Joshua Redman, and Stanley Turrentine. You can come for just the show, but those who come for a meal get better seats. ✉ *1073 Wisconsin Ave. NW, rear, Georgetown* ☎ *202/337–4141* ⊕ *www.bluesalley.com* Ⓜ *Foggy Bottom.*

Bohemian Caverns. Duck down the low-ceilinged stairway to a unique cavelike space made up of faux stalactites and stalagmites. This is a complete renovation of the Crystal Caverns, once a mainstay of D.C.'s "Black Broadway" and *the* fashionable place to see and be seen. These days Fridays and Saturdays spotlight jazz, and Wednesday's open mike night brings jazz-influenced poets to the stage. ✉ *2003 11th St. NW,*

U St. corridor ☎ *202/299–0800* ⊕ *www.bohemiancaverns.com* Ⓜ *U Street/Cardozo.*

Columbia Station. This neighborhood favorite has good food and great music. Amber lights light up the walls and the artwork, which potrays musical instruments. The nightly live music usually consists of a quality local jazz band and sometimes blues. Either way, there's usually an electric bass, rather than an upright, to help pound out tunes funky enough for dancing. ✉ *2325 18th St. NW, Adams-Morgan* ☎ *202/462–6040* Ⓜ *Woodley Park/Zoo.*

★ **HR-57 Center for the Preservation of Jazz and Blues.** Known locally as HR-57, this hot spot isn't really a club or a lounge, but a nonprofit cultural center. The warm, inviting center spotlights musicians based in the D. C. area, many of them with national followings. Beer and wine are available, or bring your own bottle ($3 corking fee per person for wine). Open Wednesday through Saturday. ✉ *1610 14th St. NW, Logan Circle* ☎ *202/667–3700* ⊕ *www.hr57.org* Ⓜ *U Street/Cardozo.*

New Vegas Lounge. This sweet dive bar is the home of Dr. Blues, and he doesn't allow any soft-jazz-bluesy-fusion in his house. Even during the weekly open-jam session, it's strictly no-nonsense wailing guitar rhythms by seasoned local players. ✉ *1415 P St. NW, Dupont Circle* ☎ *202/ 483–3971* Ⓜ *Dupont Circle.*

Takoma Station Tavern. In the shadow of the Metro stop that lends it its name, the Takoma Station Tavern hosts such local favorites as Marshall Keys and Keith Killgo, with the occasional nationally known artist stopping by to jam. The jazz happy hours starting at 6:30 Wednesday through Friday pack the joint. There's reggae on Saturday and comedy on Sunday. Sneakers and athletic wear are not allowed. ✉ *6914 4th St. NW, Takoma Park* ☎ *202/829–1999* ⊕ *www.takomastation.com* Ⓜ *Takoma.*

Twins Jazz. Twin sisters Kelly and Maze Tesfaye have made this cozy, second-floor space a haven for some of D.C.'s strongest straight-ahead jazz players, as well as for groups from New York City. On the club's menu are tasty Ethiopian appetizers along with staples like nachos, wings, and burgers. ✉ *1344 U St. NW, U St. corridor* ☎ *202/234–0072* Ⓜ *U Street/Cardozo.*

219 Basin Street Lounge. Jazz combos perform Tuesday through Saturday in this attractive Victorian-style bar, across the Potomac in Old Town Alexandria and above the 219 Restaurant. Musicians from local military bands often stop by to sit in. ✉ *219 King St., Alexandria, VA* ☎ *703/ 549–1141.*

After-Hour Restaurants

Annie's Paramount Steak House. A longtime late-night eatery, Annie's was once known only to the city's gay and lesbian population. No more. It's open until 11:30 on weekdays and 24 hours on weekends and holidays. ✉ *1609 17th St. NW, Dupont Circle* ☎ *202/232–0395* Ⓜ *Dupont Circle.*

Ben's Chili Bowl. U Street revelers can stop by this favorite among famous, infamous, and regular folks alike. Open until 4 AM, Ben's offers a glimpse of D.C. not often seen by tourists. ✉ *1213 U St. NW, U St. corridor* ☎ *202/667–0909* Ⓜ *U Street/Cardozo.*

Bistro Francais. Open until 3 AM on Tuesday through Friday mornings and until 4 AM on Saturdays and Sundays, the Bistro is a place chefs go when they're finished cooking. Expect straightforward French fare. ✉ *3128 M St. NW, Georgetown* ☎ *202/338–3830* Ⓜ *Foggy Bottom.*

Bob & Edith's Diner. This traditional diner gets crowded on weekends. If you're in Virginia after a late night of clubbing, drop by for a burger or early breakfast: it's open 24 hours. ⊠ *2310 Columbia Pike, Arlington, VA* ☎ *703/920–6103* Ⓜ *Ballston.*

The Diner. The classic diner experience is updated for the chic set at this late-night hipster hangout. ⊠ *2453 18th St. NW, Adams-Morgan* ☎ *202/232–8800* Ⓜ *Woodley Park/Zoo.*

Kramerbooks and Afterwords. This venerable standby delivers robust sandwiches like the Café Hanger Steak Sandwich and globe-trotting entries like the Café Thai Jambalaya. Not so hungry? The "Share-zies" are three lighter menu items served on a three-tiered stand for, well, sharing. Afterwords is open until 1 during the week and 24 hours on the weekend. ⊠ *1517 Connecticut Ave. NW, Dupont Circle* ☎ *202/387–1400* Ⓜ *Dupont Circle.*

Rock & Pop Clubs

Black Cat. This is the place to see the latest local bands as well as a few up-and-coming indie stars from such labels as TeenBeat and Dischord Records. Occasionally, you can see MTV acts like alt-rockers Sleater-Kinney, white-boy-funkster G. Love, or jazz-based rappers the Roots. The post-punk crowd whiles away the time in the Red Room, a side bar with pool tables, an eclectic jukebox, and no cover charge. ⊠ *1831 14th St. NW, U St. corridor* ☎ *202/667–7960* ⊕ *www.blackcatdc.com* Ⓜ *U Street/Cardozo.*

★ **Nation.** As one of the largest venues for alternative and rock music in Washington (it holds 1,000 people), Nation brings in such acts as 311, Alicia Keys, and Pink. Depending on the show, tickets are available at Ticketmaster or the door. On a separate side of the club, you can gyrate to a mix of mostly alternative dance music. On Friday night this warehouse space becomes "Buzz," a massive rave featuring the latest permutations of techno and drum-and-bass music. ⊠ *1015 Half St. SE, Southeast* ☎ *202/554–1500* ⊕ *www.primacycompanies.com* Ⓜ *Navy Yard.*

9:30 Club. An eclectic mix of local, national, and international artists (most of which fall into the alternative-music category—from the Flaming Lips and Ani DiFranco to Lucky Dube and Macy Gray) is booked at this trendy club. You can see the show from a balcony on three sides of the space or from the large dance floor in front of the stage. Vegetarian food catered from Planet X helps provide much-needed nourishment after you've been standing several hours. Get tickets at the door or through Tickets.com. ⊠ *815 V St. NW, U St. corridor* ☎ *202/393–0930* ⊕ *www.930.com* Ⓜ *U Street/Cardozo.*

Velvet Lounge. Squeeze up the narrow stairway and check out the eclectic local and national bands that play at this unassuming little joint. Indie mainstays like Adam West are regulars, but you'll also find acclaimed up-and-comers like The Bastard Sons of Johnny Cash. The bar books bands that play psychobilly, alt-country, indie pop . . . you name it, it's here. ⊠ *915 U St. NW, U St. corridor* ☎ *202/462–3213* ⊕ *www.velvetloungedc.com* Ⓜ *U Street/Cardozo.*

SPORTS & THE OUTDOORS

5

FODOR'S CHOICE

Biking and running on the C&O Canal Towpath and the Mall

D.C. United soccer team

Thompson's Boat Center's bike rentals

Tidal Basin paddleboats

HIGHLY RECOMMENDED

Bicycling at East Potomac Park

Horse races at Laurel Park

Pershing Park Ice Rink

Rock Creek Park Horse Center

Washington Wizards basketball team

By John F. Kelly
Updated by
Mitch Tropin

WASHINGTON'S 69 SQUARE MILES form a fantastic recreational back-yard. There are hundreds of grassy spaces—from the mammoth Rock Creek Park, with miles of trails for bikers, runners, joggers, and walkers, to the National Mall, where you can spike a volleyball with the monuments as a backdrop. Sports fans have a glut of professional teams on their doorstep, not to mention two spectacular stadiums: FedEx Field, where the Washington Redskins play; and the showcase MCI Center, where you can catch the NBA Wizards (and possibly Michael Jordan), the NHL Capitals, the WNBA Mystics, and a host of Division 1 college basketball teams (including the University of Maryland, 2002 NCAA National Basketball Champions).

Baseball

Washington doesn't have a professional baseball team, so fans go to Baltimore and root for the **Baltimore Orioles** (⊠ 333 W. Camden St., Baltimore, MD ☎ 410/685–9600; 410/685–9800 general information; 410/332–4633 Ext. 1.58 Warehouse ⊕ www.orioles.mlb.com). The team plays in beautiful Oriole Park at Camden Yards, which seats 48,000. Tickets range from $8 for spots in the bleachers to $40 for club level. Individual game tickets may be purchased by going to the Warehouse at Oriole Park or in Washington at the **Orioles Shop** (⊠ 925 17th St. NW, Downtown ☎ 202/296–2473). Special light-rail trains run to the stadium from the Washington's Union Station.

The **Bowie Baysox** (⊠ Prince George's County Stadium, Rtes. 50 and 301, Bowie, MD ☎ 301/805–6000 ⊕ www.baysox.com), the Orioles Class AA farm team, is in the Eastern League. They play in a 10,000-seat stadium in suburban Prince George's County, Maryland, about 45 minutes by car from Washington. Tickets range from $5 to $14 and children ages 5 and under get in free.

Head north of Washington up I–270 in Maryland to see the Oriole Class A **Frederick Keys** (⊠ Harry Grove Stadium, 6201 New Design Rd., Frederick, MD ☎ 301/662–0013 ⊕ www.keys.com), part of the Carolina League. To reach the stadium, look for the Market Street exit from Route 70 or 270. Tickets range from $5 to $11, and children ages 5 and under get in free.

To see the San Francisco Giants Class A **Hagerstown Suns** (⊠ Municipal Stadium, 274 E. Memorial Blvd., Hagerstown, MD ☎ 301/791–6266 ⊕ www.hagerstownsuns.com), take I–270 north into Maryland. Tickets for this South Atlantic League team range from $3 to $7.

About an hour south of Washington is the home of the Class A Carolina League **Potomac Cannons** (⊠ G. Richard Pfitzner Stadium, 7 County Complex Ct., Woodbridge, VA ☎ 703/590–2311 ⊕ www.potomaccannons.com). The Cannons are a farm team for the Cincinnati Reds; their tickets range from $5 to $11. Take Exit 158B off Prince William Parkway and look for the sign for Manassas; drive 8 mi and take a right onto County Complex Court.

Basketball

There are several top-flight college basketball teams here. Of the Division I men's college basketball teams in the area, the most prominent are the **Georgetown University Hoyas** (⊕ www.guhoyas.com), former NCAA national champions. Most home games are played at the **MCI Center** (⊠ 601 F St. NW, between 6th and 7th Sts., Downtown).

TICKETS & VENUES

You can buy tickets for most major sporting events at stadium box offices or from **Ticketmaster** (☎ 202/432–7328 or 410/481–7328; 800/527–6384 outside DC and Baltimore areas ⊕ www.ticketmaster.com).

Many sporting events—hockey, basketball, lacrosse, and figure skating, to name a few—take place at the modern **MCI Center** (✉ 601 F St. NW, between 6th and 7th Sts., Downtown ☎ 202/628–3200; 202/ 432–7328 box office ⊕ www.mcicenter. com). The perennially popular Washington Redskins play at **FedEx Field** (✉ Arena Dr., Landover ☎ 301/276–6070 ⊕ www. redskins.com). The **Robert F. Kennedy Stadium** (✉ 2400 E. Capitol St. NE, at 22nd St., Capitol Hill ☎ 202/628–3200) showcases some of the greatest soccer teams from Europe and Latin America, along with the D.C. United and the Washington Freedom.

The **University of Maryland Terrapins** (☎ 800/462–8377 or 301/314–7070 ⊕ www.umterps.com) won the 2002 NCAA National Basketball Championship and play in the Comcast Center at the College Park campus.

Other Division I teams include the **American University Eagles** (☎ 202/ 885–3267 ⊕ www.aueagles.com); the **George Mason University Patriots** (☎ 703/993–3000 ⊕ www.gmusports.com); the **George Washington University Colonials** (☎ 703/993–3270 ⊕ www.gwsports.com); the **Howard University Bison** (☎ 202/806–7198 ⊕ www.bisonmania.com); and the Navy team at the **U.S. Naval Academy** (☎ 410/293–4955 ⊕ www. navysports.com).

The WNBA's **Washington Mystics** (✉ 6th and F Sts., Downtown ☎ 202/ 432–7328 ⊕ www.wnba.com/mystics) play at the Metro-accessible MCI Center in downtown Washington. Ticket prices range from $8 to $37.50 and can be purchased at the MCI Center box office or through Ticketmaster. The WNBA's women's basketball season runs from late May to August.

★ The NBA's **Washington Wizards** (⊕ www.nba.com/wizards) play from October to April at the MCI Center in downtown Washington. Tickets, which can be purchased for individual games, cost from $35 to $175. You can buy them from the MCI Center box office or from Ticketmaster.

Bicycling

The numerous trails in the District and its surrounding areas are well maintained and clearly marked. For up-to-date information on biking events and other information, contact the Washington Area Bicyclist Association.

Fodor'sChoice For scenery, you can't beat the **C&O Canal Towpath** (⊕ www.nps.gov/choh),
★ which starts in Georgetown and runs along the C&O Canal into Maryland. You could pedal to the end of the canal, 184.5 mi away in Cumberland, Maryland, but most cyclists stop at Great Falls, 13 mi from where the canal starts. The occasionally bumpy towpath, made of gravel and packed earth, passes through wooded areas of the C&O Canal National Historical Park. You can see 19th-century locks from the canal's working days and, if you are particularly lucky, you may catch a glimpse of mules pulling a canal barge. The barges now take passengers, not cargo.

Suited for bicyclists, walkers, rollerbladers, and strollers, the paved **Capital Crescent Trail** (☎ 202/234–4874 Capital Crescent Coalition) stretches along the old Georgetown Branch, a B&O Railroad line that was completed in 1910 and that carried trains until 1985. The 7½-mi route's first leg runs from Georgetown near Key Bridge to central Bethesda at Bethesda and Woodmont avenues. At Bethesda and Woodmont, the trail heads through a well-lighted tunnel near the heart of Bethesda's lively business area and continues into Silver Spring. The 3½-mi stretch from Bethesda to Silver Spring is gravel. The Georgetown Branch Trail, as this section is officially named, connects with the Rock Creek Trail, which goes to Rockville in the north and Memorial Bridge past the Washington Monument in the south. On weekends when the weather's nice, all sections of the trails are crowded. For more information and to obtain free maps, call the Capital Crescent Coalition.

★ Cyclists interested in serious training might try the 3-mi loop around the golf course in **East Potomac Park** (☎ 202/485–9874 National Park Service) at Hains Point, the southernmost area of the park (entry is near the Jefferson Memorial). It's a favorite training course for dedicated local racers and would-be triathletes. If time permits, jog or bike over to the impressive Franklin Delano Roosevelt memorial. Restrict your workouts to the daytime; the area is not safe after dark. For current conditions, contact the National Park Service's East Potomac Park Office. Each

Fodor'sChoice day, bicyclists cruise **The Mall** amid the endless throngs of runners, walkers, and tourists. There's relatively little car traffic, and bikers can take in some of Washington's landmarks, such as the Washington Monument, the Reflecting Pool, the Vietnam Memorial, and some of the city's more interesting architecture, such as the Smithsonian Castle and the Hirshhorn, the "Doughnut on the Mall." A pleasant loop route begins at the Lincoln Memorial, going north past the Washington Memorial, turning around at the Tidal Basin. Along the way, there are small fountains and parks for taking a break and getting a drink of water.

Mount Vernon Trail, across the Potomac in Virginia, has two sections. The northern part, closest to D.C. proper, is 3½ mi long and begins near the causeway across the river from the Kennedy Center that heads to Theodore Roosevelt Island. It then passes Ronald Reagan National Airport and continues on to Old Town Alexandria. This section has slight slopes and almost no interruptions for traffic, making it a delightful, but challenging, biking route. Even relatively inexperienced bikers will enjoy the trail, which gives wonderful views of the Potomac. From the trail, you can take a bridge to Theodore Roosevelt Island, a relatively undeveloped area with beautiful trees. To access the trail from the District, take the Theodore Roosevelt Bridge or the Rochambeau Memorial Bridge, also known as the 14th Street Bridge. South of the airport, the trail runs down to the Washington Marina. The final mile of the trail's northern section meanders through protected wetlands before ending in the heart of Old Town Alexandria. The trail's 9-mi southern section extends along the Potomac from Alexandria to Mount Vernon.

Rock Creek Park covers an area from the edge of Georgetown to Montgomery County, Maryland. The bike path there is asphalt and has a few challenging hills, but it is mostly flat. You can bike several miles without having to stop for cars. The 15 mi of dirt trails are best for hiking. The roadway is closed to traffic on weekends. The two separate northern parts of the trail, which begin in Bethesda and Silver Spring, merge around the Washington, D.C., line. Many bikers gather at this point and follow the trail on a path that goes past the Washington Zoo and eventually runs toward the Lincoln Memorial and Kennedy Center.

Information

The **Washington Area Bicyclist Association** (WABA; ✉ 733 15th St. NW, Suite 1030, 20005 ☎ 202/628–2500 ⊕ www.waba.org) has information and puts out publications about cycling in the nation's capital. The organization's *Greater Washington Area Bicycle Atlas*, in particular, is an invaluable resource. It's available through WABA or at local bookstores.

Rentals

Bicycle Pro Shop Georgetown (✉ 3403 M St. NW, Georgetown ☎ 202/337–0254), near Georgetown University and Key Bridge by the Potomac river, rents city bikes for $20 per day.

Big Wheel Bikes, near the C&O Canal Towpath, rents multispeed bikes for $25 per day and $15 for three hours. A second location is near the Capital Crescent Trail. There's also an Alexandria branch who those who want to ride the Mount Vernon Trail. ✉ *1034 33rd St. NW, Georgetown* ☎ *202/337–0254* ✉ *6917 Arlington Rd., Bethesda, MD* ☎ *301/652–0192* ✉ *2 Prince St., Alexandria, VA* ☎ *703/739–2300.*

Bike the Sites (☎ 202/966–8662 ⊕ www.bikethesites.com) is a tour company that offers three-hour, 8-mi guided tours of downtown Washington. Costs range from $35 to $55, and bike rental is included. Advance reservations are required. Tours start from the Mall.

Bikes USA (✉ 1306-C Belle View Blvd., Alexandria, VA ☎ 703/768–3444) is a bike store near the Mount Vernon Trail in Alexandria.

Blazing Saddles (✉ 1001 Pennsylvania Ave. NW, Downtown ☎ 202/544–0055) rents all types of bikes, including tandems, and offers self-guided tours of Washington. Bikes are $5 to $9 per hour and $25 to $45 per day.

Fletcher's Boat House (✉ 4940 Canal Rd., at Reservoir Rd., Foxhall ☎ 202/244–0461), next to the C&O Towpath and Capital Crescent Trail, rents fixed-gear bikes for $8 per hour and $19 per day.

FodorsChoice **Thompson's Boat Center** (✉ 2900 Virginia Ave. NW, Foggy Bottom
★ ☎ 202/333–4861) allows easy access to the Rock Creek Trail and the C&O Towpath and is close to the monuments. Multispeed bikes are $8 per hour and $25 per day. Fixed-gear bikes are $8 per hour and $12 per day.

Washington Sailing Marina (✉ 1 Marina Dr., Alexandria, VA ☎ 703/548–9027) rents multispeed bikes for $6 per hour and $22 per day. Fixed-gear bikes are $4 per hour and $16.50 per day. The marina is on the Mount Vernon Trail off the George Washington Parkway, south of Ronald Reagan National Airport.

Boating & Sailing

The Chesapeake Bay is one of the great sailing basins of the world. For some scenic and historical sightseeing, take a day trip to Annapolis, Maryland, the home of the U.S. Naval Academy. The popularity of boating and the many boating businesses in Annapolis make it one of the best civilian sailing centers on the East Coast.

Annapolis Sailing School (✉ 601 6th St., Annapolis, MD ☎ 410/267–7205), the oldest organization of its kind in the United States is a good choice for lessons and rentals. It's world renowned.

Some of the best white-water kayakers and canoeists in the country call Washington home. On weekends they practice below Great Falls in **Mather Gorge** (☎ 703/285–2965 in Virginia; 301/299–3613 in Maryland), a canyon carved by the Potomac River just north of the city, above Chain Bridge. The water is deceptive and dangerous—only top-level kayakers should consider a run here. It's safe, however, to watch the experts at play from a post above the gorge.

Canoeing, sailing, and powerboating are all popular in the Washington, D.C., area. Several places rent boats along the **Potomac River** north and south of the city. You can dip your oars just about anywhere along the river—go canoeing in the C&O Canal, sailing in the widening river south of Alexandria, or even kayaking in the raging rapids at Great Falls, a 30-minute drive from the capital.

Rentals

Belle Haven Marina (✉ George Washington Pkwy., Alexandria, VA ☎ 703/768–0018), south of Reagan National Airport and Old Town Alexandria, rents three types of sailboats: Sunfish are $30 for two hours during the week and $35 for two hours on the weekend; Hobie Cat–style sailboats and Flying Scots are $46 for two hours during the week and $54 for two hours during the weekend. Canoes and kayaks are also available. Rentals are available from April to October.

Fletcher's Boat House (✉ 4940 Canal Rd., at Reservoir Rd., Foxhall ☎ 202/244–0461), just north of Georgetown, rents 17-foot rowboats for $19 per day.

Thompson's Boat Center (✉ 2900 Virginia Ave. NW, Foggy Bottom ☎ 202/333–4861) is near Georgetown and Theodore Roosevelt Island. The center rents canoes for $8 per hour and $22 per day. Single kayaks are $8 per hour and $24 per day, and double kayaks are $10 per hour and $30 per day. Rowing sculls are also available, but you must demonstrate prior experience and a suitably high skill level.

Fodor'sChoice   **Tidal Basin** (✉ Bordered by Independence Ave. and Maine Ave., The Mall
★   ☎ 202/479–2426), in front of Jefferson Memorial, rents paddleboats beginning in April and usually ending in September, depending on how cold the water gets. The entrance is on 1501 Maine Avenue SW, on the east side of the Tidal Basin. From around April until September you can rent two-passenger boats at $8 per hour and four-passenger boats at $16 per hour.

The **Washington Sailing Marina** (✉ 1 Marina Dr., Alexandria, VA ☎ 703/548–9027 ⊕ www.guestservices.com/wsm) rents sailboats from around mid-May to September, or until the water gets too cold. Sunfish are $10 per hour, Island 17's are $17 per hour, and the larger Flying Scots are $19 per hour. There's a one-hour minimum rental for all boats.

Barge Rides

During the one-hour rides on mule-drawn barges on the **C&O Canal** (✉ Canal Visitor Center, 1057 Thomas Jefferson St. NW, Georgetown ☎ 202/653–5190 or 301/299–2026 ☒ $8 ⊕ www.nps.gov/choh/co service.htm#george), costumed guides and volunteers explain the waterway's history. The barge rides, run by the National Park Service, depart from its visitor center Wednesday through Sunday April through November.

Bowling & Duckpin Bowling

The mid-Atlantic region is the birthplace of duckpin bowling, and among its last remaining bastions. The balls and pins are smaller than those in the standard tenpin version of bowling. John McGraw, who later went on to become a Hall of Fame baseball manager with the New York Giants, invented duckpin bowling in Baltimore around 1900 as a way to keep his players in shape during the off-season. Though this species of bowling—also known as "the ducks"—is by all accounts endangered, there are still several duckpin alleys in the area.

For those not into nostalgia who want a little more excitement, many area bowling centers now offer "cosmic" bowling, which usually starts after 10 PM and may last until 4 AM. The regular lights turn off, black lights come on, and the bowling balls and pins all begin to glow. A DJ, fog machines, and light shows are often part of the experience.

The 48 lanes at **AMF Alexandria** (✉ 6228-A North Kings Hwy., Alexandria, VA ☏ 703/765–3633) are open 9 AM–11 PM weekdays, and until 1 AM on Friday and Saturday. Games are $3.25 to $4.25. Shoe rental is $3.25.

The 40 lanes at **AMF College Park** (✉ 9021 Baltimore Blvd., College Park, MD ☏ 301/474–8282) are open 9 AM–11 PM weekdays, and until 1 AM on Friday and Saturday. Games are $2.50 to $3.25 during the week and $4 on the weekends. Shoe rental is $3.

AMF Seminary (✉ 4620 Kenmore Ave., Alexandria, VA ☏ 703/823–6200) has 40 lanes and is open 9 AM–11 PM weekdays, and until 1 AM on Friday and Saturday. Games are $3.25 to $4.25. Shoe rental is $3.24.

Bowl America Shirley (✉ 6450 Edsall Rd., Alexandria, VA ☏ 703/354–3300) has 40 lanes and is open 9 AM–11 PM weekdays, and until 4 AM on Friday and Saturday. Games are $3.75 to $4.75. Shoe rental is $2.75.

Bowl America Silver Spring (✉ 8616 Cameron St., Silver Spring, MD ☏ 301/585–6990) offers 30 lanes and is open 9 AM–11 PM weekdays, and until 1 AM on Friday and Saturday. Games are $3.75 to $5. Shoe rental is $2.75.

The **Falls Church Bowling Center** (✉ 400 South Maple St., Falls Church, VA ☏ 703/533–8131) has 32 lanes, open 9 AM to 10 PM Monday through Thursday, 10 AM to 10 PM Friday, 11 AM to 10 PM Saturday, and noon to 7 PM Sunday. Games cost $2.75. Shoe rental is $1.25.

Strike Bethesda (✉ 5353 Westbard Ave., Bethesda MD ☏ 301/652–0955 ⊕ www.strikebethesda.com) combines 34 lanes with a full restaurant, two bars, and a VIP room. Lanes are open 10 AM to 1 AM Sunday through Thursday, 10 AM to 2 AM Friday and Saturday. Games cost $4.95 to $6.95. Shoe rental is $3.

White Oak Lanes (✉ 11207 New Hampshire Ave., Silver Spring, MD ☏ 301/593–3000) has 24 lanes for duckpins and is open 9 AM to 11 PM weekdays and Sunday, and 9 AM to 1 AM Saturday. Games are $2.50 during the week and $3.25 on the weekend. Shoe rental is $2.50 for adults and $2 for children.

Fishing

The **Potomac River** is something of an environmental success story. Once dangerously polluted, it has rebounded. Now largemouth bass, striped bass, shad, and white and yellow perch are all down there somewhere, willing to take your bait. Simply renting a boat and going fishing in Washington is complicated because this stretch of the Potomac is divided among the three jurisdictions of Virginia, Maryland, and the District of Columbia. It isn't always easy to determine in whose water you're fishing or which licenses you should have. One solution: hire a guide.

One 5-mi stretch of the Potomac—roughly from the Wilson Memorial Bridge in Alexandria south to Fort Washington National Park—is one of the country's best spots for largemouth-bass fishing. It has, in fact, become something of an East Coast destination for anglers in search of this particular fish. The area around Fletcher's Boat House on the C&O Canal is one of the best spots for perch.

Information

Nationally known fishing writer **Gene Mueller** has a column that appears three times a week in the *Washington Times*. He gladly takes readers' telephone calls Thursday mornings ☎ 202/636–3268. The **"Fish Lines"** column in Friday's *Washington Post* "Weekend" section, written by Gary Diamond, outlines where the fish are biting, from the Potomac to the Chesapeake Bay.

Tackle Shop & Guides

Run by nationally known fisherman and conservationist Ken Penrod, **Life Outdoors Unlimited** (☎ 301/937–0010) is an umbrella group of the area's best freshwater fishing guides. For about $250 a day a guide sees to all your needs, from tackle to boats, and tells you which licenses are required. All of the guides are pros, able to teach novices as well as guide experts. You might be asked to leave a message; calls are usually returned the same evening.

Football

There have been many changes in the **Washington Redskins** (☎ 301/276–6000 FedEx Field stadium ⊕ www.redskins.com) since Dan Snyder became the owner in July 1999. But one thing remains the same, tickets are very difficult to get. Though FedEx Field is the largest football stadium in the NFL, all 80,000 seats are held by season-ticket holders. Occasionally you can find tickets advertised in the classifieds of the *Washington Post* or from on-line ticket vendors and auction sites—at top dollar, of course. Tickets can range from $175 to $300 for less popular opponents and as high as $800 for elite teams, like the St. Louis Rams, or Washington's biggest rival, the Dallas Cowboys. Tickets for pre-season Redskins games, played at FedEx Field in August, are easier to get.

Colleges around the capital offer an excellent alternative to booked-solid Redskins games, played from September through November: **Howard University** (☎ 202/806–7198 ⊕ www.bisonmania.com), which plays at RFK Stadium and on Howard's campus in Northwest Washington; the **University of Maryland** (☎ 301/314–7070 ⊕ www.umterps.fansonly. com), which plays in nearby College Park, Maryland; and the **U.S. Naval Academy** (☎ 410/268–6068 ⊕ www.navysports.com), which plays in Annapolis, Maryland.

Golf

Serious golfers must resign themselves to driving out of the city to find a worthwhile course. None of the three public courses in town are first-rate. Still, people line up to play here and at about 50 other area public courses, sometimes arriving as early as 2 AM to snare a tee time. Some courses allow you to make a reservation in advance.

Public Courses in the District

The claim to fame of the flat, wide, and featureless **East Potomac Park Golf Course** (✉ 972 Ohio Dr. SW, Southwest ☎ 202/554–7660) is that professional golfer and Washington resident Lee Elder got his start here. The course is 6,599 yards, par-72. Two 9-hole courses and a driving range are on the property, as well as one of the country's oldest miniature golf courses. Greens fees are $20 for 18 holes and $14 for 9 holes on weekdays—on weekends it's $24 and $17, respectively. The course is on the eastern side of the park, near the Jefferson Memorial.

The par-72, 6,300-yard **Langston Golf Course** (✉ 2600 Benning Rd. NE, at 26th St. ☎ 202/397–8638) is popular despite poorly maintained greens and fairways. Holes 8 and 9, by the Anacostia River, are challenging. Greens fees for 18 holes are $18.25 on weekdays, $11.25 for seniors; fees for nine holes are $12.50 and $9 for seniors. On weekends, the fees are $23 for 18 holds and $15.50 for 9 with no discount for seniors.

The 4,798-yard, par-65 **Rock Creek Park Golf Course** (✉ 16th and Rittenhouse Sts. NW, Northwest/upper Connecticut Ave. ☎ 202/882–7332) is the most attractive public course in the capital. The front nine holes are easy, but the tight, rolling, well-treed back nine are challenging. Greens fees are $15 for 18 holes and $9 for 9 holes on weekdays; weekend fees are $23 and $15.50.

Public Courses in Nearby Suburbs

Maryland's 6,209-yard, par-72 **Enterprise Golf Course** (✉ 2802 Enterprise Rd., Mitchellville, MD ☎ 301/249–2040) may be the best-manicured public course in the area. Its well landscaped layout wouldn't be out of place in a country club. The fee for 18 holes is $40 weekdays and $45 weekends. About 30 minutes by car from downtown Washington, the course is near the Beltway in Prince George's County.

Extremely long and winding, the 6,732-yard, par-72 **Northwest Park Golf Course** (✉ 15701 Layhill Rd., Wheaton, MD ☎ 301/598–6100) makes for slow play. It's immaculately groomed and has a short-nine course. It's about a half hour from town. The fee for 18 holes is $26 weekdays and $33 weekends; the short-nine course is $13 and $16, respectively.

To squeeze in a round of golf on the way to or from Dulles Airport, try **Penderbrook Golf Club** (✉ 3700 Golf Trail La., Fairfax, VA ☎ 703/385–3700), a short but imaginative 5,927-yard, par-71 course. The 5th, 11th, 12th, and 15th holes are exceptional. The fees for 18 holes are $55 Monday through Thursday, and $69 Friday through Sunday. Penderbrook is off West Ox Road and Route 50.

Designed by Ault, Clark & Associates, **Pleasant Valley Golfers' Club** (✉4715 Pleasant Valley Rd., Chantilly, VA ☎703/631–7902) has a 6,957-yard, par-72, 18-hole course that is pristinely landscaped with hills, hardwood trees, wildflowers, native-grass meadows, and water features. Greens fees are $60 Monday through Thursday, $70 Friday, and $85 on weekends. The club is off Route 50, south of Dulles Airport.

Though heavily wooded, the well-maintained 6,871-yard, par-71 **Reston National Golf Course** (✉ 11875 Sunrise Valley Dr., Reston, VA ☎ 703/620–9333) is not too difficult for the average player. It's about a half-hour drive from downtown Washington. Greens fees for 18 holes are $65 weekdays and $85 weekends.

Renowned landscape-architect Dan Maples designed **South Riding Golf Course** (✉ 43237 Golf View Dr., South Riding, VA ☎ 703/327–3673), an 18-hole, 7,100-yard, par-72 course off Route 50, south of Dulles Airport. Greens fees are $62 Monday through Friday, and $79 weekends and holidays.

Health Clubs

All health clubs require that you be a member—or at least a member of an affiliated club—to use their facilities. Some hotels have made private arrangements with neighboring health clubs to enable their guests to use the club's facilities, sometimes at a daily rate. If you belong to a member club of the **International Health, Racquet & Sportsclub Association** (IHRSA; ☎ 617/951–0055 or 800/228–4772 🖷 617/951–0056), you can pay by the day to use the facilities at a member club in Washington, provided that it's at least 50 mi from your home club. To access the facilities, bring your club membership card and an IHRSA "passport" from your home club. The IHRSA does not supply passports.

Guests at any Washington-area hotel may use the fabulous **Fitness Company West End** (✉ Washington Monarch Hotel, 2401 M St. NW, West End ☎ 202/457–5070) facilities for $20 per day—$10 for Monarch guests. Show your hotel-room key to the center's employees to get in. The **National Capital YMCA** (✉ 1711 Rhode Island Ave. NW, Downtown ☎ 202/862–9622) has basketball, weights, racquetball, squash, swimming, exercise equipment, and more. Some downtown hotels offer those staying with them free one-day passes. Members of an out-of-town Y show their membership card and pay a daily fee of $7 to $10, depending on the time of day, and their guests are allowed in for $15 to $20.

Hiking

Hikes and nature walks are listed in the Friday "Weekend" section of the *Washington Post*. Several area organizations sponsor outings: The **Potomac-Appalachian Trail Club** (✉ 118 Park St. SE, Vienna, VA 22180 ☎ 703/242–0965) sponsors hikes—usually free—on trails from Pennsylvania to Virginia, including the C&O Canal and the Appalachian Trail. The **Sierra Club** (☎ 202/547–2326) has many regional outings; call for details.

A self-guided nature trail winds through **Woodend** (✉ 8940 Jones Mill Rd., Chevy Chase, MD 20815 ☎ 301/652–9188; 301/652–1088 for recent bird sightings ⊕ www.audubonnaturalist.org/woodend.htm), a verdant 40-acre estate, and around the suburban Maryland headquarters of the local **Audubon Naturalist Society**. The estate was designed in the 1920s by Jefferson Memorial architect John Russell Pope and has a mansion, also called Woodend, on its grounds. You're never very far from the trill of birdsong here, as the Audubon Society has turned the place into something of a private nature preserve, forbidding the use of toxic chemicals and leaving some areas in a wild, natural state. Programs include wildlife identification walks, environmental education programs, and a weekly Saturday bird walk September through June. A bookstore stocks titles on conservation, ecology, and birds. The grounds are open daily sunrise to sunset, and admission is free.

A 1,460-acre refuge in Alexandria, **Huntley Meadows Park** (✉ 3701 Lockheed Blvd., Alexandria, VA ☎ 703/768–2525) is made for birders. You can spot more than 200 species—from ospreys to owls, egrets, and ibis. Much of the park is wetlands, a favorite of aquatic species. A boardwalk circles through a marsh, enabling you to spot beaver lodges, and 4 mi of trails wend through the park, making it likely you'll see deer, muskrats, and river otters as well. The park is usually open daily dawn to dusk.

Hockey

One of pro hockey's best teams, the **Washington Capitals** (⊕ www.washingtoncaps.com), play home games October through April at the MCI Center. Tickets range from $22 to $56 and can be purchased at the MCI Center box office, or from Ticketmaster. Tickets also can be purchased directly from the team's Web site without a service fee.

Horse Racing

★ Maryland has a long-standing affection for the ponies. You can watch and wager on Thoroughbreds at **Laurel Park** (✉ Rte. 198 and Race Track Rd., Laurel, MD ☎ 301/725–0400 or 410/792–7775 ⊕ www. marylandracing.com) from January through March, July and August, and October through December. Race days are usually Tuesday–Sunday. Simulcast wagering is available every day but Tuesday.

Mid-May brings the running of the Preakness Stakes, the second leg of horse racing's Triple Crown, at **Pimlico Race Course** (✉ Hayward and Winner Aves., Baltimore, MD ☎ 410/542–9400; 877/206–8042 Preakness information ⊕ www.marylandracing.com). The course has Thoroughbred racing from early April to late June. Race days are usually Wednesday through Sunday. Simulcast wagering is available year-round, every day but Tuesday.

Harness racing is just outside the Beltway at **Rosecroft** (✉ 6336 Rosecroft Dr., Fort Washington, MD ☎ 301/567–4000 ⊕ www.rosecroft. com). Race days are usually Thursday through Saturday, and the season runs from February to late December.

A little over an hour from downtown, just across the West Virginia border from Maryland and near scenic Harper's Ferry, **Charles Town Races** (✉ U.S. Rte. 340, Charles Town, WV ☎ 800/795–7001 ⊕ www. ctownraces.com) offers bettors who lose on the ponies the chance to win it back (or lose more) at the slot machines. Races are year-round, with evening post times Wednesday through Saturday and afternoon post times on Sunday. There's no live racing Monday through Wednesday, but simulcast wagering is available daily.

Horseback Riding

★ Lessons and trail rides are offered year-round at the **Rock Creek Park Horse Center** (✉ Military and Glover Rds. NW, Northwest/upper Connecticut Ave. ☎ 202/362–0117). The guided trail rides—for beginning riders ages 12 and up—are an hour long. Hours of operation vary with the season.

Ice-Skating

You can rent skates at all the rinks listed, which typically charge $4–$5.50 for a two-hour session, with slightly lower fees for children and seniors. Skate rentals are usually around $2 or $2.50. Some rinks charge a small locker rental fee.

The indoor rink at **Cabin John Park** (✉ 10610 Westlake Dr., Rockville, MD ☎ 301/365–0585) is open year-round.

The **Mount Vernon Recreation Center** (✉ 2017 Belle View Blvd., Alexandria, VA ☎ 703/768–3222) has an indoor rink that's open all year. It's convenient if you're staying in the lower half of Washington, D.C.

The **National Gallery of Art Ice Rink** (✉ Constitution Ave. NW, between 7th and 9th Sts., Downtown ☎ 202/289–3361) is surrounded by the gallery's Sculpture Garden, which is filled with extraordinary art sculptures on meticulously landscaped gardens. The art deco design of the rink makes it one of the most popular outdoor winter sites in Washington. In spring the rink becomes a fountain.

★ The prime location of the **Pershing Park Ice Rink** (✉ Pennsylvania Ave. and 14th St. NW, Downtown ☎ 202/737–6938), a few blocks from the White House, makes it one of Washington's most popular places to skate.

Polo

A scenic one-hour drive from downtown, in the heart of Virginia horse country, is the **Polo Great Meadow** (✉ 5089 Old Tavern Rd., Plains, VA ☎ 540/253–5156 ⊕ www.greatmeadow.org), where arena polo—a smaller-scale, more fan-friendly version of the hockey-on-horses pastime—is played each Friday night from early June through mid-September. Games start at 6 PM, weather permitting, but many folks arrive early to people-watch and to tailgate, both of which are at least as important to the polo culture as the competition. Admission is $20 per carload.

Running

Running is one of the best ways to see the city, and downtown Washington and nearby northern Virginia offer several scenic trails. It can be dangerous to run at night on the trails, although the streets are fairly well lighted. Even in daylight, it's best to run in pairs when venturing beyond public areas or heavily used sections of trails. Most city streets are safe for runs alone during the day, especially around government buildings, museums, and monuments, where there is additional police protection.

Group runs and weekend races around Washington are listed in the Friday "Weekend" section of the *Washington Post*. You can also check the Thursday calendar of events in the *Washington Times*. Comprehensive listings of running and walking events are posted on-line by the *Washington Running Report* at ⊕ www.runwashington.com and *RacePacket* at ⊕ www.racepacket.com. Another reliable source for races and casual running gatherings is the Montgomery County Road Runners—the nation's third-largest running club—at ⊕ www.mcrrc.org.

Fodor'sChoice
★ The 89-mi-long **C&O Canal Towpath** (⊕ www.nps.gov/choh) in the C&O National Historical Park is a favorite of runners and cyclists. The path is mostly gravel and dirt, making it easy on knees and feet. The most popular loop—from a point just north of the Key Bridge in Georgetown to Fletcher's Boat House—is about 4 mi round-trip. Information on the towpath and surrounding areas can be found on the National Park Service's Web site.

Fodor'sChoice
★ The most popular running route in Washington is the 4½-mi loop on **The Mall** around the Capitol and past the Smithsonian museums, the Washington Monument, the Reflecting Pool, and the Lincoln Memorial. At any time of day, hundreds of runners, speed walkers, bicyclists, and tourists make their way along the gravel pathways. For a longer run, veer south of the Mall on either side of the Tidal Basin and head for the Jefferson Memorial and East Potomac Park, the site of many races.

Across the Potomac in Virginia is the **Mount Vernon Trail**, a favorite with Washington runners. The 3½-mi northern section begins near the pedestrian causeway leading to Theodore Roosevelt Island (directly across the river from the Kennedy Center) and goes past Ronald Reagan National Airport and on to Old Town Alexandria. You can get to the trail from the District by crossing either the Theodore Roosevelt Bridge at the Lincoln Memorial or the Rochambeau Memorial Bridge, at the Jefferson Memorial. South of the airport, the trail runs down to the Washington Marina. The 9-mi southern section leads to Mount Vernon.

Rock Creek Park has 15 mi of trails, a bicycle path, a bridle path, picnic groves, playgrounds, and the boulder-strewn rolling stream that give it its name. The creek isn't safe or pleasant for swimming. Starting one block south of the corner of P and 22nd streets on the edge of Georgetown, Rock Creek Park runs all the way to Montgomery County, Maryland. The most popular run in the park is a trail along the creek from Georgetown to the National Zoo—about a 4-mi loop. In summer there's considerable shade, and there are water fountains at an exercise station along the way. The roadway is closed to traffic on weekends.

Information & Organizations

Tuesday and Thursday evenings at 6:30 PM you can join the **Capitol Hill Runners** (☎ 301/283–0821) on a 6- to 8-mi run, which begins at the reflecting pool at the base of the Capitol's west side. Most Sunday mornings the **Fleet Feet Sports Shop** (✉ 1841 Columbia Rd. NW, Adams-Morgan ☎ 202/387–3888) sponsors informal runs through Rock Creek Park and other areas. The shop's owner, Phil Fenty, leads the runs. The courses change at Phil's discretion and usually go from 5 to 7 mi. Call the **Gatorade and Road Runners Club of America Hotline** (☎ 703/683–7722) for general information about running and racing in the area.

Soccer

FodorsChoice
★

D.C. United (✉ RFK Stadium, 2400 E. Capitol St. SE, Capitol Hill ☎ 202/547–3134 ⊕ www.dcunited.com) is consistently one of the best Major League Soccer (U.S. pro soccer) teams. International matches are often played on the grass field, which is dedicated exclusively to soccer play. Games are April through September. You can buy tickets, which range from $16 to $22 and $28 to $36 for double headers or special events, at the RFK Stadium ticket office, or through Ticketmaster.

Representing D.C. in the WUSA, the professional women's soccer league, the **Washington Freedom** (✉ RFK Stadium, 2400 E. Capitol St. SE, Capitol Hill ☎ 202/547–3134 ⊕ www.washingtonfreedom.com) draws from players on the U.S. Olympic and World Cup teams. The Freedom plays at RFK Stadium April through August. Tickets range from $12 to $23 and are available through Ticketmaster.

Swimming

Washington has no beaches. If you want to swim, your best bet is to stay at a hotel with a pool. Health-club pools are open only to members, though the downtown YMCA has a pool and welcomes members of out-of-town Ys—for a fee. The District of Columbia maintains 6 public indoor pools and 19 large outdoor pools, as well as 15 outdoor pools that are smaller, but still fun for children. For information and a list of public facilities, contact the **D.C. Department of Recreation Aquatics Department** (✉ 1230 Taylor St. NW, 20011, Northwest ☎ 202/576–6436).

Tennis

The District maintains 123 outdoor courts, but because some are in seedy parts of town, check on the neighborhood in question before heading out. Contact the **D.C. Department of Recreation** (✉ 3149 16th St. NW, 20010, Northwest ☎ 202/673–7646) for a list of city-run courts and information about specific courts. **Hains Point** (✉ East Potomac Park, Southwest ☎ 202/554–5962) has outdoor tennis courts, as well as courts under a bubble for wintertime play. Fees run from $5 to $30.75 an hour depending on the time, the season, and whether it's an indoor or outdoor court. Make court reservations as early as possible—up to a week in advance.

To reach Hains Point, take 15th Street south to the Tidal Basin and then follow signs to East Potomac Park. For current conditions, contact the National Park Service's East Potomac Park Office (☎ 202/234–4874). **Rock Creek Tennis Center** (✉ 16th and Kennedy Sts. NW, Northwest/upper Connecticut Ave. ☎ 202/722–5949) has clay and hard courts. Fees depend on the time, the season, and whether you're playing indoors or out. You can make reservations up to a week in advance.

Volleyball

Possibly the most idyllic noncoastal volleyball venue you'll ever find, the **Underpass Volleyball Courts** (✉ 1100 Ohio Dr. SW, between Rock Creek Pkwy. and Independence Ave., The Mall ☎ 202/619–7225) are 11 public courts in the shadow of the Lincoln Memorial and Washington Monument and bordering the Potomac River. The courts are in an unnamed park area that's run cooperatively by the National Park Service and the D.C. government, with six of the courts reserved for organizations granted permits through the city, and the remaining five available on a first-come, first-served basis.

SHOPPING

FODOR'S CHOICE

Apartment Zero, Downtown

Child's Play, Chevy Chase

The Chocolate Moose, Dupont Circle

Neiman Marcus, Friendship Heights

Politics and Prose, Friendship Heights

Rodman's Discount Foods and Drugstore, Friendship Heights

Saks Fifth Avenue, Friendship Heights

HIGHLY RECOMMENDED

Al's Magic Shop, Downtown

April Cornell, Georgetown

Brooks Brothers, Downtown

Calvert Woodley Liquors, Tenleytown

Chanel Boutique, Downtown

Chapters, Downtown

Coach Store, Georgetown

Fahrney's, Downtown

Good Wood, U Street corridor

Home Rule, U Street corridor

Jaeger, Chevy Chase

Kramerbooks and Afterwords, Dupont Circle

Marston Luce, Dupont Circle

Miss Pixie's, Adams-Morgan

Wake Up Little Suzie, Cleveland Park

By Deborah
Papier
Updated by
Robin
Dougherty

AFRICAN MASKS that could have inspired Picasso; kitchenware as objets d'art; bargains on Christian Dior, Hugo Boss, and Burberry; paisley scarves from India; American and European antiques; books of every description; handicrafts from almost two dozen Native American tribes; music boxes by the thousands; busts of U.S. presidents; textiles by the score; fine leather goods—all this and more can be found in the nation's capital.

Discriminating shoppers can find satisfaction at Filene's Basement (the Boston-based fashion discounter) or at upscale malls on the city's outskirts. Many of the smaller one-of-a-kind shops have survived urban renewal, the number of designer boutiques is on the rise, and interesting specialty shops and minimalls can be found all over town. Weekdays, downtown street vendors offer a funky mix of jewelry; brightly patterned ties; buyer-beware watches; sunglasses; and African-inspired clothing, accessories, and art. Of course, T-shirts and Capitol City souvenirs are always in plentiful supply, especially on the streets ringing *the* Mall.

Store hours vary greatly, so it's best to call ahead. In general, Georgetown stores are open late and on Sunday; stores downtown that cater to office workers close at 6 PM and may not be open at all on weekends. Some stores extend their hours on Thursday. Sales tax is 6%, and major credit cards and traveler's checks are accepted virtually everywhere. Each shop's listing includes the nearest Metro station, although some may be as far as a 15- to 20-minute walk; we do not list Metro stops for the few stores that have no Metro nearby.

Adams-Morgan

Scattered among the dozens of Latin, Ethiopian, and Caribbean restaurants in this most bohemian of Washington neighborhoods are a score of eccentric shops. If quality is what you seek, **Adams-Morgan** and nearby Woodley Park can be a minefield; tread cautiously. Still, for the bargain hunter it's great fun. If bound for a specific shop, you may wish to call ahead to verify hours. Adams-Morganites are often not clock-watchers, although you can be sure an afternoon stroll on the weekend will find a good representation of the shops open and give you a few hours of great browsing. If you need to pick up sundries such as shampoo, a CD, or even rent a DVD, you may want to stop by the Tik Tok Easy Shop, an automated convenience store on the corner of 18th and California streets. It takes cash and credit cards. ⊠ *18th St. NW, between Columbia Rd. and Florida Ave., Adams-Morgan* Ⓜ *Woodley Park/Zoo or Dupont Circle.*

Specialty Stores

ANTIQUES & **Chenonceau Antiques.** The mostly American 19th- and 20th-century
COLLECTIBLES pieces on this shop's two floors were selected by a buyer with an exquisite eye. Merchandise includes beautiful 19th-century paisley scarves from India and Scotland, and 1920s glass lamps. ⊠ *2314 18th St. NW, Woodley Park* ☎ *202/667–1651* ☉ *Closed weekdays* Ⓜ *Woodley Park/Zoo.*

★ **Miss Pixie's.** Two levels of well-chosen collectibles include gorgeous parasols and umbrellas, antique home furnishings, glass- and silverware, vintage clothes, and hardwood bed frames. The low prices should help hold your attention. ⊠ *1810 Adams Mill Rd. NW, Adams-Morgan* ☎ *202/232–8171* ☉ *Closed Mon.–Wed.* Ⓜ *Woodley Park/Zoo.*

BOOKS **Idle Time Books.** This used bookstore sells "rare to medium rare" books with plenty of meaty titles in all genres, especially out-of-print literature. ⊠ *2467 18th St. NW, Woodley Park* ☎ *202/232–4774* Ⓜ *Woodley Park/Zoo.*

To maximize your precious shopping hours, consider following parts of the strategies below. The stores throughout the chapter are organized by neighborhood for easy planning.

Art Galleries

If it's art you're seeking (even just to look at), keep in mind that Washington has three main gallery districts, though small art galleries can be found all over the city in converted houses and storefronts. Whatever their location, many close on Sunday and Monday or keep unusual hours. For a comprehensive review of current and future exhibits, pick up a copy of *Galleries* magazine (301/270–0180, www.artline.com), available in some galleries. The ever-dependable *Washington Post* weekend section and *Washington City Paper* (published on Thursday) are also excellent sources.

6

Close to 30 galleries are in the Dupont Circle area alone. On "First Fridays," the joint open house held September through June, the streets are filled with wine-and-cheese–loving gallery hoppers. Check out **The Galleries of Dupont Circle** (🌐 www.artgalleriesdc.com) for information on all events.

Clothing & Antiques

When it comes to fashion, **Georgetown** is the place to go. You might want to start at 2000 Pennsylvania Avenue, a cluster of clothing stores and eateries a few blocks from the Foggy Bottom/GWU Metro. From the Metro it's a 10- to 15-minute walk: cross Washington Circle and walk to the 2000 block, then head up Pennsylvania Avenue (the numbered cross streets will be increasing) to M Street, where Georgetown begins with a row of antiques shops. Wisconsin Avenue—where you can find a handful of designer boutiques among the influx of trendy, youth-oriented retailers—intersects M Street. Fortify yourself at one of the area's many restaurants before heading to **upper Wisconsin Avenue** on the D.C.–Maryland border. The bus, which runs every 7–10 minutes, will take you here (or back downtown) for $1.10, or you can hop in a cab. Upscale merchants such as Saks, Lord & Taylor, and Versace are located at the northern reaches of this neighborhood. Two midsize malls, Mazza Gallerie and Chevy Chase Pavilion, contain clothing shops that range from Ann Taylor to Talbots and Neiman Marcus. Filene's Basement and T. J. Maxx offer brand-name bargains, and Lord & Taylor is right around the corner on Western Ave. Book and CD browsers may want to stop in at Borders. When you're done, the convenient Friendship Heights on the Red Line will bring you back into the city.

Retro & Eclectic Finds

Across the street from the Woodley Park Metro you'll find a shop or two selling original works of art, antiques, and vintage jewelry. From here walk to the corner of Connecticut Avenue and Calvert Street. Turn left and cross the Duke Ellington Bridge—which offers a great view of forested Rock Creek Park—into **Adams-Morgan,** where there are one-of-a-kind ethnic jewelry shops, fun restaurants, vintage-clothing stores, and boutiques. Shop your way down 18th Street to Florida Avenue. Turn left to walk toward **U Street,** where more vintage clothing and antique furniture await. Or turn right and walk to Connecticut Avenue. A left turn will lead you downhill to **Dupont Circle** and its assortment of funky book, music, and gift shops.

Yawa. Along with a large collection of African and African-American fiction and nonfiction, magazines, and children's books, Yawa also sells ethnic jewelry, crafts, and greeting cards. ⊠ *2206 18th St. NW, Adams-Morgan* ☎ *202/483–6805* Ⓜ *Dupont Circle.*

MEN'S & WOMEN'S CLOTHING

Kobos. Those looking to add traditional ethnic dress to their wardrobe may appreciate this shop's rainbow of clothing and accessories, all imported from West Africa. ⊠ *2444 18th St. NW, Adams-Morgan* ☎ *202/332–9580* Ⓜ *Woodley Park/Zoo.*

MUSIC

DC CD. The club crowd loves this music store, which has late hours and a wide selection of indie, rock, hip-hop, alternative, and soul. The knowledgeable staff often opens packages, allowing customers to listen before they buy. ⊠ *2423 18th St. NW, Adams-Morgan* ☎ *202/588–1810* Ⓜ *Woodley Park/Zoo.*

SHOES

Shake Your Booty. Trend-conscious Washingtonians come here for modish leather boots and platform shoes. ⊠ *2439 18th St. NW, Adams-Morgan* ☎ *202/518–8205* ⊘ *Closed Tues.* Ⓜ *Woodley Park/Zoo.*

Capitol Hill/Eastern Market

As the Capitol Hill area has become gentrified, unique shops and boutiques have sprung up, many clustered around the redbrick structure of **Eastern Market.** Inside are produce and meat counters, plus the Market Five art gallery. The flea market, held on weekends outdoors, presents nostalgia by the crateful. There's also a farmers market on Saturday. Along 7th Street you'll find a number of small shops, selling everything from art books to handwoven rugs to antiques and knickknacks. ⊠ *7th and C Sts. SE, Capitol Hill* Ⓜ *Eastern Market, Union Station, or Capitol South.*

Mall

Union Station. This delightful shopping enclave, resplendent with marble floors and gilded, vaulted ceilings, is inside a working train station. You'll find several familiar retailers, including Aerosole, Chicos, Swatch, and Ann Taylor, as well as a bookstore and a multiplex cinema. The east hall, which resembles London's Covent Garden, is filled with vendors of expensive and ethnic wares in open stalls. Christmas is an especially pleasant time to shop here. ⊠ *50 Massachusetts Ave. NE, Capitol Hill* ☎ *202/289–1908* ⊕ *www.unionstationdc.com* Ⓜ *Union Station.*

Specialty Stores

ANTIQUES & COLLECTIBLES

Antiques on the Hill. This store has the feel of an old thrift shop where *nothing* is ever thrown away. From floor to roof, knickknacks of every kind fill the shelves. The center of the floor is filled with furniture, and light fixtures hang from every available spot on the ceiling. ⊠ *701 North Carolina Ave. SE, Capitol Hill* ☎ *202/543–1819* ⊘ *Closed Mon. and Tues.* Ⓜ *Eastern Market.*

BOOKS

Bird-in-Hand Bookstore and Gallery. This quirky store specializes in books on art and design and also carries exhibition catalogs. ⊠ *323 7th St. SE, Capitol Hill* ☎ *202/543–0744* ⊘ *Closed Sun. and Mon.* Ⓜ *Eastern Market.*

Capitol Hill Books. Pop into this inviting store to browse through a wonderful collection of out-of-print history books and modern first editions. ⊠ *657 C St. SE, Capitol Hill* ☎ *202/544–1621* ⊕ *www.capitolhillbooks-dc.com* Ⓜ *Eastern Market.*

Fairy Godmother. This store specializes in books for children, from infants through teens. It also sells puppets, toys, craft sets, and audiotapes for those long summer-vacation car rides. ✉ *319 7th St. SE, Capitol Hill* ☎ *202/547–5474* Ⓜ *Eastern Market.*

Trover Books. Newshounds can come here to find the latest political volumes and out-of-town newspapers. ✉ *221 Pennsylvania Ave. SE, Capitol Hill* ☎ *202/547–2665* Ⓜ *Capitol South.*

CRAFTS & GIFTS **Appalachian Spring.** Head here for traditional and contemporary American-made crafts, including jewelry, pottery, blown glass and toys. ✉ *Union Station, East Hall, 50 Massachusetts Ave. NE Capitol Hill* ☎ *202/337–5780 or 202/682–0505* Ⓜ *Union Station.*

Discovery Channel Store. The products in this store, all at least loosely connected with the popular cable programmer, range from telescopes and science kits to books and amber jewelry. ✉ *Union Station, 50 Massachusetts Ave. NE, Capitol Hill* ☎ *202/639–0908* Ⓜ *Union Station.*

Woven History/Silk Road. These connected stores sell handmade treasures from small villages around the world. Silk Road sells home furnishings, gifts, clothing, collectible rugs, and accessories made in Asian mountain communities as well as such contemporary items as aromatherapy candles from not-so-rural Greenwich Village in New York. Woven History's rugs are made the old-fashioned way, with vegetable dyes and hand-spun wool. ✉ *311–315 7th St. SE, Capitol Hill* ☎ *202/543–1705* Ⓜ *Eastern Market.*

FOOD & WINE **Schneider's of Capitol Hill.** Specializing in fine wines, this Capitol Hill shop also has myriad spirits. ✉ *300 Massachusetts Ave. NE, Capitol Hill* ☎ *202/543–9300* ⊕ *www.cellar.com* ☉ *Closed Sun.* Ⓜ *Union Station.*

WOMEN'S CLOTHING **The Forecast.** If you favor classic, contemporary styles, Forecast should be in your future. It sells silk sweaters and wool blends in solid, muted tones that won't quickly fall out of fashion. ✉ *218 7th St. SE, Capitol Hill* ☎ *202/547–7337* ☉ *Closed Mon.* Ⓜ *Eastern Market.*

Downtown

The domain of the city's many office workers, **downtown** tends to shut down at 5 PM sharp with the exception of the larger department stores. Old Downtown is where you'll find Hecht's and sundry specialty stores; established chains such as Ann Taylor and the Gap tend to be concentrated near Farragut Square. Avoid the lunch-hour crowds to ensure more leisurely shopping, and keep your eyes open for a new 200,000 square foot retail area that's set to open at Gallery Place and 7th St. NW in late 2003. ✉ *North of Pennsylvania Ave. between 7th and 18th Sts., up to Connecticut Ave. below L St., Downtown* Ⓜ *Archives/Navy Memorial, Farragut North and West, Foggy Bottom/GWU, Gallery Place, McPherson Square, or Metro Center.*

Department Stores

Hecht's. Bright and spacious, this Washington favorite has sensible groupings and attractive displays that make shopping easy on both the feet and the eyes. The clothing sold ranges from conservative to trendy, with the men's department increasingly prominent. The offerings in the cosmetics, lingerie, and housewares departments are also strong. ✉ *1201 G St. NW, Downtown* ☎ *202/628–6661.* Ⓜ *Metro Center.*

Malls

Old Post Office Pavilion. This handsome shopping center, inside a historic 19th-century post office building, hasn't grown into the popular spot that developers hoped it would after renovation in the 1980s. Plans are afoot to convert the space into a hotel or other enterprise, but until that happens, you can enjoy about a dozen food vendors and 17 shops. An observation deck in the building's clock tower gives an excellent view of the city. You'll need a photo I.D. to get into the building, which also houses federal offices. ⊠ *1100 Pennsylvania Ave., Downtown* ☎ *202/ 289–4224* Ⓜ *Federal Triangle.*

Shops at National Place. The Shops takes up three levels, one devoted entirely to food stands. It's mainly youth-oriented (this is a good place to drop off teenagers weary of the Smithsonian and more in the mood to buy T-shirts), but Perfumania and clothing stores such as Casual Corner and August Max have branches here, too. Those in search of presidential souvenirs may find the White House Gift Shop quite handy. ⊠ *13th and F Sts. NW, Downtown* ☎ *202/662–1250* Ⓜ *Metro Center.*

Specialty Stores

ART GALLERIES The downtown art scene is concentrated on 7th Street between D and I streets. Redevelopment has meant that many artists have had to move their working studios from here to more affordable digs. Fortunately, the galleries, which bring foot traffic to area businesses, have managed to maintain a foothold. On the third Thursday of each month, the galleries extend their hours and offer light refreshments from 6 PM to 8 PM.

The Artists' Museum. Up-and-coming artists can rent space here from D.C. artist David Stainback; what you'll find is hard to predict. ⊠ *406 7th St. NW, Chinatown* ☎ *202/638–7001* ⊕ *www.artistsmuseum.com* Ⓜ *Gallery Place/Chinatown.*

The David Adamson Gallery. Prints, paintings, drawings, sculptures, and ceramics are shown here. ⊠ *406 7th St. NW, Chinatown* ☎ *202/628– 0257* Ⓜ *Gallery Place/Chinatown.*

Numark Gallery. This powerhouse gallery brings in established and cutting-edge artists: Peter Halley, Tony Feher, and Michal Rovner have shown their works here. International, national, and regional artists are also regularly featured. ⊠ *406 7th St. NW, Chinatown* ☎ *202/628–3810* Ⓜ *Gallery Place/Chinatown.*

The Touchstone Gallery. Minimalist paintings and photography are showcased at this gallery. ⊠ *406 7th St. NW, Chinatown* ☎ *202/347–2787* ⊕ *www.touchstonegallery.com* Ⓜ *Gallery Place/Chinatown.*

Washington Project for the Arts. Installations, films, and performances are often tied in with exhibits at this space. ⊠ *500 17th St. NW, Chinatown* ☎ *202/639–1714* Ⓜ *Gallery Place/Chinatown.*

Zenith Gallery. Founded in 1978, the Zenith exhibits indoor and outdoor sculpture, mixed media, wearable art, jewelry, crafts, and art furniture, as well as a large selection of paintings by national and international artists. ⊠ *413 7th St. NW, Chinatown* ☎ *202/783–2963* Ⓜ *Gallery Place/ Chinatown.*

BOOKS **Borders Books and Music.** In addition to a large selection of books and magazines, Borders also sells recorded music, has a café, and regularly presents book signings, free films, and jazz performances. ⊠ *1801 K St. NW, Downtown* ☎ *202/466–4999* Ⓜ *Farragut North.*

★ **Chapters.** This "literary bookstore" fills its shelves with serious contemporary fiction, classics, foreign language titles, and poetry. The store hosts author readings regularly, so check the schedule if you're spending a few days in town. ⊠ *1512 K St. NW, Downtown* ☎ *202/347– 5495* ⊕ *www.chaptersliterary.com* Ⓜ *McPherson Square.*

Olsson's Books and Records. The store stocks a large and varied collection of books for readers of all ages and a good selection of classical and folk music. Hours vary significantly from store to store. In addition to the downtown locations, there's a branch in Dupont Circle. ⊠ *1200 F St. NW, Downtown* ☎ *202/347–3686* Ⓜ *Metro Center* ⊠ *418 7th St. NW, Downtown* ☎ *202/638–7610* ⊕ *www.olssons.com* Ⓜ *Archives/ Navy Memorial.*

CRAFTS & GIFTS **Al's Magic Shop.** For professional magicians, aspiring kids, and amateur
★ pranksters, Al's has offered a full line of cards, tricks, magic wands, and
mind games for more than 65 years. Al Cohen counted Doug Henning
and David Copperfield among his customers; since Al's retirement in
2002, a new owner has kept this Washington landmark alive. ✉ *1012
Vermont Ave. NW, Downtown* ☎ *202/789–2800* Ⓜ *McPherson Square.*

★ **Fahrney's.** What began in 1929 as a repair shop and a pen bar—a place
to fill your fountain pen before setting out for work—is now a won-
derland for anyone who loves a good writing instrument. On offer are
pens in silver, gold, and lacquer by the world's leading manufacturers.
✉ *1317 F St. NW, Downtown* ☎ *202/628–9525* Ⓜ *McPherson Square.*

Indian Craft Shop. Handicrafts, such as jewelry, pottery, sand paintings,
weavings, and baskets from more than 45 Native American tribes—including Navajo, Pueblo, Zuni, Cherokee, Lakota, and Seminole—are
at your fingertips here . . . as long as you have a photo I.D. to enter the
federal building. Items range from inexpensive (as little as $5) jewelry
on up to collector-quality art pieces (more than $1,000). ✉ *U.S. De-
partment of the Interior, 1849 C St. NW, Room 1023, Downtown*
☎ *202/208–4056* ☉ *Closed weekends* Ⓜ *Farragut West.*

Music Box Center. Listen to a total of 500 melodies on more than 1,500
music boxes at this exquisite—and unusual—specialty store. One irre-
sistible item: the Harry Potter music box that plays "That's What
Friends Are For." ✉ *1920 I St. NW, Downtown* ☎ *202/783–9399*
Ⓜ *Farragut West.*

FOOD **Dean & Deluca.** This outlet of the popular New York café sells coffees and
teas, and other good reasons to take a break from shopping. ✉ *1299
Pennsylvania Ave. NW, Downtown* ☎ *202/628–8155* Ⓜ *Metro Center.*

HOME **Apartment Zero.** This swank housewares store describes itself as ap-
FURNISHINGS pealing to Frank Gehry fans, and almost everyone else who wants a leg
Fodor'sChoice up on the latest in furnishings and accessories is not likely to be disap-
★ pointed. If you're looking for pieces (or just ideas) to give your own house
a cool, downtown look, look no further. ✉ *406 7th St. NW, Downtown*
☎ *202/628–4067* Ⓜ *Gallery Place.*

JEWELRY **Pampillonia Jewelers.** Here you'll find traditional designs in 18-karat gold
and platinum as well as eye-catching contemporary designs. The selec-
tion for men is particularly good. ✉ *1213 Connecticut Ave. NW, Downtown* ☎ *202/628–6305* Ⓜ *Farragut North.*

Tiny Jewel Box. Despite its name, this shop contains three floors of precious and semi-precious wares, including unique gifts and works by well-
known designers. ✉ *1147 Connecticut Ave. NW, Downtown* ☎ *202/
393–2747* Ⓜ *Farragut North.*

MEN'S & **Brooks Brothers.** This venerable clothier has been issuing its discreet
WOMEN'S label since 1818. Men with classic tastes—gray wool suits; navy blaz-
CLOTHING ers; chinos; dignified formal wear; and of course the original, glorious
★ cotton dress shirt—can always take comfort here. And these days, so
can women: there's a selection of classic casual and work clothes for
her. ✉ *1201 Connecticut Ave. NW, Downtown* ☎ *202/659–4650*
Ⓜ *Farragut North.*

Burberry. The trench coat's still popular, but this plaid-friendly British
company also manufactures traditional men's and women's indoor ap-
parel and accessories. ✉ *1155 Connecticut Ave. NW, Downtown*
☎ *202/463–3000* Ⓜ *Farragut North.*

H&M. Situated on the former site of the Woodward & Lothrop department store, this Swedish import sells affordable and stylish casual wear
for all ages. ✉ *1155 Connecticut Ave. NW, Downtown* Ⓜ *Gallery
Place.*

J. Press. Like its flagship store, founded in Connecticut in 1902 as a custom shop for Yale University, this Washington outlet is a resolutely traditional clothier: Shetland and Irish wool sport coats are a specialty. ⊠ *1801 L St. NW, Downtown* ☎ *202/857–0120* Ⓜ *Farragut North.*

SPAS & BEAUTY
SALONS

Andre Chreky Salon. Housed in an elegantly renovated, four-story Victorian town house, this salon offers complete services—hair, nails, facials, waxing, massage, and makeup. And because it's a favorite of the Washington elite, you might just overhear a tidbit or two on who's going to what black-tie function with whom. Adjacent whirlpool pedicure chairs allow two friends to get pampered simultaneously. While you splurge on a treatment, enjoy complimentary espresso and pastries (mornings) or wine and live piano music (evenings). ⊠ *1604 K St. NW, Downtown* ☎ *202/293–9393 or 202/393–2225* Ⓜ *Farragut North.*

Victoria's Day Spa. What this spa lacks in fancy amenities it more than makes up for in homespun appeal and comparatively low prices. Special services include facials, paraffin manicures, pedicures, and body wraps as well as seaweed masks and body wraps. ⊠ *1926 I St. NW, Downtown* ☎ *202/254–0442* Ⓜ *Farragut West.*

SHOES

Church's. This top-notch English company's handmade men's shoes are noted for their comfort and durability. ⊠ *1820 L St. NW, Downtown* ☎ *202/296–3366* Ⓜ *Farragut North.*

Parade of Shoes. Under the house label at this discount women's shoe store are knockoffs of designer labels and classically styled Italian imports. During seasonal clearances, shoes are often marked down as low as $20 a pair. ⊠ *1020 Connecticut Ave. NW, Downtown* ☎ *202/872–8581* Ⓜ *Farragut North.*

WOMEN'S
CLOTHING

Ann Taylor. Young professional women head here for classy yet trendy fashions, including accessories and a small but excellent selection of shoes. There are also branches at Mazza Gallerie, Dupont Circle, Georgetown, and Union Station. ⊠ *600 13th St. NW, Downtown* ☎ *202/737–0325* Ⓜ *Metro Center.*

★ **Chanel Boutique.** The Willard Hotel annex is the place to find handbags, perfume, couture fashions, and other goodies from this legendary house of fashion. ⊠ *1455 Pennsylvania Ave. NW, Downtown* ☎ *202/638–5055* Ⓜ *Metro Center.*

Earl Allen. Many of the conservative but distinctive dresses and sportswear, wearable art, and other items at Earl Allen are made exclusively for the store. ⊠ *1825 I St. NW, Downtown* ☎ *202/466–3437* ☉ *Closed weekends* Ⓜ *Farragut West.*

Rizik Bros. This Washington institution has both designer clothing and expert advice on offer. The sales staff is trained to find just the right style from the store's inventory. Take the elevator up from the northwest corner of Connecticut Avenue and L Street. ⊠ *1100 Connecticut Ave. NW, Downtown* ☎ *202/223–4050* Ⓜ *Farragut North.*

Dupont Circle

You might call **Dupont Circle** a younger less staid version of Georgetown—almost as pricey and not quite as well kept, with more apartment buildings than houses. Its many restaurants, offbeat shops, and specialty book and record stores lend it a distinctive, cosmopolitan air. The street scene here is more urban than Georgetown's, with bike messengers and chess aficionados filling up the park while shoppers frequent the many coffee shops and stores. The farmers market, held on the Circle itself on Sundays from March through mid-December, is a popular destination for discriminating city dwellers. ⊠ *Connecticut Ave. between M and S Sts.* Ⓜ *Dupont Circle.*

Specialty Stores

ANTIQUES & COLLECTIBLES

Geoffrey Diner Gallery. This shop is a must for hard-core antiques shoppers on the hunt for 19th- and 20th-century wares, including Tiffany lamps and Arts and Crafts pieces from England and the United States. ⊠ *1730 21st St. NW, Dupont Circle* ☎ *202/483–5005* Ⓜ *Dupont Circle.*

★ **Marston Luce.** The focus is on French country furniture, but Marston Luce also carries home and garden accessories: weather vanes, stone carvings from building facades, and decorative cast-iron work. There's another outpost in Georgetown. ⊠ *1314 21st St. NW, Dupont Circle* ☎ *202/775–9460* Ⓜ *Dupont Circle.*

ART GALLERIES

America, Oh Yes! Holding one of the most extensive folk art collections in the country, this gallery is also known for its reasonable prices. The gallery represents more than 160 self-taught American artists. ⊠ *1700 Connecticut Ave. NW, Suite 300, Dupont Circle* ☎ *202/483–9644* Ⓜ *Dupont Circle.*

Anton Gallery. Paintings by Tom Nakashima and Jaune Quick-To-See Smith are regularly featured. Look for photography, mixed-media installations, works on paper, sculpture by Annella Frank, and functional ceramics by Rob Barnard to name just a few of the national and international artists who find a home here. ⊠ *2108 R St. NW, Dupont Circle* ☎ *202/328–0828* Ⓜ *Dupont Circle.*

Burdick Gallery. John Burdick's cozy gallery focuses on Inuit art and sculpture. ⊠ *1609 Connecticut Ave. NW, Dupont Circle* ☎ *202/986–5682* Ⓜ *Dupont Circle.*

Burton Marinkovich Fine Art. You know you've reached this gallery when you spot the small front yard with two distinctive sculptures (they're by Lesley Dill and Leonard Cave). The gallery has works on paper by modern and contemporary masters, including Ross Bleckner, Richard Diebenkorn, Hockney, Kandinsky, Matisse, Miró, Motherwell, Picasso, and others. Rare modern illustrated books and British linocuts from the Grosvenor School are also specialties. ⊠ *1506 21st St. NW, Dupont Circle* ☎ *202/296–6563* Ⓜ *Dupont Circle.*

Gallery K. H. Marc Moyens and Komei Wachi have devoted a lifetime to amassing a sizeable collection of contemporary art. Their spacious gallery holds a large inventory that includes works by such internationally known artists as Andy Warhol, Robert Motherwell, and Jackson Pollock. ⊠ *2010 R St. NW, Dupont Circle* ☎ *202/234–0339* Ⓜ *Dupont Circle.*

Tartt Gallery. The emphasis here is on 19th- and early-20th-century vintage photography and American contemporary folk art. ⊠ *1710 Connecticut Ave. NW, Dupont Circle* ☎ *202/332–5652* Ⓜ *Dupont Circle.*

BATH & BEAUTY

Blue Mercury. Cosmetics as well as skin cleansing products are what you'll find here. Unlike its Georgetown branch, however, there's no spa attached. ⊠ *1745 Connecticut Ave. NW, Dupont Circle* ☎ *202/462–1300* Ⓜ *Dupont Circle.*

BOOKS

★ **Kramerbooks and Afterwords.** One of Washington's best loved independents, this cozy shop has a small but choice selection of fiction and non-fiction. Open 24 hours on weekends, it's a convenient meeting place. Kramerbooks shares space with a café that has late-night dining and weekend entertainment; be prepared for a smoke-filled room. Internet café services are also available. ⊠ *1517 Connecticut Ave. NW, Dupont Circle* ☎ *202/387–1400* ⊕ *www.kramers.com* Ⓜ *Dupont Circle.*

Lambda Rising. A major player in the Dupont Circle area, Lambda carries novels by gay and lesbian writers and other books of interest to the gay community. ⊠ *1625 Connecticut Ave. NW, Dupont Circle* ☎ *202/462–6969* Ⓜ *Dupont Circle.*

Olsson's Books and Records. Like its sister stores Downtown, this branch prides itself on its wide selection of books and music. ✉ *1307 19th St. NW, Dupont Circle* ☎ *202/785–1133* ⊕ *www.olssons.com* Ⓜ *Dupont Circle.*

Second Story Books. A used-books and -records emporium that stays open late, Second Story may lead bibliophiles to browse for hours. ✉ *2000 P St. NW, Dupont Circle* ☎ *202/659–8884* ⊕ *www.secondstorybooks. com* Ⓜ *Dupont Circle.*

CHILDREN'S CLOTHING
Kid's Closet. If filling a little one's closet is on your list, stop here for quality contemporary children's clothing and toys. ✉ *1226 Connecticut Ave. NW, Dupont Circle* ☎ *202/429–9247* Ⓜ *Dupont Circle (south exit).*

CONFECTIONS
Fodor's Choice
★
The Chocolate Moose. Here's the place to stop if you're looking for the perfect molded chocolate or handmade treat. The store, which also carries nonchocolate gift items and accessories, sells its own wares as well as those of premium chocolatiers. ✉ *1800 M St. NW, Dupont Circle* ☎ *202/463–0992* Ⓜ *Dupont Circle.*

CRAFTS & GIFTS
Beadazzled. This appealing shop stocks a dazzling number of ready-to-string beads and jewelry as well as books on crafts history and techniques. ✉ *1507 Connecticut Ave. NW, Dupont Circle* ☎ *202/265–2323* ⊕ *www. beadazzled.net* Ⓜ *Dupont Circle.*

HOME FURNISHINGS
Skynear and Company. The owners of this extravagant shop travel the world to find the unusual. Their journeys have yielded a treasure-trove of rich textiles, furniture, and home accessories—all for the art of living. ✉ *2122 18th St. NW, Dupont Circle* ☎ *202/797–7160* Ⓜ *Dupont Circle.*

KITCHENWARE
Coffee, Tea and the Works. Coffee and tea lovers can find every amenity in this charmingly cluttered shop, from flavored brews to colorful ceramic pots. Also on hand is an eclectic assortment of kitchen gadgets, magnets, and other paraphernalia. ✉ *1627 Connecticut Ave. NW, Dupont Circle* ☎ *202/483–8050* Ⓜ *Dupont Circle.*

SHOES
Shoe Scene. The fashionable, moderately priced shoes for women found here are imported from Europe. ✉ *1330 Connecticut Ave. NW, Dupont Circle* ☎ *202/659–2194* Ⓜ *Dupont Circle.*

WOMEN'S CLOTHING
Betsy Fisher. Catering to women of all ages in search of contemporary styles, this store stocks one-of-a-kind accessories, duds, and jewelry. ✉ *1224 Connecticut Ave. NW, Dupont Circle* ☎ *202/785–1975* Ⓜ *Dupont Circle (south exit).*

Secondi. One of the city's finest consignment shops, Secondi well-chosen selection of women's designer and casual clothing, accessories, and shoes includes labels by such labels as Donna Karan, Prada, Ann Taylor, and Coach. ✉ *1702 Connecticut Ave. NW, Dupont Circle* ☎ *202/667–1122* Ⓜ *Dupont Circle.*

Georgetown

Georgetown remains Washington's favorite shopping area. This is the capital's center for famous citizens, as well as for restaurants, bars, nightclubs, and trendy shops. Although Georgetown is not on a subway line (the nearest Metro, Foggy Bottom/GWU, is a 10- to 15-minute walk from the shops) and parking is difficult at best, people still flock here. National chains are overtaking the specialty shops that first gave the district its allure, but the historic neighborhood is still charming, and its street scene lively. In addition to housing tony antiques, elegant crafts, and high-style shoe and clothing boutiques, Georgetown offers wares that attract local college students and young people: books, music, and fashions from familiar names like Banana Republic and Urban Outfitters. Most stores lie to the east and west on M Street and to the north on Wisconsin. ⊠ *Intersection of Wisconsin Ave. and M St., Georgetown* Ⓜ *Foggy Bottom/GWU.*

Mall

Shops at Georgetown Park. Near the hub of the Georgetown shopping district is this posh tri-level mall, which looks like a Victorian ice-cream parlor inside. The pricey clothing and accessory boutiques and the ubiquitous chain stores (such as Victoria's Secret and the Sharper Image) draw international visitors in droves. Next door is a branch of Dean & Deluca, the gourmet food store. ⊠ *3222 M St. NW, Georgetown* ☎ *202/ 298–5577* Ⓜ *Foggy Bottom/GWU.*

Specialty Stores

ANTIQUES & COLLECTIBLES **Georgetown Antiques Center.** The center, in a Victorian town house, has two dealers who share space: Cherub Antiques Gallery specializes in art nouveau and art deco, and Michael Getz Antiques sells fireplace equipment and silverware. ⊠ *2918 M St. NW, Georgetown* ☎ *202/337–2224 Cherub Gallery; 202/338–3811 Michael Getz Antiques* Ⓜ *Foggy Bottom/ GWU.*

Marston Luce. House and garden accessories are in the mix here, but the major focus is on French country furniture. There's another branch in Dupont Circle. ⊠ *1651 Wisconsin Ave. NW, Georgetown* ☎ *202/333– 6800* Ⓜ *Foggy Bottom/GWU.*

Miller & Arney Antiques. English, American, and European furniture and accessories from the 17th, 18th, and early 19th centuries give Miller & Arney Antiques a museum-gallery air. Asian porcelain adds splashes of color. ⊠ *1737 Wisconsin Ave. NW, Georgetown* ☎ *202/338–2369* Ⓜ *Foggy Bottom/GWU.*

Old Print Gallery. Here you'll find the capital's largest collection of old prints, with a focus on maps and 19th-century decorative prints (including Washingtoniana). ⊠ *1220 31st St. NW, Georgetown* ☎ *202/965–1818* ⊘ *Closed Sun.* Ⓜ *Foggy Bottom/GWU.*

Opportunity Shop of the Christ Child Society. This Georgetown landmark sells fine antiques, crystal, silver, and good-quality household goods on consignment. Prices are moderate. ⊠ *1427 Wisconsin Ave. NW, Georgetown* ☎ *202/333–6635* ⊘ *Closed Sun. and Mon.* Ⓜ *Foggy Bottom/GWU.*

Susquehanna. With three rooms upstairs, four rooms downstairs, and a garden full of benches, urns, and tables, Susquehanna is the largest antiques shop in Georgetown. Paintings cover every inch of wall space, though the shop specializes in American and English furniture. ⊠ *3216 O St. NW, Georgetown* ☎ *202/333–1511* Ⓜ *Foggy Bottom/GWU.*

ART GALLERIES Many of Georgetown's galleries are on side streets away from the main commercial strip. Their holdings are primarily made up of work done by established artists favored by serious collectors.

Addison Ripley. This well-respected gallery exhibits contemporary work by local artists, including painters Manon Cleary and Wolf Kahn and photographer Terri Weifenbach. ⊠ *1670 Wisconsin Ave. NW, Georgetown* ☎ *202/338–5180* Ⓜ *Foggy Bottom/GWU.*

Creighton-Davis. Collectors with deep pockets can pick up a Matisse at this art powerhouse, which has also been known to carry Whistlers. ⊠ *Georgetown Park Mall, 3222 M St. NW, Georgetown* ☎ *202/333– 3050* Ⓜ *Foggy Bottom/GWU.*

Galleries 1054. Several distinct galleries live under one roof at this location. With its focus on avant-garde art, **eklektikos** (☎ 202/342–1809) is one of the more daring, and exciting, galleries in the city. **Fraser** (☎ 202/ 298–6450) features contemporary realism by emerging artists. **Alla Rogers** (☎ 202/333–8595) has Eastern European and contemporary

American art and photography. **Georgetown Art Guild** (☎202/625–1470) shows international artists. **Veerhoff Galleries** (☎ 202/338–6456) presents a mix of D.C.-based and other American artists. ⊠ *1054 31st St. NW, Georgetown* Ⓜ *Foggy Bottom/GWU.*

Georgetown Gallery of Art. Off the beaten path, this cozy gallery displays paintings by Picasso, Honoré Daumier, and Marc Chagall, but emphasizes the work of British sculptor Henry Moore. ⊠ *3235 P St. NW, Georgetown* ☎ *202/333–6308* Ⓜ *Foggy Bottom/GWU.*

Hemphill Fine Arts. Near the C&O Canal, this gem of a gallery shows established artists such as Jacob Kainen and William Christenberry as well as emerging artists, including Colby Caldwell. ⊠ *1027 33rd St. NW, Georgetown* ☎ *202/342–5610* Ⓜ *Foggy Bottom/GWU.*

Spectrum. Approximately 30 artists form this cooperative gallery, which specializes in abstract and representational art. ⊠ *1132 29th St. NW, Georgetown* ☎ *202/333–0954* Ⓜ *Foggy Bottom/GWU.*

BOOKS **Barnes & Noble.** This expansive three-story chain store, housed in a former warehouse, has a coffee bar along with countless books, magazines, and CDs from around the world. ⊠ *3040 M St. NW, Georgetown* ☎ *202/965–9880* Ⓜ *Foggy Bottom/GWU.*

Bridge Street Books. This charming bookshop stocks a good selection of literature as well as books on fine arts, politics, and other subjects. ⊠*2814 Pennsylvania Ave. NW, Georgetown* ☎*202/965–5200* Ⓜ*Foggy Bottom/ GWU.*

CRAFTS & GIFTS **American Studio +.** One-of-a-kind functional and nonfunctional crafts pieces fill this wonderful place—tea kettles, corkscrews, glassware, and jewelry—all by international designers and artists. ⊠ *2906 M St. NW, Georgetown* ☎ *202/965–3273* Ⓜ *Foggy Bottom/GWU.*

The Art Store. Here you'll find three floors of artists' supplies—everything from oil paints and easels to framing supplies and portfolios. The selection of hand-made papers is quite enticing. ⊠ *3019 M St. NW, Georgetown* ☎ *202/342–7030.* Ⓜ *Foggy Bottom/GWU.*

HOME FURNISHINGS **A Mano.** The store's name is Italian for "by hand," and it lives up to its name, stocking colorful hand-painted ceramics, hand-dyed tablecloths, blown glass stemware, and other home accessories by Italian and French artisans. ⊠ *1677 Wisconsin Ave. NW, Georgetown* ☎ *202/298–7200.*

Theodore's. A Washington institution, Theodore's is the place to visit for ultra-mod housewares, from stylish furniture to accessories, leather, and upholstery that make a statement. There's an excellent selection of wall-storage units for almost all tastes. ⊠ *2233 Wisconsin Ave. NW, Georgetown* ☎ *202/333–2300.*

JEWELRY **Blanca Flor.** The specialty here is elegant, high-quality silver jewelry, mostly from Mexico. ⊠ *3066 M St. NW, Georgetown* ☎*202/944–5051* Ⓜ *Foggy Bottom/GWU.*

LEATHER GOODS **Coach Store.** Coach carries a complete (and expensive) line of well-made
★ leather handbags, briefcases, belts, and wallets. ⊠ *3259 M St. NW, Georgetown* ☎ *202/342–1772* Ⓜ *Foggy Bottom/GWU.*

MEN'S & WOMEN'S CLOTHING **Commander Salamander.** This funky outpost sells trendy clothes for the alternative set—punk kids and ravers. Sifting through the assortment of leather, chains, toys, and candy-color makeup is as much entertainment as it is shopping. The store is open till 10 PM on weekends. ⊠ *1420 Wisconsin Ave. NW, Georgetown* ☎ *202/337–2265* Ⓜ *Foggy Bottom/ GWU.*

SPAS & BEAUTY SALONS **Blue Mercury.** The retail space up front sells soaps, lotions, perfumes, cosmetics, and skin and hair care products. Behind the glass door is its "skin gym," where you can treat yourself to facials, waxing, massage, and oxygen treatments. ✉ *3059 M St. NW, Georgetown* ☎ *202/965–1300* Ⓜ *Foggy Bottom/GWU.*

L'Occitane. This French chain is known for its fine botanical fragrances, soaps, and toiletries. The scents range from classic lavender, rose, and vanilla to the more exotic lotus flower and green tea. ✉ *3106 M St. NW, Georgetown* ☎ *202/337–6001* Ⓜ *Foggy Bottom/GWU.*

Roche Salon. On the Georgetown waterfront, this salon showcases owner Dennis Roche, who has been featured in *Vogue, Harper's Bazaar,* and *Glamour* magazines. Many believe he is the city's best source for the latest hair-coloring techniques. ✉ *3050 K St. NW, Georgetown* ☎ *202/775–9775.*

Sephora. Better than any department store perfume or cosmetic counter, this candy store of beauty products offers hundreds of fine fragrances, bath products, and cosmetics from all over the world. Sephora also carries its own line of beauty products, all exquisitely packaged and quite affordable. The black-clad salespeople are pleasantly low-key. ✉ *3065 M St. NW, Georgetown* ☎ *202/338 5644* Ⓜ *Foggy Bottom/GWU.*

SHOES **Prince and Princess.** This retailer carries a full line of men's shoes and boots, including Timberland and Sebago. For women, the selection includes strappy party shoes, chunky platforms, and stylish pumps from designers such as Via Spiga and Nine West. ✉ *1400 Wisconsin Ave. NW, Georgetown* ☎ *202/337–4211* Ⓜ *Foggy Bottom/GWU.*

Shake Your Booty. The Georgetown location of this Adams-Morgan venue carries trendy, must-have footwear for women who believe that shoes, not diamonds, are a girl's best friend. ✉ *3225 M St. NW, Georgetown* ☎ *202/518–8205.*

WOMEN'S **Ann Taylor.** Like the other outposts downtown and at Union Station and CLOTHING Mazza Gallerie, this branch of the understated outfitter for young professional women sells accessories and shoes as well as clothing. ✉ *Georgetown Park, 3222 M St. NW, Georgetown* ☎ *202/338–5290.*

★ **April Cornell.** This popular designer is known for exquisite women's styles, children's clothing, and accessories. ✉ *3278 M St. NW, Georgetown* ☎ *202/625–7887* Ⓜ *Foggy Bottom/GWU.*

Betsey Johnson. The fanciful frocks here are favorites of the young and the restless. ✉ *1319 Wisconsin Ave. NW, Georgetown* ☎ *202/338–4090* Ⓜ *Foggy Bottom/GWU.*

Phoenix. Here you'll find contemporary clothing in natural fibers by designers such as Eileen Fisher and Flax, as well as jewelry and fine and folk-art pieces from Mexico. ✉ *1514 Wisconsin Ave. NW, Georgetown* ☎ *202/338–4404.*

U Street

In the '30s and '40s, **U Street** was known for its classy theaters and jazz clubs. After decades of decline following the 1968 riots, the neighborhood has been revitalized. Although the area is far from gentrified, U Street's mainstay is its devoted community, a mix of multiethnic young adults and older, working-class African-Americans. At night the neighborhood's club scene comes alive. During the day, the street scene is more laid-back, with more locals than tourists occupying the few lunch spots and distinctive shops. ✉ *U St. between 12th and 17th Sts., U St. corridor* Ⓜ *U Street/Cardozo.*

Specialty Stores

ANTIQUES &
COLLECTIBLES

★ **Good Wood.** This friendly shop sells vintage and antique wood furniture—including wonderful 19th-century American pieces—along with stained glass and other decorative items. ✉ *1428 U St. NW, U St. corridor* ☎ *202/986–3640* Ⓜ *U Street/Cardozo.*

Millennium. This eclectic shop offers a unique blend of housewares, clothing, records, books, and furniture—all of which it has dubbed "20th-century antiques." Depending on the week, you might find Bakelite silverware or an eight-track tape player. ✉ *1528 U St. NW, U St. corridor* ☎ *202/483–1218* ✪ *Closed Mon.–Wed.* Ⓜ *U Street/Cardozo.*

BOOKS **Sisterspace and Books.** Sisterspace specializes in books written by and appealing to African-American women. In addition to titles by authors such as Iyanla Vanzant, Maya Angelou, and Toni Morrison, the store offers seminars on everything from money and health to spirituality and creative fulfillment. ✉ *1515 U St. NW, U St. corridor* ☎ *202/332–3433* ⊕ *www.sisterspace.com* Ⓜ *U Street/Cardozo.*

HOME
FURNISHINGS

Habitat Home Accents & Jewelry. This store sells well-chosen desk sets, lamps, table-top items, and artist-made jewelry. ✉ *1510 U St. NW, U St. corridor* ☎ *202/518–7222* Ⓜ *U Street/Cardozo.*

★ **Home Rule.** Here you can find some of the latest design elements from Europe as well as playful sink stoppers and other fun and affordable household items. ✉ *1807 14th St. NW, U St. corridor* ☎ *202/797–5544* Ⓜ *U Street/Cardozo.*

Zawadi. The name means "gift" in Swahili, but you may want to buy the beautiful African art, home accessories, and jewelry for yourself. ✉ *1524 U St. NW, U St. corridor* ☎ *202/232–2214* Ⓜ *U Street/ Cardozo.*

MEN'S &
WOMEN'S
CLOTHING

The Boutique at U. This store caters to the club crowd, with plenty of black garb and prices that are moderate to low. Stop in here before you head out for the evening for clothing and accessories. ✉ *1100 U St. NW, lower level, U St. corridor* ☎ *202/234–2727* ✪ *Closed Mon.* Ⓜ *U Street/ Cardozo.*

Meeps Fashionette. Catering to fans of true shabby-chic and campy glamour, this shop stocks a wide selection of vintage clothes from the '40s through the '80s. ✉ *1520 U St. NW, U St. corridor* ☎ *202/265–6546* ✪ *Closed Mon.–Wed.* Ⓜ *U Street/Cardozo.*

Trade Secrets. The textured wool, velvet, and silk designs in African-inspired patterns sold here seem almost too pretty to wear. Almost. ✉ *1515 U St. NW, lower level, U St. corridor* ☎ *202/667–0634* ✪ *Closed Mon.* Ⓜ *U Street/Cardozo.*

Wild Women Wear Red. This store offers unique footwear, much of it red, for the adventurous. Featured designers include Bronx NY and Lisa Nading. ✉ *1512 U St. NW, U St. corridor* ☎ *202/387–5700* ✪ *Closed Mon.* Ⓜ *U Street/Cardozo.*

Wisconsin Avenue

A major shopping district, upper **Wisconsin Avenue** straddles the Maryland border. Between the malls, department stores, and chic, small boutiques, this area has nearly everything you could want to buy. ✉ *Wisconsin Ave. between Jennifer St. NW and Western Ave.* Ⓜ *Friendship Heights.*

Department Stores

Filene's Basement. To really appreciate the bargains here, do some window-shopping in the Mazza Gallerie mall before entering this store. In addition to big savings on men's and women's clothing by well-regarded designers such as Hugo Boss and Christian Dior, Filene's has discounts on shoes, perfume, housewares, and accessories. ☒ *Mazza Gallerie, 5300 Wisconsin Ave. NW, Friendship Heights* ☏ *202/966–0208* Ⓜ *Friendship Heights.*

Lord & Taylor. Its competition may try to be all things to all people, but Lord & Taylor focuses on classic men's, women's, and children's clothing by such designers as Anne Klein and Ralph Lauren. ☒ *5255 Western Ave. NW, Friendship Heights* ☏ *202/362–9600* Ⓜ *Friendship Heights.*

FodorśChoice ★ **Neiman Marcus.** If price is an object, this is definitely not the place to shop. Headquartered in Dallas, Neiman Marcus caters to customers who value quality above all. The carefully selected merchandise includes clothes, furs, precious jewelry, crystal, and silver. ☒ *Mazza Gallerie, 5300 Wisconsin Ave. NW, Friendship Heights* ☏ *202/966–9700* Ⓜ *Friendship Heights.*

FodorśChoice ★ **Saks Fifth Avenue.** Though technically just over the Maryland line, Saks is nonetheless a Washington institution. It has a wide selection of European and American couture clothes; other attractions are the shoe, jewelry, fur, and lingerie departments. ☒ *5555 Wisconsin Ave., Friendship Heights* ☏ *301/657–9000* Ⓜ *Friendship Heights.*

Malls

Chevy Chase Pavilion. Across from Mazza Gallerie is the newer, similarly upscale Chevy Chase Pavilion. Its women's clothing stores range from Steilmann European Selection (which carries Karl Lagerfeld's sportier KL line) to Ann Taylor Loft and Talbots. Specialty shops include Pottery Barn and J. Crew. ☒ *5335 Wisconsin Ave. NW, Friendship Heights* ☏ *202/686–5335* ⊕ *www.ccpavilion.com* Ⓜ *Friendship Heights.*

Mazza Gallerie. The four-level Mazza Gallerie is anchored by the ritzy Neiman Marcus department store and the discount department store Filene's Basement. Other stores include Williams-Sonoma for kitchenware and Villeroy & Boch for housewares, as well as Ann Taylor, Pampillonia Jewelers, and Krön Chocolatier. ☒ *5300 Wisconsin Ave. NW, Friendship Heights* ☏ *202/966–6114* Ⓜ *Friendship Heights.*

Specialty Stores

BOOKS
FodorśChoice ★ **Politics and Prose.** With a wide selection of topical novels and literary nonfiction as well as provocative author readings almost every night, this bookstore–coffeehouse lives up to its name. The nearest Metro is 15 minutes away. ☒ *5015 Connecticut Ave. NW, Friendship Heights* ☏ *202/364–1919* ⊕ *www.politics-prose.com* Ⓜ *Friendship Heights.*

CHILDREN'S
CLOTHING **Full of Beans.** This boutique sells updated classic styles, mostly in natural fibers. Sizes range from infants to boys' size 10 and girls' size 16. ☒ *5502 Connecticut Ave. NW, Chevy Chase, MD* ☏ *202/362–8566.*

FOOD & WINE ★ **Calvert Woodley Liquors.** This liquor store carries not only an excellent selection of wine and hard liquor, but also many kinds of cheese and other picnic and cocktail-party fare, as well as the legendary H&H bagels from New York. ☒ *4339 Connecticut Ave. NW, Tenleytown* ☏ *202/966–4400* Ⓜ *Van Ness/UDC.*

FodorśChoice ★ **Rodman's Discount Foods and Drugstore.** The rare store that carries wine, cheese, and space heaters, Rodman's is a fascinating hybrid of Kmart and Dean & Deluca. The appliances are downstairs, the imported peppers and chocolates upstairs. It's also a working drugstore, so you can also have a prescription filled or pick up some sinus medicine, bath bubbles, or a pair of sunglasses. ☒ *5100 Wisconsin Ave. NW, Friendship Heights* ☏ *202/363–3466* Ⓜ *Friendship Heights.*

Sutton Place Gourmet. Locals rave about the prepared foods sold at this upscale grocery, which also has premium gift baskets and a good selection of wine and beer. ⊠ *3201 New Mexico Ave. NW, Tenleytown* ☎ *202/ 363–5800* ⊕ *www.suttongourmet.com.*

GIFTS **Wake Up Little Suzie.** Clocks shaped like dogs and cats, silver jewelry,
★ funky switch-plate covers, and idiosyncratic ceramics are all here in this boutique of whimsical yet useful gifts. ⊠ *3409 Connecticut Ave. NW, Cleveland Park* ☎ *202/244–0700* Ⓜ *Cleveland Park.*

JEWELRY **Charles Schwartz and Son.** This full-service jeweler specializes in precious stones in traditional and modern settings. Fine watches are also available. ⊠ *Mazza Gallerie, 5300 Wisconsin Ave. NW, Friendship Heights* ☎ *202/363–5432* Ⓜ *Friendship Heights.*

MEN'S & **Brooks Brothers.** The oldest men's store in America, Brooks Brothers has
WOMEN'S sold traditional formal and casual clothing since 1818. Although there's
CLOTHING a small women's department, the store at this location mainly carries men's clothing. ⊠ *5504 Wisconsin Ave., Friendship Heights* ☎ *301/654– 8202* Ⓜ *Friendship Heights.*

Catch Can. Some shoppers come here for the great sales on comfortable clothing made from bright fabrics and prints. Others come year-round for the one-of-a-kind gifts for the house and closet, including stationery, furniture, and ceramics. ⊠ *5516 Connecticut Ave. NW, Chevy Chase, MD* ☎ *202/686–5316.*

Chico's. This chain store carries stylish, artful casual clothing and accessories for women. ⊠ *5418 Wisconsin Ave., Chevy Chase, MD* ☎ *301/986–1122* Ⓜ *Friendship Heights.*

Encore of Washington. This consignment shop's plentiful designer fashions, by the likes of Escada, Valentino, and Feraud, are in very good condition. ⊠ *3715 Macomb St. NW, Northwest/Upper Connecticut Ave.* ☎ *202/966–8122* Ⓜ *Tenleytown/AU.*

★ **Jaeger.** The Jaeger line of clothing, especially its knitwear, has been on the frontlines of fashion since the 1880s. This boutique store doesn't disappoint. ⊠ *5454 Wisconsin Ave., Chevy Chase, MD* ☎ *301/718– 0665.* Ⓜ *Friendship Heights.*

Micmac. At this gem of a boutique you'll find clothes by Issey Miyake and fab Arche shoes. Eye-catching displays make you want to buy one of everything. ⊠ *5301 Wisconsin Ave. NW, Friendship Heights* ☎ *202/ 362–6834* Ⓜ *Friendship Heights.*

Versace. Featuring the clothing line started by superstar Gianni Versace and now continued by his sister Donatella, this store is a favorite of the beautiful people. ⊠ *5454 Wisconsin Ave., Chevy Chase, MD* ☎ *301/ 951–4400* Ⓜ *Friendship Heights.*

SPAS & BEAUTY **Georgette Klinger Skin Care Salon.** The doyenne of spas, Georgette Klinger
SALONS specializes in skin care but can also pamper you with many other spa services. Treatments are pricey, but regular patrons say they're well worth it. ⊠ *5345 Wisconsin Ave. NW, Friendship Heights* ☎ *202/686– 8880 or 800/554–6437* Ⓜ *Friendship Heights.*

TOYS **Child's Play.** Toys are serious business in this shop. An attentive staff helps
FodorśChoice you sort through the large selection, which includes building toys, com-
★ puter software, art supplies, and classic games. ⊠ *5536 Connecticut Ave. NW, Chevy Chase MD* ☎ *202/244–3602* Ⓜ *Friendship Heights.*

Sullivan's Toy Store. Here you'll find stickers, books, learning games, costumes, stuffed animals, and just about anything else the younger set might want to play with. The art supply store adjacent to the toy space holds gifts for older recipients, from Japanese brush pens to handmade paper. ⊠ *3412 Wisconsin Ave. NW, Cleveland Park* ☎ *202/362–1343* Ⓜ *Cleveland Park.*

Tree Top Toys. This store specializes in plush dolls, European toys, and children's books and clothes. ⊠ *3301 New Mexico Ave. NW, Foxhall* ☎ *202/244–3500.*

Maryland/Virginia

It's a bit of a trek, but some of the best shopping is found on the outskirts of the city in Maryland and Virginia. Most malls are close to a Metro station, though a few are best reached by car. The Takoma Park area, on the D.C.–Maryland border, offers a concentration of charming antiques, clothing, and gift shops, which are complemented in the warmer months by seasonal street festivals with vendors and musical performances. The park itself hosts an excellent weekend farmers market in the warmer months.

By car: take George Washington Pkwy., I–495 (the Beltway).

Malls & Outlets

City Place. Discount shops such as Burlington Coat Factory and Marshall's are clustered in this mall in downtown Silver Spring, a 20-minute ride on the Metro from downtown D.C. ⊠ *8661 Colesville Rd., Silver Spring, MD* ☎ *301/589–1091* Ⓜ *Silver Spring.*

Fashion Centre at Pentagon City. Just across the river in Virginia, a 10-minute ride on the Metro from downtown, is this four-story mall with Macy's at one end and Nordstrom at the other. In between are a food court and such shops as Liz Claiborne and the Coach Store. ⊠ *1100 S. Hayes St., Arlington, VA* ☎ *703/415–2400* Ⓜ *Pentagon City.*

Tysons Galleria. Across a busy highway from Tysons Corner Center, the Galleria has 125 generally upscale retailers, including Saks Fifth Avenue, Neiman Marcus, and Macy's. ⊠ *2001 International Dr., McLean, VA* ☎ *703/827–7730.*

Potomac Mills. This mile-long mall off I–95, 30 minutes by car from the District, bills itself as Virginia's most popular attraction. There are some 220 discount and outlet stores here, including Nordstrom Rack, T. J. Maxx, Saks Off Fifth, and Linens 'N Things. Swedish furniture giant IKEA is also nearby. ⊠ *2700 Potomac Mills Circle, Woodbridge, VA* ☎ *703/490–5948.*

Tysons Corner Center. Anchored by Bloomingdale's and Nordstrom, Tysons Corner Center houses 240 other retailers. No matter when you go, be prepared to fight some of the area's heaviest traffic. ⊠ *1961 Chain Bridge Rd., McLean, VA* ☎ *703/893–9400.*

White Flint Mall. The big stores at this upscale mall are Bloomingdale's and Lord & Taylor; other stores include the Coach Store, Sharper Image, and Eddie Bauer. A free shuttle bus from the Metro is available. ⊠ *11301 Rockville Pike, North Bethesda, MD* ☎ *301/231–7467* Ⓜ *White Flint.*

Specialty Stores

ANTIQUES & COLLECTIBLES **Takoma Underground.** Descend the stairs to find yourself in the midst of vintage clothing, jewelry, books, collectibles, antique housewares, and esoteric items. ⊠ *7000 B Carroll Ave., Takoma Park, MD* ☎ *301/270–6380* Ⓜ *Takoma.*

ART GALLERIES **Torpedo Factory Art Center.** Created through the joint effort of a group of local artists and the City of Alexandria in 1974, this center has more than 80 working studios and six galleries. ⊠ *105 N. Union St., Historic District, Alexandria, VA* ☎ *703/838–4565* ⊕ *www.torpedofactory. org* Ⓜ *King St.*

CRAFTS & GIFTS **Arise.** Primarily a purveyor of Asian artifacts, antiques, and furniture, Arise also carries its own label of vibrant cotton and silk leisure clothing, as well as an astounding collection of kimonos. ✉ *6925 Willow St. NW, Takoma Park, MD* ☎ *202/291–0770* Ⓜ *Takoma.*

MEN'S & WOMEN'S CLOTHING

Amano. Not to be confused with the gift shop A Mano, this laid-back boutique sells sophisticated, funky clothing that you can wear to work or relax in at home. Accessories include cloth briefcases, silk scarves, hats, shoes, and jewelry. ✉ *7030 Carroll Ave., Takoma Park, MD* ☎ *301/270–1140* Ⓜ *Takoma.*

Glad Rags This fun vintage clothing shop often throws wacky sales, but their everyday bargains are always worth the visit. They specialize in contemporary women's clothes, with some items from recent decades. ✉ *7306 Carroll Ave., Takoma Park, MD* ☎ *301/891–6870* Ⓜ *Takoma.*

MUSICAL INSTRUMENTS

House of Musical Traditions. If you're looking for a dulcimer or a sitar, or want to learn the difference between bluegrass and blues guitar, try this nationally regarded shop. It carries uncommon instruments as well as books and recordings. ✉ *7040 Carroll Ave., Takoma Park, MD* ☎ *301/270–9090* ⊕ *www.hmtrad.com* Ⓜ *Takoma.*

SPAS & BEAUTY SALONS

Jolie, the Day Spa. Busy Washington women don't mind leaving the city behind for an appointment at Jolie. The day spa has 15 private treatment rooms and many services on offer—body treatments, massage, facials, hair, nails, and makeup. ✉ *7200 Wisconsin Ave., Bethesda, MD* ☎ *301/986–9293* Ⓜ *Bethesda.*

SIDE TRIPS

7

FODOR'S CHOICE

Mount Vernon

United States Naval Academy, Annapolis, MD

HIGHLY RECOMMENDED

Fredericksburg/Spotsylvania National Military Park

Hammond-Harwood House, Annapolis, MD

Kenmore, Fredericksburg, VA

William Paca House and Garden, Annapolis, MD

By Michael
Dolan
Updated by
CiCi
Williamson

WITHIN AN HOUR OF D.C. are numerous popular sights relating to our first president, naval history, colonial events, and famous battles. For an active side trip, you can walk or bike along the 13-mi path that parallels a section of the Chesapeake & Ohio (C&O) Canal, past Glen Echo Park, to Great Falls Tavern on the Maryland side of the Potomac. Traveling farther up the Potomac to Frederick—Maryland's second largest city—makes a pleasant day trip for antiques-hunters as well as those in search of less tangible goods, including travelers seeking a better understanding of the Civil War and its battles.

Sailing aficionados enjoy visiting the United States Naval Academy and getting out on the water in Annapolis, a major center for boating. On the Virginia side of the Potomac 16 mi from D.C. is Mount Vernon, George Washington's family home; two other interesting plantation homes—Woodlawn and Gunston Hall—are nearby. History buffs might also want to make a beeline for Fredericksburg, Virginia, to learn about the important roles this and surrounding towns played in the Revolutionary and Civil wars. The town's 40-block National Historic District contains more than 350 original 18th- and 19th-century buildings. Fredericksburg is also known for its antiques shops and its excellent, yet often reasonably priced, restaurants and hotels.

Most of these Virginia and Maryland side trips can be taken via trains, buses, and escorted tours. The most convenient way, however, is in a car.

C&O CANAL NATIONAL HISTORIC PARK & GREAT FALLS PARK

In the 18th and early 19th centuries, the Potomac River was the main transportation route between one of the most important ports on the nation's frontier—Cumberland, Maryland—and the seaports of the Chesapeake Bay. Coal, tobacco, grain, whiskey, furs, iron ore, and timber were sent down the Potomac to Georgetown and Alexandria, which served as major distribution points for both domestic and international markets.

Although it was a vital link with the country's western territories, the Potomac had some drawbacks as a commercial waterway: rapids and waterfalls along the 185 mi between Cumberland and Washington originally made it impossible for traders to travel the entire distance by boat. Just a few miles upstream from Washington, the Potomac cascades through two such barriers—the breathtakingly beautiful Great Falls and the less dramatic but equally impassable Little Falls.

To help traders move goods between the eastern markets and the western frontier more efficiently, 18th-century engineers proposed that a canal with a series of elevator locks be constructed parallel to the river. The first Potomac canal system was built at the urging of George Washington, who actually helped found the Patowmack Company for this purpose. If the firm couldn't eliminate obstacles by dredging, it built a canal around them. The five canals and other improvements were completed in 1802 (after-Washington's death), but natural variations in the river's flow—sometimes too little, sometimes too much—still interrupted river traffic, and the project, although successful for a time, failed in the long run.

Numbers in the margin correspond to points of interest on the C&O Canal National Historic Park & Great Falls Park map.

C&O Canal & Great Falls

The C&O Canal National Historic Park (on the Washington, D.C., and Maryland side of the Potomac) and the Great Falls Park (on the Virginia side) are both part of the National Park system. At a point about 9 mi west of the District line, the two parks face each other. It's here that the steep, jagged falls of the Potomac roar into a narrow gorge, providing one of the most spectacular scenic attractions in the East. Canoeing, bicycling, and fishing are popular in the parks. Within the C&O Canal National Historic Park are the Clara Barton National Historic Site and Glen Echo Park, which is notable for its whimsical architecture and its splendid 1921 Dentzel carousel.

7

Annapolis, Maryland

Maryland's capital is a popular destination for oyster catchers and boating fans. Warm, sunny days bring many boats to the City Dock, where they're moored against a background of waterfront shops and restaurants. Annapolis's enduring nautical reputation is upheld further by the presence of the United States Naval Academy. One of the country's largest assemblages of 18th-century architecture, with no fewer than 50 pre-Revolutionary buildings, the academy recalls the city's days as a major port.

Frederick, Maryland

Maryland's second-largest city is less than an hour away from Washington, D.C., and has one of the best-preserved historic districts in Maryland. There are several quirky museums in Frederick as well as a Civil War battlefield. The city and its environs also hold many antiques stores.

Potomac Plantations

Three splendid examples of plantation architecture remain on the Virginia side of the Potomac, just 15 mi south of the District. Mount Vernon, one of the most popular sights in the area, was the home of George Washington; Woodlawn was the estate of Washington's granddaughter; and Gunston Hall was the residence of George Mason, a patriot and author of the document on which the Bill of Rights was based.

Fredericksburg, Virginia

This compact city 50 mi south of Washington near the falls of the Rappahannock River played prominent roles at crucial points in the nation's history, particularly during the Revolutionary and Civil wars. A popular day-trip destination for history buffs and antiques collectors, Fredericksburg has a 40-block National Historic District containing more than 350 18th- and 19th-century buildings.

C&O Canal National Historic Park

West from Georgetown extending 13 mi to Great Falls Tavern.

C&O Canal National Historic Park originates in Georgetown and encloses a 184.5-mi towpath that ends in Cumberland, Maryland. The finest relic of America's canal-building era, its route and structures are still almost entirely intact. Construction along the Maryland bank began in

1828, using the principles of the Erie Canal in New York. When construction ended in 1850, canals stretched from downtown Washington to Cumberland through 74 locks. (The public rest room at the intersection of 17th Street and Constitution Avenue was originally a lock house of an earlier canal through Washington.) The original plan to extend a canal to the Ohio River was superseded by the economic success of the Baltimore & Ohio (B&O) Railroad, which eventually put the canal out of business.

Construction of the C&O Canal and the B&O Railroad began on the same day, July 4, 1828. Initially, the C&O provided an economical and practical way for traders to move goods through the Washington area to the lower Chesapeake. During the mid-19th century, boats carried as many as a million tons of merchandise a year. But the C&O Canal suffered a flood in late spring 1889 and couldn't recover from the financial disaster that ensued. Ownership then shifted to the B&O Railroad, the canal's largest stockholder, and operation continued until 1924, when another flood ended traffic. The railroad transferred ownership of the canal to the federal government in 1938 to settle a $2 million debt.

In the 1950s a proposal to build a highway over the canal near Washington was thwarted by residents of the Palisades (between Georgetown and the Great Falls Tavern) and others concerned with the canal's history and legacy. Since 1971 the canal has been a national park, providing a window into the past and a marvelous place to enjoy the outdoors.

❶ The towpath along the canal in **Georgetown** passes remnants of that area's industrial past, such as the Godey Lime Kilns near the mouth of Rock Creek, as well as the fronts of numerous houses that date from 1810. At the Foundry Mall, you can start a tour of the area on foot, by bike, or—from April through early November—by mule-drawn boat.

There are two visitor centers in the sections of the C&O Canal National Historic Park closest to Washington: one in Georgetown and the other in Great Falls.

At the **Georgetown Visitor Center,** National Park Service rangers and volunteers provide maps, information, and canal history. Mule-drawn canal boat rides depart from the center from about early April through early November. ✉ *1057 Thomas Jefferson St. NW, Georgetown* ☎ *202/ 653–5190* ⊕ *www.nps.gov/choh* ☉ *Apr.–Oct., Wed.–Sun. 9–4:30; Nov.–Mar., weekends 10–4, staffing permitting.*

❷ **Fletcher's Boat House,** on the D.C. side of the Potomac, rents rowboats, canoes, and bicycles and sells tackle, snack foods, and D.C. fishing licenses. Here you can catch shad, perch, catfish, striped bass, and other freshwater species. Canoeing is allowed on the canal and, weather permitting, in the Potomac. There's a large picnic area along the riverbank. ✉ *4940 Canal Rd., at Reservoir Rd., Georgetown* ☎ *202/244–0461* ☉ *Late Mar.–May, daily 7:30–7; June–Aug., daily 9–7; Sept.–Nov., daily 9–6* ☉ *Closed Dec.–early Mar. and during severe weather.*

❸ **Chain Bridge,** named for the chains that held up the original structure, links D.C. and Virginia. The bridge was built to enable cattlemen to bring Virginia herds to the slaughterhouses along the Maryland side of the Potomac. During the Civil War the bridge was guarded by Union troops stationed at earthen fortifications along what's now Potomac Avenue NW. The Virginia side of the river in the area around Chain Bridge is known for its good fishing and narrow rapids. ✉ *Glebe Rd. (Rte. 120), Arlington.*

Historical Sights

Across the Potomac and Anacostia rivers in Maryland and Virginia are places where pivotal events in U.S. history occurred. These states also have abundant colonial architecture—the real thing. Of primal importance to the shaping of the United States are spots dear to George Washington: Mount Vernon; his boyhood home at Ferry Farm near Fredericksburg; and the mansions of his relatives. Bayside Annapolis, the country's first peacetime capital, is not to be missed for its naval ties and port. A vast neighborhood of 18th-century architecture, which includes 50 pre–Revolutionary War buildings, is also here.

7

Outdoor Adventures

Hikers crossing Virginia's hills might find their senses overloaded by the beauty of flowering trees in spring or a palette of autumn leaves. Vast areas for them are in the Maryland and Virginia parks near the Great Falls.

Those who fish can stake out the numerous riverbanks and salty shores. Bikers may ride for hundreds of miles on the area's excellent, paved bicycle paths. One especially attractive route winds south along the Virginia shore of the Potomac. From it, you can view Georgetown and Washington's monuments on the opposite bank; Arlington National Cemetery; Ronald Reagan National Airport; and Old Town Alexandria. Before ending at Mount Vernon, the route runs through wildlife sanctuaries, and there are many excellent picnic spots along the way.

Where to Stay & Where to Eat

The restaurants we list are the cream of the crop in each price category. Properties indicated by an ✕⛱ are lodging establishments whose restaurant warrants a special trip. It's always a good idea to book ahead; we mention reservations only when they're essential or are not accepted. All restaurants we list are open daily for lunch and dinner unless stated otherwise; dress is mentioned only when men are required to wear a jacket or a jacket and tie.

Assume that all rooms have private baths, phones, TVs, and air-conditioning unless otherwise noted and that all hotels operate on the European Plan (with no meals) unless we specify that they use the Continental Plan (CP, with a Continental breakfast), Breakfast Plan (BP, with a full cooked breakfast), Modified American Plan (MAP, with breakfast and dinner), or the Full American Plan (FAP, with all meals).

We always list the facilities that are available—but we don't specify whether they cost extra: when pricing accommodations, always ask what's included and what costs extra. Properties indicated by a ✕⛱ are lodging establishments whose restaurants warrant a special trip.

		WHAT IT COSTS			
	$$$$	**$$$**	**$$**	**$**	**¢**
RESTAURANTS	over $32	$22–$32	$15–$22	$7–$15	under $7
HOTELS	over $270	$205–$270	$150–$205	$100–$150	under $100

Restaurant prices are per person for a main course at dinner, excluding sales tax (7.5% in VA, 5% in MD). Hotel prices are for two people in a standard double room in high season.

Glen Echo Park preserves the site of Washington's oldest amusement park (1911–68) and a stone tower from the town's earlier days. The village of Glen Echo was founded in 1891 by Edwin and Edward Baltzley, brothers who made their fortune through the invention of the egg beater. The brothers were enthusiastic supporters of the Chautauqua movement, a group begun in 1874 in New York as a way to promote liberal education among the lower and middle classes. The brothers sold land and houses to further their dream, but the Glen Echo Chautauqua lasted only one season. The National Park Service administers this 10-acre property and offers year-round dances Friday through Sunday in the 1933 Spanish Ballroom, classes in the arts, two children's theaters, two art galleries with ongoing exhibits, artist demonstrations, and a Children's Museum with environmental education workshops. You can also take a ride on a 1921 Dentzel carousel May through September. ⊠ *7300 MacArthur Blvd. NW, Glen Echo* ☎ *301/492–6229; 301/492–6282 events hot line* ⊕ *www.nps.gov/glec* ✉ *Park free, carousel ride 50¢, cost varies for dances.*

Beside Glen Echo Park's parking lot is the **Clara Barton National Historic Site,** a monument to the founder of the American Red Cross. The structure was built for her by the founders of Glen Echo, and she used it originally to store Red Cross supplies; later it became both her home and the organization's headquarters. Today the building is furnished with period artifacts and many of her possessions. Access is by a 30- to 45-minute guided tour only. ⊠ *5801 Oxford Rd., Glen Echo* ☎ *301/492–6245* ⊕ *www.nps.gov/clba* ✉ *Free* ⊙ *Tours on the hr 10–4.*

Maryland's **Great Falls Tavern,** headquarters for the Palisades area of C&O Canal National Historic Park, has displays of canal history and photographs that show how high the river can rise. A platform on Olmsted Island, accessible from near the tavern, provides a spectacular view of the falls. On the canal walls are grooves worn by decades of friction from boat towlines. Mule-drawn canal boat rides ($8), about one hour round-trip, start here between April and November from Wednesday to Monday. The tavern ceased food service long ago, so if you're hungry, head for the snack bar a few paces north. ⊠ *11710 MacArthur Blvd., Potomac 20854* ☎ *301/299–3613 or 301/767–3714* ✉ *$5 per vehicle, $3 per person without vehicle; good for 3 days at both Great Falls Park and C&O Canal National Historic Park* ⊙ *Nov.–Mar., daily 9–4:30; Apr.–Oct. daily 9–5.*

Great Falls Park, Virginia

23 mi northwest from Georgetown.

Part of the National Park System, Great Falls Park is on the Virginia side of the Potomac, across the river from C&O Canal National Historic Park. Great Falls Park's 800 acres are a favorite place for outings.

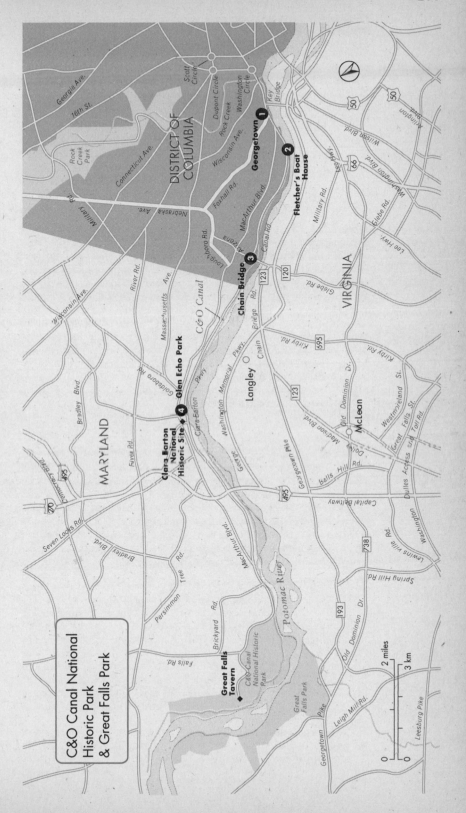

C&O Canal National
Historic Park
& Great Falls Park

DISTRICT OF COLUMBIA

MARYLAND

VIRGINIA

Rock Creek Park

Georgia Ave.

16th St.

Connecticut Ave.

Scott Circle

Dupont Circle

Washington Circle

Wisconsin Ave.

Nebraska Ave.

Military Rd.

Foxhall Rd.

Key Bridge

Georgetown 1

Fletcher's Boat House 2

MacArthur Blvd.

Arizona

Canal Rd.

Chain Bridge 3

Louisiana Rd.

River Rd.

Massachusetts Ave.

Wisconsin Ave.

C&O Canal

Goldsboro Rd.

Glen Echo Park

Clara Barton
National
Historic Site 4

Bradley Blvd.

River Rd.

Cabin John Pkwy.

495

270

Seven Locks Rd.

Bradley Blvd.

Persimmon Tree Rd.

Brickyard Rd.

MacArthur Blvd.

Falls Rd.

Great Falls
Tavern

Great Falls Park

C&O Canal
National Historic
Park

Potomac River

Clara Barton Pkwy.

George

Washington Memorial Pkwy.

Chain Bridge Rd.

Langley

123

120

Military Rd.

Glebe Rd.

Lee Hwy.

Kirby Rd.

595

Old Dominion Dr.

123

Madison Blvd.

Georgetown Pike

Balls Hill Rd.

495

Capital Beltway

McLean

Westmoreland

Great Falls St.

Dolley Madison Blvd.

Washington Lewinsville Rd.

Dulles Access and Toll Rd.

Spring Hill Rd.

738

193

Old Dominion Dr.

Georgetown Pike

Leigh Mill Rd.

Leesburg Pike

Key Hwy.

Glebe Rd.

Lee Hwy.

Wilson Blvd.

Arlington Blvd.

Washington Blvd.

50

50

66

2 miles

3 km

0

The steep, jagged falls roar into the narrow Mather Gorge—a spectacular scene. There are stunning views of the Potomac here, and a marker shows the river's high-water marks. The sites that overlook the falls date from the early 1900s, when the land was a private amusement park and visitors arrived by train. Fifteen mi of trails lead past the old Patowmack Canal and among the boulders along the edge of the falls.

Swimming, wading, overnight camping, and alcoholic beverages are prohibited, but you can fish (a Virginia, Maryland, or D.C. license is required for anglers 16 and older), climb rocks (climbers must register at the visitor center beforehand), or—if you're an experienced boater with your own equipment—go white-water kayaking (*below* the fall only). As is true all along this stretch of the river, the currents are deadly. Despite frequent signs and warnings, there are occasionally those who dare the water and drown.

A tour of the **Great Falls Park Visitor Center and Museum** takes 30 minutes. Staff members also conduct park walks year-round; the visitor center tour and guided park walks are included in the price of admission. You're encouraged to take self-guided tours along well-marked trails, including one that follows the route of the old Patowmack Canal; the visitor center provides maps for the various trails. ⊠ *9200 Old Dominion Dr., McLean, VA 22101-2223* ☎ *703/285–2966 or 703/285–2965* ⊕ *www.nps.gov/grfa* ⊠ *$5 per vehicle, $3 per person without vehicle; good for 3 days at both Great Falls Park and C&O Canal National Historic Park; annual park pass $20* ☉ *7 AM–dark; visitor center mid-Oct.–mid-Apr., daily 10–4; mid-Apr.–mid-Oct., weekdays 10–5; weekends 10–6; hrs subject to change.*

C&O Canal National Historic Park & Great Falls Park A to Z

CAR TRAVEL

To reach Great Falls Park, take the scenic and winding Route 193 (Exit 13 off Route 495, the Beltway) to Route 738 (Old Dominion Drive), and follow the signs. It takes about 25 minutes to drive to the park from the Beltway. C&O Canal National Historic Park is along the Maryland side of the Potomac and is accessible by taking Canal Road or MacArthur Boulevard from Georgetown or by taking Exit 41 off the Beltway and then following the signs to Carderock. There are several roadside stops accessible from the southbound lanes of Canal Road where you can park and visit restored canal locks and lock houses.

OUTDOORS & SPORTS

The C&O Canal National Historic Park and its towpath are favorites of joggers, bikers, and canoeists. The path has a slight grade, which makes for a leisurely ride or hike. Most recreational bikers consider the 13 mi from Georgetown to Great Falls Tavern an easy ride; you only need to carry your bike for one short stretch of rocky ground near Great Falls. You can also take a bike path that parallels MacArthur Boulevard and runs from Georgetown to Great Falls Tavern. Storm damage has left parts of the canal dry, but many segments remain intact and navigable by canoe. You can rent rowboats, canoes, or bicycles at Fletcher's Boat House, just upriver from Georgetown. 🚲 **Fletcher's Boat House** ⊠ 4940 Canal Rd., at Reservoir Rd., Georgetown ☎ 202/244-0461 ☉ Late Mar.–May, daily 7:30–7; June–Aug., daily 9–7; Sept.–Nov., daily 9–6 ☉ Closed Dec.–early Mar. or during severe weather.

TOURS

Between April and November on Wednesday through Sunday, mule-drawn canal boats leave for roughly one-hour trips from the Foundry Mall on Thomas Jefferson Street NW, half a block south of M Street in Georgetown. Reservations are not required; ticket sales begin two hours before each trip. Floods sometimes affect canal boat trips, so call the National Park Service office to check.

🚩 **National Park Service Canal Boats** ⊠ Canal Visitor Center, 1057 Thomas Jefferson St. NW, Georgetown ☎ 202/653-5190 or 301/299-2026 ⊕ www.nps.gov/choh/co service.htm#george ⊠ $8.

ANNAPOLIS, MARYLAND

In 1649 a group of Puritan settlers moved from Virginia to a spot at the mouth of the Severn River, where they established a community called Providence. Lord Baltimore, who held the royal charter to settle Maryland named the area around this town Anne Arundel County, after his wife. In 1684 Anne Arundel Town was established across from Providence on the Severn's south side. Ten years later, Anne Arundel Town became the capital of Maryland and was renamed Annapolis—for Princess Anne, who later became queen. It received its city charter in 1708 and became a major port, particularly for the export of tobacco. In 1774 patriots here matched their Boston counterparts (who had thrown their famous tea party the year before) by burning the *Peggy Stewart*, a ship loaded with taxed tea. Annapolis later served as the nation's first peacetime capital (1783–84).

Today, "Crabtown," as the city is nicknamed, is a picturesque place to stroll, shop, relax, study, or dine. It has a large assemblage of 18th-century architecture, including more surviving colonial buildings than any other place in the country. Maryland is the only state in which the homes of all its signers of the Declaration of Independence still exist. The houses are all in Annapolis, and you can tour three of the four—the homes of Charles Carroll, Samuel Chase, and William Paca.

Although it has long since been overtaken by Baltimore as the major Maryland port, Annapolis is still a popular pleasure-boating destination. On warm sunny days, the waters off City Dock become center stage for an amateur show of powerboaters maneuvering through the heavy traffic. Annapolis's enduring nautical reputation derives largely from the presence of the United States Naval Academy: its midshipmen throng the city streets in white uniforms in summer and navy blue in winter.

Numbers in the text correspond to numbers in the margin and on the Annapolis, MD, map.

a good tour

You can see Annapolis in a single well-planned day. To get maps, schedules, and information about guided tours all year round, it's best to begin your walking tour at the **Annapolis & Anne Arundel County Conference & Visitors Bureau ❶** ⌐. Exit the visitor center then turn left at West Street and walk to **St. Anne's Church ❷**, straight ahead a half block. The edifice incorporates walls from a former church that burned in 1858; a congregation has worshiped here continuously since 1692. Off Church Circle, take Franklin Street one block to the **Banneker-Douglass Museum ❸**, which portrays African-American life in Maryland, and return to the circle after a visit. Continue around the circle to the Maryland Inn and walk to the end of Main Street—passing many boutiques and small restaurants—and the **Historic Annapolis Foundation Museum Store ❹**, where you can rent audiotapes for self-guided walking tours. Farther down, past the Market House, which has many places to stop for a snack, look down to see the **Kunta Kinte Plaque and Alex Haley Memorial** ⑤, which commemorates the 1767 arrival of the slave portrayed in Alex Haley's *Roots*. On the other side of City Dock in front of the Harbor Master's office, there's an **information booth** ⑥ where you can get maps and information from April to October.

Then return to Market Square and walk down Compromise Street. Turn right at St. Mary's Street, which dead-ends at Duke of Gloucester Street. The **Charles Carroll House** ⑦ is across this street, behind St. Mary's Church. After you've made your visit, retrace your steps and turn right at Market Square onto Randall Street. Walk two blocks to the Naval Academy wall and turn right, entering the gate to the **United States Naval Academy** ⑧ and its Armel-Leftwich Visitor Center. Here you can join a tour or continue solo through the academy grounds, where future U.S. Navy and Marine Corps officers are trained. Walk toward the Naval Academy Chapel dome and turn right on Buchanan Road and again at the Tecumseh statue, figurehead of the USS *Delaware*, to visit the academy's dormitory, Bancroft Hall. Return to Tecumseh and take the curvy walkway to the left to the chapel. From the chapel entrance the Naval Academy Museum is a half block to the left in Preble Hall.

From the museum, leave through Gate 3 to your right and walk to the **Hammond-Harwood House** ⑨ and the **Chase-Lloyd House** ⑩, both designed by colonial America's foremost architect, William Buckland. The two homes are across the street from each other in the second block of Maryland Avenue. Continue on Maryland Avenue a block to Prince George Street; turn left and walk a block to the **William Paca House and Garden** ⑪, home of another signer of the Declaration of Independence. Retrace your route and continue a block past Maryland Avenue to the campus of **St. John's College** ⑫, directly ahead at the College Avenue end of Prince George Street. After touring the campus, follow College Avenue away from the Naval Academy wall to North Street and go one block to the **Maryland State House** ⑬ in the middle of State Circle. After touring the capitol, stop and visit the **Thurgood Marshall Memorial** ⑭ in State House Square, close to Bladen Street and College Avenue. Then turn back toward State Circle and turn right, exiting State Circle via School Street. Keep an eye out for the beautiful wrought iron fencing that surrounds Government House, a Georgian mansion with sculpture gardens that's the home of Maryland's governor. Walk down School Street, which leads back to Church Circle and West Street, where the tour began. From here you can drive to the **Maryland State Archives** ⑮, where you can search for family history or do historical research. It's on the right as you leave downtown on Rowe Boulevard, heading toward Route 50. Farther west on U.S. Route 50 is **London Town House and Gardens** ⑯, Maryland's largest archaeological excavation. The digging here continues in search of the abandoned town of London. The public can participate on scheduled dig days, and docents lead tours of a three-story brick home built there in 1760. To get here from Route 50, take Exit 22 onto Highway 665 and turn right onto Highway 2 south; cross the South River Bridge and turn left at Mayo Road; in less than a mile, turn left onto Londontown Road and follow it 1 mi to the site.

TIMING Walking this route will take about an hour. Budget another half hour each for tours of the smaller historic homes and an hour each for the Paca and Hammond-Harwood houses. The Naval Academy deserves about two hours, plus another half hour if you visit the museum. The capitol takes a quarter hour to see. The drive to the Maryland Archives takes about 5 minutes; it's another 15 minutes to London Town. Plan on 1½ hours for taking the tour and wandering the grounds.

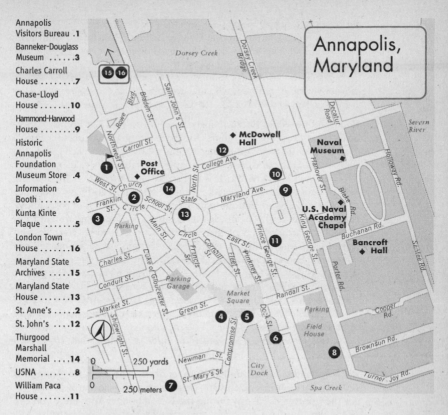

Sights to See

► **①** **Annapolis & Anne Arundel County Conference & Visitors Bureau.** Start your visit at Annapolis's main visitor center. Here you can pick up maps and brochures or begin a guided tour. ⊠ *26 West St., Historic Area* ☎ *410/ 280–0445* ⊕ *www.visit-annapolis.org* ⊙ *Daily 9–5.*

③ **Banneker-Douglass Museum.** This museum, in a former church, has changing exhibits, lectures, films, and literature about the African-American experience in Maryland. It's named for Frederick Douglass, the 19th-century abolitionist, and Benjamin Banneker, a Maryland astronomer, surveyor, and mathematician who helped Pierre-Charles L'Enfant survey what would become Washington, D.C. ⊠ *84 Franklin St., Historic Area* ☎ *410/216–6180* ⊕ *www.marylandhistoricaltrust.net* ⊠ *Free* ⊙ *Tues.–Fri. 10–3, Sat. noon–4.*

⑦ **Charles Carroll House.** This birthplace and city home of the only Catholic to sign the Declaration of Independence has 18th-century terraced gardens that overlook Spa Creek. Carroll was one of the wealthiest men in colonial America. The restored 1720 house contains a wine cellar added in the 19th century. ⊠ *107 Duke of Gloucester St., Historic Area* ☎ *410/269–1737 or 888/269–1737* ⊕ *www.carrollhouse.com* ⊠ *$4* ⊙ *Fri. and Sun. noon–4, Sat. 10–2; other times by appointment.*

⑩ **Chase-Lloyd House.** William Buckland, a prominent colonial architect, built the Chase-Lloyd House. In 1774 the tobacco planter and revolutionary Edward Lloyd IV completed work begun five years earlier by Samuel Chase, a signer of the Declaration of Independence and future Supreme Court justice. The first floor is open to the public and contains more of Buckland's handiwork, including a parlor mantelpiece with tobacco leaves carved into the marble. (Buckland was famous for his interior woodwork; you can see more of it in the **Hammond-Harwood House** across the street and in George Mason's Gunston Hall in Lorton, Virginia.) The house, furnished in a mixture of 18th-, 19th-, and 20th-century pieces, has a staircase that parts dramatically around an arched triple window. For more than 100 years the house has served as a home for older women, who live upstairs. ⊠ *22 Maryland Ave., Historic Area* ☎ *410/263–2723* ✆ *$2* ☼ *Mar.–Dec., Mon.–Sat. 2–4.*

★ ❾ **Hammond-Harwood House.** Ninety percent of this 1774 home is original. A fine example of colonial five-part Georgian architecture (a single block with two connecting rooms and wings on each side), the Hammond-Harwood House is the only verifiable full-scale example of William Buckland's work. It was also his final project, as he died the year the house was completed. Exquisite moldings, cornices, and other carvings appear throughout (note especially the garlands of roses above the front doorway). The house was meant to be a wedding present from Matthias Hammond, a planter and revolutionary, to his fiancée, who jilted him before the house was finished. Hammond died a bachelor in 1784. The Harwoods took over the house toward the turn of the 19th century. Today it's furnished with 18th-century pieces, and the garden is tended with regard to period authenticity. Tours leave on the half hour; the last begins at 3:30. ⊠ *19 Maryland Ave., Historic Area* ☎ *410/269–1714* ⊕ *www.hammondharwood.org* ✆*$6, $10 combination ticket with William Paca House* ☼ *Apr. 15–Oct., noon–5; Jan. and Feb., noon–4 weekends only; Nov.–Dec. and Mar.–mid-Apr., Mon.–Sat. 10–4, Sun. noon–4.*

❹ **Historic Annapolis Foundation Museum Store.** The Historic Annapolis Foundation operates its museum store in a warehouse that held supplies for the Continental Army during the Revolutionary War. Here you can shop, check out a diorama of the city's 18th-century waterfront, and rent taped narrations for walking tours. ⊠ *77 Main St., Historic Area* ☎*410/268–5576* ⊕ *www.hafmuseumstore.com* ✆ *Free* ☼ *Sun.–Thurs. 10–6, Fri.–Sat. 10–9. Variable extended hrs in summer.*

❻ **Information Booth.** From April to October the information booth on City Dock, adjacent to the harbormaster's office, is open and stocked with maps and brochures. ⊠ *Dock St. parking lot, Historic Area* ☎ *410/280–0445.*

> **need a break?** The reconstructed **Market House Pavilion** (⊠ City Dock, Historic Area), a collection of about 20 market stalls in the center of Market Square, sells baked goods, fast food, and seafood (either prepared or to cook at home). There's no seating; set up your picnic anywhere on the dock.

❺ **Kunta Kinte Plaque and Alex Haley Memorial.** The three-sided obelisk and plaque beyond Market Square at the head of City Dock commemorates the 1767 arrival of the African slave immortalized in Alex Haley's *Roots.* The memorial is a tribute to the author. ⊕ *www.kintehaley.org.*

⑯ **London Town House and Gardens.** This National Historic Landmark is on the South River, a short car-ride from Annapolis. The three-story waterfront brick house, built by William Brown in 1760, has 8 acres of woodland gardens. The 17th-century tobacco port of London, made up of 40 dwellings, shops, and taverns, disappeared in the 18th century, when its buildings were abandoned and left to decay. The excavation of the town is still going on. From April to September you can join the dig one Saturday each month (call for schedule). Docents conduct 30- to 45-minute house tours; allow more time to wander the grounds. From

March 15 to December, house tours leave on the hour (the last is at 3). ✉ *839 Londontown Rd., Edgewater 21037* ☎ *410/222–1919* 🖙 *$6* ☉ *Mid.-Mar.–Dec., Mon.–Sat. 10–4, Sun. noon–4; Jan.–mid-Mar., closed weekends.*

⑮ **Maryland State Archives.** Genealogists use the public search room for family history and historical research. Collections include original civic and church records, newspapers, photographs, and maps. In the lobby are changing exhibits and a gift shop. ✉ *350 Rowe Blvd., West Side* ☎ *410/ 260–6400* ⊕ *www.mdarchives.state.md.us* 🖙 *Free* ☉ *Tues.–Sat. 8:30–noon and 1–4:30.*

⑬ **Maryland State House.** Completed in 1780, the State House has the nation's largest wooden dome and is the oldest state capitol in continuous legislative use; it's also the only one in which the U.S. Congress has sat (1783–84). It was here that General George Washington resigned as commander in chief of the Continental Army and where the Treaty of Paris was ratified, ending the Revolutionary War. Both events took place in the Old Senate Chamber, which is filled with intricate woodwork (featuring the ubiquitous tobacco motif) attributed to colonial architect William Buckland. Also decorating this room is Charles Willson Peale's painting *Washington at the Battle of Yorktown,* a masterpiece of the Revolutionary War period's finest portrait artist. The Maryland Senate and House now hold their sessions in two other chambers in the building. Also on the grounds is the oldest public building in Maryland, the tiny redbrick **Treasury,** built in 1735. Note that you must have a photo I.D. to enter the State House. ✉ *State Circle, Historic Area* ☎ *410/974–3400* 🖙 *Free* ☉ *Welcome center open weekdays 9–5, weekends 10–4; ½-hr tour daily at 11 and 3.*

❷ **St. Anne's Church.** St. Anne's Episcopal parish was founded in 1692; King William III donated the Communion silver. The first St. Anne's Church, built in 1704, was torn down in 1775. The second, built in 1792, burned down in 1858. Parts of the walls survived and were incorporated into the present structure, built the next year. The churchyard contains the grave of the last colonial governor, Sir Robert Eden. ✉ *Church Circle, Historic Area* ☎ *410/267–9333* 🖙 *Free* ☉ *Daily 8–5:30.*

⑫ **St. John's College.** Here is the alma mater of Francis Scott Key, lyricist of "The Star Spangled Banner." However, since 1937, the college has been best known as the birthplace of the Great Books curriculum, which includes reading the works of great authors from Homer to Faulkner and beyond. All students at the college follow the same curriculum for four years, and classes are conducted as discussions rather than lectures. Climb the gradual slope of the long, brick-paved path to the impressive golden cupola of **McDowell Hall,** the third-oldest academic building in the country, just as St. John's is the third-oldest college in the country (after Harvard and William and Mary). St. John's grounds once held the last living Liberty Tree, under which the Sons of Liberty convened in order to hear patriots plan the Revolution against England. Wounded in a 1999 hurricane, the 400-year-old tree was removed; its progeny stands to the left of McDowell Hall. The **Elizabeth Myers Mitchell Art Gallery** (☎ 410/626–2556), on the east side of Mellon Hall, presents exhibits and special programs that relate to the fine arts. Down King George Street toward the water is the **Carroll-Barrister House,** now the college admissions office. The house was built in 1722 at Main and Conduit streets and was moved onto campus in 1957. Charles Carroll (not the signer of the Declaration but his cousin), who helped draft Maryland's Declaration of Rights, was born here. ✉ *60 College Ave., at St. John's St., Historic Area* ☎ *410/263–2371* ⊕ *www.sjca.edu.*

⓮ **Thurgood Marshall Memorial.** Born in Baltimore, Thurgood Marshall (1908–93) was the first African-American Supreme Court Justice and was one of the 20th-century's foremost leaders in the struggle for equal rights under the law. Marshall won the decision in Brown v. Board of Education, in which the Supreme Court in 1954 overturned the doctrine of "separate but equal." Marshall was appointed as United States Solicitor General in 1965 and to the Supreme Court in 1967 by President Lyndon B. Johnson. The 8-foot statue depicts Marshall as a young lawyer. ⊠ *State House Sq., bordered by Bladen St., School St., and College Ave., Historic Area.*

❽ **United States Naval Academy.** Probably the most interesting and important site in Annapolis, the Naval Academy runs along the Severn River and abuts downtown Annapolis. Men and women enter from every part of the United States and many foreign countries to undergo rigorous study in subjects that range from literature to navigation to nuclear engineering. The academy, established in 1845 on the site of a U.S. Army fort, occupies 329 waterfront acres. The centerpiece of the campus is the bright copper-clad dome of the interdenominational **U.S. Naval Academy Chapel.** Beneath it lies the crypt of the Revolutionary War naval officer John Paul Jones, who, in a historic naval battle with a British ship, uttered the inspirational words, "I have not yet begun to fight!"

Fodor'sChoice
★

Near the chapel in Preble Hall is the **U.S. Naval Academy Museum & Gallery of Ships** (⊠ 118 Maryland Ave., Historic Area ☎ 410/293–2108), which tells the story of the U.S. Navy through displays of model ships and memorabilia from naval heroes and fighting vessels. The U.S. Naval Institute and Bookstore is also in this building. Admission for the museum, institute, and bookstore is free; hours are Monday through Saturday from 9 to 5 and Sunday from 11 to 5.

On the grounds, midshipmen (the term used for women as well as men) go to classes, conduct military drills, and practice for or compete in intercollegiate and intramural sports. **Bancroft Hall,** closed to the public, is one of the largest dormitories in the world—it houses the entire 4,000-member Brigade of Midshipmen. The **Statue of Tecumseh,** in front of Bancroft Hall, is a bronze replica of the USS *Delaware*'s wooden figurehead, "Tamanend." It's decorated by midshipmen for athletics events, and for good luck during exams, students pitch pennies into his quiver of arrows. If you're there at noon in fair weather you can see midshipmen form up outside Bancroft Hall and parade to lunch to the beat of the Drum and Bugle Corps.

Adjoining Halsey Field House is the **USNA Armel-Leftwich Visitor Center** (⊠ 52 King George St., Historic Area ☎ 410/263–6933), which has exhibits of midshipmen life—including a mockup of a midshipman's room—and the Freedom 7 space capsule flown by an astronaut Alan Shepard, an Academy graduate. Walking tours of the Naval Academy led by licensed guides leave from here. You must have a photo I.D. to be admitted through the Academy's gates, and only cars used for official Department of Defense business may enter the grounds. ⊕ *www.navyonline.com* ⊠ *Grounds tour $6.50 ⊙ USNA Armel-Leftwich Visitor Center: Mar.–Dec., daily 9–5; Jan. and Feb., daily 9–4. Guided walking tours generally leave Mon.–Sat. 10–3 and Sun. 12:30–2:30; call ahead to confirm.*

★ ⓫ **William Paca House and Garden.** Paca (pronounced "PAY-cuh") was a signer of the Declaration of Independence and a Maryland governor from 1782 to 1785. His house was built in 1765, and its original garden was finished in 1772. Inside, the main floor (furnished with 18th-century antiques) retains its original Prussian-blue and soft-gray color scheme. The second floor contains a mixture of 18th- and 19th-century pieces. The adjacent 2-acre garden provides a longer perspective on the back of the house, plus worthwhile sights of its own: upper terraces, a Chinese Chippendale bridge, a pond, a wilderness area, and formal arrangements. An inn, Carvel Hall, once stood on the gardens. After the inn was demolished in 1965, it took eight years to rebuild the gardens, which are planted with 18th-century perennials. ✉ *186 Prince George St., Historic Area* ☎ *410/263–5553* ⊕ *www.annapolis.org* 🏷 *House and garden $8, house only $5, garden only $4, combination ticket with Hammond-Harwood House $10* ⊙ *House and garden mid-Mar.–Dec., Mon.–Sat. 10–5, Sun. noon–5; Jan.–mid-Mar., Fri. and Sat. 10–4, Sun. noon–4.*

Where to Stay & Eat

In the beginning, there was crab: crab cakes, crab soup, whole crabs to crack. This Chesapeake Bay specialty is still found in abundance, but Annapolis has broadened its horizons to include eateries—many in the Historic District—that offer many sorts of cuisines. Ask for a restaurant guide at the visitor center.

There are many places to stay near the heart of the city, as well as area B&Bs and chain motels a few miles outside town (some of which offer free transportation to the downtown historic area). A unique "Crabtown" option is Boat & Breakfasts, in which you sleep, eat and cruise on a yacht or schooner you've booked. Contact the visitor center for information.

Two reservation services operate in Annapolis. **Annapolis Accommodations** (✉ 41 Maryland Ave. ☎ 410/280–0900 or 800/715–1000 ⊕ www.stayannapolis.com) will book you into bed-and-breakfasts, hotels, and vacation homes. Their office is open 9–5 weekdays. **Annapolis Bed & Breakfast Association** (☎ 410/295–5200 ⊕ www.annapolisbandb.com) books lodging in the old section of town, which has many restaurants and shops as well as the Maryland State House and the City Dock. The U.S. Naval Academy and St. John's College serve as the northern and western boundaries of the territory.

$$$–$$$$ ✕ **Treaty of Paris Restaurant.** Period reproduction furniture and fabrics decorate this handsome, 18th-century dining room. For dinner, you may want to try such Continental dishes as beef Wellington or seafood choices like crab imperial, twin lobster tails, stuffed rockfish, and crab cakes. Colonial Tea Time is Wednesday from 3 to 4. The King of France Tavern next door has live jazz Friday and Saturday evenings. ✉ *Maryland Inn, 16 Church Circle, Historic Area* ☎ *410/263–2641 or 410/216–6340* 🖃 *AE, D, DC, MC, V.*

$$–$$$$ ✕ **Breeze.** In this stylish, elegant dining room, the predominantly pale-blue color scheme fits in well with the waterfront of Annapolis. On the walls are sailing scenes and soft, draped fabrics, representing sails blowing in the wind. For dinner, you may wish to try the mixed seafood grill or the New York strip steak. Daily specials use fresh, local ingredients. The quick "executive lunch" includes two courses for $10. ✉ *Loews Annapolis Hotel, 126 West St., West Side* ☎ *410/263–1299* 🖃 *AE, D, DC, MC, V.*

$–$$$$ ✕ **Middleton Tavern Oyster Bar and Restaurant.** Horatio Middleton began operating this "inn for seafaring men" in 1750; Washington, Jefferson, and Franklin were among its patrons. Today, two fireplaces, wood floors, paneled walls, and a nautical theme make it cozy. Seafood tops the menu; the Maryland crab soup and broiled Chesapeake Bay rockfish are standouts. Try the tavern's own Middleton Pale Ale, perhaps during happy hour or during a weekend blues session in the upstairs piano bar. Brunch is served on weekends, and you can dine outdoors in good weather. ☒ *City Dock at Randall St., Historic Area* ☎ *410/263–3323* ⊕ *www.middletontavern.com* ⊟ *AE, D, DC, MC, V.*

$$–$$$ ✕ **Phillips Annapolis Harbor.** With a panoramic view of the harbor, this city-dock eatery belongs to a group of popular local restaurants whose forte is Maryland-style seafood. The bar and lounge is on the ground floor; the dining room, on the second floor. The restaurant's skylights and glassed-in all-season room keep things sunny. Specialties include buckets of mussels, clams on the half-shell, lump crab cocktail, crab-stuffed flounder, seafood platters, and a clambake for two. ☒ *87 Prince George St. (12 Dock St.), Historic Area* ☎ *410/990–9888* ⊟ *AE, D, DC, MC, V.*

$$–$$$ ✕ **Ristorante Piccola Roma.** Amid the sophisticated black and white interior of the cozy "Little Rome" Restaurant, you can feast on authentic Italian food. Silva Recine prepares the recipes—specialties are antipasti, salads, pasta, veal, and fish—and supervises the fine dining staff. ☒ *200 Main St., Historic Area* ☎ *410/268–7898* ⊟ *AE, D, DC, MC, V.*

$–$$$ ✕ **Café Normandie.** Ladder-back chairs, wood beams, skylights, and a four-sided fireplace make this French restaurant homey. Out of the open kitchen comes an astonishingly good French onion soup, made daily from scratch. Bouillabaisse, lamb bean soup, puffy omelets, crepes, and various seafood dishes are other specialties. The restaurant's brunch (Friday through Sunday) includes poached eggs in ratatouille, eggs Benedict, seafood omelets, crepes, waffles, and croissants and muffins made in-house. ☒ *185 Main St., Historic Area* ☎ *410/263–3382* ⊟ *AE, D, DC, MC, V.*

$–$$$ ✕ **Cantler's Riverside Inn.** Opened in 1974, this local institution was founded by Jimmy Cantler, a native Marylander who worked as a waterman on the Chesapeake Bay. The no-nonsense interior has wooden blinds and floors, nautical items laminated beneath tabletops, and metal chairs. Food is served on disposable dinnerware; if you order steamed crabs, they'll come served atop a "tablecloth" of brown paper. Water-view outdoor dining is available seasonally. Boat owners can tie up at the dock; free parking spaces are rare during the busy summer season. Specialties include steamed mussels, clams, and shrimp as well as Maryland vegetable crab soup, seafood sandwiches, oysters, crab-cakes, and numerous finfish. To get here from Route 50, take Exit 29A onto Busch's Frontage Road. At the flashing light, turn right onto St. Margaret's Road and follow for 2.3 mi. Turn left onto Brown's Woods Road; then first right onto Forest Beach Road and follow to the end. ☒ *458 Forest Beach Rd., St. Margaret's* ☎ *410/757–1311* ⊕ *www.cantlers.com* ⊟ *AE, D, DC, MC, V* ☉ *Sun.-Thur. 11–11; Fri. and Sat. 11–midnight.*

$–$$$ ✕ **Carrol's Creek.** You can walk, catch a water taxi from City Dock, or drive over the Spa Creek drawbridge to this local favorite in Eastport. Whether you dine indoors or out, the view of historic Annapolis and its harbor is spectacular. The all-you-can-eat Sunday brunch is notable, as are the seafood specialties. A four-course prix fixe crab or bay dinner is also available. ☒ *410 Severn Ave., Eastport* ☎ *410/263–8102* ⊕ *www.carrolscreek.com* ⊟ *AE, D, DC, MC, V.*

$–$$$ ✕ **Rams Head Tavern.** A traditional English-style pub also houses the Fordham Brewing Company, which you can tour. The Rams Head serves better-than-usual tavern fare, including spicy shrimp salad, crab cakes, beer-battered shrimp, and daily specials, as well as more than 170 beers—26 on tap—from around the world. Brunch is served on Sunday. The nightclub-like Rams Head Tavern On Stage brings in nationally known folk, rock, jazz, country, and bluegrass artists. Dinner-show combo specials are offered; the menu has light fare. ☒ *33 West St., Historic Area* ☎ *410/268–4545* ⊕ *www.ramsheadtavern.com* ⊟ *AE, D, DC, MC, V.*

$-$$ ✕ **49 West Coffeehouse and Gallery.** In what was once a hardware store, this eclectic, casual eatery has one interior wall of exposed brick and another of exposed plaster, on which hang art for sale by local artists. Daily specials are chalked on a blackboard. Menu staples include a large cheese and pâté plate, deli sandwiches, soups and salads, and main dishes that include honey-garlic pork and rosemary-lime chicken. There's live music every night but Sunday. ✉ *49 West St., West Side* ☎ *410/ 626-9796* ⊕ *www.49westcafe.com* ⊟ *AE, D, DC, MC, V.*

¢-$ ✕ **Chick and Ruth's Delly.** Deli sandwiches (named for local politicos), burgers, subs, milk shakes, and other ice cream concoctions are the bill of fare at this counter-and-table institution, which has been here since 1965. ✉ *165 Main St.* ☎ *410/269-6737* ⊕ *www.chickandruths.com* ⊟ *No credit cards.*

¢-$ ✕ **El Toro Bravo.** A local favorite, this inexpensive, authentic Mexican restaurant is family-owned. The wooden colonial exterior conceals colorful, South-of-the-Border scenes hand painted on the interior walls, hanging plants, and padded aqua booths. There's usually a line but takeout is available. Lunch and dinner specials include a variety of enchiladas, fish tacos, grilled shrimp, and steak. The guacamole is made on the premises. ✉ *50 West St., 1 block from visitor center, West Side* ☎ *410/ 267-5949* ⊟ *AE, D, DC, MC, V.*

$$$-$$$$ ▥ **Annapolis Marriott Waterfront.** You can practically fish from your room at the city's only waterfront hotel. Rooms, done in a modern style with mauve quilted bedspreads, have either balconies over the water or large windows with views of the harbor or the historic district. The outdoor bar by the harbor's edge is popular in nice weather. ✉ *80 Compromise St., West Side 21401* ☎ *410/268-7555 or 800/336-0072* ☒ *410/269-5864* ⊕ *www.annapolismarriott.com* ⟿ *150 rooms* ⟁ *Restaurant, in-room data ports, gym, boating, 2 bars, laundry service, concierge, business services, meeting rooms, parking (fee), no-smoking rooms* ⊟ *AE, D, DC, MC, V.*

$$-$$$ ▥ **Loews Annapolis Hotel.** Although its redbrick exterior blends with the city's 1700s architecture, the interior is airy, spacious, and modern. Guest rooms—done in beige fabrics in various textures and shades—include coffeemakers and terry robes. A free hotel shuttle bus takes you anywhere you want to go in Annapolis, and a complimentary breakfast is served in the Corinthian restaurant for concierge guests. ✉ *126 West St., West Side, 21401* ☎ *410/263-7777 or 800/235-6397* ☒ *410/263-0084* ⊕ *www.loewsannapolis.com* ⟿ *210 rooms, 7 suites* ⟁ *2 restaurants, room service, in-room data ports, minibars, gym, hair salon, bar, laundry service, concierge, concierge floor, business services, meeting rooms, airport shuttle, parking (fee), no-smoking floors* ⊟ *AE, D, DC, MC, V.*

$$ ▥ **Governor Calvert House.** This home facing the state capitol was built in 1727 and lived in by two former Maryland governors, both of them Calverts. During its 1984 expansion, workers discovered a hypocaust (central heating system) in the basement: you can view it through a section of the floor. Rooms in the historic section are furnished with period antiques; newer rooms have period reproductions. The Governor Calvert House is one of the three Historic Inns of Annapolis. The Treaty of Paris Restaurant, the Drummer's Lot Pub, and the King of France Tavern serve all three inns. A Colonial tea is served Wednesday from 3 to 4. ✉ *58 State Circle, Historic Area 21401* ☎ *410/263-2641 or 800/847-8882* ☒ *410/268-3813* ⊕ *www.annapolisinns.com* ⟿ *51 rooms* ⟁ *In-room data ports, laundry service, concierge, business services, meeting rooms, parking (fee), no-smoking rooms* ⊟ *AE, D, DC, MC, V.*

$$ ▥ **Maryland Inn.** Eleven delegates of the 1786 U.S. Congress stayed here. Many of the guest rooms date back to the Revolutionary era (the

wooden porches and marble-tiled lobby are Victorian). Mahogany furniture and a velvet wing chair rest on aqua carpeting in the guest rooms, which also have floral wallpaper and draperies and many antique furnishings. Radiators heat the rooms. Some rooms have sitting suites or whirlpools. This is one of the three Historic Inns of Annapolis; register at the Governor Calvert House. ⊠ *16 Church Circle (entrance on Main St.), Historic Area 21401* ☎ *410/263–2641 or 800/847–8882* 🖨 *410/ 268–3813.* ⊕ *www.annapolisinns.com* 🛏 *34 rooms, 10 suites* ♦ *Restaurant, in-room data ports, some kitchenettes, gym, bar, pub, laundry service, concierge, business services, meeting rooms, parking (fee), no-smoking rooms* ⊟ *AE, D, DC, MC, V.*

$$ 🏨 **Robert Johnson House.** One of the three Historic Inns of Annapolis, this hotel is actually three cleverly integrated 18th-century houses. The front overlooks the State House. Guest rooms are furnished with 19th-century antiques, four-poster beds, and draperies matching the wallpaper. Register at the Governor Calvert House. ⊠ *23 State Circle, Historic Area 21401* ☎ *410/263–2641 or 800/847–8882* 🖨 *410/268–3813* ⊕ *www.annapolisinns.com* 🛏 *25 rooms* ♦ *In-room data ports, laundry service, parking (fee), no-smoking rooms* ⊟ *AE, D, DC, MC, V.*

$–$$ 🏨 **Sheraton–Barcelo Hotel.** Traffic and parking in downtown Annapolis can be difficult. Next to the Annapolis Mall and Westfield Shoppingtown, and near numerous chain restaurants, this large Sheraton has a free hourly shuttle bus to and from downtown. The lobby is outfitted with marble floors, fresh flowers and ferns, and two sitting areas among marble columns. The café is adjacent to the lobby. Rooms are furnished with blond woods, geometric carpeting, and burgundy-print bedspreads. ⊠ *173 Jennifer Rd., West Side 21401* ☎ *410/266–3131 or 888/627–8980* 🖨 *410/266–6247* ⊕ *www.starwood.com/sheraton* 🛏 *196 rooms* ♦ *Café, room service, in-room data ports, indoor pool, gym, lobby lounge, business services, meeting rooms, free parking, no-smoking rooms* ⊟ *AE, D, DC, MC, V.*

$ 🏨 **Hampton Inn and Suites.** A fireplace and cathedral ceiling are features of the spacious lobby in this hotel that's minutes from historic Annapolis. Choose from traditional rooms and spacious apartment-style suites, which have fully equipped kitchens. ⊠ *124 Womack Dr., Suburbs 21401* ☎ *410/571–0200 or 800/426–7866* 🖨 *410/571–0333* ⊕ *www. hamptoninn.com* 🛏 *86 rooms, 31 suites* ♦ *In-room data ports, pool, exercise equipment, billiards, shop, laundry facilities, laundry services, business center, meeting rooms* ⊟ *AE, D, DC, MC, V* ⊣⊙⊢ *BP.*

¢–$ 🏨 **Country Inn & Suites.** Within walking distance of Annapolis's largest mall, this Country Inn has a free shuttle to the historic district and to business parks. The four-story brick and wood-paneled building has interior corridors and borders a wooded area. Rooms are decorated in burgundy with floral bedspreads and dark-wood furniture. Four rooms have Jacuzzis and two have fireplaces. ⊠ *2600 Housely Rd. Suburbs 21401* ☎ *410/571–6700 or. 800/456–4000* 🖨 *410/571–6777* ⊕ *www. countryinns.com* 🛏 *100 rooms* ♦ *Microwaves, refrigerators, indoor pool, gym, laundry facilities, meeting rooms* ⊟ *MC, V* ⊣⊙⊢ *CP.*

¢–$ 🏨 **Scotlaur Inn.** On the two floors above Chick and Ruth's Delly is this family-owned bed-and-breakfast. Rooms are papered in pastel colonial prints, and hobnail-pattern bedspreads are on the beds. All rooms include irons, ironing boards and hair dryers. Breakfast is in the famous deli downstairs. ⊠ *165 Main St., Historic Area 21401* ☎ *410/268–5665* 🖨 *410/269–6738* ⊕ *www.scotlaurinn.com* 🛏 *10 rooms with bath* ♦ *Color TV* ⊟ *MC, V* ⊣⊙⊢ *CP.*

¢–$ 🏨 **Best Western Annapolis.** This two-story motel is a good value. Set away from traffic intersections but just 3 mi from the U.S. Naval Academy, it's well maintained. Guest rooms, entered from the parking lot, are decorated in forest green with quilted floral bedspreads. There's an outdoor covered deck for enjoying the Continental breakfast or your own picnic. From U.S. 50, take Exit 22 and follow the signs to Riva Road north. The motel is in a business park on your left. ⊠ *2520 Riva Rd., Parole 21401* ☎ *410/224–2800 or 800/638–5179* ▣ *410/266–5539* ⊕ *www.bestwestern.com* ⌁ *142 rooms* ᗩ *In-room data ports, pool, gym, laundry service, meeting rooms, free parking* ▤ *AE, D, DC, MC, V* ▮◯▮ *CP.*

Annapolis A to Z

To research prices, get advice from other travelers, and book travel arrangements, visit ⊕ *www.fodors.com.*

BUS TRAVEL TO & FROM ANNAPOLIS

Bus service between Washington, D.C., and Annapolis is geared toward commuters rather than vacationers. Weekday mornings and afternoons, buses arrive at and depart from the Navy–Marine Corps Stadium parking lot, from College Avenue by the state buildings, and also from St. John's College. On weekends Greyhound makes one trip daily, arriving at and departing from the stadium.

🚍 Bus Information **Dillons Bus Service** ☎ 800/827-3490 or 410/647-2321 ⊕ www. dillonbus.com. **Greyhound** ☎ 800/231-2222 ⊕ www.greyhound.com. **MTA** ☎ 410/ 539-5000 ⊕ www.mtamaryland.com.

CAR TRAVEL

The drive (east on U.S. 50, to the Rowe Boulevard exit) normally takes 35–45 minutes from Washington. During rush hour (weekdays 3:30–6:30 PM), however, it takes about twice as long. Only cars with Department of Defense stickers driven by those with military I.D.s are allowed on the Naval Academy grounds.

PARKING   Parking spots on Annapolis's historic downtown streets are scarce, but there are some parking meters for 50¢ an hour (maximum 2 hours). You can park on residential streets free where allowable; the maximum parking time is 2 hours. You can pay $4 ($8 for recreational vehicles) to park at the Navy–Marine Corps Stadium (to the right of Rowe Boulevard as you enter town from Route 50), and ride a shuttle bus downtown for 75¢. Parking is also available at garages on Main Street and Gott's Court (adjacent to the visitor center); on weekdays parking is free for the first hour and $1 an hour thereafter; on weekends it costs $4 a day.

TOURS

BOAT TOURS   When the weather's good, Watermark Cruises runs boat tours that last from 40 minutes to 7½ hours and go as far as St. Michaels on the Eastern Shore, where there's a maritime museum, yachts, dining, and boutiques. Prices range from $6 to $35. If it's wind in the sails that holds your fancy, Schooner Woodwind has two-hour sailing cruises four times daily.

🚍 Fees and Schedules **Schooner Woodwind** ⊠ 80 Compromise St., 21401; departs from Annapolis Marriott Hotel, Historic Area ☎410/269-4213 ⊕www.schoonerwoodwind. com. **Watermark Cruises** ⊠ Box 3350, 21403; City Dock, Historic Area ☎ 410/268-7600 or 410/268-7601 ⊕ www.watermarkcruises.com.

BUS TOURS   Discover Annapolis Tours leads one-hour narrated minibus tours ($12) that introduce you to the history and architecture of Annapolis. Tours leave from the visitor center daily April through November and most weekends December through March.

🚍 Fees and Schedules **Discover Annapolis Tours** ⊠ 31 Decatur Ave., Historic Area ☎ 410/626-6000 ⊕ www.discover-annapolis.com.

WALKING TOURS   The Historic Annapolis Museum Store rents two self-guided (with audiotapes and maps) walking tours: "Historic Annapolis Walk with Walter Cronkite" and "Historic Annapolis African-American Heritage Audio Walking Tour." The cost for each is $5.

Several tours leave from the visitor center at 26 West Street. On Annapolis Walkabout tours ($8), experts on historic buildings take you around the historic district and the U.S. Naval Academy. Tours are held weekends from April to October.

Guides from Three Centuries Tours wear colonial-style dress and take you to the State House, St. John's College, and the Naval Academy. The cost is $9. Tours depart daily April through October at 10:30 from the visitor center and at 1:30 from the information booth, City Dock.

🔃 Fees and Schedules **Annapolis Walkabout** ✉ 223 S. Cherry Grove Ave., Historic Area ☎ 410/263-8253 ◷ Apr.-Oct., weekends 11:30. **Historic Annapolis Foundation Walking Tours** ✉ 77 Main St., Historic Area ☎ 410/268-5576 ⊕ www.annapolis.org. **Three Centuries Tours** ✉ 48 Maryland Ave., Historic Area ☎ 410/263-5401 🖷 410/263-1901 ⊕ www.annapolis-tours.com.

FREDERICK, MARYLAND

Just 45 mi outside the District of Columbia are the rolling farmlands and Appalachian foothills of Maryland's second-largest city, which was founded in 1745. Frederick has one of the best-preserved historic districts in Maryland, topped only by Annapolis. The city was in the path of the Civil War battles of Antietam, Monocacy, and South Mountain, and exchanged hands several times during the war. Frederick would have been destroyed in 1864 had the local government not given Confederate General Jubal Early a $200,000 ransom to spare the town.

The historic downtown with its many church spires occupies a grid of one-way streets that traverse Carroll Creek. One of the bridges across the creek is painted with a large-scale mural celebrating the spirit of the community. There are several museums and homes to tour, and both Frederick and nearby towns make an excellent area for antiques shopping. Eight miles east is New Market, billed as "the Antique Capital of Maryland."

An easy day trip can be made from the Washington area, or you may prefer to spend the night at a bed-and-breakfast or motel. To the south, 27 mi, is the historic town of Harper's Ferry, West Virginia.

The most direct route to the Frederick Visitor Center—a good place to pick up free maps and begin touring the area—is to take I-270 into the city, where it becomes Highway 15 North. Exit at Rosemont Avenue and follow the signs to the visitor center. There has been some long-term construction at the Patrick Street interchange; if this exit is open, take Patrick Street East. Rosemont is the easier and best-signed way to get into town.

Sights to See

Barbara Fritchie House and Museum. This modest brick cottage was the home of the Barbara Fritchie, who, it is said, bravely defied Confederate troops from her second-floor window. The daring woman, in her 90s at the time, refused to remove her American flag and shouted at the soldiers parading by her house. John Greenleaf Whittier's poem (1863) about the incident made her famous, although another woman may have been the actual flag-waver. Over the years visitors to the house

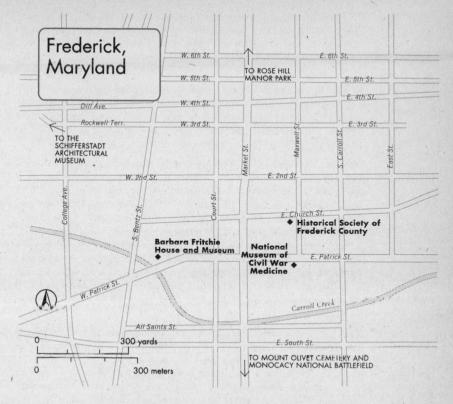

Frederick,
Maryland

W. 6th St.   E. 6th St.
TO ROSE HILL
MANOR PARK
W. 5th St.   E. 5th St.
E. 4th St.
Dill Ave.   W. 4th St.
Rockwell Terr.   W. 3rd St.   E. 3rd St.
TO THE
SCHIFFERSTADT
ARCHITECTURAL
MUSEUM
W. 2nd St.   E. 2nd St.
E. Church St.
♦ **Historical Society of Frederick County**
Barbara Fritchie House and Museum ♦
National Museum of Civil War ♦ Medicine
E. Patrick St.
W. Patrick St.
Carroll Creek
All Saints St.
0   300 yards
E. South St.
0   300 meters
TO MOUNT OLIVET CEMETERY AND
MONOCACY NATIONAL BATTLEFIELD

have included Winston Churchill and Franklin Roosevelt. ⊠ *154 W. Patrick St., Historic Area* ☎ *301/698–0630* ⊕ *www.cityoffrederick. com* ⌨ *$2* ☉ *Apr.–Sept., Thurs.–Mon. 10–4; Oct. and Nov., Sat. 10–4, Sun. 1–4.*

need a break?

Drop by the **Frederick Coffee Company** (⊠ Shab Row/Everedy Sq., 100 East St., Downtown ☎ 301/698–0039 or 800/822–0806) for pastries, soup, sandwiches, quiche, dessert, and—of course—many sorts of coffees and other beverages. As you walk in the door of this former 1930s gas station, inhale the heady fragrance of beans roasting in front of you. The Frederick Coffee Company is open 7–9 weekdays and 9–9 weekends.

Historical Society of Frederick County. A gracious 1820s Federal-style mansion helps explain what the homefront was like during the Civil War. Docent-led tours of the society's building include a room furnished as it was when the building was used as a female orphanage for 70 years. The downstairs library is invaluable to those doing genealogical research or seeking background for historical novels. The society's bookstore is next door. ⊠ *24 East Church St., Historic Area* ☎ *301/663–1188* ⊕ *www.fwp.net/hsfc* ⌨ *$2* ☉ *Historical Society: Mid-Jan.–Dec., Mon.–Sat. 10–4, Sun. 1–4; library closed Sun. and Mon.*

Monocacy National Battlefield. The Civil War battle fought here, won by the Confederates, delayed and prevented them from capturing Washington, D.C. The **visitor center** (☎ 301/662–3515 ⊕ www.nps.gov/ mono) is housed in the fieldstone Gambrill's Mill. There's an interactive computer program and electric map giving commentary about the battle. Walking trails and a self-guided auto tour take you through the July 9, 1864, clash. ⊠ *4801 Urbana Pike, north of Exit 26 of I–270* ▣ *Free* ⊘ *Apr.–late May and early Sept.–Oct., daily 8–4:30; Memorial Day–Labor Day, weekdays 8–4:30, weekends 8–5:30; Nov.–Mar., Wed.–Sun. 8–4:30.*

Mount Olivet Cemetery. Buried in this cemetery are the remains of 800 Confederate and Union soldiers killed during the Battle of Antietam as well as graves of Frederick's famous sons and daughters, including Francis Scott Key and Barbara Fritchie. ⊠ *515 S. Market St., Downtown* ☎ *301/662–1164* ⊘ *Daily dawn–dusk, chapel daily 8–5.*

National Museum of Civil War Medicine. This may be the only museum devoted to the study and interpretation of Civil War medicine. Its building was a furniture store in 1830 and then a funeral home until 1978: the dead from the Battle of Antietam (1862) were taken here for embalming. Exhibits at the museum cover "Recruitment," "Camp Life," "Medical Evacuation," and "Veterinary Medicine." More than 3,000 artifacts are on display, including a Civil War ambulance and the only known surviving Civil War surgeon's tent. Photographs and a video help explain the state of the healing arts during this period. ⊠ *48 E. Patrick St., Historic Area* ☎ *301/695–1864* ⊕ *www.civilwarmed.org* ▣ *$6.50* ⊘ *Mid-Mar.–mid-Nov., Mon.–Sat. 10–5, Sun. 11–5; mid-Nov.–mid-Mar., Mon.–Sat. 10–4, Sun. 11–4.*

ⓒ **Rose Hill Manor Park.** The former property of Maryland's first elected governor, Thomas Johnson, holds two museums. The **Children's Museum** specializes in hands-on historic educational tours targeted at elementary school ages. The **Farm Museum** offers self-guided tours of 19th- and 20th-century exhibits that include a farm kitchen, carpentry shop, harvesting equipment, and a separate carriage museum. ⊠ *1611 N. Market St.* ☎ *301/694–1646 or 301/694–1650* ⊕ *www.co.frederick. md.us/govt/parks/rose* ▣ *Donation requested; tours/programs $4* ⊘ *Apr.–Oct., Mon.–Sat. 10–4, Sun. 1–4; Nov., Sat. 10–4, Sun. 1–4.*

Schifferstadt Architectural Museum. This structure, built in 1756, is one of the finest examples of German architecture in colonial America. Inside you can see original construction elements such as a vaulted cellar, a "wishbone" chimney, hand-hewn oak beams, mud and straw insulation, and original hardware. An authentic 18th-century garden complements the story of everyday farm life. ⊠ *1110 Rosemont Ave.* ☎ *301/ 663–3885* ⊕ *www.fredericklandmarks.org* ▣ *$2* ⊘ *Apr.–mid-Dec., Tues.–Sat. 10–4, Sun. noon–4.*

Where to Stay & Eat

$$–$$$ ✕ **Bentz Street Raw Bar.** Fresh seafood and live music nightly are the hallmarks of this funky neighborhood hangout, which is Frederick's most eclectic restaurant. You can enjoy fresh Maryland crabs and oysters, steamers, soups, salads, sandwiches, and main dishes of seafood, beef, ribs and barbecue. ⊠ *6 South Bentz St., Downtown* ☎ *301/694–9134* ⊕ *www.rawbar.com* ▤ *AE, D, DC, MC, V.*

$$–$$$ ✕ **John Hagan's Tavern.** Built in 1785, this fieldstone structure has its original wooden floors: it's always been a tavern or restaurant. Staff wear period dress, and all desserts and breads are made on the premises. The regional food on the menu reveals an Early American influence: specialties include house-smoked salmon, duck, and quail; Maryland-style roast chicken with lump-crabmeat sauce; and twin grilled duck breasts in a pear–orange confit. ⊠ *5018 Old National Pike, Braddock Heights* ☎ *301/371–9189* ▤ *AE, D, DC, MC, V* ⊘ *Closed Mon.*

$–$$$ ✕ **Tauraso's.** The mouth-watering smell of pizza baked in a wood oven greets diners approaching the reservations desk of this wood-paneled, white-tablecloth trattoria. Other specialties include pasta dishes, poultry, steaks, and seafood. A favorite appetizer is Tauraso's own homemade seafood sausage. The restaurant has a bar, separate dining room, and a garden patio open seasonally. ⊠ *6 East St., Downtown* ☎ *301/663–6000* ⊟ *AE, D, DC, MC, V.*

$–$$ ✕ **Brewer's Alley.** Frederick's first brew pub was once a town hall and market building. The eatery is clean and bright, and copper brewing pots gleam next to the bar and the wooden tables. Substantial main dishes, such as large Maryland crab cakes, double-thick pork chops, steaks, and ribs are available, as are starters, salads, specialty sandwiches, pasta, and pizza. Several kinds of beer are made on the premises. ⊠ *124 N. Market St., Historic Area* ☎ *301/631–0089* ⊟ *AE, D, DC, MC, V.*

$–$$ ✕▣ **Catoctin Inn and Conference Center.** Antiques, books, family pictures, and heirlooms decorate this cozy, large house from 1790. Its well-worn original floors attest to the traffic that has come and gone in this inn a few miles south of Frederick. Three rooms have working fireplaces and hot tubs. The inn's restaurant is open to the public for dinner on Friday and Saturday with a prix-fixe menu of three courses ($26). Maryland crab soup, hickory-smoked duck, crusted rack of lamb, and bacon-wrapped pork are all specialties. ⊠ *3619 Buckeystown Pike, Buckeystown 21717* ☎ *301/874–5555 or 800/730–5550* ☎ *301/831–8102* ⊕ *www.catoctininn.com* ↪ *11 rooms, 3 cottages, 2 suites* ⌂ *Restaurant, refrigerators, in-room VCRs, outdoor hot tub, business services, meeting rooms, airport shuttle* ⊟ *AE, D, DC, MC, V* ⦿❘ *BP.*

$ $$ ✕▣ **Inn at Buckeystown.** An inviting wraparound porch fronts this bed-and-breakfast, an 1897 mansion in a village with pre-Revolutionary roots. The village is near the Monocacy River and the Civil War battlefield. Rooms are decorated in antiques and reproduction period pieces. A five-course dinner is available for an additional fee of $45; tea and lunch are offered Wednesday, Friday, and alternate Sundays. ⊠ *3521 Buckeystown Pike, Buckeystown 21717* ☎ *301/874–5755 or 800/272–1190* ☎ *301/831–1355* ⊕ *www.innatbuckeystown.com* ↪ *10 rooms, 5 with bath* ⌂ *Restaurant, bar* ⊟ *D, MC, V* ⦿❘ *BP.*

$$–$$$ ▣ **Tyler Spite Inn.** The furnishings in this federal-style mansion could tell some stories. A peace treaty was signed by General MacArthur on the check-in desk. A 10-foot-high pier mirror from the old Frederick train station was used by President Lincoln. The Chippendale-style mahogany and ebony grand piano was made in Baltimore for Francis Scott Key. Three of the guest rooms have working fireplaces. The large rooms are beautifully decorated in colors, fabrics, and wallpaper indicative of the era. Lodging price includes room tax, a walking tour of Courthouse Square, a generous breakfast, and an extensive afternoon tea. ⊠ *112 West Church St., Historic Area 21701* ☎ *301/831–4455* ↪ *5 rooms with bath* ⌂ *Pool* ⊟ *MC, V* ⦿❘ *BP.*

Frederick, Maryland, A to Z

To research prices, get advice from other travelers, and book travel arrangements, visit ⊕ *www.fodors.com.*

BUS TRAVEL TO & FROM FREDERICK
Greyhound runs daily buses between Frederick and Washington, D.C. Buses leave every two or three hours; call for schedules. The trip takes about an hour.

🚍 **Bus Information Greyhound** ☎ 301/663–3311 ⊕ www.greyhound.com.

BUS TRAVEL WITHIN FREDERICK

Frederick's historic area is compact: you can walk to most attractions. Otherwise, Frederick Transit runs frequent buses on all downtown streets and arteries.

🚌 Bus Information **Frederick Transit** ☎ 301/694-2065.

CAR TRAVEL

From Washington, the trip takes about 45 minutes. Drive north on I–270 from the Beltway I–495. The highway number changes to I–70. Frederick has several exits. To reach the historic area, use Exit 56 and follow Patrick Street west toward downtown.

TAXIS

🚖 Taxi Companies **City Cab Co.** ☎ 301/662-2250.

TOURS

The Frederick Tour & Carriage Company offers horse-drawn carriage rides through the city's historic district on weekends. Reservations are required. The company also offers historic walking tours.

🚖 Fees and Schedules **Frederick Tour & Carriage Company** ☎ 301/845-7001.

VISITOR INFORMATION

The Frederick Visitor Center is open daily 9–5 and offers brochures, walking-tour maps, and guided 90-minute tours. The Tourism Council of Frederick County can mail you brochures about the area.

🚖 Tourist Information **Frederick Visitor Center** ✉ 19 East Church St., Historic Area ☎ 301/228-2888 or 800/999-3613. **Tourism Council of Frederick County** ☎ 301/228-2888 or 800/999-3613. ⊕ www.fredericktourism.org.

MOUNT VERNON, WOODLAWN & GUNSTON HALL

Long before Washington, D.C., was planned, the shores of the Potomac had been divided into plantations by wealthy traders and gentleman farmers. Most traces of the colonial era were obliterated as the capital grew in the 19th century, but several splendid examples of plantation architecture remain on the Virginia side of the Potomac, 15 mi or so south of D.C. In one day you can easily visit three such mansions: Mount Vernon, the home of George Washington and one of the most popular sites in the area; Woodlawn, the estate of Washington's step-granddaughter; and Gunston Hall, the home of George Mason, author of the document on which the Bill of Rights was based. On hillsides overlooking the river, these estates offer magnificent vistas and make a bygone era vivid.

Numbers in the margin correspond to points of interest on the Mount Vernon, Woodlawn, and Gunston Hall map.

Mount Vernon

❶ *16 mi southeast of Washington, D.C., 8 mi south of Alexandria, VA.*

Fodor'sChoice ★

Mount Vernon and the surrounding lands had been in the Washington family for nearly 90 years by the time George inherited it all in 1761. Before taking over command of the Continental Army, Washington was a yeoman farmer managing the 8,000-acre plantation, of which more than 3,000 acres were under cultivation. He also oversaw the transformation of the main house from an ordinary farm dwelling into what was, for the time, a grand mansion.

The red-roofed house is elegant though understated, with a yellow pine exterior that's been painted and coated with layers of sand to resemble

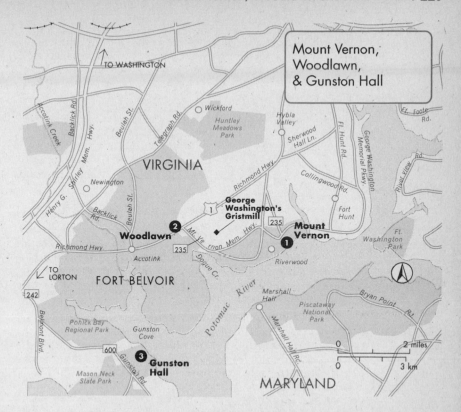

white-stone blocks. The first-floor rooms are quite ornate, especially the formal large dining room, with a molded ceiling decorated with agricultural motifs. Throughout the house are other, smaller symbols of the owner's eminence, such as a key to the main portal of the Bastille—presented to Washington by the Marquis de Lafayette—and Washington's presidential chair. As you tour the mansion, guides are stationed throughout the house to describe the furnishings and answer questions.

The real treasure of Mount Vernon is the view from around back. Beneath a 90-foot portico is George Washington's contribution to architecture: the home's dramatic riverside porch. The porch overlooks an expanse of lawn that slopes down to the Potomac. In springtime the view of the river (a mile wide where it passes the plantation) is framed by redbud and dogwood blossoms. Protocol requires United States Navy and Coast Guard ships to salute when passing the house during daylight hours. Foreign naval vessels often salute, too.

You can stroll around the estate's 500 acres and three gardens, visiting the workshops, the kitchen, the carriage house, the greenhouse, the slave quarters, and—down the hill toward the boat landing—the tomb of George and Martha Washington. There's also a pioneer farmer site: a 4-acre hands-on exhibit with a reconstruction of George Washington's 16-sided treading barn as its centerpiece. Among the souvenirs sold at the plantation are stripling boxwoods that began life as clippings from bushes planted in 1798, the year before Washington died. A tour of house and grounds takes about two hours. There's a limited number of wheelchairs available at the main gate. Private, evening candlelight tours of the mansion with staff dressed in 18th-century costumes can be arranged.

After many years of research, George Washington's Gristmill opened in 2002 on the site of his original mill and distillery. During the guided tours, led by historic interpreters, you'll meet an 18th-century miller and watch the water-powered wheel grind grain into flour just as it did 200 years ago. The mill is 3 mi from Mount Vernon on Route 235 between Mount Vernon and U.S. Route 1. Tickets can be purchased either at the gristmill itself or at Mount Vernon's Main Gate. ☒ *Southern end of George Washington Pkwy., Mount Vernon, VA* ☎ *703/780–2000; 703/ 799–8606 evening tours* 🖷 *703/799–8609* ⊕ *www.mountvernon.org* 🎫 *$9, $4 gristmill, $11 combination ticket* ⊙ *Mar. and Sept.–Oct., daily 9–5; Apr.–Aug., daily 8–5; Nov.–Feb., daily 9–4.*

Woodlawn

❷ *3 mi west of Mount Vernon, 15 mi south of Washington, D.C.*

Woodlawn was once part of the Mount Vernon estate. From here you can still see traces of the bowling green that fronted Washington's home. The house was built for Washington's step-granddaughter, Nelly Custis, who married his favorite nephew, Lawrence Lewis. (Lewis was summoned to Mount Vernon from Fredericksburg to assist his uncle with his papers and his many guests.)

The Lewises' home, completed in 1805, was designed by William Thornton, a physician and amateur architect from the West Indies who drew up the original plans for the U.S. Capitol. Like Mount Vernon, the Woodlawn house is constructed wholly of native materials, including the clay for its bricks and the yellow pine used throughout its interior. In the tradition of southern riverfront mansions, Woodlawn has a central hallway that provides a cool refuge in summer. At one corner of the passage is a bust of George Washington set on a pedestal so the crown of the head is at 6 feet 2 inches—Washington's actual height. The music room has a ceiling that's approximately 2 feet higher than any other in the house, built that way to improve the acoustics for the harp and harpsichord recitals that the Lewises and their children enjoyed.

After Woodlawn passed out of the Lewis family's hands it was owned by a Quaker community, which established a meetinghouse and the first integrated school in Virginia here. Subsequent owners included the playwright Paul Kester and Senator and Mrs. Oscar Underwood of Alabama. The property was acquired by the National Trust for Historic Preservation in 1957, which had been operating it as a museum since 1951. Every March, Woodlawn hosts an annual needlework exhibit with over 700 items on display.

Also on the grounds of Woodlawn is the **Pope-Leighey House.** Frank Lloyd Wright designed this "Usonian" modernistic home as a means of providing affordable housing for people of modest means. It was built in 1940 and moved here from Falls Church, Virginia, in 1964. ☒ *9000 Richmond Hwy., Mount Vernon, VA* ☎ *703/780–4000* ⊕ *www.nationaltrust. org* 🎫 *$7.50 for either Woodlawn or Pope-Leighey House, $13 combination ticket* ⊙ *Mar.–Dec., daily 10–5; no guided tours in Mar. due to annual needlework show; tours leave every ½ hr; last tour at 4:30.*

Gunston Hall

❸ *12 mi south of Woodlawn, 25 mi south of Washington, D.C.*

Gunston Hall Plantation, down the Potomac from Mount Vernon, was the home of another important George. Gentleman farmer George Mason was a colonel of the Fairfax militia and author of the Virginia

Declaration of Rights, the model for the U.S. Bill of Rights, which called for freedom of the press, tolerance of religion, and other fundamental democratic principles. Mason was a framer of the Constitution but refused to sign the final document because it didn't stop the importation of slaves, adequately restrain the powers of the federal government, or include a bill of rights. Mason's objections spurred the movement for the inclusion of the Bill of Rights into the Constitution.

Mason's home was built circa 1755. The Georgian-style mansion has some of the finest hand-carved ornamented interiors in the country. It's the handiwork of the 18th century's foremost architect, William Buckland, who also designed the Hammond-Harwood and Chase-Lloyd houses in Annapolis. Gunston Hall is built of native brick, black walnut, and yellow pine. The style of the time demanded absolute symmetry in all structures, which explains the false door set into one side of the center hallway. The house's interior, which has carved woodwork in styles from Chinese to Gothic, has been meticulously restored, with paints made from the original formulas and carefully carved replacements for the intricate mahogany medallions in the moldings. Restored outbuildings include a kitchen, dairy, laundry, and smokehouse. A schoolhouse has also been reconstructed.

The formal gardens, under excavation by a team of archaeologists, are famous for their boxwoods—some, now 12 feet high, are thought to have been planted during George Mason's time, making them among the oldest in the country. The Potomac is visible past the expansive deer park. Also on the grounds is an active farmyard with livestock and crops species that resemble those of Mason's time. Special programs—such as history lectures and hearth cooking demonstrations—are offered throughout the year. A tour of Gunston Hall takes a minimum of 45 minutes; tours begin at the visitor center, which includes a museum and gift shop. ✉ *10709 Gunston Rd., Mason Neck, VA* ☎ *800/811–6966 or 703/550–9220* ⊕ *www.gunstonhall.org* 💲 *$7* ⊙ *Daily 9:30–5; first tour at 10, last tour at 4:30.*

Mount Vernon, Woodlawn & Gunston Hall A to Z

BIKE TRAVEL

An asphalt bicycle path leads from the Virginia side of Memorial Bridge (across from the Lincoln Memorial), past Ronald Reagan National Airport, and through Alexandria all the way to Mount Vernon. The trail is steep in places, but bikers in moderately good condition can make the 16-mi trip in less than two hours. You can rent bicycles at several locations in Washington.

BOAT TRAVEL

The *Potomac Spirit* makes a pleasant trip from Washington down the Potomac to Mount Vernon. Tickets include admission to the estate. You can take lunch, dinner, and Sunday brunch cruises on the *Spirit of Washington*, which also departs from Washington but doesn't go quite as far as Mount Vernon. Tickets include your meal and, on the dinner and brunch cruises, live entertainment. Prices range from $32 to $71, depending on the meal served (if any) and the day of the week.
🚩 Boat Information *Potomac Spirit* and *Spirit of Washington* ⊠ Pier 4, 6th and Water Sts. SW, Southeast, Washington, DC ☎ 202/554–8000; 866/211–3811 boat reservations ⊕ www.spiritcruises.com.

BUS TRAVEL

For Mount Vernon, you can take Fairfax County Connector Bus 101 or 102 marked MT. VERNON (50¢) from Huntington. Buses leave about

once an hour—more often during rush hour—and operate weekdays 6:30
AM–9:15 PM, Saturday 7:20 AM–7:36 PM, and Sunday 9:21 AM–6:43 PM.

For Woodlawn, take Bus 105 (FT. BELVOIR; 50¢). Buses operate weekdays 6 AM–11:10 PM and weekends 6:48 AM–7:05 PM. Schedules for these
lines are posted at the Huntington Metrorail station. Buses returning to
the station have the same numbers but are marked HUNTINGTON.
🚍 Bus Information **Fairfax County Connector** ☎ 703/339-7200 ⊕ www.co.fairfax.
va.us/comm/trans/connector.

CAR TRAVEL
To reach Mount Vernon from the Capital Beltway (Route 495), take
Exit 1 and follow the signs to George Washington Memorial Parkway
southbound. Mount Vernon is about 8½ mi south. From downtown Washington, cross into Arlington on either Key Bridge, Memorial Bridge, or
the 14th Street Bridge and drive south on the George Washington
Memorial Parkway past Ronald Reagan National Airport through
Alexandria straight to Mount Vernon. The trip from Washington takes
about a half hour.

For Woodlawn, travel southwest on Route 1 to the second Route 235
intersection (the first leads to Mount Vernon). The entrance to Woodlawn is on the right at the traffic light. From Mount Vernon, travel northwest on Route 235 to the Route 1 intersection; Woodlawn is straight
ahead through the intersection.

To visit Gunston Hall, travel south on Route 1, 9 mi past Woodlawn
to Route 242; turn left there and go 3½ mi to the plantation entrance.

SUBWAY TRAVEL
From downtown D.C., Arlington, or Alexandria you can take the Yellow Line train to the Huntington Metrorail station ($1.50–$2.50, depending on the time of day and point of origin), from which you must
take a bus.

TOURS
Gray Line runs half-day trips to Mount Vernon (with a stop in Alexandria), departing daily at 8:30 AM from Union Station (from late June to
late October there's an additional trip at 2 PM). A ticket is $28 and in-
cludes admission to the mansion and grounds.

Tourmobile offers trips to Mount Vernon, April through October daily
at 10 AM, noon, and 2 PM, from Arlington Cemetery and the Washington Monument. Reservations must be made in person 30 minutes in advance at the point of departure, and the $25 ticket includes admission
to the mansion. A two-day combination ticket for Mount Vernon and
several sites in Washington is available for $45.
🚍 Fees and Schedules **Gray Line** ☎ 301/386-8300 ⊕ www.grayline.com. **Tourmobile** ☎ 202/554-5100 ⊕ www.tourmobile.com.

FREDERICKSBURG, VIRGINIA

Fifty miles south of Washington on I–95, near the falls of the Rappahannock River, Fredericksburg is a popular day-trip destination for history buffs. The town's National Historic District contains the house
George Washington bought for his mother, Mary; the Rising Sun Tavern; and Kenmore, the magnificent 1752 plantation home of George Washington's sister. The town is a favorite with antiques collectors, who enjoy
cruising the dealers' shops along Caroline Street on land once favored
by Indian tribes as fishing and hunting ground.

Although its site was visited by explorer Captain John Smith as early as 1608, the town of Fredericksburg wasn't founded until 1728. Established as a frontier port to serve nearby tobacco farmers and iron miners, Fredericksburg took its name from England's crown prince at the time, Frederick Louis, the eldest son of King George II. The streets still bear names of his family members: George, Caroline, Sophia, Princess Anne, William, and Amelia.

George Washington knew Fredericksburg well, having grown up just across the Rappahannock on Ferry Farm—his residence from age 6 to 19. The myths about chopping down a cherry tree and throwing a coin (actually a rock) across the Rappahannock—later described as the Potomac—refer to this period of his life. In later years Washington often visited his mother here on Charles Street.

Fredericksburg prospered in the decades after independence, benefiting from its location midway along the 100-mi route between Washington and Richmond—an important intersection of railroad lines and waterways. When the Civil War broke out in 1861, Fredericksburg became the linchpin of the Confederate defense of Richmond and, as such, the inevitable target of Union assaults.

Remarkably, although four major Civil War battles were fought in and around Fredericksburg, much of the city remained intact. Today the city is being overrun for a different reason. The charming, historic town is being inundated by commuters fleeing the Washington, D.C., area to kinder, less expensive environs. The railroad lines that were so crucial to transporting Civil War supplies now bring workers to and from the nation's capital an hour away, and the sacred Civil War battlegrounds share the area with legions of shopping centers.

Numbers in the text correspond to numbers in the margin and on the Fredericksburg, VA, map.

Downtown Fredericksburg

Fredericksburg, a modern commercial town, includes a 40-block National Historic District with more than 350 original 18th- and 19th-century buildings. No play-acting here—residents live in the historic homes and work in the stores, many of which sell antiques.

a good tour

Begin at the **Fredericksburg Visitor Center** ❶ ⌐ to get maps or directions or to join a tour. Walk northwest on Caroline Street three blocks to the **Hugh Mercer Apothecary Shop** ❷, where you can see tools used in 18th- and 19th-century medicine, passing numerous antiques shops and boutiques along the way. Continue another three blocks to the **Rising Sun Tavern** ❸, a house built by George Washington's brother Charles that was a popular place to converse over eat and drink. Walk back to Lewis Street, turn right, and walk two blocks to the **Mary Washington House** ❹, purchased by her famous son, where she spent the last 17 years of her life. Continue on Lewis Street and turn right on Washington Avenue to the **Kenmore** ❺ entrance. This home of George's sister contains some beautiful rooms. To see the **Mary Washington Grave and Monument** ❻, turn right on Washington Avenue and walk two blocks. Then turn around and walk back down Washington four blocks to the **Confederate Cemetery** ❼, the final resting place for more than 2,000 Confederate soldiers, including some generals. From the cemetery take William Street east (back toward the center of town) four blocks to Charles Street and turn right to the **James Monroe Museum and Memorial Library** ❽, where the fifth president of the United States practiced law in the 1780s. Walk a block down William to Princess Anne Street. The **Fredericksburg Area**

Fredericksburg, Virginia

Museum and Cultural Center ❾, on the far right corner, has artifacts that include Civil War weapons and English furniture. To return to the visitor center, walk two more blocks along Princess Anne, turn left on Hanover, and right on Caroline Street. To get to the **Mary Washington College Galleries** ❿, it's best to drive unless you want to walk almost a mile from where you are now. From the visitor center, drive five blocks northwest on Caroline Street and turn left on Amelia. Follow Amelia and turn left on Washington Avenue. One block later, turn right onto William Street. At College Avenue, turn right and drive ½ mi to the gallery on your right. Parking (on College Avenue and two reserved spots in the staff lot at the corner of College and Thornton Street) may be tight on weekdays when the college is in session. The galleries have a fine collection of Asian art, as well as works by modern masters.

TIMING   A walking tour through the town proper takes three to four hours; battlefield tours will take at least that long. (The Park Service's cassettes last about 2½ hours for an automobile tour.) A self-guided tour of the Mary Washington College galleries takes about 30 minutes. Spring and fall are the best times to tour Fredericksburg on foot, but because Virginia weather is temperate intermittently in winter, you may find some suitable walking days then. Summers—especially August—can be hot, humid, and not very pleasant for a long walk.

Sights to See

❼ **Confederate Cemetery.** This cemetery contains the remains of more than 2,000 soldiers (most of them unknown) as well as the graves of generals Dabney Maury, Seth Barton, Carter Stevenson, Daniel Ruggles, Henry Sibley, and Abner Perrin. ⊠ *1100 Washington Ave., near Amelia St., Historic District* ⊙ *Daily dawn–dusk.*

9 **Fredericksburg Area Museum and Cultural Center.** In an 1816 building once used as a market and town hall, this museum's six permanent exhibits tell the story of the area from prehistoric times through the Revolutionary and Civil wars to the present. The Civil War exhibits emphasize the civilian experience, although attention is also paid to the soldier. Military items on display include a Henry rifle, a sword with "CSA" carved into the basket, and a Confederate officer's coat. Most weapons and accessories were found on local battlefields. Other displays include dinosaur footprints from a nearby quarry, Native American artifacts, and an 18th-century plantation account book with an inventory of slaves. The first and third floors have changing exhibits. ⊠ *907 Princess Anne St., Historic District* ☎ *540/371–3037* ⊕ *www.famcc.org* ⊠ *$5* ☉ *Mar.–Nov., Mon.–Sat. 10–5, Sun. 1–5; Dec.–Feb., Mon.–Sat. 10–4, Sun. 1–4.*

▶ **1** **Fredericksburg Visitor Center.** Beyond the usual booklets, pamphlets, and maps, this visitor center has passes that enable you to park for a whole day in what are usually two-hour zones as well as money-saving passes to city attractions ($24 for entry to nine sights; $16 for four sights). Before beginning your tour, you may want to see the center's 10-minute orientation slide show. The center building itself was constructed in 1824 as a residence and confectionery; during the Civil War it was used as a prison. ⊠ *706 Caroline St., Historic District* ☎ *540/373–1776 or 800/ 678–4748* ⊕ *www.fredericksburgvirginia.net* ☉ *Daily 9–5 Closing hrs extended in summer.*

> **need a break?** Have an old-fashioned malt in **Goolrick's Pharmacy** (⊠ 901 Caroline St., Historic District ☎ 540/373–9878), a 1940s drugstore. In addition to malts and egg creams (made of seltzer and milk, not egg or cream), Goolrick's serves light meals weekdays 8:30–7 and Saturday 8:30–6. **Virginia Deli** (⊠ 101 William St., Historic District ☎ 540/371–2233 ☉ weekdays 8–4, Sat. 8–6) offers breakfast, specialty sandwiches, and Virginia favorites. For freshly made soups, sandwiches, and desserts, drop by **Olde Towne Wine and Cheese Deli** (⊠ 707 Caroline St., Historic District ☎ 540/373–7877), right across the street from the visitor center.

2 **Hugh Mercer Apothecary Shop.** Offering a close-up view of 18th- and 19th-century medical instruments and procedures, the apothecary was established in 1771 by Dr. Mercer, a Scotsman who served as a brigadier general of the Continental Army (he was killed at the Battle of Princeton). Dr. Mercer may have been more careful than other colonial physicians, but his methods might still make you cringe. A costumed hostess explicitly describes amputations and cataract operations before the discovery of anesthetics. You can also hear about therapeutic bleeding, see the gruesome devices used in colonial dentistry, and watch a demonstration of leeching. ⊠ *1020 Caroline St., at Amelia St., Historic District* ☎ *540/ 373–3362* ⊠ *$5* ☉ *Mar.–Nov., Mon.–Sat. 9–5, Sun. 11–5; Dec.–Feb., Mon.–Sat. 10–4, Sun. noon–4.*

8 **James Monroe Museum and Memorial Library.** This tiny one-story building—on the site where Monroe, who became the fifth president of the United States, practiced law from 1787 to 1789—contains many of Monroe's possessions, collected and preserved by his family until the present day. They include a mahogany dispatch box used during the negotiation of the Louisiana Purchase and the desk on which the Monroe Doctrine was signed. ⊠ *908 Charles St., Historic District* ☎ *540/654–1043* ⊠ *$5* ☉ *Mar.–Nov., Mon.–Sat. 9–5, Sun. 11–5; Dec.–Feb., Mon.–Sat. 10–4, Sun. noon–4.*

★ ❺ **Kenmore.** Named Kenmore by a later owner, this house was built in 1775 on a 1,300-acre plantation owned by Colonel Fielding Lewis, a patriot, merchant, and brother-in-law of George Washington. Lewis sacrificed his fortune to operate a gun factory and otherwise supply General Washington's forces during the Revolutionary War. As a result, his debts forced his widow to sell the home following his death. The outstanding plaster moldings in the ceilings are even more ornate than those at Mount Vernon. It's believed that the artisan responsible for the ceilings worked frequently in both homes, though his name is unknown, possibly because he was an indentured servant. Most of the lavish furnishings are in storage until 2005 while the mansion undergoes a $5 million restoration. Guided 30-minute architectural tours of the home are conducted by docents; the subterranean Crowningshield museum on the grounds displays Kenmore's collection of fine Virginia-made furniture and family portraits as well as changing exhibits on Fredericksburg life. ⊠ *1201 Washington Ave., Historic District* ☎ *540/373–3381* ⊕ *www.kenmore.org* ⊠ *$6* ☉ *Jan. and Feb. weekends 10–5; Mar.–Dec. daily 10–5.*

❿ **Mary Washington College Galleries.** On campus are two art galleries. The Ridderhof Martin Gallery hosts exhibitions of art from various cultures and historical periods. The du Pont Gallery, in Melchers Hall, displays paintings, drawing, sculpture, photography, ceramics, and textiles by art faculty, students, and contemporary artists. Free gallery-visitor parking is available in the lot at the corner of College Avenue at Thornton Street. ⊠ *1301 College Ave., Historic District* ☎ *540/654–2120* ⊠ *Free* ☉ *When college is in session, Mon., Wed., and Fri. 10–4, weekends 1–4.*

❻ **Mary Washington Grave and Monument.** A 40-foot granite obelisk, dedicated by President Grover Cleveland in 1894, marks the final resting place of George's mother. It was laid at "Meditation Rock," a place on her daughter's property where Mrs. Washington liked to read.

❹ **Mary Washington House.** George purchased a three-room cottage for his mother in 1772 for £225, renovated it, and more than doubled its size with additions. She spent the last 17 years of her life here, tending the charming garden where her original boxwoods still flourish today, and where many a bride and groom now exchange their vows. The home has been a museum since 1930. Inside, displays include Mrs. Washington's "best dressing glass," a silver-over-tin mirror in a Chippendale frame; her teapot; Washington family dinnerware; and period furniture. The kitchen and its spit are original. Tours begin on the back porch with a history of the house. From there you can see the brick sidewalk leading to Kenmore, the home of Mrs. Washington's only daughter. ⊠ *1200 Charles St., Historic District* ☎ *540/373–1569* ⊠ *$5* ☉ *Mar.–Nov., Mon.–Sat. 9–5, Sun. 11–5; Dec.–Feb.; Mon.–Sat. 10–4, Sun. noon–4.*

❸ **Rising Sun Tavern.** In 1760 George Washington's brother Charles built as his home what later became the Rising Sun Tavern, a watering hole for such patriots as the Lee brothers (the only siblings to sign the Declaration of Independence); Patrick Henry, the five-term Governor of Virginia who said, "Give me liberty or give me death"; and future presidents Washington and Jefferson. A "wench" in period costume leads a tour without stepping out of character. From her you hear how travelers slept and what they ate and drank at this busy institution. ⊠ *1304 Caroline St., Historic District* ☎ *540/371–1494* ⊠ *$5* ☉ *Mar.–Nov., Mon.–Sat. 9–5, Sun. 11–5; Dec.–Feb., Mon.–Sat. 10–4, Sun. noon–4.*

Around Fredericksburg

Surrounding the town of Fredericksburg are historic sites and beautiful vistas where, in 1862, Union forces looked over the peaceful little place with conquest on their mind. Today you see only the lively Rappahannock and beautiful homes on a lovely drive across the river.

a good drive

From downtown Fredericksburg, drive east on William Street (Route 3) across the Rappahannock River 1 mi to **George Washington's Ferry Farm** ⑪ ⌐, on the right. Living here from age 6 to 19, Washington received his formal education and taught himself surveying. Park (for free) to see the exhibits and ongoing archaeological excavations. Return on Route 3 toward Fredericksburg and turn right at the signs to **Chatham Manor** ⑫, just east of the river. This Georgian mansion has views of the Rappahannock River and Fredericksburg. From Chatham Manor take River Road (Route 607) about a mile along the river, crossing U.S. 1 (Jefferson Davis Highway) to Route 1001 and **Belmont** ⑬, a spacious Georgian house furnished with many antiques and works of art. Return to Route 1 via Route 1001 and turn right (south) and cross the river. Turn left on Princess Anne Street (Business 1, 17, and 2) and go 1½ mi to the train station. This takes you past many old homes, churches, the main business district, and the museum. Turn right on Lafayette Boulevard; the **Fredericksburg/Spotsylvania National Military Park** ⑭ and **National Cemetery** ⑮ are ½ mi ahead on the right. Exhibits, films, and ranger-led tours describe Fredericksburg's role in the Civil War.

TIMING   Allow 5 minutes to drive to Ferry Farm and 10 minutes each to drive to Belmont and Chatham Manor. A tour of Belmont takes about an hour, as does Chatham Manor if you tour the museum and gardens. The battlefields of Wilderness, Chancellorsville, and Spotsylvania Court House are each within 15 mi of Fredericksburg. It can take one to several hours to tour each one, depending on your level of interest. At the Fredericksburg Battlefield Visitor Center, allow an hour or two—there's a 22-minute video, a small museum, and frequent walking tours.

Sights to See

⑬ **Belmont.** The last owner of this 1790s Georgian-style house was American artist Gari Melchers, who chaired the Smithsonian Commission to establish the National Gallery of Art in Washington; his wife, Corinne, deeded the 27-acre estate and its collections to Virginia. Belmont is now a public museum and a Virginia National Historic Landmark administered by Mary Washington College. You can take a one-hour tour of the spacious house, which is furnished with a rich collection of antiques. Galleries in the stone studio, built by Melchers in 1924, house the largest repository of his work. An orientation movie is shown in the reception area, which was once the carriage house. ⊠ *224 Washington St., Falmouth, VA* ☎ *540/654–1015* ⊕ *www.mwc.edu/belmont* ⊠ *$6* ⊙ *Mar.–Nov., Mon.–Sat. 10–5, Sun. 1–5; Dec.–Feb., Mon.–Sat. 10–4, Sun. 1–4.*

⑫ **Chatham Manor.** A fine example of Georgian architecture, Chatham Manor was built between 1768 and 1771 by William Fitzhugh, a plantation owner, on a site overlooking the Rappahannock River and the town of Fredericksburg. Fitzhugh frequently hosted such luminaries as George Washington and Thomas Jefferson. During the Civil War, Union forces commandeered the house and converted it into a headquarters and hospital. President Abraham Lincoln conferred with his generals here; Clara Barton (founder of the American Red Cross) and poet Walt Whitman tended the wounded. After the war, the house and gardens were restored by private owners and eventually donated to the National Park

Service. The home itself is now a museum. Five of the 10 rooms in the 12,000-square-foot mansion are open to the public and house exhibits spanning several centuries. ✉ *120 Chatham La., Falmouth, VA* ☎ *540/ 373–4461* ⊕ *www.nps.gov* ✐ *$4, includes Fredericksburg/Spotsylvania National Military Park* ⊙ *Daily 9–5.*

★ ⑭ **Fredericksburg/Spotsylvania National Military Park.** The 9,000-acre park actually includes four battlefields and three historic buildings, all accessible for a single admission price. At the Fredericksburg and Chancellorsville visitor centers you can learn about the area's role in the Civil War by watching a 22-minute video at Fredericksburg and a 12-minute slide show at Spotsylvania, and by viewing displays of soldiers' art and battlefield relics. In season, park rangers lead walking tours. The centers offer tape-recorded tour cassettes ($4.95 rental, $7.50 purchase) and maps that show how to reach hiking trails at the Wilderness, Chancellorsville (where General Stonewall Jackson was mistakenly shot by his own troops), and Spotsylvania Court House battlefields (all within 15 mi of Fredericksburg).

Just outside the Fredericksburg battlefield park visitor center is Sunken Road, where from December 11 to 13, 1862, General Robert E. Lee led his troops to a bloody but resounding victory over Union forces attacking across the Rappahannock (there were 18,000 casualties on both sides). Much of the stone wall that protected Lee's sharpshooters is now a re-creation, but 100 yards from the visitor center, part of the original wall overlooks the statue *The Angel of Marye's Heights*, by Felix de Weldon (sculptor of the famous *Marine Corps War Memorial* statue in Arlington). This memorial honors Sergeant Richard Kirkland, a South Carolinian who risked his life to bring water to wounded foes; he later died at the Battle of Chickamauga. ✉ *Fredericksburg Battlefield Visitor Center, 1013 Lafayette Blvd. and Sunken Rd., Historic District* ☎ *540/ 373–6122* ✉ *Chancellorsville Battlefield Visitor Center, Rte. 3 W (Plank Rd.), Chancellorsville* ☎ *540/786–2880* ⊕ *www.nps.gov/frsp* ✐ *$4, includes all 4 battlefields, Chatham Manor, and other historic buildings* ⊙ *Visitor centers daily 9–5; driving and walking tours daily dawn–dusk.*

▶ ⑪ **George Washington's Ferry Farm.** But for the outcries of historians and citizens, a Wal-Mart would have been built on this site of our first president's boyhood home. The land was saved by the Historic Kenmore Foundation, and the discount store found a location farther out on the same road. Ferry Farm, which once consisted of 600 acres, is across the Rappahannock River from downtown Fredericksburg and was the site of a ferry crossing. Living here from age 6 to 19, Washington received his formal education and taught himself surveying while *not* chopping a cherry tree or throwing a dollar across the Rappahannock—legends concocted by Parson Weems. The mainly archaeological site also has an exhibit on "George Washington: Boy Before Legend." The ongoing excavations include a summer program for children and adults, "Digging for Young George." Colonial games are held daily June through August. Ferry Farm became a major artillery base and river-crossing site for Union forces during the Battle of Fredericksburg. ✉ *Rte. 3 E, 268 Kings Hwy., at Ferry Rd., Fredericksburg, VA 22405* ☎ *540/370–0732* ⊕ *www.kenmore.org* ✐ *$3* ⊙ *Jan. and Feb., weekends 10–5; Mar.–Dec. 20, daily 10–5.*

⑮ **National Cemetery.** The National Cemetery is the final resting place of 15,000 Union dead, most of whom were never identified. ✉ *Lafayette Blvd. and Sunken Rd., Historic District* ☎ *540/373–6122* ⊙ *Daily dawn–dusk.*

Where to Stay & Eat

For price category charts, *see* the start of this chapter.

$$–$$$ ✕ **Claiborne's.** On the walls of this swank eatery in the 1910-era Fredericksburg train station are historic train photographs. The restaurant, decorated in dark green and navy with mahogany-and-brass bars—specializes in low-country Southern dishes, including crawfish, grits, and collard greens. Accompanying the steaks, chops, and seafood are ample vegetable side dishes served family style. ⊠ *200 Lafayette Blvd., Historic District* ☎ *540/371–7080* ⊕ *www.claibornesrestaurant.com* ⊟ *AE, DC, MC, V* ⊘ *No lunch Mon.–Sat., no dinner Sun.*

$$–$$$ ✕ **Merriman's Restaurant & Bar.** Inside an old brick storefront, Merriman's dining room is painted a bright yellow. The eclectic menu includes Mediterranean dishes such as Linguine Mykonos, Greek salad, and Middle Eastern hummus jostling against classic Virginia meats and seafood. Desserts are made fresh daily. ⊠ *715 Caroline St., Historic District* ☎ *540/371–7723* ⊕ *www.merrimansrestaurant.com* ⊟ *AE, D, DC, MC, V.*

$–$$$ ✕ **La Petite Auberge.** Housed in a pre-Revolutionary brick general store, this white-tablecloth restaurant actually has three dining rooms, as well as a small bar. Specialties like house-cut beef, French onion soup, and seafood are all served with a Continental accent. A prix-fixe ($14) three-course dinner is served from 5:30 to 7 Monday through Thursday. ⊠ *311 William St., Historic District* ☎ *540/371–2727* ⊟ *AE, D, MC, V* ⊘ *Closed Sun.*

$–$$$ ✕ **Ristorante Renato.** This family-owned restaurant, decorated with lace curtains, red carpeting, and walls covered with paintings, specializes in Italian cuisine, including veal and seafood dishes. ⊠ *422 William St., Historic District* ☎ *540/371–8228* ⊟ *AE, MC, V* ⊘ *No lunch weekends.*

$$ ✕ **six-twenty-three American Bistro and Tapas.** A 1769 house once known as "The Chimneys" is now a decidedly modern place to eat. Main dishes include pasta, quail, rainbow trout, chicken adobo, flank steak, duck, and stuffed pork loin. If you are in the mood for something less imposing, look to the tapas menu, where there are almost 20 choices priced $3–$8. Brunch is served Sunday, and you can eat on the patio when the weather permits. Across from the visitor center, the restaurant shares the premises with a wine shop. ⊠ *623 Caroline St., Historic District* ☎ *540/361–2640* ⊟ *AE, D, DC, MC, V* ⊘ *Closed Mon.–Tues. No lunch Wed.–Sat.*

$–$$ ✕ **Smythe's Cottage & Tavern.** Taking a step into this cozy dining room—a blacksmith's house built in the early 1800s—is like taking a step back in time. The surroundings are colonial-style; the lunch and dinner menus, classic Virginia: seafood pie, quail, stuffed flounder, peanut soup, and Smithfield ham biscuits. ⊠ *303 Fauquier St., Historic District* ☎ *540/373–1645* ⊟ *MC, V* ⊘ *Closed Tues.*

¢–$$ ✕ **Sammy T's.** Vegetarian dishes, healthy foods, and homemade soups and breads share the menu with hamburgers and dinner platters at this unpretentious place. The bar is stocked with nearly 50 kinds of beer. There's a separate no-smoking section around the corner, but the main dining room's tin ceiling, high wooden booths, and wooden ceiling fans mean it's much chummier and more homey. ⊠ *801 Caroline St., Historic District* ☎ *540/371–2008* ⊕ *www.sammyts.com* ⊟ *AE, D, MC, V.*

¢–$$ ▥ **Richard Johnston Inn.** This elegant B&B was constructed in the late 1700s and served as the home of Richard Johnston, mayor of Fredericksburg from March 1809 to March 1810. Guest rooms are decorated with period antiques and reproductions. The aroma of freshly baked breads and muffins entices you to breakfast in the large Federal-style dining room, where the table's set with fine china, silver, and linens. The inn is just across from the visitor center and two blocks from the train station. ✉ *711 Caroline St., Historic District 22401* ☎ *540/899–7606* ⊕ *www.rjohnstoninn.com* ⚓ *6 rooms, 2 suites* ⚙ *Free parking; no TV in some rooms* ⊟ *AE, MC, V* ⵙ *BP.*

$ ⬚ **WyteStone Suites.** Near a small outlet mall, several restaurants, and the Spotsylvania County Tourism Office, this modern, all-suites hotel is 2 mi from the historic area. Each suite has king or double beds with quilted bedspreads and a sofa bed in the living room. Rooms are entered from inside walkways around the six-story atrium with indoor pool. ✉ *4615 Southpoint Pkwy., take Exit 126 off I–95, bear right onto U.S. 1 South, and turn left onto Southpoint Pkwy. to the hotel on the right, 22407* ☎ *540/891–1112 or 800/794–5005* 🖶 *540/891–5465* ⚓ *85 suites* ⚙ *In-room data ports, microwaves, refrigerators, cable TV, indoor pool, laundry facilities* ⊟ *AE, D, DC, MC, V* ⵙ *BP.*

¢–$ ⬚ **Wingate Inn.** Built in 2001, this four-story hotel has large rooms equipped for the business traveler. Free high-speed Internet access for laptop computers and coffeemakers are standard in every room. Guest rooms are decorated in a soothing cream and moss with green botanical bedspreads. The large lobby with free newspapers and large-screen TV hosts the expanded Continental breakfast and evening dessert and beverage pantry. The Wingate is set back from U.S. Route 17 (Exit 133 off I–95, north toward Warrenton). Turn left at the first signal light west of I–95. ✉ *20 Sanford Dr. 22406* ☎ *540/368–8000 or 800/228–1000* 🖶 *540/368–9252* ⊕ *www.mywingate.com* ⚓ *30 rooms* ⚙ *In-room data ports, microwaves, refrigerators, indoor pool, health club, spa, meeting rooms, free parking* ⊟ *AE, MC, V* ⵙ *CP.*

¢ ⬚ **Fredericksburg Colonial Inn.** This 1920s motel with moss-green siding and forest-green awnings contains a lobby staircase reminiscent of the one in *Gone with the Wind*'s Tara. Indeed, rooms are furnished with authentic antiques and appointments from the Civil War period, and the lobby has an old-time upright piano. Breakfast includes beverages, cereal, and coffeecake. ✉ *1707 Princess Anne St., Historic District 22401* ☎ *540/371–5666* 🖶 *540/371–5884* ⊕ *www.fci1.com* ⚓ *30 rooms* ⚙ *Microwaves, refrigerators, free parking; no smoking* ⊟ *AE, MC, V* ⵙ *BP.*

¢ ⬚ **Hampton Inn.** This may be a typical chain motel, but it's neat and clean, and the Continental breakfast is extensive. Because it's on a main artery in a busy retail area, ask for a room facing the interior courtyard. Local phone calls from your room are free, as is the HBO. Several restaurants are a block or two away. ✉ *2310 William St., Exit 130-A off I–95, Fredericksburg West, 22401* ☎ *540/371–0330* 🖶 *540/371–1753* ⊕ *www. hamptoninn.com* ⚓ *166 rooms* ⚙ *In-room data ports, cable TV, pool, laundry facilities, meeting rooms, free parking* ⊟ *AE, D, DC, MC, V* ⵙ *CP.*

Fredericksburg A to Z

To research prices, get advice from other travelers, and book travel arrangements, visit ⊕ *www.fodors.com*

BUS TRAVEL TO & FROM FREDERICKSBURG
Greyhound buses depart seven times a day from Washington to Fredericksburg between 7 AM and 5 PM. A round-trip ticket is $18.50. Buses stop at a station on Alternate Route 1, about 2 mi from the center of town; taxis and a cheap regional bus service are available there. Unfortunately, the waiting room is not open late at night. Buses are not known for their timeliness and purchasing a ticket doesn't ensure a seat.
🗐 Bus Information **Greyhound** ☎ 202/289–5160 or 800/231–2222 ⊕ www.greyhound. com.

BUS TRAVEL WITHIN FREDERICKSBURG

You can ride FRED, the city's excellent little bus, for only 25¢. Six lines—red, yellow, blue, orange, green, and purple—serve the region and stop at all historic sites as well as shopping malls and other modern areas of the city from 7:30 AM to 8:30 PM.

🚌 Bus Information **FRED** ☎ 540/372-1222 ⊕ www.efredericksburg.com/directory/transit.

CAR TRAVEL

To drive to Fredericksburg from the District, take I–95 South to Route 3 (Exit 130-A), turn left, and follow the signs. The drive takes about an hour—except during rush hour, when it's about 1½ hours.

TOURS

The tour coordinator at the Fredericksburg Visitor Center can arrange tours of the city as well as of battlefields and other historic sites. Reservations are required. The Fredericksburg Department of Tourism (in the visitor center) publishes a booklet that includes a short history of Fredericksburg and a self-guided tour covering 29 sights.

If you like to tour on wheels, take a carriage or trolley. Fredericksburg Carriage Tours depart from the visitor center for leisurely narrated tours of downtown Fredericksburg in horse-drawn carriages. Tours last about 45 minutes and cost $10.

A 75-minute narrated trolley tour takes you past most of Fredericksburg's important sights. Thirty-five monuments, markers and attractions are included, along with the Confederate and Federal cemeteries. Tours, conducted April through November, cost $12.50 and leave from the visitor center daily. Tickets may be purchased at the Fredericksburg Visitor Center.

If you'd rather stroll, try a walking tour with the Living History Company of Fredericksburg. The $15 tours covers such topics as the "Phantoms of Fredericksburg," Christmas in the 1800s, and the Civil War.

🚌 Fees and Schedules **Fredericksburg Carriage Tours** ✉ 1700 Caroline St. ☎ 540/654-5511 ⊕ www.carriagetours.com. **Fredericksburg Visitor Center** ✉ 706 Caroline St., Historic District ☎ 540/373-1776 or 800/678-4748 🖶 540/372-6587. **Living History Company of Fredericksburg** ✉ 904 Princess Anne St. ☎ 540/899-1776 or 888/214-6384 ⊕ www.historyexperiences.com. **Trolley Tours of Fredericksburg** ✉ 81 Devone Dr. ☎ 540/898-0737 or 800/678-4748.

TRAIN TRAVEL

Trains depart for Fredericksburg several times daily from Washington's Union Station, Alexandria, and several commuter stops; the trip takes an hour or less. The Fredericksburg railroad station is two blocks from the historic district at Caroline Street and Lafayette Boulevard. A round-trip ticket from Washington costs about $50 on Amtrak. The Virginia Rail Express offers workday commuter service with additional stops near hotels in Crystal City, L'Enfant Plaza, and elsewhere. A round-trip ticket from Washington's Union Station costs about $14.

🚆 Train Information **Amtrak** ✉ 200 Lafayette Blvd. ☎ 202/484-7540 or 800/872-7245. **Virginia Rail Express** (VRE) ☎ 800/743-3873 ⊕ www.vre.org/.

VISITOR INFORMATION

🚌 Tourist Information **Fredericksburg Visitor Center** ✉ 706 Caroline St., Historic District ☎ 540/373-1776 or 800/678-4748 🖶 540/372-6587 ⊕ www.fredericksburgvirginia.org.

UNDERSTANDING D.C.

THE WRITINGS ON THE WALL . . .
AND HOW THEY GOT THERE

WASHINGTON PROBABLY PRODUCES MORE WORDS than any other city in the world. Politicians orate, pundits speculate, and commentators narrate. But Washington's words have a peculiarly fleeting quality. They're copied into notebooks, transferred to computer screens, then set into type and bound into reports that are filed on shelves, placed on the Web, and then forgotten. They're printed in newspapers that yellow and turn to dust. Words are spat out in sound bites on the evening news, then released into the ether, lost forever. In the wordy war of politics, a paper trail is something best avoided.

But there's a stone trail in Washington, too: The words someone felt were important enough not just to commit to parchment, paper, or videotape but to engrave in sandstone, marble, or granite. On the buildings of Washington are noble sentiments and self-serving ones, moving odes and contemplative ones.

A reading tour of Washington's inscriptions amounts to a classical education. The inscriptions, lofty in position and tone, are taken from the Bible, from the Greeks and Romans, from poets and playwrights, from presidents and politicians. When viewing Washington's inscriptions, soaking up what is in most cases a perfect union of poesy and architecture, it's easy to see why the words "edifice" and "edify" spring from the same root.

Lesson one starts in Union Station, that great beaux arts bathhouse on Capitol Hill. Architect Daniel Burnham's 1908 train station is encrusted with carvings that do everything from romantically outline the development of the railroad to offer lessons in both humility and hospitality.

On the western end of the shining white Vermont granite structure, above the entrance to the Metro, is written (in all capital letters, as most inscriptions are):

He that would bring home the wealth of the Indies must carry the wealth of the Indies with him. So it is in travelling. A man must carry knowledge with him if he would bring home knowledge.

A bit heavy to digest when dashing for the Metroliner on a rainy Monday morning, but worth mulling over once a seat is found.

At the other end of the station is the perfect sentiment for the returning hero:

Welcome the coming, speed the parting guest. Virtue alone is sweet society. It keeps the key to all heroic hearts and opens you a welcome in them all.

These are just two of the half dozen inscriptions on Union Station. Above allegorical statues by Louis (brother of Augustus) Saint-Gaudens that stand over the main entrance are inscriptions celebrating the forces that created the railroads, including this set singing the praises of fire and electricity:

Fire: greatest of discoveries, enabling man to live in various climates, use many foods, and compel the forces of nature to do his work. Electricity: carrier of light and power, devourer of time and space, bearer of human speech over land and sea, greatest servant of man, itself unknown. Thou has put all things under his feet.

So inspirational were these and the other Union Station inscriptions that the Washington Terminal Company, operators of the station, once distributed free pamphlets imprinted with them. This probably saved more than a few sore necks.

Union Station's inscriptions were selected by Charles William Eliot, the educator and longtime president of Harvard University. According to John L. Andriot's "Guide to the Inscriptions of the Nation's Capital," Eliot borrowed from such sources as the Bible, Shakespeare, Alexander Pope, and Ralph Waldo Emerson. Eliot also penned his own epigrams, a seemingly modest skill until you start to wonder what you'd come up with when confronted with a big blank wall that will bear your words forever.

Eliot wrote the two inscriptions on the City Post Office right next to the station. The inscriptions, facing Massachusetts Avenue, describe the humble letter carrier as a:

Carrier of news and knowledge, instrument of trade and industry, promoter of mutual acquaintance of peace and of goodwill among men and nations . . .

and a . . .

Messenger of sympathy and love, servant of parted friends, consoler of the lonely, bond of scattered family, enlarger of the common life.

It's said that President Woodrow Wilson edited these inscriptions, unaware that their author was Eliot, the Ivy League wordsmith. Like all good editors, Wilson improved them.

Triangular Logic

If a walk around Washington's inscriptions is a classical education, a ramble around Federal Triangle is a civics lesson. The limestone cliffs of the Triangle, stretching from their base at 15th Street down Pennsylvania and Constitution avenues, are inscribed with mottoes that immediately conjure up a seemingly nobler time.

The walls fairly sing with inscriptions, enjoining passersby to be eternally vigilant (it's *the price of liberty; Study the past,* says the National Archives), and to heed Thomas Jefferson and *Cultivate peace and commerce with all* (on the Commerce Building, and an example of one of the tenets of good epigram selection—try to work the name of the building into at least one inscription).

The Federal Triangle inscriptions also provide justification for the buildings that they decorate and government departments they praise. The inscription on the Internal Revenue Service headquarters on Constitution Avenue is not Dante's *Abandon all hope ye who enter here* or Shelley's *Look on my works, ye mighty, and despair* but Oliver Wendell Holmes's *Taxes are what we pay for a civilized society*—just in case you were wondering what you were paying for every April 15.

Likewise, on the Justice Department we have:

Justice is the great interest of man on earth. Wherever her temple stands there is a foundation for social security, general happiness and the improvement and progress of our race.

While Justice certainly has its share of letters (including this bit of Latin: *Lege atque ordine omnia fiunt*—"By law and order all is accomplished"), the award for the most verbose structure must go to the Commerce Department Building. Stretched out along 14th Street, eight stories up and spread out over hundreds of feet, is this edifying ode:

The inspiration that guided our forefathers led them to secure above all things the unity of our country. We rest upon government by consent of the governed and the political order of the United States is the expression of a patriotic ideal which welds together all the elements of our national energy promoting the organization that fosters individual initiative. Within this edifice are established agencies that have been created to buttress the life of the people, to clarify their problems and coordinate their resources, seeking to lighten burdens without lessening the responsibility of the citizen. In serving one and all they are dedicated to the purpose of the founders and to the highest hopes of the future with their local administration given to the integrity and welfare of the nation.

It's a mouthful. But it's also redolent of a time that seems almost hopelessly naive now, a time when we could use words like "national energy" and "purpose of the founders" without smirking. This passage and two other long ones were created especially for the building, composed, it is believed, by Royal Cortissoz, for 50 years the influential art critic of the *New York Tribune.* He was also author of this much pithier epigram from the Lincoln Memorial:

In this temple as in the hearts of the people for whom he saved the union the memory of Abraham Lincoln is enshrined forever.

You can imagine Washingtonians in the 1930s watching as the inscriptions were going up in Federal Triangle, trying to guess what would be said, as if a huge game of hangman were being played. At least one Washingtonian wasn't thrilled with what he saw. In 1934, when the giant Commerce Department Building was in its final stages of construction, one Thomas Woodward wrote a letter to a friend in the Department of Justice, expressing his dismay. The letter was addressed to Charles W. Eliot II, son of the Harvard president who composed the Union Station and City Post Office epigrams. The younger Eliot forwarded the letter of complaint to Charles Moore, chairman of the Commission of Fine Arts, the body responsible—then as now—for reviewing the design of government building projects. Moore allowed as how his commission hadn't been consulted on the inscriptions. The younger Eliot followed up with a salvo of his own to Moore, stating that the inscriptions "seem to be thoroughly bromidic and uninteresting—a lost opportunity."

Eliot had a point. The Commerce Department inscriptions are lecturing rather than inspirational, long and sour rather than short and sweet. Moore must have forgotten that he once wrote: "Inscriptions are an art in themselves. They should be monumental and express in few words a great sentiment."

Still, there can be poetry in even the longest of inscriptions. Consider this moving sentiment, carved on the section of the Post Office Department Building that faces 14th Street:

The Post Office Department, in its ceaseless labors, pervades every channel of commerce and every theatre of human enterprise, and while visiting as it does kindly, every fireside, mingles with the throbbings of almost every heart in the land. In the amplitude of its beneficence, it ministers to all climes, and creeds, and pursuits, with the same eager readiness and with equal fullness of fidelity. It is the delicate ear trump through which alike nations and families and isolated individuals whisper their joys and their sorrows, their convictions and their sympathies to all who listen for their coming.

What is it about the Post Office that inspires the most poignant inscriptions? And to whom do we talk about getting "ear trump" back into common usage?

Rocks & Hard Places

Behind every inscription in Washington is the person who carved it, the man or woman who put chisel or pneumatic drill to stone and, with a sharp eye and a steady hand, made the most lasting of impressions.

Ann Hawkins is one such carver. (You can admire her chisel work throughout the National Gallery of Art. She did the names on the Patrons' Permanent Fund in the east building, a roll call of philanthropists.)

"There are two comments I get from people who watch me carve, and they make perfect symmetry," says Hawkins. "Half the people say, 'Oh, that looks so tedious. You must have a lot of patience.' But I also get 'That looks *fun.*' And they wish they could do it."

Hawkins studied for four years before she could carve well enough to take her first paying commission. She's been carving professionally since 1982, and in that time she's decided that stones are "living, breathing things." And each one is different. Sandstone is soft. Slates can be brittle and hard, with knots in them almost like wood. White Vermont marble feels sugary and crumbles a bit at the first stroke. Tennessee pink marble is chunky and firm.

There are a lot of things a stone carver has to take into account before striking the first blow, Hawkins says. "The nature of the stone, the light the inscription will receive, the weathering of the stone, how large the letters will be, what distance they'll be viewed from."

The most important part of carving, she says, is the layout of the inscription. The letters must be spaced correctly, not bunched too tightly together as if they were typeset, but spread comfortably and handsomely. The inscription must look as if it is *of* the stone, not *on* the stone.

Hawkins draws the letters on paper that—"after being measured from every direction" to make sure it's straight—is taped to the stone over sheets of typewriter carbon paper. She then outlines the inscription, transferring it to the stone. With a tungsten-carbide-tip chisel she starts hammering, sometimes working her way around the edges of the letter, sometimes starting in the center and working out. She turns and shifts the blade, roughing the letter in at first, then finishing it, aiming for the perfect V-shape indentation that is the mark of a hand-carved inscription. (Inscriptions that are machine-sandblasted through a stencil have a round center.) As with everything from squash to Frisbee, it's all in the wrist.

If the inscription is outside, the sun will provide the contrast necessary for the letters to be read. As the rays rake across the inscription, the shadows will lengthen, making the words pop. If the inscription is indoors, Hawkins paints the inside of the letters with a lacquer that's mixed with pigment, deepening the color of the stone for the eyes of the thousands who will soon be reading her handiwork.

Oops . . .

What do you do if you're a stone carver and you make a mistake? After all, the expression "carved in stone" isn't much good if fixing a typo on a chunk of marble is as easy as depressing the backspace key. Ann Hawkins: "If I got a chip, there are epoxy resins I could apply. . . . It's very rare to make a mistake, unless you do something stupid."

On big projects, boo-boos can be lopped out entirely, the offending block of stone cut out and replaced with a "dutchman," a fresh piece that's inserted like a patch and—one hopes—carved correctly. There's no dutchman in what is perhaps the city's most obvious mistake. Inscribed in three sections on the north wall of the Lincoln Memorial is Abraham Lincoln's second inaugural address. Twenty lines down in the first block of words is a phrase that concludes: WITH HIGH HOPES FOR THE FUTURE. The poor stone carver added an extra stroke to the F, transforming it into an E. Because the inscription is inside— away from the sunshine and its shadows— it would be virtually unreadable if the insides of the letters weren't painted black. And so, the bottom stroke of the E was left unpainted, making the best of a bad situation.

Back to the Stone Age

The capital's official buildings, monuments, and memorials urge us in various ways to remember the past or strive toward a more perfect future. None of the blank verse, mottoes, or maxims, though, are as moving as what appears on a V-shape set of black granite panels set into the ground near the Lincoln Memorial. The inscription isn't made up of words at all, but it's as moving as any sonnet.

Etched into the stone of the Vietnam Veterans Memorial are the names of the more than 58,000 Americans killed in that war. The names weren't carved high atop a pediment out of reach but were sandblasted delicately into the wall. Washington's other inscriptions might be meant to provide edification from a distance, but this memorial is designed to be touched, its inscriptions traced with unsteady fingers. And behind the names we see ourselves, reflected in the stone as true as any mirror.

Which leads us to the state of stone carving in Washington today. Most newer buildings in Washington aren't graced with inscriptions. While a building named after a famous American might once have warranted an inscribed quotation from that person, today we have the James Forrestal Federal Building and the William McChesney Martin Jr. Federal Reserve Board Building with nary a peep from either gentleman.

Gone, too, is the specially commissioned aphorism meant to enlighten or fire. Inscriptions like those on the Justice and Commerce department buildings— whether you consider them quaint optimism or naive bluster—are in short supply these days.

— John F. Kelly

THE FEDERAL GOVERNMENT: HOW OUR SYSTEM WORKS

"SEPARATION OF POWERS" becomes more than just a phrase in the Constitution when you visit the capital. A visit here gives you a chance to see the legislative, executive, and judicial branches of government in action, to see how checks and balances work. As Boswell put it, you have an opportunity, "instead of thinking how things may be, to see them as they are."

The Fed casts a very long shadow. It's a major employer, an important landlord, and a source of contracts, contacts, and conversation for the city. It's a patron of the arts and a provider for the needy. To some, pervasive government is what's wrong with Washington. To others, it's what's right.

The federal government occupies some of the choicest real estate in town yet pays no taxes to the District of Columbia. On the other hand, although citizens of the District *do* pay taxes, they could not vote until the 1964 elections. This has changed; now they can help elect the president, but they still have only a nonvoting delegate in Congress.

The Legislative Branch
In Pierre-Charles L'Enfant's 18th-century plan for the "Federal city," the U.S. Capitol and the White House were just far enough away from each other on Pennsylvania Avenue to emphasize the separation of powers between the legislative and executive branches. L'Enfant chose Jenkins Hill as the site for the Capitol; it's the focal point of an area now called Capitol Hill.

The Senate side of the Capitol faces Constitution Avenue, while the House side can be approached from Independence Avenue. There are two Senate office buildings at 1st Street and Constitution Avenue NE, named, respectively, for former senators Everett Dirksen and Richard Russell. A third, honoring Senator Philip A. Hart, is at 2nd Street and Constitution Avenue NE.

The House office buildings, named for former Speakers Joseph Cannon, Nicholas Longworth, and Sam Rayburn, are located in that order along Independence Avenue between 1st Street SE and 1st Street SW. It's generally agreed by residents and visitors alike that the Rayburn Building is the least attractive and, at $75 million, one of the most expensive structures in the city.

According to the Constitution, "the Congress shall assemble at least once in every year, and such meeting shall begin at noon on the 3rd day of January, unless they shall by law appoint a different day." In the years before air-conditioning, Congress usually recessed in the summer and reconvened in the fall. Today, however, with congressional calendars more crowded and air-conditioning commonplace, sessions frequently last much longer. It's not unusual for the House and/or Senate to sit through the summer and well into the fall.

Congressional sessions usually begin at noon; committee meetings are generally held in the morning. Check the *Washington Post's* "Today in Congress" listings to find out what's going on.

Don't be surprised to see only a handful of senators or members of Congress on the floor during a session. Much congressional business dealing with constituent problems is done in committees or in offices. When a vote is taken during a session, bells are rung to summon absent members to the floor. To save time, many members of Congress make the brief trip between their offices and the Capitol on a congressional subway.

There are two senators from each state, who are elected for six-year terms; the 435 members of the House serve for two years. Rank-and-file senators and members receive an annual salary of $150,000.

The Executive Branch
The White House is at 1600 Pennsylvania Avenue NW, the most prestigious address in the country. However, its first occupant, Abigail Adams, was disappointed in the damp, drafty "President's Palace." She complained that it had "not

a single apartment finished" and "not the least fence, yard, or other convenience without." On the other hand, Thomas Jefferson found the house "big enough for two emperors, one Pope, and the grand lama"—and still unfinished.

When Franklin Delano Roosevelt became president in 1932, the entire White House staff consisted of fewer than 50 people. Today, approximately 1,800 people work for the executive office of the president. They are crammed into offices in the east and west wings of the White House and in the ornate Executive Office Building (formerly the State, War, and Navy Building), adjacent to the White House to the west on Pennsylvania Avenue.

The president's annual salary is $400,000; the vice president receives $186,300. They're elected for a four-year term. If the president dies or becomes incapacitated, the vice president is next in line of succession. He is followed, in order, by the speaker of the House of Representatives; the president pro tempore of the Senate; the secretaries of state, treasury, and defense; the attorney general; the postmaster general; and the secretaries of the interior, agriculture, commerce, labor, health and human services, housing and urban development, transportation, energy, education, and veterans affairs.

The Judicial Branch

Traditionally, the opening session of the Supreme Court, on the first Monday in October, marks the beginning of Washington's social season, and the quadrennial inaugural festivities add to the excitement. The inaugural week in January usually includes a star-studded gala, as well as receptions honoring the new president, vice president, and their spouses.

The Supreme Court meets from October through June in a Corinthian-column white-marble building at 1st Street and Maryland Avenue NE. Until 1935, the justices used various rooms in the Capitol. For a while, in the 19th century, they met in taverns and boardinghouses. You can see the Old Supreme Court Chamber on the ground floor of the Capitol.

Approximately 5,000 cases are submitted for appeal each year, and the justices choose those that seem to raise constitutional questions or otherwise have a major

effect on the life or liberty of citizens. It amounts to about 160 cases a year.

Justice Felix Frankfurter said, "The words of the Constitution are so unrestricted by their intrinsic meaning or by their history or by tradition or by prior decisions that they leave the individual Justice free, if indeed they do not compel him, to gather meaning not from reading the Constitution but from reading life."

In the courtroom, the nine black-robed justices are seated in high-back black leather chairs in front of heavy red velvet draperies. Lawyers for each side present their oral arguments, with the justices often interjecting questions or comments. Generally, the court sits for two weeks and then recesses for two weeks to do research and write opinions.

They are on the bench Monday, Tuesday, and Wednesday from 10 to noon and from 1 to 2 or 3 from October through April, and they usually hear about four cases a day. During this first part of the term, the justices meet privately every Wednesday afternoon and all day Friday to discuss the cases they have heard that week and to take a preliminary vote on decisions.

The chief justice assigns different members to write the opinions. If the chief justice is on the minority side in a particular case, however, the senior justice in the majority assigns the opinion. Any justice may write his or her own opinion, agreeing or disagreeing with the majority. During the remainder of the term, in May and June, the justices usually meet every Thursday to decide on releasing their opinions.

Monday is "Decision Day," probably the most interesting time to visit the Supreme Court. That is when the justices announce their decisions and read their opinions.

Throughout the year, in the courtroom, staff members give a brief lecture about the court Monday through Friday, every hour on the half hour from 9:30 AM to 3:30 PM. Lectures are not given on holidays or on days when the justices are on the bench hearing cases.

Supreme Court justices are appointed by the president with the advice and consent of the Senate. They serve for life or, as the Constitution says, "during good behavior."

Associate justices receive $184,400 per year; the chief justice's salary is $192,600. After 10 years of service, justices may resign or retire with full pay.

Lobbyists

Virtually every special-interest group in the country, as well as a sprinkling of foreign governments, is represented by someone who "lobbies" for its cause in Washington. Some say that the word comes from President Grant's time. He used to escape the White House for brandy and a cigar in the lobby of the Willard Hotel, where interested parties would try to bend his ear. Today's lobbyists frequently conduct their business over luncheons, cocktails, and dinners, as well as on the golf courses or tennis courts of suburban country clubs.

Lobbyists' backgrounds are as diverse as the causes they represent. They are usually lawyers, public relations executives, or former congressional staff members. Many were once members of Congress or high government officials from all over the United States who have developed "Potomac fever"; that is, they do not return home but find being a Washington representative the ideal way to continue to influence public policy.

Sometimes, it appears that every group is well represented here except the average citizen. Under those circumstances, if you have a pet project, discuss it with your senator or member of Congress— he or she is your lobbyist. In doing so— like Washington's highly skilled and well-paid lobbyists—you would simply be exercising your First Amendment rights to express your beliefs and influence your government.

— Betty Ross

BOOKS & MOVIES

Books

For thorough albeit slightly outdated coverage of the hundreds of buildings that make up D.C., consult the *AIA Guide to the Architecture of Washington, D.C.* (3rd edition; 1994). *The White House: Its Historic Furnishings and First Families* (2000), by Betty C. Monkman, the curator for the White House, and photographer Bruce White, is a coffee-table book full of color and details on how the interiors of 1600 Pennsylvania have changed throughout different administrations.

Many of the biographies and autobiographies that concern major Beltway figures tell you as much about the city as they do about their announced subject. Katharine Graham's *Personal History* (1996) is a gossipy, engrossing account of the setbacks, events, and people the late publisher of the *Washington Post* encountered—and it's quite a list. In her posthumous anthology *Katharine Graham's Washington* (2002), she brought together with her own commentary first-hand accounts from those who saw the city transform itself during the 20th century: seamstresses, P. J. O'Rourke, David Brinkley, and a bevy of First Ladies all have their say.

Several bestselling mystery series use Washington and its denizens as characters. Margaret Truman, the daughter of Harry S., sets the murderous deeds covered in her Capital Crimes book in important Beltway landmarks. The Library of Congress, Ford's Theatre, and the White House itself have all served as crime scenes. For a more hardboiled take on the city, give the crime novels of George P. Pelecanos a try. The D.C. native's books are generally set in shady neighborhoods that few tourists enter. His first, 1992's *A Firing Offense*, also served as an introduction to Nick Stefanos, an ad manager turned gumshoe who knows the gritty side of D.C. quite well. A Pelecanos novel that doesn't star Nick, the stylish *King Suckerman* (1997), takes place as the city and the nation prepare for the Bicentennial. It's an effective attempt to bring the crime-ridden, tension-filled Washington of the 1970s back to life.

Movies

Hollywood has always had a hot-and-cold affair with Washington and the people that run it. When films aren't busy celebrating patriotism and the Founding Fathers, they're hard at work revealing the corruption that lies beneath the somewhat prim facade. Some movies, including Frank Capra's *Mr. Smith Goes to Washington* (1939), manage to do both. Jimmy Stewart, playing an idealistic scoutmaster, is a senatorial replacement put in place by a political machine who thinks he can be easily controlled. When he finds out about their undemocratic plotting, he has to stand up to his fellow senators. *Mr. Smith* has several scenes set at major landmarks, including the Congress and the Lincoln Memorial. The equally emblematic *Day the Earth Stood Still* (1951) gives prominence to the Washington Monument in its story of an alien who comes to earth with nothing more than peace and nuclear disarmament on its mind. The extraterrestrials in the thriller *Independence Day* and the deliberately corny *Mars Attacks!* (both from 1996) aren't so high-minded— they do considerable damage to monuments, politicians, and everyday citizens alike.

Even without the Martians, movies devote much more attention to the Executive branch than they do to the Supreme Court or those in Congress. *Dave* (1993), a farce about a presidential look-alike who's forced to impersonate a comatose president, includes cameos of some living Beltway monuments (Speaker of the House Tip O'Neill, reporters Helen Thomas and Eleanor Clift, and Senator Howard Metzenbaum) along with shots of the more inert kind. The title character of *The American President* (1995) is a widower who falls for an environmental lobbyist. He gets the girl along with the legislation he's been hoping for.

The real presidents, of course, have also come under Hollywood's gaze again and again. *All the President's Men* (1976), based on Carl Bernstein and Bob Woodward's nonfiction book, dramatizes the investigation that led the two famed reporters to unravel the Watergate scandal, an event that led to President Nixon's resignation. As you'd expect, scenes make use of the Watergate hotel complex, as well as the Department of Justice, Lafayette Square, and the exterior of the Washington Post building. The paper's offices, however, were just stage-set replicas of the real thing. (*Dick,* from 1999, is an extremely fanciful revisit of the scandal: here, "Deep Throat" turns out to be a teenage girl).

Many other Washington movies never get around to visiting the Mall or the major monuments. The scenes of Georgetown in *The Exorcist* use more than just the famous steps—there are also some shots of the Key Bridge and of Georgetown University's campus. The equally gruesome *Exorcist III* (1990), also set in Georgetown, includes cameos by such Washingtonians as Dr. C. Everett Koop, the former Surgeon General, and basketball star Patrick Ewing as the Angel of Death.

CHRONOLOGY

1608   Captain John Smith explores the Potomac.

1751   Georgetown is founded above the mouth of Rock Creek.

1775–83   Revolutionary War.

1788   The Constitution is ratified. It gives Congress exclusive legislative control of the District of Columbia.

1789   Georgetown University is founded.

1790   President George Washington chooses a site on the Potomac for the new federal capital.

1791–92   Pierre Charles L'Enfant begins planning the Federal City, and work on the White House begins.

1800   The federal capital is moved from Philadelphia to D.C.

1814   British forces raid Washington and burn the White House. President James Madison and his wife, Dolley, relocate to the Octagon until the building is restored.

1820   Washington residents are given the right to elect their own mayor.

1846   Congress passes a law returning the land southwest of the Potomac, including Alexandria and Alexandria County, to the state of Virginia.

1848   Work begins on the Washington Monument and the Mall.

1861–65   Civil War.

1862   Slavery is abolished in the federal district (the City of Washington, Washington County, and Georgetown), predating both the Emancipation Proclamation and the adoption of the 13th Amendment to the Constitution.

1867   African-American males vote for the first time.

1878   D.C. government is once again removed from the hands of its residents, this time to a municipal corporation governed by three commissioners appointed by the president.

1884   Work on the Washington Monument is completed.

1899   Congress passes the Heights of Building Act, which says that no private building in D.C. can exceed the height of the Capitol or any other important government structure. Amendments in 1910 put the restriction at 160 feet along parts of Pennsylvania Avenue and at 130 feet in the rest of the city.

1931   Hunger March on Washington.

1939   African-American opera singer Marion Anderson sings to a crowd of 75,000 on the steps of the Lincoln Memorial after being barred from the DAR's Constitution Hall.

1943   The Pentagon is completed.

1954   Racial integration is introduced to Washington schools, among the first in the nation to do so.

1961   With the passing of the 23rd Amendment, District residents get the right to vote for president.

1963 Dr. Martin Luther King Jr. delivers his "I Have a Dream" speech at National Hall after the March on Washington.

1970 D.C. gains the right of sending a nonvoting representative to the House of Representatives.

1973 Partial "home rule," including the right to vote for their own mayor, is returned to D.C. residents.

1974 General elections are held for mayor and council on November 5, 1974.

1975 Newly elected Mayor Walter Washington and the first elected council take office.

1976 Parts of the Metrorail Red Line, the city's new subway system, open.

1979 Marion Barry takes office as the mayor of D.C.

1987 Authority over and operation of two of the three D.C. area airports, Washington National and Washington-Dulles International, is transferred from the federal government to the newly created Metropolitan Washington Airports Authority.

1991 Sharon Pratt Dixon becomes the first female mayor of D.C.

1993 The Vietnam Women's Memorial is dedicated.

1995 Marion Barry is elected mayor for an unprecedented fourth term. The Korean War Veterans memorial is dedicated.

1997 Franklin Delano Roosevelt Memorial is unveiled.

1998 The Ronald Reagan Building and International Trade Center, at over three million square feet the largest federal building after the Pentagon, is dedicated on May 5.

1999 Mayor Anthony Williams takes office.

2001 A plane hijacked as part of the terrorist attacks of 9/11 crashes into the Pentagon, leaving 184 dead. The damage sustained to the building is completely repaired within 18 months.

INDEX

NOTES

NOTES

FODOR'S KEY TO THE GUIDES

America's guidebook leader publishes guides for every kind of traveler.
Check out our many series and find your perfect match.

FODOR'S GOLD GUIDES
America's favorite travel-guide series offers the most detailed insider reviews of hotels, restaurants, and attractions in all price ranges, plus great background information, smart tips, and useful maps.

COMPASS AMERICAN GUIDES
Stunning guides from top local writers and photographers, with gorgeous photos, literary excerpts, and colorful anecdotes. A must-have for culture mavens, history buffs, and new residents.

FODOR'S CITYPACKS
Concise city coverage in a guide plus a foldout map. The right choice for urban travelers who want everything under one cover.

FODOR'S EXPLORING GUIDES
Hundreds of color photos bring your destination to life. Lively stories lend insight into the culture, history, and people.

FODOR'S TRAVEL HISTORIC AMERICA
For travelers who want to experience history firsthand, this series gives in-depth coverage of historic sights, plus nearby restaurants and hotels. Themes include the Thirteen Colonies, the Old West, and the Lewis and Clark Trail.

FODOR'S POCKET GUIDES
For travelers who need only the essentials. The best of Fodor's in pocket-size packages for just $9.95.

FODOR'S FLASHMAPS
Every resident's map guide, with 60 easy-to-follow maps of public transit, parks, museums, zip codes, and more.

FODOR'S CITYGUIDES
Sourcebooks for living in the city: thousands of in-the-know listings for restaurants, shops, sports, nightlife, and other city resources.

FODOR'S AROUND THE CITY WITH KIDS
Up to 68 great ideas for family days, recommended by resident parents. Perfect for exploring in your own backyard or on the road.

FODOR'S HOW TO GUIDES
Get tips from the pros on planning the perfect trip. Learn how to pack, fly hassle-free, plan a honeymoon or cruise, stay healthy on the road, and travel with your baby.

FODOR'S LANGUAGES FOR TRAVELERS
Practice the local language before you hit the road. Available in phrase books, cassette sets, and CD sets.

KAREN BROWN'S GUIDES
Engaging guides—many with easy-to-follow inn-to-inn itineraries—to the most charming inns and B&Bs in the U.S.A. and Europe.

BAEDEKER'S GUIDES
Comprehensive guides, trusted since 1829, packed with A–Z reviews and star ratings.

OTHER GREAT TITLES FROM FODOR'S
Baseball Vacations, The Complete Guide to the National Parks, Family Vacations, Golf Digest's Places to Play, Great American Drives of the East, Great American Drives of the West, Great American Vacations, Healthy Escapes, National Parks of the West, Skiing USA.